A Brief History of American Literature

A Brief History of American Literature

Richard Gray

WILEY-BLACKWELL

A John Wiley & Sons, Ltd., Publication

Library of Congress Cataloging-in-Publication Data

Gray, Richard J.
 A brief history of American literature / Richard Gray.
  p. cm.
 Includes bibliographical references and index.
 ISBN 978-1-4051-9231-6 (alk. paper) — ISBN 978-1-4051-9230-9 (pbk.: alk. paper)
 1. American literature—History and criticism. 2. United States—Literatures—History and criticism.
I. Title.
 PS88.G726 2011
 810.9–dc22

                                                                              2010035339

A catalogue record for this book is available from the British Library.

This book is published in the following electronic formats: ePDFs 978-1-4443-9245-6; ePub 978-1-4443-9246-3

Set in 10/12.5 pt Galiard by Thomson Digital, Noida, India
Printed in Malaysia by Ho Printing (M) Sdn Bhd

1   2011

To Sheona

Contents

viii   *Contents*

Preface and Acknowledgments

In this history of American literature, I have tried to be responsive to the immense changes that have occurred over the past thirty years in the study of American literature. In particular, I have tried to register the plurality of American culture and American writing: the continued inventing of communities, and the sustained imagining of nations, that constitute the literary history of the United States. My aim here has been to provide the reader with a reasonably concise but also coherent narrative that concentrates on significant and symptomatic writers while also registering the range and variety of American writing. My focus has necessarily been on major authors and the particular texts that are generally considered to be their most important or representative work. I have also, however, looked at less central or canonical writers whose work demands the attention of anyone wanting to understand the full scope of American literature: work that illustrates important literary or cultural trends or helps to measure the multicultural character of American writing. In sum, my aim has been to offer as succinct an account as possible of the major achievements in American literature and of American difference: what it is that distinguishes the American literary tradition and also what it is that makes it extraordinarily, fruitfully diverse.

I have accumulated many debts in the course of working on this book. In particular, I would like to thank friends at the British Academy, including Andrew Hook, Jon Stallworthy, and Wynn Thomas; colleagues and friends at other universities, among them Kasia Boddy, Susan Castillo, Henry Claridge, Richard Ellis, the late Kate Fullbrook, Mick Gidley, Sharon Monteith, Judie Newman, Helen Taylor, and Nahem Yousaf; and colleagues and friends in other parts of Europe and in Asia and the United States, especially Saki Bercovitch, Bob Brinkmeyer, the late George Dekker, Jan Nordby Gretlund, Lothar Honnighausen, Bob Lee, Marjorie Perloff, and Waldemar Zacharasiewicz. Among my colleagues in the Department of Literature, I owe a special debt of thanks to Herbie Butterfield and Owen Robinson; I also owe special thanks to my many doctoral students who, over the years, have been gainfully employed in trying to keep my brain functioning. Sincere thanks are also due to Emma Bennett, the very best of editors, at Blackwell for steering this book to completion, to Theo Savvas for helping so much and so efficiently with the research and preparation, to Nick Hartley for his informed and invaluable advice on illustrations, and to Jack Messenger for being such an excellent copyeditor. On a more personal note, I would like to thank my older daughter, Catharine, for her quick wit, warmth, intelligence, and understanding, and for providing me with the very best of son-in-laws, Ricky Baldwin, and two perfect grandsons, Izzy and Sam; my older son, Ben, for his thoughtfulness, courage, commitment, and good company; my younger daughter, Jessica, for her lively intelligence, grace, and kindness, as well as her refusal to take anything I say on trust; and my younger son, Jack, who, being without language, constantly reminds me that there are other, deeper ways of communicating. Finally, as always, I owe the deepest debt of all to my wife, Sheona, for her patience, her good humor, her clarity and tenderness of spirit, and for her love and support, for always being there when I need her. Without her, this book would never have been completed: which is why, quite naturally, it is dedicated to her.

1

The First Americans

American Literature During the Colonial and Revolutionary Periods

Imagining Eden

"America is a poem in our eyes: its ample geography dazzles the imagination, and it will not wait long for metres." The words are those of Ralph Waldo Emerson, and they sum up that desire to turn the New World into words which has seized the imagination of so many Americans. But "America" was only one of the several names for a dream dreamed in the first instance by Europeans. "He invented America: a very great man," one character observes of Christopher Columbus in a Henry James novel; and so, in a sense, he did. Columbus, however, was following a prototype devised long before him and surviving long after him, the idea of a new land outside and beyond history: "a Virgin Countrey," to quote one early, English settler, "so preserved by Nature out of a desire to show mankinde fallen into the Old Age of Creation, what a brow of fertility and beauty she was adorned with when the world was vigorous and youthfull." For a while, this imaginary America obliterated the history of those who had lived American lives long before the Europeans came. And, as Emerson's invocation of "America ... a poem" discloses, it also erased much sense of American literature as anything other than the writing into existence of a New Eden.

Writing of the Colonial and Revolutionary Periods

Puritan narratives

There were, of course, those who dissented from this vision of a providential plan, stretching back to Eden and forward to its recovery in America. They included those Native Americans for whom the arrival of the white man was an announcement of the apocalypse. As one of them, an Iriquois chief called Handsome Lake, put it at the end of the eighteenth century, "white men came swarming into the country bringing with them cards, money, fiddles, whiskey, and blood corruption." They included those countless, uncounted African Americans brought over to America against their will, starting with the importation aboard a Dutch vessel of "Twenty Negars" into

---

A Brief History of American Literature. By Richard Gray
© 2011 Richard Gray

Jamestown, Virginia in 1619. They even included some European settlers, those for whom life in America was not the tale of useful toil rewarded that John Smith so enthusiastically told. And this was especially the case with settlers of very limited means, like those who went over as indentured servants, promising their labor in America as payment for their passage there. Dominant that vision was, though, and in its English forms, along with the writings of John Smith (1580–1631), it was given most powerful expression in the work of William Bradford (1590–1657) and John Winthrop (1588–1649). Bradford was one of the Puritan Separatists who set sail from Leyden in 1620 and disembarked at Plymouth. He became governor in 1621 and remained in that position until his death in 1657. In 1630 he wrote the first book of his history, *Of Plymouth Plantation*; working on it sporadically, he brought his account of the colony up to 1646, but he never managed to finish it. Nevertheless, it remains a monumental achievement. At the very beginning of *Of Plymouth Plantation*, Bradford announces that he will write in the Puritan "plain style, with singular regard to the simple truth in all things," as far as his "slender judgement" will permit. This assures a tone of humility, and a narrative that cleaves to concrete images and facts. But it still allows Bradford to unravel the providential plan that he, like other Puritans, saw at work in history. The book is not just a plain, unvarnished chronicle of events in the colony year by year. It is an attempt to decipher the meaning of those events, God's design for his "saints," that exclusive, elect group of believers destined for eternal salvation. The "special work of God's providence," as Bradford calls it, is a subject of constant analysis and meditation in *Of Plymouth Plantation*. Bradford's account of the arrival of the Pilgrim Fathers in the New World is notable, for instance, for the emphasis he puts on the perils of the "wilderness." "For the season was winter," he points out, "and they that know the winters of that country know them to be sharp and violent." The survival of the Puritans during and after the long voyage to the New World is seen as part of the divine plan. For Bradford, America was no blessed garden originally, but the civilizing mission of himself and his colony was to make it one: to turn it into evidence of their election and God's infinite power and benevolence.

This inclination or need to see history in providential terms sets up interesting tensions and has powerful consequences, in Bradford's book and similar Puritan narratives. *Of Plymouth Plantation* includes, as it must, many tales of human error and wickedness, and Bradford often has immense difficulty in explaining just how they form part of God's design. He can, of course, and does fall back on the primal fact of original sin. He can see natural disasters issuing from "the mighty hand of the Lord" as a sign of His displeasure and a test for His people; it is notable that the Godly weather storms and sickness far better than the Godless do in this book, not least because, as Bradford tells it, the Godly have a sense of community and faith in the ultimate benevolence of things to sustain them. Nevertheless, Bradford is hard put to it to explain to himself and the reader why "sundry notorious sins" break out so often in the colony. Is it that "the Devil may carry a greater spite against the churches of Christ and the Gospel here . . .?" Bradford wonders. Perhaps, he suggests, it is simply that "here . . . is not more evils in this kind" but just clearer perception of them; "they are here more discovered and seen and made public by due search, inquisition and due punishment." Bradford admits himself perplexed. And the fact that he does so adds dramatic tension to the narrative. Like so many great American stories, *Of Plymouth Plantation* is a search

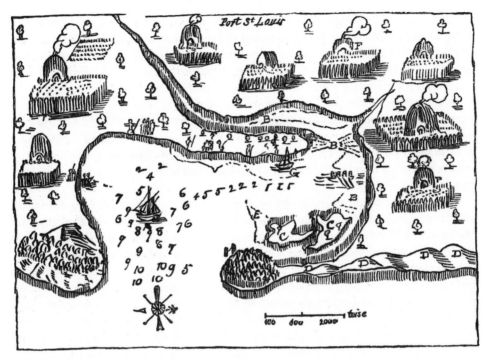

Figure 1.1   Samuel de Champlain's 1605 map of Plymouth Harbor where the Pilgrim Fathers landed. The Granger Collection/Topfoto.

for meaning. It has a narrator looking for what might lie behind the mask of the material event: groping, in the narrative present, for the possible significance of what happened in the past.

Which suggests another pivotal aspect of Bradford's book and so much Puritan narrative. According to the Puritan idea of providence at work in history, every material event does have meaning; and it is up to the recorder of that event to find out what it is. At times, that may be difficult. At others, it is easy. Bradford has no problem, for example, in explaining the slaughter of four hundred of the Pecquot tribe, and the burning of their village, by the English. The battle is seen as one in a long line waged by God's chosen people, part of the providential plan; and Bradford regards it as entirely appropriate that, once it is over, the victors should give "the praise thereof to God, who had wrought so wonderfully for them." Whether difficult or not, however, this habit of interpreting events with the help of a providential vocabulary was to have a profound impact on American writing – just as, for that matter, the moralizing tendency and the preference for fact rather than fiction, "God's truth" over "men's lies," also were.

Of Plymouth Plantation might emphasize the sometimes mysterious workings of providence. That, however, does not lead it to an optimistic, millennial vision of the future. On the contrary, as the narrative proceeds, it grows ever more elegiac. Bradford notes the passing of what he calls "the Common Course and Condition." As the material progress of the colony languishes, he records, "the Governor" – that is, Bradford himself – "gave way that they should set corn every man for his own particular"; every family is allowed "a parcel of land, according to the proportion of their number." The communal nature of the project is correspondingly diluted. The communitarian spirit of the first generation of immigrants, those like Bradford himself whom he calls "Pilgrims," slowly vanishes. The next generation moves off in search of better land and further prosperity; "and thus," Bradford laments, "was this poor church left, like an ancient mother grown old and forsaken of her children." The passing of the first generation and the passage of the second generation to other places and greater wealth inspires Bradford to that sense of elegy that was to become characteristic of narratives dramatizing the pursuit of dreams in America. It also pushes *Of Plymouth Plantation* towards a revelation of the central paradox in the literature of immigration – to be revealed again and again in American books – that material success leads somehow to spiritual failure.

Ten years after Bradford and his fellow Pilgrims landed at Plymouth, John Winthrop left for New England with nearly four hundred other Congregationalist Puritans. The Massachusetts Bay Company had been granted the right by charter to settle there and, prior to sailing, Winthrop had been elected Governor of the Colony, a post he was to hold for twelve of the nineteen remaining years of his life. As early as 1622, Winthrop had called England "this sinfull land"; and, playing variations on the by now common themes of poverty and unemployment, declared that "this Land grows weary of her Inhabitants." Now, in 1630, aboard the *Arbella* bound for the New World, Winthrop took the opportunity to preach a lay sermon, *A Modell of Christian Charity*, about the good society he and his fellow voyagers were about to build. As Winthrop saw it, they had an enormous responsibility. They had entered into a contract with God of the same kind He had once had with the Israelites, according to which He would protect them if they followed His word. Not only the eyes of God but "the eyes of all people are upon us," Winthrop declared. They were a special few, chosen for an errand into the wilderness. That made their responsibility all the greater; the divine punishment was inevitably worse for the chosen people than for the unbelievers.

Written as a series of questions, answers, and objections that reflect Winthrop's legal training, *A Modell of Christian Charity* is, in effect, a plea for a community in which "the care of the public must oversway all private respects." It is fired with a sense of mission and visionary example. "Wee shall finde that the God of Israell is among us, when tenn of us shall be able to resist a thousand of our enemies," Winthrop explained; "wee must Consider that wee shall be as a Citty upon a Hill." To achieve this divinely sanctioned utopia, he pointed out to all those aboard the *Arbella*, "wee must delight in each other, make others Condicions our owne ... allwayes having before our eyes our Commission and Community in the worke, our Community as members of the same body." This utopia would represent a translation of the ideal into the real, a fulfillment of the prophecies of the past, "a story and a by-word through the world" in the present, and a beacon for the future. It would not exclude social difference and distinction. But it would be united as the various organs of the human body were.

Along with the sense of providence and special mission, Winthrop shared with Bradford the aim of decoding the divine purpose, searching for the spiritual meanings behind material facts. He was also capable of a similar humility. His spiritual autobiography, for instance, *John Winthrop's Christian Experience* – which was written in 1637 and recounts his childhood and early manhood – makes no secret of his belief that he was inclined to "all kind of wickednesse" in his youth, then was allowed to come "to some peace and comfort in God" through no merit of his own. But there was a greater argumentativeness in Winthrop, more of an inclination towards analysis and debate. This comes out in his journal, which he began aboard the *Arbella*, and in some of his public utterances. In both a journal entry for 1645, for instance, and a speech delivered in the same year, Winthrop developed his contention that true community did not exclude social difference and required authority. This he did by distinguishing between what he called natural and civil liberty. Natural liberty he defined in his journal as something "common to man with beasts and other creatures." This liberty, he wrote, was "incompatible and inconsistent with authority and cannot endure the least restraint." Civil liberty, however, was "maintained and exercised in a way of subjection to authority"; it was the liberty to do what was "good, just, and honest." It was "the same kind of liberty wherewith Christ hath made us free," Winthrop argued. "Such is the liberty of the church under the authority of Christ," and also of the "true wife" under the authority of her husband." Like the true church or true wife, the colonist should choose this liberty, even rejoice in it, and so find a perfect freedom in true service.

Challenges to the Puritan oligarchy

John Winthrop found good reason for his belief in authority, and further demands on his capacity for argument, when faced with the challenge of Anne Hutchinson (1591–1643). A woman whom Winthrop himself described in his journal as being "of ready wit and bold spirit," Hutchinson insisted that good works were no sign of God's blessing. Since the elect were guaranteed salvation, she argued, the mediating role of the church between God and man became obsolete. This represented a serious challenge to the power of the Puritan oligarchy, which of course had Winthrop at its head. It could hardly be countenanced by them and so, eventually, Hutchinson was banished. Along with banishment went argument: Winthrop clearly believed that he had to meet the challenge posed by Hutchinson in other ways, and his responses in his work were several. In his spiritual autobiography, for instance, he pointedly dwells on how, as he puts it, "it pleased the Lord in my family exercise to manifest unto mee the difference between the Covenant of Grace and the Covenant of workes." This was because, as he saw it, Hutchinson's heresy was based on a misinterpretation of the Covenant of Grace. He also dwells on his own personal experience of the importance of doing good. In a different vein, but for a similar purpose, in one entry in his journal for 1638, Winthrop reports a story that, while traveling to Providence after banishment, Hutchinson "was delivered of a monstrous birth" consisting of "twenty-seven several lumps of man's seed, without any alteration or mixture of anything from the woman." This, Winthrop notes, was interpreted at the time as a sign of possible "error." Rumor and argument, personal experience and forensic expertise are all deployed in Winthrop's writings to meet the challenges he saw to his ideal community of the "Citty upon a Hill." The threat to the dominant theme of civilizing and Christianizing mission is, in effect, there, not only in Bradford's elegies for a communitarian ideal abandoned, but also in Winthrop's urgent attempts to meet and counter that threat by any rhetorical means necessary.

William Bradford also had to face challenges, threats to the purity and integrity of his colony; and Anne Hutchinson was not the only, or even perhaps the most serious,

challenge to the project announced on board the *Arbella*. The settlement Bradford
headed for so long saw a threat in the shape of Thomas Morton (1579?–1642?); and the
colony governed by Winthrop had to face what Winthrop himself described as the
"divers new and dangerous opinions" of Roger Williams (1603?–1683). Both Morton
and Williams wrote about the beliefs that brought them into conflict with the Puritan
establishment; and, in doing so, they measured the sheer diversity of opinion and vision
among English colonists, even in New England. Thomas Morton set himself up in 1626
as head of a trading post at Passonagessit which he renamed "Ma-re Mount." There, he
soon offended his Puritan neighbors at Plymouth by erecting a maypole, reveling with
the Indians and, at least according to Bradford (who indicated his disapproval by calling
the place where Morton lived "Merry-mount"), selling the "barbarous savages" guns.
To stop what Bradford called Morton's "riotous prodigality and excess," the Puritans
led by Miles Standish arrested him and sent him back to England in 1628. He was to
return twice, the first time to be rearrested and returned to England again and the
second to be imprisoned for slander. Before returning the second time, though, he
wrote his only literary work, *New English Canaan*, a satirical attack on Puritanism and
the Separatists in particular, which was published in 1637.

   In *New English Canaan*, Morton provides a secular, alternative version of how he
came to set up "Ma-re Mount," how he was arrested and then banished. It offers a sharp
contrast to the account of those same events given in *Of Plymouth Plantation*. As
Bradford describes it, Morton became "Lord of Misrule" at "Merry-mount," and
"maintained (as it were) a School of Atheism." Inviting "the Indian women for their
consorts" and then dancing around the maypole, Morton and his companions cavorted
"like so many fairies, or furies, rather." Worse still, Bradford reports, "this wicked man"
Morton sold "evil instruments" of war to the Indians: "O, the horribleness of this
villainy!" Morton makes no mention of this charge. What he does do, however, is
describe how he and his fellows set up a maypole "after the old English custom" and
then, "with the help of Salvages, that came thether of purpose to see the manner of our
Revels," indulge in some "harmeles mirth." A sense of shared values is clearly suggested
between the Anglicanism of Morton and his colleagues and the natural religion of the
Native Americans. There is a core of common humanity here, a respect for ordinary
pleasures, for custom, traditional authority and, not least, for the laws of hospitality
that, according to Morton, the Puritans lack. The Puritans are said to fear natural
pleasure, they are treacherous and inhospitable: Morton describes them, for instance,
killing their Indian guests, having invited them to a feast. Respecting neither their
divinely appointed leader, the king, nor the authority of church tradition, they live only
for what they claim is the "spirit" but Morton believes is material gain, the accumulation
of power and property.

   New English Canaan, as its title implies, is a promotional tract as well as a satire. It sets
out to show that New England is indeed a Canaan or Promised Land, a naturally
abundant world inhabited by friendly and even noble savages. Deserving British
colonization, all that hampers its proper development, Morton argues, is the religious
fanaticism of the Separatists and other Puritans. Morton divides his book in three. A
celebration of what he calls "the happy life of the Salvages," and their natural wisdom,
occupies the first section, while the second is devoted to the natural wealth of the
region. The satire is concentrated in the third section of what is not so much a history as

a series of loosely related anecdotes. Here, Morton describes the general inhumanity of the Puritans and then uses the mock-heroic mode to dramatize his own personal conflicts with the Separatists. Morton himself is ironically referred to as "the Great Monster" and Miles Standish, his principal opponent and captor, "Captain Shrimp." And, true to the conventions of mock-heroic, the mock-hero Shrimp emerges as the real villain, while the mock-villain becomes the actual hero, a defender of traditional Native American and English customs as well as a victim of Puritan zeal and bigotry. But that humor can scarcely conceal Morton's bitterness. Confined on an island, just before his removal to England, Morton reveals, he was brought "bottles of strong liquor" and other comforts by "Salvages"; by such gifts, they showed just how much they were willing to "unite themselves in a league of brotherhood with him." "So full of humanity are these infidels before those Christians," he remarks acidly. At such moments, Morton appears to sense just how far removed his vision of English settlement is from the dominant one. Between him and the Native Americans, as he sees it, runs a current of empathy; while between him and most of his fellow colonists there is only enmity – and, on the Puritan side at least, fear and envy.

That William Bradford feared and hated Morton is pretty evident. It is also clear that he had some grudging respect for Roger Williams, describing him as "godly and zealous" but "very unsettled in judgement" and holding "strange opinions." The strange opinions Williams held led to him being sentenced to deportation back to England in 1635. To avoid this, he fled into the wilderness to a Native American settlement. Purchasing land from the Nassagansetts, he founded Providence, Rhode Island, as a haven of dissent to which Anne Hutchinson came with many other runaways, religious exiles, and dissenters. Williams believed, and argued for his belief, that the Puritans should become Separatists. This clearly threatened the charter under which the Massachusetts Bay colonists had come over in 1630, including Williams himself, since it denied the royal prerogative. He also insisted that the Massachusetts Bay Company charter itself was invalid because a Christian king had no right over heathen lands. That he had no right, according to Williams, sprang from Williams's seminal belief, and the one that got him into most trouble: the separation of church and state and, more generally, of spiritual from material matters. Christianity had to be free from secular interests, Williams declared, and from the "foul embrace" of civil authority. The elect had to be free from civil constraints in their search for divine truth; and the civil magistrates had no power to adjudicate over matters of belief and conscience. All this Williams argued in his most famous work, *The Bloody Tenent of Persecution*, published in 1644. Here, in a dialogue between Truth and Peace, he pled for liberty of conscience as a natural right. He also contended that, since government is given power by the people, most of whom are unregenerate, it could not intervene in religious matters because the unregenerate had no authority to do so. But religious freedom did not mean civil anarchy. On the contrary, as he wrote in his letter "To the Town of Providence" in 1655, liberty of conscience and civil obedience should go hand in hand. Williams used the analogy of the ocean voyage. "There goes many a Ship to Sea, with many a Hundred Souls in One Ship," he observed. They could include all kinds of faiths. "Notwithstanding this liberty," Williams pointed out, "the Commander of this Ship ought to command the Ship's Course. This was "a true Picture of a Common-Wealth, or an human Combination, or Society."

Like Thomas Morton, Williams was also drawn to the Native Americans: those whom writers like Bradford and Winthrop tended to dismiss as "savage barbarians." His first work, *A Key into the Language of America*, published in 1643, actually focuses attention on them. "I present you with a *key*," Williams tells his readers in the preface; "this *key*, respects the *Native Language* of it, and happily may unlocke some Rarities concerning the *Natives* themselves, not yet discovered." Each chapter of Williams's *Key* begins with an "Implicit Dialogue," a list of words associated with a particular topic, the Nassagansett words on the left and their English equivalents on the right. This is followed by an "Observation" on the topic; and the topics in these chapters range from food, clothing, marriage, trade, and war to beliefs about nature, dreams, and religion. A "generall Observation" is then drawn, with cultural inferences and moral lessons being offered through meditation and analogy. Finally, there is a conclusion in the form of a poem that contrasts Indian and "English-man." These poems, in particular, show Williams torn between his admiration for the natural virtues of Native Americans, and their harmony with nature, and his belief that the "*Natives*" are, after all, pagans and so consigned to damnation. Implicit here, in fact, and elsewhere in the *Key* is an irony at work in a great deal of writing about the "noble savage." His natural nobility is conceded, even celebrated; but the need for him to be civilized and converted has to be acknowledged too. Civilized, however, he would invariably lose those native virtues that make him an object of admiration in the first place. And he could not then be used as Williams frequently uses him here, as a handy tool for attacking the degenerate habits of society. Williams's *Key* is an immense and imaginative project, founded on a recognition many later writers were to follow that the right tool for unlocking the secrets of America is a language actually forged there. But it remains divided between the natural and the civilized, the native and the colonist, the "false" and the "true." Which is not at all to its disadvantage: quite the opposite, that is the source of its interest – the measure of its dramatic tension and the mark of its authenticity.

Some colonial poetry

While Puritans were willing to concede the usefulness of history of the kind Bradford wrote or of sermons and rhetorical stratagems of the sort Winthrop favored, they were often less enthusiastic about poetry. "Be not so set upon poetry, as to be always poring on the passionate and measure pages," the New England cleric Cotton Mather warned; "beware of a boundless and sickly appetite for the reading of ... poems ... and let not the Circean cup intoxicate you." Of the verse that survives from this period, however, most of the finest and most popular among contemporaries inclines to the theological. The most popular is represented by *The Day of Doom*, a resounding epic about Judgment Day written by Michael Wigglesworth (1631–1705), *The Bay Psalm Book* (1640), and *The New England Primer* (1683?). *The Day of Doom* was the biggest selling poem in colonial America. In 224 stanzas in ballad meter, Wigglesworth presents the principal Puritan beliefs, mostly through a debate between sinners and Christ. A simple diction, driving rhythms, and constant marginal references to biblical sources are all part of Wigglesworth's didactic purpose. This is poetry intended to drive home its message, to convert some and to restore the religious enthusiasm of others. Many Puritan readers committed portions of the poem to memory; still more read it aloud to their families. The sheer simplicity and fervor of its message made it an ideal instrument for communicating and confirming faith. So it is, perhaps, hardly surprising that Cotton Mather could put aside his distrust of poetry when it came to a work like *The Day of Doom*. At Wigglesworth's death, in fact, Mather confessed his admiration for the poet: who, Mather said, had written for "the Edification of such Readers, as are for Truth's dressed up in *Plaine Meeter*."

Even more popular than *The Day of Doom*, however, were *The Bay Psalm Book* and *The New England Primer*. Only the Bible was more widely owned in colonial New England. *The Bay Psalm Book* was the first publishing project of the Massachusetts Bay Colony, and offered the psalms of David translated into idiomatic English and adapted to the basic hymn stanza form of four lines with eight beats in each line and regular rhymes. The work was a collaborative one, produced by twelve New England divines. And one of them, John Cotton, explained in the preface that what they had in mind was "Conscience rather than Elegance, fidelity rather than poetry." "We have ... done our endeavour to make a plain and familiar translation," Cotton wrote. "If therefore the verses are not always so smoothe and elegant as some may desire ..., let them consider that God's Altar need not our polishings." What was needed, Cotton insisted, was "a plain translation." And, if the constraints imposed by the hymn stanza form led sometimes to a tortured syntax, then neither the translators nor the audience appear to have minded. The psalms were intended to be sung both in church and at home, and they were. *The Bay Psalm Book* was meant to popularize and promote faith, and it did. Printed in England and Scotland as well as the colonies, it went through more than fifty editions over the century following its first appearance. It perfectly illustrated the Puritan belief in an indelible, divinely ordained connection between the mundane and the miraculous, the language and habits of everyday and the apprehension of eternity. And it enabled vast numbers of people, as Cotton put it, to "sing the Lord's songs ... in our English tongue."

The New England Primer had a similar purpose and success. Here, the aim was to give every child "and apprentice" the chance to read the catechism and digest improving moral precepts. With the help of an illustrated alphabet, poems, moral statements, and a formal catechism, the young reader was to learn how to read and how to live according to the tenets of Puritan faith. So, for instance, the alphabet was introduced through a series of rhymes designed to offer moral and religious instruction. The letter "A," for example, was introduced through the rhyme, "In *Adams* Fall/We sinned all." Clearly, the *Primer* sprang from a belief in the value of widespread literacy as a means of achieving public order and personal salvation. Equally clearly, as time passed and the *Primer* went through numerous revisions, the revised versions reflected altering priorities. The 1758 revision, for instance, declares a preference for "more grand noble Words" rather than "diminutive Terms"; a 1770 version describes literacy as more a means of advancement than a route to salvation; and an 1800 edition opts for milder versified illustrations of the alphabet ("A was an apple pie"). But this tendency to change in response to changing times was a reason for the durability and immense popularity of the *Primer*: between 1683 and 1830, in fact, it sold over five million copies. And, at its inception at least, it was further testament to the Puritan belief that man's word, even in verse, could be used as a vehicle for God's truth.

That belief was not contested by the two finest poets of the colonial period, Anne Bradstreet (1612?–1672) and Edward Taylor (1642?–1729). It was, however, set in tension with other impulses and needs that helped make their poetry exceptionally vivid and dramatic. With Bradstreet, many of the impulses, and the tensions they generated, sprang from the simple fact that she was a woman. Bradstreet came with her husband to Massachusetts in 1630, in the group led by John Winthrop. Many years later, she wrote to her children that at first her "heart rose" when she "came into this country" and "found a new world and new manners." "But," she added, "after I was convinced it was the way of God, I submitted to it and joined the church in Boston." What she had to submit to was the orthodoxies of faith and behavior prescribed by the Puritan fathers. Along with this submission to patriarchal authority, both civil and religious, went acknowledgment of – or, at least, lip service to – the notion that, as a woman, her

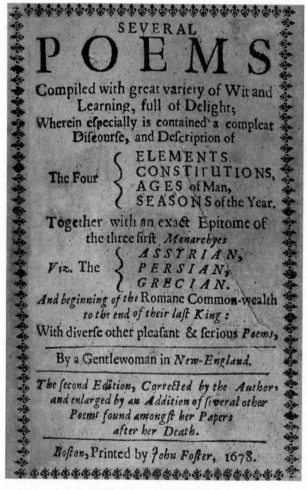

Figure 1.2 Title page of *The Tenth Muse Lately Sprung Up in America* by Anne Bradstreet, Boston, 1678. © The British Library Board. C.39.b.48(1).

primary duties were to her family, as housekeeper, wife, and mother. Bradstreet raised eight children. Despite this, she found time to write poetry that was eventually published in London in 1650 as *The Tenth Muse Lately Sprung Up in America*. Publication was arranged by Bradstreet's brother-in-law, who added a preface in which he felt obliged to point out that the poetry had not been written to the neglect of family duties.

Writing in a climate of expectations such as this, Bradstreet made deft poetic use of what many readers of the time would have seen as her oxymoronic title of woman poet. One of her strategies was deference. In "The Prologue" to *The Tenth Muse*, for instance, Bradstreet admitted that "To sing of wars, captains, and of kings,/Of cities founded, commonwealths begun," was the province of men. Her "mean pen," she assured the reader, would deal with other matters; her "lowly lines" would concern themselves with humbler subjects. The deference, however, was partly assumed. It was, or became, a rhetorical device; a confession of humility could and did frequently lead on to the claim that her voice had its own song to sing in the great chorus. "I heard the merry grasshopper ... sing,/" she wrote in "Contemplations," "The black-clad cricket bear a second part." "Shall creatures abject thus their voices raise/," she asked, "And in their kind resound their Maker's praise,/Whilst I, as mute, can warble forth higher lays?" Playing upon what her readers, and to a certain extent what she herself, expected of a female, she also aligned her creativity as a woman with her creativity as a writer. So, in "The Author to her Book" (apparently written in 1666 when a second edition of her work was being considered), her poems became the "ill-form'd offspring" of her "feeble brain," of whom she was proud despite their evident weaknesses. "If for thy father asked," she tells her poems, "say thou had'st none:/And for thy mother, she alas is poor,/Which caus'd her thus to send thee out of door." Identifying herself as a singular and single mother here, Bradstreet plays gently but ironically with Puritan sensibilities, including her own. This is a gesture of at once humility and pride, since it remains unclear whether Bradstreet's "ill-form'd offspring" have no father in law or in fact. They might be illegitimate or miraculous. Perhaps they are both.

An edition of the poems of Bradstreet was published in Boston six years after her death, with a lot of new material, as *Several Poems Compiled with Great Variety of Wit and Learning*. It contains most of her finest work. It is here, in particular, that the several tensions in her writing emerge: between conventional subject matter and personal experience, submission to and rebellion against her lot as a woman in a patriarchal society, preparation for the afterlife and the pleasures of this world, and between simple humility and pride. The focus switches from the public to the private, as she writes about childbirth ("Before the Birth of One of Her Children"), married love ("To My Dear and Loving Husband"), her family growing up ("In reference to Her Children, 23 June, 1659"), about personal loss and disaster ("Upon the Burning of Our House, July 10th, 1666") and, in particular, about bereavement ("In memory of My Dear Grandchild Elizabeth Bradstreet, Who Deceased August, 1665, Being a Year and Half Old"). What is especially effective and memorable about, say, the poems of married love is their unabashed intimacy. "If ever two were one, then surely we./If ever man were loved by wife then thee," she writes in "To My Dear and Loving Husband." And, in "A Letter to Her Husband, Absent Upon Public Employment," she consoles herself while her beloved is gone by looking at their children: "true living pictures of their father's face," as she calls them, "fruits which through thy heat I bore." There is ample time to dwell here on what Bradstreet calls her "magazine of earthly store," and to reflect that, even when she is "ta'en away unto eternity," testimony to the pleasures of the things and thoughts of time will survive – in the "dear remains" of her "little babes" and her verse. And the one dear remain will find delight and instruction in the other. "This book by any yet unread,/I leave for you when I am dead,/" she writes in a poem addressed "To My Dear Children," "That being gone, here you may find/What was your living mother's mind."

A similar sense of intimacy and engagement is one of the secrets of the work of Edward Taylor, which was virtually unpublished during his lifetime – a collected edition, *The Poetical Works of Edward Taylor*, did not appear, in fact, until 1939. Like Bradstreet, Taylor was born in England; he then left to join the Massachusetts Bay Colony in 1668. After studying at Harvard, he settled into the profession of minister for the rest of his life. Marrying twice, he fathered fourteen children, many of whom died in infancy. He began writing poetry even before he joined his small, frontier congregation in Westfield, but his earliest work tended towards the public and conventional. It was not until 1674 that, experimenting with different forms and styles, he started over the next eight or nine years to write in a more personal and memorable vein: love poems to his wife-to-be ("Were but my Muse an Huswife Good"), spiritual meditations on natural events or as Taylor called them "occurants" ("The Ebb & Flow"), and emblematic, allegorical accounts of the smaller creatures of nature and domestic objects ("Huswifery"). These poems already manifest some of Taylor's characteristic poetic habits. "Upon A Spider Catching a Fly," for instance, written around 1680–1682, begins with the kind of minute particularization of nature that was to become typical of later New England poets like Emily Dickinson and Robert Frost: "Thou Sorrow, venom elfe/Is this thy ploy,/To spin a web out of thyselfe/To catch a Fly?/For Why?" Gradually, the intimate tone of address is switched to God, who is asked to "break the Cord" with which "Hells Spider," the Devil, would "tangle Adams race." What is memorable about the poem is how closely Taylor attends to both the material facts of the spider and the spiritual truth it is chosen to emblematize: symbolic meaning is not developed at the expense of concrete event. And what is just as memorable is the way Taylor uses an elaborate conceit and intricate stanzaic form as both a discipline to his meditations and a means of channeling, then relaxing emotion. So, in the final stanza, the poet anticipates eventually singing to the glory of God, "when pearcht on high" – "And thankfully,/" he concludes, "For joy." And that short last line, consisting of just two words, at once acts as a counterpoint to the conclusion of the first stanza ("For why?") and allows Taylor to end his poem on a moment of pure, spiritual elation.

The experience of faith was, in fact, central to Taylor's life and his work. About 1647, he began writing metrical paraphrases of the Psalms. Recalling the *Bay Psalm Book*, it is nevertheless in these poems that Taylor's distinctively meditative voice starts to be given freer rein. More important, he also began to bring together his vision of the history of salvation to produce his first major work, *Gods Determinations touching his Elect*. A collection of thirty-five poems, this traces the "Glorious Handywork" of creation, dramatizes a debate between Justice and Mercy over the fate of mankind, then describes the combat between Christ and Satan for human souls. Some years after beginning *Gods*

Determinations, in 1682, Taylor turned to what is his finest longer work, *Preparatory Meditations before My Approach to the Lords Supper.* Usually composed after he had prepared a sermon or preaching notes, the 217 poems comprising this sequence are personal meditations "Chiefly upon the Doctrine preached upon the Day of administration." In them, Taylor tries to learn lessons gathered from the Sacrament day's biblical text, which also acts as the poem's title. They are at once a form of spiritual discipline, with the poet subjecting himself to rigorous self-examination; petitions to God to prepare him for the immediate task of preaching and administering the Lord's Supper; and a private diary or confession of faith. And, as in so many of his poems, Taylor uses an intricate verse form, elaborate word-play and imagery to organize his meditations and release his emotions.

Taylor belongs in a great tradition of meditative writing, one that includes the English poets George Herbert and John Donne, and an equally great tradition of New England writing: one in which the imaginative anticipation of dying becomes a means of understanding how to live. So it is perhaps not surprising that, after suffering a severe illness in 1720, he wrote three versions of "A Valediction to all the World preparatory for Death 3d of the 11th 1720" and two versions of "A Fig for thee Oh! Death." What perhaps is surprising, and moving, is how these poems acknowledge the loveliness of the world while bidding it farewell. The strength of his feeling for the things of the earth, and even more for family and vocation, becomes here a measure of the strength of his faith. It is only faith, evidently, and the firm conviction that (as he puts it in one of the *Preparatory Meditations*) his heart "loaded with love" will "ascend/Up to ... its bridegroom, bright, & Friend" that makes him content to give up all that he has not only come to know but also to cherish. In Taylor's poems, we find not so much conflict as continuity; not tension but a resolution founded on tough reasoning and vigorous emotion, patient attention to the ordinary and passionate meditation on the mysterious – above all, on a firmly grounded, fervently sustained faith. He loves the world, in short, but he loves God more.

Enemies within and without

The Puritan faith that Edward Taylor expressed and represented so vividly found itself challenged, very often, by enemies within and without. As for the enemies outside the Puritan community, they included above all the people the settlers had displaced, the Native Americans. And the challenge posed by what one Puritan called "this barbarous Enemy" was most eloquently expressed by those who had come under the enemy's power, however briefly. In February, 1676, a woman named Mary White Rowlandson (1637?–1711) was captured by a group of Narragansett Indians, along with her children. Many of her neighbors and relatives were also captured or killed, one of her children died soon after being captured, and the other two became separated from her. Rowlandson herself was finally released and returned to her husband in the following May; and the release of her two surviving children was effected several weeks later. Six years after this, she published an account of her experience, the full title of which gives some flavor of its approach and a clue to its purpose: *The Sovereignty and Goodness of GOD, Together With the Faithfulness of His Promises Displayed: Being a Narrative of the Captivity and Restauration of Mrs Mary Rowlandson.* The book was immensely popular, and remained so on into the nineteenth century; and it helped to inaugurate a peculiarly American literary form, the captivity narrative. There had been captivity narratives since the earliest period of European exploration, but Rowlandson's account established both the appeal of such narratives and the form they would usually take: combining, as it does, a vivid portrait of her sufferings and losses with an emphatic interpretation of their meaning. The moral framework of the *Narrative* is, in fact, clearly and instructively dualistic: on the one side are the "Pagans" and on the other the Christians. The Native Americans are, variously, "ravenous Beasts," "Wolves," "black creatures" resembling the Devil in their cruelty, savagery, and capacity for lying. Christians like Rowlandson who suffer at their hands are upheld only by "the wonderfull mercy of God" and the "remarkable passages of providence" that enable them to survive and sustain their faith.

As for the enemies within, nothing illustrated the Puritan fear of them more than the notorious witch trials that took place in Salem, Massachusetts in 1692, during the course of which 19 people were hanged, one was pressed to death, 55 were frightened or tortured into confessions of guilt, 150 were imprisoned, and more than 200 were named as deserving arrest. What brought those trials about, the sense of a special mission now threatened and the search for a conspiracy, an enemy to blame and purge from the commonwealth, is revealed in a work first published in 1693, *The Wonders of the Invisible World* by Cotton Mather (1663–1728). Mather, the grandson of two important religious leaders of the first generation of Puritan immigrants (including John Cotton, after whom he was named), wrote his book at the instigation of the Salem judges. "The New Englanders are a people of God settled in those, which were once the devil's territories," Mather announces. For Mather, the people, mostly women, tried and convicted at Salem represent a "terrible plague of evil angels." They form part of "an horrible plot against the country" which "if it were not seasonably discovered, would probably blow up, and pull down all the churches." A feeling of immediate crisis and longer-term decline is explained as the result of a conspiracy, the work of enemy insiders who need to be discovered and despatched if the community is to recover, then realize its earlier utopian promise. It is the dark side of the American dream, the search for someone or something to blame when that dream appears to be failing. Mather was sounding a sinister chord here that was to be echoed by many later Americans, and opening up a vein of reasoning and belief that subsequent American writers were to subject to intense, imaginative analysis.

But Cotton Mather was more than just the author of one of the first American versions of the conspiracy theory. He produced over 400 publications during his lifetime. Among them were influential scientific works, like *The Christian Philosopher* (1720), and works promoting "reforming societies" such as *Bonifacius; or, Essays to Do Good* (1710), a book that had an important impact on Benjamin Franklin. He also encouraged missionary work among African American slaves, in *The Negro Christian-ized* (1706), and among Native Americans, in *India Christiana* (1721). But here, too, in his encouragement of Christian missions to those outside the true faith a darker side of Puritanism, or at least of the Cotton Mather strain, is evident. Mather's belief in the supreme importance of conversion led him, after all, to claim that a slave taught the true faith was far better off than a free black; and it sprang, in the first place, from a low opinion of both African and Native Americans, bordering on contempt. For example, in his life of John Eliot, "the apostle of the Indians" whom Nathaniel Hawthorne was later to praise, Mather made no secret of his belief that "the natives of the country now possessed by New Englanders" had been "forlorn and wretched" ever since "their first herding here." They were "miserable savages," "stupid and senseless," Mather declared. They had "no *arts*," "except just so far as to maintain their brutish conversation," "little, if any, tradition ... worthy of ... notice." Such were "the miserable people" Eliot set out to save and, in view of their condition, he had "a double work incumbent on him." He had, Mather concluded, "to make men" of the Native Americans "ere he could hope to see them saints"; they had to be "*civilized* ere they could be *Christianized*."

Mather's account of Eliot's work among the Indians shows just how much for him, as for other early European settlers, the projects of civilization and conversion, creating wealth and doing good, went hand in hand. It comes from his longest and arguably most interesting work, *Magnalia Christi Americana; or, the Ecclesiastical History of New England*, published in 1702. This book is an immensely detailed history of New England and a series of eminent lives, and it reflects Mather's belief that the past should be used to instruct the present and guide the future. Each hero chosen for description and eulogy, like Eliot, is made to fit a common saintly pattern, from the portrait of his conversion to his deathbed scene. Yet each is given his own distinctive characteristics, often expressive of Mather's own reforming interests and always illustrating his fundamental conviction that, as he puts it, " The *First Age* was the *Golden Age*." This is exemplary history, then. It is also an American epic, one of the very first, in which the author sets about capturing in words what he sees as the promise of the nation. "I WRITE the *Wonders* of the CHRISTIAN RELIGION," Mather announces in "A General Introduction" to *Magnalia Christi Americana*, "flying from the Depravations of *Europe*, to the *American Strand*." The echo of the *Aeneid* is an intimation of what Mather is after. He is hoping to link the story of his people to earlier epic migrations. As later references to the "*American Desart*" testify, he is also suggesting a direct analogy with the journey of God's chosen people to the Promised Land. His subject is a matter of both history and belief: like so many later writers of American epic, in other words, he is intent on describing both an actual and a possible America.

Not everyone involved in the Salem witchcraft trials remained convinced that they were justified by the need to expose a dangerous enemy within. Among those who came to see them as a serious error of judgment, and morality, was one of the judges at the trials, Samuel Sewall (1652–1730). An intensely thoughtful man, Sewall wrote a journal from 1673 to 1728, which was eventually published as *The Diary of Samuel Sewall* in 1973. It offers an insight into the intimate thoughts, the trials and private tribulations of someone living at a time when Puritanism no longer exerted the power it once did over either the civil or religious life of New England. Sewall notes how in 1697 he felt compelled to make a public retraction of his actions as one of the Salem judges, "asking pardon of man" for his part in the proceedings against supposed witches, and, he adds, "especially desiring prayers that God, who has an Unlimited Authority, would pardon that Sin" he had committed. He also records how eventually, following the dictates of his conscience, he felt "call'd" to write something against "the Trade fetching Negroes from Guinea." "I had a strong inclination to Write something about it," he relates in an entry for June 19, 1700, "but it wore off." Only five days after this, however, a work authored by Sewall attacking the entire practice of slavery, *The Selling of Joseph: A Memorial,* was published in Boston. In it, he attacked slavery as a violation of biblical precept and practice, against natural justice since "all men, as they are the Sons of *Adam,* are Coheirs; and have equal Right unto Liberty," and destructive of the morals of both slaves and masters." Sewall was a man eager to seek divine counsel on all matters before acting. This was the case whether the matter was a great public one, like the issues of witchcraft and the slave trade, or a more private one, such as the question of his marrying for a third time. His journals reveal the more private side of Puritanism: a daily search for the right path to follow in order to make the individual journey part of the divine plan. They also reveal a habit of meditation, a scrupulously detailed mapping of personal experiences, even the most intimate, that was to remain ingrained in American writing long after the Puritan hegemony had vanished.

Trends towards the secular and resistance

The travel journals of two other writers, Sarah Kemble Knight (1666–1727) and William Byrd of Westover (1674–1744), suggest the increasingly secular tendencies of this period. Both Knight and Byrd wrote accounts of their journeys through parts of America that tend to concentrate on the social, the curious people and manners they encountered along the way. There is relatively little concern, of the kind shown in earlier European accounts of travels in the New World, with the abundance of nature, seen as either Eden or Wilderness. Nor is there any sense at all of being steered by providence: God may be mentioned in these journals, but rarely as a protective guide. Knight composed her journal as a description of a trip she took from Boston to New York and then back again in 1704–1705. It did not reach printed form until the next century, when it appeared as *The Journals of Madam Knight* (1825): but it was "published" in the way many manuscripts were at the time, by being circulated among friends. Her writings reveal a lively, humorous, gossipy woman alert to the comedy and occasional beauty of life in early America – and aware, too, of the slightly comic figure she herself sometimes cuts, "sitting Stedy," as she puts it, "on my Nagg." She describes in detail how she is kept awake at night in a local inn by the drunken arguments of "some of the Town tope-ers in [the] next Room." She records, with a mixture of disbelief and amused disgust, meeting a family that is "the picture of poverty" living in a "little Hutt" that was "one of the wretchedest I ever saw." Sometimes, Knight is struck by the beauty of the landscape she passes through. She recalls, for instance, how moved she was by the sight of the woods lit up by the moon – or, as she has it, by "Cynthia," "the kind Conductress of the night." Even here, however, the terms in which she expresses her excitement are a sign of her true allegiances. "The Tall and thick trees at a distance," she explains, "when the moon glar'd through the branches, fill'd my Imagination with the pleasant delusion of a Sumpteous citty, fill'd with famous Buildings and churches." Nature is most beautiful, evidently, when it evokes thoughts of culture; "the dolesome woods," as she calls them elsewhere in her journal, are at their best when they excite memories of, or better still lead to, town.

The situation is more complicated with William Byrd of Westover. Born the heir of a large estate in Virginia, Byrd was educated in England and only made Virignia his permanent home in 1726. Byrd claimed, in one of his letters (published eventually in

1977 in *The Correspondence of the Three William Byrds*), that in America he lived "like ... the patriarchs." And, to the extent that this was possible in a new country, he certainly did. For he was one of the leading members of what eventually became known as the "first families of Virginia," those people who formed the ruling class by the end of the eighteenth century – in the colony of Virginia and, arguably, elsewhere in the South. The "first families" claimed to be of noble English origin. Some of them no doubt were. But it is likely that the majority of them were, as one contemporary writer Robert Beverley II (1673–1722) put it in *The History and Present State of Virginia* (1722), "of low Circumstances ... such as were willing to seek their Fortunes in a Foreign Country." Whatever their origins, they had to work hard since as one of them, William Fitzhugh (1651–1701), pointed out in a letter written in 1691, "without a constant care and diligent Eye, a well-made plantation will run to Ruin." "'Tis no small satisfaction to me," another great landowner, Robert "King" Carter (1663–1732), wrote in 1720, "to have a pennyworth for my penny"; and to this end he, and other Virginia gentlemen like him, were painstaking in the supervision of their landholdings. Nevertheless, they were keen to use their painstakingly acquired wealth to assume the manners and prerogatives of an aristocracy, among which was the appearance of a kind of aristocratic indolence – what one writer of the time, Hugh Jones (1670–1760), described in *The Present State of Virginia* (1724) as the gentleman's "easy way of living."

Byrd, of course, did not have to struggle to acquire wealth, he inherited it. Once he had done so, however, he worked hard to sustain that wealth and even acquire more. He personally supervised his properties, once he settled in Virginia, arranging for the planting of crops, orchards, and gardens; he also attended to his duties within his own community and in the county and the colony. And he was just as intent as his wealthy neighbors were on assuming the appearance of idle nobility. When writing back to friends in England, for instance, he tended to turn his life in Virginia into a version of the pastoral. As his small hymns to the garden of the South in his letters suggest, the desire to paint plantation life as a kind of idyll sprang from two, related things, for Byrd and others like him: a feeling of exile from the centers of cultural activity and a desire to distance the specters of provincialism and money-grubbing. Exiled from the "polite pleasures" of the mother country, in a place that he once described as the "great wilderness" of America, Byrd was prompted to describe his plantation home as a place of natural abundance, ripe simplicity, and indolence. Describing it in this way, he also separated himself from the work ethic that prevailed further north. A clear dividing line was being drawn between him – and the life he and his social equals in Virginia led – and, on the one hand, England, and on the other, New England. In the process, Byrd was dreaming and articulating what was surely to become the dominant image of the South.

Byrd is mainly remembered now for *The History of the Dividing Line betwixt Virginia and North Carolina*, the account of his participation in the 1728 survey of the southern border of Virginia. In this travel journal, written in 1729 and first published in 1841, Byrd considers a number of divisions quite apart from the one announced in the title. He talks, for instance, about the difference or division between the "Frugal and Industrious" settlers of the northern colonies and the less energetic settlers to the south. "For this reason," he explains, "New England improved much faster than Virginia." He talks about the division between Indians and whites, particularly the early

European explorers. The Indians, Byrd reflects, "are healthy & Strong, with Constitutions untainted by Lewdness." "I cannot think," he adds, "the Indians were much greater Heathens than the first Adventurers." He talks about the divisions between men and women. "The distemper of laziness seizes the men," in the backwoods, he suggests, "much oftener than the women." And he talks about the differences, the division between his homeplace and North Carolina. For him, North Carolina is "Lubberland." "Plenty and a warm sun," Byrd avers, confirm all North Carolinians, and especially the men, "in their disposition to laziness for their whole lives"; "they loiter away their lives, like Solomon's sluggard, with their arms across, and at the winding up of the year scarcely have bread to eat."

Byrd's comic description of the inhabitants of North Carolina anticipates the Southwestern humorists of the nineteenth century, and all those other American storytellers who have made fun of life off the beaten track. It is also sparked off by one of a series of divisions in *The History of the Dividing Line* that are determined by the difference between sloth and industry: perhaps reflecting Byrd's suspicion that his own life, the contrast between its surfaces and its reality, measures a similar gap. Quite apart from such dividing lines, Byrd's account of his journey is as frank and lively as Knight's is. And the tone is even franker and livelier in *The Secret History of the Dividing Line*, an account of the same expedition as the one *The History of the Dividing Line* covers, first published in 1929. In *The Secret History*, as its title implies, what Byrd dwells on is the private exploits of the surveyors: their drinking, gambling, joking, squabbling and their encounters with more than one "dark angel" or "tallow-faced wench." Throughout his adventures, "Steddy," as Byrd calls himself in both histories, keeps his course and maintains his balance: negotiating his journey through divisions with the appearance of consummate ease.

Of course, the ease was very often just that, a matter of appearance, here in the histories of the dividing line and elsewhere. Or, if not that simply, it was a matter of conscious, calculated choice. As an alternative to the ruminative Puritan or the industrious Northerner, Byrd and others like him modeled themselves on the idea of the indolent, elegant aristocrat: just as, as an alternative to the noise and bustle of London, they modeled their accounts of their homeplace in imitation of the pastoral ideal. The divisions and accommodations they were forced into, or on occasion chose, were the product of the conflict between their origins and aspirations. They were also a consequence of the differences they perceived between the world they were making in their part of the American colonies and the ones being made in other parts. And they were also, and not least, a probable response to their own sense that the blood of others was on their hands. Anticipating the later Southern argument in defense of slavery, they turned their slaves, rhetorically, into "children" who positively needed the feudal institution of an extended family, with a benevolent patriarch at its head, for guidance, support, and protection. In the process, they had an enormous impact on how writers write and many others talk about one vital part of the American nation.

The trend towards the secular in the work of Knight and Byrd is also noticeable in the poetry of the period. Cotton Mather had attacked poetry as the food of "a boundless and sickly appetite," for its fictive origins and sensual appeal. Benjamin Franklin, the presiding genius of the American Enlightenment, was inclined to dismiss it because it was not immediately useful, functional. However, to this charge that poetry makes nothing happen, others replied to the contrary: that it did clear the ground and break new wood – in short, that it helped in the making of Americans. The full force of that reply had to wait until the Revolution, when writers and critics began to insist that the new American nation needed an American literature, and more specifically an American poetry, in order to announce and understand itself. But, even before that, there were poets in the colonies who were trying to turn the old European forms to new American uses. Even Cotton Mather, after all, tried to identify and celebrate the "Wonders" of the New World and so wrote a proto-epic, *Magnalia Christi Americana*. Another writer, Joel Barlow, was to make his own attempt, towards the end of the eighteenth century, at a more specifically poetic epic in *Vision of Columbus*. And two notable writers, well before that, tried their hands at producing American versions of the two other most common forms of early eighteenth-century poetry besides the epic, both of them also derived from neoclassical models, the satire and the pastoral. The two writers were Ebenezer Cook (1667–1733) and Richard Lewis (1700?–1734).

Cook divided his time between London and Maryland. He was a prolific writer, as well as a planter and tobacco merchant, but his claim to fame rests on a satirical poem he published in 1708, *The Sot-weed Factor; or, a Voyage to Maryland &c.* Written in the form of Hudibrastic verse – so named after the English poet, Samuel Butler's satire of the Puritans, *Hudibras* – *The Sot-weed Factor* presents us with a narrator who visits America only to be robbed, cheated, stripped of his guide, horse and clothes, and, in general, appalled by what he sees as the anarchy and squalor of his new surroundings. The rollicking tetrameter lines, odd rhymes and syntax help to paint a carnival portrait of life on the frontier and in the backwoods, in small towns and in "*Annapolis* .../A City Situate on a Plain." And, having left "*Albion's* Rocks" in the opening lines, the narrator eagerly returns there at the conclusion some 700 lines later. "Embarqu'd and waiting for a Wind,/I left this dreadful Curse behind," he declares, damning America as he departs. Finally, he calls on God to complete the damnation of America. "May Wrath Divine then lay those regions wast/," he prays, "Where no Mans faithful, nor a Woman Chast." The bombastic character of the curses, like the representation of the narrator throughout *The Sot-weed Factor*, alerts the reader to what is happening here. The satire apparently directed at American vulgarity is, in fact, being leveled at English snobbery, preciousness, and self-satisfaction. Cook has taken an English form and turned it to American advantage. In the process, he has developed a peculiarly American style of comedy in which the contrast between the genteel and the vernacular is negotiated, to the advantage of the latter, through a use of language that is fundamentally ironic.

Richard Lewis was just as prolific a writer as Cook; and, in the time he could spare from being a politician in Maryland, he wrote, among other things, forms of the pastoral that implied or even asserted the superiority of American nature. "A Journey from Patapsko to Annapolis, April 4, 1730" (1732), for instance, begins by acknowledging its illustrious ancestry, with a quotation from the first pastoral poem, the *Georgics* of Virgil. Lewis then includes, later on in his poetical journey, allusions to the *Seasons* by the Scottish poet James Thomson and John Dryden's translation of the *Georgics*. But, while deferring in this way to the European model he is using and the European masters who have preceded him, Lewis is nevertheless eager to insist on the specific advantages and special beauties of the countryside around him. So he dwells on the idyllic life lived here by "the *Monarch-Swain*," with "His *Subject-Flocks*" and "well-tilled Lands." In a way, this is a commonplace of European pastoral too. Lewis, however, devotes more attention than his European predecessors tended to do to the ideas of patient toil rewarded, the value of self-subsistence and the pleasures of abundance. As Lewis turns his attention from a happy farmer and his family to the burgeoning countryside around him, he espies a humming-bird, the beauty of whose "ever-flutt'ring wings" becomes a paradigm for and measure of the superiority of American nature. The phoenix, the bird of classical myth, pales beside the American bird, just as the site of pastoral in the Old World pales beside what Lewis now calls the "blooming Wilderness" of the New. Not content to stop there, the poet then asks us to behold the wonders of "the out-stretch'd *Land*" beyond wood and plantation. We turn our eyes, in effect, to what so many American poets were to take as the primary fact of their land: space, its apparent endlessness. After this, admittedly, the poetical journey concludes in conventional fashion, with references to the journey of life and prayers to the "great CREATOR." But Lewis has already staked a claim for difference. He has already, earlier on in the poem, broken new ground in the depiction of the American landscape and the development of the American pastoral form.

Although the eighteenth century in America witnessed a growing trend towards the secular, it would be wrong to deny the continuing importance and power of religious influences and writing. In the Southwest, for example, the century witnessed a significant growth of interest in and worship of the Virgin of Guadaloupe. According to legend, the Virgin appeared to a poor Indian in 1531 on a sacred site associated with an Indian goddess of fertility. She asked for a cathedral to be built to her over the site of an Aztec place of worship, which it then was. And the first account of this miraculous encounter was eventually written down a century later, in 1649, in Nahuatl, the language of the Aztecs. The Virgin was and remains a syncretic religious figure. The "somewhat dark" face and Indian features attributed to her in the original account, and in the numerous paintings and statues of her created ever since, make her a Native American Virgin; the word "Guadaloupe" is itself most probably a hybrid, derived from the Nahuatl word for "snake" and the Spanish word for "crush" and referring to a gesture often given to the Virgin Mary in statues, of crushing the snake. During the eighteenth century, however, the miscegenation of Spanish and Indian that marked the original legend became less important than the use of the Virgin of Guadaloupe as an emblem of New World hybridity, the *mestizo*. She became a potent religious, cultural, and political icon for Mexican Americans. She remains so; and she is a measure of just how far removed many Americans of the time were from the creed or even the influence of the Enlightenment.

The same is true for some American writers situated further east. In 1755, for instance, *Some Account of the Fore part of the Life of Elizabeth Ashbridge ... Written by her own Hand many years ago* was published. Little is known of its author, other than what is contained in her book, but from that it is clear that the central fact of her life was her conversion. After emigrating to America as an indentured servant, Elizabeth Ashbridge (1713–1755) discovered that her master, whom she had taken for "a very religious man" was, in fact, cruel and hypocritical. Buying her own freedom, she married a man who, she says, "fell in love with me for my dancing." But, when she embraced the Quaker religion, the dancing stopped; and her husband, in his anger and disappointment, began to beat her. The beatings only ended, Ashbridge explains, when her husband died. Then she was able to marry again, this time to someone who shared her faith. That faith, and her conversion to it, are described with simple power; just as they are in the *Journal* that another Quaker, John Woolman (1720–1772), kept intermittently between 1756 and his death – and which was published by the Society of Friends in 1774. "I have often felt a motion of love to leave some hints in writing of my experience of the goodness of God," Woolman confesses at the start of the *Journal*, "and now, in the thirty-sixth year of my age, I begin the work." What follows is the story of a life lived in the light of faith that is, nevertheless, remarkable for its simplicity and humility of tone. Woolman describes how he eventually gave up trade and his mercantile interests to devote himself to his family and farm, and to work as a missionary. He traveled thousands of miles, Woolman reveals, driven by "a lively operative desire for the good of others." The desire not only prompted him towards missionary work but also impelled him to champion the rights of Native Americans and to attack slavery, which he described as a "dark gloominess hanging over the land." Just like Ashbridge, Woolman shows how many Americans even in an increasingly secular age relied on what Woolman himself termed "the judgements of God" and "the infallible standard: Truth" to steer their lives and direct their choices, rather than the touchstones of reason and use.

The case is more complicated, however, with the greatest American embodiment of faith in the eighteenth century, Jonathan Edwards (1703–1758). Edwards was born in East Windsor, Connecticut. His father and grandfather were both clergymen and, even before he went to college, he had decided to follow their example: not least, because, as he discloses in his *Personal Narrative*, written some time after 1739, he had felt "a sense of the glorious majesty and grace of God." After that, Edwards explains, "the appearance of everything was altered" since "there seemed to be ... a calm, sweet cast, or appearance of divine glory, in almost everything." He felt compelled to meditate; he also felt compelled to review and discipline the conduct of his life. Some time in 1722–1723, he composed seventy *Resolutions* designed to improve himself in the light of his faith. "Being sensible that I am unable to do anything without God's help," he wrote at the start of them, "I do humbly entreat him by his grace, to keep these Resolutions, so far as they are agreeable to his will, for Christ's sake." What follows very much reflects the old New England habit of seeing death as the defining, determining event of life. This is a self-help manual of a special kind, shaped by a belief in human impotence and a profound sense of mortality. The experience of conversion confirmed what Edwards had, in any event, learned from his deeply orthodox religious upbringing: that God was the ground and center, not only of faith, but of all conduct and existence.

Further confirmation came when Edwards moved to Northampton, Massachusetts to become pastor there. In 1734 he preached a number of sermons stressing the passivity of the convert before the all-powerful offer of grace from God; and the sermons provoked a strong reaction among many of his congregation, who appeared to experience exactly the kind of radical conversion Edwards was preaching about and had himself undergone. Encouraged to prepare an account of this awakening of faith in his community, Edwards wrote a pamphlet that then became a book, *A Faithful Narrative of the Surprising Work of God*, published in 1737. "Some under Great Terrors of Conscience have had Impressions on their Imaginations," Edwards reported; "they have had ... Ideas of Christ shedding blood for sinners, his blood Running from his veins." But, then, having been convinced of their guilt and damnation, and resigning themselves to God's justice, these same people discovered as Edwards had the power of God's grace. Anticipating the Great Awakening that was to sweep through many parts of the American colonies in the next few years, the Northampton congregation, many of them, found themselves born again, into a new life grounded in "the beauty and excellency of Christ" just as their pastor had been before them.

Both his own personal experience, then, and the "surprising" conversions among his congregation, were enough to convince Edwards of the supreme importance of divine grace and human faith. But that did not make him averse to science and systematic thinking. On the contrary, he made his own contribution to the philosophical debates of the time. In *A Treatise Concerning Religious Affections* (1746), for instance, Edwards attempted to construct a clear theory of the place of emotion in religion, so as the better to understand the emotional experience of converts. Just how much Edwards wanted to harness reason in the service of faith and, if necessary, to defend mystery with logic is nowhere better illustrated than in his arguments – developed in such works as *The Great Christian Doctrine of Original Sin Defended* (1758) and *Two Dissertations* (1765) – concerning the total depravity of human nature and the infinite grace of God. True virtue, Edwards argued, borrowing his definitions from Enlightenment philosophers like Hutcheson and Shaftesbury, consists in disinterested benevolence towards humankind in general. It involves pure selflessness. But, Edwards then insisted, humanity can never be selfless. All human actions, no matter how creditable their effects, are dictated by self-interest. Everything a human being does springs from considerations of self because, Edwards went on, now borrowing his definitions from an earlier Enlightenment figure, Descartes, he or she can never get outside the self. A man, or woman, can never escape from their own senses and sense impressions. So, they are incapable of true virtue. Each is imprisoned in his or her own nature. Each is corrupt, fallen and evil, and the only thing that can save them is something beyond human power to control: that is, the irresistible grace of God. "All moral good," Edwards concluded, "stems from God." God is the beginning and end, the ground and meaning of all moral existence. Edwards's relation to the prevailing rationalism of his times certainly drew him towards complex philosophical argument. But it never tempted him to deviate from the straight and narrow path of faith, or to surrender a vision of human experience that was rapt and apocalyptic, swinging between the extremes of damnation and redemption.

A sermon like Edwards's most well-known piece of work, *Sinners in the Hands of an Angry God*, delivered in 1741 and published the same year, describes the alternative of damnation. In it, Edwards uses all the rhetorical devices at his disposal, above all vivid imagery and incremental repetition, to describe in gruesome detail the "fearful danger" the "sinner" is in. The other alternative, of conversions and salvation, is figured, for example, in Edwards's description in 1723 of the woman who became his wife, Sarah Pierrepoint. Like so many of Edwards's writings – or, for that matter, work by others inspired by the Puritan belief that material facts are spiritual signs – it is at once intimate and symbolic. This is, at once, his own dear beloved and an emblem of any redeemed soul in communion with God. "The Son of God created the world for this very end," Edwards wrote elsewhere, in "Covenant of Redemption: 'Excellency of Christ,'" "to communicate Himself in an image of His own excellency." "By this we may discover the beauty of many of those metaphors and similes, which to an unphilosophical person do seem uncouth," he infers; since everywhere in nature we may consequently behold emblems, "the emanations of the sweet benevolence of Jesus Christ." That belief in the spiritual and symbolic nature of the perceived world animates Edwards's writing. So does his fervent belief that all existence, natural and moral, depends on God, and his equally fervent conviction that all human faculties, including reason, must be placed in the service of faith in Him.

Towards the revolution

It is possible to see Jonathan Edwards as a distillation of one side of the Puritan inheritance: that is, the spiritual, even mystical strain in Puritan thought that empha-sized the inner life, the pursuit of personal redemption, and the ineffable character of God's grace. In which case, it is equally possible to see Edwards's great contemporary, Benjamin Franklin (1706–1790), as a distillation and development of another side: that tendency in Puritanism that stressed the outer life, hard work and good conduct, and the freedom of the individual will. Another way of putting it is to say that Franklin embodied the new spirit of America, emerging in part out of Puritanism and in part out of the Enlightenment, that was coming to dominate the culture. And he knew it. That is clear from his account of his own life in his most famous work, the *Autobiography*, which he worked on at four different times (1771, 1784, 1788, 1788–1789), revised extensively but left unfinished at the time of his death; an American edition was published in 1818, but the first complete edition of what he had written only appeared nearly a hundred years after his death, in 1867. Uncompleted though it is, the *Autobiography* nevertheless has a narrative unity. It is divided into three sections: first, Franklin's youth and early manhood in Boston and Philadelphia; second, Franklin's youthful attempts to achieve what he terms "moral perfection"; and third, Franklin's use of the principles discovered in the first section and enumerated in the second to enable him to rise to prosperity and success as a scientist, politician, and philanthropist. Throughout all three sections, Franklin is keen to present his life as exemplary and typical: proof positive that anyone can make it, especially in America, "the Land of Labour" where "a general happy Mediocrity prevails" – as long as they apply themselves to useful toil. Like the good scientist, Franklin the narrator looks at the events of Franklin the autobiographical character's life and tries to draw inferences from them. Or he tries to see how his own moral hypotheses worked, when he put them to the test of action. This means that he is more than just remembering in his *Autobiography*. He is also demonstrating those truths, about human nature, human society, and God which, as he sees it, should be acknowledged by all reasonable men.

Just how much Franklin presents his story as a prototypical American one is measured in the first section of the *Autobiography*. His "first entry" into the city of Philadelphia in 1723, for instance, is described in detail. And what he emphasizes is his sorry appearance and poverty. "I was in my working dress," he tells the reader, "my best clothes being to come round by sea." "I was dirty from my journey," he adds, "and I knew no soul nor where to look for lodging." Whatever the truth of this story, Franklin is also clearly constructing a myth here, one that was to become familiar in American narratives. This is the self-made man as hero, on his first appearance, poor and unknown and unprotected, entering a world that he then proceeds to conquer.

That Franklin was able to rise to affluence and reputation from these humble beginnings was due, he tells the reader, not only to self-help and self-reliance but to self-reinvention. In the second section of his *Autobiography*, he explains how he "conceived the bold and arduous project of arriving at moral perfection." Wanting "to live without committing any fault at any time," he drew up a list of the "moral virtues," such as "temperance," "silence," "order," "resolution," and "frugality." And he then gave "a week's attention to each of the virtues successively." A complicated chart was drawn up for the week; and, if ever he committed a least offense against that week's moral virtue, he would mark it on the chart, his obvious aim being to keep it "clean of spots." Since he had enumerated thirteen virtues, he could "go through a course complete" in moral re-education in thirteen weeks, and "four courses in a year." Springing from a fundamental belief that the individual could change, improve, and even recreate himself, with the help of reason, common sense, and hard work, Franklin's program for himself was one of the first great formulations of the American dream. Rather than being born into a life, Franklin is informing his readers, a person can make that life for himself. He can be whoever he wants to be. All he needs is understanding, energy, and commitment to turn his own best desires about himself into a tangible reality.

And that, as he tells it and indeed lived it, is exactly what Franklin did. By 1748, when he was still only forty-two, he had made enough money to retire from active business. By this time, he had also become quite famous thanks to his newspaper, *The Pennsylvania Gazette*, and a little book he published annually from 1733, *Poor Richard's Almanack*. Almanacs were popular in early America, their principal purpose being to supply farmers and traders with information about the weather and fluctuations in the currency. Franklin kept this tradition going, but he changed it by adding and gradually expanding a section consisting of proverbs and little essays, a kind of advice column that reflected his philosophy of economic and moral individualism. Eventually, many of the proverbs were brought together in one book, in 1758, that was to become known as *The Way to Wealth*; this was a nationwide bestseller and was reprinted several hundred times. Always, the emphasis here is on the virtues of diligence, thrift, and independence. "Diligence is the mother of good luck," declares one proverb. "Plough deep, while sluggards sleep," says another, "and you shall have corn to sell and keep." As a whole, the proverbs reflect the single-mindedness that had helped Franklin himself along the way to wealth. But they also show Franklin's wit. As early as 1722, Franklin had perfected a literary style that combined clarity of expression with sharpness and subtlety, and frequently humor of perception, in a series of essays called the "Silence Dogood" papers, after the name of the narrator. In these, Franklin used a fictitious speaker, the busybody widow Silence Dogood, to satirize follies and vices ranging from poor poetry to prostitution. And, throughout his life, Franklin was not only an inventor of proverbial wisdom but a masterly essayist, using his skills to promote philanthropic and political projects (*A Proposal for Promoting Useful Knowledge* (1743); *Proposals Relating to the Education of Youth in Pennsylvania* (1749)), to attack violence against Native Americans or the superstition that led people to accuse women of witchcraft (*A Narrative of the Late Massacres* (1764); "A Witch Trial at

Mount Holly" (1730)), and to satirize the slave trade and British imperialism ("On the Slave Trade" (1790); "An Edict by the King of Prussia" (1773)). Here, he developed his *persona*, "the friend of all good men," and his characteristic argumentative strategy, also enshrined in his *Autobiography*, of weaving seamlessly together the imperatives of self-help and altruism, personal need and the claims of society.

Here, and elsewhere, Franklin also elaborated his belief in America. His homeplace, Franklin explained in "Information to Those Who Would Remove to America" (1784), was a place where "people do not inquire concerning a Stranger, *What is he*? But, *What can he do*?" Anyone with "any useful Art" was welcome. And all "Hearty young Labouring Men" could "easily establish themselves" there. Not only that, they could soon rise to a reasonable fortune. They could increase and multiply, and they could live good lives. "The almost general Mediocrity of Fortune that prevails in America," Franklin explained, obliged all people "to follow some Business for subsistence." So, "those Vices, that arise usually from Idleness, are in a great measure prevented"; "Industry and constant Employment" were the "great preservatives of the Morals and Virtue" of the New World. For Franklin, America really was the land of opportunity. It was also a land of tolerance, common sense, and reason, where people could and should be left free to toil usefully for themselves and their community, as he had done. Typically, he turned such beliefs into a matter of political practice as well as principle, working on behalf of his colonial home, then his country, for most of his life. In 1757 and 1775, for example, he made two lengthy trips to England, to serve as colonial agent. After the second trip, he returned to Philadelphia just in time to serve in the Continental Congress and to be chosen as a member of that committee which eventually drafted the Declaration of Independence. Then, in 1783, he was one of the three American signatories to the treaty that ended the Revolutionary War. Finally, after some years in France as American ambassador, he became a member of that convention which drafted the Constitution of the United States. Franklin was at the heart of the American Revolution from its origins to its conclusions. And he shows, more clearly than any other figure of the time does, just how much that Revolution owed to the principles of the Enlightenment. By his presence and comments he also suggests just how much the founding documents of the American nation were rooted in a project that he himself embraced and emblematized, based on the principles of natural rights and reason, self-help and self-reinvention.

"What then is the American, this new man?" asked J. Hector St. Jean de Crevecoeur (1735–1813) in his *Letters from an American Farmer*, published in 1782. Answering his own question, Crevecoeur then suggested that "the American is a new man, who acts upon new principles; he must therefore entertain new ideas, and form new opinions." That was a common theme in the literature surrounding the American Revolution. As the American colonies became a new nation, the United States of America, writers and many others applied themselves to the task of announcing just what this new nation represented, and what the character and best hopes of the American might be. Crevecoeur was especially fascinated because of his mixed back-ground: born in France, he spent time in England and Canada before settling as a planter in New York State. He was also, during the Revolution, placed in a difficult position. As a Tory or Loyalist (that is, someone who continued to claim allegiance to Britain), he found himself suspected by the Revolutionaries; as someone with liberal

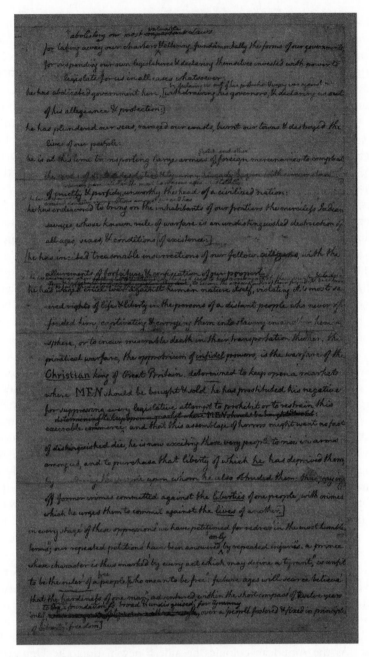

Figure 1.3   First draft of the Declaration of Independence, in the handwriting of Thomas Jefferson with alterations and corrections in the handwriting of Jefferson, John Adams, and Benjamin Franklin. Fragment (page 3) of Original Rough Draft, June 1776. Thomas Jefferson Papers, Manuscript Division. Courtesy of the Library of Congress.

sympathies, however, he also fell under suspicion among the other Tories. So in 1780 he returned to France; and it was in London that *Letters* was first published. Following a form very popular in the eighteenth century, Crevecoeuer's book (which was reprinted many times) consists of twelve letters written by a fictional narrator, James, a Quaker and a farmer, describing his life on the farm and his travels to places such as Charlestown, South Carolina. *Letters* is an epistolary narrative; it is a travel and philosophical journal; and it also inaugurates that peculiarly American habit of mixing fiction and thinly disguised autobiography. James shares many of the experiences and opinions of Crevecoeur but, unlike his creator, he is a simple, relatively uneducated man and, of course, a Quaker – which Crevecoeur most certainly was not.

At the heart of *Letters* are three animating beliefs that Crevecoeur shared with many of his contemporaries, and that were to shape subsequent American thought and writing. There is, first, the belief that American nature is superior to European culture: at once older than even "the half-ruined amphitheatres" of the Old World and, because it is subject to perpetual, seasonal renewal, much newer and fresher than, say, "the musty ruins of Rome." Second, there is the belief that America is the place where the oppressed of Europe can find freedom and independence as "tillers of the earth." America is "not composed, as in Europe, of great lords who possess everything, and a herd of people who have nothing," the narrator of *Letters* explains. "We are all animated with the spirit of an industry which is unfettered and unrestrained, because each person works for himself." "We are," the narrator triumphantly declares, "the most perfect society now existing in the world." The "new man" at the center of this perfect society reflects the third belief animating this book. The American, as *Letters* describes him, is the product of "the new mode of life he has embraced, the new government he obeys, and the new rank he holds." "Americans are the western pilgrims," the narrator proudly declaims; "here individuals of all nations are melted into a new race of men." And what lies at the end of this journey to a Promised Land, what rises out of the melting pot, is a self-reliant individual, whose "labour is founded on the basis of nature, self-interest." The American works for himself and his loved ones; he can think for himself; and the contribution he makes to his community and society is freely given, without fear or favor.

There are, certainly, moments of doubt and even despair in *Letters*. Traveling to South Carolina, James is reminded of the obscenity and injustice of slavery: not least, when he comes across the grotesque spectacle of a slave suspended in a cage in the woods, starving to death, his eyes pecked out by hungry birds. But, despite that – despite, even, the suspicion that the presence of slavery makes a mockery of any talk of a "perfect society" – the general thrust of the book is towards celebration of both the promise and the perfection of America. Crevecoeur's work is driven by certain convictions, about nature and natural rights, a new man and society, that he certainly shared with other American writers of the time – and, indeed, with some of his Romantic counterparts in Europe. But nowhere are such convictions given clearer or more charged expression. *Letters* begins with the claim that to "record the progressive steps" of an "industrious farmer" is a nobler project for a writer than any to be found in European literature. That claim is supported, and the project pursued with enthusiasm in the ensuing pages, where the hero is, quite simply, "the American."

A writer who shared Crevecoeur's belief in the possibilities of American society was Thomas Paine (1737–1809). Unlike Crevecoeur, however, Paine was unambiguously enthusiastic about the Revolution. Born in England, Paine arrived in America in 1774. He remained for only thirteen years, but his impact on America's developing vision of itself was enormous. In 1776 Paine published *Common Sense*, which argued for American independence and the formation of a republican government. "In the following pages I offer nothing more than simple facts, plain arguments, and common sense," Paine declared in the opening pages. That reflected the contemporary belief in the power of reason, which Paine shared, and the contemporary shift in political commentaries from arguments rooted in religion to more secular ones. It did not, however, quite do justice to, or prepare the reader for, the power of Paine's rhetoric. The gift for firing arguments into life, often with the help of an imaginative use of maxims, is even more in evidence in the *Crisis* papers. With Washington defeated and in retreat at the end of 1776, Paine tried to rouse the nation to further resistance in the first of sixteen papers. "These are the times that try men's souls," he began. On this memorable opening he then piled a series of equally memorable maxims, clearly designed for the nation to take to and carry in its heart: "The summer soldier and the sunshine patriot will, in this crisis, shrink from the service of their country," Paine declares, "but he that stands it *now*, deserves the love and thanks of man and woman."

The last of the *Crisis* papers appeared in 1783, at the end of the Revolution. Only four years later, Paine returned to England. There, he wrote *The Rights of Man* (1791–1792), intended as a reply to *Reflections on the Revolution in France* (1790) by Edmund Burke. It was immensely popular but, because Paine argued against a hereditary monarchy in *The Rights of Man*, he was charged with sedition and was forced to flee to France. There, his protest against the execution of Louis XVI led to imprisonment. He was only released when the American ambassador to Paris, James Madison, intervened. Paine returned to America. But the publication of his last major work, *The Age of Reason* (1794–1795), led to further notoriety and unpopularity in his adoptive homeplace. In *The Age of Reason*, Paine attacks the irrationality of religion and, in particular, Christianity. Paine did not deny the existence of "one God" and, like Franklin, he insisted that, as he put it, "religious duties consist in doing justice, loving mercy, and endeavouring to make our fellow-creatures happy." But that did not enable him to escape the anger of many Americans: he was vilified in papers and on pulpits as a threat to both Christian and democratic faiths; and he was condemned to live his last few years in obscurity.

Obscurity was never to be the fate of Thomas Jefferson (1724–1826). A person of eclectic interests – and, in that, the inheritor of a tradition previously best illustrated by William Byrd of Westover – Jefferson's very myriad-mindedness has led to quite contradictory interpretations of both his aims and his achievement. What is incontestable, however, is the central part he played in the formation of America as a nation. His *A Summary View of the Rights of British America*, for example, published in 1774, was immensely influential. In it, Jefferson argued that Americans had effectively freed themselves from British authority by exercising "a right which nature has given to all men, of departing from the country in which chance, not choice, has placed them." Such stirring words earned him a place, in 1776, on the committee assigned the task of drafting the Declaration of Independence. And, if any one person can be called the author of that Declaration, it is undoubtedly Jefferson. This founding document of the American nation enshrines the beliefs that Jefferson shared with so many other major figures of the Enlightenment: that "all men are created equal," that they are endowed with certain "inalienable rights" and notably the right to "life, liberty, and the pursuit of happiness"; and that "to secure those rights, governments are instituted among men." Like many great American documents, the Declaration of Independence describes an idea of the nation, an ideal or possibility against which its actual social practices can and must be measured – and, it might well be, found wanting.

Jefferson relied on the principle of natural rights and the argumentative tool of reason to construct a blueprint of the American nation. When it came to filling in the details, however, he relied as Crevecoeur and many others did on his belief in the independent farmer. "I know no condition happier than that of a Virginia farmer," Jefferson wrote to a friend in 1787. "His estate supplies a good table, clothes himself and his family with their ordinary apparel, furnishes a small surplus to buy salt, coffee, and a little finery for his wife and daughter, ... and furnishes him pleasing and healthy occupation." "Cultivators of the earth are the most valuable citizens," he declared in another letter, written in 1804. "They are the most vigorous, the most independent, the most virtuous, and they are tied to their country, and wedded to its interests, by the most lasting bonds." Fortunately, in his opinion, America would remain an agricultural country for the foreseeable future; small farmers would therefore remain "the true representatives of the Great American interests" and the progress and prosperity of the new republic were consequently assured. "The small landowners are the most precious part of a state," Jefferson confided in a letter to his friend and fellow Virginian James Madison in 1772. In a more public vein, he made the famous assertion that "those who labour in the earth are the chosen people of God, ... whose breasts he has made his peculiar deposit for substantial and genuine virtue": which is, perhaps, the definitive statement of a determining American myth.

That statement comes from the one full-length book Jefferson published, in 1787, *Notes on the State of Virginia*. Written in response to a questionnaire sent to him about his home state while he was serving as governor, *Notes* is at once a scientific treatise and a crucial document of cultural formation. Jefferson examines and documents the natural and cultural landscape of the New World and, at the same time, considers the promise and possibilities of the new nation. One of his several aims in the book is to rebut the argument embraced by many leading European naturalists of the time that the animals and people of the New World were inherently smaller, less vigorous, and more degenerate than their Old World counterparts This gives him the opportunity to write in praise of the Native American. Jefferson was willing to accept the idea that Native Americans were still a "barbarous people," lacking such advantages of civilization as "letters" and deference towards women. But he insisted on their primitive strength, "their bravery and address in war" and "their eminence in oratory." Rebutting European claims of this nature also allowed Jefferson to enumerate white American achievements in such fields as "philosophy and war," government, oratory, painting and "the plastic art," and to express the firm conviction that, in other areas too, America would soon have "her full quota of genius."

Like Crevecoeur, Jefferson also felt compelled to confront the challenge to his idyllic vision of America posed by the indelible fact of slavery. He condemned the peculiar institution in his *Notes* and argued for emancipation. But emancipation, for him, was linked to repatriation: once freed, the slaves should be sent to some other colony, Jefferson insisted, where they could become "a free and independent people." Removal was necessary, Jefferson felt, because the "deep rooted prejudices" of the whites and a lingering sense of injustice felt by the blacks would make coexistence impossible. Not only that, Jefferson was willing to entertain the idea that physical and moral differences between the two races further underlined the need for freed blacks to go elsewhere. "In general, their existence appears to participate more of sensation than reflection," Jefferson observed of African Americans. Among other things, this made them deficient as artists and writers. All the arguments that black people were inferior to white "in the endowments both of body and mind" were advanced, Jefferson assured the reader "as a suspicion only." But the general burden of the argument in *Notes* is clearly towards black inferiority. And the belief that, once freed, blacks should be "removed beyond the reach of mixture" is stated consistently and categorically. So, for that matter, is the belief that, if black people are not freed soon, the American republic will reap a terrible harvest. "Indeed, I tremble for my country when I reflect that God is just," Jefferson famously declared in *Notes*. There might, he thought, be "a revolution in the wheel of fortune, an exchange of situation." But then, he added hopefully, there might be a more fortunate turn of events, involving gradual emancipation. It was a sign of Jefferson's intellectual honesty that he wrestled with the problem of slavery in the first place. It was also a sign that he was, after all, a man of his times imbued with many of its prejudices that he could not disentangle the ideal of black freedom from the ideas of separation and removal. His doubts about the radical threat to the new republic posed by its clear violation of its own clearly stated belief in natural rights were, in the last analysis, subdued by his conviction that reason, as he construed it, would prevail. That is the measure of his capacity for optimism, and of his belief that, as he put it in *Notes*, "reason and free inquiry are the only effective agents against error." It is also, perhaps, a measure of a capacity for self-delusion that was by no means uniquely his.

In 1813 Jefferson began a correspondence with John Adams (1735–1826), repairing the breach in their friendship that had occurred when Jefferson defeated Adams in the presidential elections of 1800; they were published separately and in full in 1959. The first vice president and the second president, Adams was a lively intellectual of a skeptical turn of mind and the founder of a family dynasty that would produce another president, John Quincy Adams, and the historian, novelist, and autobiographer, Henry Adams. Discussing literature, history, and philosophy, Jefferson pitted his idealism against Adams's acid wit and pessimistic turn of mind. To Jefferson's insistence that "a natural aristocracy" of "virtue and talents" would replace "an artificial aristocracy founded on wealth and birth," Adams replied that the distinction would not "help the matter." "Both artificial aristocracy, and Monarchy," Adams argued, "have grown out of the natural Aristocracy of 'Virtue and Talents.'" Adams's skepticism and, in particular, his sense that in time the purest republic becomes tainted by the hereditary principle or, at least, the evolution of a ruling class, led him to think less well of the American future than Jefferson did. Part of this stemmed from a patrician distrust of the people. Whatever its sources, it prompted Adams to meet Jefferson's optimism with irony. "Many hundred years must roll away before We shall be corrupted," he declared sarcastically. "Our pure, virtuous, public spirited federative Republick will last for ever, govern the Globe and introduce the perfection of Man."

Alternative voices of revolution

The letters between Adams and Jefferson reveal two contrary visions of the new American republic and its fate. So, in a different way, do the letters that passed between John Adams and his wife Abigail. Inevitably, perhaps, the tone is more intimate, even teasing. But Abigail Adams (1744–1818) raises, consistently, the serious issue of freedom and equality for women. "I long to hear that you have declared an independency," she wrote to her husband in 1776, "and by the way in the new Code of Laws which I suppose it will be necessary for you to make I desire you would remember the Ladies." The tone was playful, but it made adroit and serious use of one of the primary beliefs of the leaders of the Revolution: that, as Jefferson put it in his *Notes*, "laws to be just, must give a reciprocation of rights . . . without this, they are mere arbitrary rules of conduct, founded on force." Unfortunately, all Abigail Adams received in response was the playful claim from John that he, and all husbands, "have only the Name of Masters." All men, he insisted, were "completely subject" "to the Despotism of the Petticoat."

Adams wrote to his wife, adding gentle insult to injury, that he could not choose but laugh at her "extraordinary Code of Laws." "We have been told that our Struggle has loosened the bands of Government everywhere," he explained: "that Children and Apprentices were disobedient – that schools and Colledges were grown turbulent – that Indians slighted their Guardians and Negroes grew insolent to their Masters." Now, he added, what she wrote to him made him aware that "another Tribe more numerous and powerfull than all the rest were grown discontented" amid the revolutionary turmoil of 1776. The remark was clearly intended to put Abigail Adams down, however playfully, to dismiss her claims for the natural rights of women by associating women with other, supposedly undeserving groups. But, inadvertently, it raised a serious and central point. "All men are created equal," the Declaration of Independence announced. That explicitly excluded women. Implicitly, it also excluded "Indians" and "Negroes," since what it meant, of course, was all *white* men. An idealist like Jefferson might wrestle conscientiously with such exclusions (while, perhaps, painfully aware that he himself was a slaveholder); a man like John Adams might insist on them, however teasingly. But they could not go unnoticed, and especially by those, like Abigail Adams, who were excluded. The literature of the revolutionary period includes not only the visionary rhetoric and rational arguments of those men by and for whom the laws of the new republic were primarily framed, but also the writings of those who felt excluded, ignored, or left out. As John Adams, for all his irony, was forced to acknowledge, the political and social turmoil of the times was bound to make disadvantaged, marginalized groups more acutely aware of their plight. After all, he had his wife to remind him.

Among the leading voices of the American Revolution, there are some who, at least, were willing to recognize the rights of women. Notably, Thomas Paine spoke of the need for female quality. "If we take a survey of ages and countries," he wrote in "An Occasional Letter on the Female Sex" (1775), "we shall find the women, almost – without exception – at all times and in all places, adored and oppressed." So, at greater length, did the writings of Judith Sargent Murray (1751–1820). Murray wrote, among other things, two plays and a number of poems; she also wrote two essay series for the *Massachusetts Magazine* from 1792 to 1794. One essay series, *The Repository*, was largely religious in theme. The other, *The Gleaner*, considered a number of issues, including federalism, literary nationalism, and the equality of the sexes. A three-volume edition of *The Gleaner* was published in 1798; and in it is to be found her most influential piece, "On the Equality of the Sexes" (1790), which establishes her claim to be regarded as one of the first American feminists. Here, Murray argued that the capacities of memory and imagination are equal in women and men and that, if women are deficient as far as the two other faculties of the mind, reason and judgment, are concerned, it is because of a difference in education. If only women were granted equal educational opportunities, Murray insisted, then they would be the equal of men in every respect.

Murray was inspired as many of her contemporaries were by the events and rhetoric of the times. Her other works include, for instance, a patriotic poem celebrating the "genius" of George Washington and anticipating the moment when the arts and sciences would flourish in "blest Columbia" ("Occasional Epilogue to the *Contrast*; a Comedy, Written by Royal Tyler, Esq" (1794)). Unlike most of her contemporaries, however, that inspiration led Sargent to consider the anomalous position of her own sex and to argue that the anomaly could and should be rectified. Appealing to the principle of equality enshrined in the laws of the new republic, to rational justice and Christian faith, she helped raise an issue that was to be foregrounded in the next century – not least, at the Seneca Falls Women's Rights Convention. There, at the Convention in 1848, a "Declaration of Sentiments" was framed that gave succinct expression to Sargent's beliefs by making a simple change to the original Declaration. "We hold these truths to be self-evident," it announced, "that all men and women are created equal."

"The great men of the United States have their liberty – they begin with new things, and now they endeavour to lift us up the Indians from the ground, that we may stand up and walk ourselves." The words are those of Hendrick Aupaumut (?–1830), a Mahican Indian educated by Moravians. They come from *A Short Narration of my Last Journey to the Western Country*, which was written about 1794 but not published until 1827. Aupaumut, as this remark suggests, was intensely loyal to the United States; and he clearly believed, or at least hoped, that his people would be afforded the same rights and opportunities as "the great men" of the new nation. Because of his loyalty, he served as an intermediary between the government and Native Americans in the 1790s. This involved traveling among the tribes; and it was evidently after a journey among the Delawares, Shawnees, and others that he wrote his book. Often awkward in style, the *Narration* reflects the desperate effort of at least one Native American, working in a second language, to record the history and customs of his peoples – and to convince them, and perhaps himself, that the leaders of the American republic would extend its rights and privileges to those who had lived in America long before Columbus landed. "I have been endeavouring to do my best in the business of peace," Aupaumut explains in the *Narration*. That best consisted, fundamentally, of assuring the Native Americans he met of the good intentions of the whites. "I told them, the United States will not speak wrong," Aupaumut recalls, "whatever they promise to Indians they will perform." The *Narrative* is, in effect, a powerful declaration of faith in the universality of the principle of natural rights, and an equally powerful statement of the belief that this principle would now be put into practice. In the light of what happened to Native Americans after this it has, of course, acquired a peculiar pathos and irony that Aupaumut never for once intended.

A Native American who was less convinced that the American Revolution was a good cause was Samson Occom (1723–1792). Quite the contrary, during the Revolutionary War Occom urged the tribes to remain neutral because that war was, he insisted, the work of the Devil. Born a Mohegan, Occom was converted by missionaries when he was sixteen. He then became an itinerant minister, devoting most of his energies to preaching and working on behalf of the Indian people. Only two books by him were published during his lifetime, but they were immensely successful. The first was a sermon written at the request of a fellow Mohegan who had been sentenced to death for murder, *A Sermon Preached by Samson Occom, Minister of the Gospel, and Missionary to the Indians; at the Execution of Moses Paul an Indian* (1722). Reflecting Occom's own evangelical convictions, and focusing, in the tradition of all execution sermons, on the omnipresence of death and the necessity for immediate, radical conversion, it was immensely popular. Its popularity encouraged the publication of the second book, *Collection of Hymns and Spiritual Songs* (1774), which became the first Indian bestseller. All Occom's work is marked by a fervent belief in the power of grace, and by his insistence that, as he put it in the execution sermon, "we are all dying creatures" who had to seek that grace at once. It is marked, as well, by a fervent rhetorical style and an equally fervent belief that all his people, the Mohegans and other tribes, were in particular need of Christian redemption. Passing through it, however, is another current, less openly acknowledged but undeniably there: the suspicion that many of the miseries of his life were there "because," as he expressed it, "I am a poor Indian," that this was true of all other "poor Indians" too, and that the way to deal with this was to build a separate community.

The rage felt by many African Americans, enslaved or freed, at the obvious and immense gap between the rhetoric of the Revolution and the reality of their condition was memorably expressed by Lemuel Haynes (1753–1833). As an evangelical minister, Haynes, along with Jupiter Hammon and Phillis Wheatley, helped to produce the first significant body of African American writing, founded on revivalist rhetoric and revolutionary discourse. His address, "Liberty Further Extended: Or Free Thoughts on the Illegality of Slave-Keeping" (written early in his career but not published until 1983), begins by quoting the Declaration of Independence to the effect that "all men are created Equal" with "Ceartain unalienable rights." Haynes then goes on to argue that "Liberty, & freedom, is an innate principle, which is unmoveably placed in the human Species." It is a "Jewel," Haynes declares, "which was handed Down to man from the cabinet of heaven, and is Coeval with his Existance." And, since it "proceeds from the Supreme Legislature of the univers, so it is he which hath a sole right to take away." Skillfully using the founding documents of the nation, and quotations from the Bible such as the pronouncement that God made "*of one blood all nations of men, for to dwell upon the face of the earth,*" Haynes weaves a trenchant argument against slavery. "Liberty is Equally as pre[c]ious to a *Black man*, as it is to a *white* one," he insists. The message is rammed home, time and again, that the white people of the new republic are in breach of divine law and their own professed allegiance to "natural rights." And

Haynes concludes with a prayer addressed to white Americans: "If you have any Love to yourselves, or any Love to this Land, if you have any Love to your fellow-man, Break these intollerable yoaks."

A similar commitment to the idea of brotherhood characterizes the work of Prince Hall (1735?–1807). Hall was a member of the Masonic order. He considered it the duty of Masons, as he put it in "A Charge Delivered to the African Lodge, June 24, 1797, at Menotomy" (1797), to show "love to all mankind," and "to sympathise with our fellow men under their troubles." The author of numerous petitions on behalf of Masons and free blacks in general, for support of plans for blacks to emigrate to Africa and for public education for children of tax-paying black people, he was also a strong opponent of slavery. His petition, "To the Honorable Council & House of Representatives for the State of Massachusetts-Bay in General Court assembled January 13th 1777" (1788), asks for the emancipation of "great number of Negroes who are detained in a state of Slavery in the Bowels of a free & Christian Country." And, in it, like Haynes, Hall uses the rhetoric of the Revolution against its authors. Slaves, he points out, "have, in common with all other Men, a natural & unalienable right to that freedom, which the great Parent of the Universe hath bestowed equally on all Mankind." Hall was tireless in his support of any scheme intended to advance the cause of black freedom and equality. He was also acutely aware of how different were the futures of the different races in "this Land of Liberty." And he was never reluctant to use republican, as well as biblical, rhetoric to point that difference out.

Haynes was born into freedom. Hall was born into slavery and then freed. Olaudah Equiano (1745–1797) was born into freedom in Africa; he was enslaved, transported first to Barbados and then to Virginia, bought by a British captain to serve aboard his ship, and then finally in 1776 became a free man again. All this became the subject of a two-volume autobiography, *The Interesting Narrative of the Life of Olaudah Equiano, or Gustavus Valla, the African, Written by Himself.* Published in 1787 and subscribed to by many of the leading abolitionists, it established the form of the slave narrative and so, indirectly or otherwise, it has influenced American writing – and African American writing in particular – to the present day. "I offer here the history of neither a saint, a hero, nor a tyrant," Equiano announces. "I might say my sufferings were great," he admits, "but when I compare my lot with that of most of my countrymen, I regard myself as a *particular favorite of heaven*, and acknowledge the mercies of Providence in every occurrence of my life." As that remark suggests, Equiano follows the tradition of spiritual autobiography derived from St. Augustine and John Bunyan and used by American Puritans and Quakers, but he adds to it the new dimension of social protest. He also begins by painting an idyllic portrait of life in Africa. Then, as Equiano tells it, came the fall. At the age of eleven, he was seized from his family and sold into slavery. Taken to the African coast, he was terrified by the sight of white people. He feared he would be eaten, Equiano tells the reader, ironically throwing back upon its authors a common European myth about other peoples; and, when he is not eaten but "put down under the decks" on ship and then transported across the ocean, his distress is hardly alleviated. Beaten savagely, chained for most of the time, gradually learning all the hardships of capture and the "accursed trade" of slavery, Equiano becomes convinced that his new masters are "savages." Preparing the ground for later slave narratives, Equiano memorably traces the major events of his enslavement and the miseries he shared with his slaves: the breaking up of families, the imposition of new names, the strangeness and squalor, the fear of the blacks and the brutality of the whites. There are, certainly, moments of relief. Aboard one ship, Equiano befriends a white man, "a young lad." Their close friendship, which is cut short by the white man's death, serves as an illustration of the superficiality of racial barriers, indicates the possibility of white kindness and a better way for free blacks and, besides, anticipates a powerful theme in later American writing – of interracial and often homoerotic intimacy. Gradually, too, Equiano manages to rise up from slavery. He learns to read. He manages to purchase his freedom. Finally, he experiences a religious vision and, as he puts it, is "born again" to become one of "God's children." But the horror of Equiano's capture and enslavement, the long voyage to America and the even longer voyage to escape from the "absolute power" exerted by the white master over his black property – that remains indelibly marked on the reader's memory. *The Interesting Narrative of Olaudah Equiano* is the first in a great tradition of American narratives that juxtapose the dream of freedom with the reality of oppression, the Edenic myth (of Africa here, of America usually elsewhere) with a history of fall and redemption – all the while telling us the story of an apparently ordinary, but actually remarkable, man.

Writing revolution: Poetry, drama, fiction

In verse, an important tradition was inaugurated by two African American poets of the time, Jupiter Hammon (1711–1806?) and Phillis Wheatley (1753–1784). Lucy Terry (1730–1821), an African slave who eventually settled as a free black in Vermont, had become known earlier for a poem called "Bars Fight," which records a battle between whites and Indians. But Terry's poem was handed down in the oral tradition until 1855. Hammon was the first African American poet to have his work published. Born a slave, Hammon published a broadside, *Evening Thought: Salvation by Christ, With Peniten-tial Cries*, a series of twenty-two quatrains, in 1760, and then a prose work, *Address to the Negroe: In the State of New York*, in 1787. The poetry is notable for its piety, the prose for its argument that black people must reconcile themselves to the institution of slavery. Some of Hammon's thinking here is registered in his poem to Phillis Wheatley, "An Address to Miss Phillis Wheatly, Ethiopian Poetess, in Boston, who came from Africa at eight years of age, and soon became acquainted with the gospel of Jesus Christ" (1778). "O Come you pious youth: adore/The wisdom of thy God,/" the poem begins, "In bringing thee from distant shore,/To learn his holy word." It then goes on to argue that it was "God's tender mercy" that brought Wheatley in a slave ship across the Atlantic to be "a pattern" to the "youth of Boston town." It is worth emphasizing that all Hammon's publications are prefaced by an acknowledgment to the three generations of the white family he served. Anything of his that saw print was, in effect, screened by his white masters, and, in writing, was probably shaped by his awareness that it would never get published without their approval. That anticipated a common pattern in African American writing. Slave narratives, for instance, were commonly prefaced by a note or essay from a white notable, mediating the narrative for what was, after all, an almost entirely white audience – and giving it a white seal of approval. And it has to be borne in mind when reading what Hammon has to say about slavery: which, in essence, takes up a defense of the peculiar institution that was to be used again by

Southern apologists in the nineteenth century – that slavery could and should be seen as a civilizing influence and a providential instrument of conversion.

African America writers of the time, and later, were, in effect, in a different position from their white counterparts. The growth in readership and printing presses, the proliferation of magazines, almanacs, manuals, and many other outlets for writing, all meant that the literary culture was changing. A system of literary patronage was being replaced by the literary marketplace. Poets like Hammon and Wheatley, however, were still dependent on their white "friends" and patrons. For Equiano, fortunately, the friends, subscribers, and readers were abolitionists. For Hammon, the friends were, quite clearly, otherwise. Phillis Wheatley enjoyed the cooperation and patronage of Susanne Wheatley, the woman who bought her in a Boston slave market when she was seven years old, and the Countess of Huntingdon. It was with their help that her *Poems on Various Subjects* appeared in 1773 in London, the first volume of poetry known to have been published by an African American. The poetry reflects the neoclassical norms of the time. It also sometimes paints a less than flattering picture of Africa, the land from which Wheatley was snatched when she was still a child. "Twas not long since I left my native shore/The land of errors, and *Egyptian* gloom," she writes in "To the University of Cambridge, in New England" (1773), adding, "Father of mercy, 'twas thy gracious hand/Brought me in safety from those dark abodes." Sometimes, however, Wheatley leans towards a more Edenic and idyllic image of her birthplace, of the kind favored by Equiano. "How my bosom burns!/" she declares in one of her poems ("Philis's [*sic*] Reply to the Answer in our Last by the Gentleman in the Navy" (1774)), "and pleasing Gambia on my soul returns,/With native grace in spring's luxurious reign,/Smiles the gay mead, and Eden blooms again." A lengthy description of "Africa's blissful plain" then follows, one that transforms it into a version of the pastoral: all of which works against Wheatley's claims made elsewhere (in "On Being Brought from Africa to America" (1773) and "To His Excellency General Washington" (1776)) that she is grateful to have been taken away from "my *Pagan* land" to "Columbia's state."

Wheatley is, in fact, a far subtler and more complicated poet than is often acknowledged. The pleas for freedom are sometimes clear enough in her prose as well as her poetry. "In every human breast God has implanted a principle, which we call love of freedom," she wrote in her "Letter to Samson Occom" (1774). That is echoed in poems like "Liberty and Peace" (1785) and "To the Right Honourable William, Earl of Dartmouth, His Majesty's Principal Secretary of State for North America, &c" (1770). In both of these, she links the longing for freedom felt and expressed by the American colonists to her own experience of oppression. On a broader scale, one of her best-known poems, "On being Brought from Africa to America," may well begin by suggesting that it was "mercy" that brought her "benighted soul" from Africa to experience "redemption" in the New World. But it then goes on to use that experience of redemption as a measure of possibility for all African Americans. "Some view our sable race with scornful eye," she admits, but then adds, pointing an admonitory figure at her, inevitably white, audience: "Remember *Christians*, *Negros*, black as *Cain*,/May be refin'd and join th' angelic train." That conclusion is a perfect example of how Wheatley could develop consciousness of self into an exploration of the black community, its experiences and its potential. It is also an illustration of how she could strike

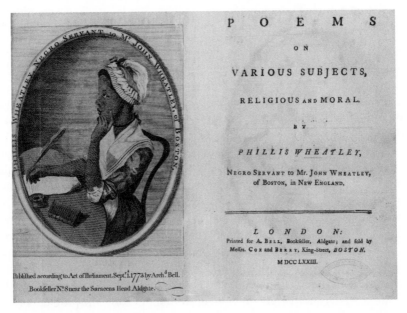

Figure 1.4 Title page and frontispiece of *Poems on Various Subjects* by Phillis Wheatley, 1773. Courtesy of the Library of Congress.

a pose, for herself and others of "*Afric's* sable race," that both deferred to white patrons and audience and subtly made a claim for dignity, even equality – that, in short, combined Christian humility with a kind of racial pride.

The difficult position of African American poets in the emerging literary marketplace is, perhaps, suggested by Wheatley's failure to find many readers for her published poetry – or, after 1773, to publish any further collections of her work. As late as 1778, she could complain about "books that remain unsold"; her *Poems* were never reprinted during her lifetime; and all her many proposals for publication in Boston were rejected. One projected volume that never saw publication was advertised by the printers with the remark that they could scarcely credit "ye performances to be by a Negro." The work was evidently too good, or too literate, to suggest such a source to them. That measures the extent of the problem poets like Hammon and Wheatley faced. Poetry, even perhaps literacy, was seen as the prerogative of white poets, like Philip Freneau (1752–1832), Timothy Dwight (1752–1817), and Joel Barlow (1754–1826). Of these three poets who set out to explore and celebrate the new republic in verse, Freneau was probably the most accomplished. Born in New York City, of a French Huguenot father and a Scottish mother, he began his poetic career as a celebrant of "Fancy, regent of the mind," and the power Fancy gave him to roam far to "Britain's fertile land," then back to "California's golden shore" ("The Power of Fancy" (1770)). Events, however, soon conspired to turn his interests in a more political and less Anglophile direction. With college friends, Hugh Brackenridge and James Madison, he wrote some *Satires Against the Tories* (1775); and with Brackenridge he also wrote a long poem in celebration of *The Rising Glory of America*. *The Rising Glory of America*,

written in 1771, published a year later, then drastically revised in 1786, marked
Freneau's full conversion to the American cause: a cause that he was later to serve
both as a satirical poet and as a strongly partisan editor and journalist. Yet, for all its
rhetorical energy, this poem about the emerging splendor of the New World is as much
a tribute to the continuing importance of the Old World, at least in matters cultural and
intellectual, as anything else. The theme may be new. The form, however, is basically
imitative. In effect, *The Rising Glory of America* tends to confirm the power of the
mother country even while Freneau and Brackenridge struggle to deny it.

Freneau was, as it happened, acutely aware of this power. A poem like "A Political
Litany" (1775) is a bitter diatribe against the political domination of Britain, "a
kingdom that bullies, and hectors, and swears." More interestingly, a poem such as
"Literary Importation" (1788) admits to a feeling of cultural domination. "Can we
never be thought to have learning or grace/," Freneau asks here, "Unless it be brought
from that damnable place." The "damnable place" was, of course, Britain; and Freneau
must have suspected that his own literary importations of style and manner answered
him in the negative. He was writing, as he perhaps sensed, in the wrong place and time.
There was the continuing cultural influence of the Old World. And there was also, as
Freneau intimates in another poem, "To An Author" (1788), the problem of writing
poetry at a moment of conflict and in a society dedicated to common sense and use. "On
these bleak climes by Fortune thrown,/Where rigid Reason reigns alone," Freneau asks
the "Author" (who is, almost certainly, himself), "Tell me, what has the muse to do?"
"An age employed in edging steel/," he adds bitterly, "Can no poetic raptures feel."
Yet, despite that, Freneau continued to indulge in "poetic raptures." There are poems
on philosophical issues ("On the Universality and Other Attributes of God in Nature"
(1815)), on politics ("On the Causes of Political Degeneracy" (1798)), on nature ("On
Observing a Large Red-Streak Apple" (1827)), and on moral and social issues such as
his attack on slavery ("To Sir Toby" (1792)). There are also pieces in which Freneau
makes a genuine attempt to arrive at universal significance in and through a firm sense of
the local. "The Indian Burying Ground" (1788) is an instance, one of the first attempts
made by any poet to understand the new country in terms of a people who had
themselves become an integral part of it – those who are called here "the ancients of the
lands." So is "The Wild Honey Suckle" (1788), in which Freneau focuses his attention
on a detail of the American scene, the "fair flower" of the title, and discovers in that
detail one possible truth about the American psyche: its fundamental loneliness and
privacy. As Freneau meditates on this one, small, frail plant, that chooses to "shun the
vulgar eye" in its "silent, dull retreat," he also adopts a quieter style, a more attentive
tone and simpler language. In some of his poetry, at least, Freneau was working towards
a form of literary emancipation, an approach and aesthetic less obviously learned from
"that damnable place."

This modest degree of success was not achieved by Dwight and Barlow, at least not in
what they considered their major work. A grandson of Jonathan Edwards, Dwight
wrote much and variously, including some attacks on slavery in both prose and verse.
His most ambitious work, however, was a poem written in imitation of the pastoral and
elegiac modes of British writers of the Augustan period like Alexander Pope and Oliver
Goldsmith. Titled *Greenfield Hill: A Poem in Seven Parts,* it was published in 1794, and
it offers an idyllic portrait of life in the American countryside. The poem becomes

a hymn to an ideal of self-reliance and modest sufficiency that Franklin and Jefferson also celebrated. Dwight describes it as "Competence." But the celebration of this particular American dream is vitiated by the fact that it is conducted in such conflicted and derivative terms. The poet endorses peace, tranquility but also necessary, sometimes violent, progress. It speaks approvingly of "Competence," modest sufficiency but also, and with equal approval, of a kind of survival of the fittest. Also, in a familiar pattern, it uses old forms to write about the new: this hymn to American virtues and uniqueness is sung in a voice that is still definitively European.

That is just as true of the attempts Joel Barlow made at an American epic, *The Vision of Columbus* (1787) and *The Columbiad* (1807). Like Dwight, Barlow was a member of a pro-Federalist group known as the "Connecticut Wits." He traveled and wrote extensively. His work includes a number of patriotic poems ("The Prospect of Peace" (1778)) and poems attacking the monarchism and imperialism of Europe ("Advice to a Raven in Russia: December, 1812" (unpublished until 1938)). His most anthologized piece is "The Hasty Pudding: A Poem in Three Cantos" (1793), a work about home thoughts from abroad that praises Yankee virtues by celebrating a peculiarly Yankee meal. *The Columbiad*, his much revised and extended version of *The Vision of Columbus*, was, however, his stab at a great work. "My object is altogether of a moral and political nature," he announced in the preface to his 1807 epic; "I wish to encourage and strengthen, in the rising generation, a sense of the importance of republican institutions, as being the great foundation of public and private happiness." Barlow was not the first to want to write an American epic. And by his time the idea of announcing the new nation in the form traditionally dedicated to such a project was becoming a commonplace. Even the congenitally cautious and skeptical John Adams could dream of such a thing. But this was the first major attempt made to realize this ambition, shared by so many, to see something that memorialized the American nation in verse just as, say, Rome and its founding had been memorialized in the *Aeneid*.

The Columbiad begins in traditional epic fashion: "I sing the Mariner who first unfurl'd/An eastern banner o'er the western world/And taught mankind where future empires lay." Contrary to the impression given by these opening lines, however, Barlow does not go on to sing of the actions of Columbus but rather of the inexorable progress of free institutions in the Americas as he anticipates them. To Columbus, in prison, comes Hesper, the guardian genius of the Western continent, who leads him to a mount of vision. The poem then proceeds in a series of visions of the American future, extending forward through colonial and revolutionary times to the establishment of peace and the arts in a new America. The final vision is of a time when the American federal system will extend "over the whole earth." Here, in the announcement of this ultimate vision, and elsewhere, the tone and style tend towards the declamatory, the derivative and didactic. What is more, the poem as a whole lacks the essential ingredient of epic: a hero, or heroic mind, engaged in heroic action. Columbus cannot be a hero. He is from the beginning completely passive. He observes, he is troubled, he hopes for the future, and he is reassured by Hesper. He cannot do anything and is, in fact, closer to being an ideal type of the reader of an American epic than to being a hero. *The Columbiad* clearly poses the problem of how to write a democratic epic, a heroic poem of the common man or woman, but it comes nowhere near solving it. That would have to wait for Walt Whitman and *Leaves of Grass*.

While Joel Barlow was busy trying to write an American epic, Royall Tyler (1756–1826) was devoting his energies to establishing an American tradition in drama. Tyler wrote seven plays, but his reputation rests on *The Contrast*, written in 1787, produced in 1790 and published two years later. The first comedy by someone born in America to receive a professional production, it was hailed by one reviewer as "proof that these new climes are particularly favorable to the cultivation of arts and sciences." *The Contrast* was written after Tyler had attended a performance of *The School for Scandal* by Richard Brinsley Sheridan and is clearly influenced by the English social comedies of the eighteenth century. It is, however, impeccably American in theme, since the contrast of the title is between Bill Dimple, an embodiment of European affectation, and Colonel Manly, a representative of American straightforwardness and republican honesty. The intensely Anglophile Dimple, described by one character as a "flippant, pallid, polite beau," flirts with two women, Letitia and Charlotte, despite the fact that a match has been arranged with a third, Maria van Rough, by her father. Manly, a patriot and veteran of the Revolutionary War, is in love with Maria. And when Dimple, having gambled away his fortune, decides to marry the wealthy Letitia instead, Maria's father, discovering Dimple's baseness, gives his blessing to Manly's suit. Dimple is then finally thwarted in his ambition to cure his insolvency when Letitia learns of his flirtation with Charlotte. And he leaves the scene, ousted but unabashed, underlining the contrast between himself and Manly as he does so. "Ladies and gentlemen," he announces, "I take my leave; and you will please to observe in the case of my deportment the contrast between a gentleman who has ... received the polish of Europe and an unpolished, untravelled American."

Manly himself underlines this contrast, through his simplicity and natural gentility of manner and through his comments on the times. The aim of the play is clearly to address the different possibilities available to the new republic and to promote civic virtue and federal high-mindedness. "Oh! That America! Oh that my country, would, in this her day, learn the things which belong to peace!" Manly prays. And he shows what those "things" are in the impeccable character of his beliefs and behavior. A subplot draws a similar lesson, by presenting another contrast in national manners, between Dimple's servant, the arrogant and duplicitous Jessamy, and Manly's servant, Jonathan, who is a plain, goodhearted, and incorruptible Yankee. In the "Prologue" to *The Contrast*, given to the actor playing Jonathan to recite, the didactic and exemplary purposes of the play are emphasized. "Our Author," the audience is forewarned, has confined himself to "native themes" so as to celebrate the "genuine sincerity" and "homespun habits" Americans have inherited from their "free-born ancestors." Tyler cannily used social comedy to explore issues that were particularly pressing for his fellow countrymen, with the emergence of a new political and social dispensation. In the process, he produced a work that answers Crevecoeur's question, "What is an American?," in a clear and thoroughly earnest way, and with an occasional wit that Crevecoeur himself could hardly have imagined.

The urge to point a moral evident in *The Contrast* is even more openly at work in those books that can lay claim to being the first American novels, *The Power of Sympathy* (1789) by William Hill Brown (1765–1793), *Charlotte Temple* (1794) by Susanna Haswell Rowson (1762–1824), and *The Coquette; or, The History of Eliza Wharton*

(1797) by Hannah Webster Foster (1758–1840). *The Power of Sympathy*, the first American novel, was published anonymously to begin with. It was originally attributed to the Boston writer, Sarah Wentworth Morton, because it deals with a contemporary scandal of incest and suicide in the Morton family. It was not until 1894 that Brown, also from Boston, was recognized as the author. An epistolary romance, its didactic purpose is announced in the preface: *The Power of Sympathy* was written, the reader is told, "To Expose the dangerous Consequences of Seduction" and to set forth "the Advantages of Female Education." The main plot deals with a threatened incestuous marriage between two characters called Harrington and Harriet Fawcett. They are both children of the elder Harrington, the first by his legitimate marriage and the second by his mistress Maria. When the relationship is discovered, Harriet dies of shock and sadness and Harrington commits suicide. Hardly distinguished in itself, the book nevertheless establishes a currency common to all three of these early American novels: a clear basis in fact, actuality (so anticipating and meeting any possible objections to fiction, imaginative self-indulgence or daydreaming), an even clearer moral purpose (so anticipating and meeting any possible objections from puritans or utilitarians), and a narrative that flirts with sensation and indulges in sentiment (so encouraging the reader to read on). Even more specifically, *The Power of Sympathy* shares the same currency as the books by Rowson and Webster in the sense that it places a young woman and her fate at the center of the narrative, and addresses other young women as the intended recipients of its message. This reflected an economic reality: in the new, vastly expanded literary marketplace of America, as in Europe, women constituted the main readership for fiction. It also, perhaps, had an ideological dimension: the novel was where women, and especially young women, could go to find a dramatic reflection of their problems, economic, social and moral – some sense, and appreciation, of the way they lived, or had to live, now.

This further dimension is more noticeable, inevitably perhaps, in novels actually written by women. Susanna Haswell Rowson's *Charlotte Temple* was published in London in 1791 and then in the United States three years later, where it became the first American bestseller. By 1933 it had gone through 161 editions; and it has been estimated that it has been read by a quarter to a half million people. In the preface to her novel, Rowson explains that the circumstances on which she founded the novel were related to her by "an old lady who had personally known Charlotte." "I have thrown over the whole a slight veil of fiction," she adds, "and substituted names and places according to my own fancy." And what she has written, she insists, has a fundamentally moral purpose. "For the perusal of the young and thoughtless of the fair sex, this Tale of Truth is designed," Rowson declares. The tale that follows this is essentially a simple one. Charlotte, a girl of fifteen in a school for young ladies, is seduced by an army officer called Montraville. Montraville is aided by an unscrupulous teacher whom Charlotte trusts, Mlle La Rue. After considerable hesitation, Charlotte elopes with Montraville from England to New York. There, she is deserted by both Montraville and Mlle La Rue, gives birth to a daughter, Lucy, and dies in poverty. What adds force, and a measure of complexity, to the tale are two things: Rowson's consistent habit of addressing the reader and her subtle pointers to the fact that, while Charlotte thinks she is in control of her fate, she fundamentally is not – she is at the mercy of male power and the machinations of others. Quite apart from establishing the American blueprint for a long line of stories about a young woman affronting her destiny, this is a subtle acknowledgment of the conflicted position in which young women, rich or poor, found themselves in the new republic. A more fluid social position for wealthy women, and relatively greater economic opportunities for the poorer ones, might persuade them all that they had more control over their destinies. Real control, however, still lay elsewhere. Coming to America does not empower or liberate Charlotte; on the contrary, as Rowson shows, it simply subjects her to the discovery of "the dangers lurking beneath" the surfaces of life. This is melodrama with a purpose. And that purpose, conceived within the sentimental constraints of the time and expressed in its conventional ethical language, is to give the people for whom it was written, the "dear girls" whom the narrator constantly addresses, a way of measuring and meeting their condition as women.

Something similar could be said about a brief novel by Judith Sargent Murray, *The Story of Margaretta* (1798), included in *The Gleaner* essays, in which, in a manner clearly meant to illustrate the author's beliefs, the heroine Margaretta manages to escape the usually dire consequences of seduction, thanks to her superiority of soul and education, and is rewarded with a loving husband. More persuasively and interestingly, it could also be said of *The Coquette*, an epistolary novel and a bestseller for which Hannah Webster Foster was not given credit until 1866. Until then, the author was known simply as "A Lady of Massachusetts." In a series of seventy-four letters, mainly from the heroine Eliza Wharton to her friend Lucy Freeman, another tale of seduction and abandonment is told. Eliza is the coquette of the title, but she is also a spirited young woman. Thoroughly aware of her own needs and charms, she is unwilling to bury herself in a conventional marriage. She is saved from a match with an elderly clergyman, Mr. Haly, when he dies before her parents can get them both to the altar. Another clergyman, the Reverend Boyer, courts her; however, she finds him dull. She would, she protests, gladly enter the kind of marriage enjoyed by her friends the Richmans, but such intimacy between equals seems rare to her. "Marriage is the tomb of friendship," she confides to Lucy; "it appears to me a very selfish state." Longing for adventure, she meets the self-confessed "rake" Peter Sanford and is entranced. Boyer, discovering the intimacy between Eliza and Sanford, gives Eliza up. Sanford deserts Eliza for an heiress. Still attracted, Eliza has an affair with Sanford; becoming pregnant, she leaves home and friends, and dies in childbirth; and Sanford, now finally admitting that Eliza was "the darling of my soul," leaves his wife and flees the country. The customary claim that the entire story was "founded on fact" is made by the author – and naturally so, since it was based on the experiences of a distant cousin. So is the customary invocation of moral purpose. What stays in the reader's mind, however, is the adventurous spirit of the heroine, despite its tragic, or rather melodramatic, consequences. "From the melancholy story of Eliza Warton," the novel concludes, "let the American fair learn to reject with disdain every insinuation derogatory to their true dignity and honor ... To associate is to approve; to approve is to be betrayed!" That may be one thematic level of *The Coquette*. But another, slyly subverting it, is Eliza's quest for freedom; her clearsighted recognition of what marriage entails for most women, given the laws and customs of the day, and her ardent longing for what she calls "opportunity, unbiassed by opinion, to gratify my disposition." On this level, *The Coquette* charts the difference between what women want and what they are likely to get. In the process, it poses a question to be explored more openly and fundamentally in many later American narratives: is it possible for an individual to remain free in society or to survive outside it?

Social questions about the new American republic were at the center of another significant prose narrative of this period, *Modern Chivalry* by Hugh Henry Brackenridge (1746–1816). Published in instalments between 1792 and 1815, *Modern Chivalry* was later described by Henry Adams as "a more thoroughly American book than any written before 1833." Its American character does not spring from its narrative structure, however, which is picaresque and clearly borrowed from the Spanish author Cervantes, but from its location and themes. The book is set in rural Pennsylvania and offers the first extended portrait of backwoods life in American fiction. Its two central characters are Captain John Farrago and his Irish servant Teague O'Regan, American versions of Don Quixote and Sancho Panza. And, as they travel around, their adventures provide an occasion for satirizing the manners of post-Revolutionary America. Farrago is a rather stuffy, aristocratic landowner, but narrative sympathy tends to be with him, or at least with his politics, since he is presented as an intelligent democrat, part Jeffersonian and part independent, inclining to the ideas of Thomas Paine. O'Regan, on the other hand, is portrayed as a knave and a fool, whose extraordinary self-assurance stems from his ignorance. At every stage of their journey, the two men meet some foolish group that admires O'Regan and offers him opportunities – as preacher, Indian treaty maker, potential husband for a genteel young lady – for which he is totally unequipped. The captain then has to invent excuses to stop such honors being bestowed on his servant; and each adventure is followed by a chapter of reflection on the uses and abuses of democracy. The satirical edge of *Modern Chivalry* anticipates the later Southwestern humorists. The disquisitions on democracy, in turn, reflect debates occurring at the time over the possible direction of the American republic. A notable contribution to these debates were the series of essays now called the *Federalist* papers (1787–1788) written by Alexander Hamilton (1757–1804), John Jay (1745–1829), and James Madison (1751–1836). The authors of these essays argued that, since people were "ambitious, vindictive, and rapacious," a strong central government was required to control "factions and convulsions." Furthermore, Madison (who was, in fact, a friend of Brackenridge) insisted that, in order to control faction without forfeiting liberty, it was necessary to elect men "whose wisdom," as Madison put it, "may best discern the true interests of their country." *Modern Chivalry* tends towards similar conclusions. The portrait of Teague O'Regan, after all, betrays the same distrust as the *Federalist* papers do of what Hamilton and his colleagues called "theoretic politicians" who believed that faction could be cured by "reducing mankind to a perfect equality in their political rights." In the novel, and in the papers, there is the same suspicion of populism, of ordinary people denied the guidance and control of their natural leaders, and a similar need to emphasize what Madison chose to term "the great points of difference between a Democracy and a Republic."

Brackenridge was not a professional author (he earned his living as a lawyer); neither were William Hill Brown, Rowson, and Foster. The person who has earned the title of first in this category in America is Charles Brockden Brown (1771–1810), although it is now fairly clear that Brown was one among several men and women who labored between 1776 and 1810 to earn their income from their writings. Under the influence of the English writer William Godwin, Brown wrote and published *Alcuin: A Dialogue*

(1798), a treatise on the rights of women. Then, further stimulated by Godwin's novel *Caleb Williams* and his own critical ideas about fiction, he wrote his four best novels in just two years: *Wieland; or, The Transformation* (1798), *Arthur Mervyn; or, Memoirs of the Year 1793* (1799–1800), *Ormond; or, The Secret Witness* (1799), and *Edgar Huntly; or, Memoirs of a Sleep-Walker* (1799). All four reveal a confluence of influences: to the moral and social purpose of Godwin was added the sentimentalism and interest in personal psychology of the English novelist Samuel Richardson and, above all perhaps, the horrors and aberrations of the Gothic school of fiction. To this was added Brown's own sense of critical mission. He believed in writing novels that would be both intellectual and popular: that would stimulate debate among the thoughtful, while their exciting plots and often bizarre or romantic characters would attract a larger audience. Brown was also strongly committed to using distinctively American materials: in the preface to *Edgar Huntly*, for example, he talks about rejecting "superstitious and exploded manners, Gothic castles and chimeras" in favor of "incidents of Indian hostility and perils of the Western Wilderness." The result of these ambitions and influences is a series of books that translate the Gothic into an American idiom, and that combine sensational elements such as murder, insanity, sexual aggression, and preternatural events with brooding explorations of social, political, and philosophical questions. These books also make art out of the indeterminate: the reader is left at the end with the queer feeling that there is little, perhaps nothing, a person can trust – least of all, the evidence of their senses.

Brown's first novel, *Wieland*, is a case in point. The older Wieland, a German mystic, emigrates to Pennsylvania, erects a mysterious temple on his estate, and dies there one night of spontaneous combustion. His wife dies soon afterwards, and their children Clara and the younger Wieland become friends with Catharine Pleyel and her brother Henry. Wieland marries Catharine, and Clara falls in love with Henry, who has a fiancée in Germany. A mysterious stranger called Carwin then enters the circle of friends; and, shortly after, a series of warnings are heard from unearthly voices. Circumstances, or perhaps the voices, persuade Henry that Clara and Carwin are involved with each other; he returns to his fiancée and marries her. And Wieland, inheriting the fanaticism of his father, is evidently driven mad by the voices and murders his wife and children. Carwin then confesses to Clara that he produced the voices by the "art" of *biloquium*, a form of ventriloquism that enables him to mimic the voices of others and project them over some distance. He was "without malignant intentions," he claims, and was simply carried away by his curiosity and his "passion for mystery." Wieland, escaping from an asylum, is about to murder Clara when Carwin, using his "art" for the last time, successfully orders him to stop. The unhappy madman then commits suicide, Carwin departs for a remote area of Pennsylvania, and Clara marries Henry Pleyel after the death of his first wife. These are the bare bones of the story, but what gives those bones flesh is the sense that the characters, and for that matter the reader, can never be quite sure what is the truth and what is not. Brown, for instance, was one of the first American writers to discover the uses of the unreliable narrator. Carwin professes the innocence of his intentions, but he also talks about being driven by a "mischievous daemon." More to the point, the entire novel is cast in the form of a letter from Clara, the last surviving member of the Wieland family, to an unnamed friend. And Clara does not hesitate to warn the reader that she is not necessarily to be trusted as a reporter of events.

The indeterminacy goes further. "Ideas exist in our minds that can be accounted for by no established laws," Clara observes. And it is never quite clear, not only whether or not she and Carwin are telling the truth, but how complicit Henry Pleyel and the younger Wieland are with the voices they hear. In his portraits of Henry and Wieland, Brown is exploring the two prevailing systems of thought in early America: respectively, the rationalism of the Enlightenment and the mysticism of Christianity. He is also casting both into doubt. Like other authors of the time, Brown liked to emphasize that his fictions were based on fact. He pointed out, in his prefatory "Advertisement" for his first novel, that there had recently been "an authentic case, remarkably similar to Wieland." Similarly, in both *Ormond* and *Arthur Mervyn*, he made use of an outbreak of yellow fever that had actually occurred in Philadelphia in 1793; and in *Edgar Huntly* he relied, not only on familiar settings, but on the contemporary interest in such diverse topics as Indians and somnambulism. What Brown built on this base, however, was unique: stories that were calculated to melt down the barrier between fact and fiction by suggesting that every narrative, experience, or judgment is always and inevitably founded on quite uncertain premises and assumptions.

Brown was read eagerly by a number of other distinguished writers of the time, among them Sir Walter Scott, John Keats, and Percy Bysshe Shelley. But he never achieved the wider popularity he desired. He wrote two other novels, *Clara Howard* (1801) and *Jane Talbot* (1801), in an apparent attempt to exploit the growing market for sentimental fiction. These were similarly unsuccessful. So, more and more, he turned to journalism to earn a living. In 1799 he founded *The Monthly Magazine and American Review*, which collapsed within a year. He then edited *The Literary Magazine and American Register* from 1803 until 1807, which was more successful. *Memoirs of Carwin*, a sequel to *Wieland*, began to appear in this periodical, but the story remained unfinished at the time of his death. In the last years of his life, his interest turned more to politics and history, a shift marked by his starting the semiannual *American Register, or General Repository of History, Politics, and Science*. Deprived of the popularity and income that he craved for during his lifetime, Brown has continued to receive less than his due share of attention. This is remarkable, not least because he anticipates so much of what was to happen in American fiction in the nineteenth century. His fascination with aberrant psychology, deviations in human thought and behavior, foreshadows the work of Edgar Allan Poe; so, for that matter, does his use of slippery narrators. His use of symbolism, and his transformation of Gothic into a strange, surreal mix of the extraordinary and the everyday, prepares the way for the fiction of Nathaniel Hawthorne and Herman Melville. Even his relocation of incidents of peril and adventure to what was then the Western wilderness clears a path for the romances of James Fenimore Cooper. Written at the turn of the century, the four major novels of Brown look back to the founding beliefs of the early republic and the founding patterns of the early novel. They also look forward to a more uncertain age, when writers were forced to negotiate a whole series of crises, including the profound moral, social, and political crisis that was to eventuate in civil war. The subtitle of the first novel Brown ever wrote, but never published, was "The Man Unknown to Himself." That captures the indeterminism at the heart of his work. It also intimates a need that was to animate so much later American writing: as it engaged, and still does, in a quest for identity, personal and national – a way of making the unknown known.

2

Inventing Americas

The Making of American Literature 1800–1865

Making a Nation

During the first half of the nineteenth century, the United States was transformed from an infant republic into a large, self-confident nation, albeit a nation divided and eventually torn apart, as Thomas Jefferson had feared, by the burning issue of slavery. The population more than trebled, from nine to thirty-one million. The rapid expansion of the railroad and manufacturing industry began shifting the national economic basis and the population from country to town. The United States itself expanded from its eastern seaboard base of sixteen states to assume continental dimensions. As the nation grew, so did the opportunities for writers. The lecture circuit generated huge audiences across the country. Newspapers and magazines proliferated. And one of the most literate populations in the world, eager for entertainment and information, opened up the possibility of writing as a means of making a living. Many pursued that possibility. Some – like Susan Warren (1839–1885), author of *The Wide, Wide World* (1850), the first American novel to sell more than a million copies – even succeeded.

The Making of American Myths

Myths of an emerging nation

One of the first writers to take advantage of the greater opportunities for publication that were opening up, and in the process become one of the first American writers to achieve international fame, was Washington Irving (1783–1859). Irving established his reputation with *Salmagundi; or, The Whim-Whams and Opinions of Launcelot Langstaff Esq., and Others* (1807–1808), a series of satirical miscellanies concerned with New York society that ran to twenty numbers. The leading essays were written by Irving, his brothers, and James Kirke Paulding (1778–1860), all members of a group known as the "Nine Worthies" or "Lads of Kilkenny" of "Cockloft Hall." Federalist in politics, conservative in social principles, and comic in tone, they included one piece by Irving, "Of the Chronicles of the Renowned and Antient City of Gotham" that supplied New York City with its enduring nickname of Gotham.

A Brief History of American Literature. By Richard Gray
© 2011 Richard Gray

Irving was now famous as an author, wit, and man of society, and to consolidate his reputation he published *A History of New York from the Beginning of the World to the End of the Dutch Dynasty* (1809) under the pen name of Diedrich Knickerbocker. Often regarded as the first important work of comic literature written by an American, it initiated the term "Knickerbocker School" for authors like Irving himself, Paulding, Fitz-Greene Hallek (1790–1867), and Joseph Rodman Drake (1795–1820), who wrote about "little old New York" in the years before the Civil War. Then, in 1820, he published his most enduring work, *The Sketch Book of Geoffrey Crayon, Gent.*, a collection of essays and sketches that was enormously successful in both England and the United States. *The Sketch Book* contains two small masterpieces that initiated the great tradition of the American short story, "Rip Van Winkle" and "The Legend of Sleepy Hollow." Four other sketches are also set in America, but most of the other pieces are descriptive and thoughtful essays on England, where Irving was still living. Both "Rip Van Winkle" and "Sleepy Hollow" have origins in German folklore. Irving admits as much in a "Note" to the first tale. Both also owe a debt, in terms of stylistic influence, to Sir Walter Scott. Nevertheless, both exploit their specifically American settings and create American myths: they explore the social and cultural transformations occurring in America at the time in terms that are at once gently whimsical and perfectly serious. In "Rip Van Winkle," the lazy, hen-pecked hero of the story ventures into the Catskill Mountains of New York State to discover there some little men in Dutch costume bowling at ninepins. Taking many draughts of some strange beverage they have brewed, he falls into a deep sleep. When he returns to his village, after waking up, he eventually realizes that twenty years have passed, the Revolution has been and gone, and that, "instead of being a subject of his Majesty George the Third, he was now a free citizen of the United States." The news naturally takes a long time to sink in; and, at first, when he is surrounded in his homeplace by people whom he does not recognize and who do not recognize him, he begins to doubt his own identity. His dilemma is a gently comic response to traumatic change; and it offers a genial reflection in miniature of the sudden, disconcerting process of alteration – and possible reactions to it – experienced by the nation as a whole. A similar transposition of American history into American legend occurs in "Sleepy Hollow." This story of how the superstitious hero, Ichabod Crane, was bested by the headless horseman of Brom Bones, an extrovert Dutchman and Crane's rival in love, allows Irving to parody several forms of narrative, among them tall tales, ghost stories, and the epic. But it also permits him, once again, to reflect on change and to present a vanishing America, which is the setting for this story, as an endangered pastoral ideal. The tendency towards a more lyrical, romantic strain suggested by Irving's evocation of the sleepy hollow where Ichabod Crane lived became a characteristic of his later work. Irving's subsequent career was erratic, and he never recovered the wit and fluency of his early style. Nevertheless, in his best work, he was a creator of significant American myths: narratives that gave dramatic substance to the radical changes of the time, and the nervousness and nostalgia those changes often engendered. Perhaps he was so effective in fashioning those myths because the nervousness about the new America, and nostalgia for the old – and, beyond that, for Europe – were something that he himself felt intensely. He was writing himself, and the feelings he typified, into legend.

The making of Western myth

Legend of a very different kind was the work of James Fenimore Cooper (1789–1851). If any single person was the creator of the myth of the American West, and all its spellbinding contradictions, then Cooper was. But he was far more than that. He was the founding father of the American historical novel, exploring the conflicts of American society in a time of profound change. He also helped to develop and popularize such widely diverse literary forms as the sea novel, the novel of manners, political satire and allegory, and the dynastic novel in which over several generations American social practices and principles are subjected to rigorous dramatic analysis. And Cooper did not begin writing and publishing until his thirties. Before that, he had served at sea, then left to marry and settle as a country gentleman in New York State. His first novel, *Precaution* (1820), was in fact written after his wife challenged his claim that he could write a better book than the English novel he was reading to her. A conventional novel of manners set in genteel English society, this was followed by a far better work, *The Spy: A Tale of the Neutral Ground* (1821). Set in Revolutionary New York State, on the "neutral ground" of Westchester County, its hero is Harvey Birch, who is supposed to be a Loyalist spy but is secretly in the service of General Washington. Birch is faithful to the Revolutionary cause but a convoluted plot reveals his emotional ties to some of the Loyalists. What the reader is presented with here, in short, is a character prototype that Cooper had learned from Sir Walter Scott and was to use in later fiction, most notably in his portrait of Natty Bumppo, the hero of the Leatherstocking novels. The hero is himself a "neutral ground" to the extent that he, his actions and allegiances, provide an opportunity for opposing social forces to be brought into a human relationship with one another. The moral landscape he negotiates is a place of crisis and collision; and that crisis and collision are expressed in personal as well as social terms, as a function of character as well as event. *The Spy* was an immediate success. One reviewer hailed Cooper as "the first who has deserved the appellation of a distinguished American novel writer." And it was followed, just two years later, by the first of the five Leatherstocking Tales, *The Pioneers* (1823).

Set in 1793 in Otsego County in the recently settled region of New York State, *The Pioneers* introduces the reader to the ageing figure of Natty Bumppo, known here as Leatherstocking. The reader also meets Chingachgook, the friend and comrade of Natty from the Mohican tribe; and, in the course of the story, Chingachgook dies despite Natty's efforts to save him. The other four Leatherstocking Tales came over the next eighteen years. *The Last of the Mohicans* (1826) presents Bumppo, here called Hawkeye, in his maturity and is set in 1757 during the Seven Years' War between the French and the British. In *The Prairie* (1827), Bumppo, known simply as the trapper, has joined the westward movement; he is now in his eighties and, at the end of the novel, he dies. *The Pathfinder* (1840) is set soon after *The Last of the Mohicans*, in the same conflict between the French and Indians and the British colonials. Here, Bumppo is tempted to think of marriage. But, when he learns that the woman in question loves another, he nobly accepts that he cannot have her. Like the many Western heroes for which he was later to serve as prototype, he recognizes that, as he puts it, it is not according to his "gifts" to love and to marry. The last novel to be written, *The Deerslayer* (1841), is, in fact, the first novel in chronological order of events. It takes the reader back to upstate New York in the 1740s. A young man here, Natty Bumppo begins the action known as Deerslayer. In the course of the story, though, he kills an Indian in a fight that approaches the status of ritual; and, before he dies, the man he has killed gives him a new name, Hawkeye. So the series ends with the initiation of its hero into manhood. It does not quite begin with his death; nevertheless, there is clearly a regressive tendency at work here. The Leatherstocking Tales, as a whole, move back in time, back further into the American past and the youth and innocence of the hero. As they do so, they move ever further away from civilization, in terms of setting and subject, and ever further away from social realism, in terms of approach. At work here, in short, is an Edenic impulse common in American writing that drives the imagination out of the literal and into romance and myth – and out of a world where the individual is defined in relation to society and into one where he or she is more likely to be situated outside it. As the conception of him alters over the course of the five Leatherstocking Tales, Natty Bumppo gravitates more and more towards the condition of an American Adam: in his comradeship with another man, his virginity, as much as in his reliance on action and instinct rather than thought and reasoning – and in his indebtedness, too, not to education or convention but to natural wisdom and natural morality.

Natty Bumppo is more than just an American Adam, however, as his recollection of earlier figures set on "neutral ground" suggests, as well as his anticipation of later Western heroes. And the Leatherstocking Tales are far more than types of the American pastoral, resituating Eden somewhere in the mythic past of the country. They are densely textured historical narratives using contrasts and conflicts both within and between characters to explore the national destiny. *The Prairie* illustrates this. The characteristically convoluted plot involves a series of daring adventures, raids, and rescues, during the course of which Bumppo saves his companions from both a prairie fire and a buffalo stampede. Woven through that plot is a close examination of human nature and its implications for human society. The original inhabitants of America, for example, are taken as instances of natural man but, the reader soon discovers, the instances are ambiguous. On the one hand, there are the Pawnees, who are "strikingly noble," their "fine stature and admirable proportions" being an outward and visible sign of their possession of such "Roman" virtues as dignity, decorum, and courage. On the other, there are the Sioux, a race who resemble "demons rather than men" and whose frightening appearance is matched only by their treachery and savagery. Nature, in turn, is represented variously, as benevolent, the source of Natty's natural wisdom ("'Tis an eddication!" he is wont to declare, while gazing at his surroundings), and the scene of a desperate internecine battle that reinforces the account of Indians as both Rousseauistic noble savages and imps of the devil. The issue of whether human beings are good, originally innocent, or evil, steeped in original sin, is sounded here. So is the issue of whether America is an Eden or a wilderness. And both those issues, Cooper realized and intimates, feed into the question of what kind of society was needed, particularly in the New World. This was a question fundamental to the infant republic, and *The Prairie* offers a fascinatingly ambivalent answer.

At his best, as in *The Prairie*, Cooper explores the basic tensions at work in American culture and history in a way that allows free play to the opposing forces. At the same time, he creates mythic figures, of whom Natty Bumppo is easily the most notable, who offer a focus for debates about the character of American democracy – and also possess the simplicity and stature required of any great epic hero. The first time we see Bumppo in *The Prairie* is typical. He appears to a group of travelers, and the reader, standing in the distance on the great plains with the sun going down behind him. "The figure was colossal, the attitude musing and melancholy," the narrator observes, and "embedded as it was in its setting of garish light, it was impossible to distinguish its just proportions or true character." Larger than life, romantic and mysterious, Natty Bumppo here anticipates a whole series of Western and American heroes. And a similarly heroic closure is given to the story of our hero. At the end of *The Prairie*, Natty dies with his gaze "fastened on the clouds which hung around the western horizon, reflecting the bright colours and giving form to the glorious tints of an American sunset." With that grand, ultimate entry into nature, Cooper may be suggesting the passing of the democratic possibilities Natty Bumppo represents. *The Prairie* certainly has an autumnal mood: it is set firmly in the past, and there are constant references to the way immigration and cultivation, the destruction of the wilderness and the scattering of the Indians have changed the West – and, quite possibly, America – between then and the time of writing. Perhaps; and, if so, the novel is as much a new Western as a traditional one, mapping out the destructive tendencies of the westward movement as well as its place in a heroic tale of national expansion. One further layer of complexity is then added to a narrative that is, in any event, a debate and a mythic drama, a great historical novel and an American epic in prose, that explores the different routes a democratic republic might take, the conflict between law and freedom, the clearing and the wilderness, communal ethics and the creed of self-reliance.

Over the three decades when the Leatherstocking series was written, many other attempts were made to translate experience in the West into literature. Notable among these were two novels, *Logan: A Family History* (1822) and *Nick of the Woods; or, The Jibbenainesay* (1837), and an autobiographical narrative first serialized in *The Knickerbocker Magazine* in 1847 and then published in 1849, *The Oregon Trail*. *Logan: A Family History* was one of the several novels and many publications of John Neal (1793–1876). It is an essentially romantic account of a noble savage, the Indian chief who gives the book its title. The reverse side of the coin is suggested by *Nick of the Woods*. An immensely popular tale in its day and also Robert M. Bird's (1806–1854) best work, it has a complicated plot involving Indian raids and massacres, a romantic heroine taken into captivity but eventually rescued, and an eponymous central character who is bent on revenge against the Indians for the slaughter of his family. Throughout all the plot convolutions, however, what remains starkly simple is the portrait of the Indians. As Bird depicts them, they are violent, superstitious, and treacherous. They may be savages but they are very far from being noble.

The Oregon Trail is another matter. For a start, it was written by someone, Francis Parkman (1823–1893), who went on from writing it to become one of the most distinguished historians of the period. Parkman was one of a generation of American historians who combined devotion to research with a romantic sweep of imagination, and a scholarly interest in the history of America or democratic institutions or both with dramatic flair and a novelistic eye for detail. Apart from Parkman himself, the most notable of these romantic historians were John Lothrop Motley (1814–1877), George Bancroft (1800–1891), and William Hinckling Prescott (1796–1859). Published before his histories, *The Oregon Trail* is an account of a journey Parkman took along the trail of the title in 1846. His purpose in taking the trip was twofold: to improve his frail health and study Indian life. Skilled in woodcraft and a decent shot, he survived the hardship of the trek, but only just: the strain of traveling eventually led to a complete breakdown in his health, rather than the recovery for which he had hoped. Incapable of writing, he was forced to dictate his story to a cousin and traveling companion. The result has been described as the first account of a literary white man who actually lived by choice for a while among Native Americans. What emerges from this account is, like the other work of Parkman and the romantic historians, an intriguing mix of fact and fiction. It is also, and equally intriguingly, double-edged. As the narrator of *The Oregon Trail*, a Harvard graduate and a member of a prominent Boston family, encounters the landscape and peoples of the West, his tone tends to hover sometimes between condescension and disgust, the style verges on the mandarin.

Yet, for all that, Parkman remembers that he found much to admire, or even cherish, in the West. The two scouts who accompanied him are portrayed in frankly romantic terms. One has the rough charm of the prairie, and an indefatigable "cheerfulness and gayety," the other a "natural refinement and delicacy of mind"; the both of them, in their different ways, are true knights of the wild. Native American life, too, is celebrated for its color and occasionally chivalric touches. "If there be anything that deserves to be called romantic in the Indian character," Parkman explains, "it is to be sought in . . . friendships . . . common among many of the prairie tribe." Parkman himself, he discloses, enjoyed just such an intimacy, becoming "excellent friends" with an Indian he calls "the Panther": "a noble-looking fellow," with a "stately and graceful figure" and "the very model of a wild prairie-rider." This is the homoerotic romance across the line between white and Indian that Cooper imagined, replayed here in however muted a key. Parkman is framing his recollections within a literary tradition that includes the author of the Leatherstocking Tales and, before him, Sir Walter Scott. Parkman is drawn to the romance of the West, what he sees as its primitive beauty, its bold colors and simple chivalry, even while he is also repelled by its rawness, its lack of refinement. So he ends up decidedly at odds with himself, when he eventually returns from the trail. "Many and powerful as were the attractions of the settlements," Parkman concludes, "we looked back regretfully to the wilderness behind us." That was a broken, uncertain note to be sounded in many later stories about going West, negotiating what the traveler sees as the borderline between civilization and savagery. Parkman was playing his part, in *The Oregon Trail*, in inaugurating the frontier as a site of imaginative adventure: with the West perceived as it was precisely because it was seen through the eyes of the East – as a place destructively, but also seductively, other.

A year after the publication of *The Last of the Mohicans*, in 1827, a very different story about the relationship between white people and Native Americans appeared, and one different in turn from the accounts of Neal, Bird, and Parkman: *Hope Leslie* by Catharine Marie Sedgwick (1789–1867). Sedgwick had already produced two best-sellers, *A New England Tale: Sketches of New-England Character and Manners* (1822) and *Redwood* (1824). She was to go on to publish many other books. The main figures in her novels tend to be women, and often women of independence and courage. *Hope Leslie*, too, focuses on the destiny of women, but in even more interesting ways than Sedgwick's other novels. There is a white heroine, whose name gives the book its title. There is also a Pequod woman, Magawisca, who saves a white man, Everell Fletcher, from execution at the hands of her father, the chief, in the manner of Pocahontas. Her act involves considerable physical, as well as emotional, courage, since she offers her body to the weapon aimed at Everell's neck and, as a result, loses her arm. Hope Leslie herself shows similar heroism when, on not one but two occasions, she frees Indian women from what she considers unjust imprisonment. And Magawisca resumes her status as an evidently "superior being" towards the end of the narrative, when she is captured by the whites. At her trial for "brewing conspiracy ... among the Indian tribes," she is defended by the historical figure of John Eliot, whom Sedgwick identifies as the "first Protestant missionary to the Indians." Magawisca, however, insists that she needs no defense, since the tribunal has no authority over her. Clearly, their heroism makes Magawisca and Hope Leslie doubles. Their primary allegiance is to conscience: what Magawisca calls "the Great Spirit" that "hath written his laws on the hearts of his original children." Obeying those laws, they defy those set in power in their respective societies, who are determinately male: Magawisca defies her father, of course, and both she and her white double Hope defy the authority of the Puritan fathers.

What is equally notable about this rewriting of Western tropes is the intimacy that evidently exists in *Hope Leslie* between white and Indian characters. Unlike Cooper, Sedgwick is perfectly willing to contemplate marriage between the two races. Faith Leslie, the sister of Hope, is carried into captivity while still a child; she marries Oneco, the brother of Magawisca; and she then refuses the chance offered her to return to the Puritan community. Sedgwick is also willing to countenance signs of kinship between women of the two races. In one narrative sequence, Hope Leslie resists the prejudices of the age and the conventions of female behavior by liberating an Indian woman called Nelena from prison. Nelena has been condemned as a witch, after she cured a snakebite with the help of herbal medicine; and she repays the debt by arranging for Magawisca to meet Hope with news of Faith. The two women, Hope and Magawisca, meet secretly in a cemetery where both their mothers are buried, and plot a way for Hope to meet her sister even though this would violate colonial law. The entire scene subtly interweaves intimations of debt and intimacy. The graves of the mothers of the two women lie side by side, the women recall how Magawisca rescued Everell Fletcher and Hope saved Nelena as they talk about the marriage between the brother of one and the sister of the other. It is a celebration of a sisterhood of the spirit and the blood.

A word of caution is perhaps necessary here. Sedgwick did not question the prevailing contemporary belief in the manifest destiny of the white race. For that matter, she did not seek to challenge the conventional notion that marriage was a woman's proper aim and reward. Within these constraints, however, Sedgwick did find a place for female integrity and for intimacy between the races; and one need only compare *Hope Leslie* with the Leatherstocking Tales to measure the difference. It is partly a matter of reversal: male transgression and bonding are replaced by, yet reflected in, their female equivalents. It is partly a matter of rewriting, radical revision: here, the connections between the races are what matter rather than the conflicts – and, whatever else may be present, there is an intensely felt sense of community and continuity. Cooper was a powerful creator of frontier myths but he was not, by any means, the only one: the legends figured in *Hope Leslie* also had a significant impact on how later Americans imagined the movement of their nation west.

The making of Southern myth

However much they differ, though, writers like Cooper and Sedgwick do have common interests and ideas, derived from the basic currency of Western myth: a belief in mobility, a concern with the future, a conviction that, whatever problems it may have, America is still a land of possibility. The counter myth to this is the myth of the South: preoccupied with place and confinement rather than space and movement, obsessed with the guilt and burden of the past, riddled with doubt, unease, and the sense that, at their best, human beings are radically limited and, at their worst, tortured, grotesque, or evil. And if Cooper was the founding father of the Western myth in literature, even though he never actually saw the prairie, then, even more queerly, Edgar Allan Poe (1809–1849) was the founding father of Southern myth, although he was actually born in Boston and hardly ever used Southern settings in his fiction or his poetry. What makes Poe a founder of Southern myth, typically of him, is not so much a matter of the literal as of the imaginative. "The Fall of the House of Usher" (1839) is set in an anonymous landscape, or rather dreamscape, but it has all the elements that were later to characterize Southern Gothic: a great house and family falling into decay and ruin, a feverish, introspective hero half in love with death, a pale, ethereal heroine who seems and then is more dead than alive, rumors of incest and guilt – and, above all, the sense that the past haunts the present and that there is evil in the world and it is strong.

Figure 2.1   Portrait of Edgar Allan Poe. Photo: akg-images.

Poe began his literary career with a volume of poetry, *Tamerlane and Other Poems* (1827). Published anonymously and at his own expense, it went unnoticed. But it clearly announced his poetic intentions: aims and ambitions that were later to be articulated in such seminal essays as "The Philosophy of Composition" (1846) and "The Poetic Principle" (1850) and further put into practice in the later volumes, *Poems by E A Poe* (1831) and *The Raven and Other Poems* (1845). The poet, Poe wrote in his essays, should be concerned, first and last, with the "circumscribed Eden" of his own dreams. "It is the desire of the moth for the star," Poe says of the poetic impulse in "The Poetic Principle." According to his prescription, the poet's task is to weave a tapestry of talismanic signs and sounds in order to draw, or rather subdue, the reader into sharing the world beyond phenomenal experience. Poems make nothing happen in any practical, immediate sense, Poe suggests. On the contrary, the ideal poem becomes one in which the words efface themselves, disappear as they are read, leaving only a feeling of significant absence, of no-thing.

Just how Poe turned these poetic ideas into practice is briefly suggested in one of his poems, "Dreamland," where the narrator tells us that he has reached a strange new land "out of SPACE – out of TIME." That is the land all Poe's art occupies or longs for: a fundamentally elusive reality, the reverse of all that our senses can receive or our reason can encompass – something that lies beyond life that we can discover only in sleep, madness or trance, in death especially, and, if we are lucky, in a poem or story. Certain poetic scenes and subjects are favorites with Poe precisely because they reinforce his ultimately visionary aims. Unsurprisingly, life after death is a favorite topic, in poems like "Annabel Lee" and "The Sleeper." So, too, is the theme of a strange, shadowy region beyond the borders of normal consciousness: places such as those described in "The City in the Sea" or "Eldorado" which are, in effect, elaborate figures for death. Whatever the apparent subject, the movement is always away from the ordinary, phenomenal world in and down to some other, subterranean level of consciousness and experience. The sights and sounds of a realizable reality may be there in a poem like "To Helen," but their presence is only fleeting, ephemeral. Poe's scenes are always shadowy and insubstantial, the colors dim, the lighting dusky. In the final instance, the things of the real world are there only to be discarded

Disengagement was not, however, something that Poe could pursue as a practical measure. He had to earn his living. He worked as an editor for various journals, including *Burton's Gentleman's Magazine* and *Graham's Magazine*; he was associated with other journals, and he was an indefatigable essayist and reviewer. What the magazines wanted, in particular, were stories; and in 1835 Poe attracted attention with one of his first short stories, "MS Found in a Bottle," which won first prize in a contest judged by John Pendleton Kennedy (1795–1870) – himself a writer and author of one of the first idyllic fictional accounts of life on the old plantation, *Swallow Barn; or, A Sojourn in the Old Dominion* (1832). This short story was followed by more and more tales appealing to the contemporary taste for violent humor and macabre incident. His first collection of stories, *Tales of the Grotesque and Arabesque*, was published in 1840; it included "Ligeia," "Berenice," and "The Assignation." In 1845 *Tales* appeared, a book that reprinted previous work. This later collection contained "The Pit and the Pendulum" and "The Tell-Tale Heart," among other notable pieces. In the earlier, in turn, Poe made his attentions as a short story writer clear in a brief preface. It was true, Poe admitted, that many of his stories were Gothic because they had terror as their "thesis." But that terror, he went on, was not of the conventional kind, since it had little to do with the usual Gothic paraphernalia; it was, instead, a terror "of the soul."

Whatever else he might have been, Poe was an unusually perceptive (if often also malicious) critic. And he was especially perceptive about his own work. Poe did not invent the Gothic tale, any more than he invented the detective story, science fiction, or absurd humor. To each of these genres or approaches, however, he did – as he realized and, in some instances, boasted – make his own vital contribution. In a detective story like "The Murders in the Rue Morgue," for example, Poe created the detective story as a tale of ratiocination, a mystery that is gradually unraveled and solved. He also created the character of the brilliant amateur who solves a crime that seems beyond the talents of the professionals. And in his Gothic stories, he first destabilizes the reader by using unreliable narrators: madmen and liars, initially rational men who have their rationalism thoroughly subverted, men who should by all commonsensical standards be dead. And he then locates the terror within, as something that springs from and bears down upon the inner life. In Poe's stories, the source of mystery and anxiety is something that remains inexplicable. It is the urge to self-betrayal that haunts the narrator of "The Tell-Tale Heart," or the cruel and indomitable will of the narrator of "Ligeia" which finally transforms reality into fantasy, his living wife into a dead one. It is the impulse towards self-destruction, and the capacity for sinking into nightmare worlds of his own creation, that the protagonist and narrator of *The Narrative of Arthur Gordon Pym* (1838) reveals at so many moments of his life. Poe tears the Gothic tale out of the rationalist framework it previously inhabited, and he makes it a medium for exploring the irrational, even flirting with the anti-rational. As such, he makes it as central and vital to the Romantic tradition as, say, the lyric poem or the dream play.

"The Fall of the House of Usher" shows how Poe makes a fictional art out of inwardness and instability. The narrator, an initially commonsensical man, is confused by his feelings when he first arrives at the home of his childhood friend, Roderick Usher. But he is inclined to dismiss such feelings as "superstition," and even when he is reunited with Usher, his response is "half of awe," suggesting a suspicion that his host might know things hidden to him, and "half of pity," suggesting the superiority of the rational man. Gradually, the narrator comes to speak only of "awe." He even admits that he feels "the wild influences" of Usher's "fantastic yet impressive superstitions" "creeping upon" him. The scene is set for the final moment, when Roderick's sister Madeline arises from her grave to be reunited with him in death, and the House of Usher sinks into a "deep and dank tarn." At this precise moment, Usher turns to the narrator and speaks to him, for the last time, addressing him as "*Madman*." The reversal is now complete: either because the narrator has succumbed to the "superstition" of his host, or because his continued rationality argues for his essential insanity, his failure to comprehend a truth that lies beyond reason. Nothing is certain as the tale closes, except that what we have witnessed is an urgent, insistent movement inward: from daylight reality towards darker, ever more subterranean levels, in the house and in the mind of the hero. And as the narrator moves ever further inward, into "Usher" the house, we the readers move ever further inward into "Usher" the fiction. The structures of the two journeys correspond. So, for that matter, do the arts of the hero and author: Roderick

Usher uses his to transform his guests' minds and expectations, so also does Poe with his imaginative guests. And at the moment of revelation at the end – when the full measure of the solipsistic vision is revealed – both "Usher" the house and "Usher" the tale disintegrate, disappear, leaving narrator and reader alone with their thoughts and surmises. In short, the house of Usher is a house of mirrors. Every feature of the story is at once destabilizing and self-reflexive, referring us back to the actual process of creative production, by its author, and re-production, by its readers. Like so many other tales by Poe, "The Fall of the House of Usher" stands at the beginning of a long line of Southern narratives that incline toward narcissism and nostalgia, the movement inward and the movement back. And it stands at the beginning, also, of an even longer line of fiction, American and European, that disconcerts the reader by jettisoning the mundane in favor of the magical and turning the literal world into a kind of shadow play.

Legends of the Old Southwest

Straddling the borders between the myth of the West and the myth of the South are those heroes and writers who are associated with the humor and legends of the Old Southwest. As for heroes, the notable figures here are Davy Crockett (1786–1836) and Mike Fink (1770?–1823?). Crockett spent a shiftless youth until his political career began when he was thirty. Serving in Congress from 1827 to 1831, and from 1833 to 1835, he was quickly adopted by Whig politicians, opposing the populist hero Andrew Jackson, who saw in Crockett a useful tool for associating their party with backwoods democracy. Davy, who boasted that he relied on "natural-born sense instead of law learning," was soon turned by skillful politicians into a frontier hero, whose picturesque eccentricities, country humor, tall tales, shrewd native wit, and rowdy pioneer spirit were all magnified and celebrated. With the help of a ghost writer, Crockett wrote *A Narrative of the Life of David Crockett, of the State of Tennessee* (1834): a book clearly designed to help him gain or retain political popularity. But soon after that, tales of the legendary frontiersman had begun to spread, by word of mouth, songs and poems, almanacs (known as Crockett Almanacs), and by such publications as *The Lion of the West* by James Kirke Paulding, *Sketches and Eccentricities of Colonel David Crockett of West Tennessee* (1833) by Mathew St Claire Clarke (1798–1842?), and *An Account of Colonel Crockett's Tour to the North and Down East* (1835). In some of these publications, Crockett may have had a hand; in many, he did not. And when he died at the Alamo in 1836, even more life was given to the legend.

As an actual historical figure, less is known of Mike Fink than of Crockett. He was a keelboatman on the Ohio and Mississippi. Before that, he had worked as Crockett had, as an Indian scout; and, when he left the river, he moved west to become a trapper. It was on the river, however, that his violence, humor, and energy made him a legend. He evidently helped to foster that legend by telling tales about himself, but it was others who wrote the tales down, among them newspapermen Thomas Bangs Thorpe (1810–1856) and Joseph M. Field (1815–1878). The stories about Fink appeared in books, the earliest of which was *The Last of the Boatmen* by Morgan Neville published in 1829. They also appeared in magazines and newspapers, like the *Spirit of the Times*, which specialized in tales of the frontier and sporting sketches, and in almanacs – among them, the Crockett Almanacs, which did not confine themselves to the exploits of Davy.

Crockett and Fink inhabit an interesting borderland between "popular" and "high" culture, the political and the legendary, oral folk tradition and published literature. The first writer to make the legends and humor of the Old Southwest part of the literary tradition was Augustus Baldwin Longstreet (1790–1870). A Georgia lawyer and academic, Longstreet published *Georgia Scenes: Characters, Incidents &c, in the First Half-Century of the Republic* in 1835. In a series of sketches varying from the descriptive to the dramatic, Longstreet presented his readers with illustrations of life in the remoter parts of the state. The sketches were linked by the appearance in nearly all of them of a narrator bearing a suspicious resemblance to the author himself – a kindly, generous but occasionally pompous and patronizing man who tended to treat his subjects as if they were specimens of some strange form of life, with a mixture of curiosity and amusement. A healthy distance was maintained from characters who were presented not so much as individuals as in terms of their common behavioral patterns; and the combined effect of the detachment, the condescension, and the generalizing tendency was to create an effect somewhere between folktale and caricature, legend and cartoon.

Longstreet's probable motives for writing in this way were ones he shared with many other Southwestern humorists: among them, Joseph Glover Baldwin (1815–1864), author of *The Flush Times of Alabama and Mississippi* (1853), Johnson Jones Hooper (1815–1862), who wrote *Some Adventures of Captain Simon Suggs, Late of the Tallapoosa Volunteers* (1845), and Thomas Bangs Thorpe, whose stories about what he called "a hardy and indomitable race" of frontier people were collected in *The Big Bear of Arkansas; and Other Sketches Illustrative of Character and Incidents in the South-West* (1845). As a professional gentleman and a Whig, Longstreet was inclined to nervousness about the crude habits of frontier life. Violent, rowdy, and anarchic, it frightened anyone used to a more stable culture with habits of deference and respect. So, in an eminently understandable way, Longstreet and other Southwestern humorists attempted to distance their frontier surroundings, to place them in a framework that would make them manageable and known. They tried, in effect, to enclose and encode them. One way of this was via the humor: by its means, violence was transformed into play. And another way of doing it was via legend: they also tried to identify the rough, rude world they saw around them with a familiar rural type – the plain farmer, with his straightforward approach to things, his raw integrity and earthy language, and above all his muscular self-reliance. By *this* means, violence could be interpreted as an excess of high spirits and honest energy; and the disruption of established social patterns could be regarded as a crucial step on the road to the recovery of a deeply traditional democratic ideal.

As time passed, though, the narrative enclosure in which Longstreet, Baldwin, and other Southwestern humorists chose to pen their frontier subjects tended to dissolve. And with dramatic results: the work that certainly represents the culmination of Southwestern humor, *The Adventures of Huckleberry Finn*, shows that. Even before that, the abolition of the conventional narrative frame was a notable feature of the comic stories and tall tales of George Washington Harris (1814–1869). Harris began writing about his backwoods hero, Sut Lovingood, as early as 1843, in pieces published in the *Spirit of the Times*. But it was not until after the Civil War, in 1867, that a full-length volume appeared, *Sut Lovingood: Yarns Spun by a " Nat'ral Born Durn'd Fool. Warped and Wove For Public Wear*. Sut tells his own tales. And all those tales are guided by his belief that, as he puts it, "Man was made a-pupus just to eat, drink, an' fur stayin' awake in the yearly part of the nites." A native of rural Tennessee, Sut is a primitive or natural man: a man who stands on the periphery of conventional society and yet still offers significant comments on it. His life, circumscribed by the animal functions, is a continual drag on our own pretensions, about the nature of our personalities and the efficacy or security of the society we have organized for ourselves. At one point in his narrative, Sut admits that he has "nara a soul, nuffin but a whisky proof gizzard"; and Harris's habitual strategy, of making us, the readers, share Sut's life and experience the connection between what he is and how he lives, leads us to suspect that in similar conditions we might be forced to say exactly the same. In effect, Sut Lovingood is one of the first in a long line of American vernacular heroes: who compel the reader to attend because, the sense is, no matter how poor or peripheral they may appear to be, they and what they have to say deserve attention – not least, because they seem to offer us a freakish mirror image of ourselves.

The Making of American Selves

The Transcendentalists

"Our age is retrospective," wrote Ralph Waldo Emerson (1803–1882) at the beginning of perhaps his most famous work, *Nature* (1836). "It builds the sepulchres of the fathers. It writes biographies, histories, and criticism," he continued. "The foregoing generations beheld God and nature face to face, through their eyes. Why should we not also enjoy an original relation to the universe?" An original relation to the universe, one founded on self-reliance and self-respect, is the key to the thought and work of Emerson. It also inspired a number of other writers at the time who saw the liberation of the self as the American imperative. For Emerson, everything served to confirm a belief in the supreme importance of the individual, the superiority of intuition to intellect (or, as he was to put it, of "Reason" to "Understanding"), and the presence of a spiritual power in both nature and the individual human being. "If we live truly," Emerson was to write in "Self-Reliance" (1841), "we shall see truly." And he dedicated himself to living and writing the truth as he saw it. He had been keeping a journal since he was a student at Harvard, in which he recorded his daily experiences and impressions, the facts of his life. He was to continue this practice until he died; and the facts he recorded there became the source of the truths he endeavored to develop in his essays and poems. From these were to be drawn pieces such as the "Divinity School Address" (1838) and "The Over-Soul" (1841), in which he rejected institutional forms of religion in favor of his belief that "God incarnates himself in man."

Emerson began to lecture regularly on the lyceum circuit, to spread his ideas as well as to make a living. He settled in Concord, Massachusetts in 1835, where he became intimate friends with other writers like Nathaniel Hawthorne, Henry David Thoreau, Bronson Alcott, and Margaret Fuller. It was here that the movement known as Transcendentalism, gathered around his ideas, took shape; and it was here also, at Emerson's home, and elsewhere that meetings of the Transcendental Club were to be held during the seven or eight years following 1836 – a group, known among its own members as the Symposium or the Hedge Club, that met together occasionally and informally to discuss philosophy, theology, and literature. Emerson himself was to become involved in the publication of the Transcendentalist quarterly magazine, *The Dial*, in 1840, assuming the post of editor in 1842, but it was in his lectures and essays that his creed of self-help and self-emancipation was most fully developed and most widely disseminated. Many volumes of essays and poems were to be published by him during the course of his life. The core of his beliefs, and of the Transcendentalist creed can, however, be found in a half dozen pieces: "The American Scholar" (1837), "Divinity School Address," "Self-Reliance," "The Over-Soul," "The Poet" (1844) – and, above all, *Nature*.

At the heart of *Nature* is an intense commitment to the power and wonder of nature and the individual and to the indelible, intimate character of the connection between the two. The self-reliance that Emerson embraced was not selfishness: since, as he saw it, to be true to the true self was to be true to the self, the spirit present in all human beings, all nature. To obey the promptings of the soul was to obey those of the Over-Soul. "Every real man must be a nonconformist," Emerson insisted, but nonconformity meant going against the superficial dictates of society, not pursuing the grosser forms of self-interest and egotism. For Emerson here, as for William Blake in *America, A Prophecy* (1793), "everything that lives is holy, life delights in life"; and to be in communion with oneself, at the deepest level, is to be in touch with what Emerson goes on to call the "uncontained and immortal beauty" that runs through the veins of everything around us. Not that Emerson neglects the material life in all this. On the contrary, in *Nature* he begins with commodity before turning to spirit: in the first instance, what Emerson considers in the relationship between human nature and nature is the circumstantial dimension, the uses and practical conquest of our surroundings. This is the element in Emersonian thought, particularly, that some of his contemporaries and subsequent generations were to distrust. But, for Emerson, use did not mean exploitation. And, while he admitted that practical use was "the only use of nature that all men apprehend," he was careful to point out that it was easily the least important.

The more important service to the soul offered by nature was, as Emerson saw it, aesthetic, intellectual, and, above all, moral. "Universe is the externization of the soul," he insisted. Nature is a product and emblem of the spirit, the Over-Soul; the true self or soul of each individual is divinely connected to it, operating according to the same rhythms and laws; so each individual, in beholding and meditating on nature, can intuit those rhythms and learn those laws. "Every natural process is a version of a moral sentence," Emerson tells the reader in *Nature*. "The moral law lies at the centre of nature and radiates to the circumference. It is the pith and marrow of every substance, every relation, and every process. All things with which we deal preach to us." The style here is characteristic. There is no visible logic to the argument. What Emerson does is to try to possess the idea by attacking it from different directions, to locate the heart or kernel of the matter by inserting various intellectual and verbal probes into its shell. The result is a series of gnomic statements, a rhetorical pattern of repetition with variation.

Emerson himself distinguished between what he called the Party of Hope and the Party of Memory among his contemporaries: the one committed to the possibilities of the future, the other wedded to the imperfections and failures of the past. And it is quite clear that Emerson saw himself as a member of the Party of Hope. This had questionable aspects for those, like Hawthorne and Melville, of a darker, more skeptical frame of mind. But it also had more unambiguously positive ones. In "The American Scholar," for instance, which Oliver Wendell Holmes called "Our intellectual Declaration of Independence," Emerson exhorted his audience to turn from imitation to originality. "We have listened too long to the courtly muses of Europe," he insists. And what the American scholar must do is become "Man Thinking" in the present, pushing beyond convention and institutions to learn, not from books, but directly from life. "Life is our dictionary," Emerson declares, offering the scholar direct rather than mediated access to the real. From this, it follows that everything in life is a source of knowledge, even the humblest, everyday subject or event. From this, it also follows that everyone can be a gatherer of knowledge, a scholar. The sources of knowledge are everywhere and are accessible to anyone who cares to attend. Americans can all be American scholars. There can be a genuine democracy, of men thinking, corresponding to the democracy of facts.

Emerson's belief in individuality led naturally, not only to a commitment to democratic equality, but to a conviction that life was process. "Nature is not fixed but fluid," he said. Change is at the root of existence, change in human beings as well as nature; and so, "a foolish consistency is the hobgoblin of little minds." This had vital consequences for Emerson's poetry. "It is not metres, but a metre-making argument that makes a poem," he insisted in "The Poet," "a thought so passionate and alive, that, like the spirit of a plant or an animal, it has an architecture of its own, and adorns nature with a new thing." For Emerson, poetry had to be as "free, peremptory, and clear" as its subject and creator, it had to be original and organic rather than imitative; it had, in short, to dramatize the liberated self. As the supreme creative power, illuminating and transforming all that comes in its orbit, the self is placed at the center of Emerson's poems. The stylistic result is something often close to free verse. As poet, Emerson does accept the preliminary discipline of a particular rhyme and rhythm scheme, but he allows himself to vary lines and meters at will; irregularity and disruption are permitted, as long as the basic sense of rhythmic speech – a speech coming directly from the primitive and oracular self – is retained.

More notable still is the effect of the ethic of self-reliance on the actual, material and moral, landscapes Emerson describes. In poem after poem, the self is shown recreating the world, transforming it into something freshly seen and fully discovered. In "The Snow-Storm" (1847), for instance, the poetic vision reshapes the scene just as "the frolic architecture of the snow" is described refashioning familiar objects into fresh and unfamiliar shapes. And in poems like "Uriel" (1847) and "Merlin" (1847), the poet is translated into an incarnation of God, whose acts of seeing and naming correspond with His original act of making the world. In effect, Emerson puts into practice here the belief he expressed in *Nature* and elsewhere that the poet does in words what everyone can do in action: that is, remake and reorder their surroundings. Emerson never ceased to believe in what he called the "infinitude of the private." Although, in his later work, there is a growing emphasis on the difficulties of knowledge, the limitations imposed by "fate" and the intimidating vastness of nature, he remained firmly convinced of the authority of the individual. He stayed loyal to the idea that every person had the power to shape and change things: which is one reason why, in the 1850s, he became involved in the movement to abolish slavery. As Emerson saw it, the permanent principles of the spiritual life were incarnated in the flux and processes of nature and the constantly changing life of the individual. To live according to those laws was to live in the present, with respect for others but without timidity or apology, in the knowledge that the final judge of any person resided in the self.

Those who pursued the Transcendentalist creed included Theodore Parker (1810–1860), who managed to remain a Unitarian minister while active in the Transcendental Club, and Bronson Alcott (1799–1888), who tried to establish a cooperative community based on Transcendentalist principles at "Fruitlands," at Harvard – it failed after only seven months. Emerson did not approve of this cooperative venture. Nor did he like another, more famous communal enterprise that lasted rather longer, from 1841 to 1847. This was Brook Farm, the cooperative community set up under George Ripley (1802–1880) nine miles outside Boston. Among those interested in the venture were Nathaniel Hawthorne, Orestes Brownson (1803–1876), Elizabeth Peabody (1804–1894), Alcott and Parker, and the person who, apart from Thoreau and Emerson himself, is now the most famous and remembered member of the Transcendental Club, Margaret Fuller (1810–1850). The work for which Fuller is now chiefly remembered is *Woman in the Nineteenth Century* (1845). The book is written in a rhetorical style similar to that of Emerson and draws its inspiration from the Emersonian and Transcendentalist belief in self-reliance and self-emancipation. What gives it its originality and impact is that Fuller, insisting that individualism and liberty are indivisible, applies the idea of self-development to "the woman question." The law of freedom, she argues, "cannot fail of universal recognition." Linking the cause of female emancipation to the abolition of slavery, she attacks all those who would try to reduce people to property, black or female, or insist that they have to be limited to a particular "sphere." It is "the champions of the enslaved African," Fuller points out, who have made "the warmest appeal in behalf of Women." This is partly because many abolitionists are, in fact, women, she explains, and see in the plight of the people whose cause they embrace a reflection of their own plight and problem. But it is also because, at the moment, neither is allowed the power and prerogatives of an adult. "Now there is no woman," Fuller remarks bitterly, "only an overgrown child."

The imperative of education is one that Fuller sees as primary. She also sees it as one that women will have to pursue for themselves. Men, she argues, have habitually kept women weak and circumscribed; it is hardly to be expected that they will now see the error of their ways and work to make women strong and free. "I wish Woman to live, *first* for God's sake," Fuller insists. "Then she will not make an imperfect man her god, and thus sink into idolatry." If she develops properly, finding her true vocation, whatever that may be, then "she will know how to love, and be worthy of being loved." What Fuller anticipates, eventually, is a partnership of equals, a time "when Man and Woman may regard one another as brother and sister." In an earlier book, *Summer on the Lakes* (1844), Fuller writes of how, when contemplating the vastness of the Midwest, she felt elated and proud. "I think," she reveals, "I had never felt so happy that I was born in America." Now, in *Woman in the Nineteenth Century*, a similarly patriotic feeling inspires her as she contemplates the possibility of a new dispensation, a new and better relation between the sexes, in the New World. "I have believed and intimated that this hope" for an equal partnership "would receive an ampler fruition, than ever before, in our own land," she informs the reader. In later life, Fuller did not confine herself to the woman question. Nor did she restrict herself to the rights of Americans.

Nevertheless, it is for her passionate commitment to the liberation of women that she is remembered today, and for her belief that the opportunities for such a liberation were greatest in the country of her birth.

"I know of no more encouraging fact," wrote Henry David Thoreau (1817–1862) in *Walden, or Life in the Woods* (1854), "than the unquestionable ability of man to elevate his life by a conscious endeavour." That was not only the creed that Thoreau preached in his writings, along with Emerson, Fuller, and the other Transcendentalists. It was also the creed that he embraced, and tried to follow, in his life. Elsewhere in *Walden*, Thoreau makes the distinction between "professors of philosophy" and "philosophers." "To be a philosopher," Thoreau suggests, "is not merely to have subtle thoughts, nor even to found a school, but so to love wisdom as to live according to its dictates, a life of simplicity, independence, magnanimity, and trust." It might seem unfair to claim that Thoreau is measuring here the difference between Emerson and himself. Nevertheless, Thoreau did try to live according to the dictates of Transcendentalism to an extent and with an intensity that Emerson never managed. Far more than his teacher, Thoreau wanted to know how it felt to live and see truly: to experience that knowledge in the body, the senses, as well as understand it in the mind. He also wanted the reader to go with him on what he called his excursions into nature, and into himself. He does not simply instruct, as Emerson does, he makes us share the experience; while we read his books, vicariously, imaginatively, we join in his life.

Thoreau pursued a pattern of alternating entry and withdrawal in relation to society. After graduating, he taught school for a time with his brother John, following the principles of Bronson Alcott. And it was with John that, in 1839, he made a trip on the Concord and Merrimack Rivers. Later, while residing at Walden, he used the journals he had kept during the trip to produce his first book, *A Week on the Concord and Merrimack Rivers* (1849). In it, Thoreau appears for the first time as a living realization of Emerson's American Scholar: in his characteristic role, that is, of "Man Thinking" on the move. The book also introduces the reader to Thoreau's characteristic style, which is essentially a rhythmic flow of description and apparent digression: a dramatic articulation of what appears to be spontaneous thought and intimate talk. "I require of every writer," Thoreau was to say in *Walden*, "a simple and sincere account of his own life"; and simplicity and sincerity were certainly his touchstones. But that should not blind us to the lyricism, the wit and panache of his writings. Like the great Romantics, Thoreau worked hard, and often artfully, to catch the casual rhythms of a mind in process – a mind that *is* process – and the moments of illumination to which its chancy, volatile movements lead.

When his brother John became fatally ill, in 1841, the school Henry had run with him was closed. Henry then lived with Emerson for ten years, serving as a general handyman. During this time, he became an intimate of the members of the Transcendental Club, and contributed work to *The Dial*; he also developed his skills as a surveyor and botanist. A period working as a tutor on Staten Island was followed by a return to Concord; and it was on his return there that he went to live at nearby Walden Pond from July 4, 1845 to September 6, 1847. Other Transcendentalists sought a communal life, at Fruitlands or Brook Farm, if they tried to live according to their principles. Characteristically, Thoreau chose to live alone, in a hut he built for himself. It was this sojourn in the woods that, several years later, Thoreau was to recreate in *Walden*, using the journals that, as a matter of habit now, he kept while he was there. Robert Frost was to call *Walden* his "favourite poem." Many other descriptions or generic titles have been applied to it: it has been called, among other things, an autobiography, a philosophical narrative, an ecological journal, a spiritual diary. It is, in a way, *sui generis*; it creates its own genre; it is unique. It is also typically American in its intense focus on the first person singular, the "I" of the narrator and author (and, in fact, its elision of narrator and author); its blend of fact and fiction, personal experience and broader reflection; and its intimacy and immediacy, the sense of a confessional raised to the level of art. *Walden*, in short, is one of the many great American books to which Walt Whitman's remark, "Who touches this book, touches a man," could act as an epigraph: because, like them, it is the utterly unrepeatable expression of the author, in a particular place and at a particular point in time. Its uniqueness, in the American context, *is* its typicality. It is, in other words, the expression of a culture committed to the idea that every person is being truly representative in being truly singular. And it belongs to a tradition of experiment, the pursuit of the personally unique and new: a tradition for which the cardinal sin is to sound like others – to imitate rather than innovate, and embrace conventional forms.

A dramatic imperative is at work in the overall structure, as well as the verbal texture, of *Walden*. Thoreau spent over two years at Walden Pond. In *Walden*, the sojourn lasts from one Spring to the next, the seasonal transit corresponding to the spiritual growth and rebirth of the hero. The first Spring is associated with youth and innocence, a spiritual equivalent of "the heroic ages." There is clearly beauty and good in this condition, as Thoreau perceives it, but there is also radical limitation. In this stage, in which "the animal man" is "chiefly developed," "the intellect and what is called spiritual man" is left "slumbering," Thoreau tells us, "as in an infant." It is necessary to develop a spiritual nature as well; and this Thoreau does through a gradual process of introspection that is associated with the seasons of Autumn and Winter. "I withdrew yet farther into my shell," Thoreau recalls of the Winter, "and endeavoured to keep a bright fire both within my house and within my breast." He drew in on himself, just as he drew in on the house and fire he built for himself; and just as the entirety of nature drew in on itself during the cold season. Thoreau deploys a complex web of natural imagery throughout *Walden* to enact the various stages in his self-emancipation. And his withdrawal into his shell is compared to the condition of a grub, or chrysalis; out of that comes eventually, in the second Spring, the butterfly, a "beautiful and winged life" that embodies the idea of resurrection, renewal. But the central image of nature, the element in the physical landscape that most fully and vividly corresponds to the spiritual landscape of Thoreau, is the pond itself. The correspondence, Thoreau points out intermittently throughout *Walden*, is intimate and extensive: making Walden Pond a type of his own spirit, or soul. Negotiating the depth of Walden Pond, Thoreau is negotiating his own possible deepnesses; contemplating its mysteries, he is also contemplating the mystery of his own individual soul. Walden *is* Thoreau, in the sense that, as he hoped when he "went to the woods," in discovering and fronting its essential facts he discovers and confronts his own – he learns of himself in learning about nature.

Since nature and human nature are coextensive in *Walden*, it is evidently appropriate that the spiritual rebirth of the hero should be announced by the coming of the second

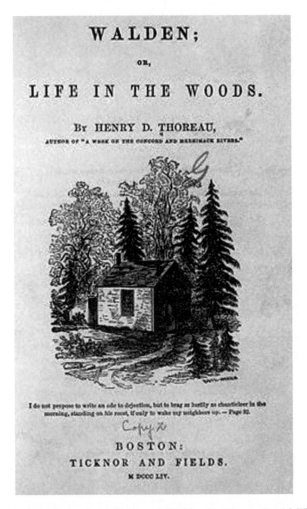

WALDEN;

OR,

LIFE IN THE WOODS.

By HENRY D. THOREAU,

AUTHOR OF "A WEEK ON THE CONCORD AND MERRIMACK RIVERS."

I do not propose to write an ode to dejection, but to brag as lustily as chanticleer in the morning, standing on his roost, if only to wake my neighbors up. — Page 92.

BOSTON:

TICKNOR AND FIELDS.

M DCCC LIV.

Figure 2.2 Title page of the first edition of *Walden* by Henry David Thoreau, with an illustration by Sophia Thoreau, 1854. © Corbis.

Spring. The ice thawing and breaking on Walden Pond is the first movement in the great drama of rebirth that concludes the book in triumph. "Walden was dead," Thoreau declares, "and is alive again." The annual resurrection of nature figures the possible resurrection of human nature, his and ours. It is not just a figure, however: the rhythms of seasonal renewal ground the rhythms of spiritual renewal, they supply a resource and correspondence for the soul. "Wildness is the preservation of the world," Thoreau insisted in a lecture titled "Walking, or the Woods" delivered in 1851. More privately, in a journal entry for the same year, he revealed: "My profession is always to be on the alert to find God in nature – to know his lurking places." Both remarks spring from the same insight and impulse as the ones enacted throughout *Walden*: a root belief in nature as a material and mystical presence, requiring our respectful attention and conscientious stewardship. To conserve nature, as Thoreau saw it and explains it throughout his writings, is to preserve human nature; to save it is to save ourselves.

"The greater part of what my neighbors call good I believe to be bad," Thoreau declares defiantly right at the beginning of *Walden*. The defiance found practical expression during his residence at Walden Pond. Refusing to pay poll tax to a government that supported the Mexican War – a war he considered merely a land-grabbing scheme for Southern slaveholders – he was imprisoned for a day. The imprisonment briefly interrupted his sojourn in the woods. More importantly, it inspired him to write "On the Duty of Civil Disobedience" (1849). For Thoreau, there was a higher law which the individual had to obey even when the government of the day violated it. If that meant breaking the laws of the day, then so be it: "under a government which imprisons any unjustly, the true place for a just man is also in prison." The doctrine of passive resistance was a natural consequence of Thoreau's belief in the ultimate authority of the self. It was to exercise a profound influence, in the next century, on Mahatma Gandhi and Martin Luther King. And, as Thoreau became increasingly involved in the antislavery movement in his later years, he became less convinced that resistance had always to be passive.

During the period 1849–1853, Thoreau made several brief trips, which supplied the material for his posthumously published books, *Excursions* (1863), *The Maine Woods* (1864), *Cape Cod* (1865), and *A Yankee in Canada* (1866). During his final years, he made further journeys to Cape Cod and Maine, then to the Great Lakes, but his increasingly failing health meant that he spent more and more time in and around Concord. Not that he minded this: his reading carried him far and wide, so that he could declare, "I have travelled a good deal in Concord." And study and writing kept him busy. He worked on a long ethnological study of the Indians, which was never completed. He continued his journal, indefatigably: by his death, he had written more than two million words, the basis of all his books. And he developed his interest in botanical science, carrying a botanical guide with him and collecting specimens wherever he went on his walks in the vicinity of Concord. That interest formed the basis of a great but unfinished project: manuscripts that were published as *Faith in a Seed: The Dispersion and Other Late Natural History Writings* (1993) and *Wild Fruits: Thoreau's Rediscovered Last Manuscript* (2000). The two books resurrect the voice and vision of Thoreau: reminding readers of why his is a central and living presence in American writing and offering again the simple lesson all Thoreau's work teaches: that, as *Walden* has it, heaven is "under our feet as well as over our heads." In lively detail, Thoreau discloses the vital thread connecting all forms of life and shows how coexistence is imperative. By unlocking the miraculous in the commonplace, here and elsewhere in his writings, he reveals its redemptive potential. Or, as he tersely puts it, at the end of *Wild Fruits*, "Nature is another name for health."

Voices of African American identity

Fuller linked the emancipation of women to the emancipation of slaves; Emerson and Thoreau found their commitment to self-emancipation leading them into support of the abolitionist movement and, in Thoreau's case, of abolition by any means necessary. Those who spoke out most powerfully against slavery, however, and the violation of selfhood it involved, were the slaves themselves. Frederick Douglass (1817–1895) was born into slavery on a plantation in Maryland. Of his birth, Douglass was later to say that he had "no accurate knowledge" as to the exact date: slaves were not regarded as important enough as individuals to warrant the recording of such details. Worse still, all he knew of his father was that he was a white man – although he had a shrewd suspicion that it was his "master." And although he knew who his mother was, he saw little of her.

Douglass knew that, as a slave, he was not truly a self, an individual, he was property. If he ever had any doubts about this, they were abolished when, as happened from time to time, he was shifted from one master to another, or witnessed the several members of his family being sold off or simply transferred. When his master died, for instance, Douglass was sent for, "to be valued with the other property," as Douglass sardonically put it. "We were all ranked together at the valuation," he recalled. "Men, women, old and young, married and single, were ranked with horses, sheep and swine." Douglass, when recollecting his life as a slave, was particularly fierce in his criticism of those arguments in defense of slavery that saw the slave plantation as an extended family, or feudal system, where the slaves were cared for by their "father," the plantation patriarch. As property, Douglass pointed out, slaves were denied their rights not only as individuals but as members of a family. At an auction or valuation, "a single word from the white man was enough ... to sunder forever the dearest friends, dearest kindred, and strongest ties known to human beings."

Douglass learned to write in a Baltimore shipyard, to which he was hired out and where he learned the trade of caulking. With that, the preliminary education that he saw as "the pathway from slavery" was complete. He found time to teach his fellow slaves to read and write. With some of them, he planned an escape that proved abortive when one of their own betrayed them. Then finally, in 1838, he escaped to pursue his vision of freedom in the North. Shortly after arriving in the North, he renamed himself: his mother's slave name was Bailey, now he was called Douglass, after a character in *The Lady of the Lake* by Sir Walter Scott. He also began reading the radical abolitionist newspaper, *The Liberator*, published by William Lloyd Garrison. This was his first step towards becoming an abolitionist leader himself and, by 1841, he had begun a career as a black leader and lecturer dedicated to the "great work" of black liberation. Encouraged by his success on the antislavery circuit, Douglass published an account of his life as a slave, *Narrative of the Life of Frederick Douglass, an American Slave* (1845). It was circulated widely, translated into several languages, and quickly helped to establish Douglass as one of the leading spokespeople for his cause. Like other slave narratives, it was primarily addressed to a white audience in the first instance; and it was mediated by white writers – William Lloyd Garrison supplied a preface and another white abolitionist, Wendell Phillips, provided an introductory letter. Like them, too, but also like *Walden*, it presents itself as at once a representative autobiography and a testament to the creed of self-emancipation. It shows how its protagonist, who is also its author and narrator, is at once extraordinary and typical – and how he found, or rather made, the means to become himself.

Among the slaveholders whom Douglass encountered was a man called Edward Covey, a notorious "Negro breaker" to whom he was hired out at the age of sixteen. It was while working for Covey, we learn, that Douglass found the basic means necessary to be himself. The discovery forms a central moment in the *Narrative*. Covey kept his slaves under constant surveillance: by adopting the habit of creeping up on them unexpectedly, he made them feel that he was "ever present," that they were ever watched. He submitted everyone to an unremitting regime of "work, work, work" in all weathers, starving them always and beating them whenever he thought necessary. Under the brutal hand of Covey, Douglass remembers, "I was broken in body, soul, and spirit"; "the dark night of slavery closed in upon me, and behold a man transformed into a brute!" But then came the turning point, introduced by a memorable rhetorical strategy. "You have seen how a man was made a slave," Douglass confides to the reader. "You shall see how a slave was made a man."

How Douglass is "made a man" is simple. He stands up for himself. When Covey tries to beat him, he resists; they fight an epic fight "for nearly two hours"; Covey gets "entirely the worst end of the bargain" and never tries to beat Douglass again. As in *Walden*, the recovery of selfhood is described as a rebirth. "It was a glorious resurrection from the tomb of slavery," Douglass recalls, "to the heaven of freedom." And just as Thoreau, after his spiritual rebirth, talks about the return of the heroic ages, so Douglass equates his own spiritual rebirth with the restoration of heroism. His emergence as an individual, capable of mental and emotional freedom now and literal freedom not long after, is the consequence of a fight worthy of one of the heroes of ancient legend. And it coincides precisely with his emergence as a man. Douglass was to spend a further four years in slavery after this. And, in describing those years, he still has plenty to tell the reader about the brutality and hypocrisy of the slave system – and, above all, about how that system dehumanizes not only the slave but also the master. He also has plenty to say about how, nevertheless, slaves make a human space for themselves, through loyalty and love, bravery and friendship. But Douglass is right to present this moment as central: since it was the moment when he was ready to express his selfhood, his sense of his own worth and dignity, at the expense of his own life if necessary. It is also the moment that expresses perfectly a belief held in common with the Transcendentalists – although, of course, Douglass was never a Transcendentalist himself: that a man could raise himself by conscious endeavor, that he could and should struggle to live freely and truly.

After the publication of the *Narrative*, Douglass spent two years promoting the antislavery cause in Britain. He returned to the United States, where he purchased his freedom; and then, in 1847, established an antislavery journal, first called *The North Star* and later retitled *Frederick Douglass' Paper*. A second journal, *Douglass' Monthly*, began in 1858. Douglass contributed a large number of editorial essays to both these publications. An enlarged autobiography, *My Bondage and My Freedom*, appeared in 1855, and a third autobiographical work, *The Life and Times of Frederck Douglass*, in 1881. In his later life, Douglass was an influential public figure. But it is for his three autobiographical books that he is a major presence in American literature. They are central texts in the linked traditions of slave narrative and American autobiography. And much of the power and popularity of the *Narrative*, in particular, stems from the way it appropriates the language and symbolism of a white, middle-class tradition while denouncing the evils of slavery and racism and while exploring the trials of Douglass's life. Douglass talks of spiritual death and resurrection, of being reborn. He also talks of a happy coincidence of divine and human purpose that both recalls the histories of the early, white settlers and anticipates many other, later American success stories: the fortunate moments in his early life, Douglass intimates, were all due to "that kind providence which has ever since attended me" – and to his own efforts, his readiness to work and fight on his own behalf. Above all, perhaps, he talks of the American ideals of self-help and self-realization, and uses the rhetoric of the American dream to distinguish between false and true Americans: between those who would destroy the dream, like the slaveholders, and those who want not only to affirm it but to live it. To that extent, the *Narrative* is a testament to the plurality of America. It is not, in other words, just a central text in this or that particular tradition; it is also an instance of how many great American texts exist at the confluence of cultures – and of how those cultures talk to each other and themselves.

Harriet Jacobs (1813–1897) also wrote at the confluence of cultures, but for her those cultures were different. "I was born a slave," Jacobs announces at the beginning of her own book, *Incidents in the Life of a Slave Girl: Written by Herself* (1861). That is the classic opening of slave narrative. Jacobs continues, however, in a different vein: "but I never knew it till six years of happy childhood had passed away." Her father was a skilled man, a carpenter, Jacobs recalls; and, on condition of paying his mistress 200 dollars a year, and supporting himself, he was allowed to manage his own trade and affairs. He and she, and her mother and brother, "lived together in a comfortable home"; and, although they were all slaves, "I was so fondly shielded," Jacobs tells her readers, that, to begin with, "I never dreamed that I was a piece of merchandise, trusted to them for safe keeping, and liable to be demanded of them at any moment." The revelation that she was, indeed, a slave came when she was six. Her mother died; and she learned from the talk around her that this was her condition. The strongest wish of her father had been to purchase the freedom of his children. But he, too, died a year later with his wish unrealized. Aside from her brother, Jacobs's closest relative was now her grandmother, Molly Horniblow, an extraordinary woman whose history had been one of betrayal.

Betrayal of different kinds lies at the heart of *Incidents*. It was an experience her grandmother had had repeatedly, Jacobs reveals; and it was an experience that then happened to her. Her mistress died when she was twelve. She had promised Jacobs's dying mother "that her children should never suffer for anything"; and, from many "proofs of attachment" the mistress had shown to Jacobs herself, she could not help "having some hope" that she would be left free in the will. She was not; she was simply bequeathed to another member of the family. So far, *Incidents* is a familiar if powerful tale: not that different from the *Narrative* of Douglass. And yet there are differences of tenor and tone that perhaps alert the reader to what is coming next. There is, first, more of an emphasis on family ties, blood relationships within the black community, than there is in the Douglass story. In addressing the reader, there is more of an appeal to sentiment, to his or her sympathy, than there is to abstract principles or emotions of anger. Men are a shadowy presence here; even the carpenter father is mentioned only in passing. It is the women who matter: heroic women like Jacobs's mother, great-grandmother and, above all, her grandmother, and evil women who betray promises, borrow money without returning it, and deny the truth of the Bible. This is a tale, in short, that concentrates on the female experience of slavery and, in doing so, appro-priates the techniques of the sentimental novel as well as using those of the slave narrative. And at the center of it is that familiar protagonist of sentimental fiction: the young woman affronting her destiny – and, in due time, faced with a dangerous seducer – the female orphan making her way in the world.

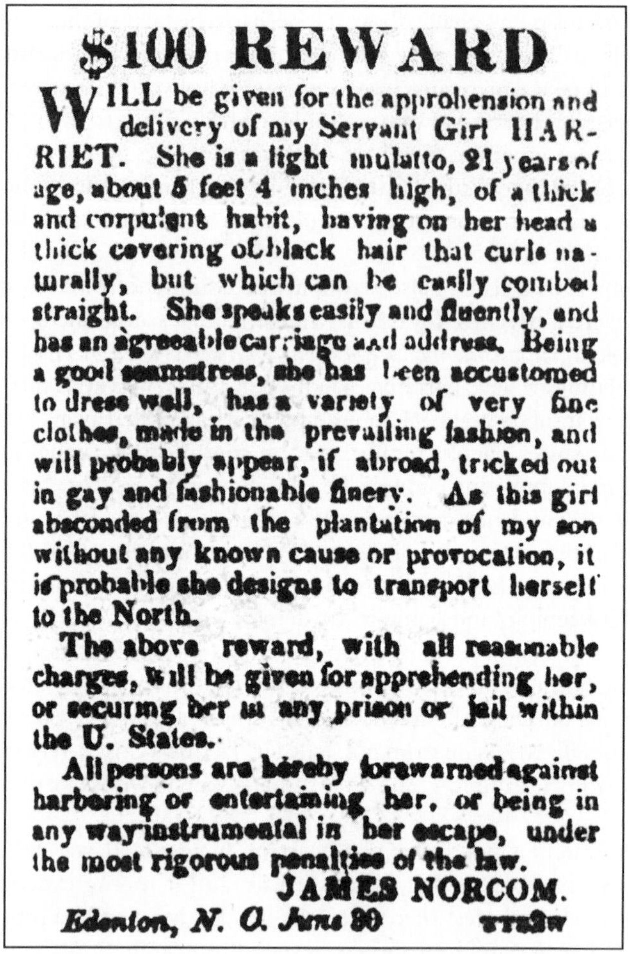

$100 REWARD

WILL be given for the apprehension and delivery of my Servant Girl HAR-RIET. She is a light mulatto, 21 years of age, about 5 feet 4 inches high, of a thick and corpulent habit, having on her head a thick covering of black hair that curls naturally, but which can be easily combed straight. She speaks easily and fluently, and has an agreeable carriage and address. Being a good seamstress, she has been accustomed to dress well, has a variety of very fine clothes, made in the prevailing fashion, and will probably appear, if abroad, tricked out in gay and fashionable finery. As this girl absconded from the plantation of my son without any known cause or provocation, it is probable she designs to transport herself to the North.

The above reward, with all reasonable charges, will be given for apprehending her, or securing her in any prison or jail within the U. States.

All persons are hereby forewarned against harboring or entertaining her, or being in any way instrumental in her escape, under the most rigorous penalties of the law.

JAMES NORCOM.

Edenton, N. C. June 30   ττₐ₃w

Figure 2.3 Reward poster for the return of escaped slave Harriet Jacobs, author of *Incidents in the Life of a Slave Girl*. Advertisement from *The American Beacon*, July 4, 1835. Courtesy of the North Carolina Office of Archives and History, Raleigh, North Carolina.

One point that has not been made about *Incidents* is now worth making. The central character in the narrative is not called Harriet Jacobs but Linda Brent. The reasons for this become obvious when Jacobs begins to describe the new household that, as an adolescent slave, she moved into. She became the object of relentless sexual pursuit by her white master, to escape which she became the lover of another white man and bore him two children. By creating Linda Brent as an alter ego, Jacobs could tell her own story as a sexual victim, move the narrative beyond the limits prescribed by nineteenth-century gentility, and yet remain safely anonymous. Here, especially, *Incidents* becomes a captivating generic mix: a slave narrative still, a sentimental story of female endeavor, a tale of sexual pursuit, attempted seduction and betrayal, and the first-person confession of a "fallen woman." "O, what days and nights of fear and sorrow that man caused me!" Jacobs confides, as she recalls how her master, here called Dr. Flint (his actual name was Dr. Norcom), tried to make her submit to him. The power, and the pathos, of this episode in *Incidents* springs from the direct address to the reader, so common in sentimental fiction, inviting us to participate in the sufferings of the heroine. Even more, it springs from Jacobs's insistence, here and throughout the book, that what she is telling is the truth – and the truth, not just for herself, but for all her "sisters."

When it comes to describing Jacobs's escape from slavery, *Incidents* again differs radically from the *Narrative* of Douglass. Jacobs did not flee northwards. Instead, as she discloses to the reader, she hid in a tiny attic in her grandmother's house for seven years. This was what she called her "loophole of retreat." "The air was stifling there," she remembers, "the darkness total" to begin with: "but I was not comfortless. I heard the voices of my children." There were, eventually, even more comforts. She succeeded in making a hole "about an inch long and an inch broad" through which she could see the daylight. Even more important, she could now see the "two sweet little faces" of her children, and more clearly hear their talk. Occasionally, she could talk to relatives and overhear conversations; regularly, from day to day, she could watch her son and daughter growing up. For Jacobs, liberation comes not in heroic battle, the recovery of manhood, and solitary flight, but in being still with her family, even if apart from them. It would be wrong to exaggerate the difference between Jacobs and Douglass here; it is certainly not absolute. Douglass, after all, spoke of being "linked and interlinked" with his fellow slaves. After seven years in hiding, Jacobs eventually fled north – where, in due course, she was reunited with her children and all had their freedom bought. But a difference there is, between these two great slave narratives.

The Making of Many Americas

"Reader, my story ends with freedom; not, in the usual way, with marriage." That conclusion to *Incidents*, playing on a conventional ending to sentimental fiction, modestly summarizes the drama of the self that inspired and intrigued so many American writers at this time: that urge towards self-emancipation that the writings of the Transcendentalists and slave narratives certainly shared. But, as Douglass and Jacobs clearly illustrate, the self could take on quite different shapes and colorations – and emancipation was far more difficult, far more of a challenge, for some. America was becoming even more of a mosaic of different cultures, colliding interests, and conflicting voices: among them, the many who wrote in and from the Native American and Mexican American communities, those who engaged in the great debate over slavery, and those who wrote about the condition of women.

Native American writing

Within the Native American tribes, so far as they were able or managed to survive, the oral traditions of folktale, legend, and poetry persisted. Some white writers like Henry Wadsworth Longfellow chose to appropriate them. Others, like William Channing, writing in the *North American Review* in 1815, even went so far as to claim that the "oral literature of the aborigines" was the only truly national literature, blessed with a common speech that was "the very language of poetry." But writing in English by

Native Americans inevitably reflected acculturation and the consequences, in particular, of removal and various assimilationist policies. Most of this writing, in fact, came from those whose tribes had been displaced in the East or forced to move to the West. That meant, mainly, the Cherokees in the South, who had acculturated rapidly, and the Six Nations and Ojibwas in the Northeast and around the Great Lakes. Such writing necessarily explored Native American interests and settings, and addressed issues of particular, often pressing importance to the tribes. But it was also likely to be written according to the conventions of the dominant, white culture of the time and, very often, reflected its tastes and habits of mind.

Nowhere is the shaping influence of white culture more evident here than in the poetry written in English by Native Americans. John Rollin Ridge (1827–1867), for instance, was a Cherokee. He was actively involved in Indian issues. But his published work is notable, not only for Ridge's insistence that his people had to become "civilized" – that is, assimilated into white society – in order to survive, but also for his wholesale adoption of white literary forms. In 1845 he published *Life and Adventures of Joaquin Murieta, the Celebrated California Bandit*. The claim made here that it is a true story is simply a bow to one of the literary conventions of the day: it is, in fact, a fairly standard popular romance. As for the poems Ridge produced at various stages in his life, they are all marked by a debt to English and American Romantic poetry. Some of these are nature poems, others are autobiographical, still others take as their subject some notable public event. All of them, however, are notable for their scrupulously exact use of traditional verse forms, and their celebration of the prevailing beliefs of white American society at the time – notably, Progress and Manifest Destiny.

Not all the work produced by Native Americans at this time conformed to white standards. On the contrary, some tried to register what was different about their people by trying to record their tales and folklore. Notable among these was Jane Johnston Schoolcraft (1800–1841). Born Jane Johnston, to an Ojibwa mother and an Irish trader father, she was educated in Ojibwa lore by the one and in English literature by the other. In 1823 she married the scholar and explorer Henry Rowe Schoolcraft (1793–1864), whose main interest was the American Indian. And from then until her death she remained his informant, guide, and assistant: interpreting native sources for him and helping him to study the Ojibwa language. Together, the Schoolcrafts began *The Literary Voyager or Muzzenyegun* in 1826, a magazine containing examples of Ojibwa folklore as well as original poems and essays, many of them by Jane Schoolcraft under assumed names. What is remarkable about the best of this work is how, in the versions of Ojibwa folklore, Jane Schoolcraft deploys her skills in English, her knowledge of English literary techniques and forms, to recreate tales in a way that encourages the (presumably, white) reader's interest and sympathy without denying cultural difference, the intrinsic characteristics of the source.

While some writers worked towards making the folklore of Native Americans available and accessible to an English speaking audience, others tried to make that audience more aware of Native American history, their rights and, often, how badly they had been treated by the white majority. Among these was the earliest significant Indian writer of the nineteenth century, William Apess (1798–?), whose paternal grandmother was a full-blooded Pequot and who claimed descent from Metacomet, the chief known as King Philip among the English. Converted to Methodism when he was fifteen, Apess became a lay preacher. Then, in 1829, his book *A Son of the Forest* appeared, the first autobiography written by a Native American to be published. Apess was raised mainly by whites, and the book is, unsurprisingly, a cultural mix. It is in the tradition of white spiritual autobiography favored by, say, Jonathan Edwards and John Woolman, but it emphasizes Apess's Indian origins and the basic humanity of the Indian people. To add to the mix, it also insists on the potential of the Indian people for adapting to white culture. This was followed by three further books: *The Experiences of Five Christian Indians of the Pecquod Tribe*, a shorter life history published in 1833 but probably written before *A Son of the Forest*, and two more historical works, *Indian Nullification of the Unconstitutional Laws of Massachusetts, Relative to the Marshpee [Mashpee] Tribe* (1835) and *Eulogy on King Philip* (1836). These three books reveal a more openly critical attitude towards whites and, in particular, a fierce critique of what Apess sees as the brutality and hypocrisy of their general behavior towards the Indian peoples. Nevertheless, Apess writes more in hope still than in sorrow or anger. His essential belief, expressed in all his books, is that, with education, the Indian can still rise; with proper observance of Christian principles, the white man can still help him; "the mantle of prejudice" will be "torn from every heart," Apess hopes – and "then shall peace pervade the Union."

An even more popular Indian autobiography than *A Son of the Forest* was *The Life, History and Travels of Kah-ge-ga-gah-bowh (George Copway), a Young Indian Chief of the Ojibwa Nation*. This was published in 1847, republished as *The Life, Letters and Speeches of Kah-ge-ga-gah-bowh, or G. Copway* in 1850 in New York, and as *Recollections of a Forest Life; or, The Life and Travels of Kah-ge-ga-gha-bowh, or George Copway* in London in the same year. In its different versions, this book had a widespread readership. And it encouraged the author, George Copway (1818–1869), in his new career as a writer and lecturer on Indian matters; prior to that, he had served as a Methodist missionary among the Indians. The book is divided into four sections. The first is an account of the Ojibwa culture into which he was born; the second rehearses how his parents were converted to Christianity in 1827 and he himself similarly converted three years later; the third describes his role as a mediator between Indians and whites; and the fourth records the recent history of relations between whites and Ojibwas. "The Christian will no doubt feel for my poor people, when he hears the story of one brought from that unfortunate race called the Indians," Copway begins. What follows is nothing if not conflicted, in ways that are a consequence of the process of acculturation Copway himself had experienced. He celebrates the blessings of white civilization but also describes how the whites robbed the Indians of their land. He rejoices in his conversion, and the conversion of others to Christianity, but he also portrays his early life with the Ojibwa, prior to conversion, as a pastoral idyll. Invoking the familiar idea of the Indian as a noble savage, Copway also taps that vein of romantic nationalism that sees American nature as superior to European culture. That does not stop him, however, from insisting on the adaptability of the Indian to what the opening of his book refers to as "the blessings of life": that is, the culture, brought to America from Europe, that he elsewhere chooses to scorn.

The autobiography of Copway, in short, is a rich mosaic of inconsistencies, precisely because Copway himself, not unusually, was trying to reconcile different cultures. He was also trying to make his way in a literary world the rules for which were largely dictated by whites. Influential white scholars supplied him with encouragement and support for his later publishing projects. *The Traditional History and Characteristic Sketches of the Ojibway Nation* appeared in England in 1850 and in the United States in 1851, and was far more critical of whites than his autobiography had been. This was followed by *Running Sketches of Men and Places, in England, France, Germany, Belgium, and Scotland* later in 1851, one of the first travel accounts written by an Indian. But gradually white interest and encouragement waned. He was adopted by a group calling themselves "native Americans" for a while. But, for them, the defining features of the "native American" were that he or she was not an immigrant nor Roman Catholic: Copway was simply a convenient tool for their purposes. Gradually, Copway dropped out of literary and political circles, and into obscurity.

The first recorded use of the term "Native American" as we understand it today, not as the group that briefly adopted Copway interpreted it, was by a Mohican, John Wannuaucon Quinney (1797–1855). In a speech to Congress in 1852, Quinney called himself "a true Native American"; and the speech as a whole reflects his passionate awareness of the Mohican presence in American history. When he delivered this speech, on Independence Day, he was coming to the end of a long career as a mediator between his tribe and the whites, a lobbyist and a political leader. And Quinney used the occasion to contrast American promise and performance. The purpose of the speech was, in fact, threefold. It was, first, to emphasize the total dispossession of his people. Second, it was to redress the balance a little by beginning to tell that story. The third purpose was to encourage a more substantial redress. Acculturation was necessary, Quinney believed, in response to white American expansionism but, for Indians to achieve this, white Americans had to be willing to accept them as equals. Even the plight of the slave, Quinney suggested, was not as bad as that of the Indian. Like many other Native American writers writing at this time, Quinney mixed pride in a tribal past with belief in a new American future, defined by the linked blessings of white civilization and Christian conversion. It was not for nothing that he was referred to, among many of his contemporaries, as "the Last of the Mohicans."

"Shall red men live, or shall they be swept from the earth?" another Indian writer of the time, Elias Boudinot (1802–1839), asked in *Address to the Whites*, delivered and published in 1826. And for Boudinot, just as for Apess, Conway, and Quinney, to live meant for the "red man" to accommodate to and be accepted by the white. Like them, too, his own story was a testament to accommodation. Born a Cherokee, he was sent to a Moravian mission school where he was educated into white values and practices. It was while traveling to solicit donations for a national academy and printing equipment for the Cherokee Nation that Boudinot delivered his *Address*. More even than the address of Quinney or the autobiography of Conway, it is a testament to the belief in a future in which Indians assume what Boudinot, at one point, calls "the mantle of civilization."

Boudinot was specifically asking for support to accelerate the process of acculturation when he gave his *Address*. That may be one reason why it is, on the whole, a hymn to the values of white culture. It is worth making two further points, however. One is that Boudinot anticipated communication between his people and the whites as a two-way process: the whites would teach the Indians about their cultural practices, and the Indians, in turn, would tell whites about their "intellectual efforts, . . . their eloquence, . . . their moral, civil, and physical advancement." The second, more important point follows from the first. Acculturation, for Boudinot and those like him, did not mean absorption. The Cherokees would become "civilized" but separate: "not a great, but a faithful ally of the United States." Following his *Address*, Boudinot was to become editor of the *Cherokee Phoenix*, the first newspaper produced by American Indians. It served a dual function: to inform local readers about events taking place in their society, and to inform whites elsewhere of the strides towards civilization being made by the Cherokee Nation. He was also to become a translator of English works into Cherokee: a perfect illustration of his hope that his people would acquire the blessings of white culture but maintain their own separate but equal integrity. Boudinot's hopes proved to be without foundation. The Cherokee Nation was forced to remove less than ten years after the *Address* was delivered, along the Trail of Tears; the consequences were little short of genocide. Ironically, Boudinot was one of those Cherokees who signed the treaty with the federal government, ceding Cherokee land in the East for Indian Territory in the West. He did so in the belief that removal was now the only way the Cherokee Nation could survive. It was a mistaken belief, and he paid for it with his life: he was killed in Indian Territory by members of his tribe, who felt that he had betrayed them by signing the treaty.

Oral culture of the Hispanic Southwest

Storytelling was not a monopoly of the Native Americans whose tales the Schoolcrafts helped to record. Apart from those who told tales of Mike Fink, Davy Crockett, and other frontier heroes or fools, there was a whole oral culture in the greater Southwest and California, those Mexican lands that prior to 1845 stretched from the Rio Grande northward as far as lower Oregon and Wyoming. This area, known among Mexicans as Mexico de Afuera, or Mexico abroad, was until quite recently the site of a vital storytelling culture. *Cuentos*, or folktales, were usually told at the end of the day as a kind of intimate performance with all the appropriate dramatic gestures, pauses, and intonation. And they could take the form of morality tales, tales of magic and enchantment, or tales in which animals speak or the dead come alive.

What is especially powerful about these tales from the Hispanic Southwest is what tends to mark out all folktales transmitted via an oral tradition: poetic repetition, narrative spontaneity and fluency, a startling generic mix, and the sense that *this* tale and tale teller form part of a continuity, a vital chain of narrative and human connection. In a story called "La Llorona, Malinche, and the Unfaithful Maria," for instance, the audience is quickly told the story of three women who killed their children. The first, La Llorona, died; her ring was taken from her dead hand and then passed on to a girl who "later became known as Malinche." After drowning all three of her children, she also died, although "even after she had died, she would cry out, 'Ohhhhh, my chilren, where are they?'" And the ring was then taken from her finger by a woman "later known as Unfaithful Maria." Obeying the instructions of an evil spirit, she killed her three children too. But her fate, we are told, was rather different from that of her predecessors. "Her head turned into that of a horse"; and, in addition, "one of her feet was that of a horse, and one was that of a chicken." After this sudden move into the grotesque, the tale is brought into the present. "This started back in 1800," we learn, "and is still going on today in Mexico." "My grandparents told me this story. Then my stepfather," the anonymous narrator explains. "Then my grandmother, my father's mother, told me this story of La Llorona who was the first. My mother told me the second story of Malinche. My stepfather told me about the third." Not only that, we are assured, the stepfather had actually seen Unfaithful Maria. One story shades into another here: so much so that, by the end, Unfaithful Maria is actually referred to as "La Llorona." And one storytelling shades into another as well, as earlier versions, earlier moments of tale telling are invoked. This insistent rhythm of repetition, accumulation, is accompanied by a narrative approach that constantly surprises: for all that one episode melts into the next, via the device of the ring, we never quite know where the story will go next or what the exact tone will be. Magic and melodrama, the sentimental and the gothic, morality and bizarre humor are mixed together to create a mood of enchantment. And, while the audience is reminded of many other occasions of storytelling, and other storytellers, they are intimately involved with this particular one. This, in short and in every respect, is a tale of community.

African American polemic and poetry

The community that aroused most debate in the first half of the nineteenth century was neither the Native American nor the Mexican American one, but the African American community of slaves. And crucial to that debate were not only the slave narratives of writers like Douglass and Jacobs but also the polemic of such African Americans as David Walker (1785–1830) and Henry Highland Garnet (1815–1882). Walker was born in North Carolina. His father was a slave but his mother was a free black woman; and so, according to the slave laws of that time, which stipulated that a child would follow the condition of their mother, Walker was born free. In 1827 he became an agent for the newly established *Freedom's Journal*. Two years later, he published the work that made him famous, and put a price on his head in the South: *David Walker's Appeal in Four Articles; Together with a Preamble, to the Colored Citizens of the World, but in Particular and Very Expressly, to those of the United States of America*. The elaborately formal title reflected Walker's aim of patterning the structure of his *Appeal* on the Constitution. But, while invoking American political precedent for his argument – and taking time to denounce Thomas Jefferson for suggesting that black people were inferior to whites – Walker also identified himself with the biblical tradition of the prophet in the wilderness, attacking the hypocrisy of contemporary religious practice and summoning up divine punishment "in behalf of the oppressed." Beginning by pointing out that "we (the colored people of these United States) are the most degraded, wretched, and abject set of beings that ever lived since the world began," Walker rejects the moderate approach of moral persuasion or an appeal to the religious sentiments of a white audience. Instead, he mocks the hypocrisy of white liberals and of white Christianity, then devotes his energies to making his black audience angry and proud. This militant document is, in effect, the first printed declaration of black nationalism in the United States.

Walker described himself as a "restless disturber of the peace," and his *Appeal* certainly created a disturbance. It went into three editions in the last two years of his life, each edition increasingly urgent in its denunciation of racial injustice – and increasingly insistent that black people should unite to take action, and be ready to kill or be killed for the cause of freedom. Walker was not thoughtlessly militant. He argued for a program of African American educational, spiritual, and political renewal so that constructive social change would follow black liberation. Nevertheless, he not only struck fear into the hearts of white Southerners, he also perturbed some white Northern abolitionists, who found the *Appeal* "injudicious." And, given the prevailing political climate of the time, it is easy to see why. Walker affirmed black citizenship in the republic at a time when many white abolitionists were arguing for the return of emancipated slaves to Africa. He insisted on black unity when many others were talking in terms of assimilation. And he made no attempt to be moderate or placatory in tone or gradualist in approach. The white South tried to suppress circulation of the *Appeal*. It may have had a hand in its author's death, since he died in suspicious circumstances; it certainly wanted him dead. But, even after Walker's sudden death, the *Appeal* continued to be reprinted and to circulate widely. Like earlier, white Americans, Walker asked to be given liberty or death – and he wanted others of his community to ask exactly the same.

Henry Highland Garnet wrote "A Brief Sketch of the Life and Character of David Walker." In 1848, with the financial aid of the militant white abolitionist John Brown, he combined his "Call to Rebellion" speech as it was known, with Walker's *Appeal* in one pamphlet. That suggests the degree of the connection between the two men, and the sense Garnet in particular had of sharing beliefs and commitments with Walker. Garnet was born a slave in Maryland, but escaped with his family in 1825. He became a Presbyterian minister and, in 1843, he attended the National Negro Convention in Buffalo, New York. There, he delivered his *Address to the Slaves of the United States of America*: his "Call to Rebellion" speech which, as the popular title indicated, argued for violent resistance if necessary in the slaves' dealings with their masters. Taking up Walker's argument that slaves should be ready to "kill or be killed" to achieve freedom, Garnet insisted that the condition of slavery made it impossible for slaves to obey the Ten Commandments. What Garnet added to the argument and language of the *Appeal* – along with pointing out, fiercely, that no Commandment required a slave to suffer "diabolical injustice" – was a perspective at once international and peculiarly American. Garnet was a traveled man: he had journeyed in America before giving his "Call to Rebellion" speech and, later, he was to journey as Consul General to Liberia, where he died. He was also widely read and informed. And he used the revolutionary ferment in Europe to support the cause of slave liberation. "The nations of the old world are moving in the great cause of universal freedom," he pointed out. Now it was time for African Americans to move in obedience to a similar impulse. They owed it to themselves, Garnet added, not only as a peculiarly oppressed people but as Americans. Garnet's peculiarly effective tactic here was to turn the white dream of American promise against white America, by claiming that it could and should be a black dream as well – and one to be realized, if necessary, by "resistance, *resistance! resistance!*" When Garnet gave his speech in 1843, it was denounced by Frederick Douglass, who at that time was an advocate of non-violent "moral suasion." And it fell short, if only by one vote, of being approved as an official resolution of the Convention. But by the 1850s, Douglass had moved towards agreement with Garnet that freedom was to be seized by any means necessary. By 1863, both men were involved in raising troops for the Union army. Even before that, in 1847, the National Negro Convention endorsed Garnet's militant stand. These were measures of how far, and how quickly, things changed.

Both Walker and Garnet addressed a black audience. On the whole, the authors of the slave narratives addressed a white one; and so did the poet George Moses Horton (1797?–1883?). That was one reason why his comments on slavery tended to be more sporadic and muted. Another, far more crucial, is that he lived for most of his life, and for all of his significant career as a poet, as a slave in the South. Born in North Carolina, Horton published his first volume of poetry, *The Hope of Liberty*, in 1829. It was published in North Carolina, with white support and financial aid; it was the first book of poetry by an African American for more than half a century, and the first book of any kind authored by a black Southerner. Most of the twenty-one poems in the volume are conventional variations on the themes of love, death, and religion. But three tentatively negotiate the issue of slavery, most notably one entitled "On Hearing of the Intention of a Gentleman to Purchase the Poet's Freedom." In this poem, Horton scarcely disguises the confession that he had been "on the dusky verge of despair" until the chance "to break the slavish bar" had been opened up to him. Horton was never freed before the Civil War, but his master did allow him to hire his time as a professional poet, waiter, and handyman, and to publish his work in such abolitionist periodicals as *The Liberator* and *The North Star*. Then, in 1845, Horton published his second volume, *The Poetical Works of George Horton, The Colored Bard of North Carolina*. Again, the poet did not risk offending his white patrons and public by openly attacking slavery. But, again, he did allow himself to comment on the sometimes bitter consequences of being a slave.

A poem called "Division of an Estate," for example, is remarkable for the sympathy it inspires for its subjects: slaves being sold at auction after the death of their master. There is irony here. The slaves, as property, are rhetorically linked to other property. And there is also pathos, as the poet asks the reader to behold "the dark suspense in which poor vassals stand" on the auction block. The mind of each, he points out, "upon the spine of chance hangs fluctuant," knowing that "the day of separation is at hand." Presumably, in this case, the distinction that many white Southerners were willing to make between slavery and the slave trade allowed Horton to emphasize the pathos. It was, at best, a false distinction, since slavery could not have existed without the slave trade, but it gave the poet some room for rhetorical maneuver. Horton was freed towards the end of the Civil War, and published a third and final volume called *Naked Genius* just after the fall of the Confederacy. This collection of 133 poems, most of them previously unpublished, continues the themes of his earlier work. In the poems on slavery, however, Horton does move from complaining about the pains and sadness the peculiar institution involves to attacking its fundamental injustice. And in one remarkable piece, "George Moses Horton, Myself," he offers a fragment of autobiography that explores the difficulties of being both a black slave and a poet. "My genius from a boy,/ Has fluttered like a bird within my heart," he tells the reader, "But could not thus confined her powers employ,/Impatient to depart." It is an apt summary of the torment he had suffered, both as a man and a poet: a torment that he hardly ever dared openly to confess. And it announces a problem, of being a black writer imprisoned in a predominantly white culture and language, that many later African American poets were to explore.

Abolitionist and pro-slavery writing

Among the white writers who were noted abolitionists were Wendell Phillips (1811–1884) and William Lloyd Garrison (1805–1879). Garrison worked with Benjamin Lundy on a periodical titled *The Genius of Universal Emancipation* for several years. But he broke with Lundy and the paper over the position Lundy held, that slaves should be emancipated gradually and removed to Africa. He began to argue for immediate emancipation, without colonization of the freed or compensation for their former masters, and to argue his case he founded *The Liberator* at the beginning of 1831. Inspired by the beliefs of the Great Awakening, Garrison was convinced that the Kingdom of God could be created on earth by men and women actively committed to eradicating evil and injustice. That led him to support the temperance movement, women's rights, and, in particular, the abolition of slavery: only by abolition, he argued, could "the 'self-evident truth'" maintained in the American Declaration of Independence, "that all men are created equal," be realized in practice. That was why, he recollected in *William Lloyd Garrison: The Story of His Life* (1885), "I determined ... to lift up the standard of emancipation in the eyes of the nation, *within sight of Bunker Hill and in the birthplace of liberty.*" Garrison was fervent in his language. He was, however, in favor of moral persuasion rather than coercion. There was, in fact, a curious gap between the violence of his words and the creed of non-violence he embraced. The violent terms in which he often expressed himself offended some, Garrison admitted. For others, though, like Frederick Douglass, who eventually broke with him over the issue, it was the belief that non-violence could defeat the power of slavery that was the problem.

The editorials and journalistic work of Garrison often possess the rhetorical power of great speeches. In the case of Wendell Phillips, it was his power as a writer and performer of public speeches that secured his place in the abolitionist movement. For twenty-five years, Phillips toured the lyceum circuit. His lectures included diverse topics but the ones for which he became and remained famous were on the subject of slavery. In his speech, "Toussaint L'Ouverture," for instance, eventually published in *Speeches, Lectures, and Letters* (1863), Phillips celebrated the black leader of the revolution against the French in Haiti. In what numerous contemporary audiences found a spellbinding account, Phillips described the courageous life and tragic death of Toussaint. "I am about to tell you the story of a Negro who has left hardly one written line," Phillips customarily began his oration. "All the materials for his biography are from the lips of his enemies." Phillips's aims were immediate: to arouse his audience to support for the abolitionist cause and the possible necessity of direct action – the oration closed, in fact, with the name of John Brown being invoked directly before that of Toussaint L'Ouverture. But in pointing out that he was unearthing a secret history, one that rarely if ever was allowed into white history books, he was curiously anticipating what was to become a resonant theme in much later, African American writing.

If Garrison was the journalist of the white abolitionist movement and Phillips the orator, then John Greenleaf Whittier (1807–1892) was its poet. Whittier had no vast ambitions. All he wanted to do was to denounce those whose preoccupations with their own selfish needs made them oblivious to the needs of others. That meant, above all, the slaveowners: he once said that he placed a "higher value" on his name appearing on the Anti-Slavery Declaration than on the title page of any book. Beyond that, he also wanted to offer as an imaginative alternative to such selfishness the kind of small and tightly knit community of interests he describes in "First-Day Thoughts" (1857) and, perhaps his most famous poem, *Snow-Bound* (1866). Whittier was born in Massachusetts to poor Quaker parents, and the Quaker experience remained fundamental to him throughout his life. It was this, in fact, which supplied him with his ideal: of a group of people held together by common values and by the belief that each member of the group is possessed of a certain "inner light."

Snow-Bound was not, of course, published until after the end of the Civil War. But it was from the experiential basis it describes, a sense of genuine contact and community, that Whittier's poetic assault on slavery was launched. And it was an assault from several directions. "The Hunters of Men" (1835), for instance, takes the path of bitter humor: a parodic hunting song, it mocks in jaunty rhyme those "hunters of men" who go "Right merrily hunting the black man, whose sin/Is the curl of his hair and the hue of his skin." "The Farewell of a Virginia Slave Mother to Her Daughters Sold into Southern Bondage" (1838) takes, as its title indicates, the path of melodrama and sentiment: as the mother of the title laments the loss of her daughters. "The Slave Ship" (1846), describing the jettisoning of slaves who, having been blinded by sickness, are no longer saleable, takes the direction of Gothic horror. And in "Massachusetts to Virginia" (1843) Whittier opts for declamation, as he denounces any attempt to return escaped slaves to the slave states. What Whittier sought in all such poems was to persuade the reader: he used whatever poetic means lay at his disposal to draw him or her into examining their conscience. Out of that, he hoped, would develop a clearer sense of personal and communal purpose. To that extent, his antislavery pieces express, just as firmly as the Quaker poems do, his belief that poetry should be no more than a means to a higher, spiritual end.

At the same time as Whittier and his colleagues were arguing for the abolition of slavery, another group in the South were arguing quite the contrary: that slavery was not only an economic necessity but a positive good. As these Southerners saw or claimed to see it, slavery was an integral part of the established, agrarian mode of life enjoyed by all the states below the Mason-Dixon line. These defenders of slavery, and by extension of the social system of the South, included the writer and social philosopher George Fitzhugh (1806–1881), the novelist William Gilmore Simms (1806–1870), the poet William J. Grayson (1788–1863), the lawyer and writer Henry Hughes (1829–1862), the scientific agriculturist and fanatical secessionist Edmund Ruffin (1794–1865), a professor of political philosophy Thomas Dew (1802–46), and the politician James Henry Hammond (1807–1864). Some of the arguments these defenders of slavery used were drawn from the Bible, purporting to find a theological warrant for the slave system. Others involved supposedly scientific theories concerning the separate, inferior origins of the "Negro race." Central to their defense, however, was the contention that Frederick Douglass, among many others, found so offensive – that the South was a feudal society, an extended family in which the master acted as patriarchal head. Everyone, black and white, had their part to play in this family. And to the slave was given the role of child, dependant. Incapable of looking after himself, the slave depended on the plantation patriarch – and, to a lesser extent, the mistress or matriarch of the house – for support and guidance: the security of work and a home, a basic moral education, and care in infancy, sickness, and old age.

Two women writers who offer intriguing variations on this idea of the pre-Civil War South as a model of paternalism are Caroline Lee Hentz (1800–1856) and Mary Boykin Chesnut (1823–1886). Hentz was born in the North; however, she moved South, to North Carolina, then later Kentucky, Alabama, and Florida. She wrote many novels to support herself and her husband: "I am compelled to turn my brains to gold and to sell them to the highest bidder," she complained once. But the novel for which she remains best known is *The Planter's Northern Bride* (1854). The interest of the novel lies in the way, in painting an idyllic portrait of life on the old plantation, it replicates the pro-slavery argument in fictional form. In this, it is typical in some ways of plantation novels from *The Valley of Shenandoah* (1824) by George Tucker (1775–1861) and *Swallow Barn* by John Pendleton Kennedy, through to many of the romances of William Gilmore Simms, such as *The Sword and the Distaff* or, as it was later known, *Woodcraft* (1852). It is typical, too, in other ways, of stories announcing the special status and even manifest destiny of the South, like *The Partisan Leader* (1836) by Nathaniel Beverley Tucker (1784–1851) and *The Cavaliers of Virginia* (1834–1835) and *The Knights of the Golden Horseshoe* (1845) by William A. Caruthers (1802–1846). Above all, though, it is typical of the legion of novels written in response to *Uncle Tom's Cabin* by Harriet Beecher Stowe. Of Stowe, Hentz once said, "slavery, as she describes it, is an entirely new institution to us." She felt she knew the institution far better than the author of *Uncle Tom's Cabin*, having lived in the South; and she was determined to show her readers how. The story contains the usual retinue of characters attending the plantation romance: including young men full of "magnanimity and chivalry," "pure and high-toned" young women, and interfering abolitionists who are determined to free the slaves even though they do not want to be freed. But what supplies the argumentative core of the book is the hero, a Southern planter called Mr. Moreland, and his faithful personal "servant," Albert, "a young mulatto." Moreland is described as "intelligent and liberal"; Albert is "a handsome, golden-skinned youth," "accustomed to wait on his master and listen to the conversation of refined gentlemen." As a result of such service, the reader is told, Albert "had very little of the dialect of the negro." This relieves Hentz of the burden of writing such dialect herself for a relatively important character with much to say. But it has the further advantage of supplying one small but crucial illustration of the benefits of slavery. The slave system, its defenders were inclined to argue, not only supported and protected the slaves, it helped to educate and refine them; and Albert's distinctive manner of speech supposedly shows just that. An alternating rhythm of action and reflection, conversation and polemic, is characteristic, not only of *The Planter's Northern Bride* as a whole, but also of other plantation and pro-slavery romances of this kind. The narrative illustrates the pro-slavery thesis; the thesis informs and shapes the narrative. And the thesis is simple: that, thanks to the paternalism of the South, "the enslaved children of Africa" are "the happiest *subservient* race ... on the face of the globe."

That, however, was not how Mary Boykin Chesnut saw it. Born in South Carolina, she married into the wealthy Chesnut family. Her husband was an influential politician, with close connections to Jefferson Davis, the President of the Confederacy during the Civil War. And, like many at the time, Chesnut kept a diary in which she recorded meetings with national figures, news of the progress of the war, and her everyday experiences and opinions. She then created a book out of the diary and her memories of the past, but died before it could be published. This composite work did not appear until 1905, then in a 1949 edition titled *A Diary from Dixie*; and the original, more highly personal diary was not published until 1984. There are many remarkable aspects to the diary, but what perhaps is most remarkable is Chesnut's commentary on slavery. "I wonder if it be a sin to think slavery a curse to my land," she muses in an entry for March 8, 1861. "Men and women are punished when their masters and mistresses are brutes and not when they do wrong – and then we are surrounded by prostitutes." That last remark picks up a recurrent theme in the diary. Chesnut was acutely aware of the brutal, ironic fact that, while the ruling white patriarchs in the Southern states insisted on their separation from, and even difference as a species to, their black slaves, they did not hesitate to have sexual contact with them. While they drew an absolute boundary between whites and blacks, they crossed the boundary constantly; and the consequences of that were large numbers of children neither "white" nor "black" but both. The most vivid example, perhaps, of slavery as a violation of humanity was offered by the white, and usually male, sexual use of their "property."

"I hate slavery," Chesnut confessed. What she hated about it, especially, was the fact that, as she put it, "our men live all in one house with their wives and concubines, and the mulattoes one sees in every family exactly resemble the white children." That inspired her sympathy for white women forced to bear daily witness to the infidelity and hypocrisy of their male kin but forced never to say anything, but it did not inspire her to any sympathy for black women who were, after all, the main victims here, subject to constant sexual coercion. As she saw it, the slave system was to blame for all this "nastiness," but so were "facile black women." Ironically, Chesnut could see through the Southern myth of the extended family far enough to notice that the white "father" was constantly violating his black "daughters": but not far enough to absolve those "daughters" of blame. She was too deeply implicated in myths about black sexuality, and the supposed animalism of the black race, for that. This is all to say that the diaries of Chesnut offer as much a symptom as a diagnosis of the moral and material brutality of slavery. What she saw was limited, as well as illuminated, by her condition as an intelligent white woman of the privileged class.

Abolitionism and feminism

The diaries of Mary Boykin Chesnut are her one contribution to American literature, but a substantial one. They illustrate just how much forms of writing often considered to be outside the parameters of literature – among them, the sermon and lecture, the diary and journal – form an integral, in fact central, part of the American tradition with its emphasis on the regulation and realization of the self. Another writer who became interested in the condition of slaves and the condition of women, Lydia Maria Child (1802–1880), was, by contrast with Chesnut, prolific in her output. And her interests led her to become an abolitionist and, for a while, attract public censure. Child first made her mark with a historical novel, *Hobomok* (1824), which dealt with the relationship between a Puritan woman and a Native American man. It offers a vision of interracial union that is closer to Catharine Maria Sedgwick, in its suggestion that such unions are eminently possible, than it is to James Fenimore Cooper. She founded and edited the first magazine for children in the United States, *Juvenile Miscellany*. She published a second novel in 1825, *The Rebels; or, Boston Before the Revolution*, about the agitation over the Stamp Tax. Then, in 1828, she married David Lee Child, a prominent abolitionist but also an impractical man, whom his wife had very often to support. Partly for financial reasons, Lydia Maria Child began writing practical advice books for women, such as *The Mother's Book* (1831) and *The American Frugal Housewife* (1831). "Books of this kind have usually been written for the wealthy," Child wrote in the opening chapter of *The American Frugal Housewife*; "I have written for the poor." Along with general maxims on health and housekeeping, and an emphasis on thrift and economy that Benjamin Franklin would have admired, the book strongly advises its women readers to give their daughters a good general education.

By 1833, Child had become actively involved in the abolitionist movement. It was that year she published *An Appeal in Favor of That Class of Americans Called Africans*. Later, in 1839, she published her *Anti-Slavery Catechism*, a pamphlet written in the form of questions and answers. What both documents reveal is that Child was a moderate abolitionist, just as she was a moderate feminist, anxious to correct the impression that as an activist, with strong social concerns, she might therefore be an irresponsible and vituperative agitator. Her aim was to persuade what she termed "our brethren of the South" to reform themselves, to reconstruct the slave system from within. This enabled her to admit that the North did not hold a monopoly on virtue. Child tried to reassure her Southern readers that, as she put it, "the abolitionists have never . . . endeavoured to connect amalgamation with the subject of abolition." But her low-keyed, conversational tone, and her presentation of herself as a sensible, humane reformer was just as obnoxious to Southerners bent on strengthening the slave system as the more openly radical approaches of Walker and Garrison were. In her later years, after she had resigned from the *Standard*, Child continued to pursue a variety of different careers as a writer and to promote several social causes. A short story, "Slavery's Pleasant Homes" (1843), explores miscegenation and its brutal consequences in terms that anticipate Mark Twain and William Faulkner. Her last novel, *A Romance of the Republic* (1867), returns to the theme of interracial marriage. Her *Letters from New York* were published in two series, in 1843 and 1845. Her *Appeal for the Indians* (1868) expressed her continuing concern for the people who had been the subject of her first long fiction. And she sustained her commitment to African Americans even after the end of slavery: *The Freedman's Book* (1865), for instance, a collection of pieces by and about black people, was printed and distributed at her expense. For Child, the cause of liberty was an all-embracing one. In particular, she saw a seamless connection between her activism as an abolitionist and her interest in the condition of women. Much the same could be said of many reformers of the time, including the Grimke sisters, Angelina Grimke Weld (1805–1879) and Sarah Moore Grimke (1792–1873). Born in South Carolina to a slaveholding family, the sisters shocked their fellow Southerners and relatives by identifying themselves with the abolitionist movement. It was while both were living in Philadelphia that Angelina wrote *An Appeal to the Christian Women of the South* (1836). "I am going to tell you unwelcome truths," she told her intended Southern white women readers, "but I mean to speak those *truths in love*." Despite the evidently modest, even apologetic beginning, the message of the *Appeal* was radical.

Southern white women, Angelina argued, should read about slavery, pray for the truth about slavery to be known, and not only speak out against slavery but also act to eradicate it by freeing their own slaves. In this *Appeal*, the cause of abolition and the cause of feminism were linked, not least because white Southern women were offered the possibility of affirming their womanhood, and their capacity for significant political action, in and through working towards the end of slavery.

Angelina Grimke also wrote more directly about the feminist cause only a year after the *Appeal*, in her *Letters to Catharine Beecher*. Here, in response to Beecher's argument that women should restrict themselves to the domestic sphere, she insisted that there were no specifically masculine and feminine rights, no such thing as "men's rights and women's rights" but only "*human* rights." Humanity was indivisible, the doctrines of liberty and equality had a universal application; and woman should be regarded "as a companion, a co-worker, an equal" of man not "a mere appendage of his being, an instrument of his convenience and pleasure." Sarah Moore Grimke was lecturing for the antislavery movement with her sister at this time; and, while Angelina was writing her *Letters to Catharine Beecher*, Sarah in her turn was preparing her *Letters on the Equality of the Sexes, and the Condition of Women* (1837–1838). The *Letters on the Equality of the Sexes* are just as resistant as the *Letters to Catharine Beecher* are to the idea that a woman's place is necessarily in the home. For too long, Sarah insisted, women had been educated "to regard themselves as inferior creatures." Like so many others concerned with the condition of American women in the nineteenth century, Sarah saw her "sisters" as fundamentally powerless and education as a vital source of empowerment. Like some of them, too, including her own sister, she saw that impotence at its most extreme in the female slaves of the South. For Sarah, as for Angelina Grimke, then, female emancipation and the abolition of slavery were intimately connected. And, in Sarah's case, that was especially so, since she saw the condition of the female slave as a paradigm, an extreme instance of the condition of all women, the subjection they all shared as the "property" of white men.

The connection between abolitionism and feminism in the nineteenth century was not, however, always seamless. In 1840 a World Anti-Slavery Convention was held in England, and those present decided on the first day not to seat women delegates. Outraged, William Lloyd Garrison joined female delegates in the gallery. And, in the same year, the American Anti-Slavery Society split mainly because the followers of Garrison insisted that women could not be excluded from full participation in the work of abolition. Among those sitting with Garrison in the gallery at the World Anti-Slavery Convention was Elizabeth Cady Stanton (1815–1902). She was similarly angered by the treatment of female delegates and decided to organize a convention, as soon as she returned to the United States, wholly devoted to the rights of women. This was the Seneca Falls Convention, which did not, in fact, take place until eight years later, when Stanton and her family moved to Seneca Falls, New York. About three hundred people attended, and a hundred of them – two thirds of them women – signed a "Declaration of Sentiments," one of the seminal documents of the century on the condition of women. Modeled, as was observed earlier, on the Declaration of Independence, and beginning by insisting that "all men and women are created equal," the document was characteristic of its time, in its mix of republican and Christian sentiment. It made no concessions at all, however, to the notion of separate spheres for men and women, or to the usual domestic pieties. And its demands were simple and radical. Women, the "Declaration" insisted, should have "immediate admission to all the rights and privileges which belong to them as citizens of the United States."

If Stanton, along with Margaret Fuller, was the philosopher of the feminist movement in America during the nineteenth century, then Fanny Fern was one of those who translated feminist principles into an enormously successful writing career. Fanny Fern was the pen name of Sara Payson Willis (1811–1872). Her first collection of articles, *Fern Leaves from Fanny's Portfolio*, appeared in 1853 and rapidly became a bestseller. *Little Ferns from Fanny's Little Friends*, a collection of essays for children, followed in the same year; next year, the second series of *Fern Leaves from Fanny's Portfolio* was published. Over the following twenty years, her essays, articles, and other writing for various journals, and collections such as *Fresh Leaves* (1857), *Folly as It Flies* (1868), and *Ginger Snaps* (1870) were to establish her as one of the most famous women writers in the nation. The essays and articles written under the name of Fanny Fern are generally marked by a lively, gossipy style, full of exclamations and rapid asides. There is plenty of sentiment, but there is also plenty of wit. There are also articles that deal in a more openly serious way with the plight of women. "The Working-Girls of New York" (1868), for instance, makes no concessions to humor as Fern describes what she calls "the contrast between squalor and splendor" in New York City: with "the care-worn working girl" and "the dainty fashionist" "jostling on the same pavement." Fern maintains a tactful balance here, between her recognition of the immense difference between these two female types, as far as their social and economic situations are concerned, and her belief that, as women, their conditions are nevertheless linked. "A great book is yet unwritten about women," Fern confides to the reader: one, presumably, that discloses both the differences and the links between rich and poor women she alludes to here.

Fern herself tried her hand at writing, if not a great, then a useful book about women: *Ruth Hall: A Domestic Tale of the Present Time* (1855). "I present you with my first continuous story," Fern wrote in her "Preface: To the Reader." "I do not dignify it by the name of 'A Novel.' I am aware that it is entirely at variance with all set rules for novel-writing." There was, as always, truth in what she said. Fern drew heavily on her own experiences in the book. *Ruth Hall* is not an autobiography, however. Neither is it a romantic or sentimental novel. Reversing the conventional pattern, the book begins with marriage (to a man who then dies leaving Ruth a widow) and ends with the heroine as a successful career woman. It focuses, not on the domestic scene, but on the literary marketplace in which Ruth must make her way. And the narrative consists, as Fern herself points out in her "Preface," not of the "long introductions and descriptions" of the traditional nineteenth-century novel but, rather, of a series of brief episodes and vignettes. There is only limited narrative exposition, character analysis, and development. What the reader is offered is a succession of brief scenes, snatches of overheard conversation, something remarkably close in many ways to the clipped, disjunctive patterns of the modern novel. *Ruth Hall* is not a modern novel, of course, and there is plenty to remind us of that. There are some remarkable plot coincidences, some Dickensian comic characters, and no less than three big deathbed scenes. Nevertheless, what Fern describes as her "primitive mode" of writing does set her at odds with contemporary convention: in tone and narrative rhythm, this is very unlike the standard "domestic tale of the present time." By the end of the novel, Ruth has made something of herself, and found that marriage and widowhood is not all life has for her.

Of Sojourner Truth (1793?–1883), someone wrote in 1881 that she "combined in herself, as an individual, the two most hated elements of humanity. She was black and she was a woman." For Truth, both elements were a matter of profound pride, and she devoted her life to proclaiming her belief that both were the source of her dignity, her worth as a human being. Much of what is known about Truth is drawn from transcriptions of her speeches, records of her public appearances, and her autobiography, the *Narrative of Sojourner Truth* (1850). She never learned to read or write. What we have are the accounts of her and her orations by others; while the *Narrative*, a contribution to both the slave narrative and the female spiritual autobiography traditions of African American literature, was dictated by Truth to Olive Gilbert, a sympathetic white woman. In 1875 the *Narrative* was reprinted with a supplement called the *Book of Life*, containing personal correspondence, newspaper accounts of her activities, and tributes from her friends. This enlarged edition of the autobiography was reprinted several times, in 1878, 1881, and 1884 under the title *Sojourner Truth: A Bondswoman of Olden Time, with a History of Her Labors and Correspondence Drawn from Her "Book of Life."* From all this, the reader learns Truth had an "almost Amazon form, which stood nearly six feet high, head erect, and eyes piercing the upper hair like one in a dream." She was born into slavery in New York State, as Isabella Baumfree, sold three times before she was twelve, and raped by one of her masters. She had five children from her union with another slave, saw one of her children sold away from her, then fled with another of her children in 1826, so seizing her freedom one year before she was formally emancipated under a New York law passed in 1827. In 1843 she received what she termed a summons from God, commanding her to go out and preach. She changed her name to reflect her new identity, as a traveler dedicated to telling people what is true, and she took to the road. By the late 1850s, she had come to embody a commitment to freedom that both contrasted with and complemented that of Douglass. With Douglass, the cause expressed itself as masculine, individualist, mythic, and literary; with Sojourner Truth it was something quite different but equally valuable – female, communal, part of an oral, vernacular tradition.

The most famous speech given by Sojourner Truth expresses this difference. In 1851, during a woman's rights convention in Ohio, she spoke on behalf of the dignity of women in response to attacks from a group of ministers. Her spontaneous oration was reported in the *Anti-Slavery Bugle*. Then, in 1878, a second and more elaborate version of the speech appeared in the *Book of Life* section of the *Narrative*; this was how the president of the convention, Frances Gage, recollected it. The rhetorical question that Gage remembered Sojourner Truth asking again and again in the speech was, "and a'n't I a woman?" That became the accepted title of the piece. It also vividly expressed Truth's commitment to the related causes of black and female liberation, black and female pride, that she saw as crucial determinants of her identity and that her admirers, similarly, saw embodied in her. Douglass enshrined his account of how "a slave was made a man" in a form that was personal, carefully articulated, and (in the sense of being written down by him) final. Truth asked the question, "a'n't I a woman?" in a forum that was communal and in a form that was spontaneous, unpremeditated, and (to the extent that it was open to the recollections and revisions of others) fluid. Both are equally memorable; and they share a basic impetus, a commitment to human dignity and natural equality, along with their differences. And both have a crucial place in the traditions of African American and American literature.

African American writing

By contrast to Sojourner Truth, who never wrote down a single one of the speeches for which she is remembered, Frances E. W. Harper (1825–1911) was one of the most prolific, as well as popular, African American writers of the nineteenth century. Over the course of her life, she produced four novels, several collections of poetry, and numerous stories, essays, and letters; she also found time to lecture widely on a whole range of reform issues, especially temperance, slavery, and racism, and the rights of women. The publication of her poem "Eliza Harris" in 1853 brought her to national attention. One of her many responses to *Uncle Tom's Cabin* by Harriet Beecher Stowe, it described a slave woman escaping across a river covered with ice, carrying "the child of her love" to "Liberty's plains." And it reflected her growing involvement with the antislavery movement. That involvement became even more marked a year later, when she inaugurated her career as a public speaker with a speech on "The Education and Elevation of the Colored Race." The lecture tour she then embarked on was grueling. But she managed to produce more poems, and essays, and to publish *Poems on Miscellaneous Subjects* (1854), which effectively began the tradition of African American protest poetry.

In 1859 Harper published her first significant fiction, the short stories "The Two Offers" and "Our Greatest Want." "The Two Offers," the first short story published by a black person in the United States, is concerned with the condition of women. It tells the tale of two cousins, one of whom suffers an unhappy marriage, and the other of whom, learning from her cousin's fate, decides to remain unmarried. Turning from marriage, as one of only several options available to a woman, the second cousin dedicates herself to "universal love and truth" – in other words, abolitionism and other reform movements. "Our Greatest Want" deals in more detail with the question of race: suggesting that, while the acquisition of wealth is necessary for African Americans, their development as "true men and true women" is more important. Both stories are characteristic, in that they are elaborately artificial in tone and sternly moral in tenor; and, together, they reflect the overriding commitments of Harper's life and work: to racial and sexual equality.

Among Harper's many other published works were a free verse narrative, *Moses: A Story of the Nile* (1869), two novels dealing with temperance (*Sowing and Reaping: A Temperance Story* (1876) and *Trial and Triumph* (1888–1889)), and a newspaper column, first called *Fancy Etchings* and then *Fancy Sketches*, in which she explored contemporary issues and moral dilemmas through the conversations and activities of various regular characters. Her two most important later works, however, were *Sketches of Southern Life* (1872) and *Iola Leroy; or, Shadows Uplifted* (1892). At the heart of *Sketches* is a series of poems narrated by an Aunt Chloe. Sixty years old, Aunt Chloe tells the reader how she learned to read, take an active interest in politics although she cannot vote, and try to make sure that the men are "voting clean." Unlike most of Harper's other poetry, these poems exploit African American oral traditions, as they tell the story of a woman who worked to gain a cabin for herself and her family and to help build schools and churches for the community. They are at once the autobiography of a former slave and a vernacular history of slavery, emancipation, and reconstruction. *Iola Leroy* is a novel with a complex plot. The earlier part of it, set in the antebellum period and during the Civil War, assaults the pro-slavery myth of the Old South, by describing the fierce desire of the slaves for freedom, then celebrates the bravery of black troops. The later part concentrates on the search of Iola Leroy and her brother for their mother, and the decision of Iola, a very light-skinned African American, not to marry a white man. Instead, she accepts the proposal of an African American and dedicates herself to building up the black community. *Iola Leroy* in effect reverses the character stereotype of the tragic mulatta and the traditional narrative device of a black person "passing" for white. Iola is in no sense a victim, and she actively refuses to take on the role of a supposedly "white" woman married to a white man. It also dramatically negotiates a range of issues that were to engage later African American women writers in particular: the separation and longing of mother and daughter, the relationship between the sexes as a cooperative, coequal one, the search for the right kind of work, role, and life for a woman.

Harper made an important contribution to African American writing; she was not, however, the first African American to publish a novel or longer fiction. In March, 1853, Frederick Douglass published his novella, *The Heroic Slave*, in his paper *The North Star*. And, in the same year, William Wells Brown (1814?–1884) published a full-length novel, *Clotel; or, The President's Daughter*. Like Douglass, William Wells Brown was born a slave, in Kentucky. His father was a white man, his mother a slave woman. He escaped from slavery in 1834, and took the name Wells Brown from a Quaker couple who assisted him in the course of his flight. Moving to Boston, he wrote his autobiography, *Narrative of William W. Brown, an American Slave*. Published in 1847, it was exceeded only in popularity as a slave narrative by the *Narrative* of Douglass, and it established Brown's reputation. Brown traveled to Europe, remaining there until 1854. In 1852 he published *Three Years in Europe*, the first African American travel book, consisting mainly of letters the author had written to friends and newspapers in America. And in 1853 he published *Clotel*. He was later to revise the novel and republish it several times: once in serial form as "Miralda; or, the Beautiful Quadroon: A Romance of Slavery, Founded on Fact" (1860–1861) and twice in novel form, as *Clotelle: A Tale of the Southern States* (1864) and *Clotelle; or, The Colored Heroine – A Tale of the Southern States* (1867). In 1848 Brown had written a piece for a compilation, *The Antislavery Harp*, entitled "Jefferson's Daughter," based on the well-established rumor that Thomas Jefferson had had a mulatto daughter by his housekeeper, an African American, who was then sold at a New Orleans slave auction. This was evidently the inspiration for *Clotel*, although in none of the different versions is Jefferson ever mentioned by name. What is notable about the novel is how openly, for its day, it explores the related themes of black concubinage, miscegenation, and the link between sexual and racial oppression. "With the growing population in the Southern states, the increase of mulattoes has been very great," the story begins. Claiming that "the real, or clear black, does not amount to more than one in four of the slave population," the narrator then goes on to consider the tragic consequences of this racially and sexually charged situation. Through several generations, black women are shown at the mercy of the arbitrary power and the sexual whims of white men and the jealousy of white women. Daughters are sold at slave auction; a black concubine is sent off to a slave trader at the insistence of a jealous white wife; one black woman kills herself rather than suffer further enslavement; another woman is put up for auction with her daughter, on the death of her husband, when it is discovered that, legally, she is black and still a slave.

To an extent, *Clotel* is a symptom of the racial blindness it diagnoses. The heroines in this story all tend to be fair-skinned, while the comic characters, the fools, tricksters, and villainous collaborators with white oppression all tend to be black. But this is something that Brown may have sensed himself. In its original version, the beloved of the heroine, Clotel, is of lighter complexion just like her. In the revised versions, however, he is described as "perfectly black." Clotel is reunited with her white father at the end of the novel; and, "having all the prejudices against color which characterizes his white fellow-countrymen," the father at first expresses his "dislike" of his son-in-law's complexion. Clotel's reply is forthright and sums up the main intended message of the book. "I married him because I loved him," she tells her father. "Why should the white man be esteemed as better than the black? I find no difference in men on account of their complexion." *Clotel* is a romantic novel but it is also a powerful assault on the slave system and, in particular, the fundamental betrayal it represented of humanity and the American dream. It was Brown's only long work of fiction, but here he mapped out much of the geography of the later African American narrative – the flight to freedom, the bitter fate of denied and mixed identities – and, in the portrait of Clotel, he created a heroine who was not just a victimized tragic mulatta but a combative spokesperson for her race.

Two other novels by African Americans to appear before the Civil War were *Blake; or, The Huts of America* (partly serialized in 1859, fully serialized in 1861–1862, and issued as a book in 1870) and *Our Nig; or, Sketches from the Life of a Free Black, in a Two-Story White House, North. Showing that Slavery's Shadows Fall Even There* (1859). *Blake* was the work of Martin Delany (1812–1885), a free black born in what is now West Virginia. In 1852 Delany published *The Condition, Elevation, Emigration, and Destiny of the Colored People of the United States*, which argued for the emigration of blacks to a state of their own creation. *Blake* continued that argument. The hero, Henry Blake, possesses many of the qualities Delany liked to identify with himself. He is "a black – a pure negro – handsome, manly, and intelligent" and "a man of good literary attainments." Born in Cuba, Blake is decoyed into slavery in Mississippi. There, he marries another slave; and, when his wife is sold and sent away from him, he runs away to begin organizing slave insurrections, first in the South and then in Cuba. "If you want white man to love you, you must fight im!" an Indian whom he meets in the course of his wanderings tells Blake. And, although Blake does not want the white man to love him, he certainly wants to fight him. The message of *Blake* is, in fact, at once revolutionary and deeply conventional, in the American grain. "I am for war – war against whites," the hero tells his allies, while insisting that they should resist amalgamation, reject life in the United States, and return to their African homeland. But Blake also advises them, "With money you may effect your escape at almost any time . . . Money alone will carry you . . . to liberty"; and money, he points out, is the reward of enterprise. Delany was a father of black nationalism who did not reject the American way but, rather, hoped to see it pursued by African Americans in Africa. The violence he embraced, and dramatized in his novel, was founded on a simultaneous alienation from and attachment to the land where he was born.

Our Nig is very different. The first published novel by an African American woman, it is also the first in black American literature to examine the life of an ordinary black person in detail. It was originally thought to be the work of a white, and perhaps even male, writer. And it was only recently established that Harriet E. Wilson (1808?–1870) was the author, drawing in part on personal experience. The central character, Frado (short for Alfrado and also called "Our Nig") is deserted by her white mother after the death of her African American father. She is abandoned in the home of the Bellmonts, where she becomes an indentured servant and is treated cruelly by her white mistress, Mrs. Bellmont, who beats her, and her daughter Mary Bellmont. The white male members of the household try to protect Frado, but they are mostly ineffectual, and Frado has to learn to protect herself. Coming of age at eighteen, she then leaves the Bellmonts and marries an African American who claims to be a runaway slave. She has a child by him, is then deserted and discovers his claim is false, experiences poverty and bad health, the result of years of abuse, and is forcibly separated from her child. As the story of Frado unfolds, some narrative attention is given to events in the Bellmont family, and to the adventures of the Bellmont children as they grow up and marry. In conventional fashion, the subsequent lives of various Bellmonts are even summarized in the closing paragraph of the novel. But the emotional center throughout is the poor black girl whose nickname – given to her, of course, by whites – provides the book with its main title. And, at the end of the story, the pathos of her plight is emphasized. "Reposing on God, she has thus far journeyed securely," the narrator advises us. "Still an invalid, she asks your sympathy, gentle reader."

Our Nig is a fascinating hybrid. Not only a sentimental novel, it is also a realist one. It focuses not so much on moments of particular brutality (although there are certainly some of them), as on the bitter daily burden of black toil and white indifference and spite. Wilson's book is many generic forms, and it is more than the sum of them: as it charts the journey of her heroine towards survival rather than satisfaction, let alone success. And, in being so, it illustrates the problem so many African American writers have faced, of trying to find a workable genre in which to express and explore themselves: a form that gives them a chance of narrating, properly, their identity. The author's identification of herself as simply "Our Nig," in the first edition of the book, was, of course, ironic; and it underlined the difficulty of finding a name for herself in a culture that tried to do that work for her – to give her, not so much a name, as a demeaning label. It is an additional irony that she was to remain unnamed, for over a hundred years, as the author, the maker of her own work: invisibility, the namelessness that is perhaps the central theme in African American writing, was to be the story of *Our Nig*, for a long time, as well as the story *in* it.

The Making of an American Fiction and Poetry

The emergence of American narratives

Our Nig had almost no impact when it was published. The reverse was true of *Uncle Tom's Cabin; or, Life Among the Lowly* by Harriet Beecher Stowe (1811–1896). *Uncle Tom's Cabin* started out, according to Stowe's intention, as a series of sketches, published in the *National Era*, an antislavery magazine, in 1851. Her aim, she told the editor of the magazine, was "to hold up in the most lifelike and graphic manner possible Slavery." When the book was published in 1852, it sold 10,000 copies in a few days, 300,000 copies in the first year, and became an international bestseller. No other book had ever sold so well, apart from the Bible. The main story is simple. Uncle Tom, a faithful and saintly slave, is sold by his owners, the Shelby family, when they find themselves in financial difficulties. Separated from his wife and children, he is taken South by a slave trader; aboard ship on the Mississippi, he saves the life of Eva St. Clare, known as little Eva, and is bought by her father, Angel St. Clare, out of gratitude. Tom is happy at the St. Clare plantation, growing close to Eva and her black playmate Topsy. But, after two years, Eva dies and then so does St. Clare. Tom is sold to the villainous Simon Legree, a cruel and debauched Yankee. The patience and courage of Tom, despite all the brutal treatment meted out to him, bewilder Legree. Two female slaves take advantage of Legree's state of mind, and pretend to escape; and, when Tom refuses to reveal their whereabouts, a furious Legree has him flogged to death. As Tom is dying, "Mas'r George" Shelby, the son of Tom's original master, arrives, to fulfill his pledge made right at the beginning of the novel, that he would one day redeem the old slave. It is too late for Tom; however, Shelby vows to fight for abolition and, as a first step, he frees the slaves on his own plantation, telling them that they can continue to work for him as "free men and free women." Woven in and around this main plot are a number of subsidiary episodes, involving a host of characters. The most important of these episodes concern Eliza Harris, a beautiful "mixed race" woman, her husband George, who lives as a slave on another plantation, and their son Harry. George is the son of a slave mother and a white father "from one of the proudest families in Kentucky." He is said to have inherited "a set of European features, and a high indomitable spirit" from his father; he has, we are told, "only a slight mulatto tinge" – and he preaches resistance, defiance. At one point, for instance, he makes what is called "his declaration of independence": he is "a free man" by natural right, he insists, and, as such, he has the right to defend his freedom, by violence if necessary. In the course of the story, George and Eliza escape. They stay at a Quaker settlement for a while, with their son Harry. Eventually, they set sail from America. On board ship, both are miraculously reunited with their long-lost mothers. They settle first in France, where George attends university for four years, and then in Africa. "The desire and yearning of my soul is for an African *nationality*," George declares. "I want a people that shall have a tangible, separate existence of its own." The final gesture of one George, Shelby, in freeing his slaves, is in effect counterpointed by the final gesture of another George, Harris, in seeking to establish what he calls "a republic formed of picked men, who . . . have, . . . individually raised themselves above a condition of slavery." Both appear to be founders of a new order.

"God wrote the book," Stowe once said of *Uncle Tom's Cabin*, "I took His dictation." Stowe was helped not only by divine intervention, though, or her sense of it, but by her reading. There are various forms of discourse at work in the novel that reflect its author's active and informed engagement with the debate over slavery. Stowe was, for example, well aware of the arguments for and against slavery. At one moment in the St. Clare episode, she comprehensively rebuts every facet of the pro-slavery argument; and, at another point, she has a family discuss the Fugitive Slave Law. The story of the flight of George and Eliza Harris clearly recalls slave narratives; the novel as a whole opens with a central situation in plantation fiction, the threatened loss of the old plantation due to debt; and, true to the conventions of sentimental fiction, there are miraculous coincidences, interminable deathbed scenes (notably, the death of little Eva), and the customary address to the gentle reader. Characters out of tall tales and frontier humor are introduced, like a comic black duo called Sam and Andy; two rough slaveholders called Tom Luker and Marks recall the rogues of Southwestern humor; various moments, such as when we are invited to enter Uncle Tom's Cabin for the first time, remind us of Stowe's participation in the local color tradition; and, along with scenes from provincial life, there are moments of pastoral and anti-pastoral – respectively, the idyllic portrait of the St. Clare plantation and detailed description of the dilapidated estate that Simon Legree owns. But Stowe does not simply imitate, she innovates. So, *this* planatation novel centers, as its subtitle indicates, not on the wealthy plantation owners but on "life among the lowly." Its hero is not some impoverished patriarch but a slave who gradually assumes the stature of a Christ figure. And the object of *this* sentimental fiction is, as Stowe declares in her "Preface," specifically moral and political: "to awaken sympathy and feeling for the African race, as they exist among us."

Those whose sympathy Stowe especially hoped to awaken were women: the narrator constantly appeals to the possible experiences of the reader as a wife and mother. To an extent, in fact, *Uncle Tom's Cabin* is a document testifying to female power as well as black possibility: the condition of women as well as that of slaves. Females are consistently better managers than men, in the novel. It is the females who offer the most fully realized vision of a redemptive society: in the Quaker settlement where George and Eliza Harris shelter – where everything runs "so sociably, so quietly, so harmoniously" thanks to the women, who run it on matriarchal and communal lines. And it is the principles identified with the feminine in the novel that we are invited to admire: the organic, creative, supportive, sympathetic impulses associated with Eva St. Clare and her "misty, dreamy" father, Angel (who is said to be more like his mother than his father). The principles identified as masculine are, by contrast, shown to be mechanized, destructive, oppressive: associated with Angel's twin brother Alfred St. Clare (who, like his father, believes in "the *right of the strongest*") and, even more, the brutal Simon Legree. Here, the contrast between Uncle Tom and George Harris is relevant. George resists, invoking the Declaration of Independence, and he is certainly admired for doing so. He is not, however, the emotional center of the novel. That is supplied by "the hero of our story," the gentle, unresistant, and feminized Uncle Tom: who invokes the Bible and only resists doing wrong – refusing to whip a fellow slave, to betray the whereabouts of two other slaves, and refusing even the chance offered him to kill Simon Legree. George is a political exemplar of a kind, but Tom is a saint, compared eventually to Christ: ready to be killed, but not to kill. Conversion not revolution is the principal subject and aim of *Uncle Tom's Cabin*; and that project is consistently associated with the feminine.

The counsel of patience embodied in its hero has earned Stowe's novel opprobrium in many quarters: "Uncle Tom," after all, has become a term of abuse, a dismissive label stuck on any African American seen to be too servile, and there is no doubt that *Uncle Tom's Cabin* often resorts to racial stereotypes. Still, the force of the attack on slavery in *Uncle Tom's Cabin* remains. And, looking at both its form and approach, it is easy to see why it made such an enormous impact on contemporary readers. Stowe took the aesthetic weaponry of several popular genres – the plantation romance, sentimental fiction, the slave narrative – and she then used them to show how the slave system violated the most sacred beliefs of her culture – the sanctity of the family and the individual soul. Stowe drew on the wealth of feeling she herself had, concerning the home and family, Christian womanhood and the Christian soul; she then appealed to that same wealth of feeling in her readers. In the process, she wrote what is, by any standards, one of the most important American books. For a while after *Uncle Tom's Cabin*, Stowe continued to write about slavery. In 1853 she wrote *A Key to Uncle Tom's Cabin*, designed to defend the accuracy of her 1852 novel. Then, in 1856, she published *Dred: A Tale of the Dismal Swamp*. This, her second story of slave society, takes a different approach from the first. It tends to concentrate on the demoralizing effects of slavery on whites. And this time the character who gives the novel its title is a fugitive and a revolutionary.

After *Dred*, Stowe steered away from the subject of slavery. *The Minister's Wooing* (1859), set in New England, uses a romantic plot to explore the limitations of the "gloomy" doctrine of Calvinism and promote belief in a redemptive Christ and a God of love and mercy. Similar themes, together with an emphasis on the power of female purity, are at work in *Agnes of Sorrento* (1862), set in the Catholic Italy of Savanarola, and *The Pearl of Orr's Island* (1862), another book set in New England which Sarah Orne Jewett credited with inspiring her own career. The local color element, which had always been there in Stowe's work, grew stronger in her later fiction. *Oldtown Folks* (1869), for instance, is set in New England in the post-Revolutionary period and has a narrator modeled on Stowe's own husband. Several of her novels resemble novels of manners more than anything else, including one called *Pink and White Tyranny* (1871). Even here, however, she was keen to announce her intention to instruct and uplift. That fierce didactic intention has meant that Stowe has often been granted less than her due as a writer. She is a didactic writer, certainly, but she is also a writer capable of combining adroit use of popular literary models with raw emotional power. Consistently, in much of her fiction and many of her sketches, she is a very good writer indeed; at her best she is surely a great one.

"Only this is such a strange and incomprehensible world!" a character called Holgrave declares in *The House of the Seven Gables* (1851), the second full-length fiction of Nathaniel Hawthorne (1804–1864). "The more I look at it, the more it puzzles me; and I begin to suspect that a man's bewilderment is the measure of his wisdom!" Hawthorne was notoriously mistrustful of all speculative schools of thought, or of anyone or any movement that claimed to have solved the mystery and resolved the contradictions of life. That included the two major historical movements associated with his native New England of which he had intimate experience: Puritanism and Transcendentalism. He was someone who managed to make great art, not so much out of bewilderment, as out of of ambiguity, irresolution – a refusal to close off debate or the search for truth. Hawthorne was undoubtedly a moralist, concerned in particular with the moral errors of egotism and pride, separation from what he called "the magnetic chain of humanity." But he was a moralist who was acutely aware of just how complex the human character and human relations are, just how subtle and nicely adjusted to the particulars of the case moral judgments consequently have to be – and how moral judgment does not preclude imaginative understanding, even sympathy. He was also someone who had inherited from his Puritan ancestors what he termed his "inveterate love of allegory." But his alertness to the dualities of experience meant that, in his hands, allegory passed into symbolism: an object or event assumed multiple possible significances, rather than correspondence with one, divinely ordained idea. Finally, Hawthorne was, he confessed in the "Preface" to *The House of the Seven Gables*, an author of romances rather than novels. But, for Hawthorne, greater imaginative freedom was a means, not an end. His aim, and achievement, was to maneuver the romance form so as to unravel the secrets of personality and history: "the truth of the human heart," as Hawthorne himself put it, and the puzzling question of whether the present is an echo or repetition of the past, a separate world "disjoined by time," or a mixture somehow of both.

In 1828 Hawthorne published his first novel, *Fanshawe: A Tale*, anonymously and at his own expense. An autobiographical work, it went unnoticed. But it did attract the attention of its publisher, Samuel Goodrich, who then published many of Hawthorne's short stories in his periodical, *The Token*. Eventually, these were reprinted in a volume, *Twice-Told Tales*, in 1837, then in a larger version in 1842. In a characteristically modest and self-critical preface, Hawthorne referred to his tales as having "the pale tint of flowers blossomed in too retired a shade." They do, however, include some of his best pieces, such as "The Maypole of Merrymount," "Endicott and the Red Cross," and "The Grey Champion." And, collectively, they explore the issues that obsessed him: guilt and secrecy, intellectual and moral pride, the convoluted impact of the Puritan past on the New England present. For the next five years, Hawthorne worked as an editor for Goodrich, then became involved briefly in the experiment in communal living at Brook Farm. Used to solitude, however, he found communal living uncongenial: its only positive result for him was the novel he published in 1852 based on his Brook Farm experience, *The Blithedale Romance*. Married now, to Sophia Peabody, he and his wife moved to Concord, where they lived in the Old Manse, the former home of Ralph Waldo Emerson. There was time for neighborly visits to Emerson, Henry David Thoreau, and Margaret Fuller, for the family – three children were born to Sophia and Nathaniel between 1844 and 1851 – and for writing: in 1846, *Mosses from an Old Manse* appeared, containing such famous stories as "Young Goodman Brown," "Rappacini's Daughter," and "Roger Malvin's Burial." There was also time, after Hawthorne left a post he had held for three years as customs surveyor, to concentrate on a longer fiction, what would turn out to be his most important work.

The germ of this work, what was to become *The Scarlet Letter* (1850), can be found as far back as 1837. In the story "Endicott and the Red Cross," the narrator describes a young woman, "with no mean share of beauty," wearing the letter A on her breast, in token of her adultery. Already, the character of Hester Prynne, the heroine of *The Scarlet Letter*, was there in embryo. And gradually, over the years between 1837 and 1849, other hints and anticipations appear in the journals Hawthorne kept. "A man who does penance," he wrote in one journal entry, in an idea for a story, "in what might appear to lookers-on the most glorious and triumphal circumstances of his life." That was to become the Reverend Arthur Dimmesdale, Hester's secret lover and the father of her illegitimate child, preaching the Election Day Sermon. "A story of the effects of revenge, in diabolising him who indulges it," he wrote in another entry. That was to be

Roger Chillingworth, Hester's husband and Dimmesdale's persecutor. Ideas for the portrait of Pearl, the daughter of Hester and Dimmesdale, often sprang from Hawthorne's observation of his own daughter, Una. As he wrote the novel, over the course of 1849 and 1850, Hawthorne was simultaneously exhilarated and wary. "*The Scarlet Letter* is positively a hell-fired story," he wrote to his publisher, when he had completed it; "it will weary very many people and disgust some."

The major tensions that Hawthorne searches out in *The Scarlet Letter* are related to his own ambivalent relationship to Puritanism, and his own Puritan ancestors in particular. As he intimates in the introductory essay to his story, he felt haunted by his ancestors yet different from them. He could experience what he calls there "a sort of home-feeling with the past," but he also suspected that his Puritan founding father might find it "quite a sufficient retribution for his sins" that one of his descendants had become a writer, "an idler" and a dabbler in fancy. *The Scarlet Letter* rehearses the central debate in nineteenth-century American literature: between the demands of society and the needs of the individual, communal obligation and self-reliance. The Puritan settlement in which the story is set is a powerful instance of community. Hester Prynne, in turn, is a supreme individualist: "What we did had a consecration of its own," she tells her lover. The conflict between the two is also a conflict between the symbolic territories that occur in so many American texts: the clearing and the wilderness, life conducted inside the social domain and life pursued outside it. And the main characteristic of Hawthorne's portrait of this conflict is its doubleness: quite simply, he is tentative, equivocal, drawing out the arguments for and against both law and freedom. As a result, the symbolic territories of *The Scarlet Letter* become complex centers of gravity: clustering around them are all kinds of often conflicting moral implications. The forest, for example, may be a site of freedom, the only place where Hester and Dimmesdale feel at liberty to acknowledge each other. But it is also a moral wilderness, where characters go to indulge in their darkest fantasies – or, as they see it, to commune with the Devil. The settlement may be a place of security, but it is also one of constriction, even repression, its moral boundaries marked out by the prison and the scaffold. Simple allegory becomes rich and puzzling symbol, not only in the mapping of the opposing territories of forest and settlement, clearing and wilderness, but in such crucial, figurative presences as the scarlet letter "A" that gives the book its title. To the Puritans who force Hester to wear the scarlet letter, it may be an allegorical emblem. In the course of the story, however, it accumulates many meanings other than "adultress." It might mean that, of course, and so act as a severe judgment on Hester's individualism; then again, as the narrator indicates, it might signify "able," "admirable," or even "angel."

The major characters of *The Scarlet Letter*, too, become centers of conflict, the debate become flesh, turned into complex imaginative action. Hester, for example, may be a rebel, modeled on the historical figure of Anne Hutchinson as well as the mythical figure of Eve. But she cannot live outside of society altogether. She is a conflicted figure, unable to find complete satisfaction in either the clearing or the wilderness; and her eventual home, a house on the edge of the forest, in a kind of border territory between the two, is a powerful illustration of this. Dimmesdale is conflicted too, but in a more spiritually corrosive way. Torn between the image he offers to others and the one he presents to himself, his public role as a revered minister and his private one as Hester's lover and Pearl's father, Dimmesdale is fatally weakened for much of the action. In his case, the central conflict of the story finds its issue in severe emotional disjunction. And Chillingworth is there to feed on that weakness, becoming Dimmesdale's "leech" in more ways than one – apparently his doctor but actually drawing sustenance from Dimmesdale's guilt and his own secret satisfying of the need for revenge. Roger Chillingworth, in turn, is more than just a figure of retribution and a possible projection of Hawthorne's own uneasy feeling that, as a writer, he was just a parasite, an observer of life. "It is a curious observation and inquiry, whether hatred and love be not the same at bottom," the narrator comments, after describing how Chillingworth declined once Dimmesdale died. The link is passion. "The passionate lover" and "the no less passionate hater" each sups voraciously on "the food of his affection"; and the hater, rather more than the lover, reminds us that laws may well be required to curb the individual appetite. Hawthorne was enough of a son of his Puritan forefathers to believe that, as he put it in his journals, "there is evil lurking in every human heart." Knowledge of evil, after all, and of her origins, is the means by which Pearl eventually ceases to be a child – a creature of the wilderness, associated with its streams, plants, and animals – and starts to become an adult, a woman in the world. And knowledge of evil renders each of the major characters even more vacillating and conflicted: ensuring that the debate between self and society that *The Scarlet Letter* rehearses remains open, for the narrator and for us, his readers.

This, perhaps, is the secret of the mysterious power of Hawthorne's major novel: it is an open text. The story explores many issues. They include, along with the central problem of law and freedom, what the narrator calls the "dark question" of woman-hood. Among many other things, *The Scarlet Letter* considers the condition of woman in and through the story of its heroine, speculating that "the whole system of society" may have "to be torn down and built up anew" and woman herself reconstructed, freed from a "long hereditary habit" – behavior instilled by social separation and subjection – before women like Hester can assume "a fair and suitable position." On none of these issues, however, and least of all on the central one, does the narrator claim to be authoritative or the narrative move towards closure. The subtle maneuvering of character, the equivocal commentary and symbolism, ensure that meaning is not imposed on the reader. On the contrary, the reader has to collaborate with the narrator, in the construction of possible meanings, every time the book is read. To this extent, for all Hawthorne's profound debt to Puritanism, *The Scarlet Letter* is an extraordinarily modern book: expressing a relativist sense of experience in a form that is more fluid process than finished product. What it offers is not, in the manner of a traditional classic text, an answer issuing out of a belief in some absolute, unalterable truth, but something more like a modern classic – a shifting, disconcerting, and almost endless series of questions.

The Scarlet Letter ushered in the most productive period of Hawthorne's life. In the next three years, he was to publish, not only the two further novels, *The House of the Seven Gables* and *The Blithedale Romance*, but another collection of stories, *The Snow Image and Other Tales* (1851), and two volumes of stories for children, *A Wonder Book* (1852) and *Tanglewood Tales* (1853). He lived in England for a while, as United States Consul, and then in Rome, returning to America in 1860. The years in Europe supplied him with the material for a novel set in Rome and dealing with the international theme that Henry James was to make his own, *The Marble Faun* (1860). They also resulted in a series of shrewd essays drawn from his observations in England, called *Our Old Home* (1863). But, back in the United States, he found it increasingly difficult to write. The writer who had once been inspired by the multiplicity of possible meanings that lay beneath the surface of things was stuck, frustrated by an apparent absence of meaning, his evident inability to strike through the surface. The "cat-like faculty of seeing in the dark" that Henry James was later to attribute to him had, Hawthorne felt, now deserted him. It was a sad ending for a great writer. But, of course, it in no way diminishes his achievement. Even the later, unfinished work is far more intriguing than Hawthorne, in his dejection, supposed. And his earlier work, above all the major stories and *The Scarlet Letter*, form an indispensable contribution to American literature.

"He can neither believe, nor be comfortable in his unbelief," Hawthorne once observed of Herman Melville (1819–1891), "and he is too honest and courageous not to try to do one or the other." For Melville, human experience was ruled by contraries. "There is no quality in this world that is not what it is merely by contraries," Ishmael declares in *Moby-Dick* (1851). "Nothing exists in itself." And those contraries were no more evident, he felt, than within each human being, as he or she struggled to find a basis for truth and faith, something that would really make life worth living. Melville could not resign himself to doubt, or a placid acceptance of the surfaces of things. He wanted to probe the visible objects of the world, to discover their animating structure, their significance. But he also sensed that the visible might be all there was – and that that, too, was a masquerade, a trick of the light and human vision. "The head rejects," the reader is told in Melville's long poem, *Clarel* (1876), "so much more/The heart embraces." That could stand as an epigraph to all Melville's work because it exists in the tension between meaning and nothingness. It bears constant and eloquent testimony to the impulse most people feel at one time or another: the impulse to believe, that is, even if only in the possibility of belief, however perversely and despite all the evidence.

Melville did not begin with the ambition to become a writer. Nor did he have an extensive schooling. His father died when he was only twelve; and, at the age of fifteen, Melville left school to support his family. Working first as a bank clerk, a teacher, and a farm laborer, he then, when he was nineteen, sailed on a merchant ship to Liverpool as a cabin boy: the voyage, later to be described in his fourth novel, *Redburn* (1849), was both romantic and grueling and gave him a profound love for the sea. Several other voyages followed, including an eighteen-month voyage on the whaler *Acushnet* in the South Seas. Ishmael, in *Moby-Dick*, insists that the whale-ship was the only Yale and Harvard he ever had; and much the same could be said of his creator, who in 1844 returned to land, where he was encouraged to write about some of his more exotic experiences at sea. Melville accordingly produced *Typee* (1846) and *Omoo, a Narrative of Adventures in the South Seas* (1847), novels that deal, respectively, with his experiences on the Marquesas and in Tahiti. They were romantic seafaring tales and, as such, proved immensely popular. But, even here, there are anticipations of the later Melville: most notably, in a narrative tendency to negotiate between contraries – youth and maturity, the primitive and the civilized, the land and the sea.

In his next novel, *Mardi: And A Voyage Thither* (1849), Melville grew more ambitious. Based in part on the author's experiences in the Marquesas, *Mardi* is an elaborate allegorical and philosophical narrative. The two novels following this concentrated on action: first, *Redburn: His First Voyage*, and then *White-Jacket; or, The World in a Man-of-War* (1850) based, like *Redburn*, on Melville's own experience. It was after completing these that Melville turned to the work that was to be his masterpiece, *Moby-Dick*, dedicated, in "Admiration for His Genius," to the man who had become his friend and neighbor, Nathaniel Hawthorne. Melville took to rereading Shakespearean tragedy at the time of preparing the story of Captain Ahab's pursuit of the great white whale; and he drew on that experience in a number of ways. There are local resemblances. Ahab addresses the skeleton of a whale, for instance, in a fashion that recalls Hamlet's famous meditation over the skull of Yorick the jester. There are stylistic resemblances. And there is, above all, the conceptual, structural resemblance. "All mortal greatness is but disease," Ishmael observes early on in the narrative. That observation, as it happens, is borrowed from an essay by Samuel Taylor Coleridge on Shakespearean tragic heroes. Even without the help of such borrowings, however, it is possible to see that the conception of Captain Ahab is fundamentally tragic. Ahab makes a choice that challenges – the gods, or fate, or human limits, the given conditions of thought and existence. That choice and challenge provoke our fear and pity, alarm and sympathy. And that leads, it seems inevitably, to a catastrophe that compels similarly complex, contradictory emotions: the suffering and death of many, including a hero who appears to exist somehow both above and below ordinary humanity.

The contradictions inherent in the portrait of Ahab spring from the dualism of Melville's own vision. Together, the narrator and the hero of *Moby-Dick*, Ishmael and Ahab, flesh out that dualism. So does the structural opposition of land and sea, which rehearses in characteristically Melvillean terms a familiar American conflict between clearing and wilderness. The land is the sphere of "safety, comfort, hearthstone, supper, warm blankets, friends, all that's kind to our mortalities"; the sea, in turn, is the sphere of adventure, action, struggle. The one maps out security, and mediocrity; the other carries intimations of heroism but also the pride, the potential madness involved in striking out from the known. The one inscribes reliance on the community, the other a respect for the self. A densely woven network of reference establishes the difference between these two territories; it also suggests the difficulty, perhaps the impossibility, of either choosing between them or finding an appropriate border area. The opposition between land and sea is made all the rawer by Melville's portrait of the ship, the *Pecquod*, on which Ahab, Ishmael, and their companions voyage. The crew are together and alone, knit into one, shared purpose yet utterly divided in terms of motive and desire. Caught each of them between the land and the sea, the social contract and isolation, they remind us that this is a ship of life, certainly, burdened by a common human problem. But it is also, and more particularly, the ship of America: embarked on an enterprise that is a curious mixture of the mercantile and the moral, imperial conquest and (ir)religious crusade – and precariously balanced between the notions of community and freedom.

All the tensions and irresolutions of *Moby-Dick* circulate, as they do in *The Scarlet Letter*, around what gives the book its title: in this case, the mysterious white whale to which all attention and all the action is eventually drawn. The reason for the mystery of the whale is simple. It "is" reality. That is, it becomes both the axis and the circumference of experience, and our understanding of it, in the novel. It is nature, and physics, a state of being and of knowing. Each character measures his understanding of the real in the process of trying to understand and explain the whale; it becomes the mirror of his beliefs, like the doubloon that Ahab nails to the mast as a reward for the first man who sights the white whale, to be valued differently by the different crew members. It is both alphabet and message, both the seeming surface of things and what may, or may not, lie beneath them. So, like the scarlet letter "A" in Hawthorne's story, its determining characteristic is its indeterminacy. How it is seen, what it is seen as being and meaning, depend entirely on who is seeing it. Three characters, in particular, are given the chance to explain what they see at some length. One offers his explanation early on in the novel, even before the voyage in quest of the white whale begins: Father Mapple, whose sermon delivered to a congregation that includes Ishmael in the Whaleman's Chapel – and forming the substance of the ninth chapter – is a declaration of faith, trust in a fundamental benevolence. It is a vision allowed a powerful imaginative apotheosis in a much later chapter entitled "The Grand Armada." However, this is not a vision in which much narrative time or imaginative energy is invested. The visions that matter here, the explanations – or, rather, possible explanations – that count, rehearse the fundamental division around which all Melville's work circulates; and they belong to the two main human figures in the tale, its hero and its teller, Ahab and Ishmael.

For Ahab, Moby-Dick represents everything that represses and denies. Believing only in a fundamental malevolence, he feels towards the white whale something of "the general rage and hate felt by the whole race from Adam down." Having lost his leg in a previous encounter with his enemy, he also desires vengeance, not just on the "dumb brute" that injured him but on the conditions that created that brute, which for him that brute symbolizes – the human circumstances that would frustrate him, deny him his ambitions and desires. Ahab is a complex figure. A tragic hero, carrying the marks of his mortality, the human limitation he would deny, he is also a type of the artist, or any visionary intent on the essence of things. An artist, he is also an American: a rebel like Hester Prynne, an enormous egotist like Ralph Waldo Emerson in the sense that he sees the universe as an externalization of his soul, and an imperialist whose belief in his own manifest destiny compels him to use all other men like tools and claim dominion over nature. "A grand ungodly, god-like man," Ahab projects his overpowering belief in himself, his will to power, on to Moby-Dick, seeing in the great white whale all that prevents a man from becoming a god. And the key to Melville's portrait of him is its dualism: it is as if the author were summoning up his, and possibly our, dark twin.

"Is it by its indefiniteness," Ishmael asks of "the whiteness of the whale," "it shadows forth the heartless voids and immensities of the universe …?" It is Ishmael who describes white as "a colorless all-color." For the narrator of *Moby-Dick*, the great white whale unveils the probability that what is disclosed when we peer intently at our circumstances is neither benevolence nor malevolence but something as appallingly vacant as it is vast, a fundamental indifference. That, though, is not all there is to Ishmael. In the course of the story, he also undergoes a sentimental education. Beginning with a misanthropy so thoroughgoing and dryly ironic that he even mocks his misanthropic behavior, he ends by accepting and embracing his kinship with the human folly and weakness he sees all around him. Specifically, he embraces Queequeg, a Polynesian harpooneer, whom initially he finds, even more than most of humanity, repellent. It is this, Ishmael's return to a specifically human sphere – expressed, in a characteristically American way, in the bonding of two people of the same sex but from different races – that enables him, quite literally, to survive. When all other crew members of the *Pecquod* are lost, and the ship itself sunk, after three days of struggle with Moby-Dick; when Ahab is destroyed by becoming one with that which he would destroy, tied by his own ropes to the great white whale; then, Ishmael floats free in what is, in effect, a reproduction of Queequeg's body – a coffin Queequeg has made, and on to which he has copied "the twisting tattooing" on his own skin. It *is* survival, not triumph. "Another orphan" of the world, Ishmael lives on because he has resigned himself to the limitations of the sensible, the everyday, the ordinary: to all that is identified, for good and ill, with the land. The difference between his own quietly ironic idiom and the romantic rhetoric of Ahab measures the gap between them: one has opted for a safety that shades into surrender, the other has pursued success only to meet with a kind of suicide. That difference also registers the division Melville felt within himself. *Moby-Dick* negotiates its way between the contraries experienced by its author and by his culture: between head and heart, resignation and rebellion, the sanctions of society and the will of the individual. And, like so many great American books, it remains open, "the draught of a draught" as its narrator puts it, because it is in active search of what it defines as impossible: resolution, firm belief or comfortable unbelief – in short, nothing less than the truth.

Moby-Dick was not a success when it was first published; and Melville felt himself under some pressure to produce something that would, as he put it, pay "the bill of the baker." That, anyway, was his explanation for his next novel, *Pierre; or, The Ambiguities* (1852). In the first year of publication, it sold less than three hundred copies. *Israel Potter: His Fifty Years of Exile* (1855), a weak historical romance set during the Revolution, was similarly unsuccessful. *The Piazza Tales* (1856) was far more accomplished, containing Melville's major achievements in short fiction, "Bartleby the Scrivener" and "Benito Cereno," but it attracted little attention. Melville did, after this, explore the issues that obsessed him in two other works of prose fiction. *The Confidence-Man: His Masquerade* (1857) offers complex multiple versions of the mythical figure of the trickster; it is at once a bleak portrait of the "Masquerade" of life, and a biting satire on the material and moral trickery of American society. *Billy Budd*, written in the five years before Melville's death and not published until 1924, in turn, reworks the traditional tale of the Handsome Sailor, so as to consider the uses of idealism, heroism, and innocence in a fallen world. However, to support himself and his family, Melville was increasingly forced to turn to other, non-writing work. And to express himself, he turned more and more to poetry. *Clarel: A Poem and Pilgrimage in the Holy Land*, based on a tour to the Holy Land the author himself had taken, was privately financed for publication; so were the poetry collections, *John Marr and Other Sailors* (1888) and *Timoleon* (1891). In his shorter poems, published here and in *Battlepieces and Aspects of the War* (1866), Melville is concerned, just as he is in his novels, with the tragic discords of experience. In "The Portent" (1886), for instance, he presents the militant abolitionist John Brown, the subject of the poem, as an alien and "weird" Christ figure. The poem, for all its ironic use of the Christ comparison, is not cynical; it does not deny Brown greatness of ambition and courage. As in *Moby-Dick*, though, admiration for such courage is set in tension with the imperative of survival: in its own small way, this poem rehearses again the issue that haunted its creator – the necessity and the absurdity of heroic faith.

Women writers and storytellers

The death of Melville went largely unnoticed by a wider public. Even those who did take note were hardly complimentary. It was not until the 1920s that his work began to be appreciated, and his stature as a major American writer was finally confirmed. Conversely, as Melville's star began to wax, the stars of other writers waned. This was notably true of those many women novelists and storytellers of the period whose work had enjoyed a wide contemporary readership. In their case, it is only in the last thirty years that reputations have been rehabilitated. Their writing has now been recognized for the pivotal cultural work it performed: the way it enabled Americans, and in particular American women, to assess their position in society and engage in debates about its prevailing character and possible development. Apart from Stowe, Fern, and Harper, those women writers whose reputations suffered for a while in this way include Caroline Kirkland (1801–1864), Elizabeth Stoddard (1823–1902), and Rebecca Harding Davis (1831–1902). Spanning the century in their lives, their work measures the range, diversity, and quality of those whom Hawthorne quite unjustly dismissed as a "damned mob of scribbling women."

Caroline Kirkland was one of the first settlers of Pinckney, Michigan, accompanying her husband there after he had acquired some land. Her ideas of the West, formed by such romantic works as *Atala* (1801) by Vicomte François-René de Chateaubriand, were radically altered by the experience. And in 1839 she published a novel, a series of scenes from provincial life on the frontier, *A New Home – Who Will Follow? or, Glimpses of Western Life* under the pseudonym of "Mrs. Mary Clavers, An Actual Settler." The book offers a version of the West that eschews romanticism, sensationalism, or even the kind of realism that emphasizes the masculine adventure and challenge of the frontier. Aiming at what she called "an honest portraiture of rural life in a new country," Kirkland begins by admitting that she has "never seen a cougar – nor been bitten by a rattlesnake." The reader must expect no more, she says, than "a meandering recital of common-place occurrences – mere gossip about everyday people." What follows is more calculated than that, however, and subtler: a portrait of "home on the outskirts of civilization" that focuses on the experience of women as they struggle to make do, and make something out of their daily lives. The majority of women in the book have to negotiate the enormity of the gap between how they and their husbands see land and life in the West. For them, the land is a place to settle, life there should be communal; for their men, however, the land is a source of status and power and life in the West is competition. For Kirkland, there is a touch of what she calls "madness" in this male attitude, but there is nothing the females can do about it. All they can do is try, as best they can, to put up with the hidden emotional costs.

Elizabeth Stoddard, born Elizabeth Drew Barstow in a small Massachusetts sea coast town, was a more unconventional person than Kirkland. In letters written in 1850, she described herself as being different from other women: someone who saw marriage as a struggle for power and motherhood as a distraction from the destiny she planned for herself. She did get married, however, to a minor poet called Richard Stoddard. And she began to write as well: poetry, short fiction, and, from 1854 to 1858, a regular column for the *Daily Alta California*. The short fiction tends to fall into one of two categories: formalized sketches like "Collected by a Valetudinarian" (1870) and tales blending realism and romance such as "Lemorne *Versus* Huell" (1863). The columns, in turn, reveal Stoddard's resistance to the received wisdom of the day. Stoddard mocked belief in manifest destiny, established religion, and the notion of a separate domestic sphere for women. She also poked satirical fun at the sentimental novel, with its "eternal preachment about self-denial." It was the 1860s, however, that were to witness her finest work. In 1862 she published her first novel, *The Morgesons*. It impressed Nathaniel Hawthorne, to whom Stoddard sent a copy, and many critics and reviewers including William Dean Howells. But it failed to secure her a reading public. Her two other novels, *Two Men* (1865) and *Temple House* (1867), suffered a similar fate. In the later two books, unlike *The Morgesons*, Stoddard adopted a male protagonist's point of view. All three, though, are characterized by an elliptical narrative style, carried along by rapid transitions of scene, conversations stripped to an explanatory minimum, and a dramatic, aphoristic, densely imagistic idiom. All three, also, reveal a world where social institutions are both repressive and in decay and religious belief is difficult, even impossible; and they also show the family as a site of struggle rather than a source of security, full of strangeness and secrecy, where passion is thwarted.

The Morgesons is exemplary in this respect. Its central character and narrator, Cassandra Morgeson, is clearly modeled on Stoddard herself; and what the book charts is a female quest for empowerment. Described as headstrong, even arrogant, by many of her acquaintances, Cassandra seeks personal autonomy. Born in a small seaport town, between land and sea, she is drawn as her great-grandfather Locke Morgeson was to "the influence of the sea": to escape, adventure, breaking away from convention and the commonplace. "The rest of the tribe" of Morgesons, Cassandra caustically observes, "inherited the character of the landscape." *The Morgesons* imitates the structure of the domestic novel, to the extent that it shows a young woman undergoing a sentimental education that ends in marriage, but it imitates it only to subvert it. Cassandra remains bold and willful, and an outsider, throughout the novel. She nurtures a dangerous attachment to a married man; she falls in love, later, with a dark, handsome stranger, called Desmond Somers, whom she eventually marries; but she always remains in control, her own woman. *The Morgesons* anticipates later fiction in its ellipses, its disjunctive, allusive idiom. It rehearses and reinvents both the gothic and sentimental fiction of its own time, in its curious, subtle mix of romance and realism. And it enters vigorously into the contemporary debate about whether there should or should not be separate spheres for women and men. But it is, above all, a book that is far more than the sum of these or any other connections: a novel that, in the spirit of those writers Stoddard most admired like the Brontës and Hawthorne, captures both the mundane and the ineffable – the materiality and the mystery of life.

Rebecca Harding Davis declared that it was her purpose "to dig into the common-place, this vulgar American life, and see what is in it." That purpose was clear enough in her first published work, "Life in the Iron Mills," which appeared in the *Atlantic Monthly* in 1861. The story was immediately recognized as an important, innovative work, introducing a new subject to American literature: the bleak lives of industrial workers in the mills and factories of the nation. "Not many even of the inhabitants of a manufacturing town know the vast machinery of system by which the bodies of workmen are governed," the narrator of the story declares near its beginning. And a major aim of Davis, in "Life in the Iron Mills," was, quite simply, to end that ignorance: to make readers aware of the oppression and the essential humanity of those workmen. Anticipating one of the major strategies of the Naturalists at the end of the nineteenth century, Davis emphasizes the typicality of her working-class characters, and the way they may be driven into crime by a system that appears to deny them any other possible avenue of escape. The tale "Life in the Iron Mills" tells is a simple one. At its center is a character called Hugh Wolfe, whose activities and fate encapsulate the aspirations and bitter reality of working people. The statue of a woman he has fashioned in his few spare moments expresses his longing for a better life, some possible source of fulfillment: "She be hungry," he says of the statue, "Not hungry for meat." The prison where he ends up, and where he kills himself, measures the cruel limitations that are his. "Was it not his right to live . . . a pure life, a good, true-hearted life, full of beauty and kind words?" he asks himself. The answer here is that it may be his right but it is not his destiny. Davis went on to write many more fictions that pursue a similarly reformist agenda. *Waiting for the Verdict* (1868), for instance, deals with the needs of the newly emancipated slaves, while *John Andross* (1874) investigates political corruption. None of her later work, however, had the impact or possesses the imaginative power of her first short story, which made her reputation and marks a turning point in American writing. In "Life in the Iron Mills," Davis's hope, as her narrator intimates, is to look "deeper into the heart of things" in a newly industrializing America. And her triumph is that she manages to do just that.

Spirituals and folk songs

Davis was writing about oppression from a position of some privilege. Among those many writers who spoke, or rather sang, from within their own oppressed condition were those slaves who handed down spirituals from generation to generation. First collected into a book by a black church leader in 1801, spirituals incorporated the secular as well as the divine and were sung not just at times of worship but throughout the day. They offered those who sang them the possibility of restitution from a life of pain: the longing to "Lay dis body down" is a constant theme. But they also offered release from the deathly definitions of their humanity forged by the slaveholders, and the possibility of resistance to and release from their enslavement. Many spirituals have call and response patterns, with lead singers setting out a line or phrase and the group responding by repeating or playing variations on it. So, the leader might call out, "Swing low, sweet chariot," and the group singers would respond, "Comin' for to carry me home." But not all do; and there are, in any event, wide variations of pace and tone. Some spirituals are dirges, lamentations, like "City Called Heaven," which begins, "I am a poor pilgrim of sorrow. / I'm in this wide world alone," or "Were You There When They Crucified My Lord?" Other spirituals are more driving and rapt, like "God's A-Gonna Trouble the Water," which repeats the title phrase seven times in five short stanzas and the phrase, "Wade in the water, children," no less than nine times. And some are jubilant, even ecstatic, like "That Great Gittin' Up Morning!," a vision of

Judgment Day that was perhaps delivered as a ring shout, with the possessed wor-shippers moving their bodies in time to its percussive rhythms.

Using such rhythms, repetitions, and imagery that anchors the mysteries of religion in the mundane realities of slave life, many of these spirituals express the dream of flying away, leaving the work and worries of the world behind. Some look to Christ and to heaven for relief and ease. Most of the spirituals are not about an easeful Jesus, however, but about the God of the Old Testament, His heroes and prophets; and many of them work towards a vision of redemption, even revenge, in this life here on earth. Songs like "Nobody Knows the Trouble I've Had" tend to elide spiritual trouble with the terrible, troublesome suffering of the slave; while songs such as "Deep River" and "Roll, Jordan, Roll" make an only slightly veiled connection between the journey into the Promised Land, made by the Chosen People, and the deliverance of slaves into their own promised land of freedom, in the Northern states or Canada. Other spirituals are even more open in expressing their dreams of liberation. "Go Down, Moses" was sufficiently frank in its demand for freedom to be banned on most slave plantations. It usually had to be sung out of earshot of the slaveholder.

As oral performances, of anonymous authorship and designed to be sung by various communities and generations, spirituals exist in many different versions. The same is true of the white folk songs of the period. "Bury Me Not on the Lone Prairie," for instance, originated as a lament about burial at sea, probably in the 1840s. It was then carried westward and, with the vastness of the open ranges of the West substituted for the vastness of the ocean, became one of the most popular early cowboy songs. The differences between spirituals and white folk songs are at least as important as the connections, however. Spirituals describe dreams of flight and the reality of "slavery chains forlorn." White songs, by contrast, are often about wandering in search of wealth or work. Other songs also tell of crossing the American continent in search of a fortune, only to give it up. And still other songs tell simply of those who travel and work: as migratory laborers, hired hands, or on the railroad.

Sometimes the wanderers of these songs find love. One of the most famous white folk songs of the period, "Shenandoah," concerns a wandering white trader who falls in love with the daughter of an Indian chief. Sometimes, as in the equally famous song about the daughter of "a miner, forty-niner," "Clementine," the subject is death. The tone of such songs can be elegiac, lyrical, as in "Shenandoah": "Oh, Shenandoah, I long to hear you –/Away, you rolling river." Alternatively, it can be sardonic, even brutal: Clem-entine, once dead, for instance, is said to have "fertilized" the many "roses and other posies" that grow above her grave. What most songs have in common, however, is an idiomatic language, images drawn from a common stock of experience available to the community, and simple compulsive rhythms, insistent repetition guaranteed to catch attention and remain stored in the memory. The songs designed for dance as well as singing are, naturally, even more captivating in their rhythms and repetitions. A "play-party song" such as "Cindy," for instance, was meant to be danced to without musical accompaniment. In turn, what were known as "answering-back songs" were meant to be sung and danced to in a call and response manner by young men and women. In one of the most famous, "Paper of Pins," for example, each of the many verses sung by the boys plays variations on the theme of offering something by way of a marriage gift. Songs like these depend more even than most on performance. Only rarely, in any event, did white folk song pass over from the process of popular transmission to the status of self-conscious, literary product. On one famous occasion it did, though. Hearing a band of Union troops singing a popular song in praise of the hero of Harper's Ferry, "John Brown's Body," the writer and lecturer Julia Ward Howe (1819–1910) rewrote the song, using its melody, rhythms, chorus, and fundamental drive, and then had it published. The result was "The Battle Hymn of the Republic" (1862).

American poetic voices

Another woman poet who achieved at least as much fame during her lifetime as Howe did with "The Battle Hymn of the Republic" was Lydia Howard Huntley Sigourney (1791–1865). Her work encompassed thousands of periodical publications and more than fifty books of poetry, autobiography, children's literature, advice writing, sketches, history, and travel. And her poetry addressed a variety of issues, many of them public ones such as slavery, the treatment of Indians, and current events, from a standpoint of compassionate Christianity and devout republicanism. Her most widely anthologized poem, "Death of an Infant" (1827), is characteristic in its use of familiar language and conventional imagery to offer a consoling portrait of a tragic event. The smile perceived on the face of the dead infant offers the consolatory assurance, to the believer, that even the power of death is circumscribed by faith. Other poems by Sigourney deal with more public issues but always, as in "Death of an Infant," in a way that consolidates faith and reassures. Any gentle interrogation of individual tragedies, or acts of injustice, is invariably framed within a fundamental acceptance of conventional Christian piety and the benevolence, the rightness of the American way, the domestic and the familial. She attacked individual acts of cruelty, against women, for instance ("The Suttee" (1827)), but she remained a firm believer in a separate sphere where women could act as guardian angels. And she expressed that belief in forms that her female audience, in particular, brought up on the popular domestic writing of the day, could readily digest and accommodate.

Two other poets of the period who explored different possibilities of expression for women were Frances Sargent Osgood (1811–1850) and Lucy Larcom (1820–1893). Osgood, a friend and quite possibly a lover of Edgar Allan Poe, was best known during her lifetime for sentimental pieces such as "The Lily's Delusion" (1846) or for more didactic works like "A Flight of Fancy" (1846). In work that remained unpublished until long after her death, however (in fact, until 1997), Osgood revealed a much bolder spirit, and a much more acid tongue, in writing of the vagaries of love. "The Lady's Mistake," for instance, deals sardonically with both the falsity of man and the flippancy of women, sometimes, in matters of the heart. In "Won't you die & be a spirit," the narrator caustically suggests that the best way to keep her lover faithful is to have him die. These are poems that actively jettison the image of woman as the angel of the house. The speaker here is a smart, knowing, world-weary but passionate creature. Domesticity is introduced here only to be scorned, turned into an acidulous joke.

Lucy Larcom was one of those who contributed work to *The Lowell Offering*, a journal containing the writings of textile mill operators working in Lowell, Massachusetts. From a middle-class background, Larcom became a "Lowell mill girl" after the death of her father. Her poems in the *Offering* soon attracted attention, and she established a career as a popular poet; a collection, *The Poetical Works of Lucy Larcom*, was eventually published in 1884. Larcom assumed a variety of voices and explored a number of subjects: there are poems on such diverse topics as the seasons ("March"), the city ("The City Lights"), young women ("A Little Old Girl"), and old ones ("Flowers of the Fallow"). "Weaving" shows what she could do at her best. Here, she uses a complex stanzaic form to explore the plight of a white girl working in a textile mill. Making a passionate connection between herself and her black sisters, the girl recognizes that, by these extreme standards at least, she enjoys a condition of relative privilege. The black women of the South suffer in ways that, according to the "web of destiny," can only terminate in "the hideous tapestry" of war. "Weaving" dramatizes the continuities and differences of oppression in a gently mellifluous, intricately patterned but nevertheless tough way. Using the activity announced in the title both literally and as a figure, it links the fate of an individual to the general, the historical. It not only intimates, it insists on interdependence, the fact that all, white women workers, black women, readers, are part of one web; and it invites sympathy, certainly, but it also contemplates, even demands, action.

For many contemporary readers, the leading American poet of the earlier half of the nineteenth century was William Cullen Bryant (1794–1878). In fact, some of his contemporaries went so far as to honor him as the founding father of American poetry. Certainly, the honor was justified as far as the subjects of Bryant's poetic landscapes were concerned. Although he was born and raised in Massachusetts and spent most of his adult life as a newspaper editor in New York City, a poem like "The Prairies" (1834) is sufficient proof of his awareness of the great lands to the West. As its opening lines indicate, it is also evidence of Bryant's realization that all the new regions of America might require the development of new tools of expression. "These are the gardens of the Desert," "The Prairies" begins; "these/The unshorn fields, boundless and beautiful,/For which the speech of England has no name." But whatever the native loyalties involved in his choice of subject, and whatever Bryant might say about the irrelevance to that subject of "the speech of England," when it came to writing rather than talking about poetry, Bryant preferred to imitate English models. Within these limitations, Bryant was undoubtedly skillful. In "To a Waterfowl" (1821), for instance, Bryant uses an alternating pattern of long and short lines to capture the hovering movement of the bird's flight. Even here, however, the poet cannot or will not resist the conventional. Most of Bryant's best poetry, like "To a Waterfowl," was written by the time he was forty, and published in two volumes, titled simply *Poems*, appearing in 1821 and 1832. He continued as an active writer and translator, though, right up until the end of his life. Notable among his many later volumes are his translations of the *Iliad* (1870) and the *Odyssey* (1871–1872), since they show Bryant's skill with the blank verse line and his ability to assume a simple, epic nobility of tone and style.

A poet who eventually outdistanced even Bryant in terms of popularity among his contemporaries was Henry Wadsworth Longfellow (1807–1882). Born in Maine, Longfellow published his first prose work, *Outre-Mer: A Pilgrimage Beyond the Sea* in 1833–1835. A series of travel sketches reminiscent of Irving's *Sketch Book*, this was followed by *Hyperion* (1839), a semi-autobiographical romance, *Voices of the Night* (1839), his first book of poetry, *Ballads and Other Poems* (1841), and *Poems on Slavery* (1842). His fame increased with the publication of a poetic drama, *The Spanish Student*

(1843), *The Belfry of Bruges and Other Poems* (1845), and *Kavanagh* (1849), a semi-autobiographical prose tale. Three long poems published at about this time also show Longfellow's ambition to create an American epic poetry by choosing domestic legends and casting them in classical forms. *Evangeline* (1847) tells the tragic story of the heroine's search for her lover. It is set in Acadie, a province of Canada roughly corresponding to present-day Nova Scotia. *The Courtship of Miles Standish* (1856) is a legend of early New England. And *The Song of Hiawatha* (1855) tells the story of a Native American hero. For all his interest in American themes and legends, however, and his dedication to the idea of an American epic, Longfellow relied on European literary forms and conventions. He did so quite deliberately, because he believed in the value, the centrality of the European-American community and its tradition. There is also a peculiar sense of self-assurance in most of his poetry: a feeling that everything that really matters, and has been found by earlier writers to matter, occurs within the compass of the respectable fireside. So, in "The Village Blacksmith" (1842), a figure actually outside the sphere of Longfellow's society and sympathy is made acceptable – to the narrator of the poem, that is, and the genteel reader – by being transformed into a rustic gentleman. There are, certainly, more poised and subtler pieces than these. "The Jewish Cemetery at Newport" (1852) uses the setting announced in the title for a mature, sympathetic meditation on the ancient Jewish experience of suffering and exile; "Aftermath" (1873) is a quiet reflection on the mixed "harvesting" of old age. But the tendency towards sermonizing remains even in these poems, as do the simply sweet idioms and rhythms and the deference to older, European forms.

Like Longfellow, Oliver Wendell Holmes (1809–1894) chose to identify with a particular group. More modest and pragmatic in his aims and intentions, however, he defined and delimited that group quite closely: to the men and women of sense and taste with whom he came into contact as a distinguished member of Boston society. Holmes is to be seen at his best in his most famous work, *The Autocrat of the Breakfast Table*. First published in *The Atlantic Monthly* in 1857–1858 and in book form in 1858, this consists of essays, poems, and occasional pieces in the form of table talk in a Boston boarding house. The wit, good sense, and moral rigor that characterizes this and later volumes such as *The Professor at the Breakfast Table* (1860) and *The Poet at the Breakfast Table* (1872) is also to be found, in miniature, in poems like "The Chambered Nautilus" (1858), with its famous concluding instruction to the poet's soul to "build thee more stately mansions."

Whereas Holmes opted for a community consisting of men of sense, however small it might have to be, a contemporary and neighbor of his chose a spiritual isolation which some of his acquaintances interpreted as madness. Jones Very (1813–1880) was a lay preacher given to mystical experiences. As a youth, he had been forced to withdraw from Harvard after experiencing a religious frenzy; and throughout his life he had visions which convinced him that his will and God's will were one. The conviction might have turned him into a fanatic or a bigot. Instead, it enabled him to write poetry which, though neglected during his lifetime, some later critics were to call great. It is, certainly, unique. The means of expression is traditional – Very rarely used anything other than the sonnet form – but this belies a poetic stance that is profoundly individualistic. In one of his poems, for instance, ordinary people in the street are transformed into "The Dead" (1839), whose grotesque and lurid shapes are an outward and visible sign of an inward and spiritual poverty. Very in effect adopts the innocent and often savage eye of the outsider, ignoring the masks people may use to evade self-knowledge. He has no connection with the world he observes and exposes, and in a sense no audience either. For as the poem "Yourself" (1839) makes clear, Very did not expect his revelations of his inner being and his secret pact with God to be properly understood by those around him.

Holmes addressing his companions at the breakfast table and Very watching the antics of the "strangers" surrounding him is a contrast played out in a different key by two other New England poets: James Russell Lowell (1819–1891) and Frederick Goddard Tuckerman (1821–1873). A member of one of the foremost families in Boston, Lowell succeeded Longfellow as professor of French and Spanish as Harvard. With Holmes, he cofounded *The Atlantic Monthly*, editing it from 1857 to 1861; with Charles Eliot Norton (1827–1898), an eminent scholar and translator, he later edited *The North American Review*. His first volume of poetry, *A Year's Life*, appeared in 1841, his second, *Poems*, three years later. Then, in a single year, 1848, he published *Poems: Second Series, A Fable for Critics, The Vision of Sir Launfal*, and the first series of *The Biglow Papers. The Vision* is a verse poem derived from the legends of the Holy Grail. *A Fable for Critics* is a verse satire containing shrewd assessments of the contemporary literary scene and its more notable figures. *Biglow Papers*, in turn, offers a series of satirical attacks on the slaveholders of the South and their political representatives. Adopting the mask of Hosea Biglow, a crude but honest Yankee farmer, Lowell attempted to fashion an authentically American voice – and to use that voice to direct people into right ways of thinking. Like Holmes, Lowell had a clear sense of his audience. Unlike Holmes, he saw this audience as a potentially large one, which he could instruct and educate. The mission of creating an audience and educating it was sustained in the second series of *Biglow Papers*. If the first series had been written in opposition to the Mexican War – seen by many as simply a means for the South to expand slavery into new territories – then the second was produced in support of the North during the Civil War. Both series were influential and immensely popular.

By contrast, Tuckerman never really attempted to cater to or create an audience and never achieved any public honors or recognition. Educated at Harvard, where Jones Very was his tutor, he withdrew before his courses were completed. He returned to take a law degree, was admitted to the bar but never practiced. Instead, he devoted most of his adult life to the study of botany and the writing of poetry. He also placed a great emotional investment in his domestic life, until the death of his wife in childbirth in 1857. This loss inspired a series of sonnet sequences, written in the period 1854–1860 and 1860–1872 and partly published in a privately financed edition in 1860. The full series of sonnet sequences was not published until the twentieth century; his long poem, *The Cricket*, did not appear in print until 1950; and *The Complete Poems* was only published in 1965. His poems are not, as Tuckerman explains in Sonnet I of the first sequence, addressed to anyone. They are, rather, an attempt to give objective life to a subjective complex of emotions. The result is, to some extent, like later poetry, Imagist poetry for instance, in which a sequence of sense impressions is presented as the equivalent of a sequence of emotions. Only to some extent, however: the poetic voice of Tuckerman also bears comparison with the voices of contemporaries, like the later Hawthorne and Melville. It is the voice of a man who feels alienated from nature, from other men, and from God: who senses that there might possibly exist "signs" in his environment that could lead him away from doubt and into philosophical certainty, but who also suspects that those signs are beyond his deciphering. For his fellow New Englander Emerson, the self, the ego, was an assertive presence. For Tuckerman, however, the self was very much on the defense and trying to make what it could of its own defensiveness – its condition of captivity.

"He is America," Ezra Pound observed of Walt Whitman (1819–1892). "His crudity is an exceeding great stench, but it *is* America." Never frightened of being called crude, Whitman would probably have appreciated the comment. And he would have liked being identified with America because that was his aim: to speak as a representative American and turn the New World into words. Whitman certainly had this aim after the day in 1842 when he attended a lecture given by Emerson, in which Emerson prophesied the imminent arrival of an American Homer to celebrate "the barbarism and materialism of the times." Whitman saw himself as the fullfilment of that prophecy. He was the man, he felt, with the courage needed to capture the ample geography of the country in lines as bold and wild as its landscape. And in the preface to the first, 1855 edition of his *Leaves of Grass* he deliberately echoed Emerson. "The United States themselves are essentially the greatest poem," he wrote, thereby alerting the reader to what he was trying to do: to invent a poetic form founded on raw experiment, and a line that swung as freely as the individual voice. There were many influences that helped Whitman to create this form and line. They ranged from Italian opera to the insistent repetitions of the King James Bible, from his interest in the spatial vastnesses of astronomy to his love of American landscape painting with its dedication to and delineation of another kind of space. But the crucial factor was Whitman's sense of himself and the potentials of his craft: for him, poetry was a passionate gesture of identification with his native land.

Like many other American writers, especially of this period, Whitman was largely self-educated. He left school at the age of eleven and learned his trade in the print shop, becoming editor of the *Aurora* in 1842 and then later of the Brooklyn *Daily Eagle*. It is in his earliest notebook, written in 1847, that Whitman breaks into something like his characteristic free verse line. Appropriately, for the poet who was to see himself as the bard of American individualism and liberty, this occurs on the subject of slavery. And, after *Leaves of Grass* was published, and enthusiastically welcomed by Emerson, Whitman was to devote his poetic life to its revision and expansion. For Whitman, poetry, the American nation, life itself were all a matter of process, energized by rhythm and change. And *Leaves of Grass* became a process too, responsive to the continuing story of personal and national identity, the poet and his democratic community. A second edition, with several new poems, appeared in 1856. While he was planning a third edition of what he called his "new Bible" of democracy, Whitman had an unhappy liaison with another man, which became the subject of several poems to be incorporated into that edition, published in 1860. The personal crisis, combined with the poet's own alarm over the threatened dissolution of the republic, casts a shadow over this 1860 version of *Leaves of Grass*, although this is balanced by Whitman's celebration of comradeship and "adhesiveness" ("the personal attachment of man to man") and heterosexual or "amative" love – in, respectively, the "Calamus" and the "Children of Adam" sequences. The role Whitman then adopted during the Civil War, as "wound-dresser" visiting sick or dying soldiers, became the source of poems for *Drum-Taps and Sequel* (1865–1866). The war poems were then appended to the next, 1867 edition of *Leaves of Grass* and incorporated into the main body of the 1871 edition. During the last two decades of his life, poems such as "Passage to India" and "Prayer of Columbus" showed Whitman moving away from the material landscapes of America to a more mystical vision of a democratic golden world that might bloom in the future. Along with this new material, the poet revised, reintegrated, and rearranged all his poetic work in the 1881 edition of *Leaves of Grass*. He then followed it a year later with what was intended as a prose companion to his poems, entitled *Specimen Days*. Even this was not the end. The final, "deathbed" edition of *Leaves of Grass* was prepared in the last years of his life, 1891–1892. It included two annexes, the "Sands at Seventy" and "Good-bye My Fancy" groups of poems. And it ended with a prose piece, "A Backward Glance O'er Travel'd Roads," in which Whitman attempted to explain both his life and his work.

Along with all the changes in the several editions of *Leaves of Grass*, though, went continuity: a commitment to the principles outlined in the preface to the very first edition. Openness, freedom, above all individualism: Whitman's aim was nothing less than to initiate a poetic tradition in which the one recognition shared is a recognition of difference, one of the few precedents accepted is the rejection of precedent, and truth and beauty are identified with a procedure of constant metamorphosis. The only genuine way in which an American could acknowledge his participation in a common cultural effort, he believed, was by behaving as a supreme individualist. He could pay his greatest respect to the past, Whitman felt, by rebelling from it, and the finest compliment he could to his nation by denying its authority over him. In doing all this, Whitman did not feel that he would be rejecting contact with others: those he lived with, those whom he observed and addressed in his poems. On the contrary, his essential purpose was to identify his ego with the world, and more specifically with the democratic "en-masse" of America. This identification on which all his poems depend, or, rather, the dialectic from which they derive their energy, is established in the opening lines of "Song of Myself": "I celebrate myself, and sing myself,/And what I assume you shall assume/For every atom belonging to me as good belongs to you." Two people, Whitman believed, could be "twain yet one": their paths could be different, and yet they could achieve a kind of transcendent contact. Equally, many people could realize a community while remaining individuals. It was Whitman's intention to state this again and again: like many other American writers, he was not afraid of the pedagogical role. His aim, though, was not merely to tell and teach but to show. He wanted to dramatize the process of contact: to make his audience aware of the fact that they could be many yet one by compelling them to feel it in the course of reading his poems.

Whitman, then, attempts to solve the problems of isolation and audience confronting the American poet, and the debate between individualism and community endemic in American literature and culture, by turning his poem into a gesture of relationship, a bridge between "I" and "you." And it is a relationship that is essentially open, the arc described by this bridge is intended at least to span past, present, and future. This comes out strikingly in the closing moments of "Song of Myself." "I bequeath myself to the dirt to grow from the grass I love,/If you want me again look for me under your boot-soles," Whitman declares; and then later, in the final two lines of the poem, he adds, "Missing me one place search another,/I stop somewhere waiting for you." Whitman identifies himself, in these lines, with the "spear of summer's grass" that, at the beginning of the poem, offered him a medium of mystical insight. The implication is clear: Whitman and his "Song" will, ideally, act as a source of continuing inspiration and contact for the reader each time he or she reads this poem. They will be an agent of vision and communion quite as inexhaustible as the leaf of grass was for the poet. The poem is transmuted, in effect, into an open field, a process – a journey that the reader is required to take on his or her own terms.

Whitman once referred to *Leaves of Grass* as "a language experiment." What is experimented with, in particular, is the possibility of an American epic. Attempts at an epic writing of the nation had, of course, been made before – by, for instance, Cotton Mather and Joel Barlow. It was, however, Whitman who discovered, or rather invented, the form epic would assume in the New World. The form is, essentially, that of the Romantic epic: as in William Blake's *Jerusalem*, there is more concern here with spiritual possibility than historical achievement and, as in Wordsworth's *Prelude*, the poet is at the center, and the growth and development of the poet's mind supplies the narrative substance. The great American epics, a poem like "Song of Myself" indicates, would follow the great Romantic epics in being plotless and without a conventional protagonist. Their strategy would be to create a hero rather than celebrate one, and to make rather than record a significant history. They would, in effect, jettison the third-person hero of traditional epic. And, in his place, they would set the poet as a representative, democratic person who discovers his or her identity and values in the course of writing, on their own and on our behalf. The essential form of such epics would have to be open, as open as "Song of Myself" or the whole "language experiment" of *Leaves of Grass* is, with the reader exploring for himself or herself the paths the poet has signposted. And, like most great long poems in the Romantic tradition, they would appear to exist in space rather than time, since they would not so much progress in a conventional, linear or logical, way as circle backwards and forwards, supplying workings of form and language in which the audience could bring their own imaginations to bear: each individual member of that audience collaborating with the poet in the creation of meaning.

"This is my letter to the World/" begins one poem (no. 441) by Emily Dickinson (1830–1886), "That never wrote to Me – ." As this poem intimates, Dickinson's condition and subject was isolation. As she put it once, in one of her letters, "My Business is Circumference"; and the circumference she was talking about was surely that of her lonely self. For her, the self was not the circumscribed Eden it was for Poe. Still less was it a matter of process, a dynamic node or source of energy capable of contact and even confluence with the other, as it was for Whitman. It was, rather, a prisonhouse, from which it was evidently impossible to escape. Her poetic mission, as she saw or sensed it, was to explore the dimensions of her cell: to find out what could be felt or known, what surmised or guessed at, and what could be said and communicated within the constraints of experience and expression that, for her, were the conditions of living. The result is a poetry that manages to be at once passionate and sly, visionary and ironic, as Dickinson tries to push perception and language to the limits while suspecting just how stringent those limits are. And it is also a voice that not only echoes the doubts of

Figure 2.4   Portrait of Emily Dickinson, daguerreotype. Amherst College Archives and Special Collections.

many of her contemporaries, about the possibility of belief and the viability of democracy, truly social living, but also anticipates the skepticism and subversiveness of later writers: those for whom any version of reality is just that, a version, a picture or figurative pattern drawn by the prisoner of what he or she sees through the bars of the prison cell.

Dickinson wrote nearly 1,800 poems, but publication was another matter. "Publication – is the Auction/Of the Mind of Man," she wrote in one piece (no. 709); and only seven of her poems were published during her lifetime, six of them without her consent. Instead of publishing her work, Dickinson collected it in packets of about twenty poems each. When she died, 814 poems bound into 40 packets were found in a box in the bottom drawer of her bedroom bureau, together with 333 poems ready for binding and numerous worksheet drafts. Selections from these were published over the next half century, but it was not until 1955 that a three-volume variorum edition was published, containing all 1,775 known poems. Three volumes of Dickinson's letters then appeared three years later. These were only a small fraction of the letters she actually wrote.

"Nature is a stranger yet," Dickinson observes in one of her poems ("What mystery pervades a well!," no. 1,400). Pushed back from nature, and from the people around her, by their irredeemable otherness, she turns to her internal geography in the belief that it is all she can ever really know. Her self and her feelings tend to encompass the world, and her recognition of this explains the extraordinary intensity with which she describes pleasure, melancholy, or despair. The eruption of pain, when it comes, becomes an apocalyptic event ("There's a certain slant of light," no. 258) and exultation, joy, as and when it occurs, seems to irradiate all existence ("I taste a liquor brewed," no. 214). Only *seems* to, however: as Dickinson is only too acutely aware, her self may be her world but that world is in no way coextensive with reality. This awareness shadows all her work. It explains, for instance, why in some poems she wryly compares her diminutive stature with the vast unknowability of nature ("Of bronze and blaze," no. 290). It also explains why, in many other poems addressed or attending to nature, she concentrates on the smaller, more elusive inhabitants of the fields and woods.

The elusive, illusive nature of reality, and the radical restraints placed on the self and its perceptions, are registered with particular force, not only in the poems about nature, but also in those about death and love. Love and death are frequently linked in Dickinson's work: "Because I could not stop for death" (no. 712), where death takes the form of a gentleman caller – taking a maiden, the narrator of the poem, on a ride that is at once a courtship ritual and a journey to the graveyard – is only one, particularly famous example. And even when they are not, they carry a comparable freight of meaning for the poet because both, for her, mark the possibility of venturing beyond the limits of the self, crossing the threshold into the unknown, into otherness. Death, especially, is an experience that is approached with a mixture of desire and fear because it might, as Dickinson sees it, lead to a "title divine" ("Title Divine – is Mine!," no. 1,072), the final escape of the self from its confinement into some more expansive, exalted state – or it might simply be a prelude to oblivion. All she can be sure of is the simple fact that she cannot be sure; on this, as on all other matters, the verdict must be left open. The self, Dickinson intimates, is fragile, evanescent, dwarfed by its sur- roundings; and the worlds it creates, the knowledge it articulates must – by the very nature of the source – remain arbitrary, temporary, and incomplete. So in poem after poem that attends to the experience of dying, the narrator approaches the gates of death only to stop short just before she enters, passes through to the other side ("A Clock stopped –," no. 287; "I heard a Fly buzz – when I died –," no. 465). The scene then goes blank, and poet, narrator, and reader alike are left gazing at the blankness, aware only that they have arrived at the boundaries of human consciousness.

The sense of the circumscriptions imposed on the isolated self, and the consequently random, truncated nature of human knowledge dictates Dickinson's poetic practice. Her poems are not just open-ended but open, and in a way that is interestingly different from Whitman. What Dickinson's work tends to do is underline its own arbitrariness, its dislocated, disjunctive character: a point that is brought out, in particularly high profile, by her disruptive use of rhythm, her frequent recourse to discords and half-rhymes, and her preference for the paratactic over more conventional forms of syntax. Dickinson subverts. She habitually uses the standard hymn stanza form, but then undermines it by lengthening or shortening lines, reversing rhythms, omitting rhymes. She opts for what might seem to be a straightforward declarative style, by placing phrases and clauses paratactically – that is, side by side in an apparently indiscriminate way. But what she is doing, it turns out, is evading the kind of finished effect that is inseparable from more sophisticated kinds of syntax. Experiences, events, expressions are set out on a level verbal landscape, separated only by the minimalist punctuation of the dash; there is no attempt made to draw things into a net of theory, an elaborate verbal plan or hierarchy. She even chooses what might be taken to be conventional subjects – love, death, nature, and so on – and may open a meditation on them in an apparently innocent, simple way, with a pretty piece of scene painting ("The pretty Rain from those sweet Eaves," no. 608) or a declaration of faith ("This World is not Conclusion," no. 501). But the scene soon becomes darker, "Faith slips" into doubt or even despair, as the poem shifts sharply from convention and the innocence assumes an ironic edge, the simplicity is exposed as fundamentally deceptive.

"I had no Monarch in my life, and cannot rule myself," Dickinson wrote once, "and when I try to organize – my little Force explodes – and leaves me bare and charred – ." In all her best work, Dickinson walks a fine line between the constraints hinted at here: between rule and chaos, "prose" and "possibility," speech and silence. But, as so often, she was being modest to the point of inaccuracy when she suggested that her poetic experiments with her self ended badly. They were explosive, to be sure, but what they did and still do is ignite awareness, compel the reader into a recognition of the magical character of experience. Here and elsewhere in her letters and poems, Dickinson also unveils a paradox, and one that is not just unique to her. It is a paradox that lies perhaps at the heart of all American writing and, certainly, at the heart of writing of this period, circulating around the idea and practice of a tradition of individualism. Dickinson had "no Monarch," nobody to tell her what and how she should write. As someone was to observe of her much later, she consequently wrote as if no one had written before. This made the tenor and texture of her work utterly hers: even the physical look of it on the page tells the reader familiar with it that *this* is the work of Dickinson. But it also established her kinship with so many others. What Dickinson and her contemporaries sustained and transmitted to their successors, in effect, was a great and continuing tradition founded precisely on the notion that there was and could be "no Monarch" for the individual: a tradition that has, as at least one of its unacknowledged aims, the forging of the uncreated conscience of a nation.

3

Reconstructing the Past, Reimagining the Future
The Development of American Literature 1865–1900

Rebuilding a Nation

The Civil War was the bloodiest conflict in American history, with over 360,000 Union soldiers and 260,000 Confederates lost on the battlefield or in military hospitals. Within a few decades after the war, however, the United States was assuming a new prosperity and developing into an industrial giant, with over half the population in the Eastern states living in towns and cities and an industrial investment of over four billion dollars. An emergent ideology of success celebrated the growth of American power and wealth. And the spread of education and literacy, the technology of mass production, the access to market opened up by the railways all meant that something like a uniform print culture was possible for the entire nation, and that specialist audiences could also be catered to or even created. There was, in short, uniformity but also diversity.

The Development of Literary Regionalisms

From Adam to outsider

Mark Twain, born Samuel Langhorne Clemens (1835–1910), called this period "the Gilded Age." "My books are simply autobiographies," Twain insisted once. True of every American writer, perhaps, the remark seems especially true of him. He relied, frequently and frankly, on personal experience: in accounts of his travels, for instance, like *The Innocents Abroad* (1869), *Roughing It* (1872), and *A Tramp Abroad* (1880). Even those books of his that were the results of strenuous imaginative effort can be read as attempts to resolve his inner divisions, and create some sense of continuity between his present and his past, his critical investment in common sense, pragmatism, and progress and his emotional involvement in his childhood and the childhood of his region and nation. The inner divisions and discontinuity were, in fact, inseparable. For all of Twain's best fictional work has to do with what has been called "the matter of

A Brief History of American Literature.   By Richard Gray
© 2011 Richard Gray

Hannibal": that is, his experiences as a child in the slaveholding state of Missouri and his years as a steamboat pilot on the Mississippi. This was not simply a matter of nostalgia for the good old days before the Civil War, of the kind to be found in other, simpler writers born in the South like, say, Thomas Nelson Page or Richard Malcolm Johnston (1822–1898). Nor was it merely another example of the romantic idealization of youth. It was rather, and more simply, that Twain recognized intuitively that his years as a boy and youth, in the pre-Civil War South, had formed him for good and ill. So to explore those years was to explore the often equivocal nature of his own vision. It was also that Twain also sensed that the gap he felt between his self and his experiences before and after the war was typical, representative. So to understand that gap was to begin at least to understand his nation and its times.

Twain first turned to the matter of Hannibal in a series of articles published in 1875 in *The Atlantic Monthly* entitled "Old Times on the Mississippi" – later revised and expanded to become *Life on the Mississippi* (1883) – and then one year later in *The Adventures of Tom Sawyer*. It was his third excursion into his and the national past, however, that produced his greatest work, *The Adventures of Huckleberry Finn*, begun in 1876 and published in 1885. Twain began *Huckleberry Finn* simply as a sequel to *Tom Sawyer*, with several narrative threads carried over from the earlier work. Even as he began it, however, he must have realized that this was a very different, more authentic work. For the manuscript shows Twain trying to catch the trick, the exact lilt of Huck's voice. "You will not know about me," the first try at an opening, is scratched out. So is the second try, "You do not know about me." Only at the third attempt does Twain come up with the right, idiomatic but poetic, start: "You don't know about me." Like a jazz musician, trying to hit the right beat before swinging into the full melody and the rhythm of the piece, Twain searches for just the right voice, the right pitch and momentum, before moving into the story of his greatest vernacular hero. The intimacy is vital too: in a way that was to become characteristic of American fiction, the protagonist addresses "you" the reader directly, in terms that appear spontaneous, sincere, unpremeditated. We are drawn into this web of words in a manner that convinces us that we are enjoying an unpremeditated, vital relationship with the hero. The spontaneity is also a function of the narrative structure. Twain once said that he relied on a book to "write itself," and that is the impression, in the best sense, given by *Huckleberry Finn*. The story has a structure, of course, that of the picaresque narrative (*Don Quixote* was one of Twain's favorite books): but that structure is as paradoxically structureless as the structure of, say, *Moby-Dick* or "Song of Myself." The book flows like the Mississippi, at a constantly altering pace, in unanticipated directions; new characters, episodes, incidents pop up without warning, old characters like Jim or Tom Sawyer reappear just when we least expect them to. Like the great works of Melville and Whitman, too, *Huckleberry Finn* remains an open field, describing an open, unstructured and unreconstructed spirit. It does not conclude, in any conventional fashion. Famously, it ends as "Song of Myself" does and many later American narratives were to do: looking to the open road, with the hero still breaking away – or, as Huck himself has it, ready to "light out for the Territory ahead of the rest."

Twain later described *Huckleberry Finn* as "a book of mine where a sound heart and a deformed conscience come into collision and conscience suffers a defeat." The central moral dilemma Huck has to face, in this deeply serious, even tragic comedy, is whether

ON THE RAFT.

Figure 3.1   Illustration from *The Adventures of Huckleberry Finn* by Mark Twain: Huck and Jim on the raft. © Bettmann/Corbis.

or not he should betray his friend, the escaped slave Jim, by revealing Jim's whereabouts to other whites, including Miss Watson, his owner. For much of the narrative, Huck is equivocal. Sometimes, he sees Jim as a slave, as property that should be returned; and sometimes he sees him as a human being and a friend, requiring his sympathy and help. And the vacillation stems from Huck's uncertainty over what takes priority: the laws of society, his social upbringing which, however patchily, has shaped his conscience, or the promptings of his own heart, his instincts and feelings as an individual. The book is about the historical injustice of slavery, of course, and the social inequity of racism, the human use or denial of human beings. But it is also about the same fundamental conflict as the one that fires *The Scarlet Letter* and so many other American narratives into life. Huck must choose between the law and liberty, the sanctions of the community and the perceptions of the individual, civil and natural justice. He chooses the latter, the lessons learned from his own experience, the knowledge of his own rebellious heart. In doing so, Huck reflects his creator's belief at the time in aboriginal innocence, the purity of the asocial – and asocial or presocial creatures like the child. And he also measures the extent of the creative triumph, since Twain manages here a miracle: that rare thing, a sympathetic and credibly virtuous character. The sympathy and credibility stem from the same source: Huck is a grotesque saint, a queer kind of savior because he does not know he is doing good. His notions of right and wrong, salvation and damnation, have been formed by society. So, when he is doing good he believes that he is doing evil, and vice versa. His belief system is at odds with his right instincts: hence, the terms in which he describes his final decision not to betray Jim. "All right, then," Huck declares, "I'll *go* to hell."

Twain's strategies for shifting Huck's conflict from the personal to the mythic are several. Easily the most important, though, is his own, almost certainly intuitive, variation on the contrast between the clearing and the wilderness: the riverbank and the river. The riverbank is the fixed element, the clearing, the community. On the riverbank, everyone plays a social role, observes a social function: either without knowing it, like the Grangerford family or the inhabitants of Bricksville, or knowing it and using it to exploit others, like the Duke and Dauphin. Everyone is obsessed with appearances and disguises, and uses language to conceal meaning and feeling from others and themselves. Everyone behaves like an actor, who has certain lines to say, clothes to wear, things to do, rather than as an independent individual. Everyone, in short, denies their essential humanity on the riverbank, and the humanity of others: here, Jim is not a human being, he is the lowest form of social function, a slave. What adds to the power of this portrait is that, as with the account of the Puritan settlement in *The Scarlet Letter*, it is simultaneously mythic and historical. This is society, the machinery of the social system seen from the standpoint of individualism. It is also a very specific society, that of the South before the Civil War. Drawing on the devices of the Southwestern humorists, but exponentially developing them, Twain offers a brilliantly detailed satirical picture of the Old South: poor whites like Pap Finn and the people of Bricksville, middle-class farmers like the Phelps family, wealthy planters like the Grangerfords – and, of course, the slaves. *Huckleberry Finn* is an unremitting comic assault on the human capacity to substitute "style" for substance, social illusion for experiential fact. But it is also a satire on one particular kind of social "style" that Twain knew only too well. It is a tragic account of what, generally, happens when people stop seeing and testing things for themselves, as individual human beings. But it is also a very American tragedy, about a moment in American history when a sense of humanity and individuality was lost, with terrible consequences for the nation.

The river, the fluid element and the medium for escape for Huck and Jim, is, of course, Twain's version of the mythic wilderness. It is a place where Huck can enjoy intimacy with Jim and an almost Edenic harmony with nature. Recasting Huck as an American Adam, Twain shows his hero attending to the moods of the river and its surroundings and, in turn, projecting his own moods in and through those natural surrounds. Huck appears to enjoy a separate peace here on the river, a world apart from rules, codes, and clock time, where "lazying" becomes a positive activity. Free from the postlapsarian compulsion to work, Huck can simply be and wonder: live, meditate, and marvel at the miracle of the particular, the minutiae of life. It is in these episodes on the river that the indelible connection between the voice of Huck and his values becomes clear. Huck scrupulously, instinctively tells it as it is. He sees things as they are, free of social pretense or disguise. So he can judge things as they are, not as the social system would tell him to judge them. It is also in these episodes that Huck's power as a syncretic figure becomes clear. Huck Finn brings together and synthesizes the warring opposites of Twain's earlier work. Huck is a focus for all his creator's nostalgia, all his yearnings for childhood, the lost days of his youth, the days before the Civil War and the Fall; and he is also, quite clearly, a projection of Twain's more progressive feelings, the belief in human development and perfectibility – he suggests hope for the future as well as love of the past. Again, this is measured in the language of the book, in that it is precisely Huck's "progressive" attention to the use and function of things that gives his observations such color and immediacy. The language Huck is given, in effect, is at once exact and evocative, pragmatic and poetic: it reveals things as they are, in all their miraculous particularity. And Huck himself, the speaker of that language, comes across as a profoundly realistic and romantic figure: a pragmatist and a dreamer, a simple figure and a noble man – a perfect gentle knight, who seems honorable, even chivalric, precisely because he sticks closely to the facts.

The deepening pessimism of Twain, in his later years, is evident from the novels *A Connecticut Yankee in King Arthur's Court* (1889) and *The Tragedy of Puddn'head Wilson* (1894), the story "The Man That Corrupted Hadleyburg" (1900), and the longer narrative, *The Mysterious Stranger*, which was published posthumously after editorial work by other hands in 1916. "I believe I can make it tell what I think of Man," he wrote of *The Mysterious Stranger*, "... and what a shabby poor ridiculous thing he is, and how mistaken he is in his estimate of ... his place among the animals." On a personal level, Twain continued to enjoy what he termed the "grace, peace, and benediction" of his family and circle of friends until the end of his life. On the social, he remained an ardent reformer and a brilliantly witty, judiciously savage critic of authority and champion of the underdog: attacking European imperialism in Africa, for instance, and American imperialism in the Spanish-American War. But his sense, most powerfully expressed in *Huckleberry Finn*, that the real could be infused with romance, that it was possible to be true to the facts and to the ideal possibilities of things: that had gone. And his eventual view of life could perhaps be summed up by a remark culled from what Twain called *Puddn'head Wilson's Calendar*: "We owe Adam a great debt. He first brought death into the world."

Regionalism in the West and Midwest

Twain has been called a regionalist, because he was born and raised in the South, lived for a while in the West, and wrote of both. Among those other writers who have been associated with the regionalist impulse was one who worked as a journalist and editor with Mark Twain in the West, Francis Bret Harte (1836–1902). Harte became editor of *The Californian* and then, in 1868, of the *Overland Monthly* in which he published the poems and stories that made him famous. Many of the stories were collected in *The Luck of Roaring Camp and Other Stories* (1870). The two most famous, the title story and "The Outcasts of Poker Flat," are typical, in that they illustrate Harte's tendency to find innocence flowering in inhospitable frontier circumstances and miners, gamblers, and whores revealing they have hearts of gold. In the same year as his most famous collection of tales appeared, Harte also published his most famous poem, "Plain Language from Truthful James." Set, like so much of his work, in a Western mining camp, it tells the story of a wily "heathen Chinee," who claims not to understand a card game then is revealed as an astute cheat.

"Plain Language from Truthful James" is also a mix of the vernacular and the more formal and rhetorical. What the narrator calls his "plain" language is not always that; and it is, in any event, set, frozen almost in an elaborate stanzaic pattern, with regular rhymes and repetitive rhythms. In this, it was typical of poems of the time about the West. Bayard Taylor (1825–1878), for example, wrote poems like "The Bison Track" (1875) and "On Leaving California" (1875) that show a similar obedience to poetic traditions, and an equally close observation of rhetorical rules, while celebrating frontier freedom. And Taylor's poems, in turn, are typical to the extent that they endorse the contemporary belief in manifest destiny – the mission of white Americans to settle and civilize the West. A similar triumphalism, couched in formal rhetoric and carefully molded verse, is to be found in the work of Joaquin Miller (1841?–1913), who became known during his lifetime as "the Byron of Oregon." The movement west was, as they saw it, a natural consequence of human evolution and national history, underwritten by both the idea of the survival of the fittest and the example of earlier explorers and settlers.

In the more settled farming regions of the Midwest, the writing tone, in both poetry and prose, tended to be quieter, the narrative vision more narrowly focused on the pieties of family and community. James Whitcomb Riley (1849–1916), for instance, achieved fame and wealth by writing a series of poems in the "Hoosier" dialect of Indiana. The poems are light and sentimental, concentrating on picturesque figures of pathos, like "Little Orphan Annie" (1883), or on the simple satisfactions of hearth and home, and the rituals of farming life, as in his most famous piece, "When the Frost is on the Punkin" (1883). Like Riley, Edward Eggleston (1837–1902) was born in Indiana and achieved fame by writing about the simplicity and community of Midwestern life and using the local dialect. He chose fiction as his way of recording and celebrating his small corner of America. But, as his most famous book, *The Hoosier Schoolmaster* (1871), shows he was similarly inclined to domesticate and sentimentalize; the tone of the narrative tends towards the pious much of the time, and both the hero and the woman he eventually marries are depicted as improbably ideal and impeccable.

African American and Native American voices

The popularity of poetry and prose that observed regionalist conventions, or what were seen as such at this time, such as the use of dialect, can be measured by the fact that a number of African American and Native American writers associated with lands to the West attempted to write in this mode. The most notable of these were the African American poet Paul Lawrence Dunbar (1872–1906), who was born in Ohio, and the Native American poet, journalist, and humorist Alexander Lawrence Posey (1873–1908), who was born in Indian Territory and raised among the Creeks. Dunbar wrote conventional verse, following the standard poetic conventions of the time, but the work that gained him national fame was his poetry written in a stereotypical Negro dialect. *Lyrics from Lowly Life* (1896), the book that brought him to the attention of the reading public, contains pieces like "A Corn-Song," which offers a dreamily elegiac portrait of life on the old plantation, and "When De Co'n Pone's Hot," which reveals even in its title just how much Dunbar owed to other dialect poets like Riley.

Alexander Posey also wrote poetry that closely observed the poetic conventions of the time. Within the limits of those conventions, however, he was able to pursue themes that reflected his sense of his Native American heritage. His "Ode to Sequoya" (1899), for example, is an elaborately formal, highly rhetorical poem, with no sense of traditions other than those of white culture in its manner of expression. But what the poem celebrates is the inventor of the Cherokee syllabary. Posey gradually moved away from conventional verse. He first tried to write poems that caught the rhythms and reflected the idioms of his native Creek; then he gradually devoted less and less time to poetry. Turning to journalism, he established the first daily newspaper published by a Native American. And, as a substitute for editorials, he began writing the Fus Fixico letters. In these, using the persona of Fus Fixico (Heartless Bird), a full-blooded Creek, Posey commented on local life, customs, and politics: satirizing those who profited from the policy of individual land allotment or Native American complicity in the greed and materialism of the times. This is dialect writing with a political purpose. It is also dialect writing that tries, more earnestly and successfully than Posey does in his poetry, to catch the rhythms of the language he heard spoken among his fellow tribesmen.

Regionalism in New England

"It is difficult to report the great events of New England; expression is so slight, and those few words which escape us in moments of deep feeling look but meagre on the printed page." The words are those of Sarah Orne Jewett (1849–1909), from the book that secured her place in American literature, *The Country of the Pointed Firs* (1896). As it happens, she made her subject, not the "great events" of her native region but little nameless acts of community, memory, or love. But she always tried to capture the speech and silence of New England: the language in which, she said, "there is some faint survival . . . of the sound of English speech of Chaucer's time," and the avoidance of any "vain shore of conversation" between people habituated to quiet and solitude – who, perhaps, "spoke very little because they so perfectly understood each other." Jewett always, too, attempted to mine the deep feelings laconically expressed in this speech and surreptitiously conveyed in this silence. "Such is the hidden fire of enthusiasm in true New England nature," the reader is told in *The Country of the Pointed Firs*, "that, once given an outlet, it shines forth with almost volcanic light and heat." One of the many achievements of her fiction, in fact, is the way Jewett maneuvers her way between what another, later New Englander, Robert Frost, was to term the fire and ice of the New England soul. This she does, not least, through her adept use of metaphoric and dramatic contrast. The remote farms and fishing towns she writes of are set between the vastnesses of the sea and the woods, "the unconquerable, immediate forces of Nature." That is part of the spirit of their inhabitants: when one of characters speaks, for instance, we are told that it is "as if one of the gray firs had spoken." But so is a "simple kindness that is the soul of chivalry," a domestic affection and a neighborliness that transforms a "low-storied and broad-roofed" house, the site of a local reunion, into the likeness of "a motherly brown hen" gathering together "the flock that came straying towards it from every direction." And so, too, is "love in its simplicity," caught in the voiceless gestures of her New England rural folk: "so moving," as we learn in *The Country of the Pointed Firs*, "so tender, so free from their usual fetters of self-consciousness."

Jewett's first stories appeared in *The Atlantic Monthly*, then a collection, *Deephaven* (1877), established her reputation. This was followed by two novels, and further collections of stories, including *A White Heron* (1886), two books for children, a historical romance and a collection of poems. She formed several important and close friendships with other women, and she encouraged the young Willa Cather to write, as she did, about her own remote homeplace. She traveled occasionally, but she always returned to her home territory in Maine. And all her best work focuses on that territory, its life, language, and landscape. This is local color writing, to an extent, but it is also writing that discovers the elemental in the local. *The Country of the Pointed Firs*, for example, uses a device common in stories normally described as regionalist or belonging to the local color school: the visitor from the city, who is gradually educated in the ways and habits of a remote community – and who encourages the reader to accompany her, to share in this sentimental education. What the unnamed female visitor and narrator of Jewett's book learns, though, is not just the peculiar customs of a particular place. She learns too, and so do we, of the deep feelings beneath the distances, the placid surfaces of communal life. She learns about the problems of women and of ageing – for this is predominantly a community of old people – and about love in a cold climate. Above all, she learns about her and our kinship with those initially strange, distant people, and the further lesson they can offer her, and us, in essential humanity.

For the narrator, the growth in understanding is also a "growth in true friendship." Arriving in the small harbor town of Dunnet Landing, she is gradually included in the lives of the townspeople; in particular, she forms a close bond with Mrs. Almira Todd, her landlady, a "herb-gatherer, and rustic philosopher." Slowly, the narrator learns about Almira's past: the man she loved but never married, the man she liked and married, and who then died at sea before he could discover where her heart truly lay. She learns about what she calls Almira's "peculiar wisdom": her habit, for instance, of explaining people by comparing them to natural objects. What she learns, in sum, is to see and appreciate Almira as an "absolute, archaic" embodiment of the life and landscape of Dunnet Landing. Departing from Dunnet Landing at the end of summer, the narrator looks back from the boat carrying her away and sees Almira on the shore. As earthy and yet as strange, miraculous as her environment, Almira Todd then vanishes into it: the narrator loses sight of her, finally, as she "disappeared … behind a dark clump of juniper and the pointed firs." The note of passing away, departure, on which *The Country of the Pointed Firs* finishes gathers up intimations of sadness and loss that quietly circulate through the entire narrative. This is a book about the ageing of life and communities. Almira Todd vanishes at the end of the story; and, equally, the life she rehearses, in all its homeliness and heroism – that is vanishing too. In this book, Jewett manages something quite remarkable, She weaves together the great theme of pastoral, that the best days are the first to flee, and a major theme in American thought and writing at the turn of the century, that an older, simpler form of society is dying.

Another woman writer who devoted herself, at least in her best work, to her New England homeplace was Mary Wilkins Freeman (1852–1930). Her finest achievements were the stories she produced for her first two published collections, *A Humble Romance and Other Stories* (1887) and *A New England Nun and Other Stories*

(1891). Set in the decaying rural communities of small New England villages and farms, these stories capture the spirit of the people through their dialect. That spirit is often dour: Freeman describes what she calls, in one of her stories, "A Church Mouse" (1891), "a hard-working and thrifty" but also "narrow-minded" group of people whose "Puritan consciences" often blight their lives. Freeman focuses, in particular, as Jewett does on the lives of women in these small communities. Exploring their interior lives and their relationships, she shows them struggling to assert themselves, and acquire some small portion of what they want, in a community dominated by male power – or, to be more accurate, grumbling male indifference. "You ain't found out yet we're women-folks. You ain't seen enough of men-folks yet to," a woman tells her daughter in "The Revolt of 'Mother'" (1891). "One of these days you'll find out, an' then you'll know we only know what men-folks think we do, so far as any of it goes," she adds with caustic irony; "an' how we'd ought to reckon men-folks in with Providence, an' not complain of what they do any more than we do of the weather."

Regionalism in the South

The writing described as regionalist or local color after the Civil War was, very often, committed to cultural restitution and recovery, the celebration of a vanishing social order or the commemoration of one that had already vanished. So it is not really surprising that much of this writing came from and concerned the South. During this period, in fact, the myth of the feudal South was modulating into the myth of the Lost Cause. The South Carolina poet Henry Timrod (1828–1867), for instance, is mainly known for poems that honor the memory of the Confederate dead. A Confederate volunteer himself, who was to see his house destroyed by the troops of General Sherman, Timrod chose to see the Civil War, as many Southerners did, as a fight for white Southern "freedom" and independence rather than as a fight to keep black Southerners in slavery. That made it easier, not only to celebrate the heroism of Confederate troops but to revere the cause for which they had fought, as in his most famous poem, "Ode: Sung on the Occasion of Decorating the Graves of the Confederate Dead, at Magnolia Cemetery, Charleston, S.C., 1867" (1872).

A more complex response to the defeat of the South is to be found in the work of another Southern poet, Sidney Lanier (1842–1881), who was born in Georgia. After writing his only novel, *Tiger-Lilies* (1867), Lanier turned to verse, much of which was published only after his death. The verse varies widely in rhythm and movement, reflecting Lanier's interest in prosody: in 1880, he published an influential work on *The Science of English Verse*. It varies just as widely in terms of genre and tone. There are, for example, accomplished polemical and satirical and dialect pieces, such as "Thar's more in the Man Than Thar is in the Land" (1877) and "Jones's Private Argument" (1877). There are also major pieces that follow the tradition of, say, "Tintern Abbey" by William Wordsworth, in combining landscape portraiture with reflection and meditation: like "Corn" (1877) and "The Marshes of Glynn" (1877). What links them, above all, is Lanier's belief in the redemptive power of the land: the conviction that the salvation of his region, and indeed his nation, lay in a return to the pieties of hearth and home, the self-reliant smallholding. Lanier was critical of both the dependence on one crop, cotton, that he felt had destroyed the Old South and still weakened the New, and the growth of a more complex, industrial society dependent on trade and capital. So, in "Corn," he moves from a richly atmospheric description of nature in all its primitive abundance, through a celebration of the culture of the independent farm and "the happy lot" of "the home-fond heart," to a critical assault on commercial farming and commerce in general. For Lanier, the choice for the South, and for America, was simple. On the one hand, as he put it in "Corn," was the pleasant mediocrity of a family supporting itself on its own land. On the other, was a culture governed by the instabilities of exchange. Despite all the evidence to the contrary, he still believed that the choice had not been made, for his nation as well as his region: and he managed to convince himself that old aptitudes and new tools could be combined to recapture the Jeffersonian dream.

Lanier was unusual among those writers concerned with the fate of the South in that he did anticipate a redemptive future. Timrod was, in this instance, more typical in that he dwelled, with an appropriate sense of pathos, on the past and loss. Writers such as Joel Chandler Harris (1848–1908) and Thomas Nelson Page (1853–1922) drew a romantic portrait of the antebellum South that presented it as a gracious, feudal civilization, peopled by stereotypes of white male nobility and white female decorum and beauty, humble black retainers notable for their simplicity and devotion to their "old massa and missis," and field-hands singing melodiously as they worked. Consistently, the Old South is seen through the receding narrative frames of the elegist. "Dem wuz laughin' times," declares one of the most famous of these elegists, Harris's Uncle Remus in *Told by Uncle Remus: New Stories of the Old Plantation* (1905), "an' it looks like dey ain't never comin' back." As the character of Uncle Remus indicates, these tales of life in the South entered into dialect through the use of African American characters and narrators. This opened up the chance, at least, of a more critical approach to slave society and its postwar residues. Some of that chance was taken up by Harris. Harris, whose Uncle Remus stories drew on African American folk sources, knew only too well why the slaves, with little means of open resistance, had celebrated the success of weak but wily characters like Brer Rabbit over the stronger but slower Brer Fox, Brer Wolfe, and Brer Bear. And in such stories as those in *Uncle Remus: His Songs and Sayings* (1880) and *Nights With Uncle Remus* (1883), he drew a contrast that had similar, and similarly hidden social and ethnic implications. Brer Rabbit is the trickster, who succeeds by playing the part of simpleton, by assuming a deceptive candor and humility. Brer Fox and others are the tricked, whose flaw is precisely their belief in their mastery, their own superior power and wisdom. The best of these tales have a subversive energy that is further informed by the colloquial vigor of the character's speech and the call and response, repetitive narrative structure – which gives the reader the sense of *this* tale being embedded in a much larger, older storytelling tradition. But like Allen, Page, and other Southern storytellers who devoted themselves to accounts of life down on the old plantation, Harris could not divorce himself from the romantic, nostalgic impulse. White Southerners of the privileged class remained resolutely noble, in his eyes. African Americans, during and after slavery, had the charm and the endearing craftiness of children: children who, like Brer Rabbit, needed some restraint, some imposed order if they were not to engineer chaos.

A more powerful sense of otherness, and the sometimes oppressive strangeness of older Southern cultures, is to be found in the work of two women writers associated with New Orleans, Grace King (1852–1932) and Kate Chopin (1851–1904). King led a curiously ambivalent life. A woman of the privileged class, she experienced poverty after the Civil War and was forced to live in a working-class neighborhood of New Orleans. A devout defender of the South, she was drawn to feminists in the North and writers interested in imaginatively exploring female disadvantage and oppression. A bilingual Protestant, she also wrote from the position of an outsider about the Roman Catholic Creoles of New Orleans, and a position that involved both identification with and critical unease about the complex racial and sexual codes she observed. Something of this mix of feelings is to be found in her story "The Little Convent Girl" (1893), which also shows how often in the South issues of race, gender, and identity become entwined. The tale is simple. A young girl travels down by riverboat to New Orleans to join her mother, after spending most of the first twelve years of her life with her father in Cincinnati and in a convent. On arrival in New Orleans, it turns out that her mother is "colored." One month later, when the riverboat returns to New Orleans, her mother takes the little convent girl on a "visit of 'How d'ye do'" to the captain. The little convent girl takes the opportunity to jump from the boat into the Mississippi, and disappears under the water. About halfway through this story, the riverboat pilot, who befriends the little convent girl, confides to her his theory that "there was as great a river as the Mississippi flowing directly under it – an underself as a river." At the end, we are told, the body of the drowned girl may well have been "carried through to the underground river, to that vast, hidden, dark Mississippi that flows beneath the one we see; for her body was never seen again." It is a perfect image for the dark, subterranean history of the South: the repressions of knowledge and feeling that eventually undermined an entire society – and here drive one young girl into a sense of abjection and then death.

The fiction of Chopin explores the racial and sexual codes of late nineteenth-century Louisiana with even greater subtlety. Chopin moved to New Orleans following her marriage. Following the death of her husband, in 1882, she moved back to St. Louis with her six children. Seven years later, she began writing, and, within ten years after that, had published twenty poems, ninety-five short stories, two novels, one play, and eight essays. Most of her stories are set in Louisiana, and cover all its social classes: aristocratic Creoles, middle and lower-class Acadians, "Americans" like Chopin herself, mulattoes and blacks. Her first two collections, *Bayou Folk* (1894) and *A Night in Acadie* (1897), established her reputation as a writer of local color. That label, however, conceals Chopin's interest, here and throughout her career, in sexual politics and, in particular, the politics of marriage. Her first two published stories, for instance, "Wiser than a God" (1889) and "A Point at Issue" (1889), concentrate on what would prove to be her dominating theme: the conflict between social demand and personal need, the social requirement that a woman should center her life on her husband and a woman's necessary obedience to her own compulsions, the impulse to express and develop her individuality. "Désirée's Baby" (1892) brings class and race into the equation. Particularly daring, for its time, is "The Storm" (1898), which uses the upheavals of a stormy day as an occasion and a metaphor for illicit sexual passion.

Not surprisingly, stories like "The Storm" were not published during Chopin's lifetime. *The Awakening* (1899) was, but it provoked enormous criticism. It was banned from the library shelves in St. Louis and, following a reprint in 1906, went out

Figure 3.2 Portrait of Kate Chopin (as Kate O'Flaherty before marriage to Oscar Chopin), 1869 carte de visite photograph by J. A. Scholten. Missouri History Museum Photographs and Prints Collections. Portraits. N11979.

of print for over fifty years. It is not difficult to see why. Edna Pontellier, the central character, a wife and a mother of two small boys, awakens to passion and herself. What that awakening involves, eventually, is a suicide that is a triumph of the will and an assertion of her own needs and strength. "I would give up the unessential; I would give my money, I would give my life for my children," she tells her friend, Adèle Ratignolle, "but I wouldn't give myself." So, in order not to surrender herself, not to lose herself in a conventional marriage or a string of more or less meaningless affairs, she swims out into the sea with no intention of returning. Edna is awoken out of what she later calls the "life-long, stupid dream" of her life during one summer at Grand Isle. Her husband, Léonce, to whom she has been married for six years, is neither a villain nor a brute, but merely an ordinary husband, a little selfish and insensitive and very conventional. There is affection between them, certainly, and the kind of understanding that often exists between married couples. But the understanding hinges on an acceptance of Edna's dependent, subsidiary status: easy enough for Léonce, of course, but something that Edna herself begins quietly to question, as she awakens to the "voice of the sea" she so loves to bathe in and, consequently, to her own spiritual and sensual impulses. Edna loves the sea. For her, it is associated with other instruments of abandon, such as art and nature. For the novel, it is the vital, untamed element, the medium of liberation, the wilderness where one can be oneself. It is everything that is the opposite of social and familial obligation. Marriage, in a sense, and dependence on men, is the equivalent of the image of the clearing that underpins so many American texts: it is the cultural space where Edna is required to obey rules that oppress her as a woman and play a role that denies her as an independent human being. Swimming in the sea, "a feeling of exultation overtook her," the reader is told, "as if some power of significant import had been given her to control the working of her body and her soul." And this feeling of power comes to her again when she flirts with Robert Lebrun, the son of the owner of the resort where she and her family are staying.

There is no doubt that Edna falls in love with Robert. There is equally no doubt that, later, she has sexual relations, not with Robert, but with another man, Alcèe Arobin, to whom she is attracted but does not love. This, however, is a story, not about illicit passion, secret affairs, and adultery, but about how all these become a means by which Edna begins, as the narrator puts it, "to realize her potential as a human being." Throughout *The Awakening*, Chopin negotiates her way between social comedy and sensuous abandon, an attention to the pressure of reality that is commonly associated with the realists and naturalists and a sense of the miraculous potential of things that invites comparison with other great narratives of romance. As the story draws to a close, and Edna commits herself to the ocean, it is, of course, the sense of the miraculous, the potential for freedom and adventure, that has the major stress. This is a death, certainly, but it is a death that is seen as a liberation and affirmation: an echo and anticipation of all those moments of breaking away that supply an open ending, a sense of continuing possibility to so many other American texts. Reading *The Awakening*, it is not hard to see why it provoked such hostility among contemporaries. Its radical character is measured by the fact that Edna's eventual suicide is depicted, not as a sacrifice, a surrender, but as a moment of self-affirmation. That character is also very American, though: since what the fate of Edna Pontellier ends by telling us is that the ultimate price of liberty – and a price worth paying – is death.

Like Chopin, George Washington Cable (1844–1925) devoted much of his fiction to his hometown of New Orleans. His earlier stories were published in periodicals between 1873 and 1879 and then gathered together in *Old Creole Days* (1879). Cable is not reluctant to portray the romance and glamour of Louisiana life in these tales: there are coquettish or courageous women, the proud or cunning men of old Spanish-French Creole society, and there are incidents of smuggling and adventure. But he is also careful to register the eccentric characteristics of the Creole dialect. And he explores the shifting character and sinister depths of old Creole society in a way that makes clear his intention of exploring the larger society of the South of his own time too. The conflicts between a harsh racial code and a history of miscegenation, between traditional customs and new laws and habits, between the pursuit of aristocratic ease and the economic imperatives of work: all these had relevance, not only for the Creole characters Cable described, trying to cope with their new American masters after the Louisiana Purchase of 1803, but for all Southerners after the Civil War. And to explore these, and similar, issues, Cable deployed a range of techniques. "It is not sight the storyteller needs," he once wrote, "but second sight. . . . Not actual experience, not actual observation, but the haunted heart: that is what makes the true artist of every sort." As it happens, Cable was very good at "sight": seeing and hearing the detail of everyday social exchange, But he was also extremely good at "second sight": exploring the haunted margins of society, and exposing its weaknesses and secrets. This made him both a political novelist and a poetic one – a writer in the great Southern tradition of using the romantic, the gothic, to reveal the repressed history of the region.

That repressed history is very much at the heart of Cable's 1880 novel, *The Grandissimes.* Here, again, he uses the medium of a romantic, at times even gothic, tale to pursue the issues that intrigued him most: pride of caste and class, resistance to necessary change, racial oppression and violence. The plot is a convoluted one, but its central premise is not. *The Grandissimes* hinges on a family feud between two old, proud Creole families: a feud for which the narrator himself finds a romantic analogy in the strife between the Capulets and Montagues in *Romeo and Juliet.* In a move characteristic of fiction generally classed as local color, the reader is introduced to the warring families, the Grandissimes and the De Grapions, both of Louisiana, by an outsider. Joseph Frowenfeld, a "young Américain," comes to the city of New Orleans with his family. The rest of his family soon dies of "the dreaded scourge," but he manages to survive. And he becomes acquainted with both Honoré de Grandissime, banker and head of his family, and the De Grapions, who nurse him during his illness. Slowly, he learns about the tangled history of the two clans, and especially the Grandissimes: he learns, for instance, that Honoré has a brother, "Honoré Grandissime, free man of color," with the same father but a different mother. He watches and witnesses the habits and eccentricities of the Creoles: their "preposterous, apathetic, fantastic, suicidal pride," their "scorn of toil," their belief that "English is not a language, sir; it is a jargon!" Cable uses his immense skill as a creator of dialect speech to introduce Frowenfeld, and the reader, to the rich plurality of cultures and traditions in old Louisiana. But he also measures the divisions of class and color that separate the different communities, and, above all, the gap that separates the white race from the black – and, in one notable instance here, brother from brother.

The Grandissimes ends on the promise of peace between the feuding families, with the marriage of Honoré Grandissime to one of the De Grapions. There is even the hope of some broader reconciliation, as Honoré has suggested that "Honoré free man of color" should become a member of the Grandissime mercantile house. But the hope is a faint one. The novel also closes with "Honoré free man of color" killing one of the haughtier white members of the Grandissime family, who has slighted him precisely because of his racial coloration. Typically of Cable, the reader is left with marriage and murder rather than marriage and music: a sense of conciliation and concord is scarred by the reminder of the deep divisions that continue to disturb this society. Cable undoubtedly felt an affection for Creole generosity, magnanimity, bravado, and glamour; this was tempered, however, by his understanding of what he saw as the disastrous consequences of Creole pride. He was a sympathetic but unremitting critic of the Creole spirit and society; and he used his imaginative analysis of old Creole days to criticize the South of his own time, which he saw as its echo and extension. That criticism, leveled aslant in his fiction and more directly in *The Silent South* (1885), a treatise advocating racial reform, made him increasingly unpopular in his own region. He moved North to Massachusetts in 1885. There, he continued to write novels, like *John March, Southerner* (1894), that dealt with the collision between Northern and Southern morals and manners. Cable was not the first writer from the South to write of his region with a mixture of sentiment and seriousness. But his work resonates with themes and imagery that were to echo in Southern fiction of the twentieth century: brothers divided by the racial barrier, the shadow of slavery, images of the plague and the swamp rehearsing the evil that surrounds and infests an entire society.

A writer who knew more than most about the dark heart of racism, North and South, and who, like Cable and Chopin, began his career as a popular "local color" writer, was Charles W. Chesnutt (1858–1932). Chesnutt was born in Cleveland, Ohio, to which his parents had recently moved. They had left Fayetteville, North Carolina to escape the repression experienced by free blacks in the South. After the Civil War, however, the family returned to Fayetteville, and it was there that Chesnutt was educated. Chesnutt first attracted attention as a writer with his story "The Goophered Grapevine," which appeared in *The Atlantic Monthly* in 1887. This was followed by many other stories set in the South, and in 1899 two collections appeared: *The Conjure Woman and Other Conjure Tales* and *The Wife of His Youth and Other Stories of the Color Line*. At the heart of *The Conjure Woman* is a picture of plantation life in the Old South, presented through the comments and stories of an ex-slave and inhabitant of the region, Uncle Julius McAdoo. Julius's tales were "naive and simple," Chesnutt was to write of them later. Their subject, he added, was "alleged incidents of chattel slavery, as the old man had known it and as I had heard of it"; and they "centered around the professional activities of old Aunt Peggy, the plantation conjure woman, and others of that ilk." Chesnutt admitted that these stories were written "primarily to amuse." But, he added, they "have each of them a moral, which, while not forced upon the reader, is none the less apparent to those who read thoughtfully." For example, Chesnutt explained, in one of the tales, "Mars Jeems's Nightmare," a cruel slavemaster is transformed into a slave for several weeks by the conjure woman so that he might have "a dose of his own medicine." The consequence is "his reformation when he is restored to his normal life."

"The object of my writings would be not so much the elevation of the colored people as the elevation of the whites," Chesnutt wrote in 1880. His way of doing this, he hoped, would be to "lead people out" to "the desired state of feeling" about black people "while amusing them." He could use the established literary genres and conventions to persuade white readers out of their prejudices "imperceptibly, unconsciously, step by step." So, the stories in *The Conjure Woman* may appear to belong to the traditions of plantation literature and dialect tales typified, on the one hand, by Thomas Nelson Page and, on the other, by Joel Chandler Harris. But they are subtly different. They introduce the lore of "conjuration," African American hoodoo beliefs and practices, to a white reading public mostly ignorant of black culture. And they offer a new kind of black storytelling protagonist: Uncle Julius McAdoo shrewdly adapts his recollections of the past to secure his economic survival in the present, sometimes at the expense of his white employer. In effect, *The Conjure Woman* quietly tells the reader about black community and humanity: the cultural forms, the strategies African Americans use to maintain their sense of identity and resist white domination. Conjure figures in these tales as a way to control property and settle disputes; above all, though, it figures as a resource, a form of power available to the powerless in oppressive, intolerable situations. So does storytelling. Julius defends himself against the superior power of the whites – whose surplus capital enables them to buy the McAdoo plantation on which he lives – with the weapon he has in evidently endless supply: the numerous tales he knows about the land that his white masters know merely as abstract property.

Following his two collections of stories, Chesnutt published three novels: *The House Behind the Cedars* (1900), *The Marrow of Tradition* (1901), and *The Colonel's Dream* (1906). *The House Behind the Cedars* is set in the same environs as virtually all his fiction: the South – the fictional town of Patesville, North Carolina again – "a few years after the Civil War." It tells the story of two African Americans, a brother and sister, who pass for white. In *The Marrow of Tradition*, Chesnutt takes a broader canvas. Basing his story on a racial massacre that occurred in North Carolina in 1898, he dramatizes the caste structure of a small town. *The Colonel's Dream*, in turn, describes the attempt of one idealistic white man, blessed with economic power and moral influence, to resist racial intolerance and help a small North Carolina town mired in economic deprivation and social injustice. Chesnutt was, in effect, contributing an African American perspective to three prominent genres of late nineteenth-century social purpose fiction in these three works: the novel of miscegenation and passing, the romance of history and politics, and the "muckraking" novel written to expose the plight of the deprived. But all three works failed to find a public, and Chesnutt largely gave up writing. In 1931, in an essay titled "Post-Bellum-Pre-Harlem," Chesnutt admitted that literary fashion had passed him by. However, he also expressed his pride that African American writing had come far since his own days of writing. For that, as he surely sensed, he had to take some credit.

The Development of Literary Realism and Naturalism

Capturing the commonplace

"The talent that is robust enough to front the every-day world ... need not fear the encounter," wrote William Dean Howells (1837–1920) in *Criticism and Fiction* (1891). "The arts must become democratic," he added, "and then we shall have the expression of America in art." For Howells, realism was the appropriate response to the drastic changes taking place in America in the late nineteenth century. And the writer who could achieve that realism could also be described as the creator of a truly democratic, essentially American art that captured the importance and the meaning of the commonplace. Howells was eventually to occupy a position at the center of literary life in America. But his own origins were, appropriately for a man dedicated to the "commonplace," quite humble. He was born in Ohio, received little formal education, and moved from town to town with his family, working for his father, a printer, as a typesetter. Beginning in 1860, he had pieces published in various national magazines. The first of his forty or so novels, *Their Wedding Journey* (1872) and *A Chance Acquaintance* (1873), made use of his travels abroad. These were followed by two fictions dealing with the contrast between Americans and Europeans, *A Foregone Conclusion* (1874) and *A Lady of Aroostook* (1879). With his first major novel, *A Modern Instance* (1882), Howells moved beyond explorations of manners to the detailed and serious consideration of wider social issues. The novel is structured around the twin themes of divorce and journalism. Howells was the first novelist to focus on journalism, and developed the theme of divorce after attending a performance of a Greek tragedy. During the composition of the book, he called it his "New Medea," a "modern instance" of what would happen to a couple whose marriage gradually deteriorates. What is remarkable about it is the way that, in a strategy characteristic of literary realism, it links the personal and the political, the emotional and the social.

Howell's 1885 novel, *The Rise of Silas Lapham,* also demonstrates what he called the "fidelity to experience and probability of motive" that he felt was an imperative for the American storyteller. More than *A Modern Instance,* it also invites the reader to what he called "the appreciation of the common." The central character here, Colonel Silas Lapham, is a Vermont farmer who has risen to wealth through his paint manufacturing business. He is a typical capitalist of the time to the extent that for him business is a sacrament. His paint is not merely "the best on the market," he declares, but "the best in God's universe," and he makes this declaration "with the solemnity of prayer," affirming the holiness of thrift and the profit motive. Lapham moves his family to Boston and begins to build a house on fashionable Beacon Hill: Howells uses the several removals of the family, as other contemporary and later realists were to do, to measure social status and upward mobility. He also encourages his wife and daughters to enter fashionable society. The Lapham family does not fit in well or easily with genteel Boston society. One member of a high-class family, however, Tom Corey, falls in love with the older Lapham daughter, Penelope. And although the match between them is delayed for a while, because the younger daughter Irene convinces herself and Penelope that Tom is in love with her, the two are eventually married. Not long after the marriage, they leave for Mexico to escape the rigid social barriers of New England. Lapham, meanwhile, has been threatened with bankruptcy due to some unsuccessful business ventures. A former partner, called Rogers, urges him to save himself by selling some property he knows to be worthless to some British investors. After a struggle with himself, Lapham decides not to make the sale. Economically bankrupt, socially disgraced, he is nevertheless morally restored, and he returns with his family to Vermont.

Structurally, with its movement towards the moral redemption of the protagonist, the moral "rise" that accompanies his social and financial fall, the story Howells devises here would have tempted other writers toward moralism and sentimentalism. But, like his hero, Howells resists temptation. As Lapham makes his decision not to sell worthless stock, what he is aware of mostly is how deeply unheroic he feels. "He had a whimsical and sarcastic sense of its being very different from the plays at the theater," the reader learns. This is a necessary choice for him, but it is not one that is accompanied by any theatrical gestures or even with much sense of satisfaction. "You've ruined me!" Rogers – who had a share in the anticipated deal – tells Lapham, when he learns of his choice. "I haven't a cent left in the world! God help my poor wife!" "This was his reward for standing firm for right and justice to his own destruction," Lapham muses, as he sees Rogers leave, "to feel like a thief and murderer." Lapham has done what he has to do but done so quietly, hesitantly, even regretfully. If there is moral grandeur here, it is no more, and no less, than the grandeur of the commonplace. "You can paint a man dying for his country," one character in the novel complains to an artist, "but you can't express on canvas a man fulfilling the duties of a good citizen." Howells can. And he leaves us with his "good citizen," Lapham, averring, with a scrupulous avoidance of heroism or sentimentalism, his humble acceptance of his citizenly duties. "I don't know as I should always say it paid," he confesses, reflecting on the choice he made; "but if I done it, and the thing was to do over again, right in the same way, I guess I should have to do it."

Three years after publishing *The Rise of Silas Lapham*, Howells himself left Boston, for New York. The move, which reflected a gradual transference of cultural power from the old New England establishment to the metropolis, was followed by a change in Howells's choice of subject and method. He was fascinated by the extremes of wealth and poverty he found in the city, and appalled by the brutal treatment of striking workers. Influenced by Tolstoy, whom he began to read in 1885, he gravitated towards socialism and to the belief that he had to adapt his realistic fiction to the problems of the machine age and the city. One result of this was a utopian fiction, *A Traveler from Altruria* (1894). Several hundred utopian fictions appeared between the 1880s and the early 1900s, as writers responded to the radical changes and social injustice of the times by imagining alternatives for America based on economic stability and principles of justice. The most famous and influential of these was *Looking Backward* (1888) by Edward Bellamy (1850–1898), which portrayed the United States in the year 2000 as a place where government ownership of the means of production and the "scientific," rational rule of a business class ensured economic equality and happiness for all citizens. Another result of the new direction in Howells's realism was the novel that deserves a place with *A Modern Instance* and *The Rise of Silas Lapham* among his major fiction, *A Hazard of New Fortunes* (1898). The most panoramic of all his works, the novel is set in the magazine world of New York City and explores the conflict between labor and capital on both a personal and a general level. On the personal level, there is, for instance, the conflict between a magazine proprietor, Dryfoos, a millionaire capitalist, and one of his employers, a socialist called Lindau. On the general, there is a vivid account of a strike of streetcar employees, in which Lindau's son is killed. Howells called *A Hazard of New Fortunes* "the most vital of my fictions." That is open to debate. What is not, however, is that it is the one among his major fictions that is most vitally concerned with social injustice – and the one most urgently and immediately directed towards the realization of what he termed "democracy in literature." Such a literature, Howells explained, "wishes to know and to tell the truth." And that truth was that "men are more like than unlike one another." That catches a note which is there in all Howells's criticism and fiction, with its primary stress on human dignity and connection. For him, as for so many realists, what was commonplace was what, in the end, was held in common and shared.

Capturing the real thing

Howells never gravitated from realism to naturalism, with its emphasis on the determining influence of heredity and environment and its harrowing depiction of landscapes, social and natural, that are at best indifferent and at worst hostile to humankind. There is a fundamental benevolence, a belief in human worth and social betterment, that is caught in one of the most famous remarks in *Criticism and Fiction*:

"our novelists concern themselves with the more smiling aspects of life, which are the more American." That remark would have elicited sardonic laughter from Ambrose Bierce (1842–1914?), who was known as "bitter Bierce" and the "the wickedest man in San Francisco" among his contemporaries, and seemed to revel in both titles. Born in Ohio, Bierce participated in the Civil War. The war disgusted him, prompting him to see soldiers as little more than paid assassins and, when it ended, he moved to California, where he established a reputation as a brilliant and caustic journalist. Living in England for four years from 1872, he returned to California. He then published *Tales of Soldiers and Civilians* in 1891, retitled *In the Midst of Life* in England and in the 1898 American edition. Another collection of stories, *Can Such Things Be?*, followed in 1893. More than half the stories in the first collection, and many in the second, deal with the Civil War; they reflect their author's feelings of revulsion for military life, and his bleak, bitterly comic view of life in general. Some of these stories capture the vicious confusion of battle, just as, say, *Miss Ravenel's Conversion from Secession to Loyalty* (1867) by John William De Forest (1826–1906) does. Others use stream of consciousness and suspense endings to explore the subjectivity of time. The same dark light that simultaneously illuminates and shadows these stories also informs Bierce's poems, and the ironic series of definitions collected in *The Devil's Dictionary* (1911). In 1913 Bierce traveled into wartorn Mexico, to escape American civilization and to seek, he said, "the good, kind darkness." He must have found it, for he disappeared.

At first sight, there are few connections between William Dean Howells and Henry James (1843–1916). But it is to Howells's credit that, as critic and editor, he was among the first to recognize James's talent. Credit is due to Howells all the more, perhaps, because as they knew, the two men came from very different backgrounds. James was born in New York City to a wealthy, patrician family, the grandson of an Irish immigrant who had amassed a large fortune. After being educated by private tutors until the age of twelve, he went to schools in Europe and the United States. Entering Harvard Law School in 1862, he withdrew after a year, and began to concentrate on writing. Reviews and essays appeared in *The Atlantic Monthly* and *The North American Review*. In 1869 he returned to Europe, his first visit as an adult, first to England and then to Italy, which made a deep impression on him. It was while he was in Europe that his beloved cousin, Mary Temple, died. How exactly this affected his later fiction is open to debate, although the situation of an attractive, lively but doomed young girl certainly recurs, in such novels as *The Wings of a Dove* (1902) and in the novella *Daisy Miller* (1878). In any event, James's first novel, *Watch and Ward*, appeared serially in *The Atlantic Monthly* in 1871 (and in volume form in 1878). This was followed by his first collection, *A Passionate Pilgrim and Other Tales* (1875) and *Transatlantic Sketches* (1875), and his first novels of real consequence, *Roderick Hudson* (1876), *The American* (1877), and *The Europeans* (1878). The story "A Passionate Pilgrim" deals with the reactions of an eager American "pilgrim" when confronted with the fascinations of the complex European world of art and affairs. And James himself during this period was something of a pilgrim in Europe, which he came to regard as his spiritual fatherland, moving there permanently in 1875. During a year in Paris, he associated with such masters of the art of fiction as Flaubert and Turgenev, who encouraged his interest in what Flaubert called "le mot juste"; the right word, the careful planning of the language and structure of the novel so as to make it an accurate register of reality.

After 1876, however, he made his home mainly in London, although he maintained an American home in Massachusetts and, much later, moved to the small town of Rye in Sussex.

In *The American*, James explores the contrasts between Europe and America through the story of a protagonist whose name betrays his origins and missions. Christopher Newman is an American who reverses the voyage of his namesake Christopher Columbus and travels from his own, New World to the Old World of France during the Bourbon period. *The Europeans* reverses this voyage, by bringing Europeans to New England. The transatlantic contrasts multiply and are more complex here, but the fundamental distinctions remain the same. The contrast between America and Europe is even more finely and fully drawn in the major work of the first period, and arguably James's greatest novel, *The Portrait of a Lady* (1881). It is, as James put it, the story of "a certain young woman affronting her destiny." Isabel Archer, a penniless orphan living in Albany, New York, is taken up by her Aunt, Lydia Touchett. She goes to England to stay with her aunt and uncle and their tubercular son, Ralph. There, she declines the proposals of both Caspar Goodwood, a rich American, and Lord Warburton, an English aristocrat. Wealthy now, thanks to an inheritance from Mr. Touchett arranged for her by Ralph, she then accepts the proposal of an American expatriate, a widower and dilettante living in Florence, Gilbert Osmond. She is introduced to Osmond by another expatriate, Madame Merle, and is impressed by his taste and refinement. Soon after marriage, however, she discovers him to be selfish, sterile, and oppressive. She also finds out that Osmond's young daughter, Pansy, is actually the daughter of Madame Merle and that this was the reason for the woman's introducing her to Osmond and promoting the marriage. Despite Osmond forbidding her, Isabel leaves for England when she hears Ralph is dying, and is at his side when he dies. Despite a last attempt from Caspar Goodwood to persuade Isabel to go away with him, though, Isabel determines to return to Osmond. And the novel closes with her accepting her destiny, or perhaps more accurately the consequences of her choices, and preparing to go back to a home that is more like a prison. Stated baldly, the story has strong elements of romance or fairytale, just like *The Scarlet Letter*: the awakening of a sleeping beauty, the three suitors, a villain whose "egotism lay hidden like a serpent in a bank of flowers," a heroine held captive in "the house of darkness, the house of dumbness, the house of suffocation," the sick young cousin who observes and admires her from afar before dying, the voyage of an American Adam – or, rather, Eve – and their exile from Paradise. But what distinguishes it, in the reading, is its adherence to the substantial realities of the social life and the subtle realities of the life of the conscious-ness. Isabel Archer is as much like the heroines of, say, *Middlemarch* or *Daniel Deronda* by George Eliot as she is like Hester Prynne: the imaginative maneuvers of the book represent as much an encounter between the American and the European as its story does. It is both of and about a collision of cultures.

One reason for the subtle but substantial reality of Isabel herself is that James focuses on her. James wanted to reveal the full implications of the developing consciousness of his protagonist. So the reader experiences a lot through her, and shares the lively animations of her mind on the move but, in addition, sees her from the outside, through the comments and often critical commentary of the narrator – and through the observations of characters like Ralph Touchett. We understand her sense of herself, her moods and changes, but we also take the measure of "the whole envelope of circumstances" in which she is implicated. Characteristically of James, the strategy is part of the debate. That phrase, "the whole envelope of circumstances," is used by Madame Merle, who has adapted to a European vision sufficiently to believe that self and circumstance are indivisible. Isabel disagrees. Subscribing to the American romance of the self, she believes in freedom as an absolute and the individual as somehow separable from circumstances. James wryly complicates the debate by intimating that his heroine's profound belief in herself, her "fixed determination to regard the world as a place of brightness, of free expansion," may itself spring from circumstance. She has grown up in a world, the new world of America, where there have been few forms or authorities, no rigidly enforced social practices, to challenge that belief. But that complication is further complicated by the clear admiration that Isabel's "flame-like spirit" inspires in the narrator, observers such as Ralph Touchett, and the reader. There is candor and honesty here, a fundamental integrity and capacity for wonder as well as innocence, an openness that leaves her vulnerable – and, by some measures at least, humanly incomplete.

With the characters surrounding Isabel, some are quietly developed, and the reader gradually comes to know them: sometimes for good, as with Ralph Touchett, and sometimes, as with Osmond and Madame Merle, for ill. Others, like Lydia Touchett, are flatter and deftly summarized when they are introduced. All, however, contribute to our understanding of the heroine and the representative character of her transatlantic encounter. A minor character such as Henrietta Stackpole, for instance, another young American woman abroad, helps the reader place Isabel further; so do the sisters of Lord Warburton, "the Misses Molyneaux." Henrietta is self-confidence and independence to the point of bluster. The Misses Molyneaux are compliant and decorous to the point of vanishing into their surroundings. The character of Isabel is mapped out using such minor characters as coordinates, in a manner James had learned from Jane Austen. And it is mapped out, too, in Isabel's perilous voyage between the possibilities represented by her first two suitors and the alternatives they vigorously embody: America, with its devotion to individual initiative, enterprise, and possibility, and Europe, with its adherence to mannerliness, custom, and tradition, the rich fabric woven out of the past. Isabel's voyage is a literal one, to begin with, when she leaves New York for England: landscapes that here, as throughout James's fiction, have a symbolic as well as a literal application, with the starkness and simplicity of the one contrasting with the opulence and grandeur of the other. But it becomes an intensely symbolic one: when Ralph Touchett tries, as he puts it, to put some "wind in her sails" by arranging for her to receive a bequest from his father.

Isabel, too, tries to put wind in the sails of someone else. She is drawn to Gilbert Osmond precisely because she believes she can help him fulfill the requirements of his imagination. With Goodwood or Warburton, she would, in a sense, be embarking on a ship that has already set sail, committing her destiny to one that had achieved full definition before she appeared; she would, perhaps, be resigning herself to the authority of another. But with Osmond, she believes, it would be she herself who would enable the voyage, create the destiny. In fact, this is not the case at all. Osmond, as it turns out, had just as firm a notion that he would be her providence when he married Isabel. What all this adumbrates is a theme interwoven with the contrast between Europe and

America, and dear to the heart of Hawthorne as much as James: the human use of human beings. The complex interplay of character focused in the figures of voyaging reminds us that to declare oneself may be to deny another.

James's response to the problem he opens up, as he examines his characters' attempts to negotiate their freedom, is a dual one, and is typical in the sense that it involves what happens in *The Portrait of a Lady* and how it is written. What happens is that Isabel decides to go back to Gilbert Osmond. To run away with Goodwood would suggest that Madame Merle had been right after all, an admission from Isabel that the "envelope" of her unfortunate circumstances was influential enough to make her evade the consequences of her own actions with a man she never loved. To return involves an acceptance of those consequences, and a fulfillment of a promise made earlier to Pansy, Osmond's daughter, that she would come back. The choice on which the novel ends depends on a subtle balance between self and circumstance, in that it involves the recognition that expression of the one properly depends on awareness of the other: that freedom is a matter of responsible, realistic self-determination. And that same balance is at work in its narrative texture. James, as he meant to, does not yield to the determining nature of circumstance here, although he admits its irreducible reality. Nor, while emphasizing the power of consciousness, does he present that power as separate and inviolable. What he does, in his fictional practice, is what he preached in his criticism. He enters into a complex series of negotiations between the "moral" and the "felt life," the messages communicated by the narrative and its status as a dramatic experience. Not only that, he shows that assertion of the one depends precisely on acceptance of the other: that, like any other living organism, the meaning of the novel *is* its being.

If the first period of James's career could be described in terms of moral realism, and the third in terms of psychological realism, then the second could be called a period of dramatic realism. James used careful manipulation of point of view, elaborate patterning of contrasting episodes and characters, and a focus on dialogue and dramatic scene to achieve here what he always sought: "the maximum of intensity," to use his own words, "with the minimum of strain." The results are powerfully evident in a novel like *What Maisie Knew* (1897) that explores adultery, infidelity, and betrayal. The entire story, although written in the third person, is told from the point of view of the perceptive but naive young girl Maisie, who is just six years old when her parents are divorced. The strategy enables James to achieve economy, intensity, and irony as he combines and implicitly compares what Maisie sees with what the narrative voice intimates.

Towards the end of his second period, James confirmed his reputation as a writer of short stories with tales many of which were about writers and writing, like "The Lesson of the Master" (1888), "The Middle Years" (1893), and "The Figure in the Carpet" (1896). In their own modest fashion, these stories prepare the way for the emotional and psychological subtleties that characterize the three major novels of the third and final period of James's career: *The Ambassadors*, written in 1901 and published in 1903, *The Wings of the Dove*, and *The Golden Bowl* (1904). In all three, James returns to the international theme. In *The Ambassadors*, for instance, Lambert Strether is sent by a wealthy widow, Mrs. Newsome, to persuade her son Chad to return to Massachusetts. Gradually, however, he grows less enthusiastic about his mission, as he becomes more and more receptive to the charms of England and France. This story of transatlantic encounters acquires some clarity by an elaborate balancing of scene and character: there are four major scenes set in a plainly allegorical garden, for instance, in which knowledge is slowly acquired and, in the course of the action, Chad and Strether change moral places. But it also acquires a certain mystery, even opacity, from James's determination to follow the smallest refinement of emotional detail, the slightest nuance of social gesture – and from a style that, in the service of this pursuit, often becomes formidably intricate.

In the last few decades of his life, James devoted much of his time to preparing the New York edition of his works. He also wrote eighteen new prefaces for his novels. He traveled widely, and wrote about his travels: in *The American Scene* (1907) and *Italian Hours* (1909). He published two volumes of autobiography, *A Small Boy and Others* (1913) and *Notes of a Son and Brother* (1914); and a third volume, *The Middle Years*, appeared posthumously in 1917. James assimilated the tendencies of his own age: the mix of realism and romance, the moral rigor, the preoccupation with selfhood. He also anticipated the direction in which many later artists were to move: towards a concern with the complex fate of being an American in an increasingly internationalized culture, the conviction that the truth of life and the truth of art are one and the same. A summative and seminal writer, he stands at the juncture between two centuries. He was also, complexly, his own man.

Towards naturalism

Of Hamlin Garland (1860–1940), Henry James once declared that he was "a case of saturation so precious as to have almost the value of genius." What James presumably meant by this remark was that Garland devoted himself to the detailed depiction of one particular area of America: the Midwest where he was born and where he spent his boyhood and youth, as his family moved between farms in Iowa, South Dakota, and his native Wisconsin. Garland is sometimes described as regionalist because of this concentration on the life and landscape of the Midwest in his fiction. At other times, he has been called a realist or even a propagandist, because of his careful but also socially committed portraits of the poverty and oppression suffered by Midwestern farming families. Garland, for his part, called himself a "veritist." The "veritist," he explained, was committed to "the truthful statement of an individual expression corrected by reference to fact." "The veritist sees life in terms of what might be, as well as in terms of what is," Garland insisted, "but he writes of what is, and, at his best, suggests what is to be, by contrast." Sticking closely to the empirical facts, but also catching or alluding to the verities, the realizable values of a life, the veritist is, in essence, a realist and a reformer. That combination of approaches is clearly at work in what is his first and, by a long distance, his finest book, *Main-Travelled Roads* (1891), a collection of stories mostly written before 1890. It contains such widely anthologized tales and sketches as "The Return of the Private," "A Branch-Road," "Up the Coulé," and "Under the Lion's Paw." All of these are powerfully informed by Garland's guilt over leaving his family, and particularly his mother, to the barren life of the farm (he departed for Boston in 1884) and by his anger over what he saw when he returned to or remembered that life, with "its sordidness, dullness, triviality, and its endless drudgeries." For Garland, the "study of sad lives" was useless unless it led to "a notion of social betterment"; the artist had to combine fact and truth, actuality and aspiration; and, in the best of his work, he did just that.

Garland's remark about the study of sad lives occurred in his review of *McTeague: A Story of San Francisco* (1899). *McTeague* was the first novel of real consequence by Frank Norris (1870–1902), who was one of those writers who gave a new and distinctly darker emphasis to American literature at the end of the century. There were poets among them. These included Edwin Markham (1825–1940), whose finest poem, "The Man With the Hoe," explored the tragic life of the farmer, "bowed with the weight of centuries" and "slave to the wheel of labor." Like Garland mixing grim realism with reforming zeal, Markham called on "masters, lords and rulers" to redeem this victim of "the world's blind greed." And, remarkably, his best work, collected in *The Man With the Hoe and Other Poems* (1899) and *Lincoln and Other Poems* (1901), struck a responsive chord, making him popular and wealthy enough to devote himself to writing. Still more notable, though, than Markham was William Vaughn Moody (1869–1910). Many poets of this period, faced with what they saw as social and moral decline, retreated into fantasy. Moody, however, was determined to explore the dislocation of his times. A poem like his "Gloucester Moors" (1901), for instance, starts from a sense of disorientation that is at once social, moral, and existential. "Who has given me this sweet,/" Moody asks, "And given my brother dust to eat?" Moody acquired fame during his lifetime from his plays, *A Sabine Woman* (1906) and *The Great Divide* (1909). They deserve a place in American literary history if only because, unlike many dramatists of the period, Moody chose for them distinctly American subjects. But it is his verse, collected in *Poems and Plays* (1912), that really takes the measure of his times. It is here that he registers, with far more resonance than most other contemporary poets, the sense of vacuum left by the disappearance of an earlier America and an older faith and by the spread of evolutionism, determinism, and relativism – and the suspicion that America had broken faith with its past by moving, in the course of a century, from liberated colony to imperial power.

The writers who contributed most to this darkening of mood, however, were novelists, like Norris. The most notable of these, apart from Norris himself, are Stephen Crane (1871–1900) and Jack London (1876–1916). They also include Theodore Dreiser (1871–1945), whose long career was to make him someone standing on the cusp between Victorianism and modernism. Like Norris, both Crane and London – and, for that matter, Dreiser – were Naturalists. That is, they subscribed to a darker, supposedly more scientific form of realism, shared with European writers like Emile Zola, that denies human agency: in these fictions, environmental forces control events and the individual is subject to the determinations of life – the elemental forces running through nature, society, and every single human being. Sharing intensely in this perception, the realization of this darker form of realism, Frank Norris had more than one term for its realization in fiction. Sometimes, he called it "naturalism with all the guts I can get into it." More often, he called it "Romance." "Realism," Norris argued in "A Plan for Romantic Fiction" (1903), "notes only the surface of things"; it "bows upon the doormat and goes away and says … 'That is life.'" "To Romance," on the other hand, "belongs the wide world for range, and the unplumbed depths of the human heart, and the mystery of sex, and the problems of life, and the black unsearched penetralia of the soul of man." What Norris was after, effectively, was a Naturalism that combined the dedication to empirical facts found in realism with the devotion to truth – which, for him, meant scientific truth – that he claimed to find in romance. In pursuing that kind of Naturalism, Norris was prepared to assault conventional taste: to show, for instance, how the brute instincts in human beings were an integral element in them, and played a necessary part in the social struggle. He was also eager to combine a detailed notation of often sordid social detail with an almost poetic celebration of the primal rhythms that, as he saw it, drove through nature and the primal urges that pulsed through man.

Norris's major project was what he called *The Epic of the Wheat*. "I've got an idea as big as all outdoors," he triumphantly announced, when he first thought of it. "There's the chance for the big, epic, dramatic thing in this." It would, he explained, be in the vein of "naturalism" but Naturalism as he understood it – and so, "the most romantic thing I've ever done." "The Wheat series" he planned was to be a trilogy. There would be first a novel focused on the production of the wheat, and the struggle between farming and railroad interests in California. This was published in 1901 as *The Octopus*: it was, as it turned out, Norris's major novel. The second was to concentrate on the distribution of the wheat and the manipulation of the wheat market in Chicago. That was published posthumously as *The Pit* in 1903. But the third, dealing with consumption and telling of a wheat famine in Europe, was never written: Norris came up with a title for it, *The Wolf*, and little more than that. The epic scale of Norris's ambition, though, is clear from *The Octopus*. The octopus of the title is the railroad – also called a "Titan" and a "colossus" – which is the most powerful vested interest in California, and spreads its tentacles all over the state. It controls the movement of prices and interest rates; it owns much of the land and dispossesses the farmers of more; it manipulates the state government and, through its power over the access to information, it ensures that, statewide, no story but its own gets told. In the course of the narrative, the farming and laboring interests are comprehensively defeated. On the naturalistic surface, *The Octopus* is the bleakest of epics. What works against the bleakness, however, and gives the novel a strangely affirmatory, even optimistic tone is Norris's belief in "force," necessity – the sense that, as the final words of this story put is, "all things, surely inevitably, resistlessly work together for good."

In effect, the social conflict of *The Octopus* is set in what Norris calls "a larger view." It is set in a frame within which, eventually, all human agents are seen as subject to "primordial energy," part of "the eternal symphony of reproduction." The narrative rhythm of the book, moving from autumn to autumn, registers this; so do the visual representations of characters, dwarfed by the vastness of the plains, and the structure of individual scenes – which habitually move from close-up into longshot, from "the minute swarming of the human insect" to "the great, majestic, silent ocean of the wheat itself." But Norris's principal means of creating this vaster perspective of endless, triumphant, primordial struggle are four characters: a writer Presley, the "seeing eye" of the novel, Shelgrim the railroad president and Behrman a railroad employee, and a strange character called Vanamee. It is Shelgrim who tells Presley that the railroad company is not in control, still less is he as president. As he explains, only "FORCE" is: on the social level, "conditions, laws of supply and demand" and on the existential level, "Nature" in its "colossal indifference." Behrman illustrates the point in one way.

Believing himself to be "the Master of the Wheat" when the railroad company triumphs, he turns out to be its victim – he is crushed, suffocated to death by "a sea" of wheat pouring down on him from a chute. And Vanamee illustrates it in another. Losing his lover, Angèle, at harvest time, she returns to him in the visionary shape of Angèle's daughter, at the same time as the recrudescence of the wheat. Above all, there is Presley. Modeled on the poet Edwin Markham, Presley begins by searching for his subject in the romance of the Old West. Becoming involved in the cause of the farmers, he then throws away his copies of Milton, Tennyson, and Browning to read Mill, Malthus, and other social philosophers. He writes a populist poem, "The Toilers," engages in political debate and violent political agitation. But neither his words nor his actions have much effect. Gradually, he withdraws into the larger view that embraces necessity. He still believes that, one day, "the People" will triumph and "rend those who now preyed upon them." But that belief involves a residual optimism that allows Presley to retain hope even in the middle of disaster. *The Octopus* is a characteristic work of American Naturalism in its potent mixture of populist political vision and an evolutionary determinism that – in its celebration of force and talk of "lower" and "higher" instincts, class, and races – teeters dangerously, sometimes, on the borders of fascism. It is also a characteristic work of Norris in its heady mix of fact and surreal fantasy and its extraordinarily cheerful nihilism.

There is little cheerfulness in the work of Stephen Crane. The tone is more muted, more quietly bleak. In prose and poetry of crystalline clarity and grimly pointed power, Crane pursues his fundamental perceptions that nature is oblivious to human need, that human beings are often relentlessly selfish or blind to circumstance, and that the two moral imperatives are humility and community. The poetry has been sadly, and unjustly, neglected. Crane published two volumes of poems during his lifetime, *The Black Rider* (1895) and *War is Kind* (1900). Stylistically, they show the influence of Emily Dickinson, by whose work Crane was much impressed. In terms of substance, they express a sense of existence that is even more cast in the shadows than that of Dickinson. It is the prose work, however, that has secured Crane's reputation. His first novel, *Maggie: A Girl of the Streets* (1893), was not widely noticed when it was first published. *The Red Badge of Courage* (1895), however, was both a critical and a popular success when it first appeared. In a characteristically pointilliste style, Crane captures here the flux and confusion of battle. Unlike Norris, Crane preferred literary impressionism, delicacy of selection and suggestion, to saturation. He picks out carefully chosen details, intimations of color and movement, apparently disconnected images and events. He then places them in juxtaposition. The result is a fictional landscape remarkable for its instability and uncertainty. Many of the scenes are set in a foggy, misty landscape, at night or in the smoke of battle. And they offer a vivid visual equivalent for Crane's view of war and life. "None of them knew the color of the sky," one of Crane's most famous short stories, "The Open Boat" (*The Open Boat and Other Stories* (1898)), begins. That is precisely the human fate, and the fate of the soldier: not to know "the color," the contours or reality of the environment. Anti-heroic, the novel also denies real human agency. For "the youthful private" whose story this is – and whose name, we eventually learn, is Henry Fleming – war is a disconcerting mix of boredom, ignorance, and fear: where long periods of waiting and wondering are punctuated by bursts of action that surprise and disconcert. War is, as Crane describes it, a paradigm of

life: not least, because it is nasty, brutish, beyond personal control, and has death – in the shape of the loathsome corpse Fleming comes across amidst "a chapel made of high arching boughs" – at its center. Characteristically, Crane draws an ironic contrast between the romance and reality of battle, the heroic fate Fleming anticipates for himself and the horrible futility, the fear and the feelings of cowardice he experiences. But he also quietly propels his young protagonist towards a kind of revelation, founded on an understanding of what his true place in war, and the scheme of things, is and what that should mean for him, in terms of judgment and conduct.

During his first encounter with the enemy, Fleming witnesses a mass retreat of his fellow soldiers. He also receives a head wound from the butt of a gun, when he grabs a deserter to try to find out what is happening. This, and his flight from a second encounter with the enemy, persuade him that he is no more than an insignificant part of a "vast blue demonstration." His dreams of glory fade into a sense of absurdity, nihilism, and hopelessness. His comrades in arms may admire the "red badge of courage" on his head, but he knows that it is not his courage, but his cowardice and confusion, that has helped put it there. Fleming has swung from romanticism to nihilism. Where Crane has him end, though, is with something like a proper human response to the bleak realities of experience. Back with his regiment, after wandering lost for some time, Fleming instinctively picks up the regimental colors when they fall from the hands of another soldier during a charge forward against the enemy. The description of this event manages a delicate balance between a sense of the fated and the chosen. Equally, the account of the aftermath is poised between pride and guilt, relief and regret. The muted moral conclusion that Crane and his young protagonist arrive at is neatly imaged in a concluding description of "a golden ray of sun" breaking for a moment "through the hosts of leaden rain clouds." Fleming, the intimation is, is "tiny but not inconsequent," he can achieve some moral agency in and through an accurate vision of where he stands, as a soldier and a man. He takes the path of realism, understanding, and humility. As a result, "the red badge of courage" of the title assumes meanings that are both ironic and serious, for him and his creator.

"Most of my prose writings," Crane declared, "have been toward the goal partially described by that misunderstood and abused word, realism." That word would not have been rejected, either, by Jack London, who, like Norris and Crane, saw reality as a naturalistic struggle for existence, dominated by what he termed – in one of his most famous stories, *The Call of the Wild* (1903) – the "law of club and fang." For London, even more ruthlessly than for Crane or even perhaps Norris, life was a battle for power. "The ultimate unit of matter and the ultimate unit of force were the same," the reader is informed in *The Iron Heel* (1908). "Power will be the arbiter," the hero of that novel declares. "It is a struggle of classes. Just as your class dragged down the old feudal nobility, so shall it be dragged down by my class, the working class."

Ernest Everhard, the hero of *The Iron Heel*, is addressing his remarks to a member of The Oligarchy, a defensive, proto-fascist conglomeration of major trusts and their private militias. The story is set in the years 1911–1932 and is supposedly a transcription of a manuscript written at the time by Avis Cunningham, the wife of Everhard and fellow revolutionary, and edited 700 years later by Anthony Meredith, who lives in what is called the fourth century of the Brotherhood of Man. It describes a violent revolutionary struggle against the iron heel of totalitarian capitalism that ends

Figure 3.3   Portrait of Jack London. © Bettmann/Corbis.

disastrously: Everhard is killed, Avis is apparently executed, and the revolution is crushed. The descriptive frame, however, offers not just hope but the fulfillment of the hero's prophecy: since the reader is told that the iron heel was finally overthrown some 300 years after the events related in what is called the "Everhard Manuscript." Like *The Octopus*, *The Iron Heel* places the specifics of political defeat within a visionary framework that proposes eventual redemption. Like *The Octopus*, too, it offers the reader a powerful mix of socialist message and proto-fascist feeling. A commitment to the political and economic jostles in London's fiction with celebration of the primitive, the morally indifferent power of nature and the beauty of blond, clean-limbed heroes: Wolf Larsen in *The Sea-Wolf* (1904), for instance, is lovingly described as being of "Scandinavian stock," "the man type, the masculine, and almost a god in his perfectness." Such heroes reflect London's overwhelming commitment to the will to power, in man, society, and nature. Even self-inflicted death can become an expression of that will, in his work. In *Martin Eden* (1909), for example, London's most autobiographical novel, the hero commits suicide by forcing himself to stay below the surface of the ocean, despite the struggle his body makes to persuade him otherwise. Suicide becomes, in these terms, a triumph of the will.

Martin Eden, Wolf Larsen, and Ernest Everhard are all men of genius from humble surroundings. Each has a touch of the rebel, the antichrist in him. Clearly, there was a sense in which London was presenting an idealized portrait of himself, and his rise from a humble background, in these portraits. London's first and second novels were published in 1902; and a year later the third, *The Call of the Wild*, catapulted him to fame. The "hero" of the story is a dog, Buck, who is kidnapped from his comfortable existence on a California estate and sold into service as a sledge dog in the Klondike. Eventually, abandoning human society and companionship altogether, Buck becomes leader of a pack of wolves. He has returned to nature, the primitive, aboriginal condition of existence. Thoreau and Twain, in their separate ways, saw nature as a fundamentally moral agency: the source of a humanly sympathetic, ethically sound life. Man, in their work, returns to nature as a means of moral instruction and regeneration. For London, however, nature is what Wolf Larsen calls it in *The Sea-Wolf*, "unmoral": it is pure precisely because it is primitive, existing apart from human judgment. His characters, human or otherwise, return to it and learn there a truth that is determinately unhuman: that life is a matter of neither emotion nor ethics but "the call of the wild," "ruthless struggle."

That truth is also learned in *The Sea-Wolf*: a novel that deserves a place with *The Call of the Wild*, *The Iron Heel*, and *Martin Eden* as one of London's major works. Here, it is a man who is suddenly removed from civilized society. In the fog on San Francisco Bay, two ferry boats collide and Humphrey Van Weyden, the narrator, is thrown overboard. He is saved by a sealing schooner, the *Ghost*, whose captain, Wolf Larsen, presses him into service. The character of Van Weyden is suggested by his interests. He is a critic who has written an essay on Poe and is planning another entitled "The Necessity for Freedom: A Plea for the Artist." Clearly, London intends the reader to regard Van Weyden as not only effete but suffering from a dangerous delusion: that human beings are capable of free will. The accident that propels Van Weyden out of society is plainly symbolic of the chance rhythms that govern all human existence. Van Weyden is first consigned to the water, the "mighty rhythm" of which offers a paradigm of the mighty rhythms ruling all things. He is then drawn into a new life on a ship the name of which suggests an afterlife, another form of existence, where he is given "new" clothes, a new name "Hump," and a new job as a cabin boy. In his "new and elemental environment" in which, he reveals, "force, nothing but force obtained," Van Weyden receives an education into the realities of power from Larsen. The lesson is learned from Larsen's instruction and example and, not least, from the sheer brute magnificence of his appearance: in terms of physique he is, we are told, like one of "our tree-dwelling prototypes," while he has a voice "as rough and harsh and frank as the sea itself." Gradually, Van Weyden changes. "It seemed to me that my innocence of the realities of life had been complete indeed," he now confesses. "I was no longer Humphrey Van Weyden. I was Hump." His muscles grow strong and hard; and his mind grows accustomed to what London and the other Naturalists saw as the essential and unavoidable truths of life: the elemental presence of force, the ineluctable nature of power, and the daily fact of brutality.

The Development of Women's Writing

Writing by African American women

The world of the Naturalists is, on the whole, a determinately male one, defined by struggle. In the work of a number of women writers of the later nineteenth century, there may be a similar interest in the allocation and distribution of power. However, it tends to express itself in different forms, less conspicuously wedded to the notion of life as war. The forms in which women writers expressed themselves during this period were several, and usually involved a continuity with writing before the Civil War. Some of the forms they took up and developed, such as spiritual autobiography, gothic, and polemic, had not been the special preserve of earlier women writers. Some, like domestic realism, had. But there was a marked tendency to use these forms to explore, as Kate Chopin did, the condition and vocation of women, their relationship to the changing worlds of home and work. And there was an equally marked tendency to look, as Mary Wilkins Freeman did, at how women could get the attention of society, and men in particular, how they could acquire a voice that mattered and get themselves heard. Such tendencies are, quite naturally, to be found with especial force in the work of those who came from, and saw themselves as representing, the most powerless, underprivileged community of women, African Americans: among them Julia A. J. Foote (1827–1900) and Pauline Elizabeth Hopkins (1859–1930). Foote, the daugh-ter of former slaves, was born in New York State and, while still only ten, began work as a domestic servant for whites. At the age of fifteen, she converted to an African Episcopal church in New York and began to devote herself to evangelical work. What she preached, above all, was the doctrine of sanctification: the belief that a Christian could be completely liberated from sin and empowered to lead a life of spiritual perfection. And her conviction that she herself had been sanctified made her sure that her destiny was to be a preacher: something that brought her into conflict with church leaders, and the general customs and prejudices of the day. This, and other notable events in Foote's life, are recounted in her autobiography, *A Brand Plucked from the Fire* (1879). To an extent, the book goes back to a tradition of spiritual autobi-ography that finds its American roots in the earliest writings of the Puritans. But it also reflects a growing commitment to the idea of spiritual androgyny, to be found in similar texts by black and white women of the time. Foote insists on her spiritual equality with men, and the spiritual equality of women in general. Citing the Bible, to the effect that "there is neither male nor female in Christ Jesus," Foote makes an eloquent case for spiritual parity that is, in her humble opinion, further proven by her witness and testimony.

Unlike Foote, Pauline E. Hopkins worked in many forms and genres, and was the most productive African American woman writer of her generation. What has secured her reputation, however, are her four novels, three of which were serialized in the *Colored American* and one of which, *Contending Forces: A Romance of Negro Life North and South* (1900), was published by the press that issued the magazine, the Colored Co-operative Publishing Company. These novels are remarkable for the use of established popular genres to explore the themes of race and gender. In *Winona, A Tale of Negro Life in the South and Southwest* (1902), for instance, a love story about a beautiful, tragic mulatta becomes a means of exploring the contentious issues of slavery and racial and sexual oppression. And in *Of One Blood; or, the Hidden Self* (1903), Hopkins produces an early example of black science fiction writing, using an imaginary underground African city as an imaginative site for exploring the racial mixing of blacks and whites. Most notable of all, in *Contending Forces*, Hopkins takes on a wide canvas and the mainstream literary genres of domestic and historical romance. The setting ranges from Bermuda in the 1790s to Boston in the late nineteenth century. Thrilling episodes involving endangered heroines and lecherous villains are juxtaposed with scenes of domestic bliss. Tragic misunderstandings and melodramatic coincidences are mingled with scenes of marriage and motherhood. And, throughout all this, Hopkins presses upon the issues of racial injustice and sexual oppression: as her black women are violated, and her black men characters brutalized and killed, by the domestic whites.

At the center of *Contending Forces* is a character called Sappho Clark. Sold into prostitution by her white uncle at the age of fourteen, she has a son who was conceived during the period when she was effectively a sexual slave. To a degree, she is the conventional romance heroine, the tragic mulatta. But Sappho is more than meets the eye. For a start, Sappho is not her real name. She has adopted it to disguise her identity, and it is a clear allusion to the ancient Greek poet who created a school of women's poetry and music on the island of Lesbos. The portrait of Sappho Clark, beneath its conventional veneer, has a definite political agenda. Her personal story exposes what Hopkins, in her "Preface" to the book, refers to as a history of "lynching and concubinage." And her declarations of independence – her insistence, for example, that she actively enjoys working outside the home for pay – add to our sense that this is a book that uses literary stereotypes, of race and gender, only to resist and subvert social ones. The domestic scenes and the eventual destiny of Sappho bring this out with particular force. While Sappho is at a boarding house, she shares in gatherings of women at sewing circles and tea parties. What at first appears a commonplace of domestic fiction, however, turns out to be much more than that. The domestic sphere was an important site of resistance, at this time, for African American women; and the black women's club movement of the 1890s, which Hopkins is effectively describing in these scenes, became a powerful collective force for change. At her best, Hopkins uses romance to make a realistic point about the present and to express hope for the future founded upon it. That is nowhere more clearly illustrated than in the fate of Sappho. Falling in love with the son of her landlady, Will Smith, she fears that her past will prevent their union and, for a while, runs away. But she is finally reunited with Will, who recognizes that she is not to blame for her life as a prostitute and is happy to marry her. The resolution may seem, and indeed is, romantic, even sentimental. But it presses home the point that woman is the victim here. In acknowledging this, and acting on the acknowledgment, Will is a romantic hero making a realistic judgment of what can happen to women, especially poor, black women, in a society dominated by men. He is doing what his creator set out to do: as she put it in her "Preface" to *Contending Forces*, "pleading for justice of heart and mind."

Writing and the condition of women

Pauline Hopkins tried to write for a living but, much of the time, had to support herself by working as a stenographer. Writing was also the means that Louisa M. Alcott (1832–1888) sought to support not only herself but her mother and sisters. During her life, she produced over 300 titles. What she is mainly remembered for, however, are her domestic novels written for children. The best known of these is *Little Women: or, Meg, Jo, and Amy*. This novel was originally published in two parts: the first, *Little Women*, appeared in 1868, the second part, *Good Wives*, was published the following year, and in 1871 the two came out as a single volume, *Little Women and Good Wives*. Alcott drew on her own life and family experiences in writing these and other domestic tales: Jo March, for instance, one of the "little women," is based on Alcott herself. But the March family live in genteel poverty, whereas the Alcotts, when Louisa was young, often suffered a fiercer deprivation. With the spectacular commercial success of *Little Women*, however, the financial security of Alcott and her relatives was assured. She continued to write domestic tales. But, before and after the publication of *Little Women*, she also continued to try her hand at other forms. And, in 1873, she published what is perhaps her most interesting book, an autobiographical fiction that covers nearly twenty years in the life of its heroine, *Work: A Story of Experience*.

Work begins with Christie, its heroine who is twenty-one, declaring her independence from her guardian, Uncle Enos. It ends with her, at the age of forty, discovering her vocation as a spokesperson for the rights of women. Christie is resolved, as she puts it, "not to be a slave to anybody." And, in pursuing that resolution, she takes jobs ranging from sewing to acting. She is also helped and inspired by the companionship and the stories of female friends, the women she meets after her declaration of independence: among them, a runaway slave and many fellow women workers. By the close of the story, Christie has a daughter, and is joined with her and other females in what is termed a "loving league of sisters." Devoted now to the cause of women, she is roughly the same age as her creator was when she published this novel; and it is hard not to see her sense of her own empowerment as something shared with Alcott. *Work* is a celebration of female liberation and labor of many kinds, including the liberation experienced in and from the labor of writing.

Harriet Spofford (1835–1921) also wrote to support herself and her family. Her reputation was established when *The Atlantic Monthly* published her short story, "In a Cellar," in 1859. She went on to write poetry, articles, and several novels. Notable among her non-fictional work is her book *Art Decoration Applied to Furniture* (1878), where she develops her belief that style in dress and furnishings reflects the people who adopt them. That belief informs what is undoubtedly her best work, her short stories, collected in such volumes as *The Amber-Gods and Other Stories* (1863), *New-England Legends* (1871), and *The Elder's People* (1920). In the title tale of her first, 1863 collection, for instance, the two major, female characters are defined by the jewelry they wear. The passionate Yon wears "pagan" amber ornaments, while the placid and patient Lu wears "light" and "limpid" aqua-marina. What also informs the best of these stories is a firm commitment to female power and community. In "A Village Dressmaker," for example, the dressmaker Susanna gives the wedding gown she made for herself to Rowena Mayhew, who is marrying the man they have both loved. And she is happy to do so because, as her two maiden aunts recognize, she has acknowledged necessity and, at the same time, she has helped another woman. That tale is from Spofford's final, 1920 collection, which is a detailed, realistic account of New England life. Some of the earlier stories are more strangely, hauntingly romantic, but they still explore the terms in which women can express and assert themselves.

Elizabeth Stuart Phelps (1844–1911) was less convinced that women would be allowed the time for their art. At least, in her best work she was. The daughter of a popular author, whose name she took as her own, she continued her mother's interest in religious fiction by writing *The Gates Ajar* (1868). This was not so much a novel as a series of conversations by fictional characters about the beauties of heaven. It was immensely popular, particularly with women readers, and was followed by a number of books, the "Gates" series, exploring the same theme. But Phelps also wrote novels that focus on the condition of women. Of these the most memorable is *The Story of Avis* (1887). At the beginning of this novel, the talented heroine, Avis Phelps, returns home to New England after training as an artist in Europe for four years. She is courted by Philip Ostrander, who has been wounded in the Civil War; and, while she is aware of the risk to her career as an artist, she marries him. She soon realizes her mistake. The care of her husband (who eventually becomes too much of an invalid to continue work), and then her son Van and daughter Wait, leave her little time for her art. In particular, she finds her work on her major project, a painting of the sphinx, constantly frustrated. Phelps uses a mixture of irony, incantation, and allusion here, to measure the losses of her heroine's life. There is an adept use of allusion, for instance, as Avis looks at her painting of the sphinx and seems to see "meanings" in its enigmatic expression. The riddle of the sphinx, for Avis, is how to be both a woman and an artist. It is a riddle she never manages to resolve for herself. All she can hope for, at the end of the novel, is that her daughter will not repeat her mistake. Her husband dead, and her son, Avis moves back into her father's house, where she will give Wait, she hopes, the training necessary not to waste her talent as she has.

A similar concern with the waste to which most women's lives are subject informs nearly all the writings of Charlotte Perkins Gilman (1860–1935). Regarded as the leading intellectual in the women's movement around the turn of the century, Gilman was mainly known during her lifetime for her non-fictional work. In *Women and Economics* (1898), she argued that the economic dependence of women on men hindered the happiness of all. *Concerning Children* (1900) and *The Home* (1904) proposed changes to liberate women to lead more productive lives; while *Man Made World* (1911) and *His Religion and Hers* (1927) anticipated a major role for women in international affairs and the church. Gilman explored similar or related themes in her fiction, which received less attention from her contemporaries. Late in her career, for example, she wrote three utopian novels that offered feminist solutions to social problems: *Moving the Mountain* (1911), *Herland* (1915), and *With Her in Ourland* (1916).

Over her lifetime, she also wrote more than 200 stories, most of them for her magazine. Of these, easily the most famous is "The Yellow Wall-Paper" (1892). Gilman based the story on her own experience of a "rest cure": a regimen of bed rest and confinement that almost drove her, she said later, to "utter mental ruin." In it, an unnamed woman records her strange experiences when she and her husband, "John," go to live in "ancestral halls" for the summer. Her husband is a physician, she tells us, so is her brother; and so, although she does not believe she is sick, when they tell her she has "a slight hysterical tendency," she feels helpless to refute them. "What is one to do?" she asks. At their new house for the summer, John chooses their room, where she is to stay to deal with her "nervous condition." She would have preferred another room, "but John would not hear of it." And the room where she is to spend most of her time she soon begins to dislike, because it is covered with a wallpaper the color of which is "repellent, almost revolting, a smouldering unclean yellow." Alone in her room, though, discouraged from writing or any other labor, she becomes obsessed with it. She first sees eyes staring from the wallpaper. Then she begins to see a "shape" behind the pattern. There is a "front pattern" and a "back pattern," she believes; the front pattern is like bars, and the shape is that of "a woman stooping down and creeping about behind." As her obsession with the paper grows, she can see the front pattern move as, she believes, "the woman behind shakes it!"

The narrator, it is clear, is starting to see the shape in the paper as a double, a secret sharer in her own imprisonment. And as that intensifies, she tears at the yellow wallpaper that constitutes her jail as well as that of her doppelganger in a desperate effort to liberate herself and her reflection. In her own eyes, that effort meets with success. The story ends with the narrator declaring to her husband – who has had to break down the door with an axe to get into the room – "I've pulled off most of the paper, so you can't put me back!" She has broken down and broken out. Under the coercive pressure of her husband, and other physicians, she has become what they prescribed her to be. They have resisted taking her, and her needs, seriously; unsympathetic and unimaginative, their best intentions have made her a prisoner. She has taken the only way out she sees or senses: through the "bars" of the wallpaper and into insanity. The power of this story stems from its mix of the surreal and the simple, the gothic and the realistic. The subtlety of the story, in turn, issues from the way the author frames the narrator: allowing us to see what she does not see, just how much her manacles are mind-forged and man-forged. Subject to the prevailing pieties about the superior wisdom of men and the necessary subordination of women, she is forced into guilt or denial. She can only write herself on the secret paper of her journal or the wallpaper. Gilman shows us all this, while never permitting us to waver in our sympathy for the narrator, or to feel the grip of her own rapt imagination upon our own.

The Development of Many Americas

Things fall apart

Henry Adams (1838–1918) was also interested in the rights and the condition of women. In 1876 he delivered an influential lecture on "The Primitive Rights of Women." His first novel, *Democracy* (1880), explores not only political life in Washington but the contemporary situation of American women; so does his second novel, *Esther* (1884). And in his two most celebrated and important works, *Mont-Saint-Michel and Chartres* (privately printed in 1904, published in 1913) and *The Education of Henry Adams* (privately printed in 1907, published in 1918), he was to explore his theory of feminine force and, in particular, the unifying cultural power embodied in the figure of the Virgin. Adams was intellectually drawn to discoveries in contemporary science and, especially, to the discovery that physical matter contained its own potential for disintegration. For him, science proved that nature was without system. "The kinetic theory of gas is an assertion of ultimate chaos," Henry Adams wrote. "In plain words, Chaos was the law of nature; Order was the dream of man." In his attempts to impose order on the flux of his experience, man was, as he saw it, like a spider snaring the forces of nature that "dance like flies before the net" of its web. That perception of disorder and entropy was to feed into later American writing; and it was memorably expressed and explored in his two major works of personal and cultural exploration.

The first of these, *Mont-Saint-Michel and Chartres*, is subtitled *A Study of Thirteenth-Century Unity*. The book is structured as a tour of medieval France, with the author acting as an expert guide. And, as Adams takes the reader around, he considers the dominant cultural power of the Middle Ages: the Catholic faith, which informed all aesthetic and intellectual endeavor as well as spiritual and ethical thought. In particular, he sees the force, the power of "the Queen Mother," the Virgin, as "absolute" during this period; adoration of the Virgin, he suggests, created a unifying ideal for the medieval sensibility, an ideal that composed life and art into a fluent harmony of sex, love, energy, and benevolence. Adams clearly sees faith in the Virgin, during the Middle Ages, as an agent of order, the "dream of man": a cohesive cultural force and, as such, in marked contrast to the disintegrative, dispersive, and essentially destructive tendencies of his own, contemporary culture. That contrast is developed in his second major work, *The Education of Henry Adams*: the contrast is even registered in its subtitle, *A Study of Twentieth Century Multiplicity*.

The *Education* has the form of an autobiography. But it is no more an autobiography than *Mont-Saint-Michel* is a travel journal. Adams remains silent about his marriage, his wife, and her eventual suicide; and he distances author from subject by describing himself in the third person. The core of the *Education*, like that of *Mont-Saint-Michel*, is intellectual and speculative: Adams is considering himself as a unique but also representative man, typical of his time, and he is using his experiences as a source of meditation, a means of considering what it is like to be alive at the turn of the nineteenth century. That strategy comes out, with particular intensity, in the chapter titled "The Dynamo and the Virgin." Here, Adams picks up his earlier meditations on the Virgin. "Symbol or energy, the Virgin had acted as the greatest force the Western world ever felt." As such, her absence from American thought and culture has a particular poignancy. "American art, like the American language, and American education," is "as far as possible sexless," Adams avers, because "this energy" embodied in her is "unknown to the American mind."

These speculations on the absence of the female principle from American life, as a source of power unity, occur during Adams's account of his visit to the Paris exhibition of 1900. Entering "the great hall of dynamos" there, Adams began, he says, "to feel the forty-foot dynamos as a moral force, much as the early Christians felt the Cross." Adams declares that those motors were unequivocally a "nightmare" for him; he had, he tells the reader, "his historical neck broken by the sudden irruption of forces totally new." "Woman had once been supreme" as an agent of social, cultural, and intellectual unity. Now, as image and instrument, of his place and time, Adams speculates, there was and is only "this huge wheel, revolving ... at some vertiginous speed," reducing matter and mind to a "sequence of force." For Adams, this experience was representative, like all the others recounted in the *Education*; and it was also seminal. All, he felt now, was a delirium of change. For the centripetal cultural energies of a female age, at once gentler and more powerful, had been substituted the centrifugal forces focused and figured in the dynamo. Adams can be faulted on particular issues. His reverence for the past, American or medieval, can be excessively uncritical. But his two major works are masterly innovations, gathering together ideas and personalities in a web of speculation. Not only that, here and elsewhere in his writings, Adams takes the measure of his times and the diminutive role to which, in his view, man as well as woman in the late nineteenth and early twentieth centuries had been relegated. His language has the wit, grace, and decorum of an earlier age of letters. His forms and feelings, however, place him decidedly at the forefront of his own times: as he contemplates a world in process with a mixture of awe and panic.

Voices of resistance

When Henry Adams wrote of multiplicity, there is no doubt that what he primarily had in mind was the disappearance of any tenable idea of order, a system of belief that would enable personal stability and cultural coherence. But inseparable from that was the sense Adams and others like him had that the Anglo-American model of civilization no longer enjoyed a monopoly on civic power. It was being challenged, more than ever, by other models. The voices of other Americans, describing other visions of America, were demanding to be heard. These included those other Americans who had been there before the whites, or those whose lands had been appropriated by the United States. They also included those who had come over, or had been brought over as slaves, before the Civil War, and those who had entered the country afterward seeking opportunity or just survival. What these voices spoke of was their need for recognition as human beings and citizens; what they raged against was injustice. Sometimes, they celebrated resistance. At other times, they anticipated an America that embraced difference, that saw multiplicity as a source of hope rather than fear.

In the Mexican-American communities of the Southwest, the most popular and compelling form for expressing racial and cultural pride and resistance to white domination during this period was the *corrido*. The *corrido* is derived from the Spanish word for "to run," and it describes the rapid pace of those narrative ballads whose roots can be traced to the romances of medieval Spain. *Corridos* first appeared, as a distinct ballad form, in Mexico during the middle of the nineteenth century. And they soon afterwards emerged in the American Southwest, assuming immense popularity in the forty or fifty years after the Civil War. *Corridos* flourished, in particular, in circumstances of cultural conflict, as an expression of a people living in a border territory. Their composers were generally anonymous, and they were transmitted by word of mouth to commemorate notable events or local heroes or to celebrate prototypical situations in the family and community. Unsurprisingly, many *corridos* focused on the conflict between Mexican-Americans and Anglo-Americans. Some, for instance, celebrated the superior prowess of Mexican-Americans as fighters or lovers, farmers or ranchers. Others spoke and sang of more open, violent conflict. In "Gregorio Cortez," for instance, a rancher shoots "the Major Sheriff" to defend his brother. Knowing that he will never receive justice in a Texas court, he flees for the Mexican border, but then gives himself up when he learns that his people are being persecuted and killed by the authorities because of him. The ballad presents Gregorio Cortez as "godlike" and heroic: "the Americans," we learn, "were whiter than a poppy/from the fear they had of Cortez and his pistol." He is presented, in effect, as an emblem of resistance to Anglo domination.

Racial pride and resistance of a different kind was expressed during this period in the speeches and songs of Native Americans who were also trying to counter white domination. Among the speeches, perhaps the most famous was the one given by Standing Bear (1829–1908), a member of the Ponca tribe, in 1881, when he persuaded the whites not to remove him and his people to Indian Territory. The speech, transcribed and translated by a native speaker, is a powerfully simple protest against racial injustice. Spare and stoical in a way characteristic of Native American oratory, it is also a vivid rehearsal of communal identity. Standing Bear successfully used persuasion, the traditional powers of Native American oratory. Others anticipated revenge and redemption. "The spirit host is advancing, they say," the "Ghost Dance Songs" declare, "They are coming with the buffalo, they say./They are coming with the new earth, they say." The Ghost Dance originated when the Paiute prophet Wovoka had an apocalyptic vision. He saw the Crow coming to bring the whirlwind and the earthquake to "the whole earth" and destroy the white invaders. The slaughtered buffalo and Indian people, the "ghosts," would then, he prophesied, return to reclaim their land, which had belonged to them at the beginning. This vision, and the hypnotic dance and song that expressed it, spread rapidly among Native American tribes from the West coast to the Midwest. It became the first genuinely intertribal experience: a dream of a time when the enemies of the tribes would be overthrown and Indians would be restored to their rightful inheritance. The song, the dance, a vision at once elegiac and apocalyptic, a mixture of memory and prophecy – all expressed powerful, communal feelings of loss and hope, betrayal and vengeance. And all created a moral panic among the whites. White fear about the Ghost Dance was, in fact, to lead directly to the massacre of 150 Indian men, women, and children at Wounded Knee in the Badlands of Dakota. With that, the dream of Wuvoka was dead.

Figure 3.4   Arapaho Ghost Dance. Illustration by Mary Irvin Wright, ca. 1900, after a photograph by James Mooney. © Bettmann/Corbis.

Voices of reform

For other American voices of the time, the vision of the future involved neither resistance nor revenge, however, but restoration of natural rights and reform. These included the Cuban immigrant essayist, journalist, and activist José Martí (1853–1895), the African American writer and scholar Anna Julia Cooper (1858?–1964), and the Native American historian and folklorist Charles Alexander Eastman (1858–1939). Martí described his vision in "Our America," an essay published in 1891. "The government must originate in the country," he argued in this essay. For him, that meant that European models of government had to be jettisoned. Identifying the United States as "Anglo-Saxon America," Martí pleaded for "Our America": a multicultural, multiracial community founded on the aboriginal uniqueness of the New World. Martí was well aware of the forces that threatened the realization of his vision, and, in particular, the residual forces of colonialism which he identified as "the tiger." But he believed fiercely in that vision of an America that recognized its indigenous roots and its multiple identity: an America, in short, that was not "theirs" but "ours."

The aims of Anna Julia Cooper were rather more modest, or at least moderately stated. In her book, *A Voice from the South* (1892), she declared that she wanted to break the silence, to give voice to the "hitherto voiceless Black Woman of America." And she wanted to do this, she explained, because "the fundamental agency under God in the regeneration, the re-training of the race ... must be the *black woman*." Cooper subscribed to the contemporary belief in "true womanhood," woman as the conscience of society. But she also insisted that the black woman, in particular, had a pivotal role to play in the regeneration of American society: because, as a black person as well as a woman, she knew with special intensity what was wrong and needed to be put right. For her, freedom was indivisible; and the black woman, doubly denied her freedom, was in a special position to know. Cooper was a devout believer in equality but not integration; and she argued from the standpoint of gentle feeling and faith rather than from that of politics or principle. Within these constraints, though, which were partly ones she shared with her times, Cooper offered a quiet plea for what she called "courteous contact, which is naught but the practical application of the principle of benevolence."

Although he too hoped for a time when his people would be assimilated into a broader, more benevolent form of American society, Charles Alexander Eastman was more troubled and conflicted than Cooper. A member of the Sioux tribe, he was educated in white schools; and living, after that, on the margins of both societies, he was never really comfortable in either. Although Eastman accepted the assimilationist ideas of his white educators, his early work is marked by nostalgia for the simplicities of tribal life. His account of the years before he was sent to school, *Indian Boyhood* (1902), was immensely popular. This was soon followed by several books on Sioux history and folklore, including *Old Indian Days* (1907) and *Wigwam Evenings* (1909). Later work signaled Eastman's own sense that he was working on the border between two cultures, trying to bring them closer together. In *The Indian Today: The Past and the Future of the American Indian* (1915), he considered the past and possible contributions of his people to American society as a whole. In the autobiographical work, *From the Deep Woods to Civilization* (1916), he presented his own career as exemplary, charting the route to assimilation. And in *The Soul of the Indian: An Interpretation* (1911), he tried to interpret Indian culture for his white readers. The portrait Eastman paints here of Indian "worship of the 'Great Mystery'" is intensely idealized and clearly designed to invite sympathy. "The spirit of Christianity and of our ancient religion is essentially the same," Eastman suggests. What stands out in marked contrast to both is the Christianity of his own day which, with its brute materialism, has lost touch with the primitive purity of its origins. Eastman hoped to draw the two cultures between which he existed closer together, by making connections such as this. His hope, and that project, were both sorely tested by his witnessing the carnage left after the massacre at Wounded Knee: an experience he recalls in *From the Deep Woods to Civilization*. But neither was ever really abandoned. Even in his last years, Eastman was still writing books like *Indian Heroes and Great Chieftains* (1918), aimed at youthful readers now. He still believed, perhaps desperately, that Indians could assimilate and that whites would welcome them, once they recognized the noble traditions they brought with them into American society.

A similar predicament, a sense of belonging neither in the white world fully nor in the Indian, haunted Gertrude Bonnin or Zitkala-Sa (Red Bird) (1876–1938). The daughter of a white man, of whom little is known, and a Sioux woman, Bonnin left the reservation to attend a Quaker school in Indiana, "the land of red apples" as she called it. She returned to the reservation but found herself culturally without anchorage: "neither a wild Indian nor a tame one," as she described herself in an autobiographical essay, "The Schooldays of an Indian Girl," published in *The Atlantic Monthly* in 1900. Feeling herself separate from her mother but also outraged by mistreatment of her people by white America, she began to write articles denouncing racial injustice and describing her own sense of cultural disorientation. Bonnin never lost the sense of being a stranger in two strange lands, an alien living between cultures. Her aim, like Eastman's, was somehow to mediate between them: by explaining to whites the Indian need for justice, by revealing to anyone the power of the Indian traditions. So, in 1901, she published *Old Indian Legends*. And twenty years later, she produced a larger, revised work, *American Indian Stories*, in which she used both fiction and autobiography to pursue her project of transplanting one culture, translating one language into another. The first Native American woman to write her own story without assistance, Bonnin stood, not only between Indian and white societies, but between the oral culture of the Indian past and the literate culture that would dominate its future. To that extent, she was building a bridge between separate generations as well as divided cultures.

Mary Austin (1868–1934) was born into a typical Midwestern family in Illinois. But like José Martí, she saw it as her mission to turn American culture away from the Anglo-American traditions of the East coast and towards the Native American and Indian traditions of the Southwest. Like Gertrude Bonnin and Charles Eastman, she saw herself as a mediator between cultures. She collected, preserved, and encouraged the continuation of American Indian and Hispanic folk arts; she published studies of American Indian songs in *The American Rhythm* (1923); and collected Indian songs and original poems in *Children Sing in the Far West* (1928). Like many regionalists of the time, she saw place as a profound determinant of character. Moving to California at the age of eighteen, living after that in New Mexico (where she continued her study of the Indians), she wrote continually and lovingly about life and landscape in the West.

And like many writers of the period, especially female ones, she wrote about the condition of women and how to change it. Her novel, *A Woman of Genius* (1912), for instance, describes how a woman escapes from her restricted life through art. Her two major books reflect the range of her commitments and her interest, in particular, in the liberatory impact of the West and the necessary liberation of women. *The Land of Little Rain* (1903) is an evocative account of the beauties and mystery of Western desert life. It was one of the earliest books to suggest that the true story of the West resided in its wilderness condition rather than in ideas of rugged individualism, empire, and conquest. Responsive to her own feelings expressed here, Austin herself became an activist for environmental causes. *Earth Horizon* (1932), in turn, her other major work, is an autobiography with a revolutionary form. Austin records how she felt herself "marked" by a sense of special mission. She remembers how she was mocked and criticized by her family for her "individual divergences" from the norms of female behavior. And to register the tensions inherent in this conflict between the demands of society and her own needs, or what she terms "tradition and realism," she distinguishes between her socially ordained self and her true self in an innovative way. Her true self, which finds fulfillment in intimate contact with the Western landscape, is "I" or "I-Mary"; the false self that others would wish to impose upon her is "she," "you," or simply "Mary." Austin sees her story as special, but also typical. She constantly reminds the reader that other women felt and fought as she did. And she argues for another America in which "I-Mary" might be comfortable: where the centers of power and place have radically shifted.

The immigrant encounter

From the land of little rain to the South Side of Chicago is an enormous leap, in terms of landscape, life, and language. But that in itself suggests just how many Americas were demanding to be heard at this time. Chicago's South Side, and in particular the Irish working-class neighborhood of Bridgeport, was where Finley Peter Dunne (1867–1936) located his most famous creation, Mr. Dooley, an Irish saloon keeper, who was never reluctant to voice his opinions on life, current events, and the social scene. Dunne, a journalist and editor of the Chicago *Evening Post*, wrote a series of monologues for his paper. They were rich in dialect, a genuine and on the whole successful attempt to catch Irish vernacular in print; and the monologues delivered by Dooley became a Chicago tradition. About 300 Dooley pieces appeared between 1893 and 1900 in Chicago newspapers. In these, Dooley came across to the reader as a man of shrewd native wit, and the place where he lived became a solidly realized social fabric. Dooley himself rarely, if ever, descends into the caricature of a stage Irishman: his fatalism, his dark side that views the world as irredeemably fallen as well as the sheer energy of his speech, prevent that. And Bridgeport itself never becomes mere background or local color. It is rich with life and a sense of urban neighborliness, a genuinely working-class, ethnic community. In 1900 Dunne moved to New York, where Dooley quickly became the most popular figure in American journalism. The satirical bent became stronger, as Dooley's inherently skeptical mind addressed the notable events of the day. The majority of the law, for instance, he described in these terms: "America follows th' flag, but th' Supreme Court follows th' illiction returns." The Dooley pieces were published as a series: *Mr. Dooley in Peace and War* (1898) was the first, *Mr. Dooley on Making a Will* (1919) the last. Together they represent, not just a major contribution to realism and the vernacular in literature, but the voice of yet another America.

The dilemma the newer immigrant communities faced, over whether to assimilate or resist assimilation to the norms of the dominant American culture, lies at the heart of the writings of Abraham Cahan (1860–1951). Having emigrated to the United States from Russia, Cahan founded the *Jewish Daily Forward*, which became a mass circulation market leader in the Yiddish Press. His first novel, *Yekl, a Tale of the New York Ghetto* (1896), won him national prominence. It tells the story of an immigrant who transforms himself from "Yekl" to "Jake": compromising his religion and traditions, his dress and behavior, so as to become an "American." Three years after his arrival in the New World, his wife Gitl follows him. On first seeing her at the Immigration Bureau of Ellis Island, Jake feels himself ashamed of her "uncouth and un-American appearance." "Jake the Yankee," as our hero describes himself, is now part of the mainstream; he does not wish to be associated with any kind of marginalized culture. Eventually, Jake leaves Gitl for an Americanized Jewish woman called Mamie. The novel ends with Jake, now divorced, setting off to remarry. But the irony is that, by this stage, Gitl herself is becoming assimilated too, as Jake observes with some irritation. Not only that, as he prepares to marry Mamie, he feels, "instead of a conqueror," like "the victim of an ignominious defeat." He has lost more than he has gained by becoming what he defines as an American. Similar feelings of loss haunt Cahan's other major novel, *The Rise of David Levinsky* (1917), in which a rich but deeply dissatisfied garment manufacturer looks back at his rise from poverty in Russia and in the ghettos of New York. It is another variation on the theme of the high price of success and Americanization.

A more optimistic version of the encounter with the immigrant is offered in the work of Mary Antin (1881–1949). Born in the Jewish Pale, the area of Russia where Jews were permitted to live, Antin arrived in America when she was thirteen. While still young she wrote *From Plotz to Boston* (1899), an impressionistic account of the emigration of her family. And in 1912 she extended her early book to make *The Promised Land*, a fuller account of the hardships of European Jews and the freedom and opportunity they discovered in America. Loosely structured around the Book of Exodus, from which its title is drawn, *The Promised Land* tells of the rebirth of its author in the New World. In America, Antin tells the reader, she was granted new clothes. She was given a new name to replace her "impossible Hebrew" one, Mary for Maryashe, and allowed to "wear" the "dignified title" of her surname "even . . . on week days." Above all, she was offered a new life, the core and agent of which was education. For Antin, "the essence of American opportunity" was, she explains, that "education was free." At school, she learned the new language, the knowledge, that would enable her to become an American, a free, self-reliant citizen. The moment when she entered school for the first time, accompanied by her siblings and led by her father, is rehearsed in reverent detail. It is, as Antin portrays it, the crossing of a threshold. "I am wearily aware that I am speaking in extreme figures, in superlatives," Antin confesses, but these were her thoughts at the time. And, "what the child thinks and feels," she adds, "is a reflection of the hopes, desires, and purposes of the parents who brought him overseas." Antin never lost her belief in the immigrant dream, as her later work *They Who*

Knock at Our Gates (1914) also testifies. For her, passage to America was genuinely passage into another, finer level of experience.

   Probably no writer is further from this optimistic view of the passage to America, the immigrant encounter and the condition of the poor, than Upton Sinclair (1878–1968). Born to a prominent but impoverished family in Maryland and educated in New York City, Sinclair wrote six novels before publishing the book that made him famous, *The Jungle*. *The Jungle* first appeared serially in *Appeal to Reason*, a weekly socialist journal, and then was released in book form in 1906. Sinclair had joined the Socialist Party of America in 1904; and, in the same year, he had spent seven weeks living among the men and women who labored in the stockyards of Chicago. A powerful study of the inhuman living and working conditions of the workers, and the unsanitary methods of production in the stockyards, *The Jungle* clearly reflected Sinclair's commitment to socialism, and it was enormously successful. On its release date, such was the anticipation caused by its serialization in *The Appeal to Reason*, the story of its publication was splashed on the front pages of newspapers from coast to coast. And in the next several decades it was translated into forty-seven languages in thirty-nine countries, making Sinclair equally famous abroad and at home. As the portrait of another America than the commonly accepted and celebrated one, *The Jungle* is the most vivid and lasting example of what was called, at the time, the muckraking movement. The term described those writers who, around the turn of the nineteenth and twentieth centuries, devoted themselves to the exposure of corruption in politics and business. Several leading periodicals of the time lent their pages to the muckrakers, among them *McClure's*, *Collier's*, and *Cosmopolitan*. And among the most influential and popular muckraking writers were Ida Tarbell (1857–1944), Lincoln Steffens (1866–1936), and David Graham Phillips (1867–1911). A prolific writer, Sinclair was to produce more than a hundred works, many of which could be seen as part of the muckraking movement, but he never surpassed the book that made him famous and stands as a monument to the muckraking movement.

   The Jungle is the story of Jurgis Rudkus, a Lithuanian peasant, and a group of his relatives and friends, all immigrants, who live, work, and die in the stockyard industry. At the beginning of the book, Jurgis is young, energetic, and optimistic. He is fascinated by stories of America, "where a friend of his had gotten rich." So, Jurgis resolves to go to this "place of which lovers and young people dreamed." Taking various members of his family with him, including his new wife Ona, he sets out for Chicago. Arriving "in the midst of deafening confusion," the noise and bustle of the big city, Jurgis and his companions are "utterly lost." With few words of English, it takes some time for them to find their way to the stockyards, Packingtown. And what they find, as they approach them, is that the atmosphere grows "darker all the time," and there is "an elemental odor, raw and crude" in the air. The vision is one of hell. There is an "endless vista of ugly and dirty little wooden buildings": the tenements in which, Jurgis will discover, people are crowded sometimes "thirteen or fourteen to a room." There are larger buildings from which smoke billows, "thick, ugly, black as night"; "it might have come from the centre of the world, this smoke"; in fact, it comes from the slaughterhouses. Lodged in Packingtown, in one of the tenement houses, Jurgis and his companions soon discover that America is a land of high prices as well as high wages. And, instead of the land of plenty he had anticipated, Jurgis encounters an economic jungle. "Here in this huge city, with its stores of heaped-up wealth," Jurgis gradually realizes, "human creatures might be hunted down and destroyed by the wild-beast powers of nature." The realization comes to him as he and his fellow immigrants encounter virtually every evil to be found in American industry, politics, and society. With poor English, they are easily exploited by those in power: the packers and their foremen, the police, the political bosses, the real-estate dealers, and all the rest of the "upper-class." The catalogue of suffering is remorseless. Sinclair does not spare the squeamish reader and his narrative approach is the reverse of subtle. Each episode is packed with what seems like redundant detail, to emphasize the point and ensure an air of authenticity. Each character, even Jurgis, is drawn in plain, strong terms rather than in delicate nuances, since the focus is on action and argument rather than personality. Each moment is unashamedly melodramatic and didactic. Yet the accumulative power of the novel is undeniable. Like many other, major works of realism or Naturalism, *The Jungle* achieves its impact from its sheer remorselessness, using the technique of the sledgehammer rather than the rapier. By the end of the story, the reader feels that he has suffered the burden of Jurgis's life with him. And, characteristically, Sinclair turns despair into hope in the final chapters. Broken, Jurgis discovers socialism, which mends him and makes him a "new man." He is "delivered from the thralldom of despair," we learn; and the final words of the novel, "CHICAGO WILL BE OURS!," anticipating the day when socialism will prevail in the city, look to the triumphs of the future rather than the tragedies of the past.

Other immigrant groups might be exploited, in the way Jurgis Rudkus was; Chinese immigrants fared even worse. They were exploited, abhorred, and attacked; then, under the terms of an act of government in 1882, almost all further Chinese immigration was banned. It was in this climate that two of the earliest Asian American writers began their work. Edith and Winnifred Eaton were the daughters of a Chinese mother and an English father. It was a measure of the complex racism of the times that, when she began to write, Winnifred Eaton (1875–1954) assumed a Japanese pseudonym. As her sister, Edith, was to observe, Americans had "a much higher regard for the Japanese than for the Chinese." Edith was not referring to Winnifred when she said this; the observation occurs in her autobiographical essay, "Leaves from the Mental Portfolio of an Eurasian" (1909). But, under the name of Onoto Watanna, Winnifred certainly found success. She wrote hundreds of stories and seventeen bestselling novels, most of them set in Japan. In some of the stories, such as "Two Converts" (1901) and "The Loves of Sakura Jiro and the Three Headed Maid" (1903), she explores the situation of the emigrant with verve and sly wit, emphasizing in particular the confusions involved in belonging to two cultures. But, perhaps because it never really challenges racial or sexual stereotypes, her stories and novels earned Winnifred Eaton considerable popularity and wealth – and, eventually, a ticket to Hollywood.

Edith Maud Eaton (1865–1914), on the other hand, adopted a Chinese pseudonym, Sui Sin Far, and wrote specifically about Chinese people and the Chinese experience in America. Born in England, she spent her early childhood in Canada. She traveled back and forth across the United States between 1898 and 1912, supporting herself with her journalism. And her stories and articles soon began appearing in popular magazines like *Good Housekeeping*. "Leaves for the Mental Portfolio of an Eurasian" describes the position from which she wrote. A tireless campaigner for social and racial justice, Eaton describes in this piece how she gradually came, not only to accept, but proudly to embrace the Chinese part of her identity. "Some day," she declares, "a great part of the world will be Eurasian." That was the positive side of her predicament. In her better moods, Eaton could see her dual inheritance, and her "Chinese instinct" in particular, as something that made her "a pioneer"; "and a pioneer," she reflected, "should glory in her suffering." The more problematical side was not just the slights and humiliations she tells us she experienced when she refused to "pass" as white or Japanese, although, given her appearance, she could have. It was her sense that she inhabited a neutral territory. "I have no nationality," she admits, but her consolation is that, with her equivocal cultural status she may, after all, supply a "connecting link" between cultures, giving, as she puts it, "my right hand to the Occidentals and my left to the Orientals."

The achievement of the stories Eaton wrote for the magazines, and collected in *Mrs. Spring Fragrance* (1912), is that they negotiate the cultural hinterland inhabited by their author with wit, passion, and pathos. With their shifting narrative perspectives, fragmented structures, and rapid changes of mood, as well as with their preference for allusion and intimation rather than emphatic statement, these tales tell us what it is like to be a person of multiple identities in a racist society. One story, "Its Wavering Image," for instance, tells of "a half-white, half-Chinese girl" called Pan who lives in the Chinatown district of San Francisco. She meets a young white journalist called Mark Carson, her "first white friend." "Born a Bohemian," as indeed Eaton was, "exempt from the conventional restrictions imposed upon either the white or Chinese woman," Pan introduces Carson to Chinatown, the neighborhood, family, and friends. Slowly, affection grows between them. As it does so, Carson sings to her a song about the "wavering image" of the moon in the water, a "symbol of love." He also tells her that she has to decide what she will be, "Chinese or white," adding, for her benefit, "you do not belong here. You are white – white." Pan resists his persuasions. "I was born here," she reflects, "and the Chinese people look upon me as their own." Carson leaves for two months and, while he is away, an article by him titled "Its Wavering Image" appears in the newspaper. It is based on all he has learned with the help of Pan during their times together. Pan sees it as a betrayal of confidence, the trust that she and her Chinese friends and relatives had placed in Carson. She "would rather that her own body and soul had been exposed," we learn, "than that things, sacred and secret to those who loved her, should be cruelly unveiled and ruthlessly spread before the ridiculing and uncomprehending foreigner." We do not learn what those things are – that is typical of Eaton's delicate, allusive art. But they are enough to make Pan rebuff a plainly bewildered Carson on his return. Appearing before him in a Chinese costume, rather than the American dress she had habitually worn in his company, she now insists, "I am a Chinese woman." The strength of this story derives from its imagining a clash of cultures that is none the less definite for being delicately stated. Its pathos and quiet wit stem, in turn, from our sense that Pan has not resolved her predicament by her act of will. She may say, and even think, that she is "a Chinese woman" but, as the story intimates, she is rather more conflicted than that. In tales like this, Eaton used her own divided self to explore the divided state of Chinese Americans. To that extent, she not only added another chapter to the story of immigrant encounter; she prepared the way for other, later writers, particularly Asian American ones, who have found themselves in exile in two different cultures.

4
Making It New
The Emergence of Modern American Literature 1900–1945

Changing National Identities

By the second decade of the twentieth century, the United States had become the most powerful industrialized nation in the world, oustripping Britain and Germany in industrial production. From a debtor nation, it emerged from World War I as a creditor nation, with loans to Europe worth thirteen billion dollars. By 1920, the majority of Americans lived in towns and cities, and all Americans had new forms of mobility and access to the national culture opened up to them by the spread of car ownership and mass communication. Many people were to face hardship after the Wall Street Crash of 1929. But if the 1930s, the period that became known as the Great Depression, were a time of crisis, they were also a time of renewed hope, as the United States government implemented policies, under what was known as the New Deal, to try to get Americans back to work.

Between Victorianism and Modernism

The problem of race

Among those who were hardest hit by the economic crisis that followed the Wall Street Crash were African Americans, many of whom had migrated northwards during the first two decades of the twentieth century. Even before that, as the century began, many Americans saw race as the most pressing problem they faced. Certainly, this was true of those African American writers who initiated debate about the "color line" as W. E. B. Du Bois (1868–1963) termed it: Du Bois himself, Booker T. Washington (1856–1915), and James Weldon Johnson (1871–1938).

Washington was born in Virginia, the son of a slave mother and a white father, in what he termed "the most miserable, desolate and discouraging surroundings." Gradually rising to national eminence, he consistently argued that "in all things that are purely social" blacks and whites could be "separate as the fingers, yet one as the hand in all things essential to mutual progress." He saw "the agitations of questions of social

A Brief History of American Literature.   By Richard Gray
© 2011 Richard Gray

equality" as "the extremest folly." Progress would come for African Americans as and when it was earned by hard work, diligence, and thrift: as it had for him, he pointed out, because he had been "determined to succeed." The core text here, for explaining Washington's gospel of progress and his own career as a demonstration of that gospel, was *Up From Slavery* (1903). It is a slave narrative of a kind, at the beginning. But it more clearly resembles the *Autobiography* of Benjamin Franklin, as it describes the rise of its hero from humble beginnings to fame and fortune – and prescribes the same route for other men and women like him. Washington even recalls Franklin in specific episodes. His account of his arrival in Richmond, Virginia to enrol in Hampton Normal Agricultural Institute, penniless, anonymous, and painfully hungry, echoes Franklin's description of his own first entry into Philadelphia. And he models the narrative on the archetypal American success story that Franklin initiated: our representative man rises to prominence thanks to hard work, thrift, and diligence and then, relentlessly optimistic, divulges the agenda he followed that enabled him to rise and will now enable his reader to rise as well. It is hardly surprising that *Up From Slavery* was an enormous success, becoming the most famous book by an African American for half a century after its publication. For it formulates a myth of black effort and achievement that slotted neatly into the prevailing white myths of the time. It was a book that white readers could find appealing, because it was unthreatening, even eager to please: "I believe it is the duty of the Negro . . . to deport himself modestly in regard to political claims," Washington concluded on the crucial issue of enfranchisement, "depending upon the slow but sure influences that proceed from property, intelligence, and high character for the full recognition of his political rights." It was also one that many black readers could find attractive because it offered a measure of hope, however limited.

Not all black readers, however: in *The Souls of Black Folk* (1903), W. E. B. Du Bois offered a comprehensive criticism of Washington's modest stance on black disenfranchisement as well as his emphasis on vocational instruction. In the first stages of his career, Du Bois devoted himself to the scholarly study of the status and condition of black people in the United States. His books during this period included *The Suppression of the African Slave Trade to the United States of America* (1896) and *The Philadelphia Negro: A Social Study* (1899). But Du Bois wanted to reach a wider audience. For him, racial prejudice was a national issue and an intensely urgent one. As he put it, "the problem of the twentieth century is the problem of race." And he wanted to make as many people as he could, black and white, aware of it. So he began to experiment with different forms. These included general studies of black people in the United States, such as *The Negro* (1915), *The Gift of Black Folk* (1935), and *Black Reconstruction* (1935). They included essays, poems, short stories, plays, and sketches, many of which were published in two magazines he edited, *The Moon* and *The Horizon*. They included a novel, *Dark Princess* (1928), and an autobiographical work, *Dusk of Dawn* (1945), which Du Bois described as "the autobiography of a concept of race." Du Bois's activism led him to help found the National Association for the Advancement of Colored People in 1909, and to edit its magazine, *The Crisis*, from 1910 until 1934. But his most influential work was the one in which he launched his attack on Booker T. Washington, *The Souls of Black Folk*.

At the heart of *The Souls of Black Folk* is Du Bois's seminal account of the "double-consciousness" of "the Negro." When he was young, Du Bois recalls, a "shadow" suddenly swept across him. It dawned upon him that he was different from others, "shut out from their world by a vast veil." In this, he suggests, he was and is like all others of his race. He, and they, have been "born with a veil, and gifted with second-sight in this American world": a world that yields them "no true self-consciousness," but only lets them see themselves "through the revelation of the other world." "It is a peculiar sensation, this double-consciousness," Du Bois confides, "this sense of always looking at one's self through the eyes of others." The African American "ever feels his two-ness, – an American, a Negro: two souls, two thoughts, two unreconciled strivings; two warring ideals in one dark body." For Du Bois, "the history of the American Negro is the history of this strife." It gives him or her, certainly, a special knowledge, the "second-sight" of the secret sharer. But it also leads to a potentially disabling ambivalence: "the contradiction of double aims" as an African and an American. The African American longs "to merge his double self into a better and truer self," a merging in which "he wishes neither of the older selves to be lost." That, however, still remains mainly a longing. Despite the end of slavery, the shadow still falls across every back man and woman in America. Du Bois weaves together autobiography and analysis, meditation and incantation in this seminal account of African American dualism, the veil of invisibility thwarting identity and true community. Gathering together intimations dimly perceived and expressed in earlier works by black Americans, it was to exercise a profound influence on later writing.

The notion of the "double-consciousness" of the African American found an immediate echo in the work of James Weldon Johnson. In his first novel, *The Autobiography of an Ex-Colored Man* (1912), the protagonist suggests that "every colored man" in the United States has, "in proportion to his intellectuality, a sort of dual personality." "He is forced to take his outlook on things, not from the viewpoint of a citizen, or a man," he explains, "but from the viewpoint of a *colored* man." This gives the African American a certain insight, what Du Bois had termed "the gift of second-sight": "I believe," the "ex-colored man" declares, "that the colored people of this country know and understand the white people better than the white people know and understand them." But it can also be a source of deep confusion: in the course of his life, as he tells it, Johnson's "ex-colored" hero crosses the racial barrier no less than four times because, being to all appearances white, he can effectively act out his own ambivalence. Unlike his protagonist, Johnson had no doubts about his identity or aims. For all of his career as a writer, he sought what he described as "a form that will express the racial spirit." And he sought in more than one form. Pursuing his quest to express the racial spirit in verse, he wrote poems addressed to the anonymous authors of blues and spirituals ("O Black and Unknown Bards" (1908)) or written in imitation of black musical forms ("Sence You Went Away" (1900)). The most powerful poetic realization of this quest, however, was *God's Trombones: Seven Negro Sermons in Verse* (1927): a series of poems in which Johnson attempted to recreate the passion and power of black sermons using polyrhythmic cadences, vivid diction, and a technique of intensification by repetition. The most powerful prose realization, in turn, and his most influential work, was *The Autobiography of an Ex-Colored Man*. Published anonymously at first, it was reissued under Johnson's own name in 1927, at the height of what was known as the Harlem Renaissance, to become a model for later novelists ranging from Zora Neale Hurston to Richard Wright and Ralph Ellison. Born to a black mother and a white father, a "tall man" whom he sees only twice during his life, the narrator begins by telling the reader that he is about to divulge the "great secret" of his life, the one he has guarded more carefully than any of his "earthly possessions." The secret is that he is "colored." *The Autobiography of an Ex-Colored Man* could be considered the first instance in African American fiction of a first-person narrator, although Harriet Wilson had employed the first person in the opening chapters of *Our Nig*. It stands, in this way, as a bridge between nineteenth and twentieth-century black literature; and that is a considerable achievement in itself. But to that achievement can be added several others. It dramatizes the dualism Du Bois had spoken of in *The Souls of Black Folk*. It captures the inner rituals of the black community, what is called here "the freemasonry of the race," in a way that had rarely been done before. It uses a picaresque form, a narrative of wandering around and beyond America, to enact a search for black identity. Above all, it presents us with a flawed hero. The subjects of earlier black autobiographies had tended towards the sensitive, the sympathetic, even the noble. The "ex-colored man" is not that at all: on the contrary, he is proud and rendered unattractive by his pride. And pride comes here before a fall. In the end, he has to recognize his error: that, as he puts it, "I have sold my birthright for a mess of pottage." Sometimes, he reflects bitterly in the final chapter, "it seems to be that I have never really been a Negro, that I have been only a privileged spectator of their inner life." At other time, he adds, "I feel that I have been a coward and a deserter, and I am possessed by a strong longing for my mother's people." But such feelings come too late. Trapped in the white world now, with two children who are to all appearances white, the "ex-colored man" cannot escape; and he can only reveal his "secret" covertly, anonymously, in the pages of this book. It is a remarkable conclusion to a story that plays subtle variations on the themes of black duality and invisibility – and that makes its points about race by something new in African American writing, a sadly contracted, alien hero.

Building bridges: Women writers

At the same time as African American writers like Washington, Du Bois, and Johnson were carving out new territory in black literature, a number of women writers were building a bridge between the preoccupations of the nineteenth century and those of the twentieth. These included three major novelists: Edith Wharton (1862–1937), Ellen Glasgow (1873–1945), and Willa Cather (1873–1947). Each of these three dedicated herself to the imaginative exploration of one or two particular areas of the United States. For Wharton, this was New York, for Glasgow the South, and for Cather it was the West and Southwest. And each was preoccupied with the social and moral transformations they saw occurring in their particular corner of the nation, and the clash between old customs and the new, that those transformations engendered.

Wharton was born Edith Jones into a wealthy New York family. In 1885 she married Edward Wharton, a man considerably older than her from her family's circle of acquaintances. The marriage, never a happy one, ended in divorce. She was in love for some time with another man, Walter Berry, an expatriate. Berry, however, made it clear that he did not want marriage, and she never married again. The themes of frustrated love and unhappy marriage became common ones in her fiction. Her first book, however, was a non-fictional work, *The Decoration of Houses*

(1897). It anticipated at least some of the interests and strategies of her later novels to the extent that it explored status and snobbery in old New York, and furnishings in particular and taste in general as an index to character. Her first full-length novel, *The Valley of Decision* (1902), was set in eighteenth-century Italy. But then followed subjects closer to home. As a wife and hostess at this time, Wharton belonged to New York society. As a novelist, however, she analyzed its customs with irony. Her New York novels, which are her best work, present a changing society and an internecine conflict between an old, patrician upper-middle class rather like her own and a newly rich upper-middle class for whom traditional ideas of culture were losing their sanctity. They also consider, in particular, the position of women in New York society: torn as Lily Bart, the heroine of her first major novel, *The House of Mirth* (1905), is between personal desire and social law – the need to fulfill the requirements of the imagination and the need to make a good marriage. *The House of Mirth* was a popular success, but it shocked many contemporary readers because of its inwardness, realism, and inclination towards tragedy: in the end, Lily Bart dies from an overdose of a sedative. In 1911 Wharton turned from a New York setting to explore the themes of thwarted love and failed marriage in a rural New England setting, in *Ethan Frome* (1911). But in both *The Reef* (1912) and the moral satirical novel, *The Custom of the Country* (1913), she returned to her fictional investigation of the habits and hypocrisies of the New York social world.

Wharton's closest examination of old New York, however, and her finest novel, is *The Age of Innocence* (1920). Set in 1870, *The Age of Innocence* tells the story of Newland Archer, a lawyer, and his involvement with two women: May Welland, who becomes his wife, and her cousin Ellen Olenska, the wife of a Polish count. Having left her abusive husband, Ellen appears in New York society, where her unconventional behavior causes ripples of concern. Attracted by her exoticism, her difference from the social norms of old New York, Newland falls in love with her, but the constraints of society and his impending marriage to May keep them apart. Still, his interest in Ellen continues after his marriage. This prompts May to disclose to her cousin that she is pregnant; Ellen then leaves New York to live alone in Paris. It is not only external constraints and May's maneuverings that frustrate Newland and Ellen. They are also separated by the very things that attract them to each other. Newland is drawn to Ellen because of her candor, sensitivity, and grace: qualities that are proven by her resistance to the idea of any hole-in-the-corner affair, her pointing our realistically to Newland that there is no "other place" that they can flee to, and, above all, by her departure when she learns May is pregnant. Ellen, in turn, is attracted to Newland by his fineness of spirit and his making her realize that, as she puts it, "under the dullness" of New York life "there are things so fine and sensitive and delicate that even those I cared for in my other life look cheap in comparison." He belongs in New York, she realizes, with its dull veneer and its finely tuned spirit; and he proves this finer side by renouncing her and accepting what he sees as his "obligations." The paradox of a love of such a kind is caught in Ellen's simple declaration to Newland: "I can't love you unless I give you up." That statement takes the measure of a society founded on notions of duty, the many shades of which are caught in Wharton's detailed portrait of old New York. It is also a register of Wharton's own, fundamentally bleak view of existence: that repression just might render the emotional life more intense, that an experience unrealized but imagined might be "more real" than one simply lived through, and that the denials practiced in a closed society breed the suffering which in the long run breeds character.

As a Southern writer, Ellen Glasgow bridged the gap between the hopefulness of the Reconstruction era and the traditionalism of what became known as the Southern renaissance. As a woman writer, she divided her attention between affectionately satirical accounts of the Southern cult of white womanhood, in novels like *Virginia* (1913), and heroic portraits of women redeeming themselves through stoical endurance of suffering and stubborn labor in the soil, in such books as *Barren Ground* (1925) and *Vein of Iron* (1935). The stance from which Glasgow started her career was a simple one. This was to work from the premise that the old feudal order was decaying, in the South and elsewhere, and that the "plain man" was "building the structure of the future" that would replace it. From that premise, she developed two fictional strategies to explain its implications. One was the strategy of comedy: a satirical inventory of the weaknesses of the "aristocratical" person, to show how "stationary and antiquated" he was. The other was more in the heroic line. It required Glasgow to concentrate her attention on the poorer white and the qualities, latent in his character, that appeared to guarantee eventual success – and this as a prelude to the presentation of his success story. The result was to create two different types of novel. Glasgow herself liked to refer to them as "novels of history" or "of the town," on the one hand, and "novels of the country" on the other. Among the books in the first mode, along with *Virginia*, were *Life and Gabriella* (1913), *The Romantic Comedians* (1926), and *The Sheltered Life* (1932). Among those in the second, together with *Barren Ground* and *Vein of Iron*, were *The Voice of the People* (1900), *The Romance of a Plain Man* (1909), and *One Man in His Time* (1922). For all the differences between the two veins of writing, though, the same optimism managed to shine through them both and betray their common authorship; satire and heroic tale were equally shaped by the conviction that the small farm was about to secure the state.

Glasgow once declared that "what the South needs now is – blood and irony." Irony there is, in plenty, in the satirical novels. The blood is shed, spent imaginatively, in the heroic novels: where the reader encounters men and women of such nerve and resolve that, we are told, their "secret self" "could not yield, could not bend, could not be broken" even under enormous pressure. Of the novels of this kind, the most powerful is *Barren Ground*, which Glasgow called "the truest novel ever written." It tells the story of Dorinda Oakley. Forsaken by the man she loves, suffering poverty and injury, she fights back. She restores the family farm, which because of all its barren ground has fallen into decay. She shelters the man she once loved when he returns, degenerated and desperate. But she no longer loves him; and, having been married once, to a man whom she liked rather than loved who has now passed away, she plans never to marry again. She is, she reflects, thankful "to have finished with all that." "I'm through with croft things," Dorinda tells local people, who complain that she has become hard as stone. She is barren since, although she nurtures other people's children and restores fertility to the family farm, she has no offspring of her own. In this, her most successful fictional account of personal and social change, Glasgow has her central character gravitate, according to the gendered terms that lurk just beneath the surface of this and all her work, from what is perceived as the female principle to the male. From the soft, yielding, and passive, to the stalwart, unbending, and rock-ribbed: to adopt the vocabulary only partly hidden in these narratives celebrating the "vein of iron" in human character, Dorinda affirms her "secret self" and, in the process, becomes a man.

"I was a radical when everyone else was a conservative," Glasgow declared in her autobiography, written towards the end of her life, "and now I am a conservative when others appear to be radical." That comment certainly located a change that took place in her thinking. Her last full-length novel, *In This Our Life* (1941), measures the change. Its central character, Asa Timberlake, an older person like Glasgow herself, is a gentleman of the old school and he is allowed to offer a largely negative judgment on his children and grandchildren – and also on contemporary life. Whatever she might like to think, however, Glasgow was no more exceptional in this, her old age, than she had been in the her youth. Her earlier books shared the optimism of those writers, at the turn of the century, who saw the general social changes that were taking place as potentially liberating, not least for women. Her last few works, in turn, belong to that vein of writing, from the South and elsewhere, that sought in the past and tradition a refuge from, and possible corrective to, the upheavals of modernity. At every stage of her career, in fact, Glasgow was very much as a writer of her times: someone writing of social alterations that affected her, especially, because she had been brought up when the terms "writing," "career," and "woman" were just about mutually exclusive.

Like Glasgow, Willa Cather was born in Virginia. Only her last novel, *Sapphira and the Slave Girl* (1940), is set there, however. And in 1883, when she was only ten, she moved with her family to Nebraska. Webster County, where they settled, was still on the frontier and there her father farmed for a year. But then, to Cather's regret, the family moved into the small town of Red Cloud. Cather was an unconventional child, a tomboy inclined to dress in boy's clothes, and she found the small town atmosphere stifling. To escape it, she went to Lincoln, to the University of Nebraska, and then to Pittsburgh where she worked as a journalist and then a teacher. She also found the time to write: a book of poems was published 1903 and then a collection of short stories, *The Troll Garden*, appeared two years later, showing the influence of Henry James. Derivative though they were, they earned her a job on a magazine in New York City. She moved to New York in 1908 and stayed there for the rest of her life. Then, in 1908, she met Sarah Orne Jewett, who offered her the example of someone writing about their own homeplace: an example Cather followed in her second novel, *O Pioneers!* (1913). Cather had found her subject: the West, its life and landscape, its place in American history, the American character and imagination. She had also found, again with the help of Jewett, a way of writing, a narrative structure that was right for her: which was not Jamesian elaboration but what Cather herself termed the "novel demeublé." The novel, she decided, should be without obvious artifice, free from the clutter of well-made, highly wrought fiction. The writer's best material, Cather felt, was there in the novelist, already molded.

Cather had come home to her subject, her source of inspiration. And, although based in New York, she often returned to her imaginative homesite to stimulate her imagination. *O Pioneers!* was written after a trip to the Southwest; and, after visiting the Southwest again in 1915, she produced *The Song of the Lark* (1915), which is partly set in the ancient cliff-dwellings of Arizona. Then, in 1916, on a trip back to Red Cloud, Cather visited a Bohemian woman, Anna Pavelka, whom she had known and admired in her youth. She found Anna serene and happy, and surrounded by children; it seemed to Cather that Anna's story ran close to the central stream of life in Nebraska and the West; and she decided to write about her. The result was her masterpiece, *My Ántonia* (1918). The novel is divided into five sections. In the first, the narrator Jim Burden recalls his early life in the Nebraskan countryside, his relationship with the Shimerda family and the daughter in that family, Ántonia Shimerda in particular. The second records how Burden moves into the small town of Black Hawk, clearly modeled on Red Cloud, and renews his acquaintance with Ántonia, who is now one of the "hired girls" working for a local family. In the third section, Jim, as Cather once did, moves to the university in the state capital of Lincoln, where he forms a close friendship with another Bohemian girl, Lena Lingard. The brief fourth section tells the story of Ántonia's betrayal by Larry Donovan, from one of the "native" or non-immigrant families. And, in the fifth, Burden remembers how, on a return West, he saw Ántonia again after many years, happily married now to a Czech called Cuzak and surrounded by children. Apparently, while she was writing *My Ántonia*, Cather told an old friend that she wanted her "new heroine" to be "like a rare object in the middle of a table, which one may examine from all sides." This, however, is misleading. Ántonia is not seen from all sides; the reader is offered only the dimmest conception of certain moments of her life. What is seen from all sides is not Ántonia herself but the memory of Ántonia carried by the appropriately named Jim Burden. It is not for nothing that, in the short, fictional "Introduction" to *My Ántonia*, another, anonymous narrator remembers being presented with the manuscript of this book by Burden; and, as Burden handed it over, (s)he recalls, he carefully added "My" to "Ántonia" in the title. This, the memory, becomes a thing complete in itself: which is why the reader is never worried by the missing pieces in Ántonia's own story.

A complex pastoral, *My Ántonia* mixes its meditations on the past, American history and myth with a telling exploration of gender. This is a book in which a woman writes about a man writing about a woman. Playing on the ironic possibilities opened up by this, Cather quietly juxtaposes Burden's mythologizing of Antonia with the mundane labor of her life: the role of the woman in the making of Western myth and her role, more fundamentally, in the making of the West. This is a book, also, that pulls no punches in its account of the tensions between "natives" and "immigrants," the "cramped" atmosphere of the provincial smalltown, and the gradual transformation of the American landscape under the pressure of agribusiness. Cather never allowed her tenderness for the uses of the past, or her tactful appreciation of the power of Western legend, to undermine her sense of just how small, plain, and mean life in the West could sometimes be. Her finest books, consequently, maintain a fine balance between romance and realism, elegy and analytical insight. Along with *My Ántonia* and *O Pioneers!*, those books include *A Lost Lady* (1923), *The Professor's House* (1923), *Death Comes for the Archbishop* (1927), and *Shadows on the Rock* (1931). Generally, the later fiction is sparer, leaner, a little more inclined towards the occasional allegorical detail and the moment of epiphany. Occasionally, it also dips further back into the past than *My Ántonia*. *Death Comes for the Archbishop*, based on the careers of two actual French missionaries, is set in the New Mexico territory in the nineteenth century; *Shadows on the Rock* moves further back and afar, into the seventeenth century and the French Canadian frontier. But the determining rhythm of these later narratives remains the same as the one rehearsed in the story of Ántonia. And there is the same densely woven texture of remembrance, personal, familial, and cultural: a shared sense that what matters to people is what they carry from their predecessors, engraved on their hearts and minds.

Critiques of American provincial life

"Too much detail," Cather once observed, "is apt, like any form of extravagance, to become slightly vulgar." Theodore Dreiser (1871–1945) would scarcely have agreed. Detail, for him, was the essence of life, and fiction. Of man Dreiser once declared, "his feet are in the trap of circumstance; his eyes are on an illusion." All Dreiser's major protagonists suffer from a need that their lives should assume dramatic form; and they suffer, not so much because they cannot fulfill this need, but because they do not really understand it. Wealth, worldly success, sexual gratification are the only aims they can know or name, but none of these reassure them or curb their restlessness. They grapple for money, they wound themselves trying to climb to fame and fortune, yet they remain outcasts: always hopeful for some sign that will release them from their craving for a state of grace or, at least, illumination. In his emphasis on man as the naturalistic victim of circumstance, Dreiser bears a close resemblance to such early contemporaries as Crane and Norris. It was Norris, in fact, who recommended that Dreiser's first novel, *Sister Carrie* (1900), should be accepted for publication. In his interest in human yearning, however, Dreiser more nearly resembles his later contemporaries, like Fitzgerald. His other major book besides *Sister Carrie*, *An American Tragedy* (1925), was actually published in the same year as *The Great Gatsby*, although Dreiser had been preparing for it for nearly twenty years.

In *Sister Carrie*, which begins in Chicago and ends in New York, Dreiser recorded his impression of cities that, like life itself, glitter, beckon, seduce, and destroy without reference to notions of justice and desert. The result was and remains a novel remarkably free from moralizing. Carrie Meeber, a Midwestern country girl, moves to Chicago, becomes the mistress of a salesman, Charles Drouet, then the mistress of a middle-aged, married restaurant manager, George Hurstwood. Hurstwood embezzles money; they flee to New York, where Hurstwood gradually sinks into failure, becoming a drunken beggar on Skid Row. Carrie, meanwhile, becomes a chorus girl, deserts Hurstwood; and, although she fails to find the happiness of which she dreams, not only survives but is launched on a successful career. With a natural buoyancy, like a cork bobbing on water, Carrie is ambitious and, like so many of Dreiser's outcasts, given to moral expediency. When, for instance, her "average little conscience" questions her about what she is doing, the reply is simple: "the voice of want made answer for her." By the end of the novel, Carrie is still longing, destined to know "neither surfeit nor content" as she sits dreamily in her rocking chair. But that, Dreiser intimates, is the human condition, not a punishment for the errant protagonist.

Continuing to work as a journalist, Dreiser took ten years to publish his next novel, *Jennie Gerhardt* (1911). This was followed by what Dreiser called his "Trilogy of Desire": *The Financier* (1912), *The Titan* (1914), and *The Stoic* (published post-humously in 1947). The "survival of the fittest" ideas that he had gathered from Herbert Spencer and T. M. Huxley led Dreiser not only to sympathize with the weak and victimized but also to place a heavy emotional investment in the Nietzschean business superman of this trilogy. Based on the character of the business magnate Charles T. Yerkes, Frank Cowperwood, the hero of all three novels is a man with a simple motto: "I satisfy myself." The tone of the trilogy is set early on in *The Financier*, when the ten-year-old Cowperwood, already a "natural leader," sees a glass tank at the local fishmarket. In it are a lobster and a squid; and, every day he passes by, Cowperwood notices that the lobster has devoured just as much as it needs for its nourishment. "That's the way it has to be," Cowperwood comments to himself. Having "figured it out" to his own satisfaction, Cowperwood resolves to be quick enough, and to be like an animal that can "adapt itself to conditions." He rises to power in terms that are both economic and erotic. But he, too, is eventually defeated by the "trap of circumstance": when, at the end of *The Titan*, his business plans are defeated. There is no moral to this, his fall, Dreiser intimates, any more than there is to his rise. The time has come, quite simply, for the pendulum to swing against him.

Despite their obvious differences, both Cowperwood and Carrie are described as innocents and soldiers of fortune, destined to make their way in a world they never made, to fight in the name of aspirations they can feel but cannot name – and, eventually, to lose. That destiny also belongs to Clyde Griffiths, the protagonist of *An American Tragedy*. This novel, inspired by an actual murder case that occurred in 1906, tells the story of how Clyde falls in love with Sondra Finchley, a rich girl who represents the elegance and wealth to which he has always aspired. A poor boy himself, he hopes to marry Sondra, What stands in his way is that another woman, Roberta Alden, just as poor as him, is carrying his child. She demands that Clyde marry her; Clyde plans to murder Roberta and takes her boating to fulfill his plans. He lacks the resolution to carry it through but, when the boat accidentally overturns, Clyde swims away leaving Roberta to drown. Clyde is not tragic in any traditional sense; that is the irony of the title. He has almost no assertive will, the pivotal event of his life, the death of Roberta, is an accident; in his passivity, rootlessness, and alienation he is no more, and no less, than any other man, and, in particular, any other American. With a compelling mixture of sympathy and criticism, Dreiser moves Clyde, in the first half of *An American Tragedy*, toward a moment in his life that, while an accident, seems inevitable, the sum of all his failures of will and understanding. Then, in the second half, he shows in relentless detail how the trap of circumstance closes more tightly and literally on his protagonist: as he faces indictment, trial, conviction, and execution. The result overall is a book that, like *Sister Carrie*, captures both the real conditions of life, as Dreiser saw them, and what he termed "the restless heart of man." It is a tragedy, not in the traditional sense, but because it registers what its author called "the essential tragedy of life," that man is "a waif and an interloper in Nature." And it is an American tragedy because it gives us a protagonist who is the victim, not just of circumstance, but of his own circumscribed dreams.

While his rejection of conventional morality earned Dreiser the disapproval of many readers and reviewers of the time, he was stoutly defended by such leading cultural commentators as H. L. Mencken (1880–1956). Mencken was chiefly notable for founding the detective magazine *The Black Mask* in 1920 and the influential periodical *The American Mercury* in 1924, and for producing numerous caustic essays collected in six volumes called *Prejudices* (1919–1927). He delighted in attacking middle-class

America, or what he termed the "booboisie"; and the defense of Dreiser gave him the opportunity to do so. So, for that matter, did his support and encouragement of other writers of the day who sometimes aroused antagonism: notably Sinclair Lewis (1885–1951) and Sherwood Anderson (1876–1941). Lewis and Anderson are both sometimes associated with what has been called "the revolt from the village": that reaction against smalltown values which characterized many American writers early in the twentieth century. That, however, masks many differences. Sinclair Lewis, for instance, chose the path of satire, a critique of provincial American life, and the middle-class in particular, that became the more tempered the older he grew. His first successful novel, *Main Street* (1920), tells the story of Carol Kennicott, the young wife of the local doctor in the small town of Gopher Prairie. For her, Gopher and its main street are the epitome of the dullness, the mediocrity of American provincialism: what another character calls "the Village Virus." Carol revolts against the Village Virus, even fleeing to Washington for a while. But, returning to Gopher Prairie eventually, she admits the dashing of her hopes for reform. So the pattern that characterizes all Lewis's satires of American provincialism is established: the impulse to escape the restrictions of class or routine leads to flight, but the flight meets with only partial success and is followed by a necessary compromise with convention. In the end, the critique is muted, not least because the last word is given to Carol's husband, Will Kennicott who, for all his stolidity, is portrayed as honest, hard-working, kindly, and thrifty.

In *Babbitt* (1922), Lewis continued his critique of the American provincial. This time, the setting is Zenith City, boasting three or four hundred thousand inhabitants and towers that "aspired above the morning mist." But the satirical thrust remains much the same. The central character, George F. Babbitt, is a hollow man, defined by the objects that surround him, his possessions, and determined, in every detail, by the conventions of middle-class dress and behavior and the dull aim of material success. Babbitt is a typical Lewis hero: someone who can neither give himself wholly over to the business of being a businessman nor commit himself fully to the more difficult business of being a man. He has dreams of escaping, which for him are expressed in the feebly romantic visions of a "fairy child" that come to him at random moments. He even makes gestures towards escape. But, like Carol Kennicott, he is eventually absorbed back into the provincial. Defined, once again, by a world of convention and commodity, all he can hope is that his son Ted will not surrender like him.

What is striking about *Babbitt* is that its satirical account of middle-class boosterism and provinciality hovers close to the affectionate. Lewis seems half in love with the thing he mocks. More to the point, there are no values in the book beyond those of the protagonist; and all he has to offer, by way of resistance to the normality of Zenith City, is feeble dreams, sad moments of escape. By the time Lewis came to write *Dodsworth* (1929), a novel about a retired automobile manufacturer traveling in Europe, the muted, compromised criticism of the middle class that characterized his earlier novels had taken a further turn. The central character, Samuel Dodsworth, is almost wholly admirable. A man who embodies all the solid, practical virtues of the provincial middle class, it is he who truly values not only American sense but European sensibility. By contrast, his wife Fran is Carol Kennicott or the "fairy child" of the earlier novels seen through a glass darkly. It is she at whom the satire is leveled because of her preten-tiousness, her failure to appreciate all that is best about her husband and her homeplace.

Lewis continued to write novels committed to the idea of social and political change: such as *Asa Vickers* (1933), about a Midwestern girl who becomes a social worker, and *It Can't Happen Here* (1935), a warning about the possibility of fascism in the United States. But, by now, he had returned to a reassertion of those very middle-class, middle-brow, and middle-western standards he had begun by satirizing.

Lewis has been called one of the worst writers in modern American literature, yet someone without whose books that literature cannot be imagined, not least because he opened up a new world, that of the middle-class Midwest, to American literature. By contrast, Sherwood Anderson was a deliberate stylist. But he, too, focused his best work on the provincial life of the West. And without that work, too, modern American literature is difficult to imagine, because he introduced new methods of storytelling, in terms of style and narrative focus, and new ways of structuring stories into a cycle. Anderson's finest book, *Winesburg, Ohio*, a linked collection of stories, was published in 1919. Set in the small town of the title, the stories in the book acquire some unity through the character of George Willard, a reporter for the local newspaper who has literary ambitions, to whom all the characters gravitate at one time or another. And they gain further unity still from the "hunger" which becomes both narrative source and subject. *Winesburg, Ohio*, the reader is told, is "The Book of the Grotesque." Initially, the word grotesque appears to mean some incongruity or other that characterizes all the people the narrator has met. But then, curiously, he suggests that grotesqueness is the product of truth or truths. The different characters whose stories are told in this volume all hunger for something, some "truth" to live by and communicate. Snatching up "the truth of virginity and the truth of passion, the truth of wealth and of poverty," they take their singular truth, their partial reading of reality as the complete text of the world. Winesburg is a town full of people who have overdeveloped one "truthful" aspect of themselves until it has achieved a disproportion that amounts to falsehood. Such people long to be and belong, to know the love that would give them identity and communality. They also long to communicate their longing, to George Willard in particular; to speak the needs that their "strained, eager" voices and strange behavior can only articulate in a distorted fashion. They are alienated, not only from others, but themselves; and it is this that distresses and disfigures them. What they want, Anderson intimates, is all that is at odds with the piety and provinciality of life in smalltown America.

The style in which Anderson tells the stories of the people of Winesburg, or the story of Hugh McVey, the Midwestern protagonist of his best novel, *Poor White* (1920), is often described as naturalistic. It is, however, more than that. Quiet and modest in tone, idiomatic in diction, attentive to the minute surface details of gesture and behavior, Anderson's style also makes a virtue of its own awkwardness. And, at its best, as in *Winesburg, Ohio*, that style enacts the problem of communication while solving it: it dramatizes the hunger to speak of what lies beneath the surface of life, in this case to the reader, and it describes a hunger satisfied. In short, it acknowledges both the difficulty and the possibility of telling the truth. It is this acknowledgment, rather than any particular stylistic traits, that was Anderson's principal gift to writers like Hemingway and Faulkner, who were to offer, in their work, far more intense but nevertheless related explorations of both the problems and the potential of language. And as with style, so with narrative structure: what Anderson offered here, to the storytellers who followed him, was a fundamental breakaway from plot into mood and meaning. Individually, the stories in *Winesburg, Ohio* break with the tradition of tightly plotted, linear narrative, in order to tell and retell moments glowing with possible significance. Collectively, they work as a cycle, a group of tales that, to use Anderson's phrase, "belong together" thanks to their intimations, their latent meaning. Anderson was never to write so well again as he did in his book about Winesburg, although there were some fine collections of stories like *The Triumph of the Egg* (1921) and *Death in the Woods* (1933), and novels that made a considerable impact at the time of publication, such as *Many Marriages* (1923) and *Dark Laughter* (1925). But with that book, and many of his other tales, he made a difference to American writing: he showed both how minimalist and how meaningful a style could be, and how stories could brim with quietly revealed meaning.

Poetry and the search for form

The twentieth century was to witness an explosion of poetry in America. The modernist experiment was to be sustained through such poetic movements as Imagism, Vorticism, and Objectivism. The traditionalist search for a past and precedent was to be maintained, not just by the Fugitive group, but in other ventures into formalism. There was to be a fresh outburst of poetry of politics or prophecy, poetry with a mystical aim and poetry of minimalist experiment and pragmatic measure. African American and Native American poets, in particular, were to tap the rhythmic sources of their culture. Bridging the gap between all these later tendencies and the verse, innovative or otherwise, of an earlier period are several poets whose work reflects the search for form, and forms of belief, that characterizes so much of the writing around the turn of the nineteenth and twentieth centuries. With poets like Edwin Arlington Robinson (1865–1935), Robert Frost (1874–1963), and Robinson Jeffers (1887–1962), in particular, the reader is confronted with work that negotiates its way between the solidity and the subversion of the moral self and poetic structure, the pursuit of form, discipline and the impulse towards fragmentation, doubt. Their work, with its intense seriousness of moral purpose, and its questioning rather than collapsing of traditional measures, shades into the old modes of writing as much as into the new.

Nothing perhaps illustrates the transitional status of Edwin Arlington Robinson more than his own description of himself, as someone "content with the old-fashioned way to be new." Robinson's first and last love was what he called "the music of English verse." As he explained it, he was "a classicist in poetic composition" who believed that "the accepted media for masters of the past" should "continue to be used for the future." However, he was far from being one of the "little sonnet-men" as he contemptuously referred to them, mere imitators of English fashion and forms. On the contrary, he was deliberately local: many of his poems are set in Tilbury Town, a fictive place based on his boyhood home of Gardiner, Maine. And he was a genuine original, obsessed with certain personal themes: human isolation, the tormented introversions of the personality, the doubts and frustrations of lonely people inhabiting a world from which God appears to have hidden His face. Few poets have ever understood loneliness better than Robinson: perhaps because he suffered from it severely himself. The early death of his mother, and then of his father in ghastly circumstances, helped make life "a living hell" for him, Robinson said, while he was young. In his adult years, Robinson was to enjoy considerable success. His early work, published in such volumes as *The Children of Night* (1897), earned him wide recognition. His 1910 collection, *The Town Down the River*, was popular enough to allow him to devote himself to writing. His later work, like *The Man Against the Sky* (1916), won him critical acclaim. His trilogy of poems based on the Arthurian legend, published between 1917 and 1927, *Merlin*, *Lancelot*, and *Tristram*, enjoyed a wide readership; and his *Collected Poems* (1921) was a awarded a Pulitzer Prize. Yet he struggled against depression and alcoholism all his life. And his perennial subject became what he termed "the slow tragedy of haunted men" – those whose "eyes are lit with a young light," illusions that at once cripple and save them – and "The strange and unremembered light that is in dreams" – the obsessive effort to make sense of experience when there is perhaps no sense to made. "The world is not 'a prison-house,'" Robinson insisted, "but a kind of spiritual kindergarten, where millions of infants are trying to spell 'God' with the wrong blocks." Robinson saw himself and his poetic characters as notable members of that kindergarten: people whose minds and language, their "words," can never quite encompass the truth about the universe, the "Word," but who nevertheless keep on trying.

Quiet desperation is a distinguishing feature of many of Robinson's characters. The despair may come, apparently, from emotional poverty ("Aaron Stark"), the pain of loss and bereavement ("Luke Havergal"), or the treadmill of life ("The Clerks"): whatever, it is palpably there in an awkward gesture, a stuttered phrase, a violent moment as in "Richard Cory" or, as in "The House on the Hill," the sense that behind the stark, simple words lies an unimaginable burden of pain. Many of Robinson's poems, in fact, derive their power from reticence, a positive refusal to expand or elaborate. In "How Annandale Went Out," for example, the reader only gradually realizes that "Annandale" is the name of a man who has been reduced by some incurable disease, or accident, to the vegetable state, and that the narrator is a doctor who has evidently been merciful enough to relieve him of his life. Such is the cryptic indirection of lines like "They called it Annandale – and I was there/To flourish, to find words, and to attend," that the meaning is not immediately clear. New Englanders, Robinson observed, are not like "those/Who boil elsewhere with such a lyric yeast," at least not on the surface. Their dramas, whatever they may be, are enacted within. So the power of many of his poems stems from the reader recognizing just how much emotional pressure there is behind the spare diction, the poignant contrast between the enormity of feeling implied and the bare, stripped manner of implication. In effect, the reader is often asked to conjecture, just as so many of Robinson's narrators conjecture about the lives of those they hardly know except as inhabitants of the same town. The poem becomes an act of commemoration, in which the speaker recalls and rehearses a life with the discomforting sense that he can only offer some provisional notes towards understanding it.

In his later years, Robinson tended to concentrate on the more positive implications of the human capacity for dreaming dreams of a better life. It was in a series of longer poetic narratives, however, rather than in short pieces like "Mr. Flood's Party," that the later Robinson moved towards affirmation: poems such as the Arthurian trilogy. "The Man Against the Sky," written at about the midpoint in Robinson's career, illustrates the change; in a reflective poem over 300 lines long, the poet sketches out the mature philosophical attitude implicit in later and even longer works. The opening lines establish the basic image, of a man making the upward climb over the hill of life to death, in a way that suggests both the man's diminutiveness and his possible grandeur. This image then leads the poet to speculate on the various attitudes of people as they face death. Representing different philosophies of life as well as death, they describe a scale of increasing negation, from faith to doubt to denial, and are roughly chronological, moving from primitive religious belief to contemporary materialism. Having pushed the argument this far, the poet then develops it a little further. We no longer believe in the "two fond old enormities" of heaven and hell, he acknowledges, but that is no reason for assuming that life is meaningless and death an annihilation. Perhaps there is an order in the universe. Perhaps the simple human will to live and to look for meaning provides a basis for belief. Despite their isolation, and the acute limitations imposed on them, people continue to search for value; they remain dreamers. And perhaps their dreams, together with the instinct to continue, bring them closer to the truth than they can ever know. The world may well be "a spiritual kindergarten," Robinson concedes, but it can offer occasional lessons, moments of illumination however dim and inadequate. We, its members, may not be able to spell the "orient Word" of belief with the few words available to us, but the failure to spell it does not disprove its existence – it may still be lurking there, somewhere.

Like Robinson, Robert Frost was drawn towards traditional forms. "I had as soon write free verse," he once declared, "as play tennis without a net." For him, traditional meters were a necessary discipline, something against which he could play off the urgencies of his own speaking voice, the chance movements of his emotions, the catch and tilt of his breath. Like Robinson, too, Frost acquired fame but never shed what he referred to as his "daily gloominess." His first volume of poetry, *A Boy's Will* (1912), was published in England, where he lived for a while. *North of Boston* (1914), his second collection, became a bestseller; *Mountain Interval* (1916), the third collection, attracted national attention; and his *Collected Poems* (1930) won national prizes. By 1955 he had so many honorary degrees that he could have his doctoral hoods sewn together to make a quilt for his bed. And by the 1960s, he was sufficiently famous to be invited to read a poem at the inauguration of President Kennedy. Yet, through all this, he was haunted by personal misfortune. Two children died in infancy, a son committed suicide, and one of his daughters was committed to a mental institution. And, not just at moments of crisis such as these, he sprinkled his journals with remarks such as: "one of the hardest disciplines is having to learn the meaningless," or, more simply, "nature is chaos."

"I've wanted to write down certain brute throat noises," Frost said, "so that no one could miss them in my sentences." Those noises, he felt, acquired additional pungency and point from being placed in tension with established rhythms and rhymes: what he was after, in effect, was a casual but crafty play of speech and song. That play, as it emerges in his poems, is not just a matter of voice, however, but of vision. By means of it, he explores the paradox implicit in one of his most famous lines: "The fact is the sweetest dream that labor knows." "The poem is the act of having the thought," Frost insisted; it is process rather than product, it invites us to share in the experiences of seeing, feeling, and thinking, not simply to look at their results. So the most his poetry will offer – and it is a great deal – is an *imaginative* resolution of its tensions: the sense that its conflicts and irresolutions have been given appropriate dramatic expression, revelation and equipoise.

"It begins in delight and ends in wisdom," said Frost in his definition of "the figure a poem makes." "The figure is the same for love. It begins in delight . . . and ends . . . in a momentary stay against confusion." The incessant coupling of opposites, the felicitous, serious play that ends in "a momentary stay against confusion" is precisely what characterizes Frost's work. It makes all his best lyrics, like "Stopping by Woods," essentially dramatic in that they enact internal conflicts, savage dualisms of thought and feeling. In turn, it makes all of his best dramatic poems, like "The Death of the Hired Man" and "West-Running Brook," essentially lyrical in that they reproduce, in beautifully individualized form, those same conflicts, turning them into intimate human communication. In "The Death of the Hired Man," for example, the event that gives the poem its title is merely the occasion for a loving argument between husband and wife that brings out their differences of speech and approach. Very different in character, and in their reactions to the hired man who returns to them after a long absence looking for work, they are nevertheless in intimate touch with each other; and they are drawn even closer together by the hired man's sudden death. They never entirely agree but their affectionate interaction, their loving war, suggests the possible coexistence of their differences – a marriage or, to use Frost's own phrase, "happy-sad blend," of realism and romance.

Another, simpler way of describing the circuitous, serpentine character of Frost's work is to say that he is the supreme example of the skeptic in modern American poetry: the person who mistrusts categorical answers, utopian solutions, and who, for reasons he thoroughly articulates, cannot or will not make up his mind. In "For Once, Then, Something," for instance, he plays on the traditional idea of looking down into a well in search of the truth. The narrator, we are told, once peered into the subterranean darkness and, for a moment, saw "a something white, uncertain": but then a ripple in the water "Blurred it, blotted it out." "What was that whiteness?" the narrator asks himself, and can find an answer only in his own indecision: "Truth? A pebble of quartz? For once, then, something." "Something" might be everything or nothing. Having wound through the mysteries of exploration, the poem ends in a series of questions that only underline the difficulties of knowing. The limits to perception, the accessibility of truth: these things remain hidden from the narrator of the poem, and so he falls back on the ultimate weapon of the irresolute, irony.

Irony is by no means Frost's only weapon, though. As his autobiographical poem "The Oven Bird" makes clear, he is a poet struggling to find "what to make of a diminished thing." Transcendence is not available for him in the way it was for earlier writers like Emerson and Whitman. Consequently, he must do what he can with what has been called "a minimal case." This sometimes involves ironic meditations on the human pursuit of knowledge, as it does in "For Once, Then, Something" or "Neither Out Far Nor In Deep." But just as often it precipitates tentative inquiry into the mysteries that hover on the edges of experience, the possible sources of fear and wonder. Fear and dread lurk close to the surface of a poem like "Design," certainly: but, in other poems, Frost's playfulness, his willingness to entertain all kinds of doubts and possibilities leads him in the contrary direction – not to transcendence of facts, perhaps, but to a wondering, joyful apprehension of their potential, to the sense that nature might after all be whispering secret, sympathetic messages to us. "The Most of It" belongs in this second group. It presents us with a situation familiar enough in Romantic literature: the protagonist – the "he" of the poem – stands looking across a lake towards some distant hills, seeking comfort and instruction from nature. In accordance with the tradition, Frost's protagonist cries out to the hills, seeking what the poet calls "counter-love, original response": some sign that nature sympathizes and that he has not "kept the universe alone." But, in this case at least, there is no clear reaction. All he seems to get back is the "mocking echo" of his own voice, confirming him in his isolation. Or does he? Perhaps all the protagonist apprehends is the echo of his voice. However, that echo is described with such dramatic bite, such vitality, that perhaps he apprehends more: perhaps he has glimpsed, if not the Emersonian Over-Soul, then at least some of the strange, animistic forces that give life dimension and energy, that transform "fact" into "dream." He, and we, cannot be sure, and it is the achievement of the poem that we cannot be: that we are left with a feeling of mystery.

Although Frost was born in San Francisco, he spent most of his life in New England, and, like Robinson, his poetry is indelibly marked by the vocal habits of that region and an ingrained regional tendency to fluctuate between irony, melancholy, and wonder. Robinson Jeffers was born in Pittsburgh and studied in Europe. After he married, however, he went to live on the sparsely populated coast of California, where he built a granite house and tower on cliffs facing the sea. Jeffers found his poetic voice with *Tamar and Other Poems* (1924). Reaction to the volume, published privately, was enthusiastic, and a commercial edition with new poems added, *Roan Stallion, Tamar, and Other Poems*, was published in 1925. Many other volumes followed, among them *The Women at Point Sur* (1927), *Give Your Heart to the Hawks and Other Poems* (1933), and *Hungerfield, and Other Poems* (1954). Together, they established Jeffers as the supreme poet of the Far West of his time: a man whose work both imitates and celebrates the vast, elemental tendencies of the Western landscape and the sea beyond. Jeffers declared that his aim was to "uncenter the human mind from itself." He wanted his verse to break away from all the versions of experience which emphasized its exclusively human properties, and to rediscover our relationship with the foundations of nature. Man, Jeffers insisted, must acknowledge the superior value of the instinctive life. He must try to imitate the rocks in their coldness and endurance, the hawks in their isolation, and all physical nature in its surrender to the wild, primeval level of being. This necessarily meant a repudiation of all humanistic philosophies in favor of what the poet liked to call "Inhumanism." It meant, he admitted, "a shifting of emphasis and significance from man to notman," with a consequent loss of those values which, for centuries, we have learned to cherish – among them, reason and self-restraint, urbanity and decorum. But, Jeffers hastened to add, it also meant the discovery of an older liberty, aligning us with the people of ancient cultures; and it involved, too, an escape from the involuted self-consciousness that makes our modern world such a painful one.

Towards the end of Jeffers's life, however, there was a distinct shift of emphasis away from the tragic and towards the mystical. The sense of an inescapable conflict between nature and human nature became of less concern; and the poet concentrated more than ever before on the possibility of union. Of course, union as an idea, as in "Divinely Superfluous Beauty," or a momentary experience, as in "Roan Stallion," is often present in his earlier work, but there it is normally qualified by a recognition of the needs and limits of the human character. In the work of Jeffers's last years, by contrast, this recognition tends to lose its power, and the poet is consequently left freer to contemplate those occasions when, as he put it once, there is "no passion but peace." In "The Eye," for instance, the poet finds refuge from the horrors of World War II in a feeling of identification with "the staring unsleeping/Eye of the earth": the poem is a perfect illustration of Jeffers's claim that Inhumanism is "neither misanthropic nor pessimistic" but "a means of maintaining sanity in slippery times," because it fosters "reasonable detachment as a rule of conduct." In "My Burial Place," in turn, Jeffers anticipates the moment at which the union between himself and nature will be complete, when his body will be compounded into dust. Like Robinson and Frost, Jeffers contemplates mortality here, in severe and immaculate lines that register how absurd and petty the human animal is, and how everything is dwarfed by the enigmatic beauty, the intrinsic perfection of nature. More starkly even than they do, he also reminds the reader that words are nothing but a temporary bridge erected over a vacuum. He recalls his audience to the thought that all human ceremonies are no more than fragile defenses against the time when we must shed our humanity, returning to the earth, our origins.

The Inventions of Modernism

Imagism and Objectivism

The beginnings of Imagism can be traced to the feeling, common among young writers in the first few years of the twentieth century, that poets were playing for safety and sentimentality. In reaction to this, a group began to gather in London dedicated, among other things, to the aim of reproducing "the peculiar quality of feeling which is induced by the flat spaces and wide horizons of the virgin-prairie" – and to the belief that "poetic ideas are best expressed by the rendering of concrete objects." They were joined, in April 1909, by the young expatriate Ezra Pound, whose own ideas about poetry had been outlined in a letter to William Carlos Williams six months earlier: "1. To Paint the thing as I see it. 2. Beauty. 3. Freedom from didacticism. 4. It is only good manners if you repeat a few other men to at least do it better or more briefly." In 1911 Pound then renewed acquaintance with Hilda Doolittle, newly arrived from the United States and calling herself H.D. and informed her, apparently to her surprise, that she was an Imagist.

Among the poems included in the first Imagist anthology, published in 1915, was "Oread" by H.D. (1886–1961). Cited by Pound as the supreme example of an Imagist poem, it is besides an illustration of what has been described as the "accurate mystery" of H.D.'s work:

Whirl up, sea –
Whirl your pointed pines,
Splash your great pines
On our rocks,
Hurl your green pine over us,
Cover us with your pools of fir.

There is a pellucid clarity of diction here, and a rhythm that is intrinsic to the mood of the poem; there is a vivid economy of language, in which each word seems to have been carefully chiseled out of other contexts, and there is a subtle technique of intensification by repetition – no phrase is remarkable in itself, but there is a sense of rapt incantation, an enthralled dwelling on particular cadences that gives a prophetic power, to the whole. It is the entire poem that is experienced, not a striking line, a felicitous comparison, or ingenious rhyme; the poem has become the unit of meaning, not the word, so each single word can remain stark, simple, and unpretentious. In "Oread," the image that constitutes the poem becomes not merely a medium for describing a sensation but the sensation itself. The sea *is* the pinewood, the pinewood *is* the sea, the wind surrounds and inhabits both; and the Greek mountain-nymph of the title becomes identified with all three elements. There is an ecstatic fusion of natural and human energies; and the image represents the point of fusion, "the precise instant" (to quote Pound) "when a thing outward and objective transforms itself, or darts into a thing inward and subjective."

"Oread" is typical of H.D.'s work. "I would be lonely," she once admitted, while living at the heart of literary London, "but for the intensity of my . . . inner life." And this became the subject of her writing, from the early Imagist verse to the later, more oracular poems: the secret existence that cast her, in the midst of company, into permanent but willing exile. The earlier work is what she is most well known for. But the later poems, although less well known, are as notable; since they represent a more open, and frequently moving, attempt to discover what H.D. called "the finite definition/of the infinite." In making this attempt, she drew on Greek and Egyptian mythology, her own Moravian heritage, astrology, psychoanalysis, and numerology, and then fashioned out of those diverse sources a poetry that is at once crystalline and prophetic: a tough, muscular, and yet mystical verse to which she gave the title "spiritual realism." All through her life, H.D. retained an intense belief in the religious possibilities of art. Her great war trilogy makes this especially clear. Written in London during World War II, the three books that comprise the trilogy – *The Walls Do Not Fall* (1944), *Tribute to the Angels* (1945), and *The Flowering of the Rod* (1946) – represent a search for "ancient wisdom," the still, generative center at the heart of the contemporary turbulence. Firm in the belief that "every concrete object/has abstract value," she attempts to fashion the mystery of personality, to recreate her own identity – to write herself by reinventing her life in the process of remembering and rehearsing it. The activity recalls Whitman's in "Song of Myself" as, indeed, does H.D.'s firm denial of egocentricity: "my mind (yours)," she insists, "/your way of thought (mine)." Each individual imagination has its "intricate map," we are told, but each map charts the same "eternal realities"; as in all great American epics, to sing and celebrate oneself is also to sing and celebrate others.

H.D.'s trilogy is an American epic, then, but it is also an Imagist epic: it does not, even in its form, represent a departure from her poetic beginnings. The reason is simple. Like Whitman, H.D. dispenses with narrative; far more than Whitman, however, she depends on what Pound called the ideogrammic method – which involves, essentially, a rapid association of images. Images are, in H.D.'s own words, "superimposed on one another like a stack of photographic negatives": one image or perception leads into another and the reader's imagination is actively engaged, making the connections. Instead of a story, in which events occur in time, or a process of logical argument, there is a juxtaposing of different images or impressions; and their interaction, the energy that passes between them, constitutes the "argument" of the poem. In her trilogy, H.D. characteristically uses an image to describe this Imagistic technique – of the many colors which, at their point of intersecting, become one color. In this sense, H.D.'s trilogy stands, along with Pound's *Cantos* and William Carlos Williams's *Paterson*, as a major work of the Imagist genius and a modernist epic.

As H.D.'s work suggests, Imagism could lead off in a number of different directions. One of these was Objectivism, associated in particular with William Carlos Williams, George Oppen (1908–1984), and Louis Zukofsky (1904–1978). The main differences between Imagism and Objectivism were a greater emphasis on the formal structure of the poem, its physical contours, and a more intense interest in its musical properties, the aural dimension as compared with the visual. But it seems fairly obvious that Objectivism grew dialectically out of Imagism – not in opposition to it but in fruitful tension with it, not least because both movements shared the core modernist beliefs: precision, exactitude, experience rendered rather than stated, the imperatives of organic rhythm and form.

Making it new in poetry

Of all the writers of this period associated with Imagism and Objectivism, none revealed fuller commitment to poetic experiment – a greater belief in the need, as he put it, to "make it new" – than Ezra Pound (1885–1972). Pound's commitment to poetry was total: to poetry as a craft, as a moral and spiritual resource, and eventually as a means of salvaging culture, redeeming history. His disinterested belief in the poem was proved by his dedicated support of other poets. "Il miglior fabbro," Eliot called him, borrowing the phrase from Dante, "the better artist," in recognition of Pound's help in transforming *The Waste Land* into the dense, allusive, and elliptical poem that we have today. Pound was the great evangelist for poetry, and he was also the great assimilator: absorbing and imitating the work of other imaginations so as to make it available for his own audiences. Starting from the premise that the state of art in a culture, and the state of poetry and language in particular, is a measure of its health, he attempted to mediate the achievements of other, earlier periods – to offer the best that had been thought and said in the past as an example and agent of recovery for the present. This was not an antiquarian enterprise; Pound was not simply trying to write "like" earlier poets. His aim, rather, was to reclaim the *principles* implicit in the work of other people: principles that were expressed, and could only be expressed in specific, material terms, according to the language and conditions of an individual culture. "Poetry is a sort of inspired mathematics," Pound said, "which gives us equations ... for human emotions." Human emotions, for Pound, remained the same, but the equations used to uncover them altered with time and place. Each poet, in this sense, had to contrive his own mathematics; no matter how much he might derive from others, he had ultimately to forge his own style – a voice that was more than just the sum of the myriad voices he echoed.

Pound's early poetry, in *A Lume Spento* (1908), *Personae* (1912), and *Exultations* (1912), is saturated in the kind of *fin-de-siècle* romanticism he was later to abjure. There are the familiar poetic subjects: songs in praise of a lady ("Ballatetta"), songs concerning

Figure 4.1 Wyndham Lewis: Portrait of Ezra Pound, 1939, oil on canvas, Tate Gallery N05042. © Tate, London, 2010. © Reproduced by kind permission of the Wyndham Lewis Memorial Trust (a registered charity).

the poet's craft ("And Thus In Nineveh"), love and friendship ("The Altar"), death ("For E. McC."), the transience of beauty and the permanence of art ("No Audiart"). Not unrelated to these, there are some of the subjects that Pound was to make peculiarly his own: the pain of exile ("In Durance"), metamorphosis ("The Tree"), the "delightful psychic experience," the ecstatic moment that is nonetheless perfect for being just that, a moment ("Erat Hora"). There are elaborate conceits, images that call attention to their own *bravura*, poetic inversions, self-conscious archaisms of word and phrasing. What saves these poems, however, is Pound's consummate sense of rhythm. From first to last, Pound was blessed with the gift of what he called "melopoeia": "wherein the words are charged, over and above their meaning, with some musical property, which directs the bearing or trend of that meaning." Most of these early poems are written according to an established metrical pattern, and Pound turns the form into an instrument on which he can play his own music: an apparently inevitable medium for his own voice.

Ripostes, published in 1912, reveals the poet's discarding of metrically regular unrhymed verse in favor of free verse. A poem like "The Return" shows this and also illustrates Pound's growing ability to write pieces that are not necessarily "about" anything in any traditional sense but are, rather, equations for a mood or an emotion. As Pound's work grew in authority, he retained this understanding of the possibilities of rhythm and image but coupled it with a growing distinctiveness of voice and a greater alertness to the problems of modern culture. A poem like "The Garden," for instance, published in *Lustra* (1916), shows Pound becoming distinctly "modern," using unromantic similes drawn from contemporary life. More to the point, it shows him developing his own language: a combination of the mandarin and the demotic, the passionate, the satirical, and the self-critical, that serves to express both his own deracination and the precarious, polyglot character of the society through which he moves.

So, in effect, Pound gradually added to his gift of melopoeia the two other necessary constituents of good poetry, as he saw it: "phanopoeia," which he described as "a casting of images upon the visual imagination," and "logopoeia," "the dance of the intellect among words." As far as phanopoeia is concerned, Pound was helped, not only by his formulation of "do's" and "dont's" for Imagists, but by his interest in Japanese and Chinese poetry. His *haiku*, "In a Station of the Metro," illustrates the Japanese influence and how it helped Pound pursue brevity and imagistic indirection. And the poems collected in *Cathay* (1915) reveal the importance of Chinese verse for him. They were written after he had read the work of a distinguished Chinese scholar, Ernest Fenollosa. Fenollosa pointed out that the Chinese language is made up of characters, each simple character representing a "particular," an image. Each complex character is then made by combining simple characters and, in this sense, Chinese remains anchored in concrete, perceptual reality; it can never lose itself in vague abstraction. Not surprisingly, Pound with his hatred of abstract discourse jumped at this; and, without knowing a word of the language, he began working on a set of versions from the Chinese which, as Eliot has said, have made him "the inventor of Chinese poetry for our time."

Taken together, the poems in *Cathay* are not just a reinvention of a particular language and culture, however, and more than new chapters in the story of Imagism. Their pervasive themes are loneliness, loss, exile: absence from home and from loved ones through some accident, from human choice or historical necessity. Which is to say that these pieces offer impersonal and objective stories through which the poet can express his feelings of uprootedness and isolation. In its own, quiet way, each voice in *Cathay* is a mask, a persona: just as, for that matter, the multiples voices in another, very different poem are – *Hugh Selwyn Mauberley*, published in 1920. *Mauberley* has been variously described as Pound's departing address to England and his farewell to aestheticism. But it could be more accurately described as a packed, allusive, and notably modernistic look both at his own plight and the plight of modern culture. In effect, the dance of the intellect in *Mauberley* is at once lively and complicated. Writing in the aftermath of the Great War (which is very much a presence in the poem), Pound analyzes the plight of modern society in and through an investigation of the plight of its writers, who are tempted, he suggests, either to give in to society's claims, or to withdraw from it completely. Going back into the previous century, focusing power-fully on recent symptoms of cultural decline, moving like quicksilver between different personae and poetic forms, he offers us the poetic equivalent of Henry Adams's *Education*: an ironic, self-critical, third-person account of a multiple, modern person-ality that is also a radical dissection of the miscellaneousness of modern culture.

Mauberley follows Pound's customary route, from analysis of the state of language to analysis of the state of the culture. So, too, do the *Cantos*, which Pound began very early in his career (the first four were published in 1919) and was still writing shortly before his death. Only now the analysis is far more complex because Pound is openly concerned, not just with contemporary cultural decay, but with the possible sources of cultural renewal. The *Cantos* are Pound's epic. Following in the tradition of Whitman, he attempts to tell the "tale of the tribe" in and through the story of an epic hero or wanderer who is, first and last, the poet himself. In doing so, however, his poetic imagination ranges a good deal further than Whitman's, to embrace multifarious examples of humanity, multiple ideas of order. There is a quest at the basis of the *Cantos* which, as Pound suggests from time to time, can be likened to Odysseus' ten-year quest in search of his home. The difference is that this quest is unending, involving as it does the human being's perpetual search for civilization, his constant attempts to rediscover the springs of skill or delight.

It is not difficult to see how the *Cantos* grew out of Pound's earlier work. The imagistic form of discourse, the linking of ethics, politics, and aesthetics, the founding of correct principles on correct language, and, not least, the belief that poetry can offer a verbal equation for those moments when, metaphorically, the human encounters the divine – all these are as basic to his poetic beginnings as they are to his tale of the tribe. Nor is it difficult to see the connections with American epic: a language experiment more radical than anything Whitman ever dreamed of, the *Cantos* set within their open-ended structure a poet who is at once a representative person, a prince, and a pedagogue, a voyager and a visionary, who tells us about good citizenship and offers us its appropriately heroic model. Whether the *Cantos* are a great single poem or a series of magnificent fragments is open to debate. Pound himself seems to have been undecided. How much the *Cantos* are damaged by Pound's espousal of Fascism, which led him to be arrested at the close of World War II (he was declared unfit to stand trial on the grounds of insanity): that, too, is a deeply serious question. What is indisputable, is that, if there is coherence, it is of a different kind than that to be found in traditional epics, and that, even if there is not – and even if Pound held some opinions that were obscene – there is still poetry here that is the fruit of a lifetime's experience, and lines that are among the finest in the language.

Pound was an expatriate. He left the United States in 1908 and, apart from the thirteen years he was in confinement after being declared insane, he spent most of his life in England, France, and Italy. Despite that, he remained a definitively American poet. The case of T. S. Eliot (1888–1965) is more complex, and raises the whole question of literary nationality – what it means to call a writer American or British or whatever, especially at times of increasing internationalism. Born in St. Louis, Missouri, a Midwestern city that Eliot chose to see as a Southern one, Eliot was descended on both sides of his family from early English settlers in New England. "Some day I want to write an essay about the point of view of an American who wasn't an American," he said in 1928, "and who . . . felt himself to be more a Frenchman than an American and more an Englishman than a Frenchman and yet felt that the USA up to a hundred years ago was a family extension."

Southerner, Northerner – and, surely, Midwesterner – by birth and background, Eliot transformed himself into "a Frenchman" and "an Englishman" by a subtle and yet strenuous act of will. After a thorough reading of poets like Jules Laforgue, Arthur Rimbaud, and Paul Verlaine, and a year studying at the Sorbonne, he succeeded in assimilating the achievements of French symbolism into English-speaking poetry. "The Love Song of J. Alfred Prufrock" (1915), for example, his first major poem, employs the Laforgian dramatic monologue, unfolding the fragmentary consciousness of its narrator (whose name, it turns out, is borrowed from a firm of furniture wholesalers in St. Louis) in a way that locates him as a name plus a voice rather than a character. Like so many poems derived from the Symbolist experience, the poem offers us not a verifiable description of the world, nor the depiction of a "real" character, but a zone of consciousness which each of us, as readers, has to pass through for himself or herself. The scene is, perhaps, initially American but it, and the narrator who dissolves into it, are presented in those disintegrative, dream-like terms that characterize many of the best French poets of the late nineteenth century. The name and voice are, in this sense, unlocated: the "one-night cheap hotels/And sawdust restaurants" that are recalled could be part of any unreal city, Paris or London as much as (or perhaps even more than) St. Louis.

After his stay in Paris, from which he returned "perceptibly Europeanized" according to a friend, Eliot spent three more years in the United States before embarking for England in the summer of 1914. Apart from a brief trip back a year later, he did not revisit the United States until 1932; and, although Eliot was to continue these visits almost annually from the late 1940s until his death in 1965, he came to look on England as his home. This was confirmed in 1927 when, in the same year that he announced his conversion to Anglo-Catholicism, Eliot became a British citizen. Almost from the beginning, he had been convinced of the necessity of a literary tradition. Slowly, this idea of a specifically literary tradition enlarged so as to acquire social, political, and theological implications. The individual was to shuffle off the constraints of the self, to find freedom in service to his culture, just as the poet, Eliot had once said, was to "escape from personality" in obedience to the demands of an impersonal art. How Eliot himself did this, as individual and poet, is the story of his career. He moved from *The Waste Land* (1920), where he uses a cunning mixture of Symbolist, Imagist, and dramatic strategies to expose the rootless, sterile nature of his own, immediate culture, through the spiritual voyagings of *Ash Wednesday* (1938) to the more achieved, if still tentative spiritual wisdom of the *Four Quartets* (1943). And in the course of this career he raised, in a particularly sharp way, the problem of his and others' literary nationalism.

The problem can be stated simply. Eliot "became" an Englishman and an English poet, but he did so in a fashion that is characteristically American, that betrays his origins in the New World. His earlier poetry demonstrates that concern with the isolated self, the lonely "I" which is perhaps *the* predominant theme in American writing. Only it demonstrates it in what was to become known as a characteristically Eliotic way: refracted through a fragmented *persona*, the self being dissolved into a series of objective correlatives. At its most obvious – in, for example, the opening line of "Prufrock," "Let us go then, you and I" – "I" becomes "you and I" to dramatize the narcissism of isolation; and the narcissistic ego translates the blank stare of reality into, alternatively, a mirror of its own concerns or a threat to its purity, or even its existence.

And in a very real sense, *The Waste Land* continues this lonely drama of the self. Of course, any genuinely imaginative reading of Eliot's most famous poem is likely to yield larger cultural inferences. Like the *Cantos, The Waste Land* uses a form of the ideogrammic method, dense patterns of imagery and a disjunctive narrative sequence, a radical juxtaposition of different perspectives and languages, to solicit an active response, a collaboration in the creation of meanings; and the meanings so created will probably include commentary on the decay of contemporary civilization. It is, however, worth recording Eliot's own comment here. "I wrote *The Waste Land* simply to relieve my own feelings," Eliot said; and there can be little doubt that a sense of sterility is so powerful in the poem precisely because its ultimate source is personal. At its inception, *The Waste Land* was a cry from the lonely self. Characteristically, Eliot then transformed this cry into a dramatic, imagistic, objective work of art that each reader can experience according to his or her own terms of reference, personal *and* cultural.

The search for otherness, some order that denies and disciplines the lonely self that cries out in *The Waste Land*, is at the heart of Eliot's later poetry. That search is there in *Ash Wednesday*, which marks Eliot's turning towards specifically religious, determinately Christian and Anglo-Catholic forms of belief to provide emotional rescue, something to shore against what he saw as the ruins of modern culture. It is also there in the *Four Quartets*, in which at times the American Adamic mode of Whitman is adopted in order to deny the cogency and truth of all that Whitman believed and said. Whereas Whitman would absorb everything into the image of himself, Eliot organizes everything – and denies the presence, or at least knowledge, of himself – so as to catch a hint, or a glimpse, of otherness. The "I" in the *Four Quartets* is not, as it is in Whitman and so much American writing, the active and reactive core of the poem, its vital center and source of creative energy. It is, at its best, a linguistic convenience, a way of locating the initial source of perception and, at worst, a kind of spiritual undertow that those following the "way of dispossession" must resist. Here, a wholly personal style takes on a grand impersonality: the language and line of Whitman are used against themselves. And here, too, the illusion of personality is raised for a moment only to be dismissed as just that, an illusion: the words "you" and "I" become floating signifiers, which can never be anchored in any meaningful, moral reality.

Whitman does not represent all of American poetry, of course. Still, the basic point remains the same: Eliot was and was not an American writer precisely because the confluence of cultures required him, he believed, to make a deliberate choice. He was an American by birth and an Englishman by force of will. Brought up in St. Louis, where the South meets the Midwest, deeply affected by the introspective inheritance of New England, he became a European, and more specifically an English, poet. Yet, while doing all this, he retained the marks of his American upbringing, as he had to, on his imagination and memory. Commonly identified with the British tradition as he is now, all he wrote can nevertheless be seen in terms of an irreconcilable conflict with his birthplace – and what he believed were the limited terms of American culture. There is no easy definition of Eliot, as there cannot be of any writers of clearly mixed nationality like him. But not just of such writers: others, many of whom never even left their native shores, have found themselves caught in the borderlands between several homes and histories. To be an American has always been a complex fate. And to be an American writer has, nearly always, been a matter of living in the encounter between different cultures, trying to dramatize and resolve the differences.

Not that William Carlos Williams (1883–1963) would have entirely agreed. When *The Waste Land* was first published, Williams recalled in his *Autobiography* (1951), "I felt that it had set me back twenty years." What Williams was disconcerted by was Eliot's academicism: his commitment to a highly wrought poetics that dismissed the pleasures of the local, the pressures of the particular and personal. Allied to this, what frightened Williams was what he saw as Eliot's yearning for otherness: for more traditional forms of culture than anything his American inheritance could supply. Formally and intellectually, Williams believed, *The Waste Land* implied a rejection of its creator's birthplace. Inscribed in its subtext was a denial of the New World, both as a fact and an idea. And, for him, this was anathema. Born in Rutherford, New Jersey, he spent time elsewhere in the United States and in Europe, studying medicine and meeting poets, but he eventually returned to his birthplace to work as a doctor there. And that movement back, not just to America but to one special American locality, expresses his allegiances. For Williams was, above all, a poet of the local, concerned with the specifics of a specific place. In Williams's work, there are, to quote a famous injunction of his, "no ideas but in things." Attention is concentrated on the individual object or emotion or event, caught at a particular moment in time and a particular point in space. Our yearning towards the abstract, what might be, is quietly checked in Williams's poems; and, instead, we are reminded of the homely beauty of the actual, what *is*.

Williams, then, is the great populist in American poetry, for whom the world is a democracy of objects. There are no hierarchies, no one thing is more important than another, each is to be valued for itself. And there are no allegories: no one thing is to be used as a tool, a vehicle to refer to another thing – it does not mean, it simply exists. Whether it is a woman lamenting the loss of her husband as in "The Widow's Lament in Springtime" (1921), a natural object as in "Sea-Trout and Butterfish" (1917), a strange moment of happiness as in "The Revelation" (1917), a street scene as in "Proletarian Portrait" (1917), or an instance of intimacy as in "This Is Just To Say" (1934), whatever it may be Williams's purpose remains the same: to emphasize or identify with the thing, not just to describe it but to imitate it in words, to allow it to express itself, to give it verbal shape, a voice. And the immediate consequence of this is, not surprisingly, a commitment to free verse: rhythms that follow the shape of the object and that respond to the exigencies of a specific occasion.

Individualism of word, object, and person: it is a very American concept, and Williams was, in fact, among the most self-consciously American of modern poets. This was not a matter of narrow nationalism. It was simply because of his firm belief in the particular and local. "Place is the only reality," he insisted: "the true core of the individual. We live in one place a one time, but . . . only if we make ourselves sufficiently aware of it, do we join with others in other places." To be an individualist meant, for Williams, to attend to one's individual locality: not to turn away from even its most alienating features but to try to understand and achieve communion with it. The aim, Williams argued, was not to "run out –/after the rabbits" as Pound and Eliot did, deserting American nature in search of European culture. It was to stay as and where one was, as Poe and Whitman had: to "return to the ground" in order truly to know the "new locality" of America, the particulars of the here and now – which, in Williams's own case, meant his hometown of Rutherford.

There was a potentially debilitating side to this approach to poetry, of which Williams himself was well aware. Poems might resolve themselves into a series of isolated instances, fragments that could not develop beyond the pressure of the immediate moment nor comment beyond the demands of the singular experience. Williams began to feel that he wanted more opportunity to comment and a chance, too, to develop his poems beyond the moment, eliciting and perhaps quietly stating principles that had only been implicit in the earlier work. Sometimes, in his later poetry, the desire to comment on issues is just that, comment. "Asphodel, That Greeny Flower" (1955) illustrates this. Addressed to the poet's wife, it weaves a lyric meditation out of the flower of its title: a meditation on love, empathy, and memory and on the human being's destructive and creative capacities – "the bomb" and the "grace of the imagination." Certainly, the asphodel supplies the occasion for all this: the poet never strays very far from it, or from the sphere of domestic affection. But there is a degree of generalization springing from the occasion, and the experience of affection, that the younger Williams would probably never have allowed himself.

There are other ways in which these later poems begin to comment and expand, though. One, also illustrated by "Asphodel, That Greeny Flower" or, for that matter, by the opening poem in *Spring and All* (1923), was symbolism: in both these poems, particular natural objects come to embody the power of love and the creative cycle. Another, and probably the crucial way in which Williams allowed his later poetry to expand, had to do with his growing concern with structure. "It is a design," concludes "The Orchestra" published in *The Desert Music* (1954), and that precisely is what many of the later poems are. They are, in the first instance, aural designs that permit radical variations of rhythm within coherent and often quite complex musical patterns and, in the second, imaginative designs, verbal tapestries or mosaics that allow within their framework for significant combinations of detail. As far as imaginative design is concerned, the exemplary instance is Williams's epic poem, *Paterson*. Like so many American epics, *Paterson* is unfinished: Book One was published in 1946, and Williams was still working on Book Six at the time of his death in 1963. Long before he died, though, Williams had anticipated this. There would never be an end to the poem, he explained, because it had to remain open to the world of growth and change. This was something his epic shared with all his work, and so too was its general approach; for, in its own way, *Paterson* is as much concerned with a reverent investigation of the particular as Williams's other poems are. The basic particulars in this case are Paterson the town, an imaginative space not unrelated to Rutherford, and Paterson the man who is, like other protagonists in American epic, at once the poet himself and all democratic individualists. The two identities of Paterson are, in any case, related; since from the very beginning of his career Williams had insisted that personality was inextricable from place. So to descend into locality, in this case Paterson, was consequently also to descend into character; to investigate the city, with the help of the imagination, was necessarily to investigate the man.

The notion of "design," however, is not so much a matter of subject as of form, the terms in which this investigation is conducted. During the course of his epic, Williams uses verse, prose, drama, dialogue, excerpts from books, letters, interviews, anecdotes, history, and fable. Every experience recorded, every event or person recreated, is studied closely, permitted the dignity of close attention. Yet out of this conglomerate of individual moments and objects, Williams manages to fashion a total pattern of meaning, a vision of life that draws its energy and coherence from the poet's reverence for simple things, the pleasures, pains, and dreams of ordinary people. "This is a POEM!" Williams insists at one point in Book Four. *Paterson* is that, although it should perhaps be added that it is a poem set firmly within the twin traditions of American epic and Imagist method. "Unless there is/a new mind there cannot be a new line," says Williams elsewhere, in Book Two. *Paterson* is a testament to that, as well: Williams's lifelong belief in the necessity of personal experiment. Perhaps the final emphasis, though, should be on something else characteristic of the poet that this great personal epic of his reveals: which is, quite simply, his capacity for imaginative understanding. For some reason, Williams was able to feel a sense of kinship with any particular thing, to appreciate and imitate its particularity: which makes him, after Whitman, the finest American poet of the democratic impulse.

Of Wallace Stevens (1879–1955), Williams once wrote: "He was the well-dressed one, diffident about letting his hair down. Precise when we were sloppy. But we all knew, liked, admired him. He really was felt to be part of the gang." Stevens was a lawyer, a successful businessman, but he was also a poet. Four of his poems appeared in *Poetry* as early as 1914. His first collection, *Harmonium*, was published in 1923; and, although its relative lack of success discouraged Stevens from further publication for some time, twelve years later a second collection, *Ideas of Order*, did appear. And this was quickly followed by a succession of volumes, among them *The Man With the Blue Guitar and Other Poems* (1937), *Notes Towards a Supreme Fiction* (1942), *Esthétique du Mal* (1944); a *Collected Poems* was published in 1954 and *Opus Posthumous* two years after his death. What the poems collected in these volumes offer is a series of meditations on the nature of reality; its relationship to human knowledge, human need, human belief, and human art. Like many great artists in different fields during the earlier twentieth century – like Joyce, for instance, or Picasso or Stravinsky – Stevens was fascinated by the interplay between the mind and the world, particularly as that interplay was expressed and explored in the different languages of literature, music, and the visual arts. He was obsessed with what he called, in "The Idea of Order at Key West" (1935), the "blessed rage for order": the human desire for form and a sense of meaning recovered, however temporarily, from the essential chaos of life. And he made that, the struggle between word and world, mind and its surroundings, the source, subject, and inspiration of his work.

Another way of putting this is to say that Stevens believed, as did the great Romantic poets, in the power of the imagination. Reality, Stevens felt, was not something given to us, which our minds receive passively, but on the contrary something made, the product of an interchange between our minds and our given circumstances. Or, as Stevens himself put it, "the imagination is the power of the mind over the possibilities of things," "like light, it adds nothing, except itself." Stevens also believed, as writers like William Blake and Samuel Taylor Coleridge did, in the power of the artistic imagination, its ability to create what he called a "supreme fiction" that could give some sense of order, however fleeting and provisional, to life. Stevens, in fact, saw the fabulator, the maker of poems, as a latter-day prophet: someone who creates the myths that give meaning to people's lives and so enables them to survive – and who offers an example to his audience, by showing them how to devise their own myths as well as listen to his. The poet's function, Stevens insisted, "is to help people live their lives." In effect, he returned the poet to his ancient role of bard or myth-maker, offering purpose and a sense of meaning to his tribe. And to this he added another, more peculiarly Romantic and American dimension, which was that of the hero. For the poet, Stevens suggested, is his own hero because his mind, his representative imagination, is the catalyst of events.

"Poetry," Stevens declared in "The Man With the Blue Guitar" (1937), "... must take the place/Of empty heaven and its hymns." Like so many of his great, nineteenth-century predecessors, Stevens was convinced that the old religious myths had crumbled into irrelevance. So poetry had to act now as an agent of redemption. The poet had to replace the priest, Art had to replace the liturgy of the church, Imaginative belief – "belief ... in a fiction, which you know to be a fiction" – had to replace religious faith. And a possible earthly paradise, created here and now out of the marriage between mind and world, had to replace the vision of a heavenly paradise, situated in some great hereafter. "The great poems of heaven and hell have been written," said Stevens, "and the great poem of earth remains to be written." The opposition this announces is at once the motive and the subject of much of his work. It is, for example, central to "Sunday Morning," one of the finest pieces in *Harmonium*. In it the poet conducts a meditation through a woman whose mind is the scene, which has as its focus the choice between two alternatives. One alternative is the vision of paradise proposed to us by the Christian faith, "the holy hush of ancient sacrifice": a vision founded upon the belief that since this is a universe of death, never answering to our desires, then we must look for our satisfactions in another dimension. The other alternative is the vision of an earthly paradise. The universe, the poet admits, may well be a universe of death when looked at in its pristine state, but it can perhaps be transformed into a living, constantly changing "mundo" with the help of the active imagination. It is, of course, the second alternative that is ultimately preferred. Believing that "The greatest poverty is not to live/In a physical world," the poet ends his meditation with a hymn to the earth: the possibilities of our environment, out of which – aided by the power of the imagination – we can fashion, however temporarily, some sense of meaning and order.

The particular spot of earth that Stevens hymned in "Sunday Morning" and elsewhere was almost exclusively American: an important point because, as Stevens put it in one of his very last poems, "a mythology reflects its region." "The gods of China," he insisted in "A Mythology Reflects its Region" (1957), "are always Chinese": that is, the world the imagination embraces is always a local one, and the fictions created out of that embrace must bear the stamp of their locality. As Stevens saw it, this marriage between a particular person and place, was "a vital affair ... an affair of the whole being." It was not simply a matter of idiom and gesture, in other words, but of identity and vision. Of course, the paraphernalia of American culture is there in Stevens's poems – things like coffee, saxophones, and large sombreros – and, like Whitman, Stevens uses a rich, polyglot language that shows he has fallen in love with American names. But these things matter less, as a mark of origin, than the fact that Stevens chose as his starting point what he called in "The Sail of Ulysses" (1957) "human loneliness/A part of space and solitude." Like every great American poet, in fact, he began with the isolated consciousness – Whitman's "essential Me" – and then progressed from there to the new dimensions, the moments of self-assertion or communion, which that consciousness struggles gamely to create.

Just how Stevens made and dramatized the dialectic between self and world, isolation and communion, is illustrated by poems like "Anecdote of the Jar" (1923) or "Thirteen Ways of Looking at a Blackbird" (1923). Both pieces work through repetition and echo, a series of significant if often subterranean connections. Complex designs of word, sound, and image, they offer readers a special world, which may be abstracted from and so depend upon our given surroundings but which has its own innate structure and system of cross-reference. Both adopt a serio-comic, slippery, slyly evasive tone, discouraging us from taking them too solemnly, simply or literally and inviting us, on the contrary, to participate in their verbal and imaginative play. Both, too, are written in such a way as to seem complete and incomplete: so imitating in their form, as well as describing in their content, the continuing act of the imagination, by which worlds are created that are closed yet open, sufficient in themselves and yet subject to change.

It would be wrong, however, to dwell on any one poem as if it summed up the whole of Stevens's work, even in its paradoxes and ambiguities. No one poem could do that. One reason is that the later poetry is, on the whole, less spry and balletic than the earlier – more meditative and austere, more discursive and openly philosophical. And another is that Stevens rarely allowed himself to be contained by a particular idiom even within the space of one poem. Each of his pieces is complexly layered, moving almost casually and without warning between high rhetoric and the colloquial, foreign borrowings, and native slang. As a result, each seems unique, with its own particular rhythms and adjustments – its own special way of turning the world into words. One of the finest of Stevens's later poems, for example, *Notes Toward a Supreme Fiction*, explores his familiar subject: "The imagination, the one reality/In this imagined world." But it creates its own separate "mundo," full of noise, color, and movement; and, rather than any argumentative structure, it is this "mundo," strange, illogical, and unpredictable, which enables the reader to see the world in a new light. It ends, as "Sunday Morning" does, with a hymn to the earth, the "fat girl" as Stevens calls her. Her changeableness, her extraordinary vitality and variety, he concludes, can be caught for a moment in a single, crystalline image. With that image, "my green, my fluent mundo," he says, "will have stopped revolving except in crystal." The revolving crystal is, of course, an image of an image. It summarizes in the only way possible for Stevens (that is, in an imaginative way) what was for him the central fact of life: the ability of the mind to achieve a kind of redemption – by working *with* the world to abstract something of value out of that world, and so, as Stevens himself put it once, build a bridge between fact and miracle.

Marianne Moore (1887–1972) knew both Stevens and Williams well and commented acutely on their work. Of Williams, for example, she observed that he was a poet supremely "able to fix the atmosphere of a moment." But she was very much her own woman and her own poet. "We must," she once declared, "have the courage of our peculiarities"; and she showed that courage herself. She was always willing to be different and to embody that difference in poetry. Born in Missouri and brought up in Pennsylvania, Moore published her first poems in 1915. Three years later, she moved to New York City and remained there for the rest of her life. Her first volume, *Poems,* was published in London in 1921 without her knowledge by two friends, one of them being H.D. Several other collections followed, among them *Observations* (1924), *Selected Poems* (1935), and *What Are Years?* (1941); and her *Collected Poems* (1951) was followed by three further collections and a *Complete Poems* five years before her death. All of her work demonstrates that stubborn determination to be oneself that she saw as the core of personality and poetry. She was willing to risk eccentricity, if it meant the creation of her own measure, and the results were original and inimitable. Just as in life she had her own vivid, odd presence, instantly recognizable because of the black cape and black tricorn hat she habitually wore, so, in her own work, she had her own distinctive, unique voice.

The peculiar quality of Moore's poetic voice, poised as it is between the controlled and the spontaneous, largely results from Moore's use of the medieval device of "rime-breaking." The formal outlines are severe: the stanzas based on syllable count, the lines so arranged on the page as to repeat specific and often quite complicated patterns. But these strict proportions are rendered much less strict by making the stanza, instead of the line, the basic unit. Rhymes are sparse, enjambement the rule, and the sense of run-on lines is increased by ending lines with unimportant words and hyphenations. The mixed feelings of order and spontaneity generated by this complex verse structure are then underlined by Moore's special way with images and words. The descriptive detail is extraordinarily, almost gratuitously, specific, asking us to look closely at the object. Moore, like Williams, tried to capture the exact contours of things in a painterly, microscopic manner, but not because, like Williams, she wished to be appropriated by them or live their life. On the contrary, her firm belief was that, by observing an object lovingly, she could discover significance *in* it which extended *beyond* it. Precision liberated the imagination, she felt; the discipline of close observation was, for her, a means of imaginative release.

There is a peculiar correspondence between Moore's voice and her vision: for the patterns of her verse embody and reinforce our sense of a world where spontaneity and order are not at odds and where the marriage between them results in spiritual poise. All Moore's poems start from a belief in discipline, the acceptance of boundaries. This acceptance was necessary, she felt, for two reasons. In the first place, the mind could discover a safeguard against danger by accepting limitations. A good deal of Moore's poetry is about armor, protection, places to hide; and it is so probably because Moore saw life in terms of risk. The second reason is more significant, however: Moore also clearly believed that, in accepting limitations, the mind discovers fulfillment. Freedom, and happiness, she felt, are to be found only in the service of forms: in an acknowledgment of the needs and restrictions of our natures, the scope of our particular world. For Moore, as she puts it in "To a Snail" (1935), "Contractility is a virtue/as modesty is a virtue" and just as "compression is the first grace of style": as poets, and as people, we need discipline to realize our best possibilities.

On the subject of poetry, Moore declared, in a poem simply called "Poetry" (1935), "I, too, dislike it: there are things that are important beyond all this fiddle." But, then, she added: "Reading it, however, with a perfect contempt for it,/ . . . one discovers in/it after all, a place for the genuine." For Moore, as she goes on to explain, "genuine" poetry is the absolute of the "high-sounding"; it is "useful" just as Whitman believed it was – in the sense that all things necessary to the perpetuation of life are. Everything is the stuff of poetry, even "business documents and/school-books." "All these phenomena are important," she says; only "half poets" make the mistake of thinking otherwise. The range of Moore's work shows how closely she followed her own prescription for "genuine" poetry. Each of her best pieces constitutes an act of imaginary possession, in which she perceives an object carefully, and then attempts to absorb it – to grasp its significance in her mind. There is no imperialism of the intellect here. The essential properties of the object are not denied; on the contrary, it is precisely because the poet acknowledges them that she can then go on, in language that is all sinew, severe and pure, to discover ulterior meaning. Many of her poems concerned with inanimate objects, such as "An Egyptian Pulled Glass Bottle in the Shape of the Fish" (1935), are what William Carlos Williams called "anthologies of transit ... moving rapidly from one thing to the next" and thereby giving "the impression of a passage through ... of ... swiftness impaling beauty." They depend, in effect, on their deftness of vision and lightness of touch, their absolute refusal to moralize in the conventional way. In turn, her animal poems are notable for the refusal to anthropomorphize. In "The Frigate Pelican" (1935), for example, Moore first insists on the bird's remoteness from man, "a less/limber animal." Only when Moore has established this difference does she then go on to make the moral discovery. "The unconfiding frigate bird," the poet tells us, "hides/in the height and in the majestic/display of his art." The creature may exist apart from human concerns but in the very act of doing so he seems to offer an example: his capacity for going his own way can, after all, be translated into *strictly human terms*. He has the courage of his own peculiarities: he follows the truths and limitations of his nature. So, paradoxically, the bird is "like" the good man in being so "unlike" him: like the good man and, Moore might have added, like the good poet.

"To be nobody-but-yourself in a world that is doing its best, night and day, to make you everybody else – means to fight the hardest battle which any human being can fight." Marianne Moore would undoubtedly have approved of this remark made by e.e. cummings (1894–1962). Perhaps she knew of it, since the two were friends. But, whereas Moore's individualism led her towards a firm (if idiosyncratic) belief in discipline, cummings's individualism led him towards a kind of imaginative anarchism. To be "nobody-but-yourself," he felt, you had to achieve liberation from the "unworld," the mind-forged manacles of society and culture. You would then become "incorrigibly and actually alive," experiencing everything with a "unique dimension of intensity"; and you could begin to discover a world in which love transcends time, natural spontaneity prevails over the demands of habit and convention, and the dreams of each particular person are the supreme reality. According to cummings, freedom was not easy: especially, freedom in poetry. "As for expressing nobody-but-yourself in words," he declared, "that means working just a little harder than anybody who isn't a poet can possibly imagine." His aim was to create a unique, and where necessary eccentric, voice to express his unique, sometimes eccentric, personality; and, in order to fulfill this aim he armed himself with a whole battery of technical effects – free verse or, on occasion, a highly original development of traditional verse forms, irregular typography, startling imagery, word coinages, and syntactical or grammatical distortions.

Like Twain and Whitman, cummings chooses "roughs and little children" for his heroes: outsiders who, according to the Romantic and American notions of things, have achieved absolute selfhood. Among the roughs is Buffalo Bill, a typically Western hero associated with the careless energy of the frontier: "he was a handsome man," cummings tells us, in "Buffalo Bill's, defunct" (1920), who used to "break onetwothreefourfivepigeonsjustlikethat." And among the other exceptional individuals and supreme individualists is cummings's own father, celebrated in one of his most famous poems, "my father moved through dooms of love" (1954). cummings has also written frequently about love: in part because, as he sees it, love offers access to that dimension of intensity needed to be "incorrigibly and actually alive." And his best love poems are precisely those that combine intense personal feeling with intelligence and verbal felicity. In "since feeling is first" (1926), for instance, the poet wittily mocks the rules and regulations of language, the very disciplines he is using: "who pays any attention/to the syntax of things," he insists, "will never wholly kiss" the woman he is addressing. Similarly, in "somewhere i have never travelled, gladly beyond" (1958), cummings alters the conventional word-order and employs a delicate mixture of adverbs, repetition, and nicely placed parentheses to create a gently ruminative tone. We are obliged to pause while we read this poem, and so experience that attitude of patient meditation which is, apparently, one of the special blessings of love.

Closely related to cummings's poetry of love are his erotic poems. cummings's erotic verse is at its best when it is at its funniest, as in "she being Brand/– new." In fact, a lot of his poetry generally is at its best in this vein. He is probably the finest American comic poet of the twentieth century because his comedy issues from serious commitments: a dedication to Eros, the intensities of physical love, and a hatred of "manunkind" – those people who reject such intensities in favor of the language and instincts of the crowd. In his best comic poems, he fuses swingeing comic polemic and verbal jugglery, trenchant satire and typographical play. "next to of course god america;" (1926), for instance, is a brilliant parody of patriotic cant that makes a powerful point about people who prefer to lose their identity in some anonymous nationalistic mass. At its most extreme, cummings's commitment to individualism and anarchic experiment can lead to difficulties of interpretation. At its best, though, his writing blends the visual dimension with the aural: as in "enter no (silence is the blood whose flesh" (1963), written towards the end of his life, in which the poet asks the "terrible anonymity" of death to "enfold" him. Characteristically, cummings responded to death, with fear certainly, but also with wonder: to be enfolded in "terrible anonymity," he felt, was a unique experience that nevertheless deserved comparison with other, unique moments of intensity in life.

It would be an exaggeration to say that, in his later poems, cummings was edging towards mysticism; it was more a sense of death as an adventure. Other modernist poets were, however, driven towards the mystical impulse: among them, Muriel Rukeyser (1913–1980), Laura (Riding) Jackson (1901–2000) and, above all, Hart Crane (1899–1932). Crane never lost his belief in the religious possibilities of poetry. It became and remained for him a means of absolute vision. Poems should, he felt, carry their readers alike "toward a state of consciousness," an "innocence" or "absolute beauty": a condition in which "there may be discoverable new forms, certain spiritual illuminations." Crane may have been driven toward this pursuit of what he termed "a more ecstatic goal" by the pain and tragedy of his life. As a child, he suffered from what he later described as "the curse of sundered parenthood": his parents separated, his mother was admitted to a sanatorium, and he went to live with his grandparents. As an adult, he enjoyed some success as a poet: his first volume, *White Buildings*, appeared in 1926, and was reasonably well received; his most famous poem, *The Bridge*, was published privately in 1929 and then in a general edition in 1930. But he had to cope with being a homosexual at a time when homosexuality was against the law. And, as he grew older, he was increasingly dogged by a sense of failure, alcoholic dependency, and a breakdown in personal relationships. While still only thirty-two, Crane disappeared from the ship returning him from Mexico to New York, and it is probable that he committed suicide by leaping into the sea. It is perhaps no wonder, then, that he sought in his work, not so much escape as a means of mystical redemption. Each of his poems, Crane hoped, would supply the reader with "a single new word, never before spoken, and impossible to enunciate but self-evident in the consciousness henceforward." Each, in supplying an access to purer vision, would create a language rather than just use one.

"As a poet," Crane declared, "I may very probably be more interested in the so-called illogical impingements of the connotations of words on the consciousness . . . than I am interested in the preservation of their logically rigid signification." He saw each word as a cumulus of possibilities and latent associations many of which could be fired into life by their verbal surrounds – by the words, and combinations of words, with which they were juxtaposed. The overtones of his language, consequently, tend to matter more than its strictly denotative meaning. This is as true of the earlier poetry as it is of the later. But in the earlier, as in, say, "Chaplinesque," the positive overtones – the feelings of redemptive possibility generated by the words – tend to be tentative and partial. These gradually disappeared, as Crane went in search of what he called "the metaphysics of absolute knowledge." The immediate cause of this alteration was a personal experience. Crane apparently enjoyed a moment of vision, or mystical seizure, which opened fresh possibilities in himself, and convinced him that "we must somehow touch the clearest veins of eternity flowing through the crowds around us." His long poem "For the Marriage of Faustus and Helen" grew directly out of his mystical experience and tried to recover it, making it available to every one of his readers. Faustus, Crane explained, is "the symbol of . . . the poetic and imaginative man of all times," Helen the symbol of an abstract "sense of beauty"; and the marriage between them is seen, not as an event really, but as a continuing possibility – the moment of communion between the soul and the spirit of Beauty which illuminates all existence afterwards.

The poetry that followed "Faustus and Helen" includes "At Melville's Tomb," a hymn of praise to the prophetic author of *Moby-Dick*. But perhaps the most powerful and moving expression of Crane's visionary impulse in his lyric poetry is to be found in "Voyages." A series of six poems written over three years, these are, as Crane explained at the time he was writing them, "love poems" and "sea poems" too: the sea appears in them as a threat to the poet-lover and as a rival, as a partner, an enemy, and eventually as a source of comfort and vision. One reason for the constant presence of the sea in the sequence is that the person to whom they are addressed was a sailor living temporarily in New York; another, that the poet and his lover stayed together in an apartment overlooking the harbor; and still another, that the sea was always a suggestive image for Crane. Like Whitman and Melville, he used the sea to describe both the cruelty of this "broken" world and the mysterious "answers" that ultimately might make the world whole again.

Apart from "Voyages," Crane's greatest achievement of his visionary years was his attempt at what he termed a "Myth of America," *The Bridge*. "I am concerned with the future of America," Crane wrote, "not because I think America has any so-called par value as a state.... It is only because I feel persuaded that there are destined to be discovered certain as yet undefined spiritual qualities ... not to be developed so completely elsewhere." It is the old problem of the American dream the poet poses, in a series of eight poems that follow the westward thrust of the bridge into the body of the continent. The movement is one in time as well as space; and as Crane moves across the continent he continually presents the reader with the same question. How, he asks, can the ideal possibilities of people be liberated so as to recover the kingdom of heaven on earth? How can a bridge be constructed between the world in which we live and the world of the imagination, so that the life of the individual may assume a fresh nobility and the forms of the community approximate to the divine? Having asked the question, he also tries to answer it. For Crane is no less visionary in that he sees himself as an agent of liberation, formulating in his work the new relationship between consciousness and reality which will make the changes he requires possible. *The Bridge*, like so much of Crane's verse, offers a series of visionary acts intended to alter our minds as a preliminary to altering our surroundings. Elliptical and allusive in texture, associative and disjunctive in structure, *The Bridge* is clearly much more of a *modern* epic than "Song of Myself," "Crossing Brooklyn Ferry," or *Leaves of Grass* as a whole. Yet it is, finally, in that great tradition initiated by Whitman, in that it is, above all, an *American* epic, concerned with spiritual possibility rather than historical achievement, creating a hero or heroic consciousness instead of simply celebrating one. Like all other major attempts at American epic, *The Bridge* is responsive to the material pressures of the nation and its promise – which, for Crane, means its mystical potential. And it remains open, requiring the reader to complete it – by continuing the spiritual journey begun by the poet.

Making it new in prose

As Gertrude Stein (1874–1946) was dying, she asked those with her, "What is the answer?" There was no reply and, after a short pause, she laughed and added, "Then what is the question?" Those last words were characteristic of a writer who was committed to experiment and inquiry, and in particular to asking fundamental questions about the relationship between language and reality. "Beginning again and again is a natural thing," she wrote in *Composition as Explanation* (1926). As she saw it, innovation was necessary because it was the "business of art" to live in "the complete and actual present." The enemies were traditional narrative, with its reliance on habit and continuity rather than instantaneousness, and memory. "It is very curious," she declared in *What Are Masterpieces* (1940), "you begin to write something and suddenly you remember something and if you continue to remember your writing gets very confused." To see the thing as it is, the thing-in-itself rather than the thing in history, was her aim: and that meant clearing away the grime of old emotions and associations. "After all," she suggested in *Picasso* (1938), "the natural way to count is not that one and one make two but go on counting one and one and one." Applied to prose, this would mean no "assembling," no comparison, no increasing density of significance; it would mean a style that, literally, was not additive. Language should become a recreation of each perception ("now and now and now"), "composition" rather than "description." It should involve, fundamentally, repetition, with small additions and modifications catching the differences as well as the similarities between each separate moment. For Stein, this project, not only to live in the actual present but "to completely express that actual present" (as she put it in her *Lectures in America* (1935)), was an aesthetic imperative but also, critically, an American one. This was because Americans were, supremely, of the present. "It has always seemed to me a rare privilege, this, of being an American, a real American, one whose tradition it has taken scarcely sixty years to create," she confessed in *The Making of Americans* (1906–1908, published in 1925). "If you are an American," she added in *Narration* (1935), "gradually you find that really it is not necessary . . . that anything that everything has a beginning a middle and an ending." You return to "the simplicity of something always happening," the purity of what is existing in the present and for itself, and to a language that evokes the sheer quality of the here and now.

Whitman was singled out as exemplary here: "he wanted really wanted to express the thing," Stein insisted in *Lectures in America*. So too were the modernist visual experiments of Picasso and the contemporary cinema. Picasso, Stein suggested, was trying to look at things as if for the first time: like a child who sees only vivid fragments – one side of its mother's face, for example – and has not yet learned to infer the whole. What she found in Picasso was what she wanted in her own work, "things seen without association but simply as things seen." And she also found it in the cinema. "The cinema has offered a solution of this thing," she explains in *Lectures in America*: the thing, that is, of simulating people, objects, emotions, "as they are existing" and without having recourse to "remembering." Reading her prose is sometimes like holding a strip of movie film and looking at each frame separately. There is stillness, newness, difference in each frame or phrase but there is also the impulse towards process, motion – registered, in Stein's work, in particular, in her preference for verbs and participles over nouns and adjectives, and her minimal use of punctuation. The present and process: that was a very American coupling, as well as a modernist one, as Stein knew well. "It is something strictly American to conceive a space that is filled with moving," she observed in *Lectures in America*, "a space of time that is filled always with moving."

Stein herself left America in 1903. Having spent her early years in Vienna and Paris as well as the United States, she moved back to Paris where she lived until her death, except for the years of Nazi occupation, when she moved to the south. A lesbian, she lived with another expatriate American, Alice B. Toklas, from 1907. A friend of such painters as Picasso, Matisse, and Braque, she established a salon in the 1920s that became a gathering place for both European artists and American expatriates like Hemingway and Fitzgerald. Her first published work, *Three Lives: Stories of the Good Anna, Melanctha, and the Gentle Lena* (1904–1905, published 1909), shows some of the influence of Naturalism. But already the hallmarks of Stein's mature style are there, especially in the second section concerning the black woman Melanctha. Melanctha is defined by her excited involvement in the present moment. And to capture this, Stein uses a style marked by repetition, that moves ever forward in a rhythmic pattern with an emphasis placed on the verb. Nouns being names, Stein observed in *Lectures in America*, "things once they are named the name does not go on doing anything to them and so why write in nouns." With poetry, however, she held a different theory of language. Although nouns did not carry prose forward, Stein argued, "you can love a name and if you love a name then saying that name any number of times only makes you love it more." And poetry is "really loving the name of anything," she said. So in *Tender Buttons* (1914), her prose and poetry meditation on "Objects: food: rooms," she sometimes dwells upon nouns: repeating one as if, each time it is repeated, a bit of inertia and impercipience is shaken loose off it and the reality is freshly brought to our

Figure 4.2 Portrait of Gertrude Stein and Alice B. Toklas. Carl Mydans/Time & Life Pictures/ Getty Images.

minds. That strategy is at work in what is perhaps her most famous phrase: "a rose is a rose is a rose is a rose." "I caressed completely caressed and addressed the noun" here, she later explained, so as to take the reader away from the common word and towards the rare reality. It was her way of pursuing a strategy common in American writing: to reassert the presence of the miraculous in the commonplace and so replace habit with wonder.

Altogether, Stein produced over 500 titles: novels, poems, plays, articles, memoirs, and portraits of the famous. These included *The Geographical History of America* (1935), *Ida: A Novel* (1940), a relatively straightforward account of a contemporary American woman, and *The Mother of Us All* (1945–1946), a portrait of the nineteenth-century American leader Susan B. Anthony. One of her best-known works from her later period is *The Autobiography of Alice B. Toklas* (1933), a fictionalized account of her own life from the point of view of her companion and partner. Stein had a high opinion of her own work that has not always been shared. She claimed that only three writers of her time were being true to the writerly imperatives she outlined: Proust, Joyce, and herself. No matter the debate over her achievement, though, there is no doubt that she was a major innovator, one of the leading figures in American literary modernism. Ernest Hemingway confessed that he was grateful to Stein "for everything I learned from her about the abstract relationship of words." Many other writers said, or could have said, the same. There may be doubts about the aesthetic answers she came up with, but there can be no doubt that she always asked the right questions.

Three modernist writers who asked questions, in particular, about the condition of being a woman were Elizabeth Madox Roberts (1881–1941), Djuna Barnes (1892–1982) and, above all, Katherine Anne Porter (1890–1980). Porter, born in

Texas, worked on a newspaper in Colorado before spending many years in Mexico and Europe. It was the experience of foreign cultures that supplied the catalyst for her first collection of stories, *Flowering Judas and Other Stories* (1930). Several of these stories are set in Mexico and, whatever the setting, they explore the theme that was to dominate her writing: a woman's search for independence, the conflict between this and, on the one hand, the pressures of custom and tradition, and, on the other, her own desire for love and the conventional security of home and family. That theme is dramatized with particular subtlety and passion in *Pale Horse, Pale Rider* (1939), a volume consisting of three short novels, and also in the stories collected under the title "The Old Order" in *Collected Stories* (1965). Miranda Rhea, the central character in "The Old Order" and two of the narratives in the 1939 collection, is semi-autobiographical. Growing up in the South, she has to learn simultaneously about the limitations inherent in the codes transmitted to her by her family and about the scope of her responsibilities. Eventually, these two levels of her story, the examination of impersonal myth and the issue of personal development, become inseparable, since the static and disciplined world into which Miranda is born is seen to be typical of the Old South and of childhood; while Miranda's gradual freeing of herself from her environment and the forms of behavior it dictates is, Porter intimates, as much the consequence of its general decay as of her own increasing maturity. Becoming an adult, she becomes less of a conventional Southerner; forsaking childhood and childish things, she forsakes along with them the codes and ceremonies of the old plantation. The lessons learned by Miranda in growing up are confirmed in a story like "Pale Horse, Pale Rider." Set during World War I, it is nominally about her love for a soldier who dies in an epidemic. More fundamentally, it is about Miranda learning to rely on nobody but herself because, in the final analysis, everyone is alone. Experiencing near-fatal illness, she sinks deliriously "through deeps under deeps of darkness," until she reaches one "minute fiercely burning particle of being . . . that relied upon nothing beyond itself for strength." It is her self, her individual consciousness and her stubborn will to live: "Trust me, the hard unwinking angry point of light said. Trust me. I stay." That trust in an independent consciousness is the core value in Porter's stories; and it is expressed not only in what Porter says but how she says it. Her finest pieces demonstrate that agility and luminosity of mind apparently so essential to travelers along what she called "the downward path to wisdom." All her characters need to guide them through their lives is shown to be there in the controlling intelligence of the narrative; in this sense, as in so many instances of modernism, the medium of Porter's work *is* its meaning.

Of all American writers concerned with the inventions of modernism, F. Scott Fitzgerald (1896–1940) was the most autobiographical. Finding in the compulsions of his life the contours of his fiction, he sustained for his generation the great American romance of the self. It was a romance, however, that was alive to the dissonances and disjunctions of the modern age and that was refracted through Fitzgerald's own sense of the porous, plural nature of his personality. "Sometimes," Fitzgerald once said, "I don't know whether I'm real or whether I'm a character in one of my own novels." And there is no doubt that the protagonists of books like *This Side of Paradise* (1920), *The Great Gatsby* (1926), *Tender is the Night* (1934), and *The Last Tycoon* (1941) bear an extraordinary resemblance to their creator. In each case, there is the same commitment to flamboyant excess, combined with a very personal kind of idealism; in each case, too, there is a testing, a trying out taking place – of the dreams of power, possibility, and wealth that have fueled America and individual Americans and of how those dreams can be negotiated in a world dedicated to consumption, a surfeit of commodities. "There never was a good biography of a good novelist," Fitzgerald observed in his notebooks. "There couldn't be. He is too many people." And, as usual, when he was being most perceptive, that comment sprang from observation of himself. Fitzgerald was, as he once put it, "a cynical idealist." He could maneuver his way through the dreams and realities that captivated him and his fellow Americans and moderns: he could measure both the necessity and the impossibility of idealism, the "green light" in the distance that heroes like Jay Gatsby stretch out towards and never quite reach. Easily as much as any American writer, and more than most, Fitzgerald demonstrates the paradox that self-revelation, ultimately, can be a revelation of humanity.

That comes out with particular clarity in Fitzgerald's finest novel, *The Great Gatsby* (1926). In writing *The Great Gatsby*, Fitzgerald set out, as he put it, to "make something *new* – something extraordinary and beautiful and simple and intricately patterned." And, to achieve this, the first and most important choice he made was to drop the third-person narrator of his two previous novels: *This Side of Paradise* and *The Beautiful and Damned* (1922). Instead of an omniscient viewpoint, there is a fictional narrator: Nick Carraway, a man who is only slightly involved in the action but who is profoundly affected by it. To some extent, Nick is quite like the protagonist Jay Gatsby. Like so many representative figures of the 1920s, including Fitzgerald himself, both are young people from the Midwest trying to prove themselves in the East. The East, and in

Figure 4.3 F. Scott and Zelda Fitzgerald in a car in front of their Westport home, photo 1920, taken on their honeymoon. Princeton University Library. F. Scott Fitzgerald Papers. Manuscripts Division. Department of Rare Books and Special Collections.

particular its cities, have become for them a new frontier, a neutral space in which their dreams of wealth, measureless power, and mobility may perhaps be realized. Both Nick and Gatsby, too, have a love affair with a charismatic woman that ends in disillusion: Gatsby with Daisy Buchanan (a character modeled in part on Fitzgerald's wife, Zelda Sayre) and Nick with a glamorous golf professional called Jordan Baker. This creates a bond of sympathy between the two men. Part of the immense charm of this novel is inherent in its tone, of elegiac romance. Nick is looking back on an action already completed that, as we know from the beginning, ended in disaster, some "foul dust that floated in the wake" of Gatsby's dreams; he is also recording how he grew to sympathize, like and admire Jay Gatsby – on one memorable level, this is the story of a love affair between two men. Liking, or even loving, does not mean approval, however; and it does not inhibit criticism. Nick has had "advantages" that Jay Gatsby, born to poverty as James Gatz, has not had. He has a reserve, a common sense, and even an incurable honesty that make him quite different from the subject of his meditations. That helps to create distance, enables him to criticize Gatsby and the high romanticism he embodies, and it makes his commentary vividly plural; Nick is, as he himself puts it, "within and without, simultaneously enchanted and repelled" by the hero he describes. The use of Nick Carraway as a narrator, in effect, enables Fitzgerald to maintain a balance for the first time in his career between the two sides of his character. The idealist, the romantic who believed in perfectibility and the pragmatist, the realist convinced that life is nasty, brutish, and short: these opposing tendencies are both allowed their full play, the drama of the narration *is* the tension between them.

The story Nick Carraway proceeds to tell is about the reinvention of the self: the poor boy James Gatz who renamed and recreated himself as Jay Gatsby, and who sees a woman as the crown and confirmation of this process. Daisy Buchanan is the dream girl whose voice, sounding like both music and money, measures the contradictions of the dream, its mix of mystery and the material. Gatsby had known Daisy when he was younger, Nick and the reader learn, before she was married to Tom Buchanan. Tom, incidentally, is a man born into wealth and a former football hero, whose sense of anticlimax since his days of sporting glory has tempted him to embrace racist ideas for explanation and excitement, to convince himself that he is not stale and finished; Fitzgerald is a brilliant analyst of the political through the personal and his story, lightly sketched, is a brief history of what tempts people into fascism. But Gatsby now wants to win Daisy back: to "repeat the past," as Nick characterizes it, and "fix everything just the way it was before." The erotic mingles with the elevated in this strange but somehow typically American desire to remold the present and future in the shape of an imagined past: looking backward and forward, Gatsby embodies a national leaning toward, not just the confusion of the ethical with the economic, but a peculiar form of nostalgic utopianism. Quickly, subtly, the dream Gatsby cherishes begins to fray at the edges. The narrative moves forward on an alternating rhythm of action and meditation, a series of parties or similar social occasions around which the moments of meditative commentary are woven; and Gatsby's parties – which he approaches with the air of an artist, since they are momentary realizations of his dream of order, glamour, and perfection – deteriorate ever more quickly into sterility and violence. Daisy becomes less and less amenable and malleable, less open to Gatsby's desire to idealize or, it may be, use her (part of the subtle ambivalence of the novel is that it can, and does, include the possibilities of both idealism and use). Quite apart from anything else, she refuses to declare that she has never loved her husband: something that may seem perfectly reasonable but that Gatsby takes as proof of her contaminating contact with a world other than his own.

Economical but also elegant, *The Great Gatsby* rapidly moves towards catastrophe. It is a catastrophe that draws together many of the pivotal images of the book. The initial setting for this concluding sequence is the Valley of Ashes, a waste land that embodies "the foul dust floating in the wake of Gatsby's dreams": not least, because it reminds the reader that success is measured against failure, there is no victory in a competitive ethos without a victim. Among the victims in this valley, presided over by the eyes of Dr. T. J. Eckleburg – an enormous advertisement that somehow sees the realities Gatsby is blinded to – is Myrtle Wilson, a resident of the place and the mistress of Tom Buchanan. Her victim status is only confirmed when she runs out in front of a car being driven by Daisy and is immediately killed. Wilson, Myrtle's husband, makes the easy mistake of thinking Gatsby (whose car it is) is responsible for his wife's death. Tom and Daisy, when he asks them where Gatsby lives, do not disabuse him. So, although it is Wilson who actually kills Gatsby at the end of the story, the Buchanans are morally responsible too. They retreat "back into their money, or their vast carelessness." And, with Gatsby destroyed with the tacit connivance of the "very rich" he has always admired, his dream shattered thanks to the quiet agency of the woman he wanted to dwell at its center, the story is almost over.

Almost, but not quite. At the funeral of Gatsby, Nick meets Henry C. Gatz, the father of the man who tried to reinvent himself. What he learns about, among other things, is the scheme of self-improvement that Gatsby drew up when he was still James Gatz and only a boy. The scheme is written on the fly-leaf of a copy of "Hopalong Cassidy." And, although it is an anticipation of the later ambitions of the hero, it is also clearly a parody of the manual of self-help that Benjamin Franklin drew up. By extension, it is a parody of all those other manuals of self-help that have thrived in American writing ever since. It does not take much ingenuity to see that a link is being forged between Gatsby's response to life and the frontier philosophy of individualism. The link is confirmed when Nick confesses that he now sees the story of Gatsby as "a story of the West after all"; in a sense, Gatsby and the Western hero are one. But this is not only a story of the West, Nick intimates, it is also a story of America. That is powerfully articulated in the closing moments of the story, when Gatsby's belief in "the green light, the orgiastic future that year by year recedes before us" is connected to "the last and greatest of all human dreams" that "flowered once for Dutch sailors' eyes" as they encountered the "fresh green breast of the new world." Gatsby believed in an ideal of Edenic innocence and perfection, Nick has disclosed. So did America. Gatsby tried to make the future an imitation of some mythic past. So did America. Gatsby tried to inform his life into an ideal, that strangely mixed the mystic and the material. So did America. Gatsby's dream is, in effect, the American dream.

But who are the "we" in the famous ending sentence of the novel? "So we beat on, boats against the current, borne back ceaselessly into the past." Americans, certainly, dreaming of the West in particular, but also surely anyone who tries to search for meaning, realize an ideal, or just make sense of their life: which includes just about everyone. Even the brutely material Tom Buchanan tries to grope for an explanation, something to help him feel that his life is not just decline and waste. What he finds, to help him explain things, may be absurd and obscene, but it shows that even he is trying to make sense of things. Within the confines of the story, though, the person who matters here, along with Gatsby, is the teller of the tale. Nick is the crucial other member of the "we," the company of those driven by the desire to shape experience into some meaningful pattern. All the while, the reader is reminded, it is Nick's consciousness that is recalling and rehearsing the past in *The Great Gatsby* – trying to discover its shape and meaning. Nick replicates in his telling of the tale what, fundamentally, Gatsby is doing in the tale being told: there is a shared need for order here, a pursuit of meaning that is definitively human. To that extent, Gatsby's project is Nick's; the form of the book dramatizes its theme. And both form and theme point to a paradox that is basic to Fitzgerald's life and writing. As Fitzgerald saw it, "we" must try to pursue the ideal; in this sense, "we" are romantics, and on this capacity depends our survival as moral beings. But "we" must always remember that the ideal will remain beyond our reach; in this sense, "we" are realists, and on this capacity depends our simple continuation and our grasp on sense. No matter how hard "we" try to reach out to the green light, it will continue to elude us; but "we" must keep on trying. That is the paradox that fires Fitzgerald's work into life. Or, as Fitzgerald put it, in his autobiographical essay "The Crack-Up" (*The Crack-Up* (1945)): "one should ... be able to see that things are hopeless and yet be determined to make them otherwise."

"Christ, Man," wrote John Dos Passos (1896–1971) to Fitzgerald, after he had read "The Crack-Up," "how do you find time in the middle of the general conflagration to worry about all that stuff?" Dos Passos was clearly baffled by Fitzgerald's preoccupation "with all that stuff" about the meaning of his personal experience. For him, what mattered was the "general conflagration," the crisis of capitalism, in the 1930s; and he directed all his energies, and his skills as a modernist innovator, to depicting that conflagration in his greatest work, *U.S.A.* (1930–1936), a trilogy consisting of *The 42nd Parallel* (1930), *1919* (1932), and *The Big Money* (1936). Dos Passos explained, in a brief preface to the trilogy, that he was intent on producing a new language. "Mostly *U.S.A.* is the speech of the people," Dos Passos declares. And that speech is meant to capture the discontinuous movement of city life, the noise, pace, and claustrophobia of modernity, the sense of many different messages, images, and impressions all bombarding the consciousness at the same time. *U.S.A.* is, definitively, of and about modern America. To be exact, it covers the period from 1900 to 1930, the period which, Dos Passos felt, witnessed the emergence of modern American society. Beginning roughly with the Spanish-American War of 1898 and ending with the Wall Street Crash and its aftermath, it dramatizes the lives of a large array of characters. Although several of these characters appear in all three novels, their activities do not constitute a unified plot. As in Dos Passos's other novels, they are types rather than fully developed individuals and, rather than agents, they are subjects; things happen to them, they do not so much have lives as destinies; acts, emotions, ideas suddenly settle within them, then disappear, without their having much to say in the matter. It is almost as if Dos Passos is anticipating the existentialist belief that experience precedes essence. But, unlike the existentialist, he has another, social point to make. All the people in these three books are evacuated of character, choice, and individuality precisely because they are social victims. They are destroyed by a society that has become totalizing in its opposition to human freedom. And this, Dos Passos insists, is the social tragedy of our times.

Interspersed between Dos Passos's panoramic account of his many characters are other sections, using techniques specifically invented for *U.S.A.* One is called "Newsreel." It is a mixture of newspaper headlines and advertising slogans, snatches of political speeches and popular songs, all drawn from the moment in social history that is being recorded in the main narrative. The Newsreel is a verbal collage, rehearsing in particular the war between capital and labor. And, just as it makes poems out of the public experience of America, so Dos Passos's second technical invention, "The Camera Eye," makes poetry out of the private feelings of the author at the time. In a charged, lyrical prose, Dos Passos recalls how he saw and reacted to the major historical events that bear down on the lives of his characters. Along with these two kinds of narrative intervention, there is also a series of sections titled "Biography." These are brief, socially charged accounts of major public figures of the time. All three innovations – Newsreel, Camera Eye, Biography – are, first of all, devices for highlighting the general social significance of an individual's experience. Dos Passos does not stop there, however, since he is not simply trying to show the reader that the public life is inseparable from the private, as if they were equals. He is, in addition, trying to suggest that – in an urban environment such as that of *U.S.A.* – the public life dominates and controls the private. He is repeating the point made in his portrait of his evacuated characters: that modern society overwhelms the individual. What Newsreel, Camera Eye, and Biography tell the reader, in effect, is what all the characters in *U.S.A.* also do: that America has become a total institution, a prisonhouse for the mind as well as the body.

During the 1920s and 1930s, Dos Passos aligned himself politically with the left. He became disillusioned with communism, however, and broke completely with his left-wing friends and allies at the time of the Spanish Civil War. His later fiction, such as the trilogy *District of Columbia* (1939–1949) and the novel *Midcentury* (1961), continue his stylistic innovations but show an increasingly conservative political stance. He was always, first and last, an individualist: concerned with the threat to the individual posed first, as he saw it, by capitalism and then, in his later work, by communism. To that extent, he belonged in the American Adamic tradition, with its commitment to the primacy of the individual, the supreme importance of the single, separate self. Consistently, Ernest Hemingway (1899–1961) belonged to that tradition too. For Hemingway, as for many earlier American writers, the essential condition of life is solitary, and the interesting, only really serious business, is the management of that solitude. In this respect, the first story, "Indian Camp," in his first book, *In Our Time* (1925), is exemplary. Young Nick Adams, the protagonist, witnesses a birth and a death. The birth is exceptionally agonizing, with the mother, an Indian woman, being cut open by Nick's father and sewn up with a fishing line. And the death too is peculiarly awful, the husband in the bunk above, listening to the woman in her agony, and responding by cutting his throat. "Why did he kill himself, Daddy?" Nick asks. "I don't know, Nick," comes the reply. "He couldn't stand things, I guess." Although this is the only significant, foreground suicide in Hemingway's fiction, the terms have been set. "Things" will remain to the last hurtful and horrible, to be stood with as much dignity and courage as possible. For the moment, though, these things of horror are too much for Nick to dwell on. He must bury them far down in his mind and rest secure in the shelter of the father. "In the early morning on the lake sitting in the stern of the boat with his father rowing," the story concludes, "he felt quite sure that he would never die."

Such are the good times of boyhood in Hemingway: not mother and home, but out in the open with father, recreating a frontier idyll. So, in the second story in *In Our Time*, to escape his wife's nervous chatter, Nick's father goes out for a walk. "I want to go with you," Nick declares; "all right," his father responds, "come on, then." Soon, when Nick is older, in the later stories "The End of Something" and "The Three-Day Blow," father will be replaced as companion by his friend Bill. But only the counters have altered, not the game. As the title of his second collection of stories, *Men Without Women* (1927), indicates, the best times of all for Hemingway, because the least complicated and most inwardly peaceful, are had by men or boys together, preferably in some wide space of land or sea, away from the noise, pace, and excitement of cities: Jake Barnes, the hero of *The Sun Also Rises* (1926), fishing with his companions Bill Gorton and Harris; Thomas Hudson and his three sons in *Islands in the Stream* (1970); and from *In Our Time*, in "Cross-Country Snow," Nick and his friend George skiing in Switzerland one last time before Nick commits himself to the trap of marriage and fatherhood. "Once a man's married, he's absolutely bitched," is Bill's drunken wisdom in "The Three-Day Blow": bitched by responsibilities, domesticity, but above all by the pain locked in with a love that may easily be broken or lost. And a man's world, although safer from certain kinds of anxiety or threat, is for Hemingway only relatively so. A man will lose his wife but he will also lose his father, not just in death but in disillusionment. Near the end of *In Our Time*, an exemplary father dies; not Nick's but the jockey, "My Old Man," with whom, around the race-courses of France and Italy, the young narrator has had a perfect time out, with no mother or woman in sight. When his father falls in a steeplechase and is killed, the son is left to bear not just his grief but also the discovery that his father had been crooked. It is more than a life that has been lost. As he overhears the name of his father being besmirched, it seems to the boy "like when they get started, they don't leave a guy nothing."

"It was all a nothing," observes the lonely protagonist of "A Clean Well-Lighted Place" (*Winner Take Nothing* (1933)), "and man was a nothing too." In the face of palpable nothing, meaninglessness, there are, finally, only the imperatives of conduct and communion with one's own solitariness. "I did not care what it was all about," Jake confides in *The Sun Also Rises*. "All I wanted to know was how to live in it." One way to "live in it," in some of Hemingway's novels, has a political slant. *To Have and Have Not* (1937) is an emphatic protest against corruption, political hypocrisy, and the immorality of gross inequality. *For Whom the Bell Tolls* (1941) commemorates three days of a guerrilla action in the Spanish Civil War and celebrates the republican fight against fascism. "I suppose I am an anarchist," Hemingway had written to Dos Passos in 1932; and the novel, like *To Have and Have Not*, shows a lonely individualist fighting while he can, not for a political program, but for the simple humanist principles of justice and liberty. But a more fundamental way to "live in it" is to live alone. In "Big Two-Hearted River," the story that concludes *In Our Time*, Nick starts out from the site of a burned-out town in Michigan. The disaster that has annihilated the town aptly crowns the world of violence revealed in the vignettes that have interleaved the stories of *In Our Time*. For

Hemingway, wounded in World War I, life *was* war, nasty, brutal, and arbitrary; and that is a lesson Nick has now learned. Putting this stuff of nightmares behind him, Nick heads away from the road for the woods and the river. Far from other human sound, he fishes, pitches a tent, builds a fire, prepares himself food and drink. "He was there, in the good place," the reader is told. "He was in his home where he had made it." It is a familiar American moment, this sealing of a solitary compact with nature. It is also a familiar concluding moment in Hemingway's work: a man alone, trying to come to terms with the stark facts of life, and of death – sometimes the death of a loved one, as in *A Farewell to Arms* (1929), other times, as in "The Snows of Kilimanjaro" (1938), his own inevitable and imminent dying. And what seals the compact, and confirms the starkness is, always, the pellucid clarity of expression, the stark, simple economy of the terms in which Hemingway's lonely heroes are rendered to us. "A writer's job is to tell the truth," Hemingway observed. And he told that truth in a style that was a verbal equivalent of the grace under pressure shown by his finest protagonists: concrete, contained, cleaving to the hard facts of life, only disclosing its deeper urgencies in its repetitions and repressions – in what its rhythms implied and what it did not say.

Hemingway called this verbal art the art of omission. "You could omit anything if you knew that you omitted," Hemingway reflected in *A Movable Feast* (1964), his memoir of his years in Paris after World War I; "and the omitted part would strengthen the story and make people feel something more than they understood." He had begun to develop this art as a newspaperman on the *Kansas City Star*, where he worked before World War I. The "real thing," Hemingway remembered, was "something I was working very hard to try to get": first, in Kansas, and then in Paris, where he received encouragement in his pursuit of concrete fact, and an example of how to do it, from Ezra Pound and, even more, Gertrude Stein. The experience of war was also vital here. Like so many of his generation, Hemingway learned from war not just a distrust but a hatred of abstraction, the high-sounding generalizations used as an excuse, or justification, for mass slaughter. "I was always embarrassed by the words sacred, glorious, and sacrifice and the expression, in vain," says the protagonist Frederic Henry in *A Farewell to Arms*, set, of course, in the Great War: "the things that were glorious had no glory and the sacrifices were like the stockyards of Chicago." "There were many words that you could not stand to hear and finally only the names of places had dignity." Like Frederic Henry, Hemingway came to feel that "abstract words such as glory, honor, courage, or hallow were obscene"; the simple words, those that carried the smallest burden of stock attitudes, were the safest ones. What the individual, and the writer, had to respond to were things and experiences themselves, not ideas about them; and the closer he stuck to them, the less risk there would be of losing what was truly felt under a mass of evasions and abstractions. The real thing the person or writer must pursue, Hemingway felt, is the truth of the individual, immediate experience and emotion. That truth is discovered by the Hemingway hero in *seeing* and *responding to* things for himself. And it is expressed by Hemingway in *describing* things for oneself, things as they are, not mediated by convention or abstraction. The style, in fact, is a measure of a commitment; it is the proper reaction to the world translated into words.

"I am telling the same story over and over," William Faulkner (1897–1962) admitted once, "which is myself and the world." That remark catches one of the major compulsions in his fiction: Faulkner was prone to interpret any writing, including his own, as a revelation of the writer's secret life, as his or her dark twin. By extension, he was inclined to see that writing as shadowed by the repressed myths, the secret stories of his culture. Repetition was rediscovery, as Faulkner saw it: his was an art, not of omission like Hemingway's, but of reinvention, circling back and circling back again, to the life that had been lived and missed, the emotions that had been felt but not yet understood. Shaped by the oral traditions of the South, which were still alive when he was young, and by the refracted techniques of modernism, to which he was introduced as a young man, Faulkner was drawn to write in a way that was as old as storytelling and, at the time, as new as the cinema and cubism. It was as if he, and his characters, in T. S. Eliot's phrase, had had the experience but missed the meaning; and telling became an almost obsessive reaction to this, a way of responding to the hope that perhaps by the indirections of the fictive impulse he could find directions out. That the hope was partial was implicit in the activity of telling the story "over and over": Faulkner, like so many of his protagonists and narrators, kept coming back, and then coming back again, to events that seemed to resist understanding, to brim with undisclosed meaning. There would always be blockage between the commemorating writer and the commemorated experience, as Faulkner's compulsive use of the metaphor of a window indicated: the window on which a name is inscribed, for instance, in *Requiem for a Nun* (1951), or the window through which Quentin Compson gazes at his native South, as he travels home from Massachusetts, in *The Sound and the Fury* (1929). Writing, for Faulkner, was a transparency and an obstacle: offering communication and discovery to the inquiring gaze of writer and reader but also impeding him, sealing him off from full sensory impact.

Faulkner began his creative life as a poet and artist. He published poems and drawings in student magazines in his hometown of Oxford, Mississippi; his first book, *The Marble Faun* (1924), was a collection of verse that showed the influence of an earlier generation of British and French poets, like Swinburne and Mallarmé. His first two novels, *Soldier's Pay* (1925) and *Mosquitoes* (1927), are conventional in many ways: the one, a tale of postwar disillusionment, the other a satirical novel of ideas. *Sartoris* (1929), his third novel, is the first to be set in his fictional county of Yoknapatawpha (although it was not given this name until *As I Lay Dying* (1930)). "Beginning with *Sartoris*," Faulkner later recalled, "I discovered that my own little postage stamp of native soil was worth writing about, and that by sublimating the actual into the apocryphal I would have complete liberty to use whatever talent I might have to its absolute top." This was followed by a series of major modernist novels over the next seven years: *The Sound and the Fury, As I Lay Dying, Sanctuary* (1931), *Light in August* (1932), and *Absalom, Absalom!* (1936). These were, eventually, to secure his reputation, if not immediately his future. Although highly regarded, by other writers in particular, he was frequently in financial trouble. The restoration of Faulkner's reputation, and his financial health, began with the publication of *The Portable Faulkner* in 1946; it was consolidated by the award of the Nobel Prize in 1950. By this time, Faulkner had produced fiction reflecting his concerns about the mobility and anonymity of modern life (*Pylon* (1935); *The Wild Palms* (1939)), and his passionate interest in racial prejudice and social injustice in the South (*Go Down, Moses* (1942); *Intruder in the Dust* (1948)). He had also written *The Hamlet* (1940), a deeply serious comedy focusing on social transformation in his region. This was to become the first book in a trilogy dealing with the rise to power of a poor white entrepreneur called Flem Snopes, and his eventual fall; the other two were *The Town* (1957) and *The Mansion* (1959). Generally, the later work betrays an inclination towards a more open, direct address of social and political issues, and a search for some grounds for hope, for the belief that humankind would not only endure but prevail. This was true not only of the later fiction set in Yoknapatawpha, like *Requiem for a Nun*, but also of his monumental *A Fable* (1954), set in World War I, which uses the story of Christ to dramatize its message of peace. Like his other later work, *A Fable* shows Faulkner moving away from the private to the public, away from the intimacies of the inward vision towards the intensities of the outward – to put it more simply, from modernism to modernity.

Faulkner's favorite among his novels, and arguably his greatest work, is *The Sound and the Fury*. The novel is concerned with the lives and fates of the Compson family, who seem to condense into their experience the entire history of their region. Four generations of Compsons appear; and the most important of these is the third generation, the brothers Quentin, Jason, and Benjy and their sister Candace, known in the family as Caddy. Three of the four sections into which the narration is divided are consigned to the voices of the Compson brothers; the fourth is told in the third person and circles around the activities of Dilsey Gibson, the cook and maid-of-all-work in the Compson house. The present time of *The Sound and the Fury* is distilled into four days: three of them occurring over the Easter weekend, 1928, the Quentin section being devoted to a day in 1910 when he chooses to commit suicide. There is, however, a constant narrative impulse to repeat and rehearse the past, to be carried back on the old ineradicable rhythms of memory. The memories are many but the determining ones for the Compson brothers are of the woman who was at the center of their childhood world, and who is now lost to them literally and emotionally: their sister, Caddy Compson.

Caddy is the source and inspiration of what became and remained the novel of his closest to Faulkner's own heart. Trying to tell of Caddy, to extract what Faulkner called "some ultimate distillation" from her story, is the fundamental project of the book. And yet she seems somehow to exist apart from it or beyond it, to escape from Faulkner and all the other storytellers. To some extent, this is because she is the absent presence that haunts so many of Faulkner's other novels: a figure like, say, Addie Bundren in *As I Lay Dying* or Thomas Sutpen in *Absalom, Absalom!*, who obsesses the other characters but very rarely speaks with his or her own voice. Even more important, though, is the fact that she is female, and so by definition someone who tends to exist for her creator outside the parameters of language: Faulkner has adopted here the archetypal male image of a woman who is at once mother, sister, daughter, and lover, Eve and Lilith, virgin and whore, to describe what Wallace Stevens once referred to as "the inconceivable idea of the sun" – that is, the other, the world outside the self. And while she is there to the extent that she is the focal point, the eventual object of each narrator's meditations, she is not there in the sense that she remains elusive, intangible.

Not that Faulkner ever stops trying to bring her into focus – for himself, his characters, and of course for us. Each section of the book, in fact, represents a different strategy, another attempt to know her. Essentially, the difference in each section is a matter of rhetoric, in the sense that each time the tale is told another language is devised and a different series of relationships between author, narrator, subject, and reader.

When Benjy occupies our attention right at the start, for instance, we soon become aware of a radical inwardness. Profoundly autistic, Benjy lives in a closed world where the gap between self and other, being and naming cannot be bridged because it is never known or acknowledged. The second section, devoted to Quentin, collapses distance in another way. "I am Quentin," Faulkner once admitted. And, as we read, we may feel ourselves drawn into a world that seems almost impenetrably private. With Jason, in the third section of *The Sound and the Fury*, distance enters. Faulkner is clearly out of sympathy with this Compson brother, even if he is amused by him. Jason, in turn, while clearly obsessed with Caddy, never claims any intimacy with her. And the reader is kept at some remove by the specifically public mode of speech Jason uses. The final section of the novel offers release, of a kind, from all this. The closed circle of the interior monologue is broken now, the sense of the concrete world is firm. Verbally, we are in a more open field where otherness is addressed. Emotionally, we are released from a vicious pattern of repetition compulsion, in which absorption in the self leads somehow to destruction of the self, and invited into the world of Dilsey, the only member of the Compson household who has a sure sense of the world outside herself or any understanding of Caddy as an individual – not just a sister or mother figure, but a separate person with needs and desires of her own.

   The closing words of *The Sound and the Fury* appear to bring the wheel full circle. As Benjy Compson sits in a wagon watching the elements of his small world flow past him, "each in its ordered place," it is as if everything has now been settled and arranged. Until, that is, the reader recalls that *this* order is one founded on denial, a howl of resistance to strangeness. The ending, it turns out, is no ending at all; it represents, at most, a continuation of the process of speech – the human project of putting things each in its ordered place – and an invitation to us, the reader, to continue that process too. We are reminded, as we are at the close of so many of Faulkner's stories, that no system is ever complete or completely adequate. Something is always missed out it seems, remaining unseen. Since this is so, no book, not even one like this that uses a multiplicity of voices – a plurality of perspectives, like a cubist painting – can ever truly be said to be finished. Language can be a necessary tool for understanding and dealing with the world, the only way we can hope to know Caddy; yet perversely, Faulkner suggests, it is as much a function of ignorance as of knowledge. "Sometimes," Faulkner admitted, "I think of doing what Rimbaud did – yet I will certainly keep on writing as long as I live." So he did keep on writing: his final novel, *The Reivers* (1962), was published only a month before he died. To the end, he produced stories that said what he suggested every artist was trying to say: "*I was here.*" And they said it for others beside himself: others, that is, including the reader.

Making it new in drama

Modernism came late to American drama. So, for that matter, did realism, experimentalism, and even, with the notable exception of *The Contrast* by Royall Tyler, Americanism. Theatrical experiment only became common in the first decades of the twentieth century, sometimes inspired by the cinema and sometimes by other forces, such as German expressionist drama. The first play of Elmer Rice (1892–1967), *On Trial* (1914), for example, employs the technique of the motion picture "cutback" to present scenes that are described by trial witnesses. With his works for the Morningside Players, a little theatre group, published in *Morningside Plays* (1917), Rice then scored a second success in experimental drama with *The Adding Machine* (1923). Here, he used the expressionist techniques of fantasy and symbolism to satirize the reduction of individuals, in the machine age, to "waste product." Rice continued to experiment with different styles. His other most notable play, *Street Scene* (1929), for instance, may be more geared towards empirical realism in its presentation of slum life. But it still uses a panoply of sound effects to get its message across.

Thornton Wilder (1897–1975) borrowed from an entirely different theatrical tradition in *Our Town* (1938). Born in Wisconsin, but raised in China, Wilder dispensed with scenery in his most famous play, and used the Chinese theatrical convention of the property man as narrator to portray life in a small town in New England. Wilder also achieved fame with his novel, *The Bridge of San Luis Rey* (1927), about a South American bridge disaster and the ironic way providence directs disparate lives to one end. And he experimented with several different dramatic forms, including comedy (*The Merchant of Yonkers* (1938)), a play inspired by Joyce's *Finnegans Wake* (*The Skin of Our Teeth* (1942)), and a tragedy inspired by Euripides' *Alcestis* (*A Life in the Sun* (1955)).

The theatrical experiments of Maxwell Anderson (1888–1959) were similarly various. After achieving success with a bluntly realistic war play, *What Price Glory?* (1924), he wrote, among many other things, a series of blank verse dramas in which the innocent and idealistic wage a bitter fight, sometimes successful and sometimes not, against the political, the economic, and the mundane. Among these dramas were *Night Over Taos* (1932), which dramatizes the end of the feudal era in New Mexico, and *Winterset* (1935), also in verse, which is set in contemporary America and was clearly suggested by the trial and execution of the anarchists Sacco and Vanzetti – a gross miscarriage of justice that became a *cause célèbre* for the left during the 1930s.

Night Over Taos was produced by the Group Theatre, *Winterset* was rejected by the Group. That is a measure of what the most influential American production company of the 1930s was after. Its aims were social as well as artistic. Although it was never a doctrinaire political theatre, the Group did see itself as a community of artists working to say something useful about society. It tended to favor a series of styles that could be handily described as left-wing symbolism; and it preferred optimism and hope over pessimism and despair. Which is, perhaps, why *Night Over Taos*, with its resonant theme of the old giving way to the new, found favor, while *Winterset*, in which the two leading characters choose to die rather than live in a corrupt world, did not. The Group Theatre grew out of the Theatre Guild of New York, the leading drama company of the 1920s. It was in operation from 1931 to 1941 and has been described as the most successful failure in the history of American theatre. Except for a couple of years when one of its plays, *Golden Boy* (1937) by Clifford Odets (1906–1963), scored a big success, it was always in financial difficulties. Nevertheless, in the ten seasons it existed, it managed to get twenty-two new productions on stage. There were occasional revivals, tours, second companies, and experimental evenings, but the main aim of the Group as a production company was to get something of dramatic and social value into performance each Spring – and, in the process, keep the Group alive. Its first production was *The House of Connelly* (1931) by Paul Green (1894–1981), a searing account of an old Southern family that is a combination of Greek tragedy and regional folk play. Its last was *Retreat to Pleasure* (1940) by Irwin Shaw (1913–1984). In between it produced plays in a wide variety of styles. All of them are driven, though, by an optimistic energy, a desire to find some grounds for belief. "We'll never lose our faith and hope and trust in all mankind," *Johnny Johnson* (1936) by Paul Green concludes. "The world is at its morning . . . and *no man fights alone!*" declares a character in *Paradise Lost* (1935) by Odets. Two other characters in another play by Odets, *Night Music* (1940), sum up the positive feelings with which these plays are charged. "Where there is life there is hope," observes one. "Only the living can cry out against life." The other's comment, or cry, is much simpler: "*Make this America for us!*"

Of all the dramatists associated with the Group Theatre, Odets is the most significant and symptomatic. He was a member of the company from the beginning, an actor in many of the earlier productions. When he finally convinced the directors that he was a playwright, his name became almost synonymous with the Group. They produced seven of his plays, where no other dramatist had more than two: *Waiting for Lefty* (1935), *Awake and Sing!* (1935), *Till the Day I Die* (1935), about the struggle of the German communists at the beginning of the Hitler regime, *Paradise Lost, Golden Boy*, about a young Italian-American violinist whose desire for wealth leads him into boxing and then into death, *Rocket to the Moon* (1938), and *Night Music*. Odets continued his career after the Group broke up. Among his later plays are *The Big Knife* (1948), which explores power and corruption in the film industry, and *The Country Girl* (1950), a backstage drama about an alcoholic actor's return to theatre life. But the plays written for the Group Theatre represent his major achievement. They are marked by a language that captures a particular urban rhythm and utilizes a tough, oblique way of speaking, a hardboiled mask for sentiment. Like a skillful cartoonist, Odets exaggerates milieu-oriented metaphor ("I wouldn't trade you for two pitchers and an outfielder"), uses repetition and the clichés of everyday speech ("So go fight City Hall!"). The result is a stylized language that feels realistic, while avoiding the flatness of most real speech or the fixed exaggerations of dialect. It is the perfect tool for his purpose: which is to capture the humor, gloomy fatality, and burning beliefs of the ordinary people who are his subjects – the urban lower-middle class from which Odets himself came.

"Most modern plays," Eugene O'Neill (1888–1953) once declared, "are concerned with the relation between man and man, but that does not interest me at all. I am interested only in the relationship between man and God." That is not strictly true, for two reasons. The first is that, in many of his plays, like *Lazarus Laughed* (1927) and *The Hairy Ape* (1922), he does move towards the condition of social drama to the extent that he explores the contemporary emphasis on acquisition and material standards or the plight of those at the bottom of the social and economic ladder. And, in all of them, he is drawn into intensely poetic, often erotic accounts of the tentacular relationships to be found, say, in families (*Mourning Becomes Electra* (1932), *Long Day's Journey into Night* (1956)), among confined groups at sea or in a bar (*Bound East for Cardiff* (1916), *The Iceman Cometh* (1946)), or in local communities and neighborhoods (*All God's Chillun Got Wings* (1924)). The second is that it was not so much God, as the absence of God that preoccupied O'Neill. O'Neill was born into a generation that included Joyce, Eliot, and Stevens, profoundly concerned with the death of the old grounds for belief. He was affected by European expressionism, with modern psychology seen as an instrument to analyze human nature, and by a Nietzschean philosophy which reinforced a characteristically American tendency to explore heroic individuals and their search for self-realization. The fundamental problem O'Neill dramatizes in all his work is the problem of the relation of the human being to something outside himself, to which he can belong and in which he can ground his life and discover a purpose: something that saves him from feeling lonely, lost, an existential exile – or, as one of his characters puts it, "a stranger in a strange land."

The younger son of a popular actor, O'Neill began writing drama when he was confined in a sanatorium. During this period of enforced rest and reflection, he produced a series of one-act plays based on his life at sea and among the outcasts in many places: he had been, at various times, a prospector for gold, a merchant seaman, and a beachcomber. His first play, *The Web* (1913–1914), was followed by nine others. Gaining further dramatic experience with George Peirce Baker's 47 Workshop at Harvard in 1914–1915, he then spent a winter in Greenwich Village, New York. Then, in 1916, his involvement with the Provincetown Players brought him, and the company, to the attention of the New York public, initially with a series of plays about the *S.S. Glencairn* and its crew, among them *Bound East for Cardiff* and *The Moon of the Caribbees* (1918). With the production of his *Beyond the Horizon* in 1920, O'Neill was acknowledged as the leading American playwright of his day. For a while, from 1923 to 1927, he helped manage the Greenwich Village Theatre; he was also a director of the Provincetown Players and a founder of the Theatre Guild, which produced his later plays. But he devoted more and more of his time to writing, in a variety of styles, to express and explore his view of life. Plays that gravitated toward naturalism included *Chris Christopherson* (1920), rewritten as *Anna Christie* (1921), *All God's Chillun Got Wings*, and *Desire Under the Elms* (1924). As such plays revealed, O'Neill was not afraid to explore difficult and, for their time, even controversial subjects. Anna Christie is a prostitute, *All God's Chillun* is concerned with interracial marriage, in *Desire Under the Elms* a woman bears a child by her stepson only to kill the child when her husband, learning that it is not his son, repudiates and disinherits him. A similar daring, a willingness to test and extend the boundaries, is also a feature of O'Neill's more experimental and expressionist work. Only now the boundaries that are tested are as much a matter of dramatic form as social norm. In *The Hairy Ape*, for example, the fall of the central character into consciousness, exile, and death is charted in eight scenes that, as O'Neill explains at the beginning, "should by no means be naturalistic."

O'Neill's interest in experiment drew him towards the use of symbolic masks for the actors in *The Great God Brown* (1926), a play that fuses symbolism, poetry, and the affirmation of a pagan idealism in an ironic critique of the materialism of the modern world. It also led him to experiment with a dramatic form of stream-of-consciousness in *Strange Interlude* (1928), where conventional dialogue is juxtaposed with stylized internal monologue to reveal the inner lives of the characters. The more romantic impulse in O'Neill, that straining towards affirmation, some source of hope, that is typical of so many of O'Neill's characters is given freer play in *The Fountain* (1925), which is dominated by a celebration of what is called here "the Eternal Becoming which is Beauty." The comic impulse, in turn, is more evident in *Ah, Wilderness* (1933), a gently humorous, nostalgic portrait of New England life that draws on O'Neill's memories of his own family. More generally typical, though, of his use of drama as a means of exploring human abandonment are *Dynamo* (1929), *Days Without End* (1934), and the trilogy *Mourning Becomes Electra* (1931). In *Mourning Becomes Electra*, the *Oresteia* of Aeschylus is retold as a story of the Civil War, with the classical sense of fate replaced by an emphasis on character conceived of in Freudian terms. The essential elements of the ancient Greek story of the curse on the house of Atreus are retained here in this story of a New England family called the Mannons: a woman in love with her father, a man in love with his mother, the wife who kills her husband as an act of vengeance, the son who kills similarly in vengeance and is consumed by the "furies." These elements, however, are redrawn in modern terms, theatrical and conceptual: the chorus, for example, is replaced by choric characters and the "furies" that pursue the son, leading him in this case to commit suicide, come from within, his own devouring sense of guilt. More to the point, there is no final tragic recognition, no sense of an ultimate resolution. At the end of *Mourning Becomes Electra*, the surviving member of the Mannon family, the daughter Lavinia Mannon, simply shuts herself up in the house, to live with the ghosts of her father, mother, and brother.

After the failure of *Days Without End*, O'Neill maintained a long theatrical silence, during which he suffered mental and physical ill health. The silence was broken by *The Iceman Cometh*, his first new play to be produced after a gap of twelve years. Set in a run-down New York bar, it is a tragi-comic exploration of O'Neill's obsessive theme, the need for meaning expressed here as the human need for a saving illusion: as one of the bar-room regulars puts it, "the lie of the pipe dream is what gives life." Many other plays written following this were only produced after O'Neill's death. Most notable of these is *Long Day's Journey into Night*, probably O'Neill's finest work, which appeared in the theatre in 1956. Set over the course of one long day in August, 1912, *Long Day's Journey into Night* tells the story of the Tyrone family: James Tyrone, a former matinee idol, his wife Mary, a nervous, sickly woman addicted to morphine, their older son Jamie, a hard-drinking cynic, and their younger son Edmund, who has literary aspirations and suffers from tuberculosis. O'Neill was drawing on his own life, and the life of his family, when he wrote this play. Edmund, for example, is an exercise in self-portraiture. But he was drawing on this for a deeper purpose. What is on offer here is a study of lives in disintegration, people without something to give shape and significance to their lives. They have lost that something, anything that might have convinced them once that life made sense; that is, even if they ever had it. As a result, they are left astray and anxious. "It was a great mistake, my being born a man. I would have been much more successful as a sea-gull or a fish," Edmund observes, and, in doing so, speaks for all the Tyrone family. "As it is, I will always be a stranger who never feels at home," he explains, "who must always be a little in love with death!'

"Stammering is the native eloquence of us fog people," Edmund says, shortly after this. The Tyrones are divided, disintegrated people. Lacking belief, grounding, they lack a sense of community, stability. They are at odds with themselves and each other; and this is expressed in the words they use, their reflections and conversations, which are characterized by a continual oscillation, an ebb-and-flow movement in which one statement will cancel out another. There is no continuity here because there are no grounds for it, no foundations in faith or conviction. The characters are aimless, without anchor in anything except their dreams of what they might have been (a nun, a concert pianist, a great Shakespearean actor) or what they might be (a great writer, a success), and no forms of emotional rescue other than those offered by various narcotics – drugs, alcohol, poetry, the blanketing numbness of the fog. What they all long for is described when Edmund recalls his life as a seaman. At sea once, he remembers, he felt that he had "dissolved in the sea." "For a second you see –," he explains, "– and seeing the secret, are the secret. For a second there is meaning!" "I belonged," he insists, "within something greater than my own life . . . to Life itself! To God, if you want to put it that way." But such moments of union are rare here. "The hand lets the veil fall," Edmund concludes bitterly, "and you are alone, lost in the fog again." That is the condition of the Tyrones, and the human condition in O'Neill's plays. The secret of joy, losing oneself in "a fulfillment beyond men's lousy, pitiful, greedy fears and hopes and dreams," is professed, if at all, only for a moment. Before and after, there is only waste and exile.

O'Neill is essentially a religious writer without a religion. The power and pain of his best work is a measure of that paradox. *Long Day's Journey into Night* achieves a tragic pathos precisely because it requires the audience both to see and share in the disintegration of the Tyrones: to recognize that they are "fog people," stammering for something they can never possess, but also to share their need, feel compelled by their "native eloquence." What is especially remarkable about this portrait of a family being borne towards extinction is how intricately O'Neill weaves the familial web. Like Faulkner, he believed that, as he has one of the characters say here, "the past is the present"; like Faulkner, too, he uses that belief to present the family as an elaborate network of blame and dependence, in which the family members both resist and rely on each other – feel isolated and betrayed, yet also feel an intense need to be with one another. The Tyrones are constantly accusing one another, blaming one another for the damage done to their own lives. They are also, constantly, relying on one another: not just for advice or assistance, nor even just for conversation or comfort, but to bolster their image of themselves through the rehearsal of shared memories and illusions – by seeing themselves, as they would like to be, in the mirror of the past or the gaze of a husband or wife, father or mother, son or a brother. *Long Day's Journey into Night* represents a seminal moment in American theatre. An American family of ordinary means inspires the awe, the fear and pity, that used to be reserved for the special few, in traditional drama. It is also a key moment in American literary modernism. The insignificant life becomes here the significance of literature, the common the uncommon and even tragic.

Traditionalism, Politics, and Prophecy

The uses of traditionalism

Not everyone during this period went after the strange gods of modernism. On the contrary, responding to that yearning for the past to be found in writers as otherwise different as Wharton and Cather, Robinson and Frost, and that preoccupation with cultural loss notable in writers as otherwise modern as Pound, Faulkner, and O'Neill, many writers sought refuge in traditionalism. Of those who pursued this belief, actively and with passion, none were so influential as those gathered in the South, initially around what was termed the Fugitive movement. Meeting in Nashville, Tennessee from 1915 on, the Fugitive group was composed of Southerners, many of them associated with Vanderbilt University. The Fugitives saw themselves as fleeing from Southern romanticism, nostalgia for the region's past. And they saw themselves fleeing, too, from the dehumanizing environment that they saw all around them – in Nashville, the modern South, and the United States.

The Fugitive, the magazine produced by the group, lasted for only three years from 1915 to 1918. It never sold more than a few hundred copies, and the quality of the poetry published in it was not particularly high. Yet this little magazine, and the Fugitive movement itself, are of real importance in the story of twentieth-century American poetry. This was because they provided a nursing-ground for a number of exceptional writers. It is also because the Fugitives offered a contrast or counterweight to the Imagists, in their emphasis on tradition rather than experiment and their commitment to the local and regional rather than the international. The impulse towards tradition-alism assumed a more regional character among those who had made up the Fugitive group after their magazine ceased publication. Moving away from the South, as many of them did, it became a faraway country for them: an attractive alternative to the urban, cosmopolitan centers, where they were now living – a place idealized by memory and distance. With allies old and new, they began to argue the case not only for tradition-alism but regionalism. The result was the formation in 1926 of a loose but mutually supportive association of individuals who shared concerns that were distinctively Southern; they were eventually to be known as the Agrarians. Of all the writers nurtured by the Fugitive and Agrarian movements, John Crowe Ransom (1888–1974) is among the most interesting, as his poetry, gathered together princi-pally in *Chills and Fever* (1924), *Two Gentlemen in Bonds* (1927), and then in *Selected Poems* (1945, 1963, 1969), attests. He is also among those most firmly committed to the belief that only a traditional society, through its myths and ceremonies, can promote human wholeness. Contemporary society, on the contrary, the one Ransom saw all around him in America, left people divided, disassociated, their personalities fragmen-ted or underdeveloped. The desperation of many of Ransom's poetic characters springs from the fact that they cannot achieve unity of being. They are like the narrator of "Winter Remembered" who, separated off from his beloved, comes to typify the sense of fragmentation, estrangement, and sheer vacuum which all those who have failed to attain wholeness of being must experience. Lonely old spinsters ("Emily Hardcastle, Spinster"), young scholars ("Persistent Explorer"), old eccentrics ("Captain Carpenter"), thwarted lovers ("The Equilibrists"), abstract idealists and optimists ("Man Without Sense of Direction"): they all illustrate that "old illusion of grandeur" which Ransom explores in one of his later poems, "Painted Head" – the belief, that is, that the mind can exist apart, "play truant from the body bush."

This, certainly, is one of Ransom's favorite themes: that "cry of Absence, Absence in the heart" which charts out a more general situation of emptiness and loss. Others are death and the world of the child, which are often treated together: as in "Dead Boy," "Bells for John Whiteside's Daughter," and "Blue Girls." "Death is the greatest subject for poetry," Ransom insisted, "... there's no recourse from death, except that we learn to face it." As such, it provides modern man with a timely reminder of his limitations: the most powerful example possible of all that the reason cannot encompass or control.

And when that subject is the death of a child then, for Ransom, a further dimension is added: because, in a fragmented society such as our own, only the child's world is whole. Only this world does not suffer from dissociation, Ransom believed, and a consequent feeling of spiritual absence; and even so it presents a less than satisfying possibility because – as the very facts of transience and mortality indicate – it is innocent, limited, and frail. Not that it is always left to the child's world to perform the positive function in Ransom's poetry: occasionally he is more explicit. This is the case with one of the few poems where he is directly concerned with the Southern tradition, "Antique Harvesters." Set on the banks of the Mississippi, the poem presents Ransom's native region as a place where wholeness of being is still available. "Antique Harvesters" is, in fact, not so much a portrait from life as a minor historical myth in which the process of creation, the act of making a landscape and then attaching to it the idea of unity of consciousness is the intent of the poem – and constitutes a vital part of its *content* too.

In some ways, Allen Tate (1889–1979) bears a haunting resemblance to Ransom. He was similarly preoccupied with the radical discontinuities of modern existence; and he also longed for a traditional society in which moral unity was the norm. But there were differences too. The volume of Ransom's creative work is relatively small; after 1927, he committed only four new poems to print, concentrating instead on public affairs and aesthetics and founding and editing the *Kenyon Review*. Apart from a year in England as a Rhodes scholar in 1913, he spent his life in America, teaching first at Vanderbilt and then at Kenyon College, Ohio. And the whole tone and texture of his poetry was highly wrought but resistant to experiments associated with modernism. Tate, on the other hand, was prolific. From *The Golden Mean and Other Poems* (1928) to *The Swimmers* (1971) he produced a steady stream of verse over six decades, brought together in *Collected Poems* (1977). He wrote interpretive biographies of Stonewall Jackson (1928) and Jefferson Davis (1929) and several volumes of comment and criticism, from *Reactionary Essays on Poetry and Ideas* (1936) to *Memoirs and Opinions* (1975). He also produced one, major novel, *The Fathers* (1938). Set in Virginia before and during the Civil War, it tells the story of two families, the Buchans of Pleasant Hill and the Poseys of Georgetown. Major Lewis Buchan, patriarch of the one family, is the consummate Southern aristocrat. George Posey, his son-in-law, is the modern man, steeped in Southern tradition but restless and outside it. Young Lacey Buchan, son of Lewis and just coming into manhood, narrates a sequence of events that tear his father and brother-in-law apart and his family asunder. These events are coincident with and inseparable from events on a larger canvas: where the South experiences comprehensive defeat and division. The personal is the political here, and vice versa.

Tate was different from Ransom, too, in that he was affected by the poetic experiments of Eliot and Crane. He even defended *The Waste Land* against Ransom's dismissive criticisms. This is reflected in the tone, and sometimes the structure, of Tate's own poetry. Freer forms alternate with metrical patterns. Logical connections are omitted, sentences inverted, and scenes changed rapidly. The distance between Tate and Ransom is measured with particular force in Tate's most famous poem, "Ode to the Confederate Dead." In some ways, "Ode" operates within the same series of assumptions as "Antique Harvesters." It, too, is a profoundly traditionalist poem which attempts to create a myth, an ideal version of the past, as a corrective to the present. The narrator, a man who characterizes the modern failure to live according to principle, stands by the monuments raised to those killed fighting for the South during the Civil War; and as he describes their lives, or what he imagines their lives to have been, the description is transmuted into celebration. The voice of "Antique Harvesters," however, is the voice of all Ransom's poems: accomplished, witty, serene – the voice of someone who can, apparently, fathom and perform his nature. The voice of "Ode," by contrast, is uncertain, feverish, disoriented – the voice of the "locked-in ego" as Tate puts it elsewhere, of a man unable to liberate himself from a sense of his own impotence and fragmentation.

Tate's search for a traditional order eventually led him away from the South and into religious faith. And he gradually turned, for the promise of moral unity, to the Roman Catholic Church. Out of the actual process of conversion came poems like "Seasons of the Soul," a powerful and often pained sequence that ends with a prayer to a mysterious "mother of silences" who seems to combine intimations of the spiritual and the sensual, the Virgin Mary and the carnal knowledge that concludes in death. After the conversion, in turn, came poems like "The Swimmers." Relaxed, fluent, idiomatic, such poems reveal a new willingness to submit to the material rather than force it into a new mold – and, in particular, to submit to the sanctions of memory and the compulsions of personality. Tate was neither the first nor the last writer to feel that ultimate salvation for the traditionalist was to be found in religion. This, in turn, enabled him to relax his tone and recall the more personal details of his past life.

The path of another notable Fugitive writer, Robert Penn Warren (1905–1989), was different, in turn, from that of Ransom or Tate. Warren was a genuine and various man of letters. His literary criticism, identifying him as one of the founders of the New Criticism, won him enormous influence: along with *Understanding Poetry* (1938) and *Understanding Fiction* (1943), co-authored with Cleanth Brooks (1906–1994), critical works written by him include the studies collected in *New and Selected Essays* (1989). An early biographical study exploring the dangers of idealism, *John Brown: The Making of a Martyr* (1929), betrays the conservative stance that aligned the younger Warren with the Agrarians. Even here, though, he took a more interrogative stance than most of his colleagues. Two later works of social and historical meditation, *Segregation: The Inner Conflict in the South* (1956) and *Who Speaks for the Negro?* (1965), measure Warren's progress towards a more liberal position and a dispassionate advocacy of civil rights. *The Legacy of the Civil War* (1956) reveals its author's lifelong interest in history as a subject and a moral discipline and his particular concern with how the war has shaped American society and sensibilities. As one of the speakers in Warren's long dramatic poem, *Brother to Dragons: A Tale in Verse and Voices* (1953; revd. edn., 1979) puts it: "without the fact of the past, no matter how terrible,/We cannot dream the future."

As a poet and novelist, above all, Warren was constantly concerned with the indelible fact of the past. That is not the entire story, though: as Warren indicated, there is also the dream of the future. Past and future, fact and idea, father and son, the traditionalist sense of what has been and the utopian feeling for what might be: the process is a dialectical one and there is no end to the growth and discovery of the self, other than that offered to each of us individually by death. Much of Warren's finest poetry and fiction is concerned with the failure to realize this dialectic. His poetry, from *Eleven Poems on the Same Theme* (1942) through such seminal volumes as *Promises* (1957) and

Audubon: A Vision (1969) to *New and Selected Poems* (1985), has returned again and again, in lyric, narrative, and meditative modes, to what one poem, "I Am Dreaming of a White Christmas: The Natural History of a Vision," calls the "process whereby pain of the past in its pastness/May be converted into the future tense/Of joy." Like Ransom, Warren has his own gallery of betrayed idealists, and many of his poems offer secular versions of the Fall. At its worst, this fall into experience provokes nihilism, surrender to the brute materiality of things. But, at its best, it leads on to a kind of redemption, expressed sometimes in terms of a rediscovery of the father.

Given that Warren is so committed, in principle, to the notion of change, it is hardly surprising that his writing bears witness to some remarkable alterations of language, tone, and vision. In his poetry, for example, the early work tended towards the highly wrought and frigidly impersonal: crabbed, allusive, and sometimes rather too know-ingly ironic, it seemed to be borrowing a manner – from Ransom and Tate, in particular – instead of shaping one in response to personal needs. The later work, by contrast, was more expansive and open: a richer, more variable idiom was combined with fluent, muscular rhythms to create a sense of energetic composure, disciplined ease. The development in the fiction was less marked, but there was still a general tendency noticeable over the course of Warren's ten novels, from *Night Rider* (1939) to *A Place to Come To* (1977), to move from the more highly wrought to the more expansive and openly personal. *All the King's Men* (1946), his most famous and accomplished novel, shows precisely how he gave his fundamental ideas fictional life. At its center is a division typical for Warren between an idealist and an opportunist: Adam Stanton, whose forename suggests his prelapsarian innocence, and Willie Stark, whose equally epon-ymous surname indicates just how far he is committed to stark fact. The protagonist and narrator, Jack Burden, is the man who must face and heal this division by coming to terms with the burden of his past, specifically in the shape of his father, and so enjoy the chance of a purely secular redemption. All this makes *All the King's Men* sound schematic. Like all Warren's fiction, the novel does veer towards the heavily freighted, a narrative so loaded with significance that it threatens to sink its surface naturalism. Like the best of it, though, it is rescued by its personal specificity and social density – and because Warren obeys his own injunction to immerse himself in history. The personal detail comes from Jack Burden, who is both man acting and man narrating. As for the immersion in society and history: that comes from the understanding of place the novel reveals, the peculiar, polyglot culture of early twentieth-century Louisiana with its mix of populist enthusiasm and easygoing cynicism, romanticism and money-grabbing. Something of this culture is caught in the rich variety of idioms Warren deploys, from the hardboiled to the dreamlike and lyrical. But even more to the point here is Warren's reimagining of a pivotal moment in Louisiana history. The character of Willie Stark is clearly based on Huey Long, the populist politician elected governor in 1928 who ran the state as his own personal fiefdom, and, just before being assassinated, was preparing to run for President on a "Share Our Wealth" program that made the New Deal look conservative. What Warren does is to take this story, the facts in the case of Long, and set it in the kind of dialectical relationship with the shaping idea of *All the King's Men* that creates a new shape and meaning for both. *All the King's Men* is consequently an apt realization of Warren's project: to remain true to the imperatives of the past and the needs of the present and future. It is also that rare thing, a philosophical novel that makes its discoveries in the welter of politics and social conflict. Not only that, it is a genuinely historical fiction in a dual sense: because it tries to come to terms with the stark facts of historical experience, and because it tries to formulate an idea of history.

Ransom, Tate, Warren: together, these three major figures chart the various possibilities of traditionalism, and in particular Southern traditionalism. Outside the South, the convictions to which the Fugitives gave such spirited expression animated many writers, among them Yvor Winters (1900–1968), J. V. Cunningham (1911–1965), and, above all, Richard Eberhart (1904–2005). The wit and sadness, and the preoccupation with mortality that characterize so many traditionalist writers are especially noticeable in Eberhart's work. The author of more than thirty volumes of poetry, among them *A Bravery of Earth* (1930), *Selected Poems 1930–65* (1965), *The Long Reach: New and Uncollected Poems, 1948–84* (1984), and *Collected Poems 1930–1986* (1988), he is someone who has been important both in his own right and as an influence on others. "We are/Betrayed by time, which made us mortal," Eberhart declares in "Anima"; and nearly all his work starts from this recognition. The structure of the world is "hard"; we all fall from "the pitch that is near madness," the "violent, vivid" and "immaculate" state of childhood, "into a realm of complexity .../Where nothing is possible but necessity"; and only a willingness to see things "in a hard intellectual light" can restore the "moral grandeur of man." These beliefs feed into Eberhart's writing, so that even his simpler poems become striking for their intellectual dexterity and rigor: ideas or experiences are introduced in a straightforward fashion and then cunningly extended, in ways that often rely on allusion or verbal or metaphoric tension for their impact. Eberhart's aim is not only to see things clearly, however, but also with "the supreme authority of the imagination" as his guide. He uses wit and dexterity, not as a substitute for vision, but as a means of liberating it, of discovering what he calls "The truth of the positive hour": which, for him, consists of "love/ Concrete, specific," "the grace to imagine the unimaginable," and the "Inescapable brotherhood of the living."

Populism and radicalism

Of those who, contrary to Eberhart, did think that a looser form and fierce belief were appropriate responses to a time of change and challenge, none were more committed than Carl Sandburg (1878–1967). The son of Swedish immigrants, Sandburg left school at the age of thirteen. Traveling though the West and taking a variety of jobs, he worked on a newspaper in Chicago, then as secretary to the socialist mayor of Milwaukee, then returned to Chicago in 1913. There, one year later, some of his poems were published in *Poetry*, the magazine founded and edited by Harriet Monroe (1860–1936). Shortly after, *Chicago Poems* (1916) and *Cornhuskers* (1918) established him as a major poet of the Midwest and Chicago renaissance. His poem "Chicago" (1916) announced the nature of his vision. "Hog Butcher for the World/Tool Maker, Stacker of wheat,/," it began, "Stormy, husky, brawling,/City of the Big Shoulders." "Chicago," like so many of Sandburg's poems, is at once a description of the newly emergent economic center of the Middle West and a celebration of the common people, its inhabitants. Its direct, unanalytical populism is reflected in the style, in which a rhetorical and flexible line, an idiomatic language and bold rhythms, all become part of the attempt to create a poetic equivalent of folk speech. Chicago, in turn, seems to be transformed into a folk hero, along the lines of Paul Bunyan or Mike Fink; and at certain points the narrator seems a folk hero too, responding to everything with an equal feeling of wonder, a reverence for its power and particularity. This is a simple poem, but it is also a remarkable one, because its celebration of the Middle West and America in general is a matter of vision and voice. It is a song both in praise and in imitation of American energy, the sense of possibility that an almost unlimited amount of living space can bring.

Sandburg's response to America was not uncritical, however. He could be hard, when he turned from celebration of the energies of the people to an attack on those who would suppress such energies or divert them to their own ends. Nor does he confine himself to the city scene; on the contrary, some of his finest poems, like "Sunset from Omaha Hotel Window" (1918) and "More Country People" (1918), are concerned with the signs, sounds, and the people of the prairies. All of his work, though, whatever its subject or treatment, is shot through with his democratic populist values; and none more so than two monumental works, his biography of Abraham Lincoln begun in 1919 and not finished until 1939, and his reworking of folk song and idiom in *The People, Yes*, a long poem that appeared in 1936. In the biography, Lincoln appears as an embodiment of the American dream; while, in the poem, Sandburg declares his faith in the democratic experiment. This is American epic at its most straightforward: plotless, concentrating more on natural potential than on cultural attainment, and ending on a note of hope. At its center is what Sandburg calls "a polychrome,/a spectrum and a prism": a mysterious, multifarious figure who is at once everybody and nobody in particular – nobody apart from that representative of his nation the writer knows best, himself.

"Oh, the great poem has yet to be written … Jeffersonian democracy as an art is a thing to be desired." The words are those of another poet associated with Chicago, Vachel Lindsay (1879–1931). Like Sandburg, Lindsay was devoted to Abraham Lincoln: "The prairie-lawyer," he called him, "master of us all." He was equally devoted to Andrew Jackson (a man for whom, as he saw it, "Every friend was an equal"), and to William Jennings Bryan. Bryan, in particular, was a charismatic figure for him: the Democratic Presidential candidate of 1896 who, for a time, made it seem possible that the farming interests of the West might yet prevail over the business interests of "the dour East." Lindsay was, in fact, raised in Illinois during the period of agrarian and populist revolt against the emergent urban-industrial economy; and it left an indelible mark on him. So, too, did the walking tour of the United States that he undertook in 1912. Out of both experiences grew a determination to create an "American" rhythm, related to the sounds of galloping herds and shrieking motors, black music and what he called "vaudevilles" and "circuses." And out of this, in turn, came poems like "General William Booth Enters Into Heaven" (1913) (which reveals his commitment to the social gospel of the underprivileged), "In Praise of Johnny Appleseed" (1913) (the mythical American hero for whom, Lindsay suggests, "the real frontier was his sunburnt breast"), and, perhaps his most famous work, "Bryan, Bryan, Bryan, Bryan" (1913). The two collections that brought Lindsay fame were *General William Booth Enters Into Heaven and Other Poems* (1913) and *The Congo and Other Poems* (1914). Whatever may be thought of his work and aims, he remains a curiously noble figure: someone who took the populist fervor and the pedagogical impulses implicit in the American tradition to their logical extreme.

A third memorable writer associated with the Chicago "renaissance" was a populist in a different sense, in that he wanted to record the real lives of people as they were lived in the Middle West, without heroic or romantic decoration. Edgar Lee Masters (1868–1950) aimed, he said, to write "a sort of Divine Comedy" of smalltown life: its minor tragedies, its melancholy and frustrations. Like Sandburg and Lindsay, he received the encouragement of Harriet Monroe; and it was still early on in his career when the major fruit of his labors appeared, *Spoon River Anthology* (1915). Using a loose verse form and spare, dry language, Masters presents the reader with a series of self-spoken epitaphs. The tone is sometimes elegiac, very occasionally lyrical and affirmative, but the major impression left by the book is one of waste. Men, women, and children reveal what happened to them and what happened was, for the most part, shame and disappointment. Gradually, the poems overlap to produce a composite picture of Spoon River: one that recalls Tilbury Town and Winesburg, Ohio, but without the passion, or Robinson's and Anderson's sense that something more lies beneath the monotonous surface. Masters is remembered now as another example of that reaction against smalltown values which characterized so many early twentieth-century American writers. It would be more useful, though, to remember him as someone who attempted to honor the stoicism of ordinary people, their laconic idioms and the harsh rhythms of their existence – and who consequently achieved one of the aims of American populist writing – of speaking not only to the people but for them.

Implicit in the work of Sandburg, Lindsay, and even Masters is the radicalism that Whitman gave voice to when he declared that "our American republic" was "experimental ... in the deepest sense." It was left to some other writers, however, to give free rein to this radical feeling: with them, the populist strain was sometimes still evident but, when it was, it was absorbed into a larger structure of feeling that anticipated political, social, and perhaps moral change. To be politically engaged, even an activist, did not, however, prescribe one style or subject: something that is clear from the work of the two most accomplished radical poets of the period, Kenneth Rexroth (1905–1982) and Archibald MacLeish (1892–1982). With Rexroth, the nature of his political commitment is clear from the conclusion to a poem called "New Objectives, New Cadres," one of the many gathered together in *The Collected Shorter Poems* (1967) (*The Collected Longer Poems* was published a year later, to be followed by several other volumes, including *The Morning Star: Poems and Translations* (1979)). The narrator describes an "activist and lecturer "drawing pointless incisive diagrams" for an audience of "miners and social workers." "We do not need his confessions," the narrative voice observes: "The future is more fecund than Molly Bloom –/The problem is to control history,/We already understand it." This has many of the trademarks of Rexroth's poetry, and indeed of his prose in *An Autobiographical Novel* (1966) and his critical essay collections, *The Bird in the Bush* (1959) and *Assays* (1961): a cool, sardonic yet passionate tone, a fierce commitment to the community of ordinary people and an equally fierce hatred of intellectuals ("spectacled men," as he calls them in another poem), the sense of a spirit as flinty and tenacious as the Western landscape where the writer made his home. There is nothing strained or artificial about such lines. "Poetry,"

Rexroth insisted, "is the living speech of the people," elsewhere adding, "I have spent my life trying to write the way I talk." Consequently, he disdained elaborate rhetoric in favor of clarity of speech, a poised syntax, and simple, lucid images. Rexroth's phrasing is organically determined by his own speaking and breathing, so a powerful sense of Rexroth the individual emerges from his work – humorous, honest, irascible, passionate, proud. William CarlosWilliams called him "a moralist with his hand at the trigger ready to fire at the turn of a hair"; he was also a poetic prophet whose prophecies were shaped by an indestructible optimism.

A similar optimism characterizes another poet for whom the idea of the writer as agent of social change was crucially important: Archibald MacLeish. MacLeish's early work, written mostly while he was in Europe, is preoccupied with the plight of the artist and is full of unassimilated influences: notably Eliot, Pound, and the French Symbolists. On his return to the United States, however, at about the time of the Depression, he became increasingly interested in social issues and began to work towards a poetic diction closer to common speech. A series of poems followed examining the problems and possibilities of his native country (*New Found Land* (1930)). These were followed, in turn, by an epic poem describing the attempted conquest of the Mexican Aztecs by the Spanish Cortéz (*Conquistador* (1932)) and by other poems satirizing the excesses of American capitalism (*Frescoes for Mr. Rockerfeller's City* (1933)) or chastising American writers for their withdrawal from what MacLeish saw as their social responsibilities (*The Irresponsibles* (1940)). "Instead of studying American life," MacLeish declared of the writers of the 1920s, "literature denounced it. Instead of working to understand American life, literature repudiated it." His clearly stated aim was to reverse this trend: "This is my own land," he announced in "American Letter" (*Collected Poems, 1917–52* (1952)). "It is a strange thing – to be an American." For MacLeish, as for many of his predecessors, this strangeness resided in the idea of America rather than the historical fact: the New World as a place of freedom and solitude, a site of possibility. "America is neither a land nor a people,/" he insisted in "American Letter," "America is West and the wind blowing/America is a great word and the snow."

Although MacLeish produced notable prose works, his energies, like those of Rexroth, were mostly devoted to poetry. There were, however, many radicals who turned to prose to examine the contemporary crisis and to express their convictions. Among the most notable of these were Randolph Bourne (1886–1918) and Michael Gold (1893–1967). Bourne established his reputation as an essayist in *The New Republic* and other magazines. His work reveals an interest in education (*Education and Living* (1917)), and a firm commitment to the development of a socially responsible fiction (*The History of a Literary Radical* (1920)). As America entered World War I, he also became an increasingly isolated advocate for pacifism and non-intervention (*Untimely Papers* (1919)). A theoretical piece entitled "The State" (1919) was left unfinished, leaving many to speculate about his possible political influence had he lived longer to complete it and other similar pieces. However, his essay on an ethnically diverse American culture, "Trans-National America" (1916), shows his perception and prescience. In it, Bourne attacked the idea of "the melting-pot": which, he said, reflected "English-American conservatism." America, he argued, was destined to be "the first international nation," "not a nationality but a trans-nationality, a weaving back and forth – of many threads of all sizes and colors." It was a potent expression of the belief in a multicultural community that has sustained many American writers.

Michael Gold was born Yitzhak Granich to Jewish immigrants on the Lower East Side of New York City. The major themes of his work are derived from that background. Yitzhak was anglicized to Isaac; then, in adolescence, evidently dreaming dreams of glory of the kind that persuaded James Gatz to rename himself Jay Gatsby, he took the name Irwin. It was in 1919–1920 that he took the name Michael Gold, in honor of a Jewish veteran of the Civil War who, he said, had fought to "free the slaves." And already, embittered by the failure of his father's business and aroused by a demonstration he witnessed in Union Square in 1914, the commitment suggested by this final name change had prompted him to write. As a youth, Gold recalled, he had "no politics ... except hunger," but now he gravitated to the political left and lifelong involvement with the Communist Party. His first piece was published in 1914 in *The Masses*. It was, typically, a poem about three anarchists who had died in a bomb explosion. Not long after, he was to publish a more important piece, an essay entitled "Toward Proletarian Art" arguing for a literature by workers rather than bourgeois leftists, about workers and for workers. If any single work was responsible for initiating the proletarian movement in American literature, then this was. Moving to Greenwich Village from the Lower East Side, Gold became involved in leftist literary circles centered around Eugene O'Neill and John Reed (1887–1920), the writer and activist whose most important work was an eyewitness account of the Russian Revolution, *Ten Days That Shook the World* (1919). He left the United States for a while to avoid the draft, but, on returning in 1920, he became editor of *The Liberator*, the successor to the suppressed *Masses*. Then, when *The Liberator* became wholly political, he helped found *The New Masses*, becoming editor-in-chief of the new magazine in 1928. His fiery columns, notable for their polemical communist views and their espousal of the cause of proletarian literature, were to be collected in *The Mike Gold Reader* (1954) and *Mike Gold: A Literary Anthology* (1972).

Throughout the 1920s, Gold had been working on a fictionalized autobiography. It was published in 1930 as *Jews Without Money*, just at the right time for such a fiercely political novel, and was an immediate success. Based on the author's early life in a Jewish ghetto, it describes in detail the degradation of poverty. It also offers a ferocious arraignment of capitalism: a system in which "kindness is a form of suicide." The father of a family is overwhelmed by the depression and dispossession he sees all around him. It is the mother, Katie Gold, who is the cornerstone of the family and the heroic center of the book. Standing up to landlords and other class enemies, struggling to survive and support her family, she offers a paradigm for the revolution of the proletariat. She also offers an example to her son, the protagonist. The story ends with his conversion to the cause of communist revolution. Stylistically, *Jews Without Money* moves between expansive, exclamatory prose, which recalls the fact that Whitman was the American writer Gold admired most, and a more journalistic idiom, with short, punchy sentences, paragraphs, and chapters, snappy vignettes and dramatic moments. And thematically it blends its revolutionary message, just as the plays of Odets do (Gold, in fact, also wrote several one-act plays for the Provincetown Players), with a vivid account of Jewish family life. Gold remained a loyal communist throughout his life, despite the manifest brutality of Stalinism. He became a daily columnist for the mass circulation communist newspaper, *The Daily Worker*, in 1933, and in 1941 he published the anti-Trotskyite *The Hollow Men*, a collection of his newspaper articles attacking the political errors of such former allies as Ernest Hemingway. He is perhaps the archetypal twentieth-century American literary radical. He is, however, also a writer who had an instinctive understanding, not just of the generalized plight of the workers, but of the needs of individual members of the dispossessed.

Like so many writers of the time who concerned themselves with the condition of the poor, Gold has sometimes been dismissed as a producer of social protest. That ignores the fact that such writers might have felt drawn to portray, and maybe protest, the social conditions around them but did so in different forms. Those forms range from the energetic rewriting of Southwestern humor for social purposes in *Tobacco Road* (1932) and *God's Little Acre* (1933) by Erskine Caldwell (1903–1987) to a more literally realistic fiction like the Studs Lonigan trilogy (*Young Lonigan* (1932), *The Young Manhood of Studs Lonigan* (1934), *Judgement Day* (1935)) by James T. Farnell (1904–1979), which doggedly charts the representative life and death of a young urban Irishman. What blanket references to social protest also manage to conceal is that, for many, commitment remained an inspiration throughout their career but inspired a rich variety of expression. Among these was Lillian Smith (1897–1966), the leading Southern white liberal of the mid-twentieth century, who devoted her life to lifting self-deception in the South about race, class, gender, and sexuality. Born into an upper-class family in the Deep South, Smith emerged into public debate in opposition to the Agrarians. She produced a small literary magazine, *Pseudopodia* (later, *North Georgia Review*), and then *South Today*, which she co-edited with Paula Snelling. Then, in 1945, she produced her most famous book, *Strange Fruit*. At once the love story of a mulatto girl and a powerful critique of racial prejudice, it became a bestseller. Her other novel, *One Hour*, appeared sixteen years later; it is about the response of a Southern town to the hysterical accusation of immorality that a young girl makes against an older man. But her notable work, apart from *Strange Fruit*, is her journalism, her works on civil rights, *Now is the Time* (1955) and *Our Faces, Our Words* (1964), and, above all, her autobiographical critique of Southern culture, *Killers of the Dream* (1949). "By the time we were five years old," Smith recalls in *Killers of the Dream*, "we had learned . . . that masturbation is wrong and segregation is right." That is characteristic of Smith at her best throughout her varied career. She recognized that her society's concepts of race invariably interacted with those of gender, sexuality, and class. And although she rarely considered class apart from race, issues of gender and sexuality are persistent in her work

Three other writers whose concern with social issues was woven through the varied tapestry of their careers are Lillian Hellman (1905–1984), Mary McCarthy (1912–1989), and Meridel Le Sueur (1900–1996). Hellman came to public attention with a series of successful plays. Her first, *The Children's Hour* (1934), shows the havoc caused by a malicious girl's invention of a lesbian relationship between her two teachers. *The Little Foxes* (1939) concerns the struggle of a reactionary Southern family to retain wealth and power despite internal feuds and the encroachments of modern society. *Watch on the Rhine* (1941) and *The Searching Wind* (1944) are two openly political dramas, dealing with the fight against Nazism. And other, later plays include *Toys in the Attic* (1964), which deals with the theme of miscegenation. "I am a moral writer," Hellman once wrote; and, in her drama, she used the conventions of the well-made play to compel her mainly middle-class audience to confront questions of justice, social equality, and personal responsibility. The crises her characters face are, invariably, ones that force them to choose between the imperatives of conscience and the demands of society. Hellman was eventually made to make that choice herself when, in 1952, because of her political activities, she was called to testify before the House Un-American Activities Committee. And, courageously, she told the committee that, while she was willing to speak about her own activism, she would not say anything about the activities of others. For this, although she was not jailed, she found herself blacklisted. However, she responded by launching a new career as a writer of autobiographical memoirs. *An Unfinished Woman* (1969) and *Pentimento* (1973) are largely concerned with her childhood experiences and early personal and political involvements. In *Scoundrel Time* (1976), however, she returned to the period when, as she put it, thanks to the Un-American Activities Committee, "truth made you a traitor as it often does in a time of scoundrels." Hellman shows that it is necessary to look backward honestly in order to go forward. If America does not acknowledge its errors, it will simply go on repeating them; if Americans do not accept their responsibilities as individuals and citizens, then they will get the kind of scoundrels to rule them they deserve.

A similar concern with moral and social responsibility lies at the heart of all Mary McCarthy's work. McCarthy began her career by writing reviews for *The New Republic*, *The Nation*, and *The Partisan Review*; she then turned to writing fiction that has often been close to the autobiographical bone. *The Company She Keeps* (1942), for instance, is a witty portrait of a bohemian, intellectual young woman; while *The Groves of Academe* (1952), a satirical portrait of faculty life at a liberal college for women, is based on McCarthy's experiences of teaching at Bard and Sarah Lawrence colleges. Her most famous novel, *The Group* (1963), in turn, springs from its author's experiences as a student at Vassar in the early 1930s. Beginning with the inauguration of Franklin Roosevelt and ending with that of Harry Truman, *The Group* follows the lives of eight Vassar women. McCarthy commented that the book was "about the idea of progress really, seen in the female sphere"; and what it reveals, fundamentally, is a lack of progress, thanks to the damaging norms of masculine aggression and feminine passivity. Among McCarthy's other novels are *Birds of America* (1971), which explores both the contemporary gap between the generations and the cultural collision between Europe and America, and *Cannibals and Missionaries* (1979), which confronts the moral and social issue of terrorism. But at least as important as her fiction is her political commentary, in works like *Vietnam* (1967), *Hanoi* (1968), and *The Mask of State: Watergate Portrait* (1974), her travel books with their accompanying social comment, such as *Venice Observed* (1956), her critical work and journalism collected in *Occasional Prose* (1985) and other volumes, and her autobiographical writing. Of the autobiographical work, *Memories of a Catholic Girlhood* (1957) is the most significant. After she was orphaned at the age of six, McCarthy was sent to Catholic schools by relatives; and *Memories* describes how, at convent school, she felt herself to be "an outsider." "I did not fit into the convent pattern," she recalls and, in order to give the appearance at least of fitting in, she was forced to pretend. Leaving convent school for "public high school," McCarthy gave up her nickname of "Cye" that had been forced on her by her Catholic classmates, along with her Catholicism and, with them both, her "false personality." "I got my own name back," McCarthy informs the reader; she "sloughed off" the mask she had been forced to wear, the spurious title she had been forced to accept, and the pretence she had been forced to live. And she became herself. It is the perfect illustration in miniature of the prevailing theme in McCarthy's work, and the one she summed up quite simply when she said that it is necessary "to choose the self you want."

Meridel Le Sueur is less well known than McCarthy, Hellman, or even Smith. Nevertheless, she is an important radical voice in American writing, speaking in particular for the social and mythic possibilities of women. The work that Le Sueur wrote and began to publish during the 1920s explored subject matter and themes that she has pursued throughout her work. Central to these explorations in the early writing is the figure of a "raw green girl," lonely, curious, seeking. Sometimes this figure is connected, as in a story called "Persephone" (1927), to a mythic formulation of experience: the separation from the mother, the plunge into the darkness of the underground, the woman (or the earth) as wounded, invaded, and raped. In time, the further, more positive implications of the myth of Persephone and her mother Demeter would be explored too: the rebirth from the darkness and the return to the mother and the world of women. "People are ready to flower and they cannot." That comment in "Annunciation" (1935) suggests just how closely the political and the personal, the social and the mythic, are interwoven in Le Sueur's work. She is perpetually concerned with how "the body repeats the landscape" ("The Ancient People and the Newly Come" (1976)) and how, in recognizing the imperatives of the body, it is possible to resist and triumph over a "society built upon . . . a cut-throat competition which sets one man against another" ("I Was Marching" (1934)). Le Sueur explored these notions in her short stories, her novel *The Girl* (written in 1939, published in 1978) based on tales of women she had known, her history of the Midwest based on folk materials, *North Star Country* (1945), and her autobiographical pieces, some of which were collected in *Salute to Spring* (1940). She also explored them in her journalism, some of which is also found in *Salute to Spring*. "I Was Marching," for example, perhaps Le Sueur's most famous piece of reportage, recalls her involvement in the Minneapolis truckers' strike in 1934. Mixing political comment and narrative cunning, the report is a startling anticipation of later new journalism; it is also animated, as all her work is, by a belief in what she later described as the "circular" and the "continuous" – the repetition of each life in every other, the sourcing of all bodies in the one. In her later work, this belief in circularity is often reflected in the form: borrowing from Native American traditions, Le Sueur tends to reject linear narrative in favor of repetitive, cyclical structures. For all the alterations of form, though, and the expansion of source and subjects, Le Sueur's central concerns remain the same: women and the land, their centuries of parallel suffering and exploitation, the hope of rebirth and renewal offered by both.

Prophetic voices

"I believe that we are lost here in America," wrote Thomas Wolfe (1900–1938) once, "but I believe we shall be found. And this belief . . . is not only our hope, but America's everlasting, living dream." That remark captures the abiding romanticism of Wolfe's work, its concern with loss and prophecy, and its search for a self-realization that is coextensive with the discovery of national identity. It also captures its dualism. All Wolfe's writing weaves its way between an intricate pattern of opposites: the rural past and the urban future, rootedness and escape, the "lonely austerity of the dark earth" where Wolfe and his protagonists grow up and "the powerful movement of the train" carrying them away from that place to wider horizons. Wolfe claimed "the enormous space and energy of America as a whole" as his subject. He also described his first novel, *Look Homeward, Angel* (1929), as "the story of a powerful creative element trying to work its way toward an essential isolation, a creative solitude." There was no contradiction here for him, however, because, like so many other American writers, he saw the story of the nation as the story of his individual self – for he was his hero Eugene Gant, he was the "powerful creative element," the source and subject of his fiction. And in working out his own perplexities, in prose that moves back and forth between rhetoric and reportage, he was trying to confront and resolve the problem of the nation as it vacillated between its historical failure and its "everlasting, living dream."

Wolfe was born and raised in the mountain town of Asheville, North Carolina, the place that became the "Old Catawba" of his fiction. With the publication of *Look Homeward, Angel*, he was able to devote himself to his writing, since it was an immediate success. A vast, sprawling book, like all Wolfe's major novels, it follows the contours of the author's early life closely. Eugene Gant grows up in a household torn between restlessness and rootedness. His father has a love of rhetoric, craft, and a demonic passion for adventure; his mother is wedded to her ancestry, place, making money and finding security; and they quarrel constantly. Eugene reads voraciously, attends school, then state college where, while he continues to feel "different" and lonely, he is beginning to fulfill his desire for "getting away." The pilgrimage Eugene is embarked on, in search of "the lost lane-end into heaven, a stone, a leaf, an unfound door," is continued in *Of Time and the River* (1935), which covers Eugene's experiences at Harvard and abroad and his teaching in New York. Together, the two narratives move outward in a series of concentric circles – from provincial hometown to state college to cosmopolitan centers and the wide world beyond – just as Wolfe's own life did. And, as they do, they chart that restless desire to break away that, like Whitman, Wolfe saw as the source of American culture. What Wolfe adds to this, however, like Cather, is a backward glance, a centripetal impulse that is a matter of emotion rather than action. Neither Gant nor America can properly escape, Wolfe suggests, since they are "acted upon by all the accumulated impact" of their ancestral experience. For Gant, as for Wolfe and America, the past is a part of their blood. They cannot go home again, but they can never entirely leave either.

You Can't Go Home Again (1940) is, in fact, the title of a novel by Wolfe that was published posthumously. It is the sequel to *The Web and the Rock* (1939), which also appeared after Wolfe died suddenly at the age of thirty-eight. In these two books, which were edited from material that Wolfe left behind at his death, the hero is called George Webber. He is, however, indistinguishable from Eugene Gant, and he continues Wolfe's project of turning his life into a national epic and himself into a representative man. The title of the first novel symbolizes the problem of its protagonist and recalls the dualism of all Wolfe's writing. George Webber is caught between the web of environment, experience, ancestry and the rock, the original strength, adventure, and beauty of the vision of his father. He is also, like his creator, torn between a sense of loss and hope. He recognizes that a corrupt society destroys the individual, but he still believes that "the true fulfillment of our spirit, of our people ... is yet to come." So Wolfe remained true, throughout his life, to that nostalgic utopianism so characteristic of American thought, that scores a corrupt present by measuring it against what has been irretrievably lost and what might still be gained. Yesterday is gone, leaving only its failures, today is a tale of waste and want, but there is still tomorrow; which might become a bright mirror of a more mythic past.

A similar vein of prophecy is at work in the fiction of John Steinbeck (1902–1968), although, in this case, prophecy is more closely wedded to political vision. Born in California, Steinbeck studied marine biology at university: a subject that may have later helped shape his interest in humanity as a collective biological organism, and the mass movement of that mass humanity as the fundamental condition of life. It was *Tortilla Flat* (1935), a vivid portrait of life among the poor in Monterey, that brought Steinbeck to prominence. And it was *In Dubious Battle* (1936), the story of a strike among migratory workers in the California fruit orchards, that brought a new political edge to his work. With *Of Mice and Men* (1937) Steinbeck firmly established himself as the novelist of the rural poor. It is the tale of two itinerant farm workers, drawn into a brotherhood of suffering with each other, who yearn to find a home. With the Depression wreaking economic havoc and drought turning vast swathes of agricultural land into a Dust Bowl, farmers and their families were reduced to absolute poverty, forced out of their homes and buildings. As they traveled across America in search of work, they needed to find a voice, someone to make the nation aware of their suffering. And they found it in Steinbeck, particularly with the publication of his most famous novel, *The Grapes of Wrath*, in 1939.

The origins of *The Grapes of Wrath* lie, typically for the time, in a series of newspaper articles Steinbeck wrote about migratory laborers. Published in 1936, they were reprinted as a pamphlet, *Their Blood is Strong*, with an epilogue added, in 1938. It was then that Steinbeck decided to turn fact into fiction to gain maximum impact: to tell a story that would enable his readers to experience the suffering he had seen. So he invented the Joad family, Oklahoma farmers who are driven off their land by soil erosion, and who drive to California hoping to take advantage of what they imagine to be a land of plenty. The migration of the Joad family is punctuated by interchapters, written in lyrical prose, that generalize the experience of the family, and force us to see what happens to them as representative of what was happening to all the rural poor of the time. Steinbeck plays cunningly with different mythical structures, too, to add resonance and representativeness to his story. The journey of the Joads recalls many other earlier, epic migrations: notably, the biblical journey to the Promised Land and the westward movement that helped shape the history of the American nation. What the Joad family find when they reach California, however, is no land of promise. For these Western adventurers, there is no realization of a dream of freedom. There is only more poverty and pain. Tom Joad, the older son in the Joad family and the epic hero, joins with Jim Casy, a minister turned labor organizer, to try to build resistance to the exploitation of the "Okies," as they are dismissively called, and other migrant laborers. Casy is killed; Tom kills to avenge his death; those few members of the Joad family who have survived try to hide Tom. But then Tom leaves, telling his mother, "I'll be ever'where – wherever you look. Wherever they's a fight so hungry people can eat, I'll be there." Casy has died but the spirit of Casy, his belief in collective identity and action, lives on in Tom. Not only that, the intimation is, it will soon be "ever'where," just as the spirit of Jesus Christ (whose initials are recalled in Casy's) spread everywhere after his death. That spirit is evidently at work in the last, symbolic moment of *The Grapes of Wrath* when Rose of Sharon, Tom's sister, who has just given birth to a stillborn child, nurses an anonymous starving man with the milk meant for her baby. She has recognized, as Tom has, her involvement in a communal identity larger than her own immediate family; and she has realized that her giving of herself to that communality is the source of renewal.

As its title indicates, as well as its narrative drive, *The Grapes of Wrath* is an angry but also an optimistic book. Recalling "The Battle-Hymn of the Republic" with its prophecy of truth marching to victory, and recollecting an earlier triumph over another kind of oppression, that title announces what the book will say: that the oppressors will be conquered, with a crusade to end poverty succeeding in the twentieth century, just as the crusade to end slavery triumphed in the nineteenth. Steinbeck acknowledges the power of the oppressors and catalogues the destitution and defeats of their victims, but he also anticipates the trampling under of that power. Weaving together the literal and the legendary, he outlines not only what America is but what it might be. And what it might be is registered, not just in conversion of people like Casy, Tom, and Rose of Sharon, or in the comments of other characters, as they grope towards political consciousness, or in the transformation of the religion of Christ on the cross into one of man on the move. It is there, also, in the sheer sweep of Steinbeck's prose as he describes the vastness of the American continent. In terms of narrative fact, the westward movement of *The Grapes of Wrath* may meet with closure. But, as far as narrative feeling is concerned, there remains something else: the conviction that there is still space, and time, to find a true West. The betrayal of the American dream may be what gives the novel its quality of barely controlled rage. But the belief in the continuing presence of that dream, as a source of renewal, is what gives it also a prophetic fervor. Steinbeck was never to write anything as powerful as his story of the Joads, although there were to be many further novels about the poor (*Cannery Row* (1945)), family troubles and tensions (*East of Eden* (1952)), and a book about Steinbeck's own journeying across America (*Travels with Charley* (1962)). *The Grapes of Wrath* stands, though, as a worthy equivalent in the twentieth century of *Uncle Tom's Cabin* in the nineteenth: a work founded on the conviction that things should and could change which, thanks to its author's mixing of the documentary and the visionary, managed to ensure that many others were equally convinced.

Community and Identity

Immigrant writing

"Where is America?" asks the narrator of "America and I" (1923), a short story by Anzia Yezierska (1885–1970). "Is there an America? What is this wilderness in which I'm lost?" The teller of the tale is, she informs the reader, an immigrant who has fled from "the airless oppression of Russia" to what she believes will be "the Promised

Land." Her dream, which mirrors the dream of Steinbeck's migrants, begins to be challenged when she arrives in the New World. Working first as a servant and then in a sweatshop, she cannot find what she calls "*my America*, where I could work for love and not for a living." Still, it encourages her to read American history. There she discovers that "the great difference between the first Pilgrims and me was that they expected to make America ... I wanted to find it ready made." "Then came a light – a great revelation!" the narrator reveals. "I saw America – a big idea ... a world still in the making." She realizes, at last, that "it was the glory of America that it was not yet finished." So she concludes, she began to play her part in the creation of "the America that is every day coming to be." And she began "to build a bridge of understanding between the American-born" and herself by opening up her life and the lives of her people to them. "In only writing about the Ghetto I found America."

The story speaks for many immigrants of the time, who wanted to play their part in the creation of what Randolph Bourne had called a "trans-national America." It also speaks for those immigrant writers who wanted to write that America into existence, by sharing their world with "the American-born." Yezierska was better educated and more experienced than most of her ghetto characters. Nevertheless, her emotional experiences as an immigrant were her inspiration. They were the source of her stories, many of them collected in *Hungry Hearts* (1920) and *Children of Loneliness* (1923), and several novels, including *Salome of the Tenements* (1922) and *Bread Givers* (1925); and they formed the basis of her fictionalized autobiography, *Red Ribbon on a White Horse* (1950). Her narrators and characters range from feisty immigrant girls to older women, isolated, disenfranchised, frustrated by years of demeaning labor. Always, though, there is the same vision shaping them as there is in the creation of the characters of Wolfe and Steinbeck, of an America still ripe with promise.

That hopeful message does not shape all immigrant writing of the period. It is not there, for instance, in the fiction of Pietro Di Donato (1911–1992), a self-taught son of Italian immigrants who described the lives of exploited workers in a rich, lyrical prose. Di Donato was haunted by the central, personal experience of his young life that came to express for him the full measure of suffering, the crucifixion suffered by the poor. When he was only eleven, his father was killed in a terrible accident, drowning in cement on a construction job; and he was suddenly forced to take over his father's role of bricklayer and financial support for his family. Laid off from work in the 1930s, Di Donato found, he said, "the leisure to think" and to read "the immortal minds of all countries." "That gave me freedom," he remembered. He began to write a short story, "Christ in Concrete," based on the death of his father. Published in 1937, it supplied the germ of a novel, also called *Christ in Concrete*, which appeared two years later. Centered on a man like his father, an immigrant caught between two worlds and in captivity to his job, it was greeted with acclaim. Success rendered Di Donato silent for nearly twenty years; and his later books, two novels and two biographies, never received the same reception or a wide readership. But the story of the life of his father, the "Christ in concrete," remains a central event in immigrant writing of the time.

Significant immigration into the United States from Asia began in 1849, when Chinese men began to arrive. Early Chinese American literary production was mainly limited to a few autobiographies and oral testimonies. Much of this literature was influenced by Chinese literary traditions, which incorporated elements from oral culture, and was often imitative of Chinese literary forms. Using China as their formal source and America as their subject, these texts were introducing a new sensibility into the American literary tradition, that of the Chinese American. Of course, something of that sensibility had already been registered in the published writing of Sui Sin Far. Something more of it was caught in the work of Jade Snow Wong (1922–2006). In her autobiographical *Fifth Chinese Daughter* (1945), she described her experience of growing up in America as the daughter of traditional and strict Chinese parents. What her parents wanted, Wong recalls, was adherence to the Chinese understanding of the female role. And, while Wong herself was not totally resistant to these expectations, she did find it difficult to reconcile them with her need to assimilate into American society. As Wong describes it, she never really resolved this dilemma. Part of her was drawn to traditional Chinese life: to its emphasis on the family, inherited customs and rituals. And part of her was eager for acceptance into white society and ready to adopt white habits of thought and belief. The ambivalence of her position was caught, not only in her book, but also in how Wong came to write it. She was encouraged to write her story by a white publisher, who wanted the voice of this second generation immigrant to be heard. But the part played by the publisher was interventionist: Wong was advised what to include, her manuscript was extensively edited to make it supposedly more palatable to white audiences, and two-thirds of it were cut. In terms of its literary production, as well as its content, *Fifth Chinese Daughter* is a formative document confirming what was to be a presiding theme of so much immigrant literature – the condition, and sometimes the curse, of living more than one history.

Japanese people began emigrating to the United States in significant numbers in the 1880s, Koreans at the end of the nineteenth century, and Filipinos from about 1900. Although the majority of immigrants from these Asian American groups tended to be single men, some were married and brought their wives with them: with the result that a second generation born in the United States – called *nisei* among the Japanese – appeared earlier than it did among the Chinese. Here, the formative writers in the earlier part of the twentieth century, respective to the different cultural groups, were Etsu Sugimoto (1873–1950), Younghill Kang (1903–1972), and Carlos Bulosan (1917–1956). Etsu Sugimoto produced what was possibly the first of a substantial amount of *nisei* writing that appeared in the 1920s and 1930s, an autobiographical novel titled *A Daughter of the Samurai* (1925). True to the rich mixture of cultural influences at work in these texts, the book juxtaposes the American life of its author with portraits of Japan that are both actual and fictional. Sugimoto has been called an ambassador of goodwill, writing to promote understanding and appreciation of Japanese Americans; and she combines a mostly favorable portrait of Japanese life with a complimentary account of America.

Younghill Kang was born in Korea, educated first in the Confucian tradition and then in Christian mission schools, and emigrated to the United States in 1921. Unlike Sugimoto, who tended to see herself as a guest in the United States, Kang desperately desired acceptance and to make America his home. Describing himself as self-educated, Kang read English and American classic literature voraciously, and attended classes at Harvard and Boston universities while working to support himself. With the help of his American wife, he began writing in English in 1928; then, while he was teaching at New York University, he became friends with Thomas Wolfe. Wolfe read some of the book

Kang was working on at the time, and took it to his own editor. It was published in 1931 as *The Grass Roof*. A novel about the life of a young man in Korea up to his departure for America, it had plainly autobiographical roots. Well received, it was followed by *East Goes West* (1937), the story of the life of a Korean in America. But, while the portrait of Korea as a "planet of death" in *The Grass Roof* had been applauded, Kang's account of American prejudice and Korean problems in America hit a less responsive chord.

Carlos Bulosan also emigrated to America while he was a young man. In 1930 he left his birthplace in the Philippines, after an impoverished childhood. He worked in the United States as an itinerant laborer and union activist. Eventually, he became one of the best-known Filipino writers in the United States, writing poetry, short stories, and essays about Filipino American life between the 1930s and the 1950s. His fame grew during and after World War II, when he produced such works as *Letter from America* (1942), *The Voice of Bataan* (1944), *Laughter of My Father* (1944), and *The Dark People* (1944). But it is for his autobiographical narrative, *America is in the Heart* (1943), that he is best known. Divided into four parts, the book opens in 1918 with the young Carlos sharing the extreme economic hardship of his family. Aware of the gross inequities of Filipino society, American cultural imperialism in the Philippines, and the need for "radical social change," Carlos embarks for the United States. Part two then sees him arrive in Seattle. Traveling around, eking out a meager existence in a series of seasonal jobs, he comes into contact with the Filipino labor movement. Forced into a ghettoized existence, he also becomes aware of just how hostile and racist a society America is. The second part of *America is in the Heart* ends, though, with a clear articulation of hope from another character, who tells Carlos, "America is a prophecy of a new society of men." And part three documents Carlos's transformation into a radicalized union activist, working for the Filipino labor movement. The short, final section, in turn, shows Bulosan achieving some literary success. Reading *The Grass Roof*, he reflects, "Why could I not succeed as Younghill Kang had?" This spurs him on to write his own story: an act which he sees as his means of fighting for a better life in America. "The time had come, I felt, for me to utilize my experiences in written form," Bulosan explains. "I had something to live for now, and to fight the world with." Writing also becomes his means of feeling he belongs. "It came to me that no man ... could destroy my faith in America again," he concludes his narrative. "It was something that grew out of the sacrifices ... of my brothers ... I know that no man could destroy my faith in America."

Native American voices

Among Native American writers, the first flourishing of literature written in English came in the 1920s and 1930s. Of the several Native American authors who began exploring the plight of their people in fiction, during the earlier part of the twentieth century, the most notable were Thomas S. Whitecloud (1914–1972), John Joseph Matthews (1894–1979), D'Arcy McNickle (1904–1977), and Mourning Dove (1888–1976). Necessarily, they focused on different aspects of the Native American experience. What they had in common, however, were certain fundamental concerns relating to the crisis in their culture. Whatever their approach, all of them were preoccupied with the debate over personal and tribal identity in the face of land loss, radical social and cultural change, and the pressure from white society to assimilate and acculturate Native Americans. The struggle of Native peoples to reconcile their ancient tribal traditions with the forces of American modernity became a dominant theme in their fiction, explored, very often, through the plight of an Indian of mixed race who, as Thomas S. Whitecloud observes of his narrator and protagonist in "Blue Winds Dancing" (1938), "don't seem to fit in anywhere." It is a struggle that, only rarely, meets with a successful outcome. The portrait of Archilde, the young male protagonist of *The Surrounded* (1936) by D'Arcy McNickle, being shackled and taken away by white law officers concludes the novel with an image of resistance and criminalization that is repeated in other works of Native American fiction of the time. It is only rarely that the leading characters in these stories find a way home.

In "Blue Winds Dancing," the hero does so, however. A semi-autobiographical account of a man caught between two cultures, the narrative is simple. A man of Indian origin dreams of home. He sees the geese going southward. "They were going home," he observes. So he leaves his white school, to return to his people, who, he reflects, "have many things that civilization has taken from the whites." On the road, he is fearful that, once returned to the reservation, he will not fit in. "Am I Indian, or am I white?" he asks himself. His question is answered for him when he finishes his journey: "I am one with my people," he finally reflects. "I am home." The fiction of D'Arcy McNickle is similarly autobiographical in origin and, in being concerned with reaffirming traditional, indigenous values, equally at odds with the popular contemporary belief that Indians should be assimilated into the dominant Anglo-American culture. McNickle also strove, in this fiction, with even more perseverance than Whitecloud, to resist the conventions of the Western narrative, popular images of Native American life, and what he called "the sentimental and inept efforts that have been made on behalf of the Indian in the past." McNickle became an influential academic and activist, writing books on Native American history (*They Came Here First* (1949), *Native American Tribalism: Indian Survival and Renewals* (1973)), numerous stories (*The Hawk is Hungry and Other Stories* (1992)), and three novels (*The Surrounded, Runner in the Sun: A Story of the Indian Maize* (1954), *Wind From An Enemy Sky* (1978)). What his many works have in common is pride in Native American traditions and a persistent belief in the right of Native Americans to self-determination. His fiction, in particular, combines a critique of Anglo-Americans, and their myopic attempts to impose their values, with a detailed portrait of Native American resistance. In *The Surrounded*, for instance, all the major Native American characters renounce their Catholicism and return to the life they lived before the missionaries arrived. As McNickle insists time and again in his work, what Native Americans want is a basic human right. But it is a right that is often denied them. And, in trying to assert it, they may be branded by white society as criminals.

Like Whitecloud and McNickle, John Joseph Matthews was of mixed-blood status. His first book, *Wah'kon-tah: The Osage and the White Man's Road*, was published in 1929 and was immensely successful; his only novel, *Sundown*, appeared five years later. As the title suggests, *Sundown* is colored by the melancholy reflection that the old tribal life is passing away. Founded in the experiences of its author, the novel tells the story of young Challenge "Chal" Windzer, the son of a progressive, optimistic man who believes Chal will become strong and talented enough to deal with change and an uncertain future. Chal starts off well. Educated at the University of Oklahoma, he is then involved in the early days of aviation. But, after World War I, he is unable to find a place in his community or a satisfying vocation; and he succumbs to the seductive attractions of white society, notably alcohol. This account of the personal failure of the protagonist is framed by a narrative of social decline: as the tribe, in general, succumbs to the corruptions of white society. "The black derricks crept further west," the reader is told. And those oil derricks represent the terrible consequences of instant wealth brought by the exploitation of resources on the reservation. The tribe becomes rich for a while and then, as the oil money runs out, falls into poverty, cultural dereliction and despair. Both the protagonist, and his tribe, have lost touch with the old, indigenous culture and found no true place in the new.

While Matthews, along with McNickle and Whitecloud, concerned himself with the dilemma of living in the collision of cultures, Mourning Dove was more interested in trying to recover the culture of her ancestors. Her maternal grandmother, with whom she lived for much of her adolescence, taught Mourning Dove about the oral traditions of her people. Mourning Dove received little in the way of a formal education from white society but, from the stories her grandmother told her, she developed an interest in her indigenous culture. And one early result of that interest was *Cogewea, the Half-Blood: A Depiction of the Great Montana Cattle Range* (1927), the first novel written by an American Indian woman. The book was produced in collaboration with a white friend and mentor, Lucullus McWhorter, a scholar of Indian traditions. The book that Mourning Dove published six years after *Cogewea*, *Coyote Stories*, was also produced with the help of McWhorter. Nevertheless, this second publication bears much more clearly the marks of Mourning Dove's own personality and is stamped with the authority of her knowledge, To that extent, this collection of folktales is much more unambiguously her own work. "The Animal People were here first – before there were any real people," Mourning Dove announces in her preface. "Coyote was the most important," she explains, "because . . . he did more than any of the others to make the world a good place to live." Before rehearsing a series of stories that have Coyote as their protagonist, she then goes on to explain her own involvement: how she was told them as part of her heritage and how she learned from them of the subtle connections between her people and the vitality and the mystery of their natural surroundings. Coyote emerges from these stories as a sharer in the vitality and mystery. A comically cunning but vulnerable trickster, he is also a being of divine power. Showing how such rituals as the sweat-house, a mystic shrine for physical and spiritual cleansing, emerged, thanks to the activities of its protagonist, *Coyote Stories* is at once a series of lively tales and a passionate affirmation of tribal identity.

The literature of the New Negro movement and beyond

Among those other Americans who had, for many years, formed part of the nation, the African Americans, a pivotal event in literature was the publication of *The New Negro* in 1925. Conceived and edited by Alain Locke (1886–1954), it grew out of a special issue of the *Survey Graphic* magazine in March of that year devoted to the district of Harlem in Manhattan. And it served as a catalyst for a growing sense of confidence that black America was on the verge of a second Emancipation: the consequence this time, not of government action, but of the will and the achievements of the people, and, in particular, the artists and intellectuals. Migration from the South into such urban centers as New York, Chicago, and Detroit, and the opening up of new economic and cultural opportunities, the challenge of continued racism and racial violence: all this served as a stimulus, and a challenge, to those who wanted to make the voice of African Americans heard. The term "the New Negro" was not coined by Locke, nor did it appear for the first time in print in his anthology. It had been in use since at least the late 1890s. Nevertheless, it was this book that gave it currency, as the term of choice to describe a new sense of racial pride. *The New Negro* was the first major literary attempt to revise the collective portrait of black America painted by W. E. B. Du Bois in *The Souls of Black Folks.* Others had an equal claim to be seen as promoters of the new movement in black cultural self-consciousness. But it was Locke who, through his landmark anthology and his energetic championing of the intellectual achievement of African Americans in the 1920s, received most of the credit. As a result, he became known as the father of the New Negro movement and dean of the Harlem Renaissance. And *The New Negro* performed the remit Locke had set for himself: to announce, as he put it, "a dramatic flowering of a new race-spirit . . . among American Negroes."

A very different perspective on the Harlem Renaissance, however, is offered in *Infants of the Spring* (1932), a satirical roman à clef by Wallace Thurman (1902–1934). Thurman was a talented poet, playwright, editor, and literary critic, as well as a novelist. Joining with a handful of other young black writers and artists in 1926, he helped to publish *Fire!!*, the most iconoclastic magazine black America had ever produced. Its many scandalized critics extinguished *Fire!!* after only one issue. But, undaunted, Thurman went on to experience success in 1929 with his play *Harlem*, which ran for over ninety performances at the Apollo Theatre, and to write three notable novels: *The Blacker the Berry* (1929), an exploration of a subject taboo in most earlier African American fiction, intraracial prejudice and the self-hatred engendered by it, *The Interne* (co-authored with A. L. Forman (1929)), and *Infants of the Spring*. In *Infants of the Spring* and elsewhere, Thurman was a scathing critic of the bourgeois attitudes that, he believed, motivated Harlem Renaissance old guards like Locke and Du Bois, claiming they proclaimed aesthetic and intellectual freedom while seeking white approval with slanted portraits of African Americans. His aim, he declared, was to create black characters "who still retained some individual race qualities and who were not totally white American in every respect save skin color."

Satirized by Thurman, celebrated by Locke, the New Negro movement of the 1920s and beyond helped to produce a host of writers. Many of them were good, and some of them were surely great. Among the most remarkable was Claude McKay (1890–1948). Born in Jamaica, McKay became known as "the *enfant terrible* of the Harlem Renaissance" after the publication of his most famous poem, "If We Must Die" (1919), established him as a militant. In the poem, written in response to the race riots that erupted in Chicago and other cities, McKay advocated violent resistance to violence. Other poems attacked lynching ("The Lynching" (1920)), slavery and its heritage ("In Bondage" (1920)), or revealed an intense love-hate relationship with his adoptive home ("America" (1920)). But, as his collection of poems *Harlem Shadows* (1922) reveals, McKay was also inclined towards more sensuous, romantic, and nostalgic modes. And the mixture of racial concern and sensuous impulse comes out, with especial clarity and intensity, in his three novels: *Home to Harlem* (1928), *Banjo* (1929), and *Banana Bottom* (1937).

In *Home to Harlem*, for example, the portrait of the hero, Jake Brown, was controversial at the time, especially in the eyes of African American reviewers. Jake is a freewheeling ex-soldier returning to the "mad riotous joy" of Harlem after World War I. Some critics of this, McKay's most successful novel, argued that Jake was a stereotype of black vagrancy. That, however, ignored what McKay presented as the positive side of Jake's character: his freedom from pretence, his vigorous assertion of his own manhood, and his instinctive distrust of the seductions of white society. It also ignored the importance of another major character, an alienated Haitian intellectual called Ray, who is both attracted to and disturbed by the hedonism of Jake – and who consistently expresses his impatience with what he calls "the contented hogs in the pigpen of Harlem." The narrative maneuvers its way between the figures of Jake and Ray, who clearly express the two sides of their creator, the sensuous and the reflective, the man who feels at home in Harlem and the one who feels at home nowhere. McKay was to continue the story of Jake and Ray in his two later novels. These were never as successful. Nor was his autobiography, *A Long Way from Home* (1937), or his sociological study, *Harlem: Negro Metropolis* (1940), or his memoir *My Green Hills of Jamaica* (completed in 1946, published in 1979). He remains, however, one of the most significant figures of the Renaissance.

So, for that matter, do two African American women writers of the period who, like McKay, suffered neglect during their later years only to be rediscovered after their deaths: Zora Neale Hurston (1891–1960) and Nella Larsen (1891–1964). Hurston was born, as she tells the reader in her autobiography *Dust Tracks on a Road* (1942), in Alabama. Her family then moved, while she was still an infant, to Eatonville, Florida, the first incorporated black community in America. In 1925 she moved to New York, where she began to study anthropology at Barnard College. This revitalized her interest in the black folklore of the South. So, in 1927, reversing the tide of the Great Migration, she returned to the South, with the help of a scholarship, to research that folklore. The result of her research was *Mules and Men* (1935), a collection of tales, songs, and games that presented African-American folklore as a lived culture. In a way that was innovative at the time, but later common practice among ethnographers, Hurston placed folklore texts in their communal context so as to demonstrate the process of their creation. Another result of Hurston's field work was her first novel, *Jonah's Gourd Vine* (1934). Based to an extent on the lives of her parents, the novel tells the story of a poet-preacher who defines himself through his art. This was followed by her masterpiece, *Their Eyes Were Watching God* (1937). Women, Hurston had noticed, were denied access to the pulpit and the porch, the privileged sites of storytelling and, to that extent, denied the chance of self-definition. Her aim, here and elsewhere in her work, became to revise and adapt vernacular forms to give voice to women: to create a genuinely democratic oral culture, or, as she put it, "words walking without masters." "Two things everybody's got tuh do for theyselves," the central character of *Their Eyes Were Watching God*, Janie Crawford, concludes. "They got tuh go tuh God, and they got tuh find out about livin' fuh theyselves." The conclusion is hard earned. Janie has to win the right to see and speak about living for herself. She has to resist the demeaning definitions her society would impose on her, as a black person and a woman. She has to defy the instructions of one of her husbands not to engage in "porch talk." She has to claim her own voice, and in the process her own self and rightful place in the vocal community. Raised by her grandmother Nancy, an ex-slave who has suffered most of the abuses heaped on black women in slavery, she is told by the old woman, "De nigger woman is de mule uh de world." But Janie holds on to her dignity, and her desire to realize herself, through two loveless marriages. And in her third marriage, to an itinerant laborer and gambler much younger than her, Tea Cake Woods, she finds love, laughter, and the opportunity to be and speak for herself. The marriage ends tragically, with the violent death of Tea Cake. Janie, however, a "born orator," has now claimed her birthright. She returns to her hometown of Eatonville, at the end of the novel, a single and singular woman: where she can now participate in the "porch talk," the "big stories" of the community. She has come home to her true speech, and her true self.

The triumph of *Their Eyes Were Watching God* is that its language is the literary equivalent of the oral performances Hurston studied as an ethnographer. Vernacular voices speak in and through the narrative, informing its dialogue and narration. Hurston evokes a community in the act of making and remaking itself; and she links that to the endless activity of talk. She shows how a small group of people ground themselves, begin to make sense of their trials and changes through the maneuverings of speech and ceremony. She discloses how one remarkable woman fulfills the promise of her life by insisting on her own right to participate in the speaking and the ceremonials. And she opens up the chance to the reader as well, of finding ground and definition, by inviting us into the process of debate. In the years immediately following *Their Eyes Were Watching God*, Hurston published another novel, *Moses, Man of the Mountain* (1939), exploring the story of Moses as recorded in the Bible and African oral traditions. She also produced another collection of folklore, *Tell My Horse* (1938). But the quality and quantity of her work began to wane. A novel about white life in Florida published in 1948, *Seraph on the Sewanee*, did nothing to prevent her sinking from public notice. By the time Hurston died, in poverty in a Florida welfare home, all her books were out of print. Her rediscovery came at the hands of a later generation of African American women writers. She is now appropriately seen, not only as a crucial figure in the literature of the "the New Negro," but as a vital link in the chain of African American writing that emphasizes continuity and community

With some justification, Nella Larsen has been called the mystery woman of the Harlem Renaissance. She produced only two novels, *Quicksand* (1928) and *Passing* (1929). *Quicksand* was hailed by W. E. B. Du Bois as "the best piece of fiction" by an African American since Charles Chesnutt. With *Passing*, Larsen became one of the first African American women to win a Guggenheim Fellowship for literature, which enabled her to spend a year researching further novels in Europe. But no more books were to appear. Larsen lived the final years of her life in greater obscurity, even, than Hurston. Her two remarkable long fictions, which were rediscovered after her death, are, however, very different from *Their Eyes Were Watching God*. Her location is a more bourgeois, educated, confined world than the one Hurston wrote about; her major characters, intelligent, sophisticated women of mixed race, are caught up in trouble-some confusions of race, gender, and class, as they try to negotiate their way through a complex social milieu. And the disjunctive, episodic structure of her narratives creates a multiple subjective space for those characters, as they search for a means of realizing identity and achieving personal fulfillment in a world that seems intent on denying them as individuals. *Quicksand* maneuvers the traditional theme of the tragic mulatto into a poignant, pioneering portrayal of a modern woman – and, in the process, offers one of the first serious studies of those aspiring to the African American middle class. *Passing*, in turn, rewrites the story of crossing the color line in psychological terms. Both are major novels of racial and sexual identity, in the modernist vein.

The work of Jean Toomer (1894–1976) can also be seen as a bridge between the New Negro movement and modernism. A contributor during the 1920s to such black journals as *Opportunity* and *Crisis*, as well as *The New Negro*, Toomer published as well in such experimental magazines as *Broom* and *The Little Review*. Toomer saw himself as a confluence of different races and influences. "In my body were many bloods, some dark blood, all blended in the fire of six or more generations," he recollected. "I was then, either a new type of man or the very oldest. In any case, I was inescapably myself." Confluence is as much a characteristic of Toomer's masterpiece *Cane* (1923) as it is of its creator. An innovative hybrid of prose and poetry, the book is divided into three sections. The first section is set in the South, in Georgia, and it concentrates on women, especially women whose thoughts and behavior set them at odds with the expectations of society. Punctuating their stories are poems written in a rapt, incantatory style, marked by repetition and recurrent images of dusk, pines, cane, and fire. The overall effect is haunting: this is a South that comes across to the reader as a dreamscape and a very real place of racial prejudice and violence. Not the least of the achievements here is the way Toomer weaves together intricate misunderstandings of race, sex, and gender: the misrecognition of women as well as the mistreatment of black people, male and female. A similarly rich tapestry of different but interconnected themes characterizes the second section. Here, the scene drifts to the North, to Washington, DC. It begins with a lyric account of black settlement in the city, marked by more syncopated rhythms and harsher imagery. It continues with a surreal portrait of Rhobert, a man sinking under the weight of his own poverty. Following this, a series of intercalated poems and prose passages explore the dreams and the disintegrative impact of city life. This is a more brutally material world than the one evoked in the first section – all sense of folk culture has evaporated – but here, too, finally, is a society marked by racial conflict, without even the balm of custom to alleviate its more bigoted practices.

The final section of *Cane* was the first to be written, and it clearly has a more autobiographical base than the others. It describes how an educated African American from the North, called Ralph Kabnis, visits the South. Written partly in the form of a story, partly in dramatic form, it shows him witnessing racial prejudice and violence, measuring the decline of the old ways, and wondering if he could become the "face" of the South and sing its songs. Frustrated in his search for a way of life, he ends by experiencing a dark night of the soul: a party in a cellar, full of drinking and sex that offers him not even a moment of relief. However, Toomer is not content to leave the reader on this dying fall. The third section, and *Cane* as a whole, ends with Kabnis crawling out of the cellar, as the sun rises. The hint of a new beginning is slight, but it is still there. And it helps make the closing moments of *Cane* as much of a confluence, an innovative mix, as the rest of this extraordinary book: poised as it is on the cusp between darkness and light.

Langston Hughes (1902–1967) was the most eminent poet associated with the New Negro movement, or what Hughes himself later called "the years of Manhattan's black Renaissance," "when the Negro was in vogue." He was not just a poet. He wrote novels (*Not Without Laughter* (1930), *Tambourines to Glory* (1958)), plays (collected in *Five Plays* (1963)), short stories (*The Ways of White Folks* (1934), *Laughing to Keep From Crying* (1952), *Something in Common* (1963)), and autobiography (*The Big Sea* (1940), *I Wonder as I Wander* (1956)). He wrote numerous essays on social, historical, and musical subjects, edited collections of black folklore, poetry, and stories. In the latter part of his life he devoted his energies to writing the "Simple Stories," involving an apparently slow, even dull-witted black character who always manages to outwit his antagonists (*Simple Speaks His Mind* (1950), *Simple Stakes a Claim* (1957), *Simple's Uncle Sam* (1965)). But it is for his poetry that he is likely to be remembered. His first collection of poems, *The Weary Blues*, was published in 1926. Other collections that appeared over the next forty years include *Fine Clothes to the Jew* (1927), *Harlem* (1942), *Montage of a Dream Deferred* (1951), and *Ask Your Mama* (1961). And all of it is marked by a powerful commitment to the notion of a separate and distinctive black identity, a sense of the shared presence of African Americans, that Hughes announced in his seminal essay, "The Negro Artist and the Racial Mountain" (1926). "To my mind, it is the duty of the young Negro artist," Hughes wrote in this essay, "to change through the force of his art that old whispering 'I want to be white' hidden in the aspirations of his people, to 'Why should I want to be white? I am a Negro – and beautiful.'" This does not mean, Hughes said, that the black writer should simply idealize black life. But it did mean that black writers should devote themselves to uncovering the power and glory of African American traditions, the "heritage of rhythm and warmth" and "incongruous humor that, so often, as in Blues, becomes ironic laughter mixed with tears."

True to this formula, Hughes made black people his subject, especially "low-down folks, the so-called common element." His poetry shows him more interested in the ordinary men and women of the fields and streets, and in particular of Harlem, than in the black bourgeoisie – who, on the few occasions when they do appear in his work, are "buked and scorned." Like Whitman, Hughes's aim is clearly identification, imaginative empathy with these people. He is, above all, a dramatic poet, speaking through a multiplicity of voices – a young schoolchild, perhaps ("Theme for English B"), a smart and sassy older woman ("Madam's Past History"), or a dying man ("Sylvester's Dying Bed") – so as to capture the multiple layers of black life. Like Whitman, too, although in a much more specific sense, Hughes is a socially committed poet. "The major aims of my work," he declared, "have been to interpret and comment upon Negro life, and its relations to the problems of Democracy." This commitment is most evident in the work that permits itself overt social comment: some of the poems written within a Marxist frame in the 1930s, say ("Christ in Alabama"), or, more generally, his bitter attacks on "The lazy, laughing South/With blood on its mouth." But it is just as powerful a shaping force in works dramatizing the petty frustrations and particular oppressions of individual black people ("Ballad of the Landlord"), their dreams of liberation ("Dream Variations") or their stony endurance ("Life is Fine").

"Most of my . . . poems are racial in theme," Hughes said. "In many of them I try to grasp and hold some of the meanings and rhythms of jazz." The latter remark suggests another, crucial way in which consciousness of the black tradition enters into his work.

Hughes may have learned a great deal about free verse from Sandburg, Lindsay, and Whitman, but he learned even more from African American music. "Jazz is a heartbeat," Hughes argued, "its heartbeat is yours." By "jazz" Hughes meant black musical culture in general; and the essence of jazz, Hughes believed, was that it was open-ended and improvisational and as such challenged the closed structures of the dominant white culture. Hughes's exploitation of black music takes many forms. Sometimes, he uses the classic, three-line blues form ("Seven Moments in Love"); sometimes, as in "Still Here," he employs fragments of blues themes and vocabulary; sometimes, as in "The Weary Blues," he mixes classic with other forms. Elsewhere, as in a poem titled "The Cat and the Saxophone," he tries to imitate the energy, the frenetic excitement of instrumental jazz. And in one of his most impressive works, *Montage of a Dream Deferred*, Hughes employs the free associations and abrupt rhythms of boogie-woogie and "street poetry," rapping and jive-talk, to create a verbal portrait of Harlem. His use of black religious music is less frequent, but a poem like "Fire" shows how he could turn to it to dramatize the spiritual side of his culture. Whatever form Hughes utilizes, he demonstrates an intimate knowledge of its intricacies – "The rhythm of life," he said, "/Is a jazz rhythm" and this is the rhythm of his poetry.

While emphasizing his commitment to black community and culture, though, Hughes was always willing to acknowledge his debt to certain white writers and, in particular, the author of *Leaves of Grass*. He saw no contradiction here, because what Whitman offered him above all was the example of self-discovery. The ways Hughes plays his variations on American themes, singing his own "Song of Myself," is suggested by two of his finest poems, "I, Too" and "The Negro Speaks of Rivers." "I, Too" involves a clear echo of Whitman. "I, too, sing America," it begins, then plays on two themes. The first is the ancient theme of dispossession: the "darker brother" who is banished from the table of communion for a while but, growing strong, prepares to reclaim his rightful inheritance. And the second is the more recent American theme of the poet as democratic hero, the representative of his culture: not, however, as it is but as it might be. Even more firmly than Whitman, Hughes seems to declare, "I project the history of the future." "The Negro Speaks of Rivers" is more concerned with the past than the future, the heritage that is the black American's special strength. "I've known rivers," its narrator reveals, "I've known rivers ancient as the world and older than the flow of human blood in human veins." The vision unfolded is at once accurately historical and elemental, since the rivers, as they are named in order, recall some of the civilizations the black race has helped build, while rehearsing the ancient idea that the same deep forces run through the body of the earth and the bodies of men and women. Knowing the rise and fall of cultures, black people have known the tale of time; they have seen once proud civilizations pass away and will see others follow eventually. Hughes's poems are always asking the reader to consider this, the mysterious essences of black life as well as its jazzy surfaces. As in the best black music there is energy, sensuality, humor, certainly, but also soul.

Other poets roughly contemporary with Hughes shared a similar desire to voice the separateness of black culture. Notable among these were Sterling A. Brown (1901–1989) and Gwendolyn Bennett (1902–1981). Not everyone did, however. Among those who were skeptical, at least, about the idea of a specifically black aesthetic were William Stanley Braithwaite (1878–1962), Anne Spencer (1882–1975) and, above all, Countee Cullen (1903–1946). Cullen was certainly a complicated case, since he did explore race in some of his work. A poem like "Incident" (1924), for instance, recalls the first time when he was called "nigger," when he "was eight and very small"; and the title piece in *The Black Christ, and Other Poems* (1929) recounts the lynching of a black youth for a crime he did not commit. Cullen, however, was inclined to place his poems about his African American heritage in a kind of ghetto: in each of his first three collections, there is a section specifically entitled "Color." And even these poems, although *about* that heritage, are not definitively *of* it. "What is Africa to me," begins one piece actually called "Heritage" (1925): "One *three centuries removed / From the scenes his fathers loved, / Spicy grove, cinnamon tree, / What is Africa to me?*" Cullen wanted, he said, to be "a poet, not a Negro poet." So, for the forms and language of his verse, he was content to follow Romantic convention. Sometimes, the pain involved in his struggle always to sound non-racial, and usually to concentrate on non-racial subjects, breaks through the discreet surfaces of his work. "My color shrouds me," he admits in "Heritage"; and in "Yet Do I Marvel" (1925), he laments, "Yet do I marvel at this curious thing:/To make a poet black and bid him sing!" But, as a rule, he refused to think in terms of a distinctive ethnic heritage.

In the transitional generation of African American poets following Hughes and Cullen, the most articulate spokesmen for Cullen's position were Melvin B. Tolson (1898–1966) and Robert Hayden (1913–1980). Opposed to this position, in turn, in this transitional generation is Gwendolyn Brooks (1917–2000). Born in Kansas, but "a Chicagoan" as she calls herself in terms of upbringing and commitment, Brooks published her first collection, *A Street in Bronzeville*, in 1945. Prior to that, she had published more than a hundred poems in her weekly column in the *Chicago Defender*. Following that, she published numerous collections: among them, *Annie Allen* (1949), *Bronzeville Boys and Girls* (1956), and *In the Mecca* (1968). In her early work, while her main subject was black life, her style was mannered, academic, and sometimes difficult. Gradually, however, as Brooks absorbed herself more into the lives of urban blacks, particularly of the South Side of Chicago, the style became looser, more idiomatic, incorporating such diverse influences as free verse, black vernacular, and the blues. A catalyst for change was her association with the Black Arts movement in the 1960s, which helped Brooks develop a more committed stance. She became one of the most visible articulators of "the black aesthetic." This reinforced her lifelong interest in social issues, in street life and supposedly insignificant, everyday characters. It sharpened her style, making it flintier, edgier. And it prompted her to be more challenging, provocative – because, as she put it in 1967, "Art hurts. Art urges voyages." Like Hughes, she often adopts the voice of the poor and dispossessed ("the mother"), but she can, just as easily, assume that of the more articulate and self-conscious ("Negro Hero"). There is little sense of victimization in her work, even though many of her subjects are social victims: these are people who manage to get by, achieving the dignity of survival. A hard, stony idiom, taut syntax, and primitive, urgent rhythms are harnessed to a recreation of black street life that combines sympathy for the oppressed with a sardonic appreciation of the sources of their oppression.

Like so many African American writers of this and later periods, Brooks was influenced by African American musical forms, and in particular by the blues. Among others who were affected by the blues, and black cultural and musical forms, were some other African American writers of the transitional generation writing mostly in prose: Dorothy West (1907–1998), Ann Petry (1911–1997) and, above all, Margaret Walker (1915–1998) and Richard Wright (1908–1960). Margaret Walker had a career that extended from the last days of the Harlem Renaissance in the 1930s to the Black Arts movement of the 1960s. Even before her first book of poetry, *For My People*, was published in 1942, she had won national attention for her work: the title poem, for example, had been published in Chicago five years earlier. And with its publication her reputation was secured. "For My People," in particular, was acclaimed as a significant piece for African Americans. Deploying the long line of Whitman here, the cadences learned from her preacher father and the rhythms of the new American poetry encountered in Chicago, Walker sang, as she put it, "for my people everywhere." Mixing piety with prophecy, she also combined commemoration of the black past with lively anticipation of the future. Despite the success of *For My People*, Walker did not publish anything else for over twenty years. Her novel, *Jubilee*, appeared in 1966. Based, Walker has explained, on the tales of her great-grandmother told to her by her grandmother, it tells the story of Vyry, the child of a white plantation owner and his black mistress. To the extent that the book is built around the seminal events of Southern history – the days of the old slave order, the Civil War, and Reconstruction – *Jubilee* replicates the structure of the traditional plantation romance. To the extent that it tells of one powerful woman in particular, committed to her own passionate needs, it recollects one famous version of plantation romance in particular, *Gone With the Wind*. But this is a radical rewriting of plantation romance and the myths of black and white womanhood. In her revisionist account of the Southern past, Walker exposes the rigid barriers of race, gender, and class that scarred slave society and were perpetuated after the Civil War. And the dramatic setpieces here tend to be incidents of racial violence and oppression rather than the traditional tableaux of the banquet, the wedding party, and the hunt ball. At the center of all this is an intelligent, energetic young woman. Unlike Scarlett O'Hara, however, this young woman is born black and a slave. Dreaming "confused dreams in which she struggled to be free," Vyry has to deal with chains that are all too literal and brutal, but her will and determination are never defeated. Neither is her belief, not only in herself, but in human nature. This is a book that preaches, not so much revolution, as the imperative of black resistance and the possibility of white redemption. As such, it helped to initiate a new tradition in tales about the South.

Like Margaret Walker, Richard Wright was born in the South, in Natchez, Mississippi. His childhood was spent in poverty. His formal education ended when he left junior high school. Worse still, as he reveals in the first of his two autobiographical volumes, *Black Boy* (1945), he was denied a sense of his own humanity and identity as he grew up. Wright traveled north to Chicago in 1927. "I dreamed of going north and writing books, novels," Wright remembered. "The North symbolized for me all that I had not felt and seen." Like so many others involved in the Great Migration, Wright had his dreams of a better life shattered, encountering only new forms of racial oppression and economic deprivation when he went northwards. He did, however, find comradeship in the Communist Party, which he joined in 1936. That comradeship was short-lived. Within a year, he had broken with the party because of its attempts to control his creative freedom. But he continued to work with others, black and white, of similar social and political commitment. So, as well as editing *New Challenge* with

Dorothy West, he wrote proletarian poetry for *New Masses* and *Partisan Review*; he served as a correspondent for the *Daily Worker*; and well up to the publication of *Twelve Million Black Voices* (1941), an illustrated folk history of African Americans, he tried to work out the relationship between the techniques of fiction and the tenets of Marxism.

For Wright, the best way of working out that relationship was in his own fiction. Even before moving to New York City in 1937, he had written most of his novel *Lawd Today*, which was published posthumously in 1963. And in 1938, his first book, *Uncle Tom's Children*, was published. A collection of four novellas set in the Jim Crow South, the book casts an ironic light on its own title by showing a series of protagonists becoming increasingly rebellious as they find the collective means to resist. "I wanted to try to build a bridge of words between me and the world outside, that world which was so distant and elusive that it seemed unreal," Wright recalled in the second volume of his autobiography, *American Hunger* (1977). And bricks for that bridge were found, not only in certain systems of thought he found congenial, particularly the Marxist analysis of society and the Freudian system of psychology, but in literary naturalism.

Despite the success of *Uncle Tom's Children*, Wright was uneasy about its potential for sentiment. It was, he suspected, a little too like the work the title of which it parodically echoed, *Uncle Tom's Cabin*: one that "even bankers' daughters could read and weep and feel good about." So, he resolved that his next fiction would be so "hard and deep" that readers "would have to face it without the consolation of tears." The result was his most important book, *Native Son* (1940). Set in the black ghetto of the South Side of Chicago, it presents a protagonist who would deny any attempt to see him as a figure of pathos. Bigger Thomas kills two women, one white and one black. The first killing is an accident but, recalling the pivotal murder in *An American Tragedy* by Theodore Dreiser, it is seen as an accident waiting to happen. It issues out of the fear that is the emotional condition of Bigger's life; it is seen as the product, not of will, but of circumstance and the desperate violence it engenders. And the second, more deliberate killing follows from this. Waiting in prison for his trial, Bigger feels for the first time a sense of freedom because, he believes, he has broken out of the prison of himself. Previously, there had been "two worlds" for him, "something the *world* gave him and something he *himself* had"; "never in all his life," he senses, "with this black skin of his, had the two worlds . . . been together; never had he felt a sense of wholeness." Now, he begins to feel it. So, despite the attempts of his communist lawyer, Max, to move him from a sense of identity built on "hate," "resistance and defiance," to one founded on "hope," a recognition of others similarly suffering, he cannot do so. He cannot deny what he sees as the logic of his actions, the imperative of violence. He lacks the social consciousness, the capacity for articulation that Max requires of him. All he can say is "what I killed for, I am!"

Native Son is a story that combines intense involvement with interrogation. The reader shares the fear of the protagonist, can understand the reasons why Bigger revels in his violence but can also see exactly how and why he is in error. It also mixes naturalism with the gothic, even surreal. The irreality of Bigger's life, on the shadowy edges of white society, lends a dreamlike quality to many of his experiences. Standing at the narrative center, although by no means limiting the narrative perspective, is a character who gradually assumes multiple dimensions. Bigger is "a scared colored boy from Mississippi," as his lawyer calls him. He is a modern instance, a product of certain

Figure 4.4 Scene from the film version of *Native Son* by Richard Wright, with Richard Wright as the main character, Bigger Thomas. Film directed by Pierre Chenal, US/Argentina, 1951. Source: BFI Stills.

racial, social, and economic practices. He is a historical paradigm, in that Wright clearly asks us to connect the paths of "hate" and "hope" to the larger, historic possibilities of fascism and socialism. He is even a classic American hero to the extent that the "two worlds" between which he is divided recall the two that have divided many other American protagonists, traditionally figured as the wilderness and the clearing. All of which is by way of saying that *Native Son* is as rich in meaning as it is in terms of narrative medium. A fiction burning with a fierce sense of racial and social injustice, it is also a major historical novel and a narrative fully in the American grain.

Following the publication of *Native Son*, Wright left the United States for Mexico. Then, in 1946, he moved to Paris, where he spent the rest of his life. In Paris, he became associated with Jean-Paul Sartre, Albert Camus, and Simone de Beauvoir. They may have influenced his gravitation towards forms of existentialism noticeable in his 1953 novel, *The Outsider*, about the search of a self-conscious black intellectual for identity. Other fiction followed: *Savage Holiday* (1954) and *The Long Dream* (1958). So did works of non-fiction that placed social oppression in a global context, linking racism in America to colonialism in Africa and Asia: *Black Power* (1954), *The Color Curtain* (1956), and *White Man Listen!* (1957). The move towards black nationalism in many of these later works was to attract the Black Aesthetic writers of the 1960s, who claimed Wright as a favored ancestor. What they valued in these works, and in another way in *Native Son*, was what they saw as Wright's militancy: his willingness to use art as a weapon. For Wright, literature was coextensive with life. And the major task in each was to make a mark, establish a sense of wholeness and presence. They were coextensive but not, however, to be confused with each other, because, as Wright put it, those staples of literature, "image and emotion possess a logic of their own." "Every first rate novel, poem, or play," Wright argued in "Blueprint for Negro Writing" (1937), "lifts the level of consciousness higher." It was in this sense, as he saw it, that imaginative writing got its social work done: as a vital agent of awareness.

Mass Culture and the Writer

Western, detective, and hardboiled fiction

The first half of the twentieth century witnessed an exponential increase in the production and consumption of fiction. Compulsory education in most American states had created a growing number of readers hungry for escapist entertainment. And, from the 1860s, mass market publishing, in the form of slender, cheaply printed booklets known as dime novels, fed that hunger. Dime novels thrived on melodramatic adventure. Some had historical or sea settings. But of all the genres the new mass readership and mass methods of production generated, none was more popular, to begin with, than the cowboy tale. Very early on, too, the dime-novel Western became formulaic. There was a hero who represented a synthesis of civilization and the wilderness; there was an emphasis on action, progress, and the blessings of manifest destiny; and the settings were appropriately epic, with vast, wild, open spaces. The dime novel operated at the level of fantasy, where conflicts that could not be resolved in the real world could find appropriate resolution. It celebrated the self-reliance, natural nobility and individuality of a modern American whose daring actions confirmed the inevitable onward march of his nation. In the first half of the twentieth century, three novels in particular were to underwrite the romance of the West, and acquire enormous popularity. They were *The Virginian* (1902) by Owen Wister (1860–1938), *Riders of the Purple Sage* (1912) by Zane Grey (1872–1939), and *Shane* (1949) by Jack Schaefer (1907–1991).

Among other genres popular in dime novels were detective stories. From the 1870s on, stories of street life in New York City, Philadelphia, and elsewhere came into fashion, and soon afterwards the mass-audience tale of detection emerged. These dime-novel detective stories offered little in the way of character complexity; they were convenient vehicles for carrying a plot full of action and adventure to its inevitable conclusion. Contrivances though they were, however, they signaled the beginning of the transference of the hero from the open spaces of the West to the cavernous streets of the city. Following on them, the detective in American twentieth-century fiction would slowly supplant the cowboy as a mythic embodiment of national values: an urban individualist whose commitment to his own code was more internalized, more a matter of maneuvering his way within the labyrinth of society rather than operating outside it. From 1915, prototypical detective stories also began to appear in the pulp magazines that, within a few years after this, had replaced dime novels and story-paper weeklies as the staple source of cheap fiction. What was notable about these stories is that the best of them – with their hardbitten protagonists and tough-minded narratives – reflected the gritty realities of post-World War I America. Many writers were to experiment with writing in this vein, but easily the most important were Dashiell Hammett (1894–1961) and Raymond Chandler (1888–1959).

Dashiell Hammett had worked as a private detective for the Pinkerton Agency in San Francisco, shortly before serving in the army in World War I. That experience served him well in his early stories, set in a sharp and credibly drawn northern California landscape. Beginning in 1923, they featured a character called the Continental Op, the toughest and shrewdest investigator in an outfit called the Continental Detective

Agency. Altogether, the Op was to appear in two dozen stories, and in the serialized versions of the novels, *The Dain Curse* (1929) and *Red Harvest* (1929). His other, hugely influential heroes were the mildly inebriate husband and wife team of Nick and Nora Charles, in *The Thin Man* (1934), and the protagonist in what may be the single most important private-eye novel, *The Maltese Falcon* (1930), Sam Spade. Raymond Chandler wrote of Hammett and his followers that they were responsible for "taking murder out of the library and putting it back on the streets where it belonged." Hammett created heroes who were not merely cool, tough, cynical; they confronted the conditions surrounding them with a full knowledge of their latent violence and their pervasive corruption. Favoring a rapid tempo and economy of expression, a tough, brittle, unadorned prose that came to be known as the "hardboiled style," Hammett nevertheless wove elaborate patterns of intrigue and deceit. His novels became narrative labyrinths, replicating the literal labyrinths of the city streets and the social labyrinth of urban power, in which it became just about impossible to know whom to trust – other than oneself. Pursuing the fabulous jewel-encrusted black bird that supplies the title of *The Maltese Falcon*, "the stuff that dreams are made of," Sam Spade discovers what in a sense he has always known: that there is little he can rely on, apart from his own nerve and work – and the simple code that tells him, "when a man's partner is killed he's supposed to do something about it," even if he did not like him.

The fiction of Hammett brims with undisclosed romanticism. In the work of Raymond Chandler, that romanticism is more or less disclosed. Many of the familiar elements of the hardboiled detective story, as perfected by Hammett, are still there: the setting in an urban labyrinth, the sense of a conspiratorial network of evil, the terse dialogue, rapid narrative tempo and flashes of violence. What is relatively new with Chandler, however, is a more highly wrought style and more open concern with a code of honor. Chandler was born in Chicago, educated in England, and only began writing fiction at the age of forty-five. When he began, he mixed the hardboiled with other idioms, which he saw as the product of his European education. "All the best American writing," Chandler argued, "has been done by cosmopolitans. They found freedom of expression, richness of vocabulary" in the United States. "But they had to have European taste to use the material." That taste, in his case, led to a vivid use of metaphor and allusion, sharp street language and a trenchant use of wisecracks. It also led to evocative scene-setting: creating the sense of a neon-lit jungle. Chandler helped create what later became known as a noir world: rainswept streets, dark, empty buildings, shadows and fog punctuated by the occasional streetlamp, light from the window of a lonely room or an all-night café. This is the world in which Chandler's solitary detective makes his way. Usually, as in *The Big Sleep* (1939), *Farewell My Lovely* (1940), and *The Long Goodbye* (1953), that hero is Philip Marlowe. Marlowe, more than most detectives of his kind, is a man of honor, committed to justice, a righter of wrongs as well as an agent of the law. As Chandler was well aware, he bears little resemblance to any real private detectives. Marlowe is more like the familiar figure of the American Adam, redrawn and resituated in California. Surrounding him are vicious villains, corrupt cops, avaricious businessmen and politicians, and usually decadent women. Somehow, he manages to keep his integrity in the midst of all this. He is as much alone as the mythic cowboy is: that is the source of his pride, as well as his strange pathos.

Not all writers associated with the hardboiled school concentrated on stories with detectives at their center. Particularly as the Depression set in, many turned their attention to the lives of apparently average people caught up in a cycle of deprivation – turning to sex or violence or both in a desperate attempt to break that cycle. At the core of these hardboiled or noir novels is a myth of success with no social world to sustain it. That is especially true of the fiction of one hardboiled writer, James M. Cain (1892–1977), who for a while, in the 1930s and 1940s, was the most notorious writer in the United States. Cain published his first novel, *The Postman Always Rings Twice*, in 1934. It tells the story of Cora Papadakis and a drifter Frank Chambers, lovers who murder Cora's wealthy husband for his money, making it look like an accident. Cora then dies in a car crash, and ironically Frank is convicted of murder for her death when it was in fact an accident. Other novels followed, notably *Double Indemnity* (1936), in which again an unmarried man and a married woman plan and execute the husband's "accidental" death, this time for the insurance money. They established Cain as a master of what became known as hardboiled eroticism: with sex, presented with a frankness unusual for the time, seen as a primary motive, the instinct driving people to escape from their mean, petty lives. However, Cain himself insisted that he made "no conscious effort to be tough, or hardboiled, or grim … I merely try to write as the character would write." In this sense, his work is a version of the American demotic tradition in literature. In prose rhythms that imitate those of ordinary American speech, he shows "the average man" and woman caught up in the dullness of their lives and dreams of leaving: destroyed by the very passions that, however perversely, they see as their avenues of escape.

Humorous writing

Far removed from the cold eye that many hardboiled novelists like Cain cast on American society were the more affectionate, even accepting perspectives of contemporary humorists. Notable among these was Ring Lardner (1885–1933), who excelled in the kind of short sketch or story that was more than half in love with the thing it satirized. With Lardner, however, there was something more: a remarkable ear for American speech and an extraordinary capacity for catching the rhythms of the vernacular. Lardner was an established sports journalist before he began writing a series of letters in the disguise of "Jack Keefe," a newcomer to a professional baseball team. Published first in the Chicago *Tribune*, they brought him fame as an explorer of semi-literate idiom and an exposer of demotic vanity, incompetence, and self-deception. They were published in 1914 as *You Know Me, Al: A Busher's Letters*. Other subsequent volumes included *Bib Ballads* (1915), a collection of verse, *The Big Town* (1921), a humorous novel, and the collections, *How to Write Short Stories* (1924) and *The Love Nest* (1926). Americans of all walks of life appear in his writing, their personalities defined by their utterances. And, although that writing appears to obey the conventional limits of contemporary American humor, it is in fact unusually mordant, even cynical. The people to whom Lardner gives voice are reduced to their essential banality or dullness, cruelty, violence, or stupidity. The sardonic surfaces of his fiction only partially conceal a deeply pessimistic viewpoint, as Lardner allows his "average" characters to condemn themselves out of their own, forever open mouths.

Apart from Lardner, the two most notable humorous writers in the first half of the twentieth century were James Thurber (1894–1961) and Dorothy Parker (1893–1967). Thurber was a regular contributor to *The New Yorker* for many years, both as a cartoonist and a writer. His sketches and stories were collected in such volumes as *The Owl in the Attic, and Other Perplexities* (1931) and *My World – and Welcome to It!* (1942). The strange and whimsical characters Thurber describes, some of them animals and many of them people, respond to upsets with a sad persistence. They all seem repressed and misshapen, subject to malignant circumstances that somehow they survive. "Humor is a kind of emotional chaos told about calmly and quietly in retrospect," Thurber observed. And the victims of chaos who receive his special attention are his sad middle-aged men, caught by the dreariness of their lives, custom, and predatory women – and quietly dreaming of escape into a world of adventure, where they can perform feats of daring that range from the quaintly romantic to the bizarre.

The humor of Dorothy Parker was considerably more acerbic. Her writing career began as a literary critic in her native New York City; and she soon acquired an almost legendary reputation for her malicious and sardonic wisecracks. Then, in 1926, she published her first book of poems, *Enough Rope*. A bestseller, it was followed by two other books of verse and, in 1936, by her collected poems, *Not So Deep As a Well*. The poems show that Parker was just as skeptical about relations between the sexes as Thurber was. Only, whereas Thurber tended to show feckless husbands at the mercy of tyrannical wives, Parker was more cynically evenhanded. She simply dismissed the possibility of romantic fulfillment for either sex. Parker pursued similar caustic variations on the frustrations of love and the futility of idealism in her prose work. The short stories and sketches collected in *Laments for the Living* (1930), for example, *After Such Pleasures* (1933) and *Here Lies* (1939) are marked by their wry wit, their economy and polish, but, above all, by their refusal to take any prisoners. Parker could be tough on herself; she could write successfully in many different genres, But it was with her epigrammatic wit, that usually instilled fear in those around her, that she made her mark – a wit that moved between the cool, the clever, and the cynical.

Fiction and popular culture

Margaret Mitchell (1900–1949) would never qualify as a humorist. The closest she came to humor, outside of *Gone With the Wind* (1936), was her sardonic comment that "long ago" she gave up thinking about her long romantic tale set in Georgia during the Civil War and Reconstruction as her book. "It's Atlanta's, in the view of Atlantians." That says something about the phenomenal success of her novel. An instant bestseller, at least twenty-five million copies have so far been sold. *Gone with the Wind* is a fundamentally simple tale: one that, in the tradition of plantation and Civil War romance, tells the story of the South from the point of view of the middle-class planters. More specifically, it is the tale of Scarlett O'Hara: a heroine who, under the pressures of war and hardship, grows from a girl to a woman, a Southern belle to a matriarch. Many of the familiar, stereotypical characters of Southern plantation romance are here. There is the world-weary plantation Hamlet, played here by Ashley Wilkes, the roguish, dangerous plantation Hotspur, a role taken by Rhett Butler. There are, inevitably, a "Mammy," various "Uncle Tom" figures who faithfully serve and save their white masters, a vicious white overseer, melodious field hands and women like Scarlett's friend, the gentle Melanie Hamilton who fulfill Southern expectations of what it means to be "a very great lady." What ignites *Gone With the Wind*, however, is its heroine. Here, with Scarlett O'Hara, Mitchell revisits a familiar character type, the strong woman – particularly popular in the 1930s, when such characters were often seen as potential redeemers of a barren land – and gives that character type new complexity and depth, not least through subtle inflections of gender.

Like the heroine of many popular female narratives, from romance through the early feminist novel to soap opera, Scarlett O'Hara is an initially unexceptional girl who is forced into an exceptional maturity. Like them, she is torn in her affections between respectability and risk, in the respective figures of Ashley and Rhett. However, while she possesses some of the stereotypical "feminine" characteristics, such as a lack of interest in war and politics, what makes her remarkable is her possession of other, supposedly "masculine" traits. As she develops, during the course of the narrative, she shows herself to be tough, ruthless, competitive. She is committed to the land, her property, and money as a means to keep that land. Like the central character of the classic historical novel, too, she herself becomes a site of struggle between the old order and the new. Or, as the narrative puts it, "her mind pulled two ways," between nostalgia for the past and the necessities of the present and future. At the end of the novel, Scarlett does turn back, to Tara, her homeplace. But in going back, Scarlett is also going forward, trying for a synthesis of the new aims and the old values: a balance between past and future registered in her famous closing remark, "After all, tomorrow is another day." What is notable, and regrettable, about this most popular of American romances, however, is that it combines this relatively sophisticated representation of gender with a presentation of race that is regressive to the point of obscenity. The humanity of black men is a conspicuous absence in the novel. So, too, are the humanity and sexuality of black women, since the only black women who receive any attention are asexual. *Gone With the Wind* is certainly an inescapable fact of American literary history; it represents a confluence of narrative traditions; and it has at its center one of the most memorable heroines in American fiction. But that fact is an ugly one, in some ways. Recalling an American dream, Mitchell inadvertently exposes an American nightmare and, in the process, shows how romance may have its dark side.

Despite the enormous success of the film of her book, Mitchell had very little interest in Hollywood. In fact, she rarely strayed outside Atlanta. Unlike her, though, one thing many humorists and hardboiled writers did have in common was precisely their experience of the film capital of the world. Of those who came to Hollywood, and registered the impact of popular culture generally in their writing, no writer was more perceptive than Nathanael West (1903–1940). Born Nathan Wallenstein Weinstein in New York City, West lived in Paris for two years, where he completed his first novel, *The Dream Life of Balso Snell* (1931). A surrealist fantasy, it was completely ignored. The subsequent fiction, written after West returned to the United States in the early 1930s, occupies a strange border territory between the surreal and the naturalistic, drawing its peculiar character from a confrontation with America at its most meaningless. Something of this is registered in West's third book, *A Cool Million: The Dismantling of Lemuel Pitkin* (1934), a brutally comic attack on the American myth of success, the rise of the self-made man from rags to riches. But the works in which West explored and exploited the absurd – as the essential narrative of life and entire story of America – were his second and fourth and final ones: *Miss Lonelyhearts* (1933), written just after he returned from Europe, and *The Day of the Locust* (1939), written while he was working as a scriptwriter in Hollywood – and published just a year before his sudden death.

The hero of *Miss Lonelyhearts* is – Miss Lonelyhearts. The reader never learns his real name. He is the agony aunt on the New York *Post-Dispatch*, which tells its customers: "Are-you-in-trouble? – Do-you-need-advice? – Write-to-Miss-Lonelyhearts-and-she-will-help-you." The trouble is, the people who write to Miss Lonelyhearts really do need help. He is appalled and obsessed by their sufferings. "For the first time in his life," as he explains to his girlfriend Betty, he is forced "to examine the values by which he lives." And, finding nothing, he realizes that his taking on of the agony column as a kind of joke has backfired: "he is the victim of the joke and not its perpetrator." Life, Miss Lonelyhearts knows, has always been meaningless; and "men have always fought their misery with dreams." "Although dreams were once powerful," Miss Lonelyhearts realizes, "they have been made puerile" by the mass media; "among many betrayals, this is the worst." Miss Lonelyhearts himself is among those who feel most fiercely betrayed. In his agony, Miss Lonelyhearts is, he senses, "capable of dreaming the Christ dream," passionately embracing a saving fiction. He is also, West intimates, as an agonized agony aunt, something of a Christ figure himself, even if an absurd and impotent one. The climax comes when Miss Lonelyhearts has a religious experience. Succumbing to the temptation of the "Christ dream," he is convinced he has become one with God. Driven by that conviction, he holds out his arms Christlike to a cripple, one of those whom he sees as the wretched of the earth. But the cripple fights to escape from his embrace. In the struggle that follows, the gun the cripple is carrying suddenly goes off, and Miss Lonelyhearts is killed. Miss Lonelyhearts's bid to become a savior ends in black farce.

When writing *Miss Lonelyhearts*, West gave it the provisional title: "a novel in the form of a cartoon strip." That suggests the tone of this book, which turns a potentially tragic theme into a comedy of the absurd. Beneath the surface of the narrative, West makes sly, allusive play with all manner of myths that other, earlier cultures have used to endow their fundamentally meaningless lives with a sense of meaning. Along with being a mock Christ, for instance, Miss Lonelyhearts is a mock Oedipus, a mock quester, and a mock hero of vegetation myth. On the surface, however, what the reader is presented with is precisely that: a world of surfaces. The characters are, intentionally, ciphers, caricatures, identified by one or two exaggerated features; and each short, sharp chapter is a comic routine, a cartoon strip the nature of which is announced by its title. With characters reduced to objects, objects are magnified, take on a life of their own. This is a world in which things are more animated than people, where character is commodified and commodities assume – an often malevolent – character. It is also a world stripped of meaning. In its self-evident artifice, *Miss Lonelyhearts* effectively reminds the reader what its protagonist learns, and then forgets: that nothing can explain things – least of all, a story like the one we are reading. To that extent, West was writing here on the borderline between modernism and postmodernism: negotiating a move from art as explanation to art as game, a verbal playfield. *Miss Lonelyhearts* anticipates many books written several decades later that play with the premise that everything, including the book before us, is insignificant, a play of signs – in a word, a fiction.

For West, the difference with popular culture was not that it was superficial – in a depthless world, nothing was more or less superficial than anything else; it was that, in its pursuit of the appearance of depth, popular culture succeeded only in being, as Miss Lonelyhearts puts it, "puerile." That puerility is the subject of *The Day of the Locust*. The novel opens with a brief impression of a film set. The reader then accompanies the central character, Tod Hackett, through Los Angeles, past "Mexican ranch houses, Samoan huts, Mediterranean villas . . . Tudor cottages, and every possible combination of these styles." So, it is clear, what is depicted in the studio is no more unreal than what lies outside. This is a place where "the need for beauty and romance" has issued in "the truly monstrous," and nothing is what it seems. Its inhabitants are those who hang about the studios, waiting for a break. They are also the nameless crowd, the spectators: the retired, middle class, who have traveled to southern California at the end of years of "dull, heavy labor" in the Middle West, in search of "the land of sunshine and oranges." Once there, they have become overwhelmed by a sense of betrayal. At the end of *The Day of the Locust*, the hopeless hordes of Midwesterners who have poured locust-like into California now pour into Hollywood to gaze at the celebrities arriving at a movie premiere. There, the crowd becomes a mob, goes berserk; and Tod, crushed almost to death, sees in a kind of vision the canvas he has been working on, "The Burning of Los Angeles," as if it were completed. It is an appropriately apocalyptic note on which to end a story that announces the selling and subversion of the American dream. The America West describes is one that has lost touch with the real. All it has left is boredom and fear, the resignation and rage of the mob: the both of them signs of a culture that has no sustaining connection with the past – and no adequate means of imagining its future.

5
Negotiating the American Century
American Literature since 1945

Towards a Transnational Nation

The United States emerged from World War II a global superpower. By the end of the twentieth century, with the collapse of the Soviet Union, it had also become the only superpower in existence. Despite social conflict – notably in the 1960s over civil rights and the war in Vietnam – and occasional downturns in the economy, the general direction of American wealth and power was upwards. The same is true for population growth: Americans numbered 180 million in 1960; within thirty years that had increased to 250 million. America, by the year 2000, had become internationally dominant; so had American culture. At the same time, however, the United States had become, more than ever, internationalized: so much so, it has been calculated, that by the middle of the twenty-first century "non-white" and third world groups will outnumber whites. America is, in effect, on its way to becoming even more of a multicultural society than it ever was – or what one contemporary writer has called "the first universal nation."

Formalists and Confessionals

From the mythological eye to the lonely "I" in poetry

In the period immediately following World War II, American writers looked back on a conflict that had threatened to engulf humankind. Among these were the many poets who wrote of their own involvement in conflicts for which – as one of them, Randall Jarrell, put it – "The soldier sells his family and his days." "It is I who have killed,/" declared Karl Shapiro (1913–2000). "It is I whose enjoyment of horror is fulfilled," and, for a while, this sense of having participated in a great historical crisis nurtured a poetry that was notable for its direct address to public issues and events. In 1945, for instance, two substantial collections of war poems were published: *The War Poets* edited by the influential anthologist Oscar Williams and *War and the Poet* edited by Richard Eberhart. Not long after this, Louis Simpson (1923–), in poetry included in *The Arrivistes: Poems 1940–9* (1949), produced work that spoke sardonically of "war-heroes, . . . wounded war-heroes," "packaged and sent home in parts," and that tried,

A Brief History of American Literature. By Richard Gray
© 2011 Richard Gray

too, to capture the tension, the actual experience of war. Shapiro, for his part, in early collections like *Person, Place and Thing* (1942), produced plangent memorials for the unknown soldier ("Elegy for a Dead Soldier"), bitter accounts of a war machine ("Troop Train"), and vivid descriptions of the life of an ordinary conscript during battles ("Full Moon: New Guinea"), and on the return home ("Homecoming"). "Lord, I have seen too much," begins one of Shapiro's poems; and that remark suggests the documentary accuracy, tinged with a bitter knowingness that characterizes many of these pieces.

But if documentary accuracy was the primary aim of most of these poets, this did not necessarily preclude other ambitions. In particular, many writers were keen to see the war in mythological terms. "Lord, I have seen too much," for example, ends with the poet-combatant comparing himself to Adam "driven from Eden to the East to dwell"; and the legend of the Fall became a favorite way of adding a further resonance to global conflict. This was especially true of Randall Jarrell (1914–1965), whose volumes of poetry began with *Blood for a Stranger* (1942), and whose *Complete Poems* was published in 1969. Innocence, and its loss, obsessed him; and the war became for him a powerful symbol of loss, a reversal of the westward myth in that his combatants invariably "fall to the East" from innocence to suffering and experience. This does not mean that his war poems are lacking in documentary detail. What is remarkable, however, is Jarrell's capacity for capturing the dual nature of the experience of war. As he presents it, war makes life more "real" – in the sense that it brings people closer to the pressures of history and the physical acts of living and dying – and more "unreal" – in that it cuts them off from everyday routine, propelling them into a world of potential nightmare. "The soldiers are all haunted by their lives," Jarrell remarks in one piece; and it is this feeling of moving through experience half-asleep, together with imagery of a fall in which innocence is violated, that distinguishes his most famous war poem, "The Death of the Ball Turret Gunner."

The work of Randall Jarrell in fact indicates the direction in which American poetry was to go within ten years of the end of the war: towards mythology, the use of dream and archetype. His poems are intimate and idiomatic. In all of them, however, and especially the earlier ones, the lively texture is complicated by the use of legends, dreams, and fairytale. "All this I dreamed in my great ragged bed .../Or so I dreamed," he says in one piece; in another, he refers to a young girl reading in a library as "An object among dreams." Frequently, the dream convention or the structure of fairytale enables him to edge between the real and the surreal; soldiers mingle with figures from the gospels in his work, ordinary people rub shoulders with angels, devils, or characters from the Brothers Grimm. "Behind everything," Jarrell insists, "There is always/The unknown unwanted life"; and his capacity for combining what he called "the plain/Flat object-language of a child" with the vocabulary of dream registers this.

Writing in 1952, W. H. Auden commented on this interest in legends and archetypes that seemed to characterize a new generation of poets. Auden's remarks were written as a preface to the first volume of W. S. Merwin (1927–), *A Mask for Janus* (1952); and Merwin, in his earlier work, illustrates this mythologizing tendency even more clearly than Jarrell. With Jarrell, the impulse towards the legendary is tempered by his use of peculiarly fluent, even flat forms of speech and his professed commitment to the lives and dreams of ordinary people. In the early poetry of Merwin, however, the landscape is stylized and anonymous (there are, in fact, no references to the United States in the 1950s); the language is elevated and often archaic; and the tone is distant. Exploiting traditional meters, populated by archetypal figures and ancient myths, this is a poetry that refuses any accommodation to the contemporary. Its subjects are the perennial ones of birth, death, and renewal, and it deals with them in terms of allegory and parable, a vocabulary as old as the human race.

If the early poetry of Merwin reveals a characteristic feature of American poetry at the beginning of the 1950s, then the work of Richard Wilbur (1921–) illustrates analogous ones. For Wilbur, the appropriate way of acknowledging discordancy in verse is to accommodate it within an elaborate formal structure. The poet, he argues, has to convert "events" into "experiences," and he does this through a skillful application of form; the poet's forms supply a context, while his ironic yet steady voice draws disparate elements together, relates them and holds them in equilibrium. "Poems are not addressed to anybody in particular," Wilbur declared. "The poem . . . is a conflict with disorder, not a message from one person to another." He committed himself, early on in his career, to the idea of the poem as object, rather than vehicle of communication, with its own "strictness of form." Having made that commitment, he has stuck to it, from the early poems gathered in *The Beautiful Changes and Other Poems* (1967), through *The Poems of Richard Wilbur* (1963), to later collections such as *The Mind-Reader* (1970). Others of roughly his generation have done so too: among them, in her own inimitable way, Elizabeth Bishop. After the early 1950s, however, many American poets rejected formalism, and the mythologizing tendency. Some of them, at least, turned towards autobiography; in their hands, poetry became, once again, not a flight from personality but a dramatization of the personal. The first person was restored to the poetic center.

This rediscovery of the personal in American poetry assumed many forms – as various, finally, as the poets involved. At one extreme are poets who attempted to plunge into the unconscious: in the work of Robert Bly (1926–) (whose best collection is *The Light Around the Body* (1967)), Robert Kelly (1935–) (some of whose best work is in *Finding the Measure* (1968)), Galway Kinnell (1923–) (whose *Selected Poems* appeared in 1982), and James Wright (1927–1980) (*Collected Poems* (1971)), for example, the poet dives down beneath the level of rational discourse, using subliminal imagery and a logic of association to illuminate the darker areas of the self, the seabed of personal feeling, dream, and intuition. Others have dramatized the personal in more discursive, conscious forms. These include poets like Richard Hugo (1923–1982), Karl Shapiro, and Louis Simpson, who explore the self's discovery of the outer world and its reaction to it and, rather more significant, those like Adrienne Rich (1929–), Anne Sexton (1923–1974), and W. D. Snodgrass (1926–2009), who incorporate elements of their personal histories in their poems. The voice of W. D. Snodgrass, and his stance towards nature, is notable for being at once controlled and intense. His finest work is "Heart's Needle" (1959), a series of poems which have as their subject his daughter and his loss of her through marital breakdown. "Child of my winter," begins the first poem, "born/When the new fallen soldiers froze/In Asia's steep ravines and fouled the snows." Cynthia, the poet's child, was born during the Korean War and she is, he suggests, the fruit of his own "cold war": the static, frozen winter campaign is also Snodgrass's marriage. The allusions to the war, and descriptions of the season, are there, not because of any intrinsic interest they may possess, but because they image the poet's personal feelings.

"My poems . . . keep right on singing the same old song": the words could belong to Snodgrass, but in fact they were spoken by Anne Sexton, whose first two collections, *To Bedlam and Part Way Back* (1960) and *All My Pretty Ones* (1962), established her reputation and her intensely personal stance. Even those pieces by Sexton that appear not to be concerned with herself usually turn out to be subjective, to have to do with her predicament as a woman. "The Farmer's Wife," for instance, begins as a description of someone in rural Illinois, caught up in "that old pantomime of love," and then concludes with lines that suddenly switch the focus from farmer and wife to the poet and her lover. Elsewhere, when the narrative mask is dropped, the tone can be painfully raw and open, and given a further edge by elaborate rhyme-schemes or tight stanzaic forms. "All My Pretty Ones" is a good illustration of this. Addressed to the poet's father, the contrast between the passion and intimacy of the address and the strictness of the given measure only exacerbates the situation, intensifies the feeling of the poem. However, she was not only concerned with the pain of being daughter, wife, mother, lover. She also sang, as she put it, "in celebration of the woman I am," in praise of her distinctive identity as an American *female* poet.

A similar pride in the condition of being a woman characterizes the poetry of Adrienne Rich. Rich's early work in *A Change of World* (1951) and *The Diamond Cutters* (1955) is decorous, formal, restrained. But even here there is a sense of the subversive impulses that lie just below the smooth surfaces of life. In "Aunt Jennifer's Tigers," for example, the character who gives the poem its title seems to be crushed beneath patriarchal authority. However, the tigers she has embroidered "across a screen" suggest her indomitable spirit. Polite on the surface, passionate beneath, Aunt Jennifer's art is, at this stage, Adrienne Rich's art. Gradually, though, Rich came to feel that "instead of poems *about* experience," she was, as she put it, "getting poems that *are* experiences." A work like "Diving into the Wreck," the title poem in her 1973 collection, measures the change. In it, the poet tells of a journey under the sea, during which she has to discard all the conventional supports on which she has leaned in the upper world. Diving deep into the deepest recesses of her being, exploring the "wreck" of her own life, Rich feels compelled to jettison inherited techniques. A more open, vulnerable, and tentative art is required, she feels, to map the geography of her self: a feeling that is signaled in this poem, not only by its argument, but by its directness of speech, its stark imagery and idiomatic rhythms, above all by the urgency of its tone. The map is not just for her own use. "We are confronted," Rich has declared in the preface to *On Lies, Secrets and Silence: Selected Poems 1966–1978* (1979), "with . . . the failure of patriarchal politics." In Rich's later work, the confrontation with herself is inseparable from her broader, feminist purposes.

From formalism to freedom in poetry

The example of Adrienne Rich is symptomatic in several ways. In the first place, her later poetry shows how ready American poets have become to take risks. "I have been increasingly willing," she has said, "to let the unconscious offer its material." In the second, she illustrates the particular triumph of the better poets of the personal. Her best work is squeezed out of her own intimate experience; it can be painfully straightforward and frank, but it can also be surreal and political. Finally, Rich is representative in that she was far from alone in terms of her stylistic development from formal to freer verse forms. Not everyone ceased to be a formalist. But, whether interested in personal confession or not, many poets turned, at about the same time as Rich, towards a more open, idiomatic poetry.

Among the poets who show this alteration is Donald Hall (1928–) (the range of whose work is shown in *The Alligator Bride: Poems New and Selected* (1969)), who moved from traditional forms, as in "My Son, My Executioner," to the more fluent and relaxed measures of poems like "The Town of Hill" and "Maple Syrup." There is Robert Bly, who began by writing short, quiet, carefully constructed portraits of rural life and landscapes in the West, before graduating to a more sensuous, various, and insinuating music. There is also Delmore Schwartz (1913–1966), who began by exploring his own suffering and isolation in strict, formal meters and conventional structures, as his first collection *In Dreams Begin Responsibilities* (1938) illustrates, but then, in poems like "Seurat's Sunday Afternoon along the Seine," gravitated to a looser idiom and a rambling longer line meant to reflect the rhythms of ordinary, everyday speech. A similar transfiguration of restless life into mobile language is noticeable in the later work of W. S. Merwin. His earlier poetry is formal and mythological. From this, Merwin moved, in collections like *The Moving Target* (1963) and *The Carrier of Ladders* (1970), to more contemporary, sometimes personal subjects, though mostly written in fairly regular iambics, and then on, in turn, to the angular, radically disruptive rhythms of "Morning": "The first morning/I woke in surprise to your body/for I had been dreaming it." This is not confessional verse, but it represents a departure from Merwin's earlier work: an interest in the more obviously permanent forms of human vision has been replaced by a pursuit of life as it passes.

As American poets gravitated, during this period, towards more flexible verse forms, many of them also went in search of a more idiomatic vocabulary. With Alan Dugan (1923–2003), whose *Collected Poems* appeared in 1969, the result has been a tough, brittle, determinedly populist style. "Here the world is," he declares in "Prayer," "/enjoyable with whiskey, women, ultimate weapons, and class"; and he does his best to express that world as it is. Dugan frequently tries to shock the reader into attention, whereas the poems of William Stafford (1914–1993) (included in *Stories That Could Be True: New and Collected Poems* (1977)) tend to open quietly ("They call it regional, this relevance –/the deepest place we have"), then move towards some muted discovery of a small truth, a partial explanation of things. "The signals we give – yes or no, or maybe –/should be clear," Stafford says at the conclusion to "A Ritual to Read to Each Other," adding "the darkness around us is deep." Clarity of language, verbal modesty, is for him a stay against oblivion, something to illuminate or hold back the surrounding dark.

"Dispossess me of belief/between life and me obtrude/no symbolic forms": this request, made by another postwar poet, A. R. Ammons (1926–2001), repeats the aims of Stafford, but in a different key. It also exposes a further way in which American verse has removed itself from formalism: by dispensing, not only with conventional meters and "signatory" language, but with the "symbolic forms" of narrative closure. Revitalizing the earlier American interest in "organic form," Ammons is one among many recent writers who want the radiant energy they perceive at the heart of the natural world to become the energy of the poem, "spiralling from the center" to inform every line. There are, Ammons suggests in "Corson's Inlet," "no/. . . changeless shapes": the poet-seer must invent structures that imitate the metamorphic character of things. The organisms he creates must respond to life as particularity and process; they must be dynamic, unique to each occasion; above all, they must be *open*. "There is no finality of vision," Ammons concludes (with deliberate inconclusiveness), "... I have perceived nothing completely,/... tomorrow a new walk is a new walk." Echoing a whole series of great American texts, Ammons also speaks here for another generation of poets who respond to "The wonderful workings of the world" with their own workings of the imagination. "*Ecology* is my word," Ammons affirms in another, longer poem published in 1965, "Tape for the Turn of the Year." "My other word is *provisional*," he continues, "... you may guess/the meanings from *ecology*/.../the center arising/form/adapts, tests the/peripheries, draws in/.../responds to inner and outer/change." Those lines could act as an epigraph to many volumes of American verse published during the 1960s and later, in which the poet tries to insert himself into the processes of life, and the reader is asked to insert himself into the processes of the work.

The uses of formalism

There are many ways of being a formalist poet. One way is illustrated by the subtle, serious wit of Richard Wilbur. Another, by the passionate, metaphysical sensibility of Stanley Kunitz (1905–2006), whose *Collected Poems* appeared in 2000. In a poem like "Foreign Affairs," for instance, Kunitz develops the conceit of lovers as "two countries girded for war" to examine the intricacies and erotic heat of a relationship. The poem is at once cerebral and sensuous, turning what could have been merely an intellectual *tour-de-force* into a sensitive analysis of the way "fated and contagious selves" can somehow be "separated by desire." It represents a mentally energetic kind of formalism, whereas the reverence for form that characterizes, say, the work of Howard Nemerov (1920–1991) is calmer, more reflective, expressive of Nemerov's belief that a poem should mean as well as be: even great poems, he suggests, unlike the things of nature, "tell ... rather than exemplify/What they believe themselves to be about."

Still other varieties of formalism, different in turn from those of Wilbur, Kunitz, and Nemerov, are illustrated by the idiomatic, often bizarre wittiness of Reed Whittemore (1919–2000), the incisive, sardonic tones of Weldon Kees (1914–1955), and the patient concern with getting it right, trying to put things properly, that characterizes the work of Donald Justice (1925–2004). At one extreme is the dispassionate reflectiveness of Edgar Bowers (1924–2000) or the equally dispassionate elegance of X. J. Kennedy (1929–). At the other is the poetry of Anthony Hecht (1923–2004), whose measured, ironic voice becomes a medium for passionate explorations of the fear and darkness at the heart of things. In recent times, however, the most memorable lesson in the uses of formalism has been given by Elizabeth Bishop (1911–1979), whose *Complete Poems* were published in 1969, followed by *Geography III* (1976). Of her good friend Marianne Moore, Bishop said, "The exact way in which anything was done, or made, was poetry to her." The same could be said of Bishop herself: "all her poems," Randall Jarrell once suggested, "have written underneath, *I have seen it*." Bishop's aim is to attend carefully to the ordinary objects around her; and then, through that gesture of attention, to catch glimpses of what she calls "the always-more-successful surrealism of everyday life." The more closely she observes something, the more it seems to become arrested in time, translated for a moment into a world of stillness and dream. This resembles Moore's habit of using close attention as a means of imaginative release. However, Bishop's poetic voice is quite unlike Moore's. Strongly musical rhythms, unexpected but inevitably recurring rhymes, wit and clarity of idiom, above all a use of inherited formal structures that is characterized by its elegance and tact – all help to create a poetry that balances itself between mellow speech and music, the lucidity of considered thought and the half-heard melodies of a more sensuous, magical vision.

For Bishop the poem is, above all, a symbolic journey, an excursion that is perhaps promising and perhaps not. Her poetry is full of travel, literal and otherwise. There are poems about travelers ("Crusoe in England"), poems that recall things seen while traveling ("Arrival at Santos"), poems that ask the question, "Should we have stayed at home and thought of here?" One of her pieces has as its epigraph a quotation from *Landscape into Art* by Kenneth Clark: "embroidered nature . . . tapestried landscape"; and this suggests the peculiar ability she possesses to mingle landscapes literal and imagined, or to find the sources of art and inspiration in the most unpromising and mundane of surroundings. Typically, the revelations her poetic journeys achieve are joyful but also sad: with the sadness of rootlessness, perhaps, and isolation. Bishop's watching eye and musing voice are kept at one remove; the quality of distance is always there, enabling wonder certainly but also loss. As some of Bishop's personae learn, the solitude that is a prerequisite of attentiveness, and so imaginative discovery, promotes absence: to look and see is, after all, to stand apart.

One of Bishop's poems, "In the Waiting Room," actually describes how the poet learned about this apartness. While sitting in a dentist's waiting room, she recalls, "I said to myself: three days/and you'll be seven years old." "I felt: you are an *I*," she goes on, "you are an *Elizabeth*": "I knew that nothing stranger/had ever happened, that nothing/stranger could ever happen." The position realized here is the site of most of her work, whether she is attending to objects, people, or events. Her explorer's eye transforms ordinary creatures into extraordinary characters, the stuff of artifice and legend. The aim is not to be merely fanciful, even in more openly bizarre poems such as "The Man-Moth." What Bishop is after is a deeper realism. She is trying to reveal things that may be most available to the unhabituated eye: to uncover the peculiar strategies we and other animals use to confront and defy the forces that govern us ("The Armadillo"), or the strange communications that can occur between the different dimensions of life, the earth and the sea, waking and sleeping. In one of her most famous poems, the insight such communication can offer is compared to the drinking of "Cold dark deep and absolutely clear water" – so cold, in fact, that it seems to "burn your tongue." "It is like what we imagine knowledge to be," she declares of such a draught: "dark, salt, clear, moving, utterly free,/drawn from the cold hard mouth/of the world." It is not stretching a point to say that it is exactly this kind of knowledge Bishop realizes in her own work: where truth slips in through the cold peculiarities of fact and then quietly slips away again.

Another poet who began as a formalist of sorts was Theodore Roethke (1908–1963). His first volume of poetry, *Open House* (1941), used traditional verse structures and depended on the then fashionable mode of tough intellectualism. The opening lines of the first, and title, poem show that this was no ordinary formalist, however. "My secrets cry aloud," Roethke declared. "I have no need for tongue./My heart keeps open house." "I'm naked to the bone," Roethke declares later in this poem, "Myself is what I wear": that is almost, but not quite, true. He is still, after all, dressed in the uniform of inherited poetics. But beginning with his second volume, *The Lost Sea and Other Poems* (1948), this too was to be discarded in the search for the subrational, prehistorical roots of being. "Cuttings (later)" bears witness to the change: "I can hear, underground, that sucking and sobbing,/In my veins, in my bones I feel it, –" Roethke confesses here – "The small waters seeping upward,/The tight grains parting at last."

Much of his verse after the first volume, Roethke explained, "begins in the mire." There is a new rooting of poetry in sensuous experience here, the "greenhouse" world or natural landscape of the poet's childhood (Roethke's father was owner of over twenty-five acres of greenhouses). Along with this, there is a new search for some dynamic concept of correspondence between the human and vegetable worlds. Roethke felt that he had to begin at the beginning, with primitive things: to journey into the interior of the natural order, and into himself as part of that order. This required, in turn, a more primitive voice. So, Roethke uses the free verse line, long, elaborately alliterated, with a preponderance of heavy stresses, open vowels, and participles, to create an effect of enormous effort and evolutionary struggle; instead of imposing order on experience, he tries to discover the order latent in it. This ties in with an alteration of idiom. As he dwelt on primeval life, so Roethke naturally gravitated towards a more subliminal language: the intuitions of folklore, fairytale, and myth, shapes that lurk "Deep in the brain, far back."

"Often I think of myself as riding – " observes the narrator of one of Roethke's later poems, "/Alone, on a bus through western country." "All journeys, I think, are the same," she says a little later. "The movement is forward, after a few wavers." The narrator here is an old woman, modeled on the poet's mother; and the poem from which these observations are taken, "Meditations of an Old Woman," illustrates two ways in which the poet, even as he grew older, continued to change and grow. One way involved an intensified interest in the people around him. The other way was towards a creative analysis of ultimate questions: about God, Eternity – above all, about "Death's possibilities" and their significance for the living. As the old woman meditates, she considers the imminence of her death and the disappointments of her past: but she remembers positive moments as well, when she achieved growth by realizing a harmonious relationship with all that is. Such moments more than make up for others, she believes: they are blessed with a special perfection of their own that no deity can ever supply. "In such times," she says, "lacking a god/I am still happy." It seems appropriate that even this poem, the product of "an old crone's knowing," should end on a note of affirmation and possibility. For Roethke, as the work gathered in his *Collected Poems* (1966) shows, life was a continual wayfaring, an expedition into the grounds of being that offered joy or wonder as a reward. It was a process of constant beginnings, "many arrivals," whereby, the poet felt – to quote from one of his most famous pieces, "The Waking" – "I learn by going where I have to go."

Confessional poetry

"Alas, I can only tell my own story." The words could be those of many American poets; in fact they were written by Robert Lowell (1911–1977), and sum up his work. Despite the touch of regretfulness noticeable in this remark, Lowell did seriously believe that his story needed to be told; and for this there were two good reasons. One was Lowell's characteristically American tendency to see himself as a representative of his culture; the other was his willingness, or rather determination, to assume the role of scapegoat – to challenge, confront, and expose himself, for the purposes of revelation and discovery, to the major pressures of his times.

In his early work, collected in *Lord Weary's Castle* (1946), Lowell's painful awareness of self, together with his anxiety over a world that seemed to him to be corrupted by egotism, led him towards a consciously Catholic poetry. Poems like "The Holy Innocents" and "The Quaker Graveyard in Nantucket" juxtapose the self-absorption of the isolated individual with the selflessness of true faith. The introspective and fragmentary nature of the New England and American traditions is contrasted with the serenity and coherence of the Roman Catholic order. The language of these poems is packed and feverish, the syntax often contorted, the imagery disruptive: all is barely kept in control by the formal patterns of the verse. Like an unwilling disciple, the poet seems to be trying to force himself into accepting the rigors of inherited form and faith; he has to will his speech and his spirit into submission. For all the fierceness of his initial conversion, in fact, Lowell was too much a part of New England – too solitary, introspective, and individualist – to be comfortable as a Catholic; and it was only his rage for order that made him try for a while to compel himself into submission.

"It may be," Lowell wrote once, "that some people have turned to my poems because of the very things that are wrong with me. I mean the difficulty I have with ordinary living." By the time he wrote this, Lowell had had several nervous breakdowns and left the Catholic Church. More to the point, this difficulty he had with "ordinary living" had helped turn his poetry in a new direction: for in the hope, apparently, that he might resolve his problems he had begun writing, first in prose and then in poetry, about his life and family. In part, Lowell was prompted to take this change of course by his reading of other poets, notably William Carlos Williams; but in part it seemed a natural course for him to take, not only because of its possibly therapeutic function but also because it enabled him to pursue his search for a satisfactory voice and place. In the event, in the poems that were eventually published in *Life Studies* (1959), Lowell discovered not just a medium for expressing his devouring inwardness but a way of fulfilling his desire for spiritual anchorage as well: something that, besides offering him the opportunity for emotional release, described a fleeting sense of stability and order.

As the reader compares the poems in *Life Studies* – like "Memories of West Street and Lepke" or "Skunk Hour" – with the earlier work, the contrast could hardly be more striking. Gone is the Catholicism; in its place is a different, more muted and ironic kind of belief, in the imaginative and moral power of faithful speech. Gone, too, are the tortuous language and elaborate arrangements of line and rhythm; in their place are lines that are limpid and flexible, a syntax and idiom that play cunning variations on the colloquial, and rhymes that when they do occur are invariably unexpected and elusive. The poet no longer begins with a predetermined structure for his material, but tries to discover structure and immutability in the actual processes of remembering and articulating. The only order now tolerated is the order of literature; the poem recreating the experience becomes the one acceptable means of refining and shaping it.

The success of *Life Studies* helped turn Lowell into a public figure, the most visible American poet of his generation. And it was partly in response to this enhanced status that he began taking a public stand on some of the major issues of the day, such as the war in Vietnam. At the same time, his poetry, while remaining profoundly personal, addressed problems of history and culture: in his own way, like Whitman he tried to consider what it was like to be an American at mid-century. "Waking Early Sunday Morning" (1967) gives one illustration of how Lowell wedded his intense inwardness of impulse to historical event and contemporary crisis. Another is offered by "For the Union Dead," the title poem in his 1964 collection. In this poem, the civic disorder of the present is contrasted with two alternative ideas of order. One is the public order of the past: old New England, conceived of in consciously mythological terms and figured in the statue of a Colonel Shaw, who commanded a black regiment during the Civil War. The other is the only possible order for the present: a personal one, registered here in the architecture of the poem. Shaw's statue, a monument to public principle, has to be replaced by acts of private judgment which, like this poem, may then furnish others with the vision and vocabulary necessary to change their own lives.

For many of the last years of his life, Lowell concentrated on a series of unrhymed and irregular sonnets, collected in books like *Notebook 1967–1968* (1969, augmented edition 1970), *The Dolphin* (1973), and *History* (1973). Talking about these sonnets, Lowell explained that they were "written as one poem, intuitive in arrangement"; they were, he added, "less an almanac than the story of my life." As a whole, they are further proof of their creator's belief in the power and efficacy of literature: in an almost manic way, the poet seems intent on metamorphosing all his life into art, endowing his every experience, however trivial, with some sort of structure and durability. They are also proof of his Americanness; for, taken together, they constitute another epic of the self. Less openly responsive to the problems of political society than the *Cantos*, less deliberately preoccupied with the future of America than "Song of Myself," *Notebook* and the succeeding volumes nevertheless share with those poems a concern with the life-in-progress of the protean poet, as representative of his time and place.

After the sonnets, Lowell published only one further volume, *Day by Day* (1977). The poems here, which show him returning to freer, more varied verse-forms, are elegiac, penitential, and autumnal, as if the poet were trying to resolve ancient quarrels and prepare himself for death. With storybook neatness, Lowell did die very shortly after the book was published: his life and his life's work were completed at almost exactly the same time. In reading these final poems, the reader is likely to be reminded again just how much faith in the self provided the bedrock value in all Lowell's writing: at times challenged, as in his earlier poetry, occasionally questioned or qualified, as in the later, but always, incontestably there. Like other great American poets, Lowell learned how to translate what he called the "poor passing facts" of autobiography into "the grace of accuracy." Consequently, his story becomes history: he told true tales of his life which have become true tales for all of us.

"Really we had the same life," Lowell wrote in his elegy for John Berryman (1914–1972), "the generic one/our generation offered." Lowell recognized in Berryman a fellow explorer of dangerous psychological territory. What is more, he learned from Berryman: *Notebook*, he acknowledged, bore the imprint of Berryman's *The Dream Songs* (1969). But *The Dream Songs* was by no means Berryman's first work:

like Lowell again, "cagey John" (as he was later to call himself) began under the burden of alien influences, particularly Yeats and Auden. On the whole, his earlier poetry is constricted by its formal quality and attentiveness to established models. *Berryman's Sonnets*, for instance, written in the 1940s although not published until 1968, start from an intensely personal base, an adulterous love affair the poet had with an unspecified woman. But everything is distanced by the use of the strict Petrarchan form, archaic language, and a conventional argument that leads us through love and loss to transference of affection from woman to muse. Only now and then do we get glimpses of the vain, sad, drunken, lustful, comic, and pathetic "I" that dominates the later work.

"I want a verse fresh as a bubble breaks," Berryman declared in one of his sonnets; and the fresh style came in *Homage to Mistress Bradstreet* (1956), which the poet called a "drowning" in the past. In this long poem of fifty-seven stanzas, the "benevolent phantom" of the seventeenth-century poet, Anne Bradstreet, is conjured from the grave; she speaks, through the voice Berryman gives to her, of her emigration to New England and her hard life there; in a moment of intense communion, at once spiritual and erotic, the two poets from different centuries engage with each other; then Bradstreet succumbs to the pull of the past, and she and Berryman are once more imprisoned in their own times. The basic pattern of the poem is one of defiance followed by submission or reconciliation: a pattern Berryman saw as the basic rhythm of life. "We dream of honor, and we get along," he was to say later: existence is a series of small, proud assertions made within the shadow of death, little victories in the face of ultimate defeat. Undoubtedly, *Homage* is a work of the historical imagination, but it is also a personal poem in that it enables Berryman to realize his own voice by making the dead speak and tell their story.

"Man is entirely alone/may be," Berryman remarks just over midway through *Homage*, then adds, "I am a man of griefs & fits/trying to be my friend." This anticipates the tone and vision of Berryman's major work, the *Dream Songs*, the first of which were published in 1964 and the last of which he was still writing just before his death by suicide in 1972. "I am obliged to perform in great darkness/operations of great delicacy/on my self," Berryman admits in one of these songs, and this suggests their essential thrust. Like *Notebook*, they document, in the manner of a journal, the chaotic growth of a poet's mind: the processes of his life, in all their absurdity, fear, pain, and wonder. Unlike *Notebook*, however, the story is told with the help of a character, a person called Henry who is "at odds wif de world and its god." Along with his creator, Henry is many things: transient, willful, lustful, tired, ridiculous, stricken; and he is aided and abetted, particularly in the earlier songs, by another character called Tambo who speaks in a thick, stage-Negro dialect. If Henry, and by extension, Berryman, is "a divided soul," then Tambo helps to dramatize that division. And, as he does so, the reader is reminded of earlier dialogues of self and soul, or mind and body, but with the suspicion that those dialogues have been transposed here into a more contemporary and disjunctive key. The shifts of mood are kaleidoscopic. Certain themes or obsessions recur, such as the suicide of Berryman's father, then, later, the pleasures of his new marriage and the birth and growth of his child, his "heavy daughter": but no particular theme is allowed to dominate. "These songs are not meant to be understood, you understand," warns Berryman, "/They are only meant to terrify and comfort." They are "*crazy* sounds," intended to give tongue to life as it passes: hell-bent on resisting any notions of "ultimate structure" or any suggestion of a stable, unitary self.

The triumph of the *Dream Songs* is that they are deeply intimate, but also the product of cunning and craft. The tragedy of most of Berryman's last poems, in *Love & Fame* (1970; revd. edn. 1972) and *Delusions* (1972), is that they are merely intimate. "I wiped out all the disguises," he said of these poems, ". . . the subject was . . . solely and simply myself." "I am not writing autobiography-in-verse," Berryman insists: unfortunately, he is at least trying to, and very little is added to the meanings or measure of his autobiography by the use of verse. This is not so much confessional poetry, in fact, as pure confession: moving, sometimes, in the way that the confidences of any stranger might be, but not something in which we can begin to share.

"I've been very excited by what is the new breakthrough that came with, say, Robert Lowell's *Life Studies*," said Sylvia Plath (1932–1963). "This intense breakthrough into very serious, very personal emotional experience, which I feel has been partly taboo." Plath's excitement grew from a sense of kinship. Even her earlier poems are marked by extremism of feeling and melodic cunningness of expression. But it was in the poems published after Plath's suicide, in *Ariel* (1966), that the impulse towards oblivion, and the pain that generated that impulse, were rendered in inimitably brutal ways: in terms, at once daring and deliberate, that compel the reader to participate in the poet's despair. The suffering at the heart of her work has received ample attention; however, the craft that draws us into that suffering is sometimes ignored. Her later poetry is a poetry of the edge, certainly, but it is also a poetry that depends for its success on the mastery of her craftsmanship, her ability to fabricate larger, historical meanings and imaginative myth out of personal horror. And it is a poetry, as well, that draws knowingly on honored traditions: the Puritan habit of meditation upon last things, the American compulsion to confront the abyss of the self – above all, the burning conviction felt by poets as otherwise different as Poe and Dickinson that the imagining of death is the determining, definitive experience of life.

"Dying/Is an art, like everything else," Plath remarks in "Lady Lazarus," "I do it exceptionally well." Her poetry is artfully shaped: setting stark and elevated imagery of the sea, fire, moon, whiteness, and silence – all suggestive of the purifying, peaceful nature of oblivion – against figures of domesticity and violence – the pleasures and the pains of living in the world. Everything is incorporated within a habit of intense personal meditation, conversation with the self: "I've got to . . . speak them to myself," Plath said of these later poems. "Whatever lucidity they may have comes from the fact that I say them aloud." The poems concerning the affections that tie us to this world, like "Morning Song" (about the birth of her daughter), are notable for their wry tenderness and wonder; those that describe the false self the world requires us to construct, such as "The Applicant," are marked by a corrosive wit; while the pieces that concentrate on the ambiguous nature of death ("Death & Co.") or the perfecting of the self in the experience of dying ("Fever 103," "Edge") are more rapt and bardic, singed by the fire of prophecy. What characterizes all this work, however, despite evident differences of tone, is the sheer seductiveness of Plath's voice: she conjures up the roots of her own violence, and the reader is caught in the spell.

The artful way in which Plath immerses the reader in her experience is illustrated by "Daddy": a poem that in addition measures the distance between her use of the

Figure 5.1 Portrait of Sylvia Plath. © Bettmann/Corbis.

confessional mode and, say, Lowell's. "Daddy," Plath said, "is spoken by a girl with an Electra complex." More to the point, it is based on her own ambivalent relationship with her father (who died when she was still young), her tendency to recreate aspects of that relationship in later, adult relationships, her attempts at suicide, and her desperate need to come to terms with all these things. The secret of the poem lies in its tension. There is the tension of the narrator's attitude to her father and other men, between fear and desire, resentment and tenderness. There is tension beyond this, the poet intimates, in all human connections: the victim both detests and adores the victimizer, and so is at once repelled and attracted by the brutal drama of life. Above all, there is tension in the poem's tone. The banal horrors of personal and general history that Plath recalls are rendered in terms of fairytale and folk story; while the verse form is as insistently jaunty as that of the nursery rhymes it invokes. This manic gaiety of tone, at odds with the bleak content, has a curiously hypnotic effect on the reader, who feels almost caught by a contagion, compelled to surrender to the irresistible litany of love and hate. Nor do the closing lines bring any release. "Daddy, daddy, you bastard, I'm through," Plath concludes, but the impression is more that she is "through" in the sense of being over and done with than "through" to and with her father. Like scratching a wound, the speaking of her relationship seems only to have exacerbated the pain. There is an art of reconciliation and an art of resistance. There are confessional poets who discover peace, therapeutic release in the disciplines of writing and those, equally disciplined, whose writing only pushes them further towards the edge. If Lowell is an example of the former, then Plath is an illustration of the latter: in the interests of her art she ventured to the point where there was nothing left but the precipice and little chance of a return.

New formalists, new confessionals

Since the deaths of Plath, Berryman, and Lowell, new generations have been busy redrawing the map of American poetry. Among these generations are some notable formalists, poets who necessarily derive their inspiration from personal experience but use a variety of means to distance things and disengage their work from autobiography. The personal stimulus and the desire for disengagement are particularly remarkable in the work of Charles Wright (1935–) (a selection of which is to be found in *Country Music* (1982) and *Scar Tissue* (2007)). "I write poems to untie myself, to do penance and disappear/Through the upper right-hand corner of things," he declares in one poem, "Revision"; other typical lines are, "I am weary of daily things," "I'm going away now, goodbye." If the first person enters Wright's poetry, it does so only to be erased. His poetry is poetry of an "I" yearning for transcendence and its own obliteration. It is a poetry of spiritual hunger, rather than fulfillment, expressed sometimes directly, as in "Next," and sometimes, as in "Spider Crystal Ascension," through symbolism. The structures Wright chooses – the three stanza form of "Tattoos," for instance, or the twelve and fourteen line forms of "Skins" – are clearly a part of this larger project: seeking the still point of the turning world, he commits himself to spatial forms, a frozen moment, arrested motion.

Subtly different kinds of distancing are to be found in the work of Amy Clampitt (1920–1994) and Louise Glück (1943–). Clampitt has a habit of weaving the phenomenal world into an artful piece of embroidery. In "The Kingfisher," for example, the title poem of her 1983 collection, the calculated play of imagery, a strict and quite complex stanzaic form, winding syntactical shapes and a feeling for words as distinctly odd artefacts: all help transmute the story of a love affair into a tapestry, rich and strange – or, as Clampitt herself puts it, into "an illuminated manuscript in which all the handiwork happens to be verbal." With Glück, the effect is not so much of a mosaic as of ritual. Glück's poems (in collections like *The First Four Books* (1995) and *Averno* (2006)) deal with themes that are intensely personal in origin: family life ("Poem," "Still Life"), motherhood and children ("All Hallows," "The Drowned Children"), a lost sister ("Descending Figure"), love between a man and a woman ("Happiness"). But everything is rendered in an oblique, impersonal manner, seen as if through the wrong end of a telescope. The actors in these human dramas are usually anonymous; there is a timeless quality to their actions; and the terms in which they are rescued for our attention possess the stark inevitability of fable.

Along with these new departures in formalism, however, poetry of the personal has continued unabated. In several instances, recent writers have developed the tradition of relating identity to landscape. John Haines (1924–), for instance, connects the wintry surroundings of Alaska, and the Middle West "with its trodden snow/and black Siberian trees," to harsh visions of himself and his culture; in such collections as *News from the Glacier* (1982) and *For the Century's End* (2001) the natural world is seen in terms of internecine conflict and so too is America. His aim, evidently, is to identify himself with these conflicts: to participate in a struggle that is at once elemental and political. The tone of this involvement is sometimes celebratory, sometimes meditative or angry. Whatever, it constantly recalls that great poet of participation, Whitman: for Haines shares with Whitman not only a populist impulse and a feel for organic rhythms but also a radicalism that is both personal and political. Similar echoes of Whitman, tracing a correspondence between inner and outer worlds, are to be found in the work of Robert Pinsky (1940–), a poet who tries to capture what he calls the "mothlike" life hovering behind "The glazed surface of the world." Pinsky's voice, quieter than Haines's, may sound ordinary, but that is precisely the point: like Whitman, he is obsessed with the heroism of the ordinary – or even of the apparently banal. So, in volumes that include *The Figured Wheel* (1996) and *Gulf Music* (2007), he describes "the tyranny of the world visible," and in particular the suburban landscapes of New Jersey, and hints at the "unique/Soul" beneath this, the "hideous, sudden stare of self" that can be glimpsed by the sympathetic imagination. American life is marked for him by its doubleness; a favorite setting, the seashore, implies this duality of perspective. Set between the mysterious ocean and "vast, uncouth houses," Pinsky and his characters inhabit a border area. They live and work "For truth and for money" – two very different yet related "stays/Against boredom, discomfort, death and old age."

Dave Smith (1942–) also secretes the poetry of the personal in the poetry of place: "Grandfather," he declares in one poem, "Cumberland Station," "I wish I had the guts to tell you this is a place I hope/I never have to go through again." Only in this case the place is Southern: the "anonymous fishing village" where he lives, perhaps, the woods and rivers ("The Last Morning"), a disused railway ("Cumberland Station"), or a Civil War cemetery ("Fredericksburg"). His poetry, gathered in collections like *The Wick of Memory* (2000), is saturated in locality, focusing in particular on what most art, in its pursuit of an "entirely eloquent peace," "fails to see": the disinherited, those victimized by society and often excluded from its frames of reference. And through this landscape moves the poet himself, trying to "hold . . . obscure syllables/one instant." He, it seems, is given presence by the "eye," the observation of extrinsic detail. So, for all his interest in the personal, Smith – like Haines and Pinsky – chooses to refract personality: to clothe the naked self in the warm details of circumstantiality.

Public and Private Histories

Documentary and dream in prose

"Our history has moved on two rivers," Norman Mailer (1923–2007) wrote in *The Presidential Papers* (1963), "one visible, the other underground; there has been the history of politics which is concrete, practical . . . and there is the subterranean river of untapped, ferocious, lonely and romantic desires, that concentration of ecstasy and violence which is the dream life of the nation." That may sound like a reformulation of a perennial American dialectic: the clearing and the wilderness, fixity and fluidity, the strictures of society and the subversive impulses of the self. If it is, then it was certainly given additional impetus in many prose texts in the three decades or so after

World War II, when writers struggled to negotiate what they saw as an increasingly baffling and bizarre world.

For Mailer himself, the American history that mattered for him personally began with World War II. That war inspired a powerful vein of fiction. Some of it was written in what Gore Vidal (1925–), commenting on his own war story *Williwaw* (1946), called "the national manner ... a simple calculated style." Apart from *Williwaw*, such novels included *From Here to Eternity* (1951), a grimly realistic story of army life in Hawaii on the eve of the attack on Pearl Harbor, by James Jones (1921–1977), and *The Gallery* (1947) by John Horne Burns (1916–1953). But Vidal himself, as his remark suggests, did not remain long within the constraint of realist simplicity. His later work shows him using a mixture of realism and satire, sardonic comment and acerbic wit, sometimes surreal fantasy and always irony, to explore such disparate subjects as homosexuality (*The City and the Pillar* (1948)), politics ancient (*Julian* (1964), *Creation* (1981)) or modern (*Washington D.C.* (1967), *Hollywood* (1990)) or both (*Two Sisters* (1970), *Live from Golgotha* (1992)), transsexuality and the media *(Myra Breckinridge* (1968), *Myron* (1974)), and the heroes and villains of American life and society (*Burr* (1973), *1876* (1976), *Lincoln* (1984)). And two of the most notable novels to come out of the war exploited the techniques of the absurd to capture the bleak, bitter absurdities of that conflict: *Catch-22* (1961) by Joseph Heller (1923–1999) and *Slaughterhouse-Five; or The Children's Crusade* (1969) by Kurt Vonnegut (1922–2007). *Catch-22* shows its protagonist, Yossarian, as the victim of mad, conspiratorial military and political systems: caught in a closed system (the military, the war machine, society), his simple desire to escape from which proves his sanity and so his fitness to go on serving it. And *Slaughterhouse-Five* circulates around the firebombing of Dresden, which as a prisoner of war Vonnegut had witnessed. The Heller novel uses a disjointed narrative technique, nightmare sequences, and bleak humor to depict a world gone crazy. The Vonnegut novel goes further. Mixing science fiction with satire, comedy with determinism, it shows its protagonist, Billy Pilgrim, inhabiting different zones of time and space. Haunted by a punitive air raid that burned to death more people than died at Hiroshima, Billy plods through dull middle age in suburban America while simultaneously alive and comfortable on the distant planet of Tralfamadore. The time-warp technique allows Vonnegut simultaneously to offer ironic commentary on our inhumanity and the opportunity for destruction provided by twentieth-century technology to satirize middle America and the bourgeois standards of suburbia, and to explore human inconsequence. Vonnegut has written many other fictions that move between satirical humor and surreal fantasy: among them, *Player Piano* (1952), *The Sirens of Titan* (1959), *Cat's Cradle* (1963), *Breakfast of Champions* (1973), *Bluebeard* (1987), and *Timequake* (1997). Heller also wrote several other novels, including *Something Happened* (1974) and a sequel to *Catch-22, Closing Time* (1994). Neither of them, however, equaled their absurd comedies set in the nightmare of war. In *Catch-22* and *Slaughterhouse-Five*, human beings grapple to find meaning in the meaningless, and fail; and the conflicts that haunt them seem illogical as well as obscene.

Mailer wrote his own war novel, *The Naked and the Dead* (1948), he said, as "a parable about the movement of man through history." His book, he explained, explored "the outrageous proposition of cause and effect ... in a sick society." The parable is executed in terms of flesh and blood, depicting the capture of the island of

Anopopei from the Japanese. There are two levels to the action. There is the actual fighting of the reconnaissance platoon under Sergeant Croft, which gives us the view on the ground of the combatant soldier. And there is the strategic view of the operation as conceived by General Cummings. Connecting these two levels is the middle-class liberal, Lieutenant Hearn, who will not agree with Cummings's fascist beliefs, is humiliated by him and eventually killed by the agency of Croft. There is a bleak irony at work throughout the narrative; we are in the realm of the absurd. The island is captured. But that is thanks, not to the strategy of Cummings, but to the actions of the incompetent Major Dalleson. The capture of the island serves no useful purpose. And what prevails in the end is the desperate obstinacy of oppressed men, who reach the point where they can be oppressed no further. The ultimate irony is the way in which the members of the platoon turn. Pushed by Croft almost to the top of Mount Anaka, they stumble into a nest of hornets, from which they flee in terror down the mountainside. Discarding their weapons as they go, they suddenly understand that "if they threw away enough possessions, they would not be able to continue the patrol."

The eight men of the reconnaissance platoon are clearly meant to be a representative cross-section of American society. They are drawn from different places and ethnic groups; their backgrounds and prewar lives, however, represented in inter-chapters that Mailer calls "The Time-Machine," have a grim similarity about them. These are the wretched of the earth, conceived in terms that recall the fiction of Dos Passos. The energy of the book does not lie here, but in the portraits of the two men of power. Croft is the natural fascist, a sadist who kills for the thrill of killing. Cummings is the intellectual fascist, who not only enacts but expresses his beliefs. "The only morality of the future," he tells Hearn, "is a power morality." "There is one thing about power," Cummings adds. "It can flow only from the top down." So, with its rigid hierarchies and distinctions, "you can consider the Army as a preview of the future." That remark made by Cummings was seminal for Mailer, since much of his work – extraordinary in its range as it is – can be seen as an exploration of power: its different manifestations, how it expresses itself in individuals and society. His second novel, *Barbary Shore* (1951), set mostly in a run-down boarding-house in Brooklyn, is about power and politics. His third novel, *The Deer Park* (1955), set around Hollywood, is more about power and sex. A later book, in turn, *Why Are We in Vietnam?* (1967), is about those national fantasies of power that prompted America into its imperialist venture in Southeast Asia.

What *Why Are We in Vietnam?* also suggests is the willingness of its author to incorporate fact and dream, the documentary and the demonic modes, in his imaginative investigation of power. It may be a war novel of a kind, but that is a very different kind from *The Naked and the Dead*, which, for all Mailer's talk of it as a parable, is clearly in the tradition of American naturalism. A master storyteller in the realist and naturalist vein, Mailer has also excelled at the New Journalism, a form he helped create, which takes actual events and submits them to imaginative transformation. *Armies of the Night* (1968), for instance, which is subtitled "History as a Novel, The Novel as History," has as its subject a 1967 protest march on the Pentagon. *Miami and the Siege of Chicago* (1969) deals with the Republican and Democratic conventions of 1968; *The Prisoner of Sex* (1971) is Mailer's encounter with feminism; *Marilyn: A Biography* (1973) is a study of the life and meaning of Marilyn Monroe; and *The Executioner's Song* (1979) is at once an account of the events surrounding the execution of the convicted killer Gary Gilmore and an investigation into the roots of American violence. An essay like "The White Negro" (1957), in turn, shows Mailer becoming part of the beat movement, calling on his contemporaries to resist corporate America and pursue a radical, more spontaneous alternative. *Of Women and Their Elegance* (1980) returns to Marilyn Monroe, whom Mailer sees as both an American icon and an embodiment of the power and potential corruptibility of sex, but this time in the form of fantasy, an "imaginary memoir" of the star. And *Ancient Evenings* (1983), set in ancient Egypt, has a protagonist who is reborn three times, as he rises from a peasant childhood to become an advisor to the pharaohs. Throughout his 1965 novel, *An American Dream*, Mailer has his hero, Rojack, negotiating the edge between an America of hard facts and power politics and a nightworld America of strange, subrational or supernatural experience. It is an edge that this novel itself inhabits, as Mailer himself negotiates his way between a harsh, empirical idiom, and one that gestures towards strangeness. "I was caught" between two Americas, Rojack admits, which clearly correspond to the two rivers of American history described by his creator. All his career, Mailer has been similarly caught. Out of that capture, though, he has produced fiction and non-fiction that goes further than most in negotiating the mysterious dialectic of power that – for him, as for many others – constitutes the story of his nation.

There are many other novelists who have attempted a comparable negotiation. John O'Hara (1905–1970), from his acidic first novel, *Appointment in Samarra* (1936) to the attenuated realism of *Ten North Frederick* (1955) and *From the Terrace* (1958), has investigated the interconnections of money, sex, and social position. The bent towards satire, a mordant moralism, is strong in the fiction of John Cheever (1912–1982). *The Wapshot Chronicle* (1957), for example, his most famous work, is an account at once wistful and comic of a wealthy but declining Massachusetts family. *The Stories of John Cheever* (1978) contains many pieces that ask the question why, as Cheever himself puts it, "in this most prosperous, equitable, and accomplished world – where even the cleaning women practice the Chopin preludes in their spare time – everyone should seem to be disappointed." In turn, his last book, *Oh What a Paradise It Seems* (1982), continues the theme of the American dream, and the mystery of its unfulfillment. But this time, by focusing on an ageing man who is rejuvenated by an unusual romance, Cheever informs his usual vein of comic melancholy with a feeling of hope. Nelson Algren (1908–1981) and William Gaddis (1922–1998) offer an illustration of the different formal possibilities for rewriting contemporary America. In novels like *The Man With the Golden Arm* (1948) and *A Walk on the Wild Side* (1956), Algren uses a hardbitten prose style to narrate the lives of an American underclass, a world of dealers and dope, poker and prostitution. Gaddis, by contrast, employs a richly parodic idiom, a protean narrative idiom that insists on its own fictiveness, to play with such themes as art and illusion (*The Recognitions* (1955)), the hypocrisies of corporate empire (*J R* (1975)), ambition, loss, and the hunger for apocalypse in a world of competition (*Carpenter's Gothic* (1985)), and the complex figurations that make up the maze of American law (*A Frolic of His Own* (1994)).

A contrast of a different kind is offered by Paul Bowles (1910–1999) and William Styron (1925–2006). Bowles became an expatriate in the 1940s, and his work is generally set in Morocco where he lived most of his life. *The Sheltering Sky* (1949), for instance, *Let it Come Down* (1952), and *The Spider's House* (1955) are all set in North

Africa. Their nominal scene, however, is less important than the interior world of his characters, which is a world of nothingness. Many of them are rich American exiles and most of them have reached – to use the phrase that concludes *The Sheltering Sky* – "the end of the line." In his own cosmopolitan way, as he exposes the horror of nothing, Bowles exploits one vein of writing often associated with the South. Styron, who spent most of his life in the United States – first in Virginia, then in Connecticut – exploited others. His first novel, *Lie Down in Darkness* (1951), revealing the tragic life and suicide of a girl whose rich Southern family was unable to supply her with love and security, is almost an exercise in Faulknerian tropes and themes. While his fourth, *The Confessions of Nat Turner* (1967), concerning the life of the eponymous hero, the leader of an 1831 slave revolt, is a radical rewriting of plantation romance. It is also, as Styron explains in an "Author's Note," "a meditation on history." So, for that matter, are his 1953 novella *The Long March* (1957) and his 1979 novel *Sophie's Choice*, which deals with the historical event that has cast its shadow over all subsequent Western history, the holocaust.

Among those writers whose work cut through Western mythology during the immediate postwar period were Wallace Stegner (1909–1993) and from a later generation, Larry McMurtry (1936–). Stegner once said that he was seeking "a usable continuity between past and present." That search is most noticeable in *Angle of Repose* (1971), in which the narrator, a retired historian, sets out to write his grandparents' – and in particular his grandmother's – story chronicling their days carving a life for themselves in the West. The book subtly disposes of what the narrator calls "several dubious assumptions about the early West": pointing out, for instance, that "large parts of it were owned by Eastern and foreign capital and run by iron-fisted bosses." But it also fiercely interrogates a new West that has lost touch with its past. "I get glimpses of lives close to mine," says the narrator as he browses through his grandparents' papers. "I'd like to live in their clothes for while." He does so; and his act of research becomes an act of recovery. He discovers the continuity between his present and past, and the "angle of repose" where the lives of his ancestors came to rest in him. McMurtry has moved between very different modes. His work includes novels honoring the land and the earlier generations who were its stewards (*Horseman, Pass By* (1961), *Leaving Cheyenne* (1963)), books satirizing smalltown life or urban displacement (*The Last Picture Show* (1966), *Texasville* (1987), *When the Light Goes* (2007)), and fiction that casts a cold but not entirely unromantic eye on such traditional Western themes as the trail drive (*Lonesome Dove* (1981)) and Billy the Kid (*Anything for Billy* (1988)). Significantly, these books on old Western themes came after McMurtry himself called for writers in his home state of Texas "to turn from the antique myths of the rural past and to seek plots and characters and literary inspiration in modern Texas's urban, industrial present." Which suggests how equivocal writers of the West can be about the myths enshrined in its past.

A novelist who has negotiated his way with particular subtlety between past and present, the legends and facts, in this case of the Midwest, is Wright Morris (1910–1998). Born in Nebraska, his acutely crafted fiction observes characters often in oblique fashion as they try to come to terms with others, with the past of their family and community, and with the history and legends informing the places where they live. Morris said that his aim in many of his books was "to salvage what I considered threatened, and to hold fast what was vanishing." He pursued this aim in novels that, typically, concentrate on one situation diversely affecting the people involved in it (*My Uncle Dudley* (1942), *The Field of Vision* (1956), *Ceremony in Lone Tree* (1960)), or show characters searching for a meaningful life (*The Ways of Love* (1952)) or loving relationships (*The Huge Season* (1960)). He also did so in books like *The Home Place* (1948) that combine sharp but sensitive verbal and visual description. Typically, Morris avoids prolonged dialogue and moments of intense action in his novels. His characters are marked by their refusal to speak at length: "Cora . . . welcomed silence," we are told of one leading figure in *Plain Song* (1980). Moments of conventional crisis are less crucial to them than moments of gradual illumination, quiet or mute understanding – which are usually the gifts of maturity. "Already," we learn of a character in *Fire Sermon* (1971), "he was old enough to gaze in wonder at life." What they achieve, if they are lucky, is immersion in the land, and the habits and rituals it instills. The older characters in Morris's work are likelier to be luckier in this way. For the younger, there is the feeling of being "withdrawn from the scene." "Abstinence, frugality, and independence – the home-grown, made-on-the-farm trinity," reflects the protagonist in *The Home Place*. "Independence, not abundance, is the heart of . . . America" – or at least of the old America to which he has tried to return. But it is, he recognizes, a heart that beats less fiercely in his own generation.

Contested identities in prose

The first novel of E. L. Doctorow (1931–), *Welcome to Hard Times* (1960), was a Western of sorts. But it was also a violent demythologizing of the romance of the West which, in a manner to become typical of its author, explored the need for community in a destructively individualistic culture. Doctorow has consistently expanded or sub-verted established generic forms to explore an American paradox: the elaborate circuitries of wealth and influence that connect one thing to another in American society and its fundamental lack of cohesiveness, real bonds between people other than those of manipulation and use. In *The Book of Daniel* (1971), based on the case of Julius and Ethel Rosenberg, who were executed as convicted spies in 1953, Doctorow used the form of the political novel to consider divisions that are social, familial, and generational. For *Ragtime* (1975), an account of three fictional families at the beginning of the twentieth century intertwined with actual historical figures, he turned to a form that recalled *U.S.A.* by John Dos Passos. The social comment of Doctorow's novel, however, is edged with a sense of absurdity. *Loon Lake* (1980) is the novel as hybrid, a mix of styles and perspectives, *World's Fair* (1985) a fusion of memoir, scrapbook, and thinly disguised autobiography. In *Billy Bathgate* (1989) and *The Waterworks* (1994), Doctorow uses the generic conventions of the gangster and gothic novels to explore different moments in the life of New York City; in *The March* (2006), he deploys the form of the historical novel to explore the rupture of Civil War. Doctorow is a tireless experimenter in narrative forms. Consistently, though, he has stretched those forms to test his vision of a society that is not so much a community as a conspiracy.

"We have two lives," observes a character in *The Natural* (1952), the first novel of Bernard Malamud (1914–1986), "the life we learn with and the life we live after that.

Suffering is what brings us toward happiness." All the novels of Malamud offer variations on the theme sounded here. They are set in different times and places and have very different nominal subjects. *The Natural,* for example, deals with baseball as a realm of American heroism and myth. *The Assistant* (1957), Malamud's second novel, is about an Italian-American called Frank Alpine who becomes an assistant to a New York Jewish shopkeeper. His third, *A New Life* (1961), tells the tale of a Jewish professor of English who goes to teach in an Oregon "cow college." Among his later novels, *The Fixer* (1967), based on actual events that occurred in 1913, describes how a Russian Jew is falsely accused of and imprisoned for murder. *Pictures of Fidelman* (1969) tells of a middle-aged Bronx resident who goes to Italy to be an artist; *Dubin's Lives* (1974) is about the marriage and love affairs of a famous author; *God's Grace* (1982) is a pseudo-biblical tale about a man who is the sole survivor of a nuclear war and begins a new civilization among apes. Some of the novels are comic or satirical, others sadder, more serious. All, however, are parables: fables that are, on one level, dense with historical specificity and personal detail and, on another, placeless, timeless. And what these fables narrate is a painful progress to maturity: the process by which an individual can truly become a hero by entering into the lives of others.

"It's obvious to everyone that the stature of characters in modern novels is smaller than it once was," Saul Bellow (1915–2005) once wrote, "and this diminution powerfully concerns those who value experience." "I do not believe that human capacity to feel or do can really have dwindled or that the quality of humanity has degenerated," he went on. "I rather think that people appear smaller because society has become so immense." This catches something of the concern that lies at the heart of Bellow's own novels, which navigate the two rivers of American history in their own agonized yet corrosively comic way.

No novel by Bellow is exactly exemplary, because a key feature of his achievement is his ability to dramatize his concerns in a variety of fictional forms. His two earliest novels gravitate towards the condition of nightmare and the leading character as victim. His second novel, actually called *The Victim* (1947), is about the agonizing, equivocal relation between a Jew and Gentile who, despite their radical differences, seem "dependent for the food of spiritual life" upon each other. His first, *Dangling Man* (1944), shows us a man caught precisely between the life around him and the life within, as he waits for induction into the army. With his third novel, *The Adventures of Augie March* (1953), Bellow adopted a picaresque, more extrovert form; as he was also to do for his fifth book, *Henderson the Rain King* (1950). Adventuring through several countries, Bellow's larger-than-life mythic hero pursues, just as his other protagonists do, a search for identity. Typically of this extroverted novel, the extremes he has to maneuver between are dramatized in two characters, his brothers. His older brother has become a social success but at the expense of brutalizing, even destroying, himself. His younger brother is pure of spirit, sweet, simple-minded, and helpless – and terrified of leaving the enclosure of the self, just as much as he is of venturing outside the walls of the asylum in which he is confined. Faced with these alternatives, Augie's solution is to run and dodge: to slip between the fixities and definites of the social world and the swamplike inertia of the isolated self – and to find freedom in movement, the provisional and the possible. "Look at me going everywhere!" Augie declares at the end of the novel. "Why, I am a sort of Columbus." It is a characteristically American conclusion, as Bellow signals by making the last word of the book "America."

The novel that competes with *Augie March* as Bellow's finest, *Herzog* (1964), signals a return to a more introspective form. Moses Herzog, the narrator, is possessed of a representative modern mind, "inconstant, divided, vacillating." He is caught between the isolated ambit of consciousness, a place of retreat for the formulation of ideal patterns, and the teeming surfaces of society, where those patterns seem to be bombarded out of existence by a welter of details. "*The human soul is amphibian*," Herzog reflects, "*and I have touched its sides.*" And his own amphibious nature compels him to vacillate, hysterically but helplessly. He is torn, a man dangling between pride and humility, self-assertion and self-mockery. He makes forays into the streets, then withdraws. He writes "letters" to establish contacts with the world outside, but he does not complete or read them. No more than Augie March, or Bellow's other protagonists, does he heal this gap in himself, as well as between himself and his world. But, just as much as they, he remains convinced of the possibility of resolution. That conviction stays with him. And he closes the story with a sense of peace and promise, which seems to exist outside language. "At this time he had no messages for anyone," the novel concludes. "Nothing. Not a single word." The conclusion is equivocal. Since Herzog is our source of information here, we cannot be sure whether the peace and promise he has found is an assured discovery or a pious hope. What we can be sure of, however, is that his creator, Bellow, has taken us on one of the most revelatory explorations into a problem that has haunted so many American writers. And taken us, then, into the prospect of a solution, a resolution that lies beyond words.

No subsequent novel of Bellow's has matched the achievement of *Herzog* or *Augie March*. In their own fiercely ruminative manner, however, they have considered the same overwhelming question. His 1969 novel, *Mr. Sammler's Planet*, acquires additional urgency, as it considers the possibility of "the collapse of civilization" and the barbarous destruction of consciousness, from the fact that its protagonist, in his seventies, is a survivor of the Holocaust. *The Dean's December* (1982) places its clearly autobiographical central character between two social orders, the decaying communism of Eastern Europe and the anarchic capitalism of the United States, that seem equally repellent. Collectivism and individualism both lead here to violation of the spirit; and there is, it appears, no alternative, no third way. What is notable about these later books, among them Bellow's 1987 and 2000 novels *More Die of Heartbreak* and *Ravelstein*, is their darkening of tenor and tone. What remains for Bellow, however, is a ferocious belief in the integrity of knowledge: the imperative of looking without flinching into the heart of things – and the ineluctable nature of the truth we can find there. As Mr. Sammler, in his 1969 novel, puts it, despite all the vagaries of consciousness and violence of civilization, "we know *what is what*." That knowledge is something all Bellow's protagonists possess, at some juncture. It is also what his fiction, even at its darkest, manages to teach.

By the end of *Herzog*, the narrator has reached a point where, he tells us, he felt "a deep, dizzy eagerness to *begin*." At the end of *Portnoy's Complaint* (1969) by Philip Roth (1933–), to conclude the manic monologue that constitutes the book, his psychiatrist is permitted the final word: "Now vee may perhaps to begin. Yes?" One condition for beginning, or being able to think about doing so, is some measure of liberation from the past. Herzog perhaps achieves this by the conclusion of Bellow's novel. But Alexander Portnoy still seems to be drowning in his own subjectivity: a subjectivity which, like that of so many of Roth's protagonists, seems to be determined by other people, the larger narrative of his family, community, and culture. In an earlier Roth novel, *Letting Go* (1962), Gabe Wallach, one of the major characters, reveals some of the psychologically crippling effects of being raised in the family nest, or trap. He tells his girlfriend that he can never escape from that trap, be "off the hook," until, as he puts it, "I make some sense of the larger hook I'm on." Within the terms of the story, he never does. Similarly, in Roth's first novel, *Goodbye, Columbus* (1959), the protagonist Neil Klugman stands staring at his reflection in a library window, after the painful end of an affair. "The outside of me gave up little information about the inside of me," Klugman says; he wanted "to go behind that image and catch whatever it was that looked through those eyes." However, as he "looked hard" at his own image, he recalls, and his "gaze pushed through it," all he ended up seeing was "a broken wall of books, imperfectly shelved." The project of all Roth's fiction could be said to be precisely this: to gaze at the image of an American like himself, to discover what lies beneath. What, it asks, is the mysterious self, the subjectivity that stares back, that captivates me? There is no simple answer to this question. But as Roth's protagonists and narrators maneuver their way between the outside and the inside, they incline towards the inclination Neil Klugman offers as he looks in the library window. Perhaps selfhood is a fiction, a product of the past and the dreaming imagination, all that is recorded in books; perhaps nationhood is as well.

The earlier novels explore this enigma of subjectivity through a series of protagonists who share Roth's own Jewish upbringing, and who find it hard to escape from the narrative of the Jewish family and culture. Portnoy, for instance, is locked in a past that is circumscribed by his mother and orthodox "boundaries and restrictions," the "None Other" of traditional Jewish law. He seeks relief in obsessive masturbation and an equally obsessive masturbatory monologue. But the forms of relief, sexual and verbal, that he finds for himself only reveal his entrapment: endlessly, it seems, he circles around the past and the guilt it instills. Constantly, like so many of Roth's entrapped Jewish males, he looks with longing at the "goyim" and their world. "These people are the *Americans*," he declares; "these blond-haired Christians are the legitimate residents and owners of this place." They occupy "center-field" rather than the margins of society; and they seem to him to possess a freedom from the past, a mobility and unreflective, unconstrained subjectivity that he can only look at with envy. This perception of "the *Americans*," as Portnoy calls them, is a mirage, of course, the product of his yearning. And, in many of his later novels, Roth has explored both that mirage and the use of writing to reflect selfhood and nationhood. Much of the finest of this later fiction considers the fate of a writer, Nathan Zuckerman, very much like Roth, so that the book itself becomes a mirror – or, rather, a means of gazing through the library window at other books: among them, *The Ghost Writer* (1979), *Zuckerman Unbound* (1981), *The Anatomy Lesson* (1983), *Zuckerman Bound* (1985), *Exit Ghost* (2008). Some of it has a writer called Philip (*Deception* (1990)) or Philip Roth (*Operation Shylock: A Confession* (1993)) as a protagonist. And all of it is concerned, not just with personal identity, but with the identity of America. That concern is clear in books like *The Plot Against America* (2004), which imagines an extreme right, anti-Semitic coup in the United States. It is even clearer in *American Pastoral* (1997) where

Zuckerman, in trying to tell the story of a man he sees as an archetypal American hero, finds himself telling the story of his nation. "I dreamed a realistic chronicle," Zuckerman explains. But, as that paradoxical remark intimates, what he ends up with is fiction, myth: the pastoral story Americans have invented for themselves of their aboriginal innocence – their longing for freedom, a pure subjective space, and their feelings of dereliction and dismay when they do not have it. In an earlier novel, *The Counterlife* (1986), Zuckerman had described the womb as "the pastoral landscape par excellence"; that suggests the take on American versions of pastoralism here. *American Pastoral* is a meditation on the yearning, the looking backward that maybe determines any attempt to understand and narrate ourselves. It is also about the American inflection given to this, which claims the United States as what Zuckerman calls "desire's homeland," a state of prelapsarian grace.

Grace, or the possibility of it, is one of the concerns of John Updike (1932–2009), whose 1963 novel, *The Centaur*, has an epigraph from Karl Barth: "Heaven is the creation inconceivable to man, earth the creation conceivable to him," Barth observes here. "He himself is the creature on the boundary between heaven and earth." All Updike's major characters inhabit this boundary: between heaven and earth, the intensity of life and the inevitability of death, dreams of freedom and the comforts of a compromised, suburban environment. "I feel to be a person is to be in a situation of tension," Updike once explained. "A truly adjusted person is not a person at all." So characters like George Caldwell (*The Centaur*), Harry Angstrom (*Rabbit, Run* (1960), *Rabbit Redux* (1971), *Rabbit is Rich* (1981), *Rabbit at Rest* (1990), *Rabbit Remembered* (2001)), Piet Hanoma (*Couples* (1968)), Henry Bech (*Bech: A Book* (1970), *Bech is Back* (1982)), Roger Lambert (*Roger's Version* (1986)), even the Muslim fundamentalist Ahmad in *Terrorist* (2006) – all perform and pursue their maladjustments in what is called, in *Couples*, "a universe of timing": enacting the beauty, and the terror, of their own duality. So, in *The Centaur*, George Caldwell, an ageing schoolteacher, is having to come to terms with his own decline and imminent death. "I'm a walking junkheap," he declares, announcing an obsession with waste, human and universal, that runs through Updike's fiction. "I hate Nature. It reminds me of death," he insists bitterly. All things, cars, houses, people, landscapes, fall apart, revert to zero.

Against this entropic vision, this dread of the void, is set the possibility of love. "A man in love ceases to fear death," Updike observed in one of his essays. There is also what Updike has called the "brainless celebration of the fact of existence": like the carnival celebrations that conclude his first novel, *The Poorhouse Fair* (1959). And there are the comforts of the customary, routine and structure. Piet Hanoma, in *Couples*, for instance, is a dedicated carpenter. Grappling with materials helps him to fend off a sense of the void. "He needed to touch a tool. Grab the earth," the reader is told. "All houses, all things that endured, pleased Piet." And yet such is the duality of Updike's characters, they can also feel like a prison sometimes. The void is terrifying but maybe liberating; the structures of houses, the suburbs, suburban routine may be comforting but also claustrophobic. And Updike always returns to the fundamental intimation that structures waste away too, they are part of "the world's downward skid." "I think books should have secrets, like people do," Updike has said. And the secret his own books disclose is the imminence of the void, the dread fear of death and the dim possibility of grace: another dimension that gives depth and resonance to what might seem to be the fleeting contingencies of his suburban settings. One way he alerts the reader to this extra dimension is through sly allusion to myth, folktale and fairytale. The myth of Chiron lurks beneath the surface of *The Centaur*, to give the story what Updike called a "counterpoint of identity"; the story of Peter Rabbit underlies the Rabbit series; and the tale of Tristan and Iseult enriches Updike's 1994 novel about love and criminality, *Brazil*. Another way is through a playful mixing of genres or temporal planes. In *The Witches of Eastwick* (1984) and *The Widows of Eastwick* (2008), three mischievous suburban women enjoy adventures that are simultaneously sexual and paranormal. But the most productive way of all, for Updike, is through the severe elegance of his prose, which weaves a path between documentary and magic.

At the end of the first book in the Rabbit series, *Rabbit, Run*, the protagonist of all four novels, Harry Angstrom, finds himself confronted with a "dense pack of impossible alternatives." Standing in the street, he imagines a road leading back into the heart of the city, to his responsibilities as a husband, father, and family provider. "The other way," he reflects, leads "to where the city ends." "He tries to picture how it will end, with an empty baseball field, a dark factory, and then over a brook into a dirt road, he doesn't know." As he imagines the end to this other road, as "a huge vacant field of cinders," "his heart," we are told, "goes hollow." The field of cinders or the suburban net: it appears to him to be death either way. He cannot make a choice, as he stands poised between the two routes. All he can do is maneuver, engage in simple motion. As the final words of the novel put it, "he runs. Ah: runs. Runs." Indecision, evasion of this kind, has a long history in American writing. What is more, it is precisely running of one kind or another that becomes the tactic of so many characters in recent American fiction: as they find themselves poised between what Updike calls two roads, and Mailer the two rivers of American history. Dodging, maneuvering, balancing: these are agencies of existential deferral, means of living between the two roads or rivers. Weaving together, wavering between documentary and dream: these are devices of stylistic deferral, allowing the novel to inhabit a border territory. With his vacillating heroes and variety of styles, Updike is close to many of his contemporaries. And, like them, he sees death as the only conclusive moment. Before that, life is process, running, a series of beginnings.

Of the many other novelists who have attempted to navigate the two rivers of American history, among the most accomplished is Don DeLillo (1936–). Although not formally a postmodern novelist, DeLillo is fascinated by the condition of post-modernity. *White Noise* (1984), for instance, is an ironic comedy about the mass replication of images in modern America and the anxiety technology engenders in its characters' precarious sense of identity. With a paranoid professor of Hitler studies at a Midwestern college as its central character, *White Noise* addresses the media and the idea of mediation as it occurs in a wide range of disguises. DeLillo is concerned here, and elsewhere in his fiction, not just with the power of the media to invade consciousness, but with the idea that all contemporary American experience is informed by modes of representation which determine consciousness at every level. And not just contemporary American experience: *Mao II* (1991), for example, explores the impact of mass culture on a global level. What place is left for the individual, the novel asks, in the face of the totalizing ideologies of the media? Perhaps "the future belongs to crowds." In the fictional world of DeLillo, characters negotiate their ironic or pathetic way through a culture defined by its consumption: not so much of the actual but the imaginary, the promissory image offered to them on the television screen. DeLillo is the novelist as anthropologist: sifting through American lives as signifiers of their culture to see what place there is, if any, for the individual or the authentic. The anthropological character of his fiction is never more noticeable than in his 1997 novel, *Underworld*, which plots the course of American history from 1951 to 1992. It pivots, in particular, on the technology of waste. "Waste is the secret history, the underhistory," one character declares, "the way archaeologists dig out the history of early cultures." Future historians, the reader infers, might interpret twentieth-century America in terms of the story of its waste products. And that is DeLillo's narrative project here: to gather and study the discarded remnants of American culture, weaving historical memory and imaginative recall together to produce a secret history, an underworld narrative.

What distinguishes many of the characters of DeLillo is their subjection to the anonymizing processes of the market and certain feelings generated by that subjection – a vague anxiety (an anxiety that achieves momentary point and poignancy in his post-9/11 novel, *Falling Man* (2007)), a sense of dissatisfaction, yearning. These are precisely the distinguishing features of protagonists in a number of other late twentieth-century novels: notably, *The Moviegoer* (1961) by Walker Percy (1916–1999), *Cabot Wright Begins* (1964) by James Purdy (1923–2009), *Ironweed* (1983) by William Kennedy (1928–), *The Sportswriter* (1986), *Independence Day* (1995), and *The Lay of the Land* (2006) by Richard Ford (1944–), the "New York Trilogy" (*City of Glass* (1985), *Ghost* (1986), *The Locked Room* (1987)) of Paul Auster (1947–), *Bright Lights, Big City* (1984) by Jay McInerney (1955–), and *Less than Zero* (1985) by Bret Easton Ellis (1965–). Nominally, all these novels and their protagonists are very different. What connects all these fictions, however, is a dread of inconsequence. Their protagonists all share what one of them, Frank Bascombe in *Independence Day*, calls a fear of "the cold, unwelcome, born-in-America realization that we're just like the other schmo." What is more, most of them also share the feeling that, maybe, the fear has been realized: that they have indeed been "tucked ever more deeply," as Bascombe puts it, "more anonymously, into the weave of culture." And that culture is itself anonymous, an accumulation of insignificances, not just ordinary but blank.

Nothing could be further from all this than the world of Cormac McCarthy (1933–), whose work is marked with an indelible sense, not so much of blankness or evil, as of homelessness. There is an argument for seeing McCarthy as a Southern writer – or, rather, one of those many white male writers who have been busy recently rewriting Southern subjects and themes: among them Peter Taylor (1917–1994), Harry Crews (1935–), Barry Hannah (1942–2010), and Robert Olen Butler (1945–). The literal geography of his first four novels (*The Orchard Keeper* (1965), *Outer Dark* (1968), *Child of God* (1973), *Suttree* (1979)) is, after all, scrupulously confined to one Southern place within a 100-mile radius of Maryville, Tennessee. And they could be said to participate in one of the oldest debates in Southern writing, between pastoralism and the anti-pastoral. There is, however, equally an argument for situating McCarthy among those other white male writers who have been busy deconstructing Western myth and telling tales of a newer, truer West: among them, Edward Abbey (1927–1989), William Gibson (1944–), Frederick Barthelme (1943–), and Rick Bass (1950–). McCarthy's 1985 novel, *Blood Meridian* (1985), marks the beginning of his departure from the South into Western settings: a departure confirmed by his "Border Trilogy," *All the Pretty Horses* (1992), *The Crossing* (1994), and *Cities of the Plain* (1998) and two subsequent novels, *No Country for Old Men* (2005) and *The Road* (2006). All six later novels are characterized, not only by an inversion of traditional Western stories about crisis and redemption, but also by a sense of the bleakness of Western space. The unobstructed extension of the landscape triggers here, not the conventional feeling of freedom, but intimations of empty immensity, the denial of human value and distinction. There is even an argument for associating McCarthy with those writers who work through verbal experiment, the exploration of different styles: like Stanley Elkin (1930–1995), Harold Brodkey (1930–1996), Russell Banks (1940–), or David Foster Wallace (1962–2008). Reading his work is often like strolling through a museum of English prose styles: with, say, sentences imitating Hemingway's gift for simple words modulating into the complex rhythms of Faulknerian speech.

Perhaps the most useful way of looking at all McCarthy's work is precisely this: in terms of a confluence of styles – and in the context of his own preoccupation with homelessness, orphanhood, and wandering. McCarthy (and he is typical of his contemporaries even in this) is a literary hybrid. And he is so because he is reflecting the mixed, plural medium which, as he sees it, everyone inhabits now, and perhaps always has: the border territory that is our place of being in the world, made only the more starkly remarkable to us all by the collapse of those cultural barriers that used to provide shelter. Homelessness is the source as well as the subject of McCarthy's work, because at the heart of it lies an uncanny sense of the exile that *is* our lives, now more than ever, the displacement that turns every day into a crossing of borders.

Crossing borders: Some women prose writers

A fiction writer from the South who has believed, on the contrary, very firmly in place is Eudora Welty (1909–2001). "Feelings are bound up in place," Welty insisted in her essay on "Place in Fiction" (1962). "It is by knowing where you started that you grow able to judge where you are." For Welty, that place is the South. Some of her short stories are set elsewhere, in London, Italy, or Greece. But most of those collected in, for instance, *A Curtain of Green* (1941), *The Golden Apples* (1949), and *The Bride of Innesfallen* (1955) are situated in and around the South. So, too, are such novels as *The Robber Bridegroom* (1942), *Delta Wedding* (1946), *Losing Battles* (1970), and *The Optimist's Daughter* (1972). The tone and tenor of her fiction is remarkably various. So, *The Robber Bridegroom*, set in the Natchez Trace region of Mississippi in the late eighteenth century, based loosely on a Brothers Grimm fairytale, mixes the actual and the extraordinary to the point where the line between the two becomes indistinguishable. *Delta Wedding*, the novel that followed *The Robber Bridegroom*, is a magical but also slyly mocking plantation novel. It is set on a Mississippi plantation in 1923, a year Welty chose from an almanac as being one in which there were no wars or natural disasters to disrupt the normal pattern of domestic life. The narrative is uneventful in the conventional sense: the uneventfulness allowing Welty, she has said, "to write a story that showed life that went on on a small scale of its own."

What these two novels share, despite all their differences, is what they share with all Welty's fiction. There is, first, an understanding of place as fact and feeling: "location pertains to feeling," Welty has said, "feeling profoundly pertains to place." There is, second, a sense of the dialectics of living and of historical experience as a matter of record and myth. There is, third, a conviction that it is through language, especially, that the human animal realizes identity and community. And there is, finally, an animating belief that, as Welty herself put it once, "ambiguity is a fact of life." "All things are double," the reader is told in *The Robber Bridegroom*: so what is needed, in writing as well as living, is "the power to look both ways and to see a thing from all sides." All these habits of mind and imagination come together in all Welty's best stories: whether they are comic, like "Why I Live at the P.O.," lyrical like "A Still Moment," tragic like "Death of a Traveling Salesman," or gothic and grotesque like "Petrified Man." For that matter, they come together in a novel very different from either *The Robber Bridegroom* or *Delta Wedding*: *Losing Battles*, a comedy that, with sympathy and humor, describes people waging an unequal struggle with circumstances who remain hopeful despite everything – and who, above all, use old tales and talking as a stay against confusion. An accomplished photographer, Welty was fond of using photography as a paradigm of the human project to name and know experience: to use stories, like her own, and ceremonies, like those of her characters, to get a purchase on ourselves and our world. Just as we click the shutter, Welty intimates, the object will disappear, leaving "never the essence, only a sum of parts." Writing is a pursuit of the real, but the real will always elude us.

"Ours is the century of unreason," Welty declared once, "the stamp of our behavior is violence and isolation: non-meaning is looked upon with some solemnity." Flannery O'Connor (1925–1964) would have agreed with some of this, but not all. What troubled her was not lack of reason but absence of faith. "The two circumstances that have given character to my writing," O'Connor admitted in her collection of essays, *Mystery and Manners* (1969), "have been those of being Southern and being Catholic"; and it was the mixture of these two, in the crucible of her own eccentric personality, that helped produce the strangely intoxicating atmosphere of her work – at once brutal and farcical, like somebody else's bad dream. A devout if highly unorthodox Roman Catholic in a predominantly Protestant region, O'Connor interpreted experience according to her own reading of Christian eschatology – a reading that was, on her admission, tough, uncompromising, and without any of "the hazy compassion" that "excuses all human weakness" on the ground that "human weakness is human." With rare exceptions, the world she explores in her work – in her novels *Wise Blood* (1952) and *The Violent Bear It Away* (1960) and her stories gathered in *A Good Man is Hard to Find* (1955) and *Everything That Rises Must Converge* (1965) – is one of corrosion and decay. It is a world invested with evil, apparently forsaken by God and saved only by His incalculable grace. It is a netherworld, a place of nightmare, comic because absurd, and (as in early Christian allegory) the one path by which its inhabitants can travel beyond it is that of renunciation and extreme suffering.

O'Connor once explained her work by saying that "the novelist with Christian concerns will find in modern life distortions which are repugnant to him." His audience, though, will find those distortions "natural." So such a novelist has to make his vision "apparent by shock." "To the hard of hearing you shout," she said, "and for the almost-blind you draw large and startling figures." Her figures are grotesque, in other words, because she wants us to see them as spiritual primitives. In order to describe to us a society that is unnatural by her own Christian standards – and make us feel its unnaturalness – she creates a fictional world that is unnatural by almost any accepted standards at all. O'Connor's characters are distorted in some way, because their distortions are intended to mirror their guilt, original sin, and the spiritual poverty of the times and places they inhabit. That is only half the story, though. From close-up, these characters may seem stubbornly foolish and perverse, ignorant witnesses to the power of evil. But ultimately against their will, they reveal the workings of eternal redemption as well. As, for instance, O'Connor shows us Haze Motes preaching "the Church Without Christ" and declaring "Nothing matters but that Jesus was a liar," she practices a comedy of savage paradox. Motes, after all, relies on belief for the power of his blasphemy: Christ-haunted, he perversely admits the sway over him of the faith he struggles to deny. Every incident in *Wise Blood*, and all O'Connor's fiction, acquires a double edge because it reminds us, at one and the same time, that man is worthless and yet the favored of God. The wickedness of humanity and the grace of God are opposites that meet head on in her writing, and it is in the humor that they find their issue. What we are offered on the surface is a broken world. But the finely edged character of O'Connor's approach offers an "act of seeing" (to use her own phrase) that goes beyond that surface: turning what would otherwise be a comedy of the absurd into the laughter of the saints.

A writer whose fictional world was as strange yet instantly recognizable as O'Connor's was Carson McCullers (1917–1967). "I have my own reality," McCullers said once towards the end of her life, "of language and voices and foliage." And it was this reality, her ghostly private world, that she tried to reproduce in her stories (collected in *The Mortgaged Heart* (1971)), her novella *The Ballad of the Sad Café* (1951), and her four novels: *The Heart is a Lonely Hunter* (1940), *Reflections in a Golden Eye* (1941), *The Member of the Wedding* (1946), and *Clock Without Hands* (1961). She gave it many names, over the years, and placed it consistently in the South. Southern though its geographical location might be, however, it was like no South anybody had ever seen before. It was another country altogether, created out of all that the author had found haunting, soft, and lonely in her childhood surroundings in Georgia. It was also evolved out of her own experience of melancholy, isolation, and occasional if often illusory happiness. "Everything that happens in my fiction has happened to me," she confessed in her unfinished autobiography (*Illumination and Night Glare* (2000)). Her life, she believed, was composed of "illumination," moments of miraculous insight, and "night glare," long periods of depression, feelings of enclosure within herself. So are the lives of her characters. The people she writes about may seem or feel strange or freakish: because they belong to a marginal group, maybe, because of their awkward age, their anomalous desires or grotesque appearance. But in their freakishness they chart the coordinates of all our lives; their strangeness simply brings to the surface the secret sense of strangeness all of us share in what McCullers sometimes called our "lonesomeness." So, for example, *The Member of the Wedding* is an initiation novel in which the lonely, sensitive, twelve-year-old protagonist, Frankie Adams, is initiated into the simple ineradicable fact of human isolation: the perception that she can, finally, be "a member of nothing." At the heart of McCullers's work lies the perception Frankie comes to, just as the protagonist of *Clock Without Hands*, J. J. Malone, does when he learns that he has a few months to live. Each of us, as Malone feels it, is "surrounded by a zone of loneliness."

Whereas McCullers published only four novels in her short life, and O'Connor only two, Joyce Carol Oates (1938–) has produced more than fifty. She has also written hundreds of shorter works, including short stories and critical and cultural essays, and her plays have been produced off Broadway. Often classified as a realist writer, she is certainly a social critic concerned in particular with the violence of contemporary American culture. But she is equally drawn towards the gothic, and towards testing the limits of classical myth, popular tales and fairy stories, and established literary conventions. Many of her novels are set in "Eden County," based on the area of New York State where she was born. And in her early fiction, *With Shuddering Fall* (1964) and *A Garden of Earthly Delights* (1967), she focuses her attention on rural America with its migrants, ragged prophets, and wrecking yards. In *Expensive People* (1968), by contrast, she moved to a satirical meditation on suburbia; and in *Them* (1969) she explored the often brutal lives of the urban poor. Other, later fiction has shown a continued willingness to experiment with subjects and forms. *Wonderland* (1971), a novel about the gaps between generations, is structured around the stories of Lewis Carroll. *Childwold* (1976) is a lyrical portrait of the artist as a young woman. *Unholy Loves* (1979), *Solstice* (1985), and *Maya: A Life* (1986) cast a cold eye on the American professional classes. *You Must Remember This* (1987) commemorates the conspiratorial obsessions of the 1950s, while *Because it is Bitter, and Because it is My Heart* (1991) dramatizes the explosive nature of American race relations. Common to her fiction, including more recent novels like *Missing Mom* (2005) and *The Gravedigger's Daughter* (2007), however, is a preoccupation with crisis. She shows people at risk: apparently ordinary characters whose lives are vulnerable to threats from society, their inner selves or, more likely, both.

Violence also threatens the characters in the stories of Grace Paley (1922–2007). In this case, however, the characters seem to find the energy to resist, or at least survive. In tale after tale in her several collections (*The Little Disturbances of Man* (1959), *Enormous Changes at the Last Minute* (1974), *Later the Same Day* (1985)), the reader is presented with irrepressibly energetic children, feisty women, and tough-minded men. Supposedly ordinary working-class people, mostly inhabiting the cheaper, rougher districts of New York City, they show an extraordinary capacity to weather economic deprivation, social oppression, or familial violence. Nothing, perhaps, could be further from this than the fiction of Alison Lurie (1926–) and Anne Tyler (1941–). In novels like *Love and Friendship* (1962), *The War Between the Tates* (1974), *Foreign Affairs* (1984), and *Consequences* (2006), Lurie has marked with quiet satire the lives of academics and authors: the politics of the family and the campus, the contacts and conflicts between American and English society. Tyler has ranged more widely, in such novels as *Earthly Possessions* (1977), *Dinner at the Homesick Restaurant* (1982), *The Accidental Tourist* (1985), *Breathing Lessons* (1988), and *Digging to America* (2006). But certain preoccupations tend to recur: families and the separations they suffer through death and through the isolation of one member from another, the need to live more than a life of quiet desperation and the desperate fact of truly living, taking a risk. What these writers share is worth emphasizing, though, for all their differences. It is something shared with other recent and notable women writers, among them Ann Beattie (1947–), Gail Godwin (1937–), and Josephine Humphreys (1944–). All of them reveal, with gentle intensity, those moments in life – usually shared by a group, perhaps a family – when the familiar suddenly becomes strange. The contours of the everyday are disrupted, by bereavement maybe or betrayal; and the characters, often female, are forced to revise accepted notions about their own nature and those dear to them – and to make a choice about where they stand, even if only quietly to themselves.

One of the most remarkable groups of recent women writers to examine communities, and especially families, in crisis comes from the South. The group includes Bobbie Ann Mason (1940–), Lee Smith (1944–), Ellen Gilchrist (1935–), Dorothy Allison (1950–), Jayne Ann Phillips (1952–), and from an earlier generation, Ellen Douglas (1921–). Mason is the author of a number of remarkable short stories (*Shiloh and Other Stories* (1982)) that show, she says, how she was "haunted by the people I went to school with." Working in local dime stores or wrecking yards, perhaps, or living in rural trailer parks and frequenting shopping malls, her characters register not only the changes in their own lives but also transformations in their culture. Or, as one feisty young woman character tells her father: "Times are different now, Papa. We're just as good as the men." In novels like *In Country* (1985), *Spence & Lilla* (1988), *Feather Crowns* (1993), and *An Atomic Romance* (2006), Mason has continued her sensitive exploration of such people, as they weave their way between a vanished past, a slippery present, and an uncertain future. In her early stories in *Black Tickets* (1980), Phillips is similarly concerned with people trying to make sense of their aimless lives, their world of broken families, truck stops, strip joints, people on the move. And to do so, they seem never to cease talking, about their lives and world, to others or themselves. More ambitiously, in her novels *Machine Dreams* (1984), *Shelter* (1994), *Motherkind* (2000), and *Lark and Termite* (2009), she has woven voices together to tell stories of death and desire, the subterranean ties that bind one person to others, personality to history.

"Granny would lean back in her chair and start reeling out story and memory," recalls the protagonist in *Bastard Out of Carolina* (1992) by Dorothy Allison. That suggests something else that many of the more recent white women writers from the South share. The tales they tell are often rehearsed in oral telling, or emerge in a style that recalls the spoken word. Lee Smith, for instance, has an uncanny ear for voices and an unusual range. She catches the vocal timbre of the small town (*Fancy Strut* (1973)) and the rural community (*Family Linen* (1985)), sensitive young women (*Black Mountain Breakdown* (1986)) and indomitable older ones (*Fair and Tender Ladies* (1988)), the recent past (*The Lost Girls* (2002)) and the more distant (*On Agate Hill* (2006)). The voices that inhabit the work of Gilchrist tend to be more educated, but they carry, in their idiom, what the protagonist of *The Annunciation* (1983) calls the "cargo" of other, remembered voices that she "must carry with her always." And in *Cavedweller* (1998) by Allison the interplay between present and recollected voices is even more on the surface: as, like so many protagonists in these stories, the leading character returns to her hometown to try to come to terms with the past. Unsurprisingly, the clash of voices often encountered in these books by white Southern women has a racial inflection. In what is probably her finest novel, *Can't Quit You Baby* (1988), for instance, Ellen Douglas tells the story of two women – one rich, white, and pampered, the other poor, black, and world-weary – who share a Mississippi kitchen for fifteen years. And as the two women, the mistress of the house and the housekeeper, talk and tell stories, the reader learns of a prolonged encounter that is too complex to be described in terms of simple love and hatred.

"I am crawling through the tunnel of myself," observes a character in *The Benefactor* (1963) by Susan Sontag (1933–2004). Sontag has written in various genres and forms: essays, cultural, critical, and political (*Styles of Radical Will* (1969), *On Photography* (1977), *Under the Sign of Saturn* (1980), *AIDS and Its Metaphors* (1988)), drama (*Alice in Bed, A Play* (1993)), short stories and longer fiction (*I, etcetera* (1978), *Death Kit* (1967), *The Volcano Lover, A Romance* (1992)). All of her work, however, is concerned with varieties of alienation and mediation: the pressing, often claustrophobic relationship between reality and what she calls in one of her books "the circle of my consciousness." Her writings, fictional and non-fictional, could be described in the terms she herself used for the work of Samuel Beckett: as "delicate dramas of the withdrawn consciousness." In this, she is not alone. A number of other recent women writers have been concerned with the predicament of the trapped sensibility, often female. The problem is there in such otherwise different books as *Final Payments* (1978) by Mary Gordon (1949–) and the immensely popular novels *The Women's Room* (1977) by Marilyn French (1929–2009) and *Fear of Flying* (1973) by Erica Jong (1942–). More seriously and powerfully, it is present in the work of Joan Didion (1934–). Didion is an accomplished writer of non-fiction that explores American dreams and nightmares: that history of ecstasy and violence that Mailer spoke of, and that has led so often to political disaster or cultural breakdown (*Slouching Towards Bethlehem* (1968), *The White Album* (1979), *After Henry* (1992)). And in novels like *Play It As It Lays* (1970) and *The Last Thing He Wanted* (1996), she has taken alienation to a kind of logical conclusion. In spare, lyrical prose that works as much through its absences, the spaces between the words as the words themselves, she presents the reader with a world of vacancy: where the protagonists find it difficult to escape from emotional numbness, other characters approximate to objects, things to be manipulated, and experience is random, violent, and without meaning.

For some characters in recent novels by women, the way to escape all this is to go west: not to the coast, necessarily, but to the wide open spaces that lie between that coast and the Mississippi River. So, the protagonist in *The Bean Trees* (1989), then later *Pigs in Heaven* (1993), by Barbara Kingsolver (1955–) flees westward to Arizona, from the poverty and pressures of her life in Kentucky. There, she builds a new life for herself and a new "home" and "family" with friends and the abandoned child she takes up with her on the journey. What, however, is remarkable about the fiction of Jane Smiley (1949–) and E. Annie Proulx (1935–) is that it refuses to accommodate the West to these notions of liberatory flight. The women and men in the stories of Smiley are caught up in the conflicts of family life, condemned to see in themselves "the fusing and mixing of their parents" and to scrabble for material success or survival, even though the places where they work out their fates are vast and open. So in *A Thousand Acres* (1991), Smiley rewrites the story of King Lear and his daughters, transporting it to a farm in Iowa. The book is a subtle but radical transformation of the Shakespearean tragedy, a visionary version of the politics of the family, particularly fathers and daughters, and an unraveling of some familiar Western tropes. Life in the West, Smiley intimates, can be as embroiled in the past, disputes over blood and earth, as anywhere else: in the world of *A Thousand Acres*, we are told, "acreage and financing were facts of life as basic as name and gender."

The politics of the family have been a shaping force in the world of E. Annie Proulx, too, whatever setting she has chosen, In *The Shipping News* (1993), for example, set in

Newfoundland, she satirizes what some American politicians like to refer to lovingly as family values. Violence and abusive sex are all in the family here. Nevertheless, while the book does not idealize the family, it does suggest that coming to know one's family, even distant family, is a way to know oneself. The verdict on the family in *Close Range* (1999), a series of stories set in the West, is more corrosive. And equally corrosive is the verdict on the West. Here, families disintegrate, relationships rarely last for more than "two hours," and the culture itself seems to be given over to the abstractions of money and image. In one story, "The Mud Below," a character called Diamond Felts tries to pursue a model of cowboy masculinity that he finds seductive by joining a rodeo. He is motivated, it turns out, by the refusal of his father to accept him: "Not your father," his father tells Diamond, "and never was." But his adventure ends in a disastrous accident. Even before that, the brutal reply of his mother when Diamond asks her who his father was, "Nobody," lets us know how much this is a tale about two kinds of failed paternity. There is the failure of the literal father, but there is also the failure of the founding fathers of Western myth. Casting a cold eye on that myth, Proulx sees it as a mask and a masquerade. She is not alone in this, nor is she in the conviction that the two rivers of American history have become fatally mixed and muddied. Or, as the caustic epigraph to *Close Range* has it: "Reality never been of much use out here."

Beats, Prophets, and Aesthetes

Rediscovering the American voice: The Black Mountain Writers

In 1950 Charles Olson (1910–1970) in his essay on "Projective Verse" declared war on both the formalists and the confessionals, announcing the emergence of new forces in postwar American poetry. "Closed" verse, the structures and metered writing "which print bred," was to be jettisoned, Olson declared: so too was "the private-soul-at-any-public-wall," the lyricism of the strictly personal approach. What was required was an "open" poetry. "The line comes . . . from the breath, from the breathing of the man who writes," Olson argued, "at the moment he writes"; it was therefore unique to the poet and the occasion. The poet responded to the flow and pressure of things, he registered this in his diaphragm, and he then compelled his readers, by sharing his breathing rhythms, to feel the same pressures and participate in the flow of the moment.

"I have had to learn the simplest things/last," Olson wrote in one of his poems, "Maximus, to himself" (1953), "Which made for difficulties." The problem, as he saw it, was not that truth was intrinsically difficult: on the contrary, earlier civilizations like the Mayan had acted upon it with instinctive ease. It was that habits of mind and language that had been entrenched for centuries had to be *un*learned. The process of unlearning, and then making a new start, began with books like *Call Me Ishmael* (1947), his extraordinary critical work on Melville. It was also initiated in some of the earlier poems published in the 1940s. However, it was in the work published after this, through the 1950s and beyond, that his sense of poems as performative moral acts was fully exercised: in shorter pieces like "The Kingfishers" (1949), "In Cold Hell, In Thicket" (1950), and "As the Dead Prey Upon Us" (1956), as well as in the *Maximus Poems* (1983), written over several decades, which represent Olson's own version of the American epic.

Undoubtedly, Olson's major poetic achievement is the *Maximus Poems*. The Maximus who gives these poems their title is an "Isolated person in Gloucester, Massachusetts," the poet's home town, who addresses "you/you islands/of men and girls": that is, his fellow citizens and readers. A "Root person in root place," he is, like Williams's Paterson, a huge, omniscient version of his creator. The poet is the hero here, as he normally is in the American epic, and this poet is notable as an observer, correspondent (many of the poems are described as "letters"), social critic, historian, pedagogue, and prophet. The poems that constitute his serial epic vary in stance and tone. Nevertheless, certain themes recur, supplying a stable center to this constantly shifting work. Olson's aim is a specific reading of the history of Gloucester, and the surrounding area by land and sea, that will enable a revelation of truth: one particular "city" will then become the "City," an "image of creation and of human life for the rest of the life of the species." The opening lines of the first poem announce the quest: "the thing you're after/may be around the bend." The voyage of discovery is, in effect, in search of the near, the familiar. Such a goal is not easy, Olson suggested, at a time when "cheapness shit is/upon the world" and everything is measured "by quantity and machine." Nothing valid is easy, even love, when "pejorocracy is here," the degradations of capitalism and consumerism – and where the familiar has been contaminated by the "greased slide" of "mu-sick," the evasions of modern mass culture. But it is still possible to live *in* the world, achieving the recognition that "There are no hierarchies, no infinite, no such many as mass, there are only/eyes in all heads,/to be looked out of." It is still possible to realize contact with particular places and moments ("there is no other issue than the moment"), and to build a new community or "polis" based upon humility, curiosity, and care.

Like many other American epics, the *Maximus Poems* juxtapose America as it is with America as it might be. But "we are only/as we find out we are," and perhaps Americans can "find" a new identity and society. Certainly, Olson hoped so and worked hard, in both his art and his life, to realize that hope: he had something of the evangelical fervor of Pound, which came out in particular during the years he taught at Black Mountain College in North Carolina. Among his colleagues and pupils there were a number of poets who shared at least some of his aims, the most important being Robert Creeley (1926–2005) and Robert Duncan (1919–1988). In the case of Creeley (whose *Collected Poems* was published in 2006), an interest in open forms and the belief that "words are things too" has combined with two quite disparate but complementary influences. There is, first, his involvement with the free-flowing experiments of Abstract Expressionism and modern jazz. Along with this, there is what Creeley has termed his "New England temper." New England has given Creeley many things, including a tendency to be "hung up," to suffer from pain ("I can/feel my eye breaking") and tension ("I think I grow tensions/like flowers . . ."). Above all, though, what it has given him is two things, one to do with perception, the other with expression. "Locate *I*," declares Creeley in one of his poems; elsewhere, he insists, "position is where you/put it, where it is." He is fascinated by the perceptual position of the speaker, how the poem grows out of the active relationship between the perceiver and perceived. The preoccupation with the limits of vision that earlier New Englanders demonstrated is consequently translated into cool, modernist terms. At the same time, New England habits have, Creeley says, given him a "sense of of speech as a laconic, ironic, compressed way of saying something to someone." His poems evolve on both a sequential grammatical level and a cumulative linear level; each line reaffirms or modifies the sense of the sentence and the total argument, each word exists in tension with all the others. There is risk here, a taste for the edgy and subversive, of a kind that would be equally familiar to Thelonious Monk and Emily Dickinson. Given the habit "I" or self-consciousness has of getting in the way of revelation, Creeley tries to strip poetry of its more obtrusive, interfering devices. To capture the "intense instant" what is needed is caution, perhaps ("The Innocence"), surprise ("Like They Say"), spontaneity ("To Bobbie"): above all, a willingness to follow the peculiar shape and movement of an experience, however unpredictable it may be. Creeley's sparse, brittle poems use their silences just as effectively as their speech and present the cardinal sin as cowardice – the fear of the challenge thrown out to us by the, as yet, unseen and unarticulated.

"I like to wander about in my work writing so rapidly that I might overlook manipulations and design": that remark of Robert Duncan's suggests that he, too, saw the poem as a process, of being and knowing. However, another remark of his illustrates the mystical strain that helps distinguish him from his Black Mountain colleagues: "Poetry is the very life of the soul: the body's discovery that it can dream." With a background as a romantic and theosophist, Duncan said that he experienced from the first an "intense yearning, the desire for something else." Language, rhythm, metaphor: all these Duncan began by seeing as an access to revelation. What the Black Mountain experience added to this was the liberating influence of open forms. Duncan took the notion of the poem as field and colored it with his own original impulses: so that it became for him, the idea of the poem as a "Memory-field" in which "all parts ... cooperate, coexist" in mystical union. Past and future are folded together in the "one fabric" of his verse, with the result that what the reader sees, ideally, is "no first strand or second strand" but the "truth of that form," the timeless "design" as a whole. "There is a natural mystery to poetry," Duncan wrote in 1960; and in his poems, beginning with early collections such as *Heavenly City, Earthly City* (1949), *The Opening of the Field* (1960), and *Roots and Branches* (1964) and ending with *Ground Work II: In the Dark* (1987), he tried to announce that mystery.

Restoring the American vision: The San Francisco Renaissance

Duncan gradually moved, he claimed, from "the concept of a dramatic form to a concept of musical form in poetry." The "dramatic form" he refers to here is the one he favored when he emerged as a leading poet in the late 1940s, as part of what has become known as the San Francisco Renaissance. For the San Francisco poets, drama and performance were primary. As one of them, Lawrence Ferlinghetti (1919–), put it in 1955, "the kind of poetry which has been making the most noise here ... is what should be called street poetry." "It amounts to getting poetry back into the street where it once was," he added, "out of the classroom ... and – in fact – off the printed page." Ferlinghetti was speaking for a more demotic, populist poetry than the kind preferred by many of the San Franciscans – including Duncan, even in his early years – but he still spoke for more than himself. Immediacy, drama, language, and a line shaped by the *voice*: these were the priorities of a group of otherwise different poets who wanted to liberate poetry from the academy.

Ferlinghetti's own poems illustrate this interest in oral impact: many were conceived of as "oral messages" and have been performed to a jazz accompaniment. The line is long and flowing, the language is strongly idiomatic, the imagery colorful to the point of theatricality. As Ferlinghetti sees him, in "A Coney Island of the Mind" (1958), the poet is at once a performer, "a charleychaplin man," and a pedagogue, a "super realist" who is willing to risk absurdity as he strives not only to entertain but to instruct. Other poets associated with the Bay Area and San Francisco group – and whose work shows a similar interest in oral impact – include Brother Antoninus, who after his departure from the Dominican Order in 1970 published under the name of William Everson (1912–1994) and Michael McClure (1932–). But the most important is Gary Snyder (1930–).

Snyder was born in San Francisco and has worked as a logger, forester, and farmer in the Northwest. "As much as the books I've read the jobs I've done have been significant in shaping me," Snyder said in his book of essays *Earth House Hold* (1969). "My sense of body and language and the knowledge that . . . sensitivity and awareness are not limited to educated people." Most of his poems (gathered in such collections as *A Range of Poems* (1966), *Turtle Island* (1974), *No Nature* (1992), and *Danger on Peaks* (2004)) are direct and simple, characterized by an elemental reverence for existence and salvaging poetry from the most primitive human experiences. Unmarked by the normal tensions of language, they depend on open forms and the "rhythms of physical work . . . and life" for their impact. The simplicity of Snyder's work is not simplification, however. It derives in part from his devotion to Zen Buddhism. Zen encourages the active appreciation of the natural world as an agent of vision, transcendence and elimination of the self; and its art of deft brushstrokes dispenses with calculated technique and structured reasoning in favor of spontaneous attention to living things. "A poet faces two directions," Snyder suggests, "one is the world of people and language and society, and the other is the non-human, non-verbal world . . . the inner world . . . before language . . . custom, . . . culture." Zen has helped Snyder to bridge the gap between these two worlds.

"I hold the most archaic values on earth," Snyder insists. "They go back to the Paleolithic"; "I try to hold history and the wilderness in mind," he has added, "that my poems may approach the true nature of our times." For him, identification with "that other totally alien, non-human" can be experienced in tilling the soil, shaping word or stone, "the lust and ecstasy of the dance," or "the power-vision in solitude." And it has led him on naturally to a hatred of human assumptions of power and "the ancient, meaningless/Abstractions of the educated mind." His work celebrates such primary rituals as hunting and feasting and the mysteries of sex and birth but, with its commitment to participation in nature rather than possession of it, it is equally capable of polemic – something that is especially noticeable when Snyder directs his attention to the ecology. It is at this point, in particular, that Eastern and Western strains in his writing meet. Snyder has learned about "the buddha-nature," the intrinsic vitality lurking in all things, not just from Zen but from poets like Whitman; just as his habit of meditation rather than appropriation has been borrowed from Thoreau as well as the Buddhist tradition, and his belief in renewal springs from the spirit of the frontier as much as from oriental notions of the eternal cycle.

Recreating American rhythms: the beat generation

Snyder, Ferlinghetti, and many of the other San Francisco poets were also involved in the activities of another group that rose to prominence in the 1950s, commonly known as "the beat generation." The beat generation was initially associated with New York, but it first attracted the interest of a larger public when, in 1956, Allen Ginsberg, Jack Kerouac, and Gregory Corso joined Ferlinghetti, Snyder, and others in public reading appearances in the coffee houses and colleges of San Francisco. And national fame was guaranteed with the confiscation of copies of Ginsberg's *Howl* by the San Francisco police in the same year – on the grounds that, as the Collector of Customs put it, "The words and the sense of the writing are obscene." *Howl*, Ginsberg's first published book of poems, then sold over 50,000 copies within a brief period of time. Along with Kerouac's *On the Road*, it became what Kenneth Rexroth called "the confession of faith of the generation that is going to be running the world in 1965 and 1975 – if it is still there to run." For a while, the figure of the beat or the beatnik even attracted national media attention, although he (and it was usually a "he") tended to be considered only to be mocked and dismissed.

The greatest poet of the beat generation was Allen Ginsberg (1926–1997). When he took part in a demonstration against American involvement in Vietnam, he carried a placard that declared simply, "War is black magic." With him, as he said, poetry was "a catalyst to visionary states of mind"; and he was assisted in his pursuit of a visionary goal by a mystical experience he had while still young. At first, Ginsberg attempted to insert his prophetic vision into what he later termed "overwritten coy stanzas." He then

Figure 5.2 Beat artists in a café, New York, late 1950s. Left to right: poet Gregory Corso (back of head to camera), painter and musician Larry Rivers, writer Jack Kerouac, musician David Amram, and poet Allen Ginsberg. John Cohen/Getty Images.

recognized Whitman's long line as an appropriate precedent, a possible vehicle for what he called "my romantic-inspiration-Hebraic-Melvillian bardic breath." *His* breath, *his* speech was to be the organizer of the line, a perception to which he was helped, not only by Whitman and Williams, but by the advice of Jack Kerouac. A jazz musician, Kerouac observed – and especially a saxophone player – is "drawing breath and blowing a phrase . . . till he runs out of breath, and when he does, his sentence, his statement's been made." This sense of drawing in the breath, in a way that reminds the reader at once of Charlie Parker and an Old Testament prophet, is what is most noticeable about the famous opening line of "Howl" (1956): "I saw the best minds of my generation destroyed by madness, starving hysterical naked, dragging themselves through negro streets at dawn looking for an angry fix."

"Mind is shapely": that remark of Ginsberg's suggests how much a piece like "Howl" is committed to the discontinuities of consciousness. For all their discontinuities, though, Ginsberg's poems do have paraphraseable arguments. "Howl," for instance, is a grimly serious yet comically surreal account of the betrayal of a generation. The first part explores the denial of the visionary impulse by forces like "the narcotic tobacco haze of Capitalism" and celebrates its continuance in such subversive elements as "angelheaded hipsters," "saintly motorcyclists," and "the madman bum and angel beat in Time." In the second part, the poet denounces "Moloch the loveless," the god of power and "pure machinery," in a way that recalls earlier prophets like Isaiah. Finally, the third part concentrates on the destiny of one man, Carl Solomon, whom the poet identifies with as an archetype of suffering. Fired by this identification, Ginsberg then projects an imaginary liberation for them both, where they "wake up electrified out of coma" to their "own souls' airplanes roaring over the roof." That jubilant remark illustrates the mixture of religious intensity and wry realism which is one of Ginsberg's most memorable gifts. Poems like "Howl," "In Back of the Real" (1956), or "A Supermarket in California" (1956) work because they walk a tightrope between acknowledgment of the grubby particulars of everyday life and proclamations of the immanent presence of the ideal.

"It occurs to me that I am America,/I am talking to myself again." These lines are another example of Ginsberg's capacity for being comic and serious at one and the same time. And they also express his very American desire to celebrate and sing himself as representative man: to present his poems as what he called "a complete statement of Person." As part of this statement, Ginsberg wrote some extraordinarily powerful accounts of personal grief, like "Kaddish" (1961), his fugue-like elegy to his mother. He also produced poems of passionate sexual encounter, such as "Love Poem on a Theme by Whitman" (1956), and others like "The Reply" (1956) that describe his experience of drugs in terms that recall earlier, prophetic accounts of wrestling with God. In the 1960s, in particular, Ginsberg made his wanderings over America and the globe his subject: in poems that were, as he put it, "not exactly poems nor not poems: journal notations put together conveniently, a mental turn-on."

In his later years, as *Death and Fame: Poems 1993–97* (1998) indicates, Ginsberg gravitated closer to Buddhism. The idea of "an awakened emptiness" or "no Self" that was always lurking in his earlier work now assumed more importance, promoting what the poet himself termed "a less attached, less apocalyptic view." One side result of this was that many of his poems in later collections directed gentle mockery at his own

egotism, or surveyed the nightmares of contemporary history with a sense of acceptance, even distance. His poem about the death of his father, "Don't Grow Old,"
included in *Collected Poems 1947–1985* (1986), charts the alteration: unlike "Kaddish,"
it responds to loss, not with rage, but with a grave, melancholy quietude. This is not to
say that such poems are unfeeling, but they place human emotion within the measureless scope of "a relatively heavenly emptiness." Nor is it to ignore the continuities
that underpin evident change. The long line remains in evidence; so do humor and the
impulse to transmute verse into vision. Behind the Buddhist mask, the authentic
American rebel was still at work, demanding to be heard.

Among the other beat poets, the most memorable is probably Gregory Corso
(1930–2001). Corso has evolved a distinct identity, or rather identities, out of his
poems. "Should I get married? Should I be good?" begins one of his most famous
pieces, "Marriage" (1959), which then presents him trying out possible marriages,
inventing potential selves, only to discard each one of them in turn. Jokey at times, at
others wildly surreal, the poet is like Whitman's "essential Me": standing apart from the
game of life and the roles it prescribes, refusing to commit himself to a fixed status. The
rapidity of Corso's verse line is part of his message, as are his subversive humor and
unpredictable alterations of pace and tone: the poet will not, it seems, be tied down by
any of the institutions or forms that we use to organize life, whether they involve meter,
stability of mood, or marriage.

Reinventing the American self: The New York poets

Another, rather different vision of alternative America surfaces in the work of a group
whose main connections have been with the visual arts, the New York poets, among
them Frank O'Hara and John Ashbery. "Poetry was declining," wrote the leading
member of this group, Frank O'Hara (1926–1966), in one of his poem-painting
collaborations with the painter Larry Rivers. "/Painting advancing/we were
complaining/it was 50." O'Hara felt at odds with most of the poetry that was being
written in America in the 1950s. His aim was to "defamiliarize the ordinary," even what
he felt was the "sheer ugliness in America"; and, in order to do this, he wanted to be as
attentive as possible to the world around him. It was the artist's "duty to be attentive,"
he felt, so the artists he cherished were those like his friend Larry Rivers who, as he put it,
"taught me to be more keenly interested while I'm still alive." "Perhaps this is the most
important thing art can say," he suggested, and as a way of saying this himself he
pursued a poetic structure that was changing, shifting, quirky, quick, and immediate.
His literary mentors were people like Whitman, with whom O'Hara shared a belief in
the multiple nature of identity, and Williams, whose commitment to seeing and
mobility O'Hara appreciated. O'Hara also learned from the Surrealists and Dadaists,
who taught him how to capture the simultaneity of the instant. On a strictly literary
level, in fact, O'Hara's development could be charted through his *Selected Poems*
(1973) from his early experiments with "straight Surrealism" ("Chez Jane") and his
imitations of American writers such as Williams ("Les Etiquettes Jaunes"), to the
mature poetry of the late 1950s where the two modes are wedded. The result of this
union is a poetry that can shift, with astonishing speed, from flat literalism to fantasy
and then back again. But to talk in strictly literary terms about O'Hara or the other

New York poets is only to tell half the story. O'Hara, and his friends, were interested in an art fired into life by the moment; and that meant certain kinds of poetry certainly, but also all forms of dance, the motion picture and action painting.

O'Hara's own term for the aesthetic he shared with other poets and painters was "Personism." "Personism," the poet tells us, "puts the poem squarely between the poet and the person.... The poem is at last between two persons instead of two pages." True to this credo, there is a quality of intimate conversation to much of O'Hara's poetry – of talk "between two persons" that is at once familiar and fantastic. The voice talking here, however, is not confessional but responsive, eager to attend to the continuum of things and ready for immersion in the processes it contemplates. O'Hara does not reflect in a traditional way nor try to extrapolate significances. Instead, he swims in the medium of his feeling and being, inviting us to come into momentary awareness of things just as he does. He traces, say, the disjunctive movements of his sensibility ("In Memory of my Feelings"). Or he compels us into attention to the total environment of the city ("Rhapsody"). As he does so, he alerts us to his own instinctive belief that "the "slightest loss of attention leads to death." Life in these terms has an immanent rather than transcendent value: it is, as O'Hara himself put it once, "just what it is and just what happens."

How does O'Hara achieve this "openness," and so dodge the habitual? On a larger scale, he does so by opting for a range of tone and form. There are his "I do this, I do that" poems, like "Joe's Jacket" and "Lana Turner has Collapsed!"; and there are also more intensely surreal pieces, such as "Second Avenue," Whitmanesque odes like "To the Film Industry in Crisis," and powerfully erotic lyrics of homosexual love, the most striking of which is "You are Gorgeous and I'm Coming." On the more local level of the individual poem, O'Hara's discomposing mix of literalism and surrealism works with other strategies to strip away the veneer of habituation. His lineation for instance, with its ambivalent positioning of words, constant breaks and compulsive enjambement, generates tension, a sense of breakneck speed. Like a Cubist or Abstract Expressionist painter, O'Hara scrambles his representational clues, preferring complex effects of simultaneity, the clash of surfaces, to the illusions of depth and coherence. There are constant temporal and spatial dissolves too; the poet shifts rapidly from one place to another without the usual semantic props, such as "when," "after," or "before." Everything, as a result, is absorbed into an undifferentiated stream of activity, the flow of the now.

"O'Hara's poetry has no program," John Ashbery has insisted, "and therefore cannot be joined." This is true. Nevertheless, many poets have felt an affinity with him, and shared at least some of his purposes. Their personal affection for him has been expressed in the numerous elegies that appeared after his death: the most notable of which, perhaps, are "Strawberries in Mexico" (1969) by Ron Padgett (1942–), "Buried at Springs" (1969) by James Schuyler (1923–1991), and "Frank O'Hara" (1967) by Ted Berrigan (1934–1983). Apart from O'Hara, however, the most significant poet associated with the New York group is Ashbery himself (1927–). Ashbery has written in a variety of genres. *A Nest of Ninnies* (1969), written with James Schuyler (1923–1991), is a novel satirizing the vacuous lives of two suburban families. *The Heroes* (1952), *The Compromise* (1956), and *The Philosopher* (1956) are plays that exploit, and sometimes travesty, conventional forms from classical myth to detective story drama. The international edition of the *New York Herald Tribune* became the outlet for his extensive art criticism. But it is for his poetry that he has become well known. Ashbery published his first book of poems, *Turandot and Other Poems*, in 1953. Other notable volumes include *Some Trees* (1956), *The Tennis Court Oath* (1962), *Self-Portrait in a Convex Mirror* (1975), *A Wave* (1984), *Flow Chart* (1991), *Chinese Whispers* (2000), and *A Worldly Country* (2007). Ashbery first encountered O'Hara at Harvard, and when O'Hara moved to Manhattan in 1951 the two met regularly. The enthusiasms the two poets shared generated some similar tendencies in their poetry. But a way of signaling the difference between Ashbery and O'Hara is to say that Ashbery's is a poetry of absence. His poetry deflates our expectation of sense, or presence, by offering us the playful, fluid zone of deferred sense, suspended meaning. "Someday I'll explain" he promises jokily in "Ode to Bill," "Not today though."

Ashbery's earliest published poems, such as "Some Trees," are mainly concerned with the operations of the sleeping consciousness, and are activated by the belief that the function of the poet is, as he puts it, to "give fullness/To the dream." These were followed by his experimenting, at roughly the same time as O'Hara, in "straight surrealism." In poems like "Europe" and "They Dream Only of America," fractured images, jumbles of non-sequiturs, and techniques of verbal collage are used to dramatize the humiliating and reifying aspects of modern life. But it has been from the later 1960s on that Ashbery has hit his stride, with poems such as "The Skaters," "Self-Portrait in a Convex Mirror," "A Wave," and the 216-page poem that constitutes *Flow Chart*, as well as prose pieces like "The System." No one work is entirely characteristic of his mature writing. What is common with them all, however, as Ashbery tries to realize what he calls "the quirky things that happen to me," are certain stylistic features. An irresolute syntax, the casual use of slang, cliché and apparent redundancies, false starts and back-tracking, free associations, occasional opacity of phrasing and the equally occasional hard, focused image: all these are the verbal weapons of a mind in process – or, rather, a mind that *is* process, a medium in which disparate objects meet and merge. The long, serpentine verse paragraphs Ashbery favors hold the different elements in close physical contiguity, as if the writer were trying to create a multidimensional space, a "seamless web" in which everything could be folded into everything else. This is a poetry which insists that structures are always virtual. And this is a poet who insists on the disjunctive nature of history and personality. Historical experience, evidently, is a "tangle of impossible resolutions and irresolutions," what happens outside the neat demarcations of storytellers. Personality, in turn, is stripped of conclusive choices: "I cannot decide in what direction to walk," the poet admits in "Grand Galop," adding happily, "/But this doesn't matter to me." Lacking such determinants, the coordination of a particular road taken, it too becomes shadowy, as shifting and irresolute as the language that enacts its absence.

"All was strange": the closing remark in "A Wave" sounds a theme that resonates through Ashbery's poetry and the work of other contemporary American poets, not all of them necessarily identified with the New York group. The metamorphoses of consciousness, the absolute ravishment of the senses by the radiant surfaces of the world are, for instance, the primary intuitions of a writer who is in many respects different from Ashbery or O'Hara, James Merrill (1926–1995). Merrill is commonly associated with the New Critical school and, in a strictly formal sense, there is truth to

this association: much of his work, to be found in *Collected Poems* (2001), is characterized by a delicate, ironic verbal wit, formal prosody, careful crafting of syntax and
metaphor, and a baroque sense of decor. He betrays traces of the confessional tendency
too, in that some of his poems deal with painful autobiographical material: his tangled
erotic involvement with his mother ("The Broken Home," "Emerald"), his fiercely
oedipal relationship with his father ("Scenes from Childhood"), or the pleasures and
pains of being a homosexual ("Days of 1964," "Mornings in a New House"). That said,
it has to be added that Merrill begins and ends where Ashbery and O'Hara do: with
what Merrill himself, in "Transfigured Bird," calls "the eggshell of appearance." There
may be a perilous abyss beneath *this* surface, but what Merrill senses always is the
inevitability and necessity of masks, screens, fictions.

If Merrill's lyric poems aestheticize autobiography, reflecting what he calls "the dull
need to make some kind of house/Out of the life lived, and out of the love spent," then
his epic trilogy, *The Changing Light at Sandover* (1982), expresses a larger desire to
create an aesthetic for survival. Written in a variety of poetic forms, the trilogy was the
result, Merrill claimed, of a communion with spirits: into it he poured his beliefs and
fears, spread among passages of revelation that were spelled out to him on an ouija
board. "The design of the book swept me along," he said: this is an epic as formless and
personal as all other American epics. Along with other experiments in this genre, it is
possessed of a fierce energy, the animating conviction that there is still time to choose
between the apocalypse and the millennium. On the one hand, Merrill points out, there
is the danger of global destruction wrought by "ANIMAL SOULS," the passive victims
of technology and their own destructive impulses. On the other, there is the opportunity of a new life, a paradise on earth springing from the liberation of the imaginative
intelligence and its discovery of a redemptive fiction. The words and artefacts fashioned
by feeling were for Merrill, as for so many other American writers, an access to a saving
knowledge of our predicament; and in this sense the true opposite of poetry is, not prose
or science, but annihilation.

Resisting orthodoxy: Dissent and experiment in fiction

In prose, resistance to orthodox culture took various forms, even among those
predominantly white male writers who formed the major part of the beat movement.
Just how various these forms could be, within the ranks of the beats, is suggested by the
contrast between Jack Kerouac (1922–1969) and William Burroughs (1914–1997).
Outside the movement, a similar contrast is registered by other major figures of literary
dissent: Henry Miller (1891–1980), J. D. Salinger (1919–2010), Charles Bukowski
(1920–1994), Richard Brautigan (1935–1984), and Ken Kesey (1935–2001).

Jack Kerouac was born Jean-Louis Kerouac in Massachusetts. After a Catholic
upbringing, he roamed about the United States, taking various odd jobs, and worked
as a merchant seaman before writing the first of his semi-autobiographical novels, *The
Town and the City* (1950), about a family in his hometown of Lowell. *On the Road*
followed in 1957. It established Kerouac as the novelist of the beats, just as "Howl"
identified Ginsberg as their poet. Several books that followed were also documents of
beat consciousness, although they also reflected their author's growing interest in the
discovery of truth or "dharma" through Zen Buddhism: *The Subterraneans* (1958), *The*

Dharma Bums (1958), *Tristessa* (1960), *Big Sur* (1962), and *Desolation Angels* (1965). Other books, still beat in sensibility, were evocations of Kerouac's childhood: *Doctor Sax* (1959), *Maggie Cassidy* (1959), and *Visions of Gerard* (1963). Still others described his search for his Breton ancestors (*Satori in Paris* (1966)), his travels (*Lonesome Traveler* (1960)), his recollections of his life and friends and, in particular, of Neal Cassady, his traveling companion (*Visions of Cody* (1972)). What is common to all these books, and to his poems collected in *Mexico City Blues* (1959), is an urgent, rhythmic style, that works through repetition and an excited, evocative tone to create a feeling of spontaneity and intimacy. Kerouac pushed to an intense extreme the insight of Whitman that, ideally, who touches the book touches the man. He was also clearly inspired by the vastness, the space of the American continent: it is no accident that the final paragraph of *On the Road* has the narrator contemplating that space.

On the Road, more energetically than any of Kerouac's other novels, brings American self and American space together, in a celebration of the vastness, the potential of both. The protagonist and narrator is Sal Paradise. Clearly a self-portrait, Paradise is a struggling author in his mid-twenties. He tells of his encounters with Dean Moriarty, a teenager whose soul is "wrapped up in a fast car, a coast to reach, and a woman at the end of the road." During the next five years they travel from coast to coast, either with or to each other. Nothing substantial, in terms of plot, seems to have happened by the end: although, having been abandoned by him in Mexico, Sal continues to "think of Old Dean Moriarty, the father we never found." Plenty occurs, of course, but events possess the fluidity of a stream rather than the fixity of narrative form. Things happen, and then our heroes move on to encounter something else, something new in the experiential and fictional process. Like those heroes, the reader is initiated into a contact with the now, life as present and process. Style and structure similarly invite us to freewheel through the open spaces of personality and geography. What the book charts, finally, is what is called at one point "all the wilderness of America," at once liberating and terrifying: a world that stretches out as far as the eye can see and, within, far beyond what the mind can know.

Just as Sal Paradise is Kerouac in fictional disguise, so Dean Moriarty is Kerouac's friend, Neal Cassady. Another character in *On the Road*, Carlo Marx, is Allen Ginsberg. And another, Bull Lee, is William Burroughs. Two things were formative influences in Burroughs's life: his experiences as a drug addict and as a homosexual in the claustro-phobic moral climate of Cold War America. Among the first books Burroughs wrote, in fact, were two dealing precisely with these two circumstances: *Junkie*, published under the pseudonym of William Lee in 1953, and *Queer*, which was written in 1953 but not published until thirty-two years later. Starting from his own experiences with drug addiction, Burroughs began to develop a whole mythology of need and control. "The algebra of need," as Burroughs calls it, means that need creates subservience: allowing malign forces to enter and exploit the individual consciousness. "The face of 'evil,'" the reader is told at the beginning of *The Naked Lunch* (Paris, 1959; New York, 1962), "is always the face of total need." And his experience as a homosexual, in a homophobic postwar culture that identified gay people with other, repressed enemies of the state like communists, allowed him to recognize how forms of control could be exercised in the body politic and the American body politic in particular. For Burroughs, the malign forces bent on absorbing or exploiting the unique identity of the individual are omnipresent, waiting to do their parasitic work: "I can feel the heat closing in," *The Naked Lunch* begins, "feel them out there making their moves."

Undoubtedly, Burroughs's most powerful fictional exploration of the algebra of need and the dream of being freed from all conditioning forces is *The Naked Lunch*. An intense rendering, not only of the horrors of addiction, but also of the cultural illusions for which addiction functions as a metaphor, the book has no narrative continuity or sustained point of view. Its separate episodes are not interrelated; they simply coexist in a particular field of force, brought together by the mind of William Burroughs, which then abandons them. And its title means just what it says: "a frozen moment when everyone sees what is on the end of every fork." To produce such frozen moments, when we can see the ugly object inside the egg, the worm inside a piece of fruit – both images for the corruptions inside civilization – is the project of the narrative. This Burroughs pursues creating a series of waste lands, dark cities, and barren landscapes that hover somewhere between cartoon and nightmare. Most people, the narrative intimates, collude with or surrender to a system that reduces them to a state of inertia. What that narrative offers, as an alternative to this, is a chance to "look around with Honest Bill": to become alert, not only to the ways human identity is devoured and dissolved in the modern world, but to the possibility of resistance, even release. The reader, Burroughs insisted, could cut into *The Naked Lunch* at any point, so as to enjoy the spontaneity and independence of constituting their own system. It offers, too, a play of different language habits. No verbal code prevails, as Burroughs moves towards what he was eventually to call his goal: "the writing of silence."

That phrase suggests the predicament Burroughs faced, with increasing intensity. If he started his work out of a sense of vulnerability to drug addiction and social stigmatization, his emphasis gradually shifted to word-addiction, language as an ultimate form of control. "*Rub out the word forever*" is the call in *Nova Express* (1964). That remark registers the tension at the heart of his work: he is using language against itself. Intent on liberating the consciousness from all forms of control, the weapon he has at his disposal for this purpose has been, as he sees it, the original and ultimate controlling agent. Burroughs's response to this dilemma, this question of how to achieve "the writing of silence," took several forms. Like Pound, he became interested in other cultures and vocabularies that resist the abstractions and oppositions of Western language and thought. In his case, as *The Yage Letters* (1963) indicates, this drove him towards the Mayan codices. He also became convinced, as *The Ticket that Exploded* (1967) suggests, that, while human beings are vulnerable to damaging instructions fed into them as on to a tape recorder, the tape can be wiped clean; the ticket of entry into contemporary reality can be exploded or impounded. "Why not take over the ticket?" we are asked. And one, seminal way of taking over the ticket, a logical development of earlier verbal experiments in *The Naked Lunch*, is what Burroughs called the cut-up method. Which is just that. Words, phrases, are cut up into fragments and rearranged at random so as to create, not propositions or declarative statements, but suggestive word series. That answers to an imperative as old, at least, as the dream of America: to escape from the constraints of society, history, language, to lose even the constrictions of a particular identity in a condition of absolute space.

The resistance to orthodoxy embraced by Henry Miller and Charles Bukowski is simpler. And the nature of that freedom is suggested by the fact that both men wrote a kind of fictive autobiography. Miller was a traveler, living in various areas of the United States and for ten years as an expatriate in Europe. Among his many works, the best known is *Tropic of Cancer*, which was published in France in 1934 but not in the United States until 1961. "This is not a book," Miller declares at the beginning. "No, this is a prolonged insult, a gob of spit in the face of Art, a kick in the pants to God, Man, Destiny, Time, Love, Beauty ... what you will." "I am going to sing for you," Miller insists, "a little off key perhaps, but I will sing." What he sings of here, in a literal sense, is his life as an expatriate in Paris: his adventures in art, his sexual relations, his quasi-philosophical musings, all animated by his belief that "more obscene than anything is inertia." What he sings of, here and elsewhere, more generally, is his conviction that (as he puts it in *Tropic of Capricorn* (France, 1939; US, 1962) "there is only one great adventure and that is inward towards the self." *The Air-Conditioned Nightmare* (1945) and its sequel, *Remember to Remember* (1947), sum up his feelings about the American scene, which he describes in terms of a prison or cancer ward, a place isolated from real health and life. And works like *Sexus* (1949), *Plexus* (1953), and *Nexus* (1960), *The Rosy Crucifixion* as Miller called this trilogy, continue his fictive autobiography in a form that is, as usual, deliberately formless, obedient only to what Miller saw as the sprawling, insistent rhythms of existence, and the self.

"I AM. That covers all experience, all wisdom, all truth," Miller wrote in *Remember to Remember*. Charles Bukowski might have said something similar, although he would have said it in a much more downbeat way. The son of an American soldier and a German woman, Bukowski grew up in Los Angeles, worked mainly in unskilled jobs, and only began to write when he was thirty-five. Bukowski shared a number of impulses with Miller: a distrust of art and the artistic establishment, a commitment to living his own life outside the norms of American society, a related commitment to recording that commitment in forms that hovered between the fictive and the autobiographical. But Bukowski as he was and how he perceived himself – in, say, the fictive persona of Henry Chinaski – was much more the tough, lowbrow outsider, hard living and hard drinking, floating casually through a world of sex and violence: in short, a drifter rather than, like Miller, a seeker. Bukowski produced his first book of poems, *Flower, Fish and Bestial Wail*, in 1960. Like most of his work, it was published by a small press and reached out to an underground audience. It was followed by more than thirty poetic collections, ending with *The Last Night of Earth, Poems*, in 1992. His stories appeared in several collections, such as *Erections, Ejaculations, Exhibitions and General Tales of Ordinary Madness* (1972), as well as in little magazines. And novels like *Notes of a Dirty Old Man* (1969), *Post Office* (1971), *Women* (1978), and *Ham on Rye* (1982) turned his life on the seedy edge of things into hardboiled narratives that combine the eye of the camera, with its disposition for empirical detail, with the inner eye of the fabulist, alert to the nightmare of the streets. There are no large gestures in Bukowski's work. Using an off-hand, free-flowing line or sentence and a casual idiom he simply records things as they pass in a cryptic, sardonic way. And what passes before him is the other America: life among the underclass, the dropouts, the dispossessed who cast a shadow over the national dream of success.

A writer who made the unfulfillment of that dream of success his primary subject is J. D. Salinger. Salinger began writing stories for magazines, which he did not choose to collect, before World War II. His first book, however, and his most famous, was a novel,

The Catcher in the Rye, published in 1951. Its opening words, "If you really want to know about it, the first thing you'll probably want to know is where I was born," introduces us to Holden Caulfield. It also introduces us, in an intimate, immediate way that is characteristic of so much American writing, to the troubles and contradictions of Holden's life. Holden is an unhappy teenager who runs away from boarding school. Lonely, quixotic, compassionate, he is plagued by the "phoniness" of his environment. And in the book, he tells the story of his flight to New York and his eventual nervous breakdown. It turns out, in the end, that he is recalling all this from a sanatorium. The title of the novel refers to his desire to preserve innocence: not his own – that, he senses, is already lost – but the innocence of those still to grow up. He has to stop them from experiencing a fall that recalls both the mythical fall of Adam and Eve into knowledge and the universal fall from innocence into experience, childhood into adulthood. Images of falling and flight pervade *The Catcher in the Rye*. Holden dreams of heading West or lighting out for the country; he cherishes anywhere that time seems to stand still. Equally, he fears any kind of fall, for himself and others; at one point, he even finds it difficult, frightening, to step down from the pavement on to the street. The novel is a triumph in the vernacular and confessional modes, drawing the reader into the narrator's resistance to the world that surrounds him and, he feels, threatens to stifle him. It also offers us a hero who, in his sadly contracted way, reminds us of the many other rebels and dreamers, grotesque saints and would-be saviors that populate American fiction.

In particular, Holden recalls Huckleberry Finn. Like Huck, Holden is an outsider who dislikes system and distrusts authority; like Huck, too, he has to make his way through a world of hypocrisy and deceit that seems to threaten him at every turn. The differences between the two, however, are as important as the connections; and these have to do with the simple facts that Holden is a little older, much richer than Huck and moves in an urban environment – an America where there is no longer any frontier to which the hero can flee. Huck has an innocent eye. Holden is more knowing, more judgmental and more deeply implicated – whether he likes it or not – in the "phoney" circumstances he describes. Above all, the clarity and candor that characterize Huck, who is a truthteller, are replaced by a deep unease, uncertainty. Holden is confused; and, as his apparently spontaneous recollections of a crisis in his life make clear, he is not sure what the truth about himself and his world is. That uncertainty is in turn part of the attraction of the book, and its modernity. *The Catcher in the Rye* draws us into a sometimes painfully close relationship with a narrator, who is simultaneously confessional and defensive, longing to reveal himself but fearful of dropping the mask – and not, perhaps, sure what that self is. So, we feel, we know Holden and we do not know him: he is an intimate and a mystery.

After *The Catcher in the Rye*, Salinger produced several collections of stories (*Nine Stories* (1953), *Franny and Zooey* (1961), *Raise High the Roof Beam Carpenters and Seymour: An Introduction* (1963)). Many of them concerned the Glass family and, in particular, the lonely, brilliant eccentric individualists, Franny, Zooey, Seymour, and Buddy Glass. In the early 1960s, however, he retired to his rural home, withdrew from the literary scene, and stopped publishing his work. Richard Brautigan did not withdraw in this way but, before committing suicide in 1984, he gradually slipped from public view. Although he continued publishing into the early 1980s, his most successful work had appeared a decade or so earlier: *A Confederate General from Big Sur* (1964), *Trout Fishing in America* (1963), *In Watermelon Sugar* (1968), and *The Abortion: An Historical Romance* (1971). *Trout Fishing in America* is characteristic. It describes the search of the narrator for a morning of good fishing in a crystal-clear stream. His search takes him through a variety of American landscapes: city parks in San Francisco, forests in Oregon, a Filipino laundry, a wrecking yard that sells used trout streams by the foot. Surreal and anarchic, whimsical and nostalgic, the narrative is at once a critique of a culture that has betrayed its early promise – where the dream of trout fishing has become a purchaseable commodity – and a celebration of continuing possibility, the anarchic, unbowed spirit of the individual. This is the book as fictional play: a typographical game eschewing plot or structure of any ordinary kind, using surprise and spontaneity to make its central point. The point is a simple and very American one: we can be whatever we want to be, do whatever we want to do, whatever the destructive element that surrounds us. To that extent, thanks to the liberating imagination, trout fishing in America is still possible.

A similarly anarchic optimism characterizes the work of Ken Kesey. Born in Colorado and brought up in Oregon, Kesey worked for a while as a ward attendant in a mental hospital. This provided him with the material for his first and finest book, *One Flew Over the Cuckoo's Nest* (1962). The novel is set in a psychiatric ward that is dominated by a character called the Big Nurse, who appears to have limitless power over the inmates. Controlling her charges by subtle pressures and, wherever necessary, more aggressive measures such as electric shock treatment, she embodies the principles of behaviorism. Forcing them to adjust to a prescribed norm, she also suggests forces at work in society generally. For she is constantly referred to by the narrator as an agent of "The Combine." Society is run by some secret force, the implication is, which tries to manipulate all its members. And of that force the Big Nurse is a servant and a symptom, although by no means the only one. Then into the ward comes an authentic American rebel, Randle McMurphy, who offers the inmates the example and chance of independence. After various acts of rebellion, McMurphy is subjected to a lobotomy operation, which reduces him to a vegetable, passive and compliant. And unwilling to see him like this, his best friend in the institution, an ex-reservation Indian named Bromden, smothers McMurphy and so takes his life. The smothering is described in sexual terms, because it is an act of love. It is also an act of devotion by a disciple. For, like some of the inmates, Bromden has grown immeasurably under the influence of McMurphy. So much so that, after killing his mentor, Bromden breaks out of the mental institution to go on the road and maybe return to his tribe. McMurphy may be dead but, evidently, the spirit of rebellion that he embodied still survives.

If McMurphy is the hero of *One Flew Over the Cuckoo's Nest*, then Bromden supplies its vision. A giant, schizophrenic Indian who has pretended to be deaf and dumb to escape notice, he is the narrator. He is an outsider, an innocent eye in a way like Huck Finn: but what he sees is far stranger, more surreal. It may not be literally true but it is symbolically so. The eye of Bromden sees the inner truth. Kesey said that he was addicted to comic books, which he calls "the honest American myths." And here that addiction turns the story into a vivid mix of naturalism and carnival. Celebrating a kind of anarchic individualism, *One Flew Over the Cuckoo's Nest* has its own anarchic energy. This retelling of the combat between the self and the system is unique because it carries a comic book edge, which adds a further touch of subversion. The compelling tropes of the American drama of beset manhood are all there: the rebel in action and the rebel in vision, the bond between two men, the woman as a threatening instrument of the system, the sacrifice of the mentor, the survival of the disciple, and the final lighting out for the territory. But they are all set in their own transgressive space, an area of vulgar power and possibility that mocks claims to authoritativeness and authority of any kind – including those of high culture. Kesey was to go on to chart that transgressive space in other fiction and essays (*Sometimes a Great Notion* (1964), *Kesey's Garage Sale* (1973), *Demon Box* (1986), *The Further Enquiry* (1990)). He was also to attempt to create it for himself and others: traveling in his "Magic Bus" around America with his companions, whom he called "the Merry Pranksters," organizing psychedelic events and light shows – all of which Tom Wolfe wryly recorded in his book, *The Electric Kool-Aid Acid Test* (1968). But *One Flew Over the Cuckoo's Nest* remains his most powerful mapping of transgression, his most memorable expression of the belief that lost freedom can and must be recovered.

The Art and Politics of Race

Defining a new black aesthetic

Nobody has had to resist more in American society than African Americans. One form of resistance is illustrated by a writer whose work is part autobiography, part picaresque fiction, and part social history, Maya Angelou (1928–). In the first volume of her series of autobiographical fictions, *I Know Why the Caged Bird Sings* (1970), Angelou confers an exemplary status on the experiences of the narrator, whose childhood is spent shuttling between rural, urban, and smalltown America. Exemplary, too, is what she learned: the two major strands of the African American tradition, both of them inherited from women. From her grandmother, the narrator tells us, she absorbed the religious influences, the gospel tradition of African Americans. From her mother, she received "the blues tradition." Both elements of the black vernacular inform the account of this exceptional yet exemplary woman, and her meetings with other remarkable black women: among them, a friend who teaches her to speak again, to rediscover the beauty of the "human voice," after the shock of rape has left her temporarily dumb. They also inform the later volumes in this series, *Gather Together in My Name* (1974), *Singin' and Swingin' and Gettin' Merry Like Christmas* (1976), *The Heart of a Woman* (1981), *All God's Children Need Traveling Shoes* (1986), and *A Song Flung Up to Heaven* (2002).

Another, very different form of resistance is illustrated by Imamu Amiri Baraka (1934–). Baraka established his reputation under his given name of Leroi Jones. His first published work was a play, *A Good Girl is Hard to Find* (1958). Two other plays soon followed, *The Baptism* (1964) and *The Toilet* (1964), mostly concerned with issues of personal identity. Before them, *Preface to a Twenty Volume Suicide Note* (1961) appeared, a collection of personal and often domestic poems. In the earlier stages of his career, while he was still known as Leroi Jones, Baraka was influenced by those white American poets who, like him, saw themselves as alienated from the cultural mainstream. An alteration in Baraka's voice and vision came in the 1960s when, like many black nationalists, he dispensed with his white "slave name" and adopted a title more in keeping with his new self and mission. His work became correspondingly more radical and more involved with issues of racial and national identity. The plays *Dutchman* (1964), *The Slave* (1964), and *Slave Ship: A Historical Pageant* (1967) all deal with relations between black and white people. As works of "revolutionary theatre," they demonstrate Baraka's awareness of himself as a leader of a movement that seeks to use drama as a weapon against American racism. The episodic novel, *The System of Dante's Hell* (1965), equates the black slums of Newark, New Jersey with the Inferno. The various essays of *Home: Social Essays* (1966) trace his artistic transformation from black beat poet to father of the Black Arts movement. And the poems in *The Dead Lecturer* (1964) represent Baraka's poetic farewell to the beats. Marked by an ever-increasing preoccupation with racial issues, these lyrics crystallize his commitment to revolutionary action and his disavowal of what he saw as the political decadence of his former compatriots. Other volumes of poetry followed, including *It's Nation Time* (1970), *In Our Terribleness* (1970), and *Transbluesency: The Selected Poems of Amir Baraka/Leroi Jones* (1995). Other work, such as *Blues People: Negro Music in White America* (1963), showed his growing involvement in the African American tradition. Or, like the work published in *Four Black Revolutionary Plays* (1969), showed him reaching out to, and trying to teach, a largely unlettered audience. Around 1974, Baraka announced a further development in his political ideology and aesthetic, with a formal commitment to a Marxist-Leninist perspective: anticipating the overthrow, by blacks and whites alike, of oppressive capitalist systems. Plays such as *S-1* (1974) and *The Motion of History* (1977) testify to the change. And works like *Hard Facts* (1975), *Poetry for the Advanced* (1979), and *Daggers and Javelins* (1984) show his efforts to reconcile the more positive and useful aspects of black nationalism with what he saw as the scientific accuracy of Marxism. Later publications show that effort continuing: among them, *Eulogies* (1996), *Funk Love: New Poems, 1984–1995* (1996), and *The Autobiography of Leroi Jones/Amiri Baraka* (1997). As an organizer and activist, he has continued, ever since the 1960s, to influence immeasurably the direction of African American thought and writing.

As a writer, in particular, though, Baraka's main contribution has been to encourage a generation to be unapologetic, even proud and aggressive, about their African American heritage. Particularly in the writing of the 1960s and early 1970s, he introduced a prophetic, apocalyptic dimension into black writing: a sense of mission, the violent redemption of the sins of the past in the revolutionary future. In a way, this was the American dream in new pan-African robes: liberation from the present tyranny, the poet hoped, would be accompanied by a recovery of the perfection of the past and its restitution for an imagined future. There was no place for whites here, certainly: "white people," we are told, ". . . are full of, and made of/shit." But, ironically, Baraka still reflected the millennial tendencies of a culture he was determined to reject.

As for that determination itself, that was all real enough. Apart from certain crucial aspects of Western culture, notably Marxism and socialism, it still remains one of his dominating motives. He could not entirely unlearn his American education, but he tried hard to do so. As far as active practice was concerned, this insistence on "Black feeling, Black mind, Black judgment" led Baraka not only to political involvement but to the promotion of black community theatre. With his help, the Black Arts Repertory Theatre/School was opened in Harlem in 1965, to become of critical importance in the development of the Black Arts movement. And, following its demise, Baraka set up the Spirit House in Newark, with its troupe of actors called the Spirit House Movers. On the level of theory, in turn, it was Baraka above all who formulated the idea of a Black Aesthetic. Even the rage that has characterized so much of his work has been defended by him in terms of his moralist/nationalist aesthetics. "What I'm after is a sense of clarity," he claimed in *Black Music* (1967), "if it sounds like anger, maybe that's good."

Anger has not been Baraka's only mode, even in the more purely nationalist writing of the 1960s and 1970s. His work is also punctuated by cries for help ("S.O.S."), friendly persuasion ("Goodbye!"), above all by respect for the energy of black people ("Black Art") – something that he has identified with the ultimate agent of creativity ("God ... is energy") and as an instrument of change, to be mobilized by force if necessary ("20th-Century Fox"). There is pride here and faith in collective identity, the belief that black people "are all beautiful" ("Ka Ba"). Seeking to harness the "ancient images" and "magic" of the African inheritance to his cause, Baraka couples this with the verve he finds in all black cultural forms, from the speeches of Malcolm X to the music of Muddy Waters. "What will be/the sacred words?" he asks. His aim, which he sees himself as sharing with other black writers, is to unravel a new language and rhythm, "sacred words" that will liberate him, his work, and in the process the hearts and minds of all his "black family." In the service of that aim, as his post-9/11 collection of poems, *Somebody Blew Up America* (2001) shows, he is still willing to court controversy and provoke attacks from the white mainstream.

The Black Arts movement was, in particular, a movement that inspired poets, and among those poets who received inspiration from it, and sometimes also from Amiri Baraka, were Mari Evans (1927–), Sonia Sanchez (1934–), Nikki Giovanni (1943–), Don L. Lee/Haki R. Madhubuti (1942–), and David Nelson (1944–). These writers have shared with Baraka the belief that, as Sonia Sanchez puts it in "Right on: white america" (1969), "this country might have/been a pion/eer land once,/and it still is." By way of explanation, Sanchez then adds pointedly: "check out/the falling gun/shells/on our blk/tomorrow." In other words, they have rejected the white American dream: "The white man's heaven is the Black man's hell," we are told in *The Black Bird* (1969), a play by the poet and playwright Marvin X (1944–). But they are also trying to restore the pioneer values of liberation and mobility, once so fundamental to that dream, for their own people. This has necessarily involved them in a commitment to revolutionary struggle. "change up," Don L. Lee/Haki R. Madhubuti commands, "let's go for ourselves/.../change-up and yr children will look at u differently/than we looked at our parents." The aim is to achieve an irreversible shift of power: "I'm/gonna make it a crime to be anything BUT black," Mari Evans has announced in "Vive Noir!" (1968), "gonna make white/a twenty-four hour/lifetime/J.O.B.". Formally, this has aligned them with all those trying to "write black," to realize a verbal approximation of the energy of black speech and music: "to be black," as Lee/Madhubuti puts it in one poem ("But He Was Cool" (1970)), "is/to be/very – hot."

The women among more recent African American poets have also urged the need for another kind of change to combat not just the racism of white culture but the latent sexism of the black. Even revolutionary poets like Baraka have tended to talk in generic

terms about "the black man" and identify black women with the sexual and repro-
ductive functions. This sense of the redoubled oppression of black women, on the
grounds of gender as well as race, has led Sonia Sanchez to celebrate her attachment to
others like herself. "I cried," Sanchez declares, in "Just Don't Never Give Up on Love"
(1984), "For myself . . . For all the women who have ever stretched their bodies out
anticipating civilization and finding ruins." It has encouraged Mari Evans to celebrate
the simple fact of her own black womanhood ("I am a black woman"). For Jone Jordan
(1936–), the edge to her experience as woman is more traumatic. A victim of rape, she
has seen in the violence she has suffered a connection with other forms of violence, more
general and historical, perpetrated in Africa and America, since "*it all violates self-
determination.*" And in "Poem About My Rights" (1989) she explores and insists upon
the links between her own past and, say, "South Africa/penetrating into Namibia
penetrating into/Angola." The connection between herself and history does not stop
there, however, with the acknowledgment of the evil done to her as a black woman and
to black people in many parts of the world. She will fight back, so setting an example to
others similarly violated. "From now on," she tells all her oppressors, "my resistance/
my simple and daily and nightly self-determination/may very well cost you your life."

The violence which seeps into Jordan's work is, unsurprisingly, there in the work of
many other African American poets. It is the determining feature, for instance, in the
work of two remarkable African American poets of this period, Etheridge Knight
(1931–1991) and Michael Harper (1938–). Both Knight and Harper, like many black
writers, allow the rhythms of African American musical traditions to pulse through their
work. So, in "A Poem for Myself (Or Blues for a Mississippi Black Boy)" (1980), Knight
exploits blues forms to tell a story of wandering from Mississippi to Detroit, Chicago,
New York, then back to Mississippi. And in "Ilu, the Talking Drum" (1980) he takes the
black American experience in a full circle from Africa to the South then back to an Africa
of the spirit using an African rhythmic structure to imitate the voice of an African drum.
The titles of several of Harper's collections betray his own, similar allegiances: *Dear John
Coltrane* (1970), *Song: I Want a Witness* (1972), *Healing Song for the Inner Ear* (1985),
Songlines in Michaeltree (2000). Exploring his connection to jazz artists like Coltrane
and Charlie Parker, insisting on human and cultural continuity, his work is oriented to
performance: "blacks have to *testify*," he proclaims in "*Song: I Want a Witness*," "/and
testify and *testify*." For Harper, the violence he records is a matter of family loss and racial
history: the death of an infant son ("Nightmare Begins Responsibility" (1975)) or a
brother ("Camp Story" (1985)), the suffering inflicted upon Native Americans by "mad
Puritans" ("History as Apple Tree" (1977)), the assassinations of Malcolm X and Martin
Luther King ("Here Where Coltrane Is" (1977)). For Knight, the violence was closer to
the bone. "I died in Korea from a shrapnel wound and narcotics resurrected me," he
once confessed. "I died in 1960 from a prison sentence and poetry brought me back to
life." Many of Knight's poems were written in imprisonment – his first collection
was simply called *Poems from Prison* (1968) – and they detail the loneliness, the
bitter frustration of prison life. They work through a violence of language and verve
of movement learned from the black oral tradition, but they also work through the way
Knight links himself to a communality of suffering.

Violence, though, is no more the single defining feature of recent African American
poetry than any specific definition of race – what it means to be an African American – is.

What is remarkable about so much of this work, in fact, is the multiple forms in which African Americanism can enter into this poetry. With Rita Dove (1952–), for instance, there is an inclination toward multiculturalism. The settings of her spare, enigmatic poems range from Ohio to Germany to Israel; and in just one volume, slaves, mythological and biblical characters, and the ancestors and immediate family of the poet all jostle side by side. "I am profoundly fascinated by the ways in which language can change our perceptions," she has said. Some of her work addresses that subject head on: by exploring how a single word or image can permit a voyage into strange seas of thought ("Ö" (1980)) or how a poem can provide "a little room for thinking," a chance and space to dream ("Daystar" (1986)). Some of it approaches the liberating potential of language in a sidewise fashion: by considering how earlier generations of African Americans nurtured the "crazy feeling" that they could change their lives in the words they spoke, the songs they sang ("Kentucky, 1833" (1980)). Dove is continually trying to speak the unspoken. That includes those dimensions of experience and history that have been suppressed, most often, for reasons of gender or of race. So, in a poem called "Arrow" (1989), she quietly subverts those literary positions that reduce black people to marginal caricatures and women to convenient symbols of the ineffable. And in her long poem sequence, *Thomas and Beulah* (1987), she resurrects the rarely acknowledged contribution of working-class blacks to American life by telling the story of the courtship, marriage, and subsequent life of her own grandparents.

Defining a new black identity in prose

As far as prose is concerned, a seminal event in the history of African American writing since World War II was the publication in 1952 of *Invisible Man*. The author was Ralph Ellison (1914–1994). Born in Oklahoma and the grandson of slaves, Ellison was named Ralph Waldo after Emerson. Educated in a segregated school system, he then went south to Alabama to attend the black college of Tuskegee. In the South, in particular, Ellison recollected in his second collection of essays, *Going to the Territory* (1986), he found all "the signs and symbols that marked the dividing lines of segregation." But he also found time to read modern poetry. In New York Ellison met Richard Wright, who was then editor of the *New Challenge*. And it was while he was there that he wrote his first short story, and also worked in the black community gathering and recording folk material that was to become an integral part of his fiction. The early work Ellison produced reflected the influence of Wright and Naturalism. But Ellison slowly developed his own style, a mix of realism, surrealism, symbolism, folklore, and myth. "I was to dream of a prose which was flexible and swift, confronting the inequalities and brutalities of our society forthright," Ellison explained in his first book of essays, *Shadow and Act* (1964): "but yet thrusting forth its images of hope, human fraternity and individual self-realization." That dream was realized in *Invisible Man*: arguably the most profound and compelling novel about identity to be published during this period.

Set in the 1930s, *Invisible Man* describes the experiences of its anonymous black protagonist and narrator as he wanders through America, struggling to come to terms with the dilemma Ellison summed up in one of his essays: "the nature of our society is such that we are prevented from knowing who we are." He is "invisible," he discovers: his black skin renders him anonymous in white society. And, like so many heroes in

American fiction, black and white, he is torn between unsatisfactory alternatives: corresponding, in their own modernist, racially inflected way, to the mythic opposition of clearing and wilderness. He can either, he learns, surrender to the various demeaning roles prescribed for him by society. Or he can escape into a fluid, formless territory, a subterranean world that seems to exist outside history: where, instead of a repressed self, he seems to have no self at all.

Each stage in the journey of the invisible man, usually marked by a site and a speech, sees him trying on a new role, a fresh change of clothes and identity. He begins as a "darky," subjected to ritual humiliations and the level of a beast: forms of subjection that Ellison pointedly compares to those suffered by women. This is in the South, and still in the Southern states, he is then offered the chance to become the "college boy," following the Booker T. Washington road to success in a segregated institution. Journeying to New York City, he takes on the role of worker at a factory called the Liberty Paint Company, whose principal product is a kind of whitewash. Here, as elsewhere in the book, Ellison moves smoothly between different stylistic modes as he describes a workplace that is, quite clearly, a paradigm and parody of American society. Following his factory experience, the invisible man takes on a new role, by joining a group called the Brotherhood in New York. The Brotherhood is a thinly described version of the Communist Party, and the protagonist has now become an activist. This role is no more satisfactory than the others, though, as the continued imagery of games, blueprints, plans, repression, and castration suggest. The invisible man is still required to deny a crucial part of himself as an individual, a man, and, above all, a black man. And, at the climax of the narrative, following a race riot in Harlem, he retreats to an underground sewer, which he furnishes and lives in while, he tells us, he writes this book. He is now in a "border area" where he can understand his invisibility and ask us, the readers, the question that ends the book: "Who knows but that, on the lower frequencies I speak for you?'

What *Invisible Man* offers as a solution to the unsatisfactory alternatives of the clearing and the wilderness, a restrictive system and pure chaos, is what the protagonist realizes. He lives on the edge, a borderland where he can negotiate his way between the contingencies of history and the compulsions of himself. So, stylistically, does Ellison. Just as the hero manages to extricate himself from a series of fixed environments, so the author shows a comparable suppleness by avoiding getting trapped in one idiom, one language. The style of *Invisible Man* mixes several verbal forms and influences into one multicultural whole. The structure, in turn, offers a crafty variation on several narrative forms. This is a picaresque novel, to an extent. It is also a novel in the great tradition of American monologue. It is the novel as epic and the novel as myth. It also, in its mixture of naturalism and nightmare, recollects other great novels that have explored American society and the American racial divide: *Absalom, Absalom!*, say, or *Native Son*. Above all, it is a novel that has spoken and still speaks for more people, of any race, than its author could have imagined.

Ellison died without completing another novel. Apart from *Invisible Man*, two collections of his essays were published in his lifetime. When he died, he left behind six unpublished short stories and an uncompleted novel. These appeared in, respectively, 1996 and 1999: *Flying Home and Other Stories* and *Juneteenth*. By contrast, the productivity of a comparable figure in African American prose writing, James Baldwin

(1924–1987), was immense. Principally known as a novelist and essayist, he was also a playwright, scriptwriter, poet, director, and filmmaker. His novels and essays, and his play *The Amen Corner* (1955), revolve in particular around the themes of racial and sexual identity. "The question of color, especially in this country," Baldwin wrote in *Nobody Knows My Name: Notes of a Native Son* (1961), "operates to hide the great question of the self. That is precisely why what we like to call 'the Negro problem' is so tenacious in American life." And to the question of color, as a determinant of identity, he added the question of sexuality, since most of his intimate relationships were homosexual – and at a time when homosexuality was still criminalized. To these questions, in turn, he added the questions of family and religion. Born in Harlem when his mother was single, Baldwin suffered at the hands of his stepfather as he grew up. The stepfather, David Baldwin, an itinerant preacher, insisted that James was ugly and bore the mark of the devil. For a while, Baldwin served as a "young minister" in the Pentecostal Church. His earliest stories even reflect a religious influence. But in 1944 he moved to Greenwich Village, then began to shuffle off his church associations and to work on a novel, provisionally titled "Crying Holy" and then "In My Father's House." It was published in 1953 as *Go Tell It on the Mountain*; it immediately established Baldwin's reputation and is his most accomplished novel.

Essentially, *Go Tell It on the Mountain* is an initiation novel. Its protagonist, John Grimes, whom we first meet on "the morning of his fourteenth birthday," is modeled on the young James Baldwin. Other members of the fictional family recall other members of the Baldwin family. In particular, John's stepfather Gabriel is a recollection of David Baldwin. The book is divided into three sections. Told from John Grimes's perspective, the first section, "The Seventh Day," establishes John's marginal position in the family. "What shall I do?" John asks himself. The possible answers to that question are two: and they are investigated both in his own story and that of his family. He can either see himself as others see him and lapse into hatred and rejection of himself. The consequences of that are shame, guilt, fear, or compensatory fantasy: all of which John succumbs to for a while. Or he can struggle to accept and realize himself: to pursue the kind of self-realization that Baldwin was thinking of, on a larger, historical scale, when he wrote, "the American Negro can no longer ... be controlled by the white American image of him."

The second section of *Go Tell It on the Mountain*, concentrating on John's aunt, stepfather, and mother, offers variations on the theme of self-denial. Images of dirt, darkness, and grime (the pun on the family name is clearly intentional) evoke what is to be denied, cleared away; the dominant emotional pattern here is one of retreat, repression, since all three older people choose to suppress their true feelings, to hide their true selves behind masks. What is additionally remarkable about this second section is how Baldwin links the story of individuals to history. Informing what we hear about the three characters is the substance of the African American experience, from slavery to the Great Migration. That sense of another, racial dimension, deepening and enriching the personal fate, then feeds into the final section, "The Threshing-Floor," which recounts the struggle of John for his own self. In a complex religious experience, John moves from a sense of damnation to one of salvation: a process that is coextensive with a movement from rejection to acceptance of himself, from disgust to delight. The achievement of *Go Tell It on the Mountain* is that, as an initiation novel, it works on many levels. It records the initiation of a boy into knowledge of his own sexuality, of a black boy into realization of his own racial inheritance and identity, and of a young person into a recognition of his own humanity and presence in the community. Not only that, it registers another, parallel initiation: that of the author himself, into an understanding that would subsequently shape his career, that only in accepting himself could he express himself, only in embracing the cultural forms available to him as an African American, could he encounter and possibly transcend his own suffering and that of his race.

While he was still working on *Go Tell It on the Mountain*, in 1948, Baldwin moved to France. He was to spend the rest of his life traveling between Europe and the United States, living in France and Switzerland but never leaving the United States imaginatively. His second novel, *Giovanni's Room* (1956), openly explores homosexuality, in the story of a young white American expatriate in Paris. *Another Country* (1962), his third novel, uses New York, Paris, and elsewhere as settings for several characters trying to explore issues of racial and sexual identity. Other, later novels similarly pursue problems of race and sexuality: among them, *Tell Me How Long the Train's Been Gone* (1968), *If Beale Street Could Talk* (1974), and *Just Above My Head* (1979). His first book of essays, *Notes of a Native Son* (1955), was followed by several others: notably *The Fire Next Time* (1962), in which Baldwin insisted that America could never truly be a nation until it had solved the color problem. If it did not solve it, he warned, it would face apocalypse, "the fire next time." His play *The Amen Corner* was, in turn, followed by another three: *Blues for Mr. Charlie* (1964), *One Day, When I was Lost* (1973), and *A Deed from the King of Spain* (1974). Right up until his final book of essays, *The Price of the Ticket* (1985), Baldwin continued to be committed to what he called "the necessity of Americans to achieve an identity" and the questions of systematic racism and injustice – the active denial of black identity by white America – that this necessarily raised.

For many years, and especially during the 1950s and early 1960s, Baldwin was a political activist. He marched, talked, and worked with a number of civil rights leaders, including the two most famous, whose speeches and other writings give them a place in American literary history, Malcolm X (1925–1965) and Martin Luther King (1929–1968). Born Malcolm Little, and later also known as el-Hajj Malik el-Shabazz, Malcolm spent his earliest years in Michigan. After his father died, probably at the hands of a white racist group, and his mother was placed in a mental institution, Malcolm moved to Boston to live with his half sister. He became involved in the nightlife and underworld of Boston, then later Harlem; and in 1946 he was arrested and imprisoned for armed robbery. During his prison years, he experienced a conversion to the Nation of Islam. Upon his release, he changed his name to Malcolm X, the X signifying the unknown name of his African ancestors and their culture that had been erased during slavery. Becoming a minister for the Nation of Islam, which preached the idea that whites are devils, he helped build it into a significant force in urban black life. However, in 1963, he split from the leader of the Nation of Islam and began to move from the mainly spiritual philosophy of the Nation to a more political black nationalism. About this time, too, he began to collaborate with the author Alex Haley (1921–1992) on *The Autobiography of Malcolm X*. The *Autobiography* was published in 1965, the same year that Malcolm X was assassinated.

As an orator, especially in his last few years, Malcolm X was renowned for his quick wit, fast talk, nervy syncopated rhythms, and for his erudition. The *Autobiography* has the same oracular, oral power as the speeches. Here, in a way typical of both American and African American autobiography, Malcolm X presents his own experience as exemplary. He shows, for instance, how the demeaning label of "nigger" applied to him, when he was young, even by white liberals betrayed a general tendency to erase the humanity of African Americans. In opposition to this erasure, Malcolm X asserts his own presence, the reality of the many identities he realized during his life: the hustler, the criminal, the spiritual leader, the political activist. He also uses the autobiographical models of the slave narrative, the record of a conversion experience, and the success story of a self-made man to inform, enliven, and generalize this personal account. What he achieved in his relatively short life was considerable, making him a charismatic figure and a catalyst for political activity. And what he achieved in this, his account of that life, is just as remarkable: whatever else it is, it is one of the great American autobiographies.

Unlike Malcolm X, Martin Luther King Jr. embraced a gospel of non-violence in the quest for racial equality. Like Malcolm X, he was the son of a minister. King grew up immersed in the doctrine of Christian love and in the music and rhetoric of the Baptist Church. Both were to affect him profoundly, as did his extensive reading of theological and literary texts as a college student and afterwards. King became a minister of a Baptist church in Montgomery, Alabama in 1954. Soon after that, in 1955, he gave his first civil rights address. Between then and his assassination in 1968, he traveled the nation giving approximately 2,000 speeches and sermons: among them "I Have a Dream" (1963), the climactic speech at a massive civil rights demonstration in Washington, and "I've Been to the Mountaintop," the speech he gave in Memphis the night before he was killed. "I Have a Dream" illustrates King's characteristic rhetorical strategy, learned from the many sermons he had both heard and given, of using memorable images, verbal play, literary allusions, and biblical borrowings to communicate his message. As the insistent use of the phrase which gives that speech its title shows, it also indicates his love of incremental repetition: using a repeated phrase ("I have a dream") to build one statement, one sentence on another. It is a device at least as old as the King James Version of the Bible, as American as the poems of Langston Hughes and Whitman, and it gives to many of his speeches and sermons the irresistible force of a tidal wave. King knew exactly how to weave different traditions of thought and language, many of them black and some of them white, into a series of intricate, intense variations on the message that concludes "I Have a Dream": "Let freedom ring."

Born in Chattanooga, Tennessee and raised in Buffalo, New York, Ishmael Reed (1938–) interviewed Malcolm X for a local Buffalo radio program, as a result of which the program series was cancelled. Moving to New York City in 1962, he helped found the *East Village Other*, one of the first and best-known alternative newspapers. He also became involved in the formation of the Black Arts movement. However, his participation in that movement was both participatory and adversarial. A complex, combative thinker, Reed acknowledges that the black element reveals the permeable nature of American experience and identity. But he also insists on the permeable nature of blackness. He has made it his aim, as a poet, playwright, essayist, and, above all, a novelist, to live between cultures and dramatize the exchanges between them. And he has done so, not only in his own writing, but also in editing works like *MultiAmerica:*

Figure 5.3   Martin Luther King delivering his "I Have a Dream" speech in Washington, August 28, 1963. Rolls Press/Popperfoto/Getty Images.

Essays on Cultural Wars and Cultural Peace (1997) and in founding the Before Columbus Foundation in 1976, a multiethnic organization dedicated to promoting a pan-cultural view of America. Reed is not afraid of controversy. The first of his major novels, *The Free-Lance Pallbearers* (1967), for instance, represents a subversive departure from the autobiographical style of earlier African American narratives. It also offers a parody of *Invisible Man*, for many critics the masterwork of African American fiction. Nor is he frightened of going against the grain of any prevailing critical or creative fashion. The sheer slipperiness of his works has, in fact, led to him being given many, wildly different labels. Perhaps it would be most accurate to see him as someone who uses a mix of traditions to illuminate and invigorate: combining continuity and the impromptu in a cultural dynamic that Amiri Baraka described as "the changing room."

What all this means, for novels as otherwise diverse as *Mumbo Jumbo* (1972), *Flight to Canada* (1976), *The Terrible Twos* (1982), *The Terrible Threes* (1989), and *Japanese by Spring* (1993), is serious fun and a passionate waywardness. Voodoo, Reed has said, "teaches that past is present"; and each of these novels, and others, offers that lesson in a sly, subversive, jokily – sometimes horrifically – disjunctive way. The resistance here is to the narrow functional forms favored by what one of Reed's characters in *Mumbo Jumbo* dismisses as the "neo-social realist gang." More particularly, it is to any traditional kind of African American narrative that, as Reed himself has put it, "limits and enslaves us" by confining black experience to a singular, linear model. The writer metamorphoses into the voodoo-man, the trickster god weaving backwards and forwards in time and between different levels of narration. And the writing turns on a syncretic, multi-layered vision of reality – with the clear enemy being the idea of a master narrative. In *Flight to Canada*, for instance, Reeds picks up the old form of the slave narrative and then, through a transformation of style, changes a remembrance of servitude into an act of liberation. A flight from slavery is enacted twice in the book: the first time in a poem called "Flight to Canada" written by a character called Quicksill, the second in Quicksill's escape to Canada. But a flight from slavery also *is* the book. "For him, freedom was the writing," it is said of Quicksill. And freedom is the writing of *Flight to Canada* the novel as well as "Flight to Canada" the poem, as Reed deploys self-reflexiveness, parody, deliberate anachronism, and constant crisscrossing between different histories and cultures to maneuver himself out of the straitjacket of social realism. Through meaningful mischief, Reed slips the reader the message that freedom springs from confluence not control, an easygoing commerce between cultures. Reed refuses to be slave to his narrative, in *Flight to Canada* or elsewhere; and he resites the act of connection between living and dead in an altered demography. This is a return to origins, a flight into and out of the past that occurs within a fictional version of the uncertainty principle: an America that seems to follow no set rules, other than those of diversity, chance, and change.

Two African American writers whose return to origins is less slippery are Ernest Gaines (1933–) and Albert Murray (1916–). With Gaines, the determining factor that enables such a return is voice. So, in *The Autobiography of Miss Jane Pittman* (1971), the title character, based on Gaines's great aunt, recovers her past and that of her people in a heroic act of storytelling. In novels as otherwise different as *A Gathering of Old Men* (1983) and *A Lesson Before Dying* (1993), voice becomes a tool of empowerment for Gaines's characters; whereas for Murray's it is not so much voice as the blues idiom. Murray realized his belief in the redemptive potential of the blues in his fictional trilogy, *Train Whistle Guitar* (1974), *The Spyglass Tree* (1991), and *The Seven League Boots* (1996). The three novels trace the growth of their protagonist and narrator, Scooter, from his Alabama childhood to his maturity as a jazz musician. Along the way, he learns individual worth and communal responsibility; and he discovers that the best way to be and express oneself is in an instinctive exchange with others – an exchange something like the relationship between the jazz soloist and supporting band.

Defining a new black identity in drama

An African American dramatist who believed equally in the chance to be and express oneself was Lorraine Hansberry (1930–1965). Hansberry wanted to capture the authentic voice of the African American working class. After associating with various prominent figures in the cultural life of Harlem and working on *Freedom*, a newspaper founded by the singer and activist Paul Robeson, she began working on a play set in the South Side of Chicago. Originally titled "The Crystal Stair," after a line from a poem by Langston Hughes, it was eventually named after another line from a Hughes poem called "Harlem." "What happens to a dream deferred?" Hughes had asked. "Does it dry up/Like a raisin in the sun? .../Or does it explode?" Hansberry called her play, a dramatization of dreams deferred that threaten to explode, *A Raisin in the Sun* (1959).

A Raisin in the Sun has been compared to *Native Son*. Set in a black, Chicagoan, working-class environment, it explores, as Richard Wright's novel does, frustrations and struggles that are determined by the primary fact of race. It even opens in the same explosive way: with the sound of an alarm clock, that seems to herald crisis and call on the audience to pay attention. While Hansberry investigates many of the same issues as Wright, though – the relation of material wealth to human dignity, the crippling consequences of poverty and racial prejudice, the conflict between separation and assimilation – she does so in a more hopeful register. The dramatic premise is simple. An insurance benefit of 10,000 dollars paid on the death of the father of the household becomes the source of conflict within the Younger family: as Mama Lena Younger, the widow, beneficiary, and matriarch argues with her son, Walter Younger Jr., over its use. Not only does the premise allow Hansberry to unravel the tensions within the family, tensions that are clearly symptomatic of differences within the African American community as a whole, it enables her to suggest the intimacy of their shared experience – and their ultimate solidarity in the face of white prejudice and oppression. In the end, resisting white threats and attempts at bribery, Walter Younger Jr. goes along with his mother's desire to move from their cramped apartment into a white neighborhood. "We come from people who had a lot of pride," Walter tells a white man who tries to dissuade the Younger family from becoming his neighbors. "We have decided to move into our house because my father . . . he earned it." Working together, despite their differences, they end the play preparing for a move that will change their lives, perhaps for good, perhaps ill, probably both. The dream is no longer deferred.

Both Ed Bullins (1935–) and August Wilson (1945–2005) are also seminal figures in the story of African American drama since World War II. Bullins was brought up in a tough Philadelphia neighborhood and knows the violence of the ghetto at firsthand: he was nearly stabbed to death as a youth. The gritty existence his characters lead, in a street world that Bullins describes as "natural" rather than naturalistic, reflects the influence of that environment. He eventually settled in San Francisco, where he joined other African American writers to form Black Arts West, a militant cultural and political organization, and direct the Black House Theatre. The writer who influenced him most was Amiri Baraka. In his play *Dutchman*, in particular, Baraka had used elements of myth, mixing absurdist conventions and realistic strategies with a brittle colloquialism, to tell a fast-paced tale of a fatal encounter between a provocative white woman and a naive, middle-class black man. The woman, called Lula, turns from flirtation to taunts, as she attacks the black man, Clay, for playing the role which the dominant white society has handed him. Clay finally replies with all the force of racial hatred that he has repressed in order to survive, claiming that for a black man repression and conformity are necessary because murder is the only alternative. Furious at losing control of the situation, Lula fatally stabs Clay. She then orders the other riders on the subway train where she and Clay have met and where all the action occurs, to remove his body. As they are doing so, the play ends with another black man entering the subway car and Lula begins her act all over again. The claustrophobic physical setting, the sense of irresistible force and motion, and, not least, the constant references to Adam and Eve, fairytales, and the Flying Dutchman: all suggest the synthesis of styles at work in this tale of racial tension and sexual repression. Clearly affected by this, and other plays by Baraka, Bullins has created his own mix of the vernacular and mythic, in the more than fifty plays he has written, starting with *Clara's Old Man* (1965) and *Goin' a Buffalo* (1968).

Goin' a Buffalo, for instance, is about a group of characters living on the edge in Los Angeles, prostitutes and pimps. "This play is about some black people," Bullins tells us in the initial stage directions. For these people, money, drugs, and sex circumscribe their lives. They are caught, it seems, in enclosed spaces that reflect their captive status in society; and they are bewildered by the gap that opens out between the promise of America and the realities, the sheer violence of their everyday existence. For them, Buffalo, on the other side of the American continent, beckons as an escape, a chance to realize the dream of freedom and a fresh start. The dream, however, dissolves in conflict, manipulation, and deception. Bullins later chose to include *Goin' a Buffalo* in his Twentieth-Century Cycle, a proposed series of twenty plays on the African American experience, that deals not so much with race relations as with the everyday lives of African Americans. His plays consistently startle in their raw power of language and action, their concentration on the psychosocial anger of African American culture. The "natural" style Bullins says he follows is a product of craft, calculation. Music, particularly rhythm and blues and jazz, is used to frame the actions and focus feeling. Symbolism, such as the symbols of boxes, enclosures that run through *Goin' a Buffalo*, establishes meaning. Language, a stripped, rhythmic vernacular, discloses only what the characters want to disclose: there is no obvious attempt made to impart a message. This is an art that resists overt ideology, but that nevertheless explores the many avenues by which drama can issue out of and return to black life, carrying with it a series of potentially revolutionary ideas.

While Bullins has been central to the story of alternative theatre, success on the mainstream stage has tended to elude him. By contrast, August Wilson enjoyed mainstream popularity. His *Ma Rainey's Black Bottom* (1982), *Fences* (1983), *Joe Turner's Come and Gone* (1984), *The Piano Lesson* (1986), *Two Trains Running* (1992), and *Seven Guitars* (1995) were all produced on Broadway with some success. Born on "The Hill," a racially mixed area of Pittsburgh, Pennsylvania, to a black mother and a white father he seldom saw, Wilson encountered racial prejudice early. He also encountered two formative cultural influences: black talk and black music. Beginning to write plays in the 1970s, *Ma Rainey's Black Bottom* established his reputation. Set in 1920s Chicago, it describes the economic exploitation of black musicians by white record companies and the ways in which victims of racism are compelled to direct their rage at each other rather than at those who caused their oppression. It is also a memorable combination of the vernacular, violence, and humor. So is *Fences*, which concerns the struggles of a working-class family in the 1950s to find security. *Joe Turner's Come and Gone* is set some forty years earlier than *Fences*, in a Pittsburgh boarding house in 1911; *The Piano Lesson*, in turn, is placed in 1937. *Two Trains Running* moves forward several decades, to the late 1960s – to a coffee shop where regulars discuss their troubled relation to the times – and *Seven Guitars* then moves back to the 1940s. Wilson declared that, as a playwright, he wanted to "tell a history that has never been told." His major plays reflect this; they were all part of the "Century Cycle" of ten plays, each of them intended to investigate a central issue facing African Americans in a different decade of the twentieth century (the others are *Jitney* (1983), *King Hedley II* (2000), *Gem of the Ocean* (2003), and *Radio Golf* (2005)). He was aiming at rewriting the history of every decade so that black life would become an acknowledged part of the theatrical and general history of America.

Telling impossible stories: Recent African American fiction

If any novelist has had a project similar to that of August Wilson in drama, it is surely Toni Morrison (1931–). "For me, in doing novels about African Americans," she has declared, "I was trying to move away from the unstated but overwhelming and dominant context that was white history and to move it into another one." Her work can, in fact, be seen as an attempt to write several concentric histories of the American experience from a distinctively African American perspective. "The crucial difference for me is not the difference between fact and fiction," Morrison once admitted, "but the distinction between fact and truth. Because facts can exist without human intelligence, but truth cannot." That search for truth began with her first novel, *The Bluest Eye* (1970). It has a simple premise. A narrator, Claudia McTeer, tells the story of Pecola Breedlove, a black girl whose hunger for love is manifested in a desire for blue eyes that eventually drives her to insanity. Pecola is driven inward by the norms of white society (the bluest eye, the ideal family): to shame, the destruction and division of the self. Claudia, the narrator, finds herself directed outward, to anger against white society: finding a convenient scapegoat in the "white baby dolls" she cuts up and destroys. *The Bluest Eye* deconstructs the image of the white community as the site of normality and perfection. It also exposes the realities of life in an impoverished African American community, whose abject socioeconomic status is exacerbated by the politics of race.

Coextensive with Morrison's concern with the psychosocial consequences of racism is her interest in what she calls "silence and evasion": the gaps and omissions in American history. In her second novel, *Sula* (1973), for example, she shows how a black community evolves and shapes itself, with its own cultural resources and elaborate social structure. She rescues it from a kind of historical anonymity. Morrison's third novel, *Song of Solomon* (1977), sustains her commitment to what is called here "names that had a meaning": the evolution of a distinctive black identity and community through the habit of language. A complex tapestry of memory and myth, *Song of Solomon* tells the story of a young man, Milkman Dead, who comes to know himself through a return to origins. *Tar Baby* (1981) also pursues themes of ancestry and identity, how African Americans come to name and know themselves. It does this primarily through the contrast between two characters, Jadine Childs, a model, and William (Son) Green, an outcast and wanderer. Jadine, brought up with the help of white patrons, has been assimilated into white culture; Son remains outside, in resistance to it. The identity crisis posed by the conflict between her and Son is never really resolved; Morrison adopts her usual strategy, of leaving the narrative debate open.

With her fifth and most important novel so far, *Beloved* (1987), Morrison took the core of a real story she had encountered while working as a senior editor at Random House. It was recorded in *The Black Book* (1974), an eclectic collection of material relating to more than 300 years of African American history. And it concerned a fugitive slave called Margaret Garner who killed her daughter, then tried to kill her other children and herself rather than be returned to slavery. Morrison took this as the nucleus of her story about Sethe Suggs, who killed her own young daughter, Beloved, when faced with the same threat. Circling backwards and forwards in time, before and after the Civil War, the novel discloses how Sethe and other characters – especially, her daughter Denver and her lover, Paul D – struggle with a past that cannot but must be remembered and named. In other words, it pivots around the central contradiction in African American, and for that matter American, history: living with impossible memories. There is the need to remember and tell and the desire to forget; there are memories here with an inexhaustible power to erupt and overwhelm the mind which must somehow be commemorated yet laid aside if life is to continue. It is a contra-diction caught in a phrase repeated in the concluding section of the narrative: "it was not a story to pass on" (where "pass on" could mean either "pass over" or "pass on to others"). It is one caught, too, in the scandalous nature of the act, the killing that haunts Sethe. In that sense, the mother-daughter relationship that Morrison characteristically focuses on here is at once a denial of the institution of slavery and a measure of its power.

Beloved is an extraordinary mix of narrative genres. It has elements of realism, the gothic, and African American folklore. It is a slave narrative that internalizes slavery and its consequences. It is a historical novel that insists on history as story, active rehearsal, and reinvention of the past. It weaves its way between the vernacular and a charged lyricism, the material and magical, as it emphasizes the centrality of the black, and in particular black female, experience. This is a novel that reorients history, American history in particular, to the lived experience of black people. It is also a passionate novel that sets up a vital circuit between historical events and emotional consequences, and then connects up that circuit to any one, black or white, or whatever, who reads it. "Did a whiteman saying make it so?" Paul D asks himself at one point. The immediate answer turns out to be "yes"; the ultimate answer is "no." The novel and its characters turn out, after all, to offer another form of "saying," a more authentic way of seeing and telling the personal and historical past. That is why the last word of *Beloved* is, precisely, "Beloved"; because the whole aim of the story, and its protagonist, has been to name the unnameable.

After *Beloved*, Morrison published two books that, with it, form part of a loosely connected trilogy, *Jazz* (1992) and *Paradise* (1998). Morrison has said that the three novels are about "various kinds of love": the love of a mother for her child, romantic love, and "the love of God and love for fellow human beings." The three might equally be described as charting the history of African Americans. *Jazz*, set in Harlem in 1926, was inspired by Morrison reading in a book she was editing, *The Harlem Book of the Dead*, about a young woman who, as she lay dying, refused to identify her lover as the person who shot her. *Paradise* is set in 1976. In describing the intimate contact between two communities, though, one a black township and the other a refuge for women, it circles as far back as 1755. It also supplies another example of Morrison's characteristic strategy of giving voice to the silence while initiating its own forms of silence. That is, it brings those traditionally exiled to the margins, for reasons of race, gender, or both, to the center of the stage; it allows them to name themselves and narrate their history. But it quietly intimates its own lack of authority, the blanks and absences detectable in its own account, and the responsibility that this imposes on the reader.

In *Beloved*, for example, the reader never knows who the young girl is who returns to Sethe during the course of the story. Is she the ghost of the two-year-old daughter Sethe killed twenty years earlier? Does she recall Sethe's nameless mother, since some of her dreams and narrations seem to recall the horrors of the Middle Passage? Is she a myriad figure, a composite of all the women ever dragged into slavery? Or is she a very singular young woman who has been driven mad by her enslavement? We cannot know, for sure: all we can do is allow these possibilities to feed into our own retelling of an intolerable, impossible past, our own project of naming the unnameable. Nor, for that matter, can we be certain what happens at the end of *Paradise*. The pivotal act of this novel is the shooting, and apparent killing, of the women at the refuge by nine men from the township. *Paradise* closes, however, with the "marvelous" disappearance of the bodies of the women and the reappearance, then, of four of them. One of the several, unresolved puzzles of *this* story is, therefore, what they return *as*, ghosts or human beings who somehow survived the attack. But just as *Beloved*, for all its push beyond realism, leaves no doubt as to the monstrous *fact* of slavery and its central place in the story of America, so *Paradise* leaves no doubt about the *necessity* for the reappearance of women like these, in some form or another, for the survival of the republic. *Paradise* is a book about the failures of American democracy (hence its setting in the bicentennial). It is about the strengths and fatal flaws in the black community (hence its complicity in the shootings). It is about the core meaning of the African American story to American history (hence the narrative connections forged with key events since 1776). And it is also a book about the failure of patriarchy. Morrison has resisted the description of herself as a feminist. She is right to do so because *Paradise*, like all her novels, is so much more than a polemical statement of a position. But, in its own way, it registers a fundamentally optimistic belief in the recovery of the American republic – a belief that all her work tends to share – and, in this case, at the hands of women.

Apart from the occasional excursion into drama (*Dreaming Emmett* (1986)) and critical and social theory (*Playing in the Dark, En-Gendering Power: Essays on Anita Hill, Clarence Thomas, and the Construction of Social Reality* (1992)), Morrison has focused on the writing of novels, her most recent being *Love* (2003) and *A Mercy* (2008). By contrast, Alice Walker (1944–) has written seven novels, on which her reputation rests, but she has also produced many volumes of poetry, collections of short stories, volumes of essays, and children's books. All her work, in different genres, is dedicated to what she has come to call "womanism." In fiction, Walker inaugurated her career with *The Third Life of Grange Copeland* (1970), a realistic novel describing three generations of a family whose history is marred by racial oppression and sexual violence. It is notable for its stark account of a repetitive cycle of abuse, wife beating and sexual exploitation, within the black family and community. *Meridian* (1976), Walker's second novel, concentrates on the civil rights movement and the fight for social change. It is, however, centered on the experience of women. Its central character, Meridian Hill, lives in the North but returns to the South to help in a voter registration drive. Meridian, the reader learns, is "*held* by something in the past" that includes, above all, her mother and a church that is both her mother's church and – whether she likes it or not – her mother church. Meridian never comes to personal terms with her mother but, by returning to her mother's history and ancestry, she does experience a symbolic rapprochement. "Mama, I *love* you. Let me go," Meridian is able to whisper to the figure of her mother she sees in a dream. She has made peace with her, and can move on. Meridian is also able to make her peace and come to terms with the church, and in a less purely symbolic way. For the church she encounters in the South is one transformed by the civil rights revolution. Her return to origins has initiated change, but change that is contiguous with the earlier experiences of her community. In that way, she has come back to her own history only to transcend it, and become a whole woman.

Change, a purely secular salvation involving the discovery of identity and community, is also at the heart of *The Color Purple* (1983). At the center of this novel is Celie, the victim of racial and sexual oppression. Raped by the man she believes to be her father, she is battered and abused in a loveless marriage. Nevertheless, she gradually learns "how to do it," how to grow into being and companionship. Her mentors here are three women. One, called Sofia, teaches her by example the lesson of resistance to white and male oppression. Another, her sister Nettie, offers her a more complex lesson, primarily through her letters. A missionary who goes to work in Africa, Nettie discloses to Celie the ancient cultural and spiritual dimensions of the African American tradition: the proud inheritance they share. Through her encounters with white colonists and developers, she also quietly links the story of racial oppression in America to a larger history of imperial adventure and conquest. The third mentor Celie encounters is a blues singer, Shug Avery. The first person for whom Celie feels a definite physical attraction, Shug teaches Celie about her body, offering the possibility of sexual pleasure. She also unpacks the cultural forms that she and Celie share as African Americans: the sensual promise of jazz, the tragic melancholy of blues. And, like Sofia and Nettie, she leads by example. She is a powerful illustration of selfhood, a person who positively fills the space she occupies. More than anyone, Shug encourages Celie to believe in herself. Everything, Shug suggests, is holy. Everything is worthy of respect and wonder. The divine is to be found, not in "the old white man" worshipped in church, in this place or that, but in everything. Even the color purple. Even, and especially, Celie. It is a profoundly American sentiment, this belief in a democracy of being, a divinity that informs every individual. And it allows Celie to flower from absence into presence: to become herself.

Since writing *The Color Purple*, Walker has written several books that push at the formal boundaries of fiction while developing themes and revisiting characters first encountered in this seminal 1983 novel. *The Temple of My Familiar* (1989), for instance, explores a wide variety of subjects from a womanist perspective. It reintroduces Shug Avery; it introduces us to the granddaughter of Celie; it is, perhaps, not so much a novel as a collection of loosely related tales. In turn, *Possessing the Secret of Joy* (1992) picks up the issue of female circumcision, touched on in *The Color Purple* as a symptom of male cultural violence; *By the Light of My Father's Smile* (1998) explores the thin boundaries between different ethnic traditions, and between life and death; and *Now Is the Time to Open Your Heart* (2004) describes a woman's quest to accept the ageing process. No subsequent book, however, has matched *The Color Purple* or *Meridian* as an account of the discovery of being. And none has matched *The Color Purple* in its revelatory use of form. *The Color Purple* is not just a story of personal growth that happens to be written as a series of letters. It achieves its meaning precisely by being an epistolary novel: returning to one of the oldest forms of prose fiction and using that as the key to opening up the self. Celie writes herself into existence, into contact with herself and communion with others. And those others include the readers, since the letters are ultimately addressed to us.

Paule Marshall (1929–) and Jamaica Kincaid (1949–) approach the experiences of people of color, especially women, from a different perspective, because of their West Indian background. Kincaid was born in Antigua, leaving there for the United States when she was sixteen. Marshall was born in the United States, in Brooklyn; the influence on her of her West Indian background, however, has been profound. The daughter of second-generation Barbadian immigrants, Marshall grew up listening to the tales of her mother and her female West Indian friends, whom she has described in her non-fiction as the "poets in the kitchen." Her first novel, *Brown Girl, Brownstones*, was also a first in several different ways when it appeared in 1959. It was one of the first novels, since the time of Claude McKay, to explore the link between African American people and their West Indian counterparts, one of the first to delve into the inner life of a young black female protagonist, and one of the first to explore in detail the relationship between a black mother and daughter. Selina Boyce, the protagonist in *Brown Girl, Brownstones*, is the daughter of first-generation Barbadian immigrants. She is brought up in the brownstone buildings of Brooklyn, in an area that, as the novel opens in 1939, is experiencing a sea change in terms of its inhabitants. The whites are moving out or "discreetly dying," and West Indian immigrants are moving in. The brownstones constitute an anchor in this sea of racial change; and, as Selina grows up there, listening to the kitchen talk of her mother Silla and her friends and witnessing the reveries of her father, Deighton, in his upstairs sun room, she finds herself torn. Her mother, a powerful figure, longs to assimilate, to "buy house" as she puts it and buy into the American dream. Her father, a feckless romantic whom Selina adores, dreams of returning to Barbados. Marshall refuses to resolve the process of cultural adaptation Selina engages in as she grows up. At the end of *Brown Girl, Brownstones*, Selina is still faced with the task of coming to terms with her equivocal feelings about her mother and (now dead) father and the mixed, polyglot character of her inheritance. She plans, however, to leave Brooklyn for the "islands": not to imitate the return to origins dreamed of by her father but to retrace the diasporic wanderings of her mother. "I'm truly your child," Selina now tells Silla; and she takes up the burden, not of abandoning her American identity, but of discovering the other cultural fragments required for self-definition.

The wandering quest Selina takes up at the end of *Brown Girl, Brownstones* has become a hallmark of Marshall's fiction. It characterizes the four novellas collected in *Soul Clap Hands and Sing* (1961), and her later novels *The Chosen Place, the Timeless People* (1969), *Praisesong for the Widow* (1987), and *Daughters* (1991). Involving, very often, a reverse Middle Passage, it dramatizes a search for and reconciliation of the self with an African diasporic historical past. Wandering also marks the longer fiction of Jamaica Kincaid, such as *Annie John* (1985), *Lucy* (1990), and *The Autobiography of My Mother* (1996). In *Lucy*, the nineteen-year-old character after whom the novel is named arrives in the United States from Antigua in 1967, just after the island has received its independence from Great Britain. Working as an au pair for a white family in New York City, she finds herself, as she puts it, wrapped "in the mantle of a servant." But her position, her origins in what she calls "the fringes of the world," and, not least, her keenly ironic intelligence, enable her to cast a cold eye over the generic American household she enters (Kincaid stresses the point by supplying no family name). Observing a supposedly ideal American family from close up, she witnesses its destructive tensions and divisions. Eventually, she leaves her job as au pair; her commitment to her fashioning of herself, she feels, requires her to reject that life, just as, earlier, she had felt compelled to abandon an "ancestral past" rooted in the "foul deed" of slavery. Selfhood is now seen as a process; and Lucy prepares to pursue that process in the fluid, multicultural terrain of New York City, the ultimate metropolis. *Lucy* ends with Lucy beginning to write her story in her diary, opening with her full name, Lucy Josephine Potter. "I understood that I was inventing myself," she asserts. That is her task, and her need, as she now sees it. Which is a task that links her, as Kincaid must know, with many other travelers to and sojourners in the New World. Even in her resistance to the orthodoxies of America, Lucy is making a very American choice.

Realism and Its Discontents

Confronting the real, stretching the realistic in drama

The New York City in which Lucy decides to make her way is not just the ultimate metropolis. For many years, it has been the theatrical capital of America. Until around the end of the 1950s, it was even more localized than that. One street in particular, Broadway, was synonymous with the American theatre; and that street, together with the side streets intersecting it, dominated the theatrical activity of the nation. What is remarkable about the work produced when Broadway was at its height is its roots in domestic realism. This was not, however, a limitation, since the finest American dramatists of the period used realism as a means of exploring fundamental issues. As it happens, the careers and styles of the two greatest American playwrights of this period, Arthur Miller and Tennessee Williams, are exemplary. Those careers reveal certain parallels. Their styles, however, reveal radical differences. Miller used realism to explore wider moral and political issues; whereas Williams was more interested in deploying it to explore emotional and psychological forces. Miller concentrated on the ordinary person put under extraordinary pressure by their society. Williams, on the other hand, focused on misfits: extraordinary people trying to bear up against the ordinary pressures of life. For Miller, the orbit of attention was formed by what he called "the Common Man." To pursue this, he fashioned an idiom that replicated the clarity and misperceptions of the vernacular: the direct poetry of the street that, sometimes, people use to conceal the truth from themselves. For Williams, what mattered was the common humanity that connects the uncommon to the rest of us. And to dramatize that, he devised a language that, at its best, was subtly poetic, rhythmic, and emotional. These two major dramatists measured the diverse potential of domestic realism: stretched out, when necessary, to incorporate borrowings from other forms, notably symbolism and expressionism. They also mapped out the terrain that most subsequent American dramatists have occupied. Apart from a brief period in the 1960s and just after, when many playwrights struck out towards more radical experiment, it is the dramatic land of Miller or Williams that most continue to inhabit. The domestic setting and some form of realistic speech have continued to dominate the American stage.

The first play by Arthur Miller (1915–2005) to reach Broadway, *The Man Who Had All the Luck* (1944), closed after only four performances. His second, *All My Sons* (1947), however, achieved success and introduced themes that would dominate his work: the pursuit of success enshrined in the American dream, social and familial tension, and the conflict between competing moralities, the economic and political system as a final cause of the problems and misconceptions Miller's characters have to endure. With *Death of a Salesman* (1949), his finest play, Miller endowed similar issues and problems with a tragic dimension. It relates the story of a representative American, Willy Loman: an ordinary man, as his surname punningly indicates, but one whose choices and their consequences spell out the darker side of the national dream. A salesman who, after thirty-five years on the road, has never achieved the rewards and recognition for which he had hoped, Willy is driven to despair by his failure in a system that seems to him to guarantee success. Measuring his worth by the volume of his sales – Miller never lets us know what Willy sells because, essentially, he is selling himself – Willy withdraws from the crises and disappointments of the present into memories of the past and into imaginary conversations with his brother Ben, his symbol of success. *Death of a Salesman* is, in a sense, a memory play: a working title for it was "The Inside of his Head." And everything here is seen double, as Willy sees it and as it is: a point sounded in the initial stage description of Willy's "fragile-seeming home." "An air of the dream clings to the place," we are told, "a dream rising out of reality." This is also a tale of domestic realism in which Miller uses elements of expressionism and symbolism to transmute the story into a tragedy. The dialogue is realistic vernacular: the idiom of a society that pursues illusion rather than fact. But the "exploded house" in cross-section that appears in Act One and supplies the setting for most of the play prepares us for a revelatory intimacy. We, the audience, are drawn into the family combustion. We are drawn into the collapsing consciousness of Willy, in particular, into the past as an explanation of the present. And with the help of a rich tapestry of symbols (the symbols of success and successful father figures that haunt Willy, for instance), we are invited to see this drama as the tragic crisis of a society as well as one of one unremarkable but representative man.

Good American that he is, Willy believes that success is his birthright. He can never give up this belief, or its corollary: that, in the land of opportunity that is America, failure can only be the fault of the individual. Despite his growing sense of separation from the success ethic, he still judges himself in its terms. His wife Linda watches helplessly as he tears himself apart. All she can do is care and ask others to care: "attention," she declares, "attention must be finally paid to such a person." His son, Happy, can only surrender to the same ethic. Willy's other son, Biff, is different. Biff senses that he does not want what the world calls success. But, unfortunately, he cannot articulate, or properly know, what he does want. "I don't know – what I'm supposed to want," he confesses. All he can say to Willy, in a desperate declaration of personal love and social resistance, is "Pop! I'm a dime a dozen, and so are you!" Listening to Biff, Willy learns the value of love. Tragically, and typically, however, he then translates love into the only values he knows, the values of a salesman. What he gives Biff in return is the gift of himself, or rather his worth as an economic unit. Willy kills himself so that his family can have the insurance money and Biff, he hopes, can get a new start in life. "He had the wrong dreams, all, all, wrong," Biff observes of his father, as he stands beside his graveside. The tragedy of Willy Loman was that, and that he was tremulously aware of that. And, Miller makes it clear, it is the tragedy of a society as well.

The challenge that Willy Loman never quite meets, to know and name himself, is also the challenge that confronts John Proctor, the central character in *The Crucible* (1953), and Eddie Carbone, the protagonist in *A View from the Bridge* (1955; revised 1956). As in *Death of a Salesman*, too, that challenge is a personal one rooted in a social landscape: people in Miller's plays, especially the earlier ones, are compelled to confront themselves, and make the choices that define their lives, in terms that are determined by their history and society. Eddie Carbone cannot meet the challenge. John Proctor does meet the challenge, however. Written at the height of the hysteria whipped up by the Un-American Activities Committee, *The Crucible* explores issues of personal conscience and social suppression through the dramatic analogy of the 1692 Salem witchcraft trials. With the help of this analogy, Miller, who was himself a victim of the Committee, touches on all the consequences of McCarthyism: the exploitation of legitimate cultural fears, conspiracy theories, and social hysteria, the oppression of the innocent and the manipulation of power, the complicity of ordinary citizens and public officials in a paranoid social process that appears to take on an irresistible life of its own. When John Proctor's wife is named as a witch by a young woman, Abigail, with whom he has had an adulterous liaison, he attempts to expose the accuser. This, however, leads to his own arrest. Tempted to save his skin by confessing, he decides that honor requires his death. He has been drawn into examining his life by the accusations leveled at him; and he recognizes that, while innocent of witchcraft, he has other responsibilities to answer for. His confession of adultery with Abigail initiates an intense spiritual revaluation of himself. This leads, in turn, to the belief that even his execution for witchcraft would be unearned, since he is guilty while those he would be dying with are truly innocent. John confesses because he believes himself too ridden with guilt to die with honor. He recants, however, out of a sense of responsibility to the innocents he is to die with, and to himself. The demand that his signed confession be displayed in public is one that he feels compelled, ultimately, to resist. It would steal innocence from the truly innocent: "How may I live without my name," John asks his accusers. "I've given you my soul; leave me my name!'

After an absence of eight years from the New York stage, Miller returned in 1964 with *After the Fall* and *Incident at Vichy*. This was followed by *The Price*, in 1968, and *The Creation of the World and Other Business*, in 1972. The plays of this period are very different in terms of subject matter. *After the Fall* is a semi-autobiographical drama, based on Miller's marriage to Marilyn Monroe; *Incident at Vichy* deals with Nazi persecution of the Jews. In *The Price*, two brothers meet after the death of their father to arrange the sale of his furniture. In *The Creation of the World*, a serio-comic rewriting of the story of Adam and Eve, Adam must struggle to find a capacity for goodness, and moral responsibility in himself, to guide Eve towards forgiveness and Cain towards repentance. All of them, however, are marked by a shift from the social to the personal. Whatever the subject, the focus is on individual experience and the problem of individual guilt.

The personal resonance of plays like *After the Fall* was sustained in some of Miller's later works. *Elegy for a Lady* (1982), for example, is an elegant and ambiguous exploration of love. *Some Kind of Love Story* (1982), in a similarly intimate way, investigates the strange relationship between a private detective and a prostitute he has been questioning about a murder over the years. *I Can't Remember Anything* (1987) again concentrates on a couple, this time an elderly one, to dramatize the pleasures and the pains of old age. *Mr Peters' Connection* (2000) focuses on the title character, as he struggles to forge a connection between his past and present. A few other later dramas return, however, to the social emphasis of *Death of a Salesman* and *The Crucible*. *The Archbishop's Ceiling* (1977) uses the setting of an unnamed East European country to consider the responsibilities of the artist. Even more memorably, *The American Clock* (1986) returns to Miller's earlier dramatic explorations of the national democratic experiment. An epic history of the Depression of the 1930s, in both personal and public terms, the play focuses on the memories of two survivors. One, Les Baum, dwells on the domestic: the decline of his middle-class Jewish family into poverty. The other, a financier named Arthur Robertson, concentrates on the social: his survival, thanks to his ability to anticipate the economic crash. Together, though, the recollections of the two men register an abiding faith in the ability of the American nation to repair and redefine itself. What the Depression did ultimately, Miller suggests, was strengthen and affirm democracy, to give Americans back their belief in themselves – together with a renewed conviction that, as one character puts it, "the world was meant to be better."

For Tennessee Williams (1911–1983), too, the world was meant to be better; however, he and many of his characters believed that it had little chance of being so. "I write from my own tensions," Williams observed. "For me, this is a form of therapy." And those tensions drove him toward intensely poetic examinations of the injured spirit: the private pains and passions of lonely individuals for whom the task of living in the world is almost unendurable. "We're all of us sentenced to solitary confinement inside our own skins for life!" the main character Val Xavier in *Orpheus Descending* (1957) declares. "What does anyone wait for? For something to happen, for anything to happen, to make things make more sense." Waiting, and living in the meantime; so many of Williams's protagonists are concerned with nameless fears and insecurities – and with desperate desires, grasping at anything to offer distraction from the pain. Williams called his fragile, wounded characters "the fugitive kind."

The Glass Menagerie (1945) was the first drama to announce Williams's project of stretching ordinary domestic realism to explore extremes of sensibility and experience. The domestic setting of the play is transformed by being filtered through reminiscence. "The play is memory," Tom Wingfield, the narrator, announces at the beginning. "Being a memory play, it is dimly lighted, it is sentimental, it is not realistic." Tom's memories circulate around his family, living in genteel poverty in St. Louis during the Depression. Tom recalls his life with his mother Amanda, a faded Southern belle who clings persistently to glamorous illusions about her past, and with his sister Laura, a crippled, painfully shy young woman whose intensely private world is centered on a treasured collection of small glass animals. He recollects how he ached to leave home, but how his mother insisted he first supply a man to care for Laura in his absence. In a series of impressionistic scenes, Tim conjures up for us how he brought a visitor to the house, "an emissary from a world that we were somehow set apart from," and how the visit ended in disaster. And he remembers how he finally left home, never to return. Williams presents the Wingfield family as unable to function in reality, this "so called world of ours." But this seems more of a virtue than a weakness: the alternative space they inhabit seems as special and seductive as the world of glass animals that gives the play its title. Driven by guilt over his desertion of his mother and sister, Tom comes to realize this.

The intensely heightened realism that characterizes *The Glass Menagerie* marks all of Williams's finest work. It is there, above all, in his finest play, *A Streetcar Named Desire* (1947). Set in New Orleans, the plot is simple. Blanche Dubois visits her sister Stella and finds her married to what she calls an "animal," the crude, intensely physical Stanley Kowalski. Another faded Southern belle, Blanche has come "to the last stop at the end of the line," as the director of the first Broadway production of the play, Elia Kazan, put it. This is her last chance. She struggles for control of Stella with Stanley. She also struggles for a new life, a new romance with Stanley's friend Mitch. She fails. After a violent and sexual confrontation with Stanley, she is defeated and broken. And the play ends with Blanche being taken off to the asylum and Stella and Stanley still together. Williams explained once that the idea for the play came from a time when he himself was living in New Orleans. Near where he lived ran "two streetcars, one named DESIRE and the other named CEMETERY." For him, the "undiscourageable progress" of the two seemed to have "some symbolic bearing," to express the opposing fundamentals of experience. And they are certainly the tensions that threaten to tear Blanche apart. Blanche Dubois is torn between death and its opposite, desire, "the long parade to the graveyard" and the desperate longing to live and perhaps love. Resisting death, reaching out to desire, she engages in mortal combat with her brother-in-law for somewhere where things might make more sense. She "tries to make a place for herself," as Kazan put it. But there is no place for her.

A Streetcar Named Desire has the elemental force of a struggle for survival. It begins when Blanche invades the space occupied by Stanley and Stella. It lasts for the duration of a primitive fight for that space between Blanche and Stanley. It ends with Blanche's defeat and departure. So it signals a fundamental need that humans share with all animals, to secure territory. Building on this foundation, however, Williams weaves a complex tapestry of oppositions, as he describes the conflicting personalities of Blanche and Stanley. In a series of eleven tight, cinematic scenes, he uses every resource of theatrical language to tell us what, essentially, this man and woman are, and mean. Blanche is a Southern lady in a world with no use for ladies. Her need is to find protection, to secure her image of herself in the gaze of the, mostly male, other. Endowed with an evocative idiom, a theatricality of gesture and behavior, Blanche stands for illusion, idealism, culture, purity, love, the romance of the past. As her name intimates, she is associated with whiteness, the virgin of the zodiac, soft colors and soft lights: "I can't stand a naked light bulb," she declares as she puts up an "adorable little coloured paper lantern," "any more than I can a rude remark or a vulgar action." But, equally, she stands for "lies," falsehood, fantasy, and weakness: it is this, after all, that makes her vulnerable. "I've been on to you from the start!" Stanley declares just before the brutal climax of the play. "Not once did you pull any wool over this boy's eyes!"

That is a typical remark. Stanley is as tough and terse in words as he is in action. He believes that, as he puts it, you have "to hold front position in this rat-race" and, to do that, you need pluck and luck. His faith is in the facts, in prosaic reality rather than poetic idealism and illusion. His allegiance is to the rawly physical, the sexual rather than the spiritual. Associated with vivid colors, violent action, the goat of the zodiac and the strutting cockerel of folktale, he has no interest in the past. His commitment is to the present and the future, and what he can make out of them. "We've had this date with each other from the beginning!" Stanley says to Blanche immediately before he rapes her. It is a remark typical of the play, in its mix of brutality and mystery: suggesting, as it does, that these two antagonists are strangely fascinated with each other and with their antagonism. The "date" with each other, the conflict that is at the heart of *A Streetcar Named Desire*, operates on many levels. It is a fairytale, of beauty and the beast. It is a social history, of a declining old world and an emergent new one, translated into sexual terms. It is a mythic contest between the material and the moral, the "female" principle and the "male." It is also a painfully human tale of tension between two richly individualized characters. With its multiple levels of meaning and inflection, all of them founded on a raw base of feeling, *A Streetcar Named Desire* is a play constantly available to the discovery of fresh nuances. It is also a play that leaves its audiences torn between pity and fear as we contemplate the fate of Blanche Dubois.

Williams was only to approach the achievement of *A Streetcar Named Desire* in one or two of his later plays. *Cat on a Hot Tin Roof* (1955) is a powerful drama with a dual narrative. Big Daddy Pollitt, a Mississippi landowner, has to decide who should inherit his estate. Practical considerations clearly favor his sensible, reliable son Gooper; emotion and empathy draw him toward his childless and tortured son Brick. Brick and his wife Maggie, the "cat" of the title, have in turn to find some way of living together. Both narratives gravitate towards the discovery of emotional truth: the need to know and accept oneself. Big Daddy decides in favor of Brick, his natural heir and spiritual mirror – however warped that mirror may be; Brick and Maggie start to face the facts about themselves and their relationship. By contrast, *The Night of the Iguana* (1961) has a minimal plot. Weaving together very different characters, Williams explores his chosen theme of waiting for meaning with a characteristic mix of realism and poetic sensibility. This is not, unfortunately, the case with many of his other plays. Some, like *The Rose Tattoo* (1951) and *Period of Adjustment* (1960) are simply minor comedies. Others, such as *Suddenly Last Summer* (1958), stray into a sensationalism unanchored in emotional reality, the raw, intimate feeling that secures his best work. Still others, among them *Summer and Smoke* (1968), *Camino Real* (1953), *Orpheus Descending* (1957), and *Sweet Bird of Youth* (1959), suffer from an excess of symbolism.

Plagued by alcoholism, drugs, and depressive illness in his later years, Williams never completely lost his touch. Even in the most disappointing work, there are moments of corrosive pathos that recall the writer at his best. Such moments, however, tend to exist in a vacuum. Williams himself seemed to sense the decline in his own powers, as he compulsively rewrote material in a desperate attempt to make it work. *The Milk Train Doesn't Stop Here Anymore* (1963), for instance, was revised no less than three times. He also began to use his plays as confessionals. So, *In the Bar of a Tokyo Hotel* (1969) includes an artist suffering a mental and aesthetic breakdown: while in *Clothes for a Summer Hotel* (1980) Williams used F. Scott and Zelda Fitzgerald as barely disguised projections of his own sense of falling off and failure. The fact that he could not sustain the level of intensity that characterizes *A Streetcar Named Desire* is not perhaps remarkable. The fact that he could achieve it at all, there and in some other plays, is; and it makes him one of the two or three greatest American dramatists.

By the late 1950s, the dominance of Broadway was being challenged. Alternative theatre was appearing in New York City, first "Off-Broadway" as it was called, and then, when "Off-Broadway" came to acquire status, "Off Off-Broadway." New theatres and theatre companies were also developing in other parts of the country. By the 1980s, up to ten times as many new American plays were being produced outside Broadway as on; and the expanded theatrical arena inevitably encouraged a degree of experiment. Of the many dramatists who discovered the freedom first to experiment outside Broadway, the most notable are Edward Albee (1928–), Sam Shepard (1943–), and David Mamet (1947–). The first play by Edward Albee to be produced, first in Berlin in 1959, then in New York in 1960, *The Zoo Story*, introduced many of his obsessive themes: alienation, the human need and terror of contact, a nameless existential fear that seems to haunt all, but especially modern, life. Two plays that followed this, *The Death of Bessie Smith* (1961) and *The American Dream* (1961), give a more specifically American edge to Albee's explorations of human anxiety and alienation. The success of *The American Dream* enabled Albee to move to Broadway. There, in 1962, his best and most well received play was produced: *Who's Afraid of Virginia Woolf?* Set in a small New England college, it depicts the events of one night of passionate conflict and purgation. And, unlike Albee's earlier work, it gravitates towards domestic realism. To be more exact, this is domestic realism edged with a fiery poeticism. In this, as well as its portrait of characters who find everyday life almost unendurable, it recalls the work of Tennessee Williams: a debt that Albee slyly acknowledges through brief allusions to *A Streetcar Named Desire*. George, a history professor, and his wife Martha, bring a young colleague and his nervous wife back from a party. They involve the younger couple in a torrent of argument and abuse that appears to be a nightly ritual. After a second act that Albee has called "Walpurgisnacht," when the pain and purgation are pushed to the limit, comes the "Exorcism" of Act Three. The imaginary son that George and Martha have created, as some kind of sustenance and defense against the existential dread that haunts their lives, is declared dead by Martha. The couple acknowledge their illusions, and end the play facing an unknown future with a courage that comes from admitting their fear but not turning back, not trying to hide. To the question of who is afraid of Virginia Woolf – that is, is afraid of all the despair and insecurity of modern life, especially modern American life – the answer is that George and Martha are. But so is everybody. At least, George and Martha know they are; in that knowledge is a measure of redemption.

What is curious about *Who's Afraid of Virginia Woolf?*, in the light of Albee's subsequent development, is the way the play ultimately forces us to see George and Martha's immersion in life as strangely heroic. For them, if it hurts, it is real. Life, it seems to them and the action seems to suggest, is painful, unbearably difficult for those committed to living, rather than evading, it. The passion of that perception, however, a passion that consequently fires up the story of George and Martha, is precisely what is lacking from most of Albee's later work. Many of the later plays explore familiar themes. *Tiny Alice* (1964), for example, explores the absurd but inescapable nature of illusion. *A Delicate Balance* (1966) dramatizes human defense systems, how social and family rituals, even argument and aberrant behavior, act as temporary stays against confusion. *The Lady from Dubuque* (1980), in turn, presents dying, and the despair consequent on the knowledge of it, as a necessary adjunct of living. But none of these plays, not even the critically acclaimed *Three Tall Women* (1994) or the more recent *Me, Myself and I* (2007), has the sometimes bitter vitality of the early work. It is too intent on presenting an argument rather than a dramatic action.

Sam Shepard saw his first play performed Off Off-Broadway in 1964: *Cowboys*. Between then and 1975 he wrote more than twenty-five more. They include *Icarus's Mother* (1965), *La Tourista* (1966), *Operation Sidewinder* (1970), *Mad Dog Blues* (1971), *The Tooth of Crime* (1972), *Action* (1974), and *Geography of a Horse Dreamer* (1974). Most of them are notable for radical shifts of character, tone, and even dramatic medium, jazz-like rhythms of action and speeches resembling jazz riffs. Rarely linear, logical, or consistent, they habitually use settings and symbolism in which cowboys collide with monsters, rock mythology is mixed with religion and folklore, and the America of small farms and wide open spaces, fast cars and jukeboxes is invaded by magic and the supernatural. Certain themes recur, and were to become characteristic of Shepard's work: that, in a random, crazy world, human beings have to experiment with identity, that the failure to acknowledge magic is a fatal error of modern times – above all, that alienation from the spiritual is endemic in American culture and linked to alienation from the past. America, according to all these early plays, is heading in the wrong direction: away from the power of mystery to the power of the material. And nowhere is this clearer than in the best of them, *The Tooth of Crime*.

At the core of *The Tooth of Crime* is a mythic contest between Hoss, an ageing rock star, and Crow, a young newcomer with a new style. Typically of the work of this period, Shepard deploys a kaleidoscope of images, as his characters use a fast-talking, sharp-shooting range of styles in an attempt to impose alternative realities on each other. Hoss is a gypsy loner, a Mafia godfather, a boxing champion, the old pro; Crow is a teen gang leader, a lonely hit-man, the challenger, the new kid on the block. Above all, Hoss is a man with a history and roots, simultaneously enriched and weakened by his accomplishments and his knowledge of his art. Crow is a boy with no knowledge beyond his own limited experience, no sense of commitment to any community or communal inheritance: with the strength and freedom that his own alienation and amorality bring. Hoss is the past, Crow the future; given that, the outcome of the contest between them is inevitable. All Hoss can do, finally, to reaffirm his identity, is kill himself with a stylishness that Crow can only envy.

Not long after writing *The Tooth of Crime*, Shepard moved away from the disjunctive narrative rhythms of his earlier work. He remained committed to a theatre of extremes, emotional and actorly. But his style gravitated closer to domestic realism, the dynamics of the familiar and obsessive intimacy. Bizarre events and brutal emotional violence still occurred, but there were no longer such radical shifts in language and form. This alteration of style was announced in *Curse of the Starving Class* (1977), the first play in a trilogy exploring the relationship of Americans to their land, family, and history; the other two are *A Buried Child* (1979), probably his finest play to date, and *True West* (1980). At the center of *A Buried Child* is a family that embodies the corruption of the American spirit; a corruption that Shepard was to address more directly later, in what he called his "take-off on Republican fascism," *The God of Hell* (2007). The child that supplies the title of *A Buried Child* is the product of an incestuous union whom the family have killed. Clearly, what Shepard is rehearsing here is what he sees as a general national compulsion to bury the past, to rewrite history so as to retain the illusion of innocence. The process is not irreversible, the play intimates. In the final scene, the father of the buried child enters with its exhumed body in his arms. As he does so, the offstage voice of the mother of the family announces a miraculous abundance of vegetables springing up on a farm that, until then, had been a waste land. The resurrection of the family, and by implication America, is possible. All it needs is courage to face and embrace the past. With that, it will again be "paradise out there."

The power of *A Buried Child*, and of so many of Shepard's plays in his mature style, stems from his weaving together of the domestic and the mythic, volcanic emotions and vast landscapes. So, in *True West*, Shepard explores a uniquely American myth through the claustrophobic tale of two brothers writing a script. The script is about a chase: one man pursuing another across the country. Gradually, the two brothers become the two men in the script. The real and the fictional coalesce; and this answers the question slyly posed in the play's title. The myth of America *is* its reality, Shepard suggests, the dream of the West *is* the true West. What dream and truth, myth and reality both involve, in turn, is the immensity of human feeling and setting: drives and desires that sweep through men and women like a whirlwind. In *Fool for Love* (1983), for instance, the two central characters are lovers, half-brother and sister, who cannot live apart or together. They are victims of a passion that is like an elemental force; lurching from one extreme to another, tenderness is inseparable from violence for them, and love from hate. The motel on the margins of the desert where the passion is acted out translates their condition into material terms. It is, like each of them, each of their bodies, a small, frail enclosure in the middle of an empty immensity, which can barely contain the elements careering within it. To be human, it seems for Shepard both here and in all his work, is to be in the eye of the storm.

Like Albee and Shepard, David Mamet used the freedom of the theatre outside Broadway to find a style. Mamet first achieved success with *The Duck Variations* (1972) and *Sexual Perversity in Chicago* (1974). They introduced his characteristic style. This is not so much the vernacular, or the idiom of an actual subculture, as an intensely poetic instrument. Repetition, intensification, a shared jargon and rhythm: all are used by the characters to create the feeling of a club – a closed world, with its own games, secret signs, and codes. These two early plays also introduced Mamet's obsessive interest in how people use language, not just as a communicative tool, but to give the illusion of substance and significance, to their lives. The truth of fiction, sounding right, is similarly important to the characters in *American Buffalo* (1975) and *Glengarry Glen Ross* (1984), two plays which also take us into the dark heart, the selling of America. In *American Buffalo*, some minor criminals planning a robbery use a language that combines the mannerly and the vulgar, the precious and the obscene, while *Glengarry Glen Ross* turns from robbers planning a robbery to salesmen planning a sale. Mamet makes the one seem in no way morally superior to the other. The salesmen are selling tracts of land in Florida; and the Scottish lilt of the title refers to the fantasy names given to what are worthless pieces of real estate, virtual swamp. The distinction of the play lies precisely in its revaluation of the perverse resourcefulness of the salesmen. To earn a living, they have to combine the cynicism appropriate to their fraudulent trade with a belief in their skill, the power and value of their virtuoso sales techniques. Their language tells their story. It is the story of a club of men for whom "a great sale" is the fiction that gives false meaning to their lives. So, in its own way, the play is as devastating a critique of the American myth of success as *Death of a Salesman*. Mamet has continued to explore characters who create a local habitation and a name for themselves out of fast talk, shared slang, and smart conversation. *Speed-the-Plow* (1988) is set in Hollywood, with its flattery and fake intimacy. *Oleander* (1992) deals with the issue of sexual harassment in the story of a female student who denounces a university professor. Whether she has a legitimate grievance or is working with her "group" to achieve a kind of ethical cleansing, or whether there is a mix of both at work here, is never made clear. The audience is left in suspension; and, in a way, this is how the typical Mamet play always leaves us. All his characters are not so much liars as accomplished fantasists: who use the wiles of words, sometimes knowingly and sometimes not, to suspend disbelief in the fantasies they inhabit. As such, they offer a comment, not just on their own subcultures, but on American culture generally.

One result of the exponential growth in other theatrical arenas in America has been the increase in the production of plays by writers from previously marginalized groups. Notable here is the emergence of many women playwrights, including Marsha Norman (1947–), Wendy Wasserstein (1950–2006), and Beth Henley (1952–). Norman saw her first play, *Getting Out* (1977), produced in Louisville, Kentucky; other, later plays include *Circus Valentine* (1979) and *The Hold-Up* (1980). But it is *'Night, Mother* (1982) that has brought her her greatest success so far. At the center of the play is a woman in her forties, Jessie Cates, who tells her mother that she plans to commit suicide. Resisting every attempt her mother makes to dissuade her, she outlines her reasons for killing herself. "I'm just not having a very good time," she explains, "and I don't have any reason to think it'll get anything but worse." *'Night, Mother* is not so much about the ethics of suicide, as about the right of the individual to control her own destiny. After forty or so years, Jessie is taking control of her life. In all this, *'Night, Mother* is very much in the American grain. Very much in the Southern grain, by contrast, are the plays of Beth Henley, her most notable being *Crimes of the Heart* (1979) and *The Miss Firecracker Contest* (1981). The women who dominate her work offer variations on the Southern grotesque. Simultaneously feisty and fantastic, bold and bizarre, they tend to see life askew and respond to events in a quirky way that hardly distinguishes between the serious and the trivial. Their quirkiness turns out, however, to be a survival technique.

Survival is also an issue at the heart of the plays of Wendy Wasserstein. In *Uncommon Women and Others* (1977), *Isn't It Romantic?* (1983), *The Heidi Chronicles* (1988), and *Third* (2005), Wasserstein took as her subject her own generation of women, shaped by the feminist aspirations of the 1970s. *Uncommon Women*, for example, explores the lives of a group of ambitious young women in an exclusive college. They receive ambiguous messages about their destiny from their teachers, family, and society. Confused by these messages, they pursue different destinies, none of which seems satisfactory. In a concluding section set some six years after the main action, these "uncommon women" are still trying to find ways of expressing their uncommonness, their difference from the norm prescribed for previous generations of women. Nothing has really been resolved. "I'm afraid I haven't really been happy for some time," the main character, Heidi Holland, in *The Heidi Chronicles*, admits, "It's just that I feel stranded." That is a shared feeling among female characters in these plays: confusion, irresolution, the sense of an immeasurable gap between what they want and what their society tells them they can get. Despite that, these characters at some elemental level reveal an indestructible optimism: the belief that, as Heidi Holland puts it, "maybe, just maybe, things will be a little better."

It was not until the late 1960s that another minority group was able openly to dramatize issues of identity. Up until then, a homosexual playwright like Tennessee Williams had to explore his homosexuality by stealth and indirection. From one perspective, for example, Blanche Dubois can be seen as a mask: a concealed means of expressing what it feels like to be different from the moral majority. With plays like *The Boys in the Band* (1968) by Mart Crowley (1945–), however, the subject of male or female homosexuality came directly to be addressed. *The Boys in the Band*, although it suffers from a tendency to conform to the stereotype of the anguished, self-hating gay, was one of the first commercially successful plays to deal with its gay characters not only openly but with considerable sympathy. Other, later dramas that deal with the homosexual community and focus on homosexuals, and made their way into the mainstream theatre, include *As Is* (1985) by William M. Hoffman (1935–) and *The Normal Heart* (1985) by Larry Kramer (1935–). Above all, there is *The Torch Song Trilogy* (1981) by Harvey Fierstein (1954–). In three plays originally written and produced separately, Fierstein uses a dramatic persona, Arnold Beckoff, to consider the evolution of homosexuals to social acceptance and, more important, acceptance of themselves. A deft blend of autobiography, comedy, domestic realism, and social naturalism, the trilogy concludes with Beckoff mourning the loss of his lover and partner. By now, he has discovered that, in his own way, he is as "normal" – if that is the right word – as everyone else: wanting a home, a loving partnership, the right to mourn his loved one openly. By now his mother recognizes this, too, acknowledging that his widowhood is the emotional and moral equivalent of her own, and that his sexual preference and status have to be honored.

Apart from some of the African American playwrights discussed earlier, the most notable dramatist from the racially marginalized minorities is David Henry Hwang (1957–). His first play, *F.O.B.* (1978), deals with the cultural conflict between those of Chinese origin born in America and those "fresh off the boat," newly arrived immigrants. It was followed by *Family Devotion* (1981), which explores a similar theme, *The Dance and the Railroad* (1981), based on a strike in 1867 by Chinese workers on a railroad, *Sound and Beauty* (1983), consisting of two one-act plays, and *Rich Relations* (1986). His early plays met with varying fortunes, but in 1988 Hwang achieved major success with *M. Butterfly*. The play was inspired by a 1986 newspaper account of a bizarre relationship. A French diplomat, on trial for espionage, was revealed to have had a twenty-six year relationship with someone he believed to be a Chinese woman, whereas in fact "she" was not only a spy but also a man. From this story, Hwang got his idea for what he called "a deconstructivist *Madame Butterfly*" addressing a complex web of racial and sexual issues. The basic arc of the play, as Hwang explains in an afterword, is simple. "The Frenchman fantasizes that he is Pinkerton and his lover Butterfly," Hwang says. "By the end of the piece, he realizes that it is he who has been Butterfly, in that the Frenchman has been duped in love; the Chinese spy, who exploited that love, is therefore the real Pinkerton." What expands and enriches that arc, though, is Hwang's understanding of how issues of race and gender, cultural and imperial politics intersect here; how the tragic blindness of the Frenchman involves multiple levels of misrecognition. Hwang has the Chinese lover, Song, allude to those levels in his courtroom testimony after the two are finally caught: "The West thinks of itself as masculine – big guns, big industry, big money – so the East is feminine – weak, delicate, poor." For Hwang, as for Song, the tale of the French diplomat and his lover is not so extraordinary, given what the author calls "the degree of misunderstanding between men and women and also between East and West." "Her mouth says no but her eyes say yes," as Song puts it. "The West believes the East, deep down, *wants* to be dominated."

In *M. Butterfly*, Hwang offers a powerful metaphor for the way men misperceive women and the West misperceives the East: themes he was to continue exploring in his play *Yellow Face* (2007) and his reworking of a popular musical, *Flower Drum Song* (2003). The events of *M Butterfly* coincide with the period of the Vietnam War, alluded to several times, which gives them additional resonance. The metaphor is powerful because it is dramatic. None of this would have worked if Hwang had not fashioned a compelling action that, besides being strong on insight, is a strange kind of love story. René Gallimard, the Frenchman blinded to reality by his consuming desire *not* to see the truth, is a character who inspires sympathy as well as stupefaction. Song, besides being given to what the judge at his trial caustically terms "armchair political theory," is a man caught up in his own fantasies about women. The reason that he makes what Gallimard calls "the Perfect Woman" is precisely that he knows what men intend by that phrase. "There is a vision of the Orient that I have," Gallimard eventually confesses, "Of . . . women willing to sacrifice themselves for the love of a man." Challenged with veritable fact, Gallimard will not surrender that vision. "I've finally learned to tell fantasy from reality. And, knowing the difference, I choose fantasy," he announces. For Gallimard, "death with honor is better than life." That, in his case, means killing himself with the declaration, "My name is René Gallimard – also known as Madame Butterfly." It is a strange kind of honor that compels him to become his own fantasy. It measures just how far men see themselves and their needs in women, how far the West projects its will to power and domination on to the East. This is a genuine tragedy and, on one level, a genuinely American one.

New Journalists and dirty realists

Realism is a slippery term, but it is true to say that the realistic approach, allied to the domestic setting, has been the staple of the American theatre. In prose writing, fictional and non-fictional, it also became the weapon, in particular, of those who came to be known as the New Journalists. In fact, according to the man who has seen himself as the chief publicist for the New Journalism, Tom Wolfe (1931–), realism is now, or should be, the core of all serious writing. Wolfe's specific argument here has been with those American writers who, as he sees it, have ignored their primary obligation, to catch the manners and comment on the morals of their times, and who have instead pursued fantasy and absurdism, myth and magic. For Wolfe, the counter-revolutionary movement, a return to social realism, began in the early 1960s, with the appearance of articles and books that explored non-fictional subjects using some of the classic strategies of realist fiction. The main exponents of this new way of writing, registering the rich social fabric of contemporary America were, he suggested, him, of course, Norman Mailer, Joan Didion, and Truman Capote (1924–1984).

According to Wolfe, the good New Journalist should stick to the facts as far as he can, the ones he has gathered as a reporter. But in retelling those facts, he uses certain novelistic techniques that have helped give the realistic novel its unique power; these techniques are essentially four. First is an extensive use of dialogue: so the New Journalist needs to be a skillful interviewer and careful recorder. Second is a detailed and exact recording of the everyday gestures, habits, manners of people, their styles of clothing, furniture, and so on. Third is a careful arrangement of the narrative, scene by scene. Fourth is a consistent use of narrative point of view, so that the reader can see things just as the reporter saw them. Curiously, this formula does not precisely inform Wolfe's own non-fiction. He has published many collections of essays commenting on contemporary American culture, from its popular heroes to its alternative lifestyles. The collections include *The Kandy-Kolored Tangerine-Flame Streamline Baby* (1965), *Radical Chic and Mau-Mauing the Flak Catchers* (1970), *The Painted Word* (1975) about the pretensions of the art world, and *The Right Stuff* (1979) about the

US astronauts, "gods for a day." But, as the titles of many of these collections suggest, what most of his essays are notable for is their wit, bravura, and high octane prose: a baroque pop style that offers a sardonic comment on their subjects. His prescription for the New Journalism does not fit his own non-fiction; nor does it fit the immense Swiftian satire of his novels, *The Bonfire of the Vanities* (1987), *A Man in Full* (1998), and *I Am Charlotte Simmons* (2004). Rather, it fits perfectly some of the work of Norman Mailer (*The Armies of the Night, The Executioner's Song*) and Joan Didion (*Slouching Towards Bethlehem, The White Album*), and the later writing of Truman Capote, above all *In Cold Blood* (1966).

Capote had already acquired a reputation before he published *In Cold Blood*, with books such as *Other Voices, Other Rooms* (1948), a gothic tale about a homosexually inclined boy groping towards maturity, *The Grass Harp* (1951), and *Breakfast at Tiffany's* (1958), about a light-hearted, freewheeling, romantic playgirl living in New York City. *In Cold Blood* was something different. It was based on fact. In 1959 two ex-convicts, Perry Smith and Richard Hickock, broke into the isolated farmhouse of a respectable family called the Clutters, tied up the four family members who were there, then killed them. All they got, for loot, was between forty and fifty dollars. Having learned about the brutal incident, Capote worked on and off for five years, interviewing friends and family, surviving members, and detectives investigating the murders. Then, once Smith and Hickock were caught, Capote got to know them as well, talking to them during the trial, after their conviction, and right up until the time of their execution in 1965. Out of the mass of material he accumulated, Capote then produced what he called his "Non-Fiction Novel." His aim in writing it, he explained, was to make the cold fact of the murder understandable; by implication, it was to make the violence characteristic of contemporary society understandable. And the best way he could do this, he felt, was by presenting that cold fact in the context of other facts: above all, by avoiding anything not derived from observation, interview, and record. Capote tries to avoid commentary in the book; he also seeks to eschew analysis, social or psychological, simply presenting what he has seen or heard. He does, however, permit himself use of the four novelistic devices Wolfe prescribed for the New Journalism. In particular, the entire narrative is carefully structured scene by scene, section by section. The first section, for instance, leads slowly up to the killing, building tension by cutting between the Clutter family and Smith and Hickock driving towards them. The second concentrates on the search for the killers, the third describes them after their arrest and during their trial, and the fourth, final section brings them to death row and eventual execution.

Using this narrative arrangement, Capote avoids sensationalism. For example, the actual murders are only described in the third section, through the recollection and confessions of the murderers; there is no attempt made to step outside of this, in some kind of voyeuristic, melodramatic way. What he avoids, though, is less important than what he gains. *In Cold Blood* takes violence out of the backwoods and the city – their usual sites in American fiction – and into the heartland. In doing so, it vividly juxtaposes the contrasts and contradictions of American life. The dream and the nightmare, American normalcy and its dark underbelly: these opposites are powerfully registered, thanks to Capote's method of presentation. More than that, they come together in direct conflict in the central event of the book. Capote cannot entirely absent himself in terms of sympathy from the narrative. He was clearly drawn to one of the murderers, the misfit Perry Smith, and it shows. He was also a stranger to the kind of middle American tastes and habits the Clutters embodied, and that occasionally shows too. But this is a book that works because, most of the time, it is dispassionate. Capote captures, with a cold but uncynical eye, the bleak emptiness of life on the vast wheat plains of Kansas, that area of the Midwest where the Clutters lived and worked. With equal dispassion, he catches the quiet desperation of Smith and Hickock, as they wander across the country in search of a job or, more often, in search of someone to rob and perhaps kill. There is no explanation supplied for the killing. Things happen, people suffer; those who make them suffer must suffer in turn. That is the closest *In Cold Blood*, wedded to the cult of the fact, comes to a judgment. Otherwise, it is left to the reader to see the violence as random, gratuitous, meaningless – and, to that extent, peculiarly typical of America and the contemporary American scene.

The prose style of *In Cold Blood* is one of scrupulous meanness. Capote was to use it again, with less success, in later books like *Music for Chameleons* (1980), a collection of pieces, and his unfinished novel, *Answered Prayer* (1986). It is also a style that is favored by those writers known as dirty realists. They include Bobbie Ann Mason and Jayne Ann Phillips, at least in their early work, Larry Brown (1945–2004) and Harry Crews. What these writers honor and articulate are the lives of the working poor: people who have to sell their labor, or even their bodies, to live and who might, at any time, lose everything, including the basic dignities that make human beings human. "This is America, where money's more serious than death." That remark, coined by Harry Crews, could act as an epigraph to the work of many of the dirty realists. For that matter, it could act as an epigraph to the work of the first and finest of them, Raymond Carver (1938–1988). During his lifetime, Carver published several collections of short stories, among them *Will You Be Quiet, Please?* (1976), *What We Talk About When We Talk About Love* (1981), *Cathedral* (1984), and *Where I'm Calling From* (1988). Terse and toughly graceful, these stories sometimes recall the work of Hemingway in the way the writer uses omission, the spaces between the words to catch evanescent, elusive feelings. They also resemble the early short stories of Hemingway, in particular, in their quiet stoicism, their allegiance to the concrete, their cleaving to the stark surfaces and simple rituals of everyday life. What is remarkable about Carver's stories is the way they combine weariness with wonder: an acknowledgment of the sheer grind and cruelty of life, especially for the poor, with the occasional moment of relief, revelation. So, in a story called "A Small, Good Thing," a small boy is killed in a road accident just before his birthday. The cake ordered for the birthday celebration is, naturally enough, not picked up by the parents. The baker, not knowing the reason, is outraged, and starts making a series of abusive phone calls. Confronted by the angry, heartbroken parents at his bakery, all he can say is, "I'm just a baker," "I'm sorry. Forgive me, if you can." And a little more: he can offer them some freshly baked rolls. "Eating is a small, good thing in a time like this," he tells the mother and father of the dead boy. It is not much, next to nothing in a dark world, but it is *not* nothing. The three sit together in the clean, well-lighted place of the bakery, eating and talking. And the parents, the story concludes, "did not think of leaving."

Realism slips into stylistic minimalism in the work of Carver and the dirty realists. In *Last Exit to Brooklyn* (1964) by Hubert Selby Jr. (1928–2004), a vivid, sometimes obscene account of the violence and corruption of contemporary urban life, it slides into gothic documentary. Outside of certain genre reading, though, such as the detective story, the thriller, and the police procedural, the area where it has had most conspicuous impact in recent times is in the various accounts, fictional or non-fictional, of the war in Vietnam. Some of the best of these accounts in fiction circulate around memories of the Vietnam War: *In Country, Machine Dreams,* and *Ray* (1980) by Barry Hannah, whose protagonist, a Vietnam veteran, appears to live by the maxim, "It is terribly, excruciatingly difficult to be at peace when all our history is war." Others are devoted to the combat zone. The military experience of Tim O'Brien (1946–), for instance, has been the material of most of his novels, especially in the three most notable, thinly fictionalized ones. *If I Die in a Combat Zone, Box Me Up and Ship Me Home* (1973) is a series of linked sketches; *The Things They Carried* (1990) explores the futility of searching for the truth about what happens, or why, in war; *Going for Cacciato* (1978) stretches into magic realism as it follows a breakaway group of soldiers marching across Asia to Paris. O'Brien has also explored the legacy of the Vietnam past as it haunts the American present, in *Northern Lights* (1975) and *In the Lake of the Woods* (1994).

Among all the literary treatments of the Vietnam War, though, the one that stands out is a work of non-fiction, in the vein of the New Journalism: *Dispatches* (1977) by Michael Herr (1940–). There have been many other non-fictional accounts, notably *A Rumor of War* (1977) by Philip Caputo (1941–) – which Caputo tersely described as "simply a story about war, about the things men do in war and the things war does to them." But no account matches *Dispatches* in its narrative power, its ability to capture the brutally material yet dreamlike quality of combat, its strangely unreal reality. Herr deploys direct address, pacy language, the syncopations of jazz, rock, and pop to register a battle landscape that is also a 1960s spectacle. Here, the phrase "theatre of war" takes on a series of meanings, since this is a real conflict shot through with alternative realities: media events, bad drug trips, John Wayne movies, and rock concerts. Real and basic enough, however, are the "shitty choices" with which the "grunts" are confronted. They can have "fear and motion" or "fear and standstill," Herr observes. *Dispatches* is a great non-fiction novel about war because, caught in its panoramic field of vision, is the insanity of combat as it was experienced by men standing on the edge of death every moment of every day. And, in its dark way, the book has its own heroes: those men themselves, the "grunts," who somehow made their way through things – with the help of black humor, bleak cynicism, and the belief that, in a world without logic, the only logical thing to do was to go with the flow, stick to the job, and try to stay alive.

Language and Genre

Watching nothing: Postmodernity in prose

When Wolfe was cataloguing the forms of the contemporary American novel that, he believed, had failed in the primary duty to the real, he picked out one group for particular condemnation. They were the postmodernists. For their part, some of those writers have returned the compliment. One of them, for example, clearly thinking of figures like Raymond Carver, has referred to the school of "Post Alcoholic Blue-Collar Minimalist Hyperrealism." The opposition is not universal, nor even inevitable. Nevertheless, it has been there at times: between the New Journalists and the Fabulators, the dirty realists and the fantasists or systems builders. And it is mapped out clearly in the gap that separates Wolfe, Carver, and the Capote of *In Cold Blood* from the wholehearted postmodernists of contemporary American writing: notably, Thomas Pynchon (1937–) and John Barth (1930–). Pynchon is perhaps the most acclaimed and personally the most elusive of the postmodernists. Relatively little is known about him, which adds to the mystique his fiction projects: since that projection is of a world on the edge of apocalypse, threatened by a vast conspiracy directed by or maybe against an established power elite. This conspiracy, the intimation is, is decipherable through a series of arcane signs. The signs, however, require interpretation, decoding according to the rules of structural paranoia. And one of those rules is that structural paranoia is impossible to distinguish from clinical paranoia. So interpretation may be a symptom rather than a diagnosis. Pynchon's novels are extraordinarily intricate webs, self-reflexive halls of mirrors, because they replicate the world as text – a system of signs that must but cannot be interpreted.

Pynchon has been his own fiercest critic. In an introductory essay to his early stories, *Slow Learner* (1984), he has said that his fundamental problem when he began writing was an inclination "to begin with a theme, symbol, or other unifying agent, and then try to force characters and events to conform to it." His books are certainly packed with ideas and esoteric references; and, whether one agrees with this self-criticism or not, it is clear that Pynchon laid down his intellectual cards early. The title of his first important short story is "Entropy" (1960). It contains specific references to Henry Adams; and it follows carefully the Adams formulation, "Chaos was the law of nature; Order was the dream of man." The use of entropy as a figure for civilization running down was to become structurally formative in his later fiction. So was his use of two kinds of characters, alternative central figures first sketched out here. The situation in "Entropy" is simply and deliberately schematic. There is a downstairs and upstairs apartment. Downstairs, a character called Meatball Mulligan is holding a lease-breaking party, which moves gradually towards chaos and consequent torpor. Upstairs, another character, an intellectual called Callisto, is trying to warm a freezing bird back to life. In his room he maintains a small hothouse jungle, referred to as a "Rousseau-like fantasy." "Hermetically sealed, it was a tiny enclave in the city's chaos," the reader is told, "alien to the vagaries of the weather, national politics, or any civil disorder." The room is a fantasy, a dream of order, in which Callisto has "perfected its ecological balance."

"Entropy," in this way, mediates between binary opposites which are the opposites of modern consciousness and culture. There is the pragmatist, active to the point of excess, doing what he can with the particular scene, working inside the chaos to mitigate it. And there is the theorist, passive to the point of paralysis, trying to shape and figure the cosmic process, standing outside as much as he can, constructing patterns for the chaos to explain it. Meatball is immersed, drowning in the riotous present; Callisto is imprisoned in the hermetically sealed glasshouse of the past. The text, which here and later is the dominant presence in Pynchon's writing, is the interface between these two figures, these two systems of experience.

In his first novel, *V* (1963), Pynchon returned to two formative characters recalling Callisto and Meatball in the shape of Hubert Stencil and Benny Profane. The book confirms its author's sense of the modern world as an entropic waste land, inhabited by people dedicated to the annihilation of all animatedness. It is bounded by dead landscapes, urban, mechanical, underground. A populous narrative, it is also packed with characters who are ciphers: seeing others and themselves, not as people, but as things, objects, they lapse into roles and cliché. Blown along the mean streets, and even meaner sewers, of this story, Benny Profane is a *schlemiehl*, the suffering absurd comedian of Jewish lore. A faded copy of a picaro, he drifts through life in such enterprises as hunting alligators underneath New York City; it is there in the darkness of the sewers that he finds his greatest comfort and peace. Hubert Stencil, on the other hand, searches the world for V., the mysterious female spy and anarchist who is by turns Venus, Virgin, Void, and seems everywhere and nowhere. Stencil appears to be on a significant quest. Described as "a century's child" and born in 1901, he is pursuing the remnants of the Virgin in the world of the Dynamo. His father, a former British spy, has left behind enigmatic clues pointing to a vast conspiracy in modern history. So, whereas Profane lives in a world of sightlessness without signs or discernible patterns, Stencil enters a world of elusive signs and apparent patterns, all gravitating toward an absent presence, the lady V. His quest is for a fulcrum identity. In a sense, he is given an outline identity by his search, since he thinks of himself as "quite purely He who looks for V. (and whatever impersonations that involves)." It is also for the identity of modern times. Using the oblique strategy of "attack and avoid," Stencil moves through many of the major events of the twentieth century, seeking to recover the master plot, the meanings of modern history and this book. The only meaning found, however, is the erasure of meaning: the emptying of a significant human history and its sacrifice to mechanism and mass.

At the heart of *V* is a paradox characteristic of all Pynchon's work. Its enormous historical bulk and vast social fabric is so constructed that it may be deconstructed, so complexly created that it may be doubted then decreated. The deconstruction is there, centrally, in the controlling sign of V. herself, "a remarkably scattered concept" as we are told. A shifting letter attached to a historical process of progressive de-animation, the human figure is translated into a figure of speech. The other two compositional principles of the novel, Stencil and Profane, may apparently be opposed, just as Callisto and Meatball are, as the creator of patterns and the man of contingency, the constructive and the deconstructive, he who seeks and he who floats. They are joined, however, not only in a failure of significance but a failure of identity. Their names are parodies, their words and gestures gamesome or stereotypical, their physical bearing a series of masks. As such, they offer playful variations on a definition of life supplied during the novel: as "a successive rejection of personalities." In the simplest sense, *V* is not a book without a subject or a plot. But in another, more elemental sense, it is. Not only a text about indeterminacy, *V* is an indeterminate text: its significance, its subject is the lack, the impossibility of one.

Almost the last reported words of V. are, "How pleasant to watch Nothing." In his subsequent fiction, Pynchon has continued this watching in a variety of fictional guises. So, in both his second novel, *The Crying of Lot 49* (1966), and his third, *Gravity's Rainbow* (1973), the narrative ends with the enigma it poses unsolved, the plot and its meaning unresolved. *Gravity's Rainbow* is set in the closing years of World War II. The story, a complex web of plots and counterplots, involves a Nazi Lieutenant Weissman, disguised as a mysterious Captain Blicero, and an American sleuth, Lieutenant Tyron Slothrop, while V-2 rockets rain down on London. Weissman, it appears, was once the lover of V.: in this elaborately intertextual world, Pynchon's texts echo his own as well as the texts of others. The gravitations of mood are characteristic: from black humor to lyricism to science fiction to fantasy. So is the feeling the reader experiences, while reading this book, that he or she is encountering, not so much different levels of meaning or reality, as different planes in fictive space, with each plane in its shadow box proving to be a false bottom, in an evidently infinite regression. So, also, finally is the suspicion of conspiracy: *Gravity's Rainbow* explores the possibility that, as one character puts it, "war was never political at all, the politics was all theatre, all just to keep the people distracted."

In this fictive maze, the V-2 rocket assumes an elusive significance. The intimations of a conspiratorial system, here "dictated ... by the needs of technology" is wedded, in a way characteristic of Pynchon, to a centrally, crucially indeterminate sign. Like V., the V-2 rocket is as compelling as it is mysterious, as beautiful as it is dangerous, constantly dissolving into nothingness, deadly. Since *Gravity's Rainbow*, Pynchon has moved forward to the landscape of the 1980s and, through ample reminiscence, the 1960s in *Vineland* (1990), then back to the early twentieth century in *Against the Day* (2006). In between those two novels, he moved back to the early republic in *Mason and Dixon* (1997): to the days when men like the two famous surveyors mentioned in the title were trying to establish boundaries in the boundlessness of America, in order to appropriate it. America is memorably described in this novel as "a very Rubbish-Tip for subjunctive Hopes, for all that *may yet be true*." It is the landscape that inhabits all Pynchon's fiction. The fictive energy of Pynchon seems inexhaustible, because it careers tirelessly between contraries. And what drives it is summed up in one simple question one central character asks the other in this novel: "Good Christ, Dixon. What are we about?"

The narrator of John Barth's second novel, *The End of the Road* (1958), begins the story he is to tell with a sly parody of the opening sentence of *Moby-Dick*: "In a sense, I am Jake Horner." That use of language to set up distances is characteristic. The distances are several: between reader and character (Horner is already asking us to look at him as only "in a sense" what he names himself), narrator and character (who only "in a sense" form a negotiable, nameable identity) – above all, between the world inside the text and the world outside. Barth has proved to be his own best critic precisely because his is a fiction that continually backs up on itself, subverting any temptation to link that fiction to reality by commenting on form. His texts and characters are constantly commenting on themselves, or inviting such comment. His fourth novel, *Giles Goat-Boy* (1966), for instance, begins with fictive letters of introduction by several editors that suggest, among other things, that the author is "unhealthy, embittered, desperately unpleasant, perhaps masturbative, perhaps alcoholic or insane, if not a suicide." "This author," one editor complains, "has maintained ... that language *is* the matter of his books"; "he turns his back on what *is the case*, rejects the familiar for the amazing, embraces artifice and extravagance; washing his hands of the search for Truth, he calls himself ... 'doorman of the Muses' Fancy-house.'"

"What *is the case*" is a sly allusion to a famous remark made by the philosopher Ludwig Wittgenstein: "The world is all that is the case." The world, Wittgenstein argues, is the sum of what we take to be true and believe that others take to be true. We construct our world from the inside out; and the crucial weapon in those configurations is the system of language we have at our disposal. Inadvertently, one of the fictive editors reveals the project that is at the heart of all Barth's fiction, and all other work that is sometimes called postmodern and sometimes metafiction. Everything is only "in a sense" this or that it is named. The self is the sum of its rules, its locutions; the world is the sum of our constructions of it; any apparent essence, any "natural" being or feeling, is really a social construct, a sign of culture trying to wear the mask of nature (and "nature" is a cultural convention, too); and the text refers to nothing but itself. The ultimate postmodern protagonist is perhaps Echo in *Lost in the Funhouse* (1968), Barth's first collection of stories, who "becomes no more than her voice." That, together with the self-referential nature of his language and the self-reflexive character of his fiction, may make Barth's work sound abstract to the point of being ossified. It is not, because the voice is vital: his novels and stories are as packed with voices, energetic, comically ebullient, often ironic, as Pynchon's are with masks and figures. Not only that, in his hands, the prisonhouse of language becomes a funhouse: a place for play and passionate virtuosity.

As for voices: these range from the tones of the narrator of Barth's first novel, *The Floating Opera* (1956), recalling his experiences on the day in 1937 when he debates suicide, to the multiple voices of his fifth novel, *Letters* (1979). As its title implies, *Letters* is an unusual development of epistolary fiction. In it, seven more or less parallel narratives are revealed through correspondence written by seven characters from Barth's earlier fiction, including the author himself as just another imaginary figure. The intricate story that emerges is a characteristic enquiry into enclosure and liberation: the patterns into which all seven characters have previously been set, the degree of freedom they may possibly discover. Life equals language equals story. That is the formula animating Barth's work. To cease to narrate is to die: a point that Barth makes more or less explicit in his use of the figure of Scheherezade in the opening story in his collection, *Chimera* (1972). Scheherezade was the figure in Arabian folktale who stayed alive simply by telling stories. Telling stories, in turn, spins into fantasy. Barth is fond of creating worlds within worlds, using parody and pastiche, verbal and generic play to produce multiple, layered simulacra: that is, copies of something for which the original never existed. It could and can never exist, because there was and is no reality prior to the imitation, to tales and telling. So, in *The Sot-Weed Factor* (1960), Barth takes up the author of the 1708 Maryland poem with the same title, Ebenezer Cooke, about whom virtually nothing is known. He then uses Cooke as the hero of a lusty picaresque tale that is a pastiche of history, conventional historical fiction, autobiography, and much else besides. *Giles Goat-Boy*, after its initial framing in the debate over authorship, continues this subversion through similarly comic devices. The whole modern world is conceived of as a university campus, controlled by a computer that is able to run itself and tyrannize people. The book is, in part, a satirical allegory of the Cold War, since it is divided into East and West. It is also a characteristically layered fiction, since it parodies several genres (myth, allegory, the quest) and a variety of texts (including the Bible, *Don Quixote*, and *Ulysses*). Above all, it translates the earth into an artifice. Works written since *Giles Goat-Boy*, such as *Letters*, *Sabbatical: A Romance* (1982), *The Last Voyage of*

Sinbad the Sailor (1991), and *The Development* (2008), continue Barth's passionate play with various forms, the numerous ways in which we tell ourselves stories to live and live in them. For him, that play is imperative and inspiring, coextensive with breathing. Some of his characters, sometimes, may yearn, as one of them puts it, "to give up language altogether." But that, as Barth indicates, is to "relapse into numbness." It may seem attractive occasionally, but to evacuate voice is to erase identity, place, and presence. To abandon language is to surrender to death.

Two writers who have sketched out very different possibilities for postmodernism, and, in doing so, created distinctive fictive landscapes, are Donald Barthelme (1931–1989) and John Hawkes (1925–1998). The distances between them, despite their common allegiance to work of art as object, an opaque system of language, are suggested by two remarks. "Fragments are the only forms I trust," observes the narrator in one of the stories in Barthelme's second collection, *Unspeakable Practices, Unnatural Acts* (1968). "The need is to maintain the truth of the fractured picture," Hawkes insisted in an early interview. Hawkes is interested in creating strange, phantasmagoric landscapes, dreamscapes that evoke what he has called "our potential for violence and absurdity as well as for graceful action." Barthelme is just as committed as Hawkes is to the displacement of the writer from the work. He is also committed to the displacement of the work from the world, so that the work becomes simply, as Barthelme puts it, "something that is *there*, like a rock or a refrigerator." But, whereas Hawkes's fiction has a quality of nightmare, entropic stillness, Barthelme's stories and novels are witty, formally elegant, slyly commenting on themselves as artefacts. Hawkes began his writing, he has said, with "something immediately and intensely visual – a room, a few figures." Barthelme, however, begins *his* writing in the verbal rather than the visual. "Oh I wish there were some words in the world that were not the words I always hear," explains the title character in Barthelme's first novel, *Snow White* (1967). Barthelme obliges with a verbal collage, full of odd juxtapositions, a verbal equivalent of Pop Art, which picks up the detritus of modern life and gives it a quality of surprise. Waste is turned to magic in his work, but the sense of magic is also accompanied by unease. Barthelme's fiction constantly fluctuates between immersion in trash culture and the impulse to evade that finds its emotional issue in irony, disappointment, and a free-floating nostalgia.

"Do you like the story so far?" asks the narrator of *Snow White* about halfway through. He then helpfully provides the reader with an opportunity to answer: "Yes ( ) No ( )." This is followed by a further fourteen questions for the reader to fill in his or her preferences. Quite apart from reminding us that this book is an artefact, the product of play and planning, the questionnaire offers a slyly parodic comment on the currently fashionable ideas of the work of art as open and the reader as co-producer of the text. But the last question sounds a slightly melancholic note. "In your opinion, should human beings have more shoulders? ( )," the narrator asks. "Two sets of shoulders? ( ) Three? ( )." Any world has its stringencies, its absences, restricting the room for magic and play. Barthelme is resistant to message. One of his stories, "The Balloon" in *Unspeakable Practices, Unnatural Acts*, even toys with the absurdity of meaning. An enormous balloon appears over the city. People argue over its significance. Some manage to "write messages on the surface." Mainly what people enjoy, though, is that it is "not limited and defined." It is delightfully random, floating free above "the grid of precise, rectangular pathways" beneath it. Clearly, the balloon is a paradigm of the art object, the kind of free-form product, plastic and ephemeral, that Barthelme is interested in making: resistant to interpretation. But, in its own odd way, as it floats free over the citizens, it generates a ruefulness, a wry regret that carries over into Barthelme's other fictions. Readers can certainly walk around a Barthelme verbal object, seeing in it a model of how to free up language and feeling from stale associations. But what they are likely to catch, as they walk around, is a borderline melancholia. So, when Snow White writes a poem, the seven men who live with her have no doubt as to its theme. "The theme is loss, we take it," they ask caustically. Her reply is simple: "I have not been able to imagine anything better."

Of John Hawkes's 1961 novel, *The Lime Twig*, his fellow novelist Flannery O'Connor has observed that "You suffer it like a dream. It seems to be something that is happening to you, that you wait to escape from but can't." That is true of all his fiction. His nominal subjects range far and wide: many of them, he has said, acquired from the newspapers or from other writers. So, for instance, *The Cannibal* (1949) explores the horrors of devastation in postwar Germany. *The Lime Twig* presents the psychopathic effects on a man of life during and after the blitz on London. *Travesty* (1967) is the monologue of a Frenchman that serves as a suicide note while he prepares to kill his daughter, his friend, and himself. *Virginia* (1982) concerns a girl who has experienced two previous lives in France, both marked by strange sexual experience. And *The Frog* (1996) tells of a boy with a real or imagined frog in his stomach. What characterizes all his novels, however, is a dreamscape fractured by an appalling, yet almost ritualized violence. In *The Cannibal*, the primary act of violent negation is signaled by the controlling metaphor of the book, which also gives it its title. Although the main setting is Germany after the war, it reaches back to 1914 and forward to a future repetition of Nazi control, which will return the entire nation to an insane asylum. The dominant presence, and narrator, is Zizendorf, the leader of the Nazis. Set in contrast to him is a young girl, Selvaggia, who stands at a window in innocent, impotent terror, watching the evil that men do. By the end, she is "wild-eyed from watching the night and the birth of the Nation." Zizendorf orders her to draw the blinds and sleep. The last sentence of the book gives us her response: "She did as she was told." The return to an evidently endless sleep, a nightmare of violent repression, seems inevitable, since there is no intimation, in this or any other book by Hawkes, that things can change or get better.

The differences between Hawkes and Barthelme suggest that postmodernism is best seen, not as a unified movement, but as a cluster of possibilities, a generic field. That field includes Thomas Berger (1924–), whose finest novel, *Little Big Man* (1964), is a parodic rewriting of frontier myth, reinserting a typical protean man of postmodern fiction, the Little Big Man of the title, into the Old West. It also includes John Gardner (1933–1982), whose best work, *Grendel* (1971), retells the story of the Old English poem *Beowulf* from the viewpoint of the monster, and Robert Coover (1932–), whose best novel, in turn, *The Public Burning* (1977), transfers actual events, including the Eisenhower years and the execution of the Rosenbergs for spying, to the figurative realm. The execution of the Rosenbergs is turned into a public burning in Times Square, New York. Times Square itself is presented not just as a public meeting place but a source of a history, since it is here the records of the *New York Times* are created.

Coover goes on to analyze how historical record is made, showing that fiction can only aid facts in the rehearsal of the past; it can, and does, draw it into subjective reality. In doing so, he offers a postmodernist meditation on history, and on the origins of story.

Postmodernism also includes those writers who have chosen and pursued an absurd humor that deconstructs and demystifies all it surveys. Notable here are J. P. Donleavy (1926–) (*The Ginger Man* (1955), *The Beastly Beatitudes of Balthazar B* (1968)), Terry Southern (1926–2000) (*Candy* (1958), *The Magic Christian* (1959), *Blue Movie* (1970)), and John Kennedy Toole (1937–1969). In his posthumously published novel *A Confederacy of Dunces* (1980), Toole mocked everything to do with his region, the South and his hometown of New Orleans, making his hero, Ignatius Reilly, sound sometimes like a Southern traditionalist on speed. Postmodernism as black humor or brave fantasy tends to merge with contemporary confessional forms of male liberationists like John Irving (1942–) (*The World According to Garp* (1978), *The Hotel New Hampshire* (1981), *A Prayer for Owen Meany* (1989), *Until I Find You* 2005)) and female liberationists like Lisa Alther (1944–) (*Kinflicks* (1976), *Original Sin* (1981)). At the other edge, postmodernism as radical, metafictional experiment is more inclined to reveal its international relations. Notable instances of this are the works of the Polish-born, Russian-reared Jerzy Kosinski (1933–1991) from *The Painted Bird* (1965), through *Being There* (1971) to *The Hermit of 69th Street* (1988) and the Austrian-born, Chinese-reared Walter Abish (1931–). Abish's first novel, *Alphabetical Africa* (1974), invites a comparison with *le nouveau roman* in its stern attention to verbal structure. His second novel, *How German It Is* (1984), suggests other international relations. A postmodern political thriller, it concerns an American of German parentage who returns to a German town to investigate his father's wartime death and answer to his own question as to how German he is. The influential presences here include American writers like Pynchon, French ones like Butor, who have used popular genres to break and undercut them, and, more deeply, other European writers such as Italo Calvino and Peter Handke. As in the work of Calvino and Handke, there is a bleak detachment, a flat materialism to *How German It Is*, the presentation of a world of signs without meanings under which dark meanings may hide.

The actuality of words: Postmodern poetry

Internationalism is also a marked feature of postmodernism in poetry, especially that form of postmodernism known as language poetry. The antecedents of the language poets, for instance, include not only such American writers as Gertrude Stein, Louis Zukovsky, and John Ashbery, but also Europeans like James Joyce. Reflecting the belief of one of the leading language poets, Charles Bernstein (1950–), that "poetry, like philosophy, may be involved with the investigation of phenomena (events, objects, selves) and human knowledge of them," those antecedents and influences include a number of continental philosophers as well. Language poetry is as various in its manifestations as contemporary sculpture or photography, but one aim all language poets have in common is this: instead of employing language as a transparent window on experience, language poets insist on the materiality of words, the distance of the medium they use from whatever we think of as natural or immediate. An analogy might be made with the sculptor who draws attention to the stone with which he or she is working, its weight, texture, and cleavage. Privileging technique, resisting any temptation to present the poem as a window on experience, the language poet builds up a mosaic structure by means of seemingly unrelated sentences and sentence fragments. This progression of non-sequiturs frustrates the reader's expectations for linear development and at the same time it discloses a more complete world of reference. The stress is laid on production rather than ease of consumption, on the use of artifice in such a way as to force open given forms and break habitual patterns of attention.

Along with this emphasis on the materiality of the signifier, what language poets also have in common is the project of restoring the reader as a co-producer of the text. That follows inevitably from their resistance to closure. "The text calls upon the reader to be actively involved in the process of constructing its meaning," as Charles Bernstein puts it. "The text formally involves the process of response/interpretation and in doing so makes the reader aware of herself or himself as producer as well as consumer of meaning." Bernstein is one of the three leading exponents of language poetry. The other two are Michael Palmer (1943–) and Susan Howe (1937–). Both an accomplished poet and a leading theorist of language poetry, Bernstein's numerous collections include *Poetic Justice* (1979), *Islets/Irritations* (1983), and *Girly Man* (2006). Sometimes, the vocations of poet and theorist come together. *Artifice of Absorption* (1987), for example, is an essay in verse that makes a core distinction between *absorption* and *impermeability* in literature. Absorptive writing, Bernstein suggests, pursues the realistic, continuous, and transparent; impermeable, or antiabsorptive writing favors artifice, discontinuity, the opaque. It is the impermeable, clearly, that he prefers. His aim, Bernstein writes, is for the reader "to be actively involved in the process of constructing its meaning," and, as far as both reader and writer are concerned, "to wake/us from the hypnosis of absorption." In *Artifice of Absorption*, Bernstein cites his poem "The Klupzy Girl" as an example of his poetic technique. With typically antic humor, he takes an all-American Klutz of both French and British descent (since she bears a close resemblance to Keats's "La Belle Dame Sans Merci") as his demonic muse here. He then uses a rich mix of styles, redundancies, clichés, awkward or irrelevant constructions to create what is called, toward the end of the poem, "a manic/state of careless grace." The artifice is foregrounded by various cinematic devices: cutting and shifting focus, unanticipated breaks, disturbing and distorted perspective. It is this disjunctive rate of change that dictates the poem's rhythm, as it lurches from statements so bold that they border on parody ("Poetry is like a swoon, with this difference:/it brings you to your senses"), through disconnected snatches of conversation, phrases that might be overheard in the street, comments that float unanchored. Art, Bernstein has insisted, must be extraordinary, aberrant, abnormal; and in "The Klupzy Girl" he manages to achieve just that – with a style that distorts and a strange, disturbing lady as the poem's occasion.

Michael Palmer has said that he is "a little bit outside" "the way many of the so-called language poets work" because the way "I inhabit language, or language inhabits me, is in a sense more traditional." Certainly, his poetry betrays other debts, to the Black Mountain and New York poets in particular; and, in his critical writings, he has admitted the inevitability of narrative. But his work is fundamentally of the language movement because of his core commitment to what he calls "radical discontinuities of surface and voice" – to a poetry that resists and interrogates. He is interested, he says, in a poetry that "will not stand as a kind of decor in one's life, not the kind of thing for hammock and lemonade, where at the end everything is in resolution." He is also concerned with the political implications of style and form: his work questions the status quo on the rhetorical level, supplying a critique of "the discourses of power by undermining assumptions about meaning and univocality." He may be more interested in story than Bernstein is. However, as Palmer himself has pointed out, story, as well as autobiography, always involves a measure of concealment. So, in a work like *Notes for Echo Lake* (1981), he uses concealment devices like writing about himself in the third person, in order to disclose. But, even while disclosing, there is a hermetic quality to his writing that issues from radical skepticism: fundamental uncertainty about, as he has it, "whether I know whatever I know." Palmer is a prolific poet. His many collections include *Plan of the City O* (1971), *First Figure* (1984), and *Company of Moths* (2005). Nearly all his work is marked by a search for an evidence of order in the sound and structure of language and proof of life, love in the steadiness of companionship.

Structurally, the poetry of Susan Howe often registers her early training in the visual arts. Some of her work treats words like fragments in a collage. Others experiment with the significations that emerge from the irregular distribution of letters on the page. The lines, "Do not come down the ladder/iforI/have eaten/ita/way," from "White Foolscap: Book of Cordelia" (1983), distribute sense, a layer of potential meaning, on a specifically visual level. Howe grew up during World War II, however, and, as a young woman, came under the influence of Charles Olson. Both experiences ignited her interest in an often silenced, often slighted history. "The deaths of millions of people in Europe and Asia," Howe has said, "prevented me from ever being able to believe history is only a series of justifications, or that tragedy and savagery can be theorized away." Her books of poetry include *The Western Borders* (1976), *Defenestration of Prague* (1983), *The Europe of Trusts* (2000), and *The Midnight* (2003). And many of her poems show her ability to transform historical documents, the archive and the chronicle, into an elusive, elliptical, yet deeply personal drama: in which, say, the ancient Britain of Lear, the New England of the Indian wars, or the New England of Thoreau enters the consciousness of a woman living and working at the end of the American century, and beyond. Unlike Olson, Howe has never constructed a central persona. Instead, her poems contain lines and phrases that just will not come together in a unifying speech, form, or episode. Lines may pass with one or two others, then typically drift off by themselves or into new, temporary arrangements. A charged lyricism fuses with a critical examination of authorial voice as, using pun and wordplay, Howe calls meaning itself into question. Figures hover at the edge of memory and history in her work, and on the borderlines of speech. They seize our attention momentarily, then they are gone. "For we are language Lost/in language," one poem, "Speeches at the Barriers," declares. "Wind sweeps over the wheat/mist-mask on woods." A feeling of dissolution marks out these lines, a perpetual erasing inherent in the endless ebb and flow of human language, consciousness and history.

Signs and scenes of crime, science fiction, and fantasy

Language poetry remains the literature of a small community. As postmodernists, though, language poets resist the traditional division of culture into minority and mass, elite and popular. In their turn, writers of detective stories, thrillers, and hardboiled and science fiction have shown the same resistance over the past forty years: producing work so pervasive in its influence that it has helped erase the line of demarcation between genre fiction and literature. As far as hardboiled and detective tales are concerned, the period from roughly the 1940s to the 1960s was notable for the development of paperback original series and mystery magazines. And two very different writers who benefited from these new means of literary production and distribution were Mickey Spillane (1918–2006) and Jim Thompson (1906–1976). Spillane leaped to success in 1947, when he created the private eye Mike Hammer for *I, the Jury*. Hammer is a veteran of World War II who sets out to avenge the murder of an old army buddy who once saved his life. Assisted by his loyal, sexy secretary, Velda, he vows to let nothing stand in his way. And, at the climax of the story, he shoots his naked fiancée in the abdomen when he finds out that she has killed his buddy and five others. An untrammeled Id who is constantly exploding in messianic rage – against intellectuals and homosexuals, or anyone who oppresses the "little guy," from the Mafia to the Communist Party – Hammer continued his pursuit of vigilante justice in a series of novels whose titles suggest their tone and tenor: *My Gun is Quick* (1950), *Vengeance Is Mine* (1950), *Kiss Me Deadly* (1952).

Jim Thompson is a much darker, more impressive writer than Spillane, although he also shows a taste for psychopathic violence. His noir fiction contains few detectives. What it has in abundance is unreliable narrators and protagonists whose mental state verges on and often topples over into psychosis. The condition they inhabit is measured by the scatological mathematics of Thompson's 1959 novel, *South of Heaven*: "shit and three are nine . . . screw and two is four and frig makes ten." Typical is the narrator of *The Killer Inside Me* (1952), Deputy Lou Ford. Ford pretends to be a simple-minded hick, when in fact he is a ruthless, sadistic killer, responsible for the murders he is supposed to be investigating. The world this smiling villain inhabits is a bleak one, where human nature festers, corrupts, and disrupts. The narration is sly, fooling the reader much of the time as well as the other characters. And the narrative tone, darkening the brutal, gaudy landscapes the Deputy negotiates, is cold, comic, and caustic: exposing what looks like an almost universal hypocrisy. In other novels, Thompson introduces us to con artists (*The Grifters* (1963)), lowlife criminals (*The Getaway* (1959)), and people cracking up in a figurative prison of tough talk, "lowdown" behavior, and smalltown scheming (*After Dark, My Sweet* (1955)). The family offers no refuge here; it is riven with incestuous desires and violence. In *King Blood* (1954), for instance, the protagonist is aroused in the act of beating his mother. People are on their own in a world of "sickness," trying to cope while maybe knowing that, as Lou Ford puts it, "all of us started the game with a crooked cue."

There were several notable generic developments in crime and hardboiled fiction during the three decades or so following World War II. These included the emergence of police procedural fiction and a kind of crime novel in which motivation rather than detection was central. The police procedural form, in which the role of protagonist is given to an entire unit of police officers, was introduced by Lawrence Treat (1903–1998). However, the writer who has achieved most marked success with it is Evan Hunter (1926–2005), working under the name of Ed McBain, who produced more than forty novels set in the 87th Precinct of a thinly disguised New York City. The detectiveless crime novel, in turn, became the forte of Patricia Highsmith (1921–1995). Her first novel, *Strangers on a Train* (1950), set the pattern and established her claustrophobic fictive world. Here, and in other novels like *This Sweet Sickness* (1960), strangers are emotionally tied to each other through acts of violence. People are twinned, find themselves with secret sharers of their lives, in relationships that vacillate between love and hatred. Highsmith seems especially interested in acts of doubling and disguise that expose the darker side of life, and the murkier depths of human personality. This is especially so in her most popular books, about the pleasant, totally amoral young American Tom Ripley. The first and best of these, *The Talented Mr. Ripley* (1955), offers a sardonic variation on *The Ambassadors* by Henry James: as Ripley, despatched to rescue a wealthy young man from the cultural fleshpots of Europe, ends up by murdering him and assuming his identity. There are no puzzles in Highsmith's work, justice is rarely done, and the emphasis is on the perpetrator of the crime rather than the victim or detector. What there is, besides this shift of emphasis, is a disconcerting dissolution of the boundaries that keep society safe and ourselves comfortable: between reality and fantasy, the permissible and the forbidden, good and evil.

Other writers besides Highsmith began to explore the possibilities of crime and mystery at the same time as her, the most notable of them being Ross Macdonald (1915–1983). His main protagonist, Lew Archer, first appeared in *The Moving Target* (1949). At first, Archer was a relatively stereotypical version of the hardboiled hero. Even in this first book, however, he reflected his creator's conviction that nothing is clear-cut. "Evil isn't so simple," Archer explains here. "Everybody has it in him, and whether it comes out in his actions depends on a number of things. Environment, opportunity, economic pressure, a piece of bad luck, a wrong friend." Gradually, though, Archer evolved into a prototypical figure of the Vietnam years and after. "Not the usual peeper," as one of the characters observes in *The Far Side of the Dollar* (1965), Archer becomes more reflective and coolly perceptive. More interested in listening than detecting, understanding rather than meting out justice, in books like *The Drowning Pool* (1950) and *The Underground Man* (1971), Archer discovers the roots of present traumas in past betrayals. He exposes the schemes and self-deception concealed below the comfortable surfaces and plastic moralities of the marketplace. And he shows how the older generation have disturbed and disoriented the younger. As a quiet moral center, rather than a focus of action, Archer reflects the view, expressed in *Sleeping Beauty* (1973), that "every witness has his own way of creeping up on truth." Interrogation becomes less a matter of intimidation, more a chance for the participant to unburden knowledge, to dig up a buried past and perhaps come to terms with it. That past, invariably, has a social dimension: since what, on a deeper level, these stories dig up involves the sins of the founding fathers being visited upon the sons and daughters – the dreams of a nation turned irrevocably sour.

From the 1970s, novels written in the general generic field of crime and mystery have largely been published first in hardback. What has been remarkable about this period is the rapid growth in the use of the genre to address serious issues. At the same time, markedly more sophisticated approaches to narration and characterization shown by many American mystery novelists have further eroded the distinction between genre writing and literature. That growth of sophistication is notable in the work of three contemporary masters, Elmore Leonard (1925–), George V. Higgins (1939–1999), and James Ellroy (1948–). Leonard began by writing westerns, notable among which are *Hombre* (1961) and *Valdez is Coming* (1970). Then, after reading *The Friends of Eddie Coyle* (1972) by George V. Higgins, he turned to the mystery genre and new ways of telling stories. The work of Higgins portrays sleazy characters on both sides of the law, with a toughly realistic sympathy for their struggles. It depends, above all, on dialogue: a stylized vernacular that has the smell of authenticity and draws the reader into a world of rough justice, hard money, and fast deals. Leonard developed a similar sympathy for his morally dubious characters through an equally vigorous use of their speech. Voice is as important to him as it is to Higgins. And, in works from *Fifty-Two Pickup* (1974) through *La Brava* (1983) to *Glitz* (1985) and beyond, he has used a variety of urban settings in which to place his humanized villains. There are no true villains in the work of Ellroy either. In his case, however, it is because there appears to be no moral code here to distinguish heroes from villains, or to hint at the possibility of redemption. What Ellroy describes, with darkly comic venom and in a prose as strung out as a telegraph wire, is a world of violence and betrayal and corruption – where the ugliness just keeps on getting uglier. This is particularly noticeable in his Los Angeles Quartet, *The Black Dahlia* (1987), *The Big Nowhere* (1988), *L.A. Confidential* (1990), and *White Jazz* (1992). Written in what sometimes seems like frenetic shorthand, the quartet charts crime and corruption in the City of Angels from the end of World War II to the election of John Kennedy. It is not so much a series of mystery novels as an absurdist vision of urban hell.

Among American women writers of mystery fiction, Sara Paretsky (1947–) is particularly notable. With her first novel, *Indemnity Only* (1982), Paretsky introduced a private investigator, Victoria Iphigenia Warshawski, known as "Vic" or "V.I.," who narrates her experiences just as the traditional, hardboiled hero does. As this and the other Warshawski books, such as *Deadlock* (1984), *Blacklist* (2003), and *Fire Sale* (2005), show, though, Paretsky entered the hardboiled tradition in order to revise it. Her protagonist may be as sharply observant and harshly reflective as the traditional private eye; the prose may crackle with the same urgency; the same cool eye is cast on the grainy textures of everyday life. But this is a private eye, and private eye fiction, with a difference. For one thing, Warshawski wryly distances herself from earlier textbook heroes: "I'm no Philip Marlowe," she observes in *Tunnel Vision* (1994), "forever pulling guns out of armpits or glove compartments." For another, she is constantly concerned about her own toughness, worrying that her job diminishes human connection. And she seeks, and finds, that connection: not so much with men of her own age – her sexual relations, even her brief, past marriage seem relatively peripheral to her – but with an older, male neighbor and, even more, with other women. Her closest relation is with another, older woman, Lotte Herschel. That, perhaps, is one measure of Warshawski's own sense of female solidarity. Very much a child of the 1960s, she constantly reflects on the raw deal women still have despite the women's liberation movement in which she participated. She is also constantly trying to help other women, in her capacity as private eye and through her involvement in various causes and groups, such as a women's shelter. The feminism Paretsky embodies in her central character is neither narrow nor shrill. Warshawski is an unsentimental, acerbically intelligent character with an ironic sense of humor as well as a keen eye for injustice. And the wrongs to women Warshawski may uncover are always seen to be tied to a wider web of corruption. The specific crimes she investigates, and solves, are usually committed to preserve or consolidate power and always relate to wider social problems. The power may involve men but it is never definitively male; the problems may involve women but they are never exclusively female.

What has been described as the first African American detective story, *The Conjure-Man* by Randolph Fisher (1897–1934), appeared in 1925. Thirty years later, Chester Himes (1909–1984) published *For Love of Imabelle* (1957, reissued as *A Rage in Harlem* (1965)), the first in a series of urban thrillers, resembling the police procedural in form, whose main characters grew to be two African American police detectives: Coffin Ed Johnson and Grave Digger Jones. Himes had himself been in prison, for armed robbery. It was there that he became an apprentice writer. Once he was released, he began writing novels that reflected his preoccupation with the destructive power of racism (*If He Hollers Let Him Go* (1945)), his experiences in prison (*Cast the First Stone* (1952)), and his own problems as an intelligent, sensitive black man living in a world dominated by whites (*The Primitive* (1955)). "The American black man is the most neurotic, complicated, schizophrenic, unanalyzed, anthropologically advanced specimen of mankind in the history of the world," Himes wrote in the first volume of his autobiography, *The Quality of Hurt* (1972). It was partly to escape the predicament outlined here that he became an expatriate. Leaving for Europe in 1953, he made only occasional trips back to the United States, usually to New York City. After several lean years in Europe, Himes was given the opportunity to write for Editions Gallimard's *Série noire*, a respected series of translated American crime fiction. And so it was in Europe that his own variations on the police procedural scored their first success: among them, *The Real Cool Killers* (1959), *Cotton Comes to Harlem* (1965), and *Blind Man With a Pistol* (1969). In these novels, Himes juxtaposes absurdly comic characters with sinister situations, setting everything against the grim background of a swarming, degraded ghetto. Many of them concern a goodhearted black male, just inching along, who finds himself involved in a desperate struggle for his life. A morally equivocal light-skinned woman may be at the heart of his trouble. In any event, the scene is packed with hard-nosed gamblers, religious freaks, and drug-crazed killers. Armed with identical revolvers, dressed in black suits and driving a battered Plymouth sedan, Johnson and Jones do the best they can in this world. As they struggle to deal with the chaos and corruption that surrounds them, the two detectives inspire the same fear and awe as the "bad men" of African American folklore. For all that, their struggle seems increasingly hopeless. By the time of the last book in the series, *Blind Man With a Pistol*, chaos seems to have come to Harlem in earnest and Johnson and Jones seem unable to restore order. The final image of the novel, signaled by its title, sums it all up: people are helpless in the face of a scattershot destructiveness that is as wasteful as it is random.

Twenty years after Himes completed his series of novels with Johnson and Jones at their center, Walter Mosley (1952–) published *Devil in a Blue Dress* (1990). This was followed by several other novels, including *White Butterfly* (1992) and *A Little Yellow Dog* (1996), set in postwar Los Angeles and featuring a reluctant black investigator, Ezekiel "Easy" Rawlins. The novels unfold in a developing history: *Devil in a Blue Dress* takes place in 1948, *A Little Yellow Dog* just before the assassination of President Kennedy in 1963, *Little Scarlet* (2004) after the 1965 Watts Riot. They show an acute sense of the racism endemic in American society, not least in its police force. A migrant from the South, financially secure yet still aware of the precariousness of being black, Easy Rawlins is a World War II veteran who recalls that "the army was segregated just like the South." Easy carves out a life for himself with a home, some rental properties, and an unconventional family of two adopted children, all of it concealed from the gaze of white bureaucracy. He is socially invisible in a way, just like the protagonist of *Invisible Man*. And, as he maneuvers his way in and around the absurdities of a world dominated by whites, he attends to the voice inside to guide him. Not a detective but someone in the "favor business" of the black community, he is drawn into each adventure by attending to that voice: in order, that is, to maintain some tenuous grasp on security for him and his children. The danger Rawlins encounters comes from inside as well as around him. He is only too aware of his own capacity for violence: a capacity figured in Raymond "Mouse" Alexander, a childhood friend and sidekick whom he both loves and fears. Alexander is gleefully amoral and murderous; and his casual, conscienceless approach to things adds depth and shade to the portrait of Rawlins. Mosley has said that he owes a debt to Albert Camus in his conception of Easy Rawlins. And it is clear that, like other African American writers before him, he has used existentialism to explore the trials of race. Whatever else he is, this amateur detective (anti-)hero is a man in process: using his quicksilver sensibility, not just to get by, but to make himself and make his own morality up, as he wanders around some of the meanest streets in the city.

Native American sleuths began appearing in fiction well before their African American counterparts. Popular interest in the West, and in what was seen as the exoticism of Native American cultures, led to the wide dissemination of books with titles like *Velvet Foot, the Indian Detective, or, The Taut Tiger* (1882) in the later part of the nineteenth century. The "Indian detective" in these stories was stereotypically adept at tracking, following footprints, or investigating the scene of a crime. What is different about more recent developments in this area is that mystery writers now are far more alert to cultural difference. Writers such as Tony Hillerman (1925–2008), in novels like *The Blessing Way* (1970) and *Finding Moon* (1996), pursue their work on the intersection where Anglo and Native American cultures meet. They expand the methods of investigation to incorporate different value systems and processes of thought; they explore the uneasy meeting, the conflict and occasional congruence, between whites and Native Americans; and they open the genre to political processes, such as the rights of indigenous peoples, or the impact of commercial exploitation of the land – both on the harsh landscapes of the Southwest and on those cultures still closely tied to the earth. This opening up of the generic field of mystery to the processes of history and the problems of cultural conflict is not just the work of those who take Native Americans or African Americans as their subject. Chicano culture enters the detective genre in the fiction of Rudolph Anaya concerned with Sonny Baca, an Alburquerque private eye who first appears in *Zia Summer* (1995). It does so, again, in *Partners in Crime* (1985) by Rolando Hinojosa (1929–). In turn, immigrant culture in general and Korean culture in particular is the scarcely hidden agenda in *Native Speaker* (1995) by Chang-Rae Lee (1965–): a book that uses the mystery formula to investigate what is called the "ugly immigrant's truth" of social exploitation, cultural confusion, and, sometimes, personal self-hatred. In novels like these, it becomes impossible to preserve a distinction between mystery fiction and serious literature.

In *God Bless You, Mr. Rosewater* (1965) by Kurt Vonnegut, the protagonist drunkenly addresses a meeting of writers of science fiction. "I love you sons of bitches," he announces. "You're all I read any more. You're the only ones who'll talk about the really *terrific* changes going on." That echoes a sentiment expressed by many readers of science fiction. Given the enormous pace of technological change in the twentieth and twenty-first centuries, then, so the argument goes, science fiction is the only form of literature addressing the truth. Among recent science fiction writers, one of the most notable is Robert Heinlein (1907–1988), not least because his works negotiate a path between scientific literalism and fantasy. Heinlein is also capable of humor and social comment. *Double Star* (1956), for instance, is about a failed actor who claims to be a galactic politician. And he can use the genre to make intelligent guesses about the future – from which vantage point he can then cast a critical eye over the present. So, his best-known novel, *Stranger in a Strange Land* (1961), concerns Mike Smith, a human who has been brought up on Mars. Initiated into an unearthly way of regarding reality, Smith has also acquired suprahuman powers. On returning to Earth, he founds a new religion based on Martian habits, more pacifist and hedonist than most earthly creeds. At the end of the novel, though, he is torn to pieces by outraged humans, crucified for his beliefs and practices. *Stranger in a Strange Land* takes themes ingrained in the American experience and writing – the lonely hero, the clash with conventional society, exile, longing, and the impulse to merge with older, deeper forms of community – and gives them a new twist. This is a new siting of a series of classic tropes. So is another novel, *Childhood's End* (1954), by an equally influential science fiction writer, Arthur C. Clarke (1917–2008). This is a story about the end of the world – due, not to some humanly produced catastrophe, but because the human race achieves a total breakthrough into pure mind. It is experienced by all the children under ten, who suddenly cease to be individuals and become a vast group endowed with extraordinary powers. Jan, the last man on earth and observer of its final hours, watches the children; "their faces," he comments, "were merging into a common mold" as they metamorphose into what is called here the Overmind. The whole trajectory of the narrative is in fact distinctly transcen-dentalist: Overmind, after all, seems to echo the Emersonian notion of the Over-soul. This is another story that rewrites old American stories in new forms.

Ray Bradbury (1920–) published numerous short stories before establishing his reputation with *The Martian Chronicles* (1950). It describes the first attempts of earth people to conquer and colonize Mars, the thwarting of their efforts by the gentle, telepathic Martians, the eventual colonization and the eventual effect on the Martian settlers of a nuclear war on Earth. As much a work of social criticism as anything, the novel explores some of the prevailing anxieties of the 1950s and beyond: the fear of war, the longing for a simpler life, the resistance to racism and censorship. *Fahrenheit 451* (1953) is also a cautionary tale that uses an imagined future to critique the present. The title refers to the temperature at which books are supposed to burn; and the book is set in a future world where the written word is banned. A group of rebels resist the ban by memorizing entire works of literature and philosophy, Here, and in his other books (including numerous collections of stories like *The Golden Apples of the Sun* (1953)), Bradbury views technological change with a cautious sympathy. Not against such change in itself, he is nevertheless alert to potential dangers – above all, the possibility that the moral evolution of human beings will not keep pace with their technological development. The use of science fiction or fantasy as a critique and corrective is just as notable in the work of Ursula Le Guin (1929–). In fact, in her introduction to her novel *The Left Hand of Darkness* (1969), Le Guin has insisted that "science fiction is not predictive; it is descriptive." True to that formula, this novel describes and critically defines sexual prejudice. It is set on an imaginary planet populated by "androgynes," people who can at different times be male, female, and neuter. An ordinary human who falls in love with a member of this trisexual society is forced to examine the meaning of sexual roles. And the reader, in turn, is invited to imagine what it may mean to be simply human, living outside the social determinants of sexual identity. Other books are critical of contemporary American political and social values. *The Word for World Forest* (1972) is about Vietnam; and *The New Atlantis* (1975) presents a futuristic vision of a totalitarian United States. Her most ambitious and acclaimed work, the "Earthsea" trilogy, is more preoccupied with fundamental values: addressing, in terms of scientific fantasy, the need to face the evil in oneself (*A Wizard of Earthsea* (1968)), the need for trust and truth (*The Tombs of Atuan* (1971)), and the need to accept the fact of death (*The Farthest Shore* (1972)).

The scope of science fiction, its capacity to explore not only social and moral issues, but matters of being and knowledge is especially evident in the stories of Philip K. Dick (1928–1982), Samuel R. Delany (1942–), and Octavia Butler (1947–2006). Preoccupied with problems of perception, Dick returned obsessively to the permeable boundaries separating the real from the illusory, fact from fiction. Which is a reason for his interest in hallucinatory drugs and their impact on consciousness (*The Three Stigmata of Palmer Eldritch* (1964), *A Scanner Darkly* (1977)). As the title of his most famous novel, *Do Androids Dream of Electric Sheep?* (1968), indicates, it was also the reason for his imagining of cunning facsimiles of humanity that call into question all our ideas of what it means to be human. The work of Delaney reflects his own belief that, as he has put it, "the science fictional enterprise is richer than the enterprise of mundane fiction." An African American, Delaney began by writing relatively traditional science fiction. His first book, *The Jewels of Iptor* (1962), explores themes of quest, the capabilities of technology, and the status of the artist, to all of which Delaney would later return. *The Einstein Intersection* (1967) is an ambitious attempt to satirize forms of human life using a science fiction frame. *Nova* (1968) is a dense translation of the myths of Prometheus and the Holy Grail into futuristic terms. These novels reveal an increasing complexity. In the early 1970s, however, Delaney moved away altogether from conventional narrative logic. *Dhalgren*, published in 1975, marks the change. "A book about many things," as Delaney has described it, it presents a city that has suffered a disaster so catastrophic that the space-time continuum has been distorted. In a powerful image of society in chaos, buildings burn endlessly without being consumed; and the only possibility of redemption seems to shine in youth and art. Time, logic, and narrative viewpoints are all cut loose from their traditional literary moorings; in this and the later *Atlantis: Model 1924* (1995), they function relativistically. An additional, disconcerting factor in *Dhalgren* is that

Kid, the narrator, is dyslexic and epileptic. These later books take science fiction into the postmodern; as they do so, they carry the habit of the genre to speculate and subvert to a new extreme.

Both the earlier and later science fiction of Delaney is also notable for extending the frontiers of the genre as far as the treatment of race and sex are concerned. Those frontiers have been further stretched by Octavia Butler, who is also African American. Her Patternist series, for instance, which includes *Patternmaster* (1976), *Wild Seed* (1984), and *Clay's Ark* (1984), has as its central character a 4,000-year-old immortal, Dune, who is able to move at will from body to body. The movement is regardless of race and gender, although Dune prefers to inhabit the bodies of black males. Just how writers like Butler have stretched science fiction is suggested by her best-known book, *Kindred* (1988). This was originally meant to be a Patternist novel, but Butler found it too realistic to fit into the futurist frame of the series. Here, a young black woman called Dana is transported back in time, from the 1970s Los Angeles suburb where she lives with her white husband, to a Maryland plantation before the Civil War. She then finds herself the property of a family whose eldest son Rufus has summoned her to save him. During her journey back into the racial past, Dana loses an arm: a mark of how slavery inscribed itself on the bodies, as well as the minds and memories, of African Americans. Incorporating elements of social and historical realism, and naturalist critique, into its framework of fantasy, *Kindred* shows how adaptable the genre of science fiction can be – and just how alert, perceptive, and predictive science fiction writers can become, as they attend to what Eliot Rosewater called "the really *terrific* changes going on."

Creating New Americas

Dreaming history: European immigrant writing

Sometimes, it has seemed more appropriate to call the changes going on in and around America during the past half-century as terrible rather than terrific. Those changes, in particular, have helped account for the waves of immigration that have turned the United States into even more of a "universal nation" than it was in the first two centuries of its existence. Isaac Bashevis Singer (1904–1991), for instance, came to the United States from Poland in 1935. He became a journalist, writing in Yiddish for the *Jewish Daily Forward*. It was there also that he published most of his fiction. Dealing with the mixed inheritance of Polish Jews, their traditional faith and folkways, he combined fantasy with humor. His first major work, *Satan in Gusay*, was published in Yiddish in 1935 and in English twenty years later. The first of his books to appear in English was *The Family Muskat* (1950), a naturalistic account of the decline of a Jewish family in Warsaw from the beginning of the twentieth century until World War II. It was followed by other books set in Poland, like *The Magician of Lublin* (1960), *The Manor* (1967), and *The Estate* (1969). Throughout his life, Singer also chronicled ghetto life in wry, pungent short stories, collected in such volumes as *Gimpel the Fool* (1957), *The Spinoza of Market Street* (1961), and *Passions* (1978).

Enemies: A Love Story (1972) was the first of his novels to be set in the United States. It comprises a kind of post-Holocaust trilogy with *The Penitent* (1983) and the posthumously published *Meshugah* (1994). "Although I did not have the privilege of going through the Hitler Holocaust," Singer writes in a caustic author's note to *Enemies*, "I have lived for years with refugees from this ordeal." And, in each of these narratives, characters try to exorcize the millions of ghosts created by genocide. In *Enemies*, the protagonist, a refugee called Herman Broder, shuttles uneasily between three women: a mistress and two wives, one he married in America, the other he thought had died in Europe. At the same time, he careers between the ordeal of his European past and the challenge of his American present. Persistently reinventing himself, Herman encounters postwar culture as a mildly deranged survivor who is alienated from the grand narratives of history and trapped in wartime memories. "Where are the Nazis?" his psychotic mistress asks him, when he takes her on a trip into the American pastoral of the Adirondack mountains. "What kind of world is this without Nazis? A backward country, this America." Like her, Herman suspects trauma and disruption everywhere; he cannot reconcile the Holocaust with his American experience and so form a new cultural identity. All he can manage, finally, after his mistress commits suicide, is to set up a strange, touching *menage à trois* with his two wives. It is not a reconciliation of the warring opposites of his life, perhaps, but it is a form of survival. In *The Penitent*, the protagonist survives in another way, by leaving "the Golden Land" of America for Europe. In *Meshugah*, the narrator negotiates a sort of survival when he marries, in a muted gesture of forgiveness, a woman who had collaborated with the Nazis. It is, we are told, "the quietest wedding since the one between Adam and Eve." Despite such gently redemptive moments, though, all three books in the post-Holocaust trilogy are marked by a comic absurdism of tone and a carnivalesque nihilism of spirit. Meshugah, Singer reminds the reader, is a Yiddish word meaning "crazy, senseless, insane." That reflects the feeling, expressed by one character, that "the whole world is an insane asylum." The only genuine relief in this fiction comes from its antic narrative rhythms and mordant humor. As Singer confessed, shortly before he died, some of his characters may finally have "made peace with the cruelty of life, and the violence of man's history ... but I haven't."

Memories of the Holocaust haunt immigrant survivors in several other notable fictions of this period. Cynthia Ozick (1928–), for instance, has explored characters unwilling to accept the notion of their new home, the United States, as Eden in her novel *The Cannibal Galaxy* (1983) and her two-part novella, *The Shawl* (1980). Born in New York City, Ozick explores the dilemma of being Jewish in a Christian world. In her short stories, in particular, she expresses her oppositional difference by turning postmodernism against itself. Two of her most engaging tales, for instance, about a character called Ruth Pottermesser, included in *Levitation: Five Fictions* (1982), employ postmodernist techniques to undermine postmodernist values and reaffirm traditional Jewish values of conscientiousness and respect for the limits of the self. It is in the longer fiction, however, that the limits to imagining America are seriously addressed, through the experience of Holocaust survivors. Tortured by what are called, in *The Shawl*, "cannibal dreams," the human devastation they have witnessed, these survivors seem not only skeptical but substanceless. Ghostlike, they appear hardly to inhabit their own bodies, to be really there in a culture that their own memories turn into something irredeemably mediocre, meaningless. The vision of America nurtured by Joseph Brill, the protagonist in *The Cannibal Galaxy*, is scarcely pastoral or paradisaical. A French Jew who survived the war in hiding, he sees the United States, where he now works as a school principal, as a land of the mediocre. Obsessed with the breakdown of culture, Brill feels that he is trapped in a cannibal galaxy, a "megalosaurian colony of primordial gases that devours smaller brother galaxies." He also sees shadows of the past looming through the banal surfaces of the present. The "innocent" American architecture of the school campus, for example, with the buildings lined up symmetrically, takes on the ghostly contours of the boxcars that took his family away from Paris to death in Poland. Like Rosa Lublin, the protagonist of *The Shawl*, who treasures the shawl of her daughter, killed in a concentration camp, like a talisman, Brill is wrapped up and rapt in recollection. Rosa equates America with the trivial, the "prevalent, frivolous." So does Brill. She has no time for millennial dreams; neither does he. Lublin and Brill are fatally alike in their "secret cynicism," that sense of only half living in a banal limbo. Both of them end up married: which might suggest a kind of making do and going on. But the suitor of Rosa is comic, and acceptance of him grudging. And, after taking a wife, Joseph Brill retires to a middle-class existence in Florida that sounds like a parody of the American dream. Neither has learned more than to sojourn as a stranger in the promised land.

It is difficult to think of a European émigré writer further from all this than Vladimir Nabokov (1899–1977). In fact, the verbal shift required, from immigrant to émigré, suggests some of the difference. Nabokov's first novel in English, *The Real Life of Sebastian Knight*, was published in 1941; it concerns a young Russian in Paris, the narrator, who discovers the true nature of his half-brother, an English novelist, while writing his biography. This was followed by *Bend Sinister* in 1947, about a politically uncommitted professor in a totalitarian state who tries to maintain personal integrity. Four years later, Nabokov published his first memoir, *Conclusive Evidence*, later retitled *Speak, Memory* and, under this title, revised and expanded in 1966. Four years after that, in turn, came the book that established his fortune, his reputation for some and notoriety for others, *Lolita*, published first in France then, after censorship problems were resolved, in the United States in 1958. It tells of the passion of a middle-aged European émigré, who calls himself Humbert Humbert, for what he terms "nymphets" in general and the twelve-year-old girl he calls Lolita in particular, and their wanderings across America. It was Nabokov's first novel set in his new home in the new world; and its success allowed him to devote himself fulltime to his writing. Three more novels appeared after the first publication of *Lolita*: among them, *Pale Fire*, a postmodernist *tour-de-force* purporting to be a poem about an exiled Balkan king in a New England college town and the involved critical commentary on the poem by an academic who admits to being the king himself. Along with the two other novels, *Pnin* (1957) and *Ada, or Ardor: A Family Chronicle* (1969), there are novellas, short stories, a play, critical studies and commentary, translations of his earlier Russian novels, lectures and correspondence, and a monumental translation of Pushkin's *Eugene Onegin* (1964). All of the work reflects Nabokov's aesthetic of subjective idealism. All of it plays variations on the observation made by the academic commentator in *Pale Fire*: "'reality' is neither the subject nor the object of true art," that commentator observes, "which creates its own special reality having nothing to do with the average 'reality' perceived by the communal eye."

Which suggests the fundamental difference between Nabokov and even a writer like Singer, let alone Ozick. "To be sure, there is an average reality, perceived by all of us," Nabokov admits in *Strong Opinions* (1973), a collection of his answers to questions about himself, art, and public issues. "But that is not true reality: it is only the reality of general ideas, conventional forms of humdrummery, current editorials." "Average reality," Nabokov insists, "begins to rot and stink as soon as the act of individual creation ceases to animate a subjectively perceived texture"; any book he makes, any art anyone makes that is worth reading is "a subjective and specific affair." According to this subjective idealist creed, there can be no totalizing, totalitarian reading of experience, no monolithic entity entitled "life." There is only the "manifold shimmer" of separate, specific lives, *my* life, *your* life, *his* life, or *her* life. Nor is there some kind of absolute truth or absolute morality, a master narrative of history or ethics that the artist must discover and disclose. There is no place here for naturalism or didacticism. "I am neither a reader nor a writer of didactic fiction," Nabokov confesses. "Why do I write books, after all? For the sake of pleasure, for the sake of the difficulty." "*Lolita* has no moral in tow," he adds. "For me a work of fiction exists only insofar as it affords me what I bluntly call aesthetic bliss." That bliss is the triumph of art, for Nabokov. Its tragedy is suggested by an anecdote Nabokov tells about the original inspiration for *Lolita*. Which is a story about an ape who, after months of coaxing, produced the first ever drawing by an animal. "This sketch showed the bars of the poor creature's cage."

Lolita is certainly Nabokov's finest book. Before it was published, he wrote of it, to Edmund Wilson, "its art is pure and its fun riotous." The purity of its art has several dimensions. Structurally, Nabokov uses traditional romance patterns only to deconstruct them. Humbert Humbert reveals how he desired Lolita, possessed her, fled with her across America after the death of her mother, Charlotte Haze, lost her to a man named Quilty, then killed her new lover. It is the elemental romance structure used here to startling, inverted effect, with elements of quest, attainment, journey, loss, pursuit, and revenge. The love plot is propelled forward in a straight line, in accordance with whose unremitting extension Charlotte loves Humbert, who loves Lolita, who loves Quilty, who seems to love no one at all. And, as in the courtly love story, the desire of the narrator becomes a metaphor for other kinds of daring, transgression, and retribution. "Oh, My Lolita, I have only words to play with!" Humbert declares early on in the novel. And that discloses another kind of artfulness. The narrator is telling his story as he awaits trial for murder. A "Foreword" by one "John Ray Jr. Ph.D." informs us that Humbert died "in legal captivity" after writing this "Confession of a White Widowed Male" "a few days before his trial was scheduled to start." Humbert is a peculiarly knowing narrator. "I shall not exist if you do not imagine me," he tells the reader. "I am writing this under observation," Humbert admits. Within the narrative, this is literal, since he is in the psychiatric ward of the prison and his cell has an observation window. But Humbert is additionally aware of being under our observation as well. That helps make his story slippery, his character protean, and his language radically self-referential. Like all Nabokov's novels, but even more than most, *Lolita* is a verbal game, a maze: what one character in *Pale Fire* christens a "lexical playfield."

The lexical playfield belongs to the author eventually rather than the narrator. It is Nabokov who discovers pleasure and difficulty in the complex web of allusion and verbal play – "the magic of games," as Humbert calls it – that constitutes the text. There is, however, a distinct difference between the games of the narrator and those of the author, "Lolita" the confession and *Lolita* the novel. It is this. Humbert remains so trapped in his words, the "signposts and tombstones" of his story, that he does not realize he is using Lolita. Nabokov does. A great deal of intercultural fun is derived from the contrast between the "old-world politeness" of Humbert and what he perceives as the intriguing banality of America. This is an international novel, in one of its dimensions; and it offers a riotously comic collision between different languages, different voices. And that collision has the dramatic advantage of allowing Lolita, as she is to herself, to escape through the chinks of the narrative. Perversely, Nabokov once claimed that "one day a reappraiser will come and declare that I was a rigid moralist kicking sin … and assigning sovereign power to tenderness, talent, and pride." That reappraisal is clearly required here, for what we as readers witness is Humbert committing the cardinal sin in the subjective idealistic moral lexicon: he takes another human being as a means rather than an end. In the process, he commits child abuse and statutory rape. But that is subsumed, for Nabokov, under the determining, damning fact that he has acted like a moral totalitarian with Lolita. He has imprisoned her within his own reality, denying her right to herself. Momentarily, Humbert senses this: when, in the last chapter of *Lolita*, he hears from his cell sounds coming from the valley below. "What I heard was but the melody of children at play," he confesses; "and then I knew that the poignant thing was not Lolita's absence from my side, but the absence of her voice from that concord." The note of longing, loss, was one that Nabokov was particular apt to sound. What charges it with a tragic pathos here, however, is the pain of knowing, as Humbert does for a brief moment, that there is nothing worse than this: to rob someone of their childhood – to steal from them the chance to say this is *my* reality, *my* life.

Remapping a nation: Chicano/a and latino/a writing

Different, in turn, from those who came to the United States from the East or West are those who entered from the South: the Mexican Americans. Living in what has become known as occupied America, formerly Mexican land now owned and controlled by the United States, they form a richly hybrid culture: one founded on *mestizo* or mixed origins. Mexican Americans negotiate a border territory, *la frontera*, where competing languages and cultures encounter each other. "Every Mexican knows there are two Mexicos," one Mexican American commentator has observed, "– the real one and Mexico de Afuera (Mexico abroad) as Mexicans call it, composed of all the persons of Mexican origin in the United States." And nowhere has this awareness of duality, two Mexicos, been more apparent than in the distinctive body of Chicano writing that began around 1960.

The term *chicano* probably derives from the sixteenth-century corruption in pronunciation of *mexicano* or *meschicano* which then, with the dropping of the *mes*, becomes *chicano* – or, for the female equivalent, *chicana*. Gaining momentum from the widespread civil rights activism of the 1960s, the chicano movement found expression in both poetry and prose. Chicano poets have been linked with the performance poetry movement, through their multiculturalism and their attachment to a past when the oral was primary. Among the most notable performance poets have been two, in particular, who reveal very clearly the priorities, formal and ideological, of chicano poetry: Gary Soto (1952–) and Jimmy Santiago Baca (1952–) – who is, in fact, half chicano and half Apache. The formal priorities are a clear, uncomplicated language, concrete imagery, a driving rhythm, and a linking of personal experience to the social. The ideological ones are plain enough from Soto's declaration, "I believe in the culture of the poor," and what he has to say, in turn, about the work of Baca. Of the two long narrative poems that comprise *Martin and Meditations on the South Valley* (1987), Soto has said, "What makes this story succeed is its honesty, a brutal honesty, as well as Baca's original imagery and the passion of his writing." "A history is being written of a culture of poverty," Soto added of his fellow chicano, "which, except for a few poets, is absent from American poetry." Those few, of course, include the author of these words, Soto himself, in works that commemorate and celebrate personal memories ("Bealy Street" (1977)), his family ("The Cellar" (1978)), and the Mexican American community ("Kearney Park" (1985)).

What the poetry of Soto and Baca does not possess is suggested by someone else who maps out *la frontera*, the border territory inhabited by Mexican Americans: the chicana poet Lorna Dee Cervantes (1954–). Certainly, Cervantes can rise to a powerful performance rhetoric just as Soto and Baca do. She is acutely aware, as other chicano/a poets are, of division and dispossession. What Cervantes adds to this, however, is a subtle use of speech and symbol, and an even subtler understanding of tensions sometimes within Mexican American culture. Specifically, these tensions have to do with machismo, the tradition of male dominance. Sometimes, as in a poem with the tell-tale title "Macho" (1991), she exposes those tensions simply and directly. At others, she links them with her notion of struggle as the sign and support of all life. What is the enemy is also the guide, Cervantes intimates. What is other to us can enslave or, through struggle, it can liberate. In personal terms, that other for her is men; in ethnic terms, it is machismo. In social terms, it is Anglo-America, in aesthetic terms, it is the English language. In the most elemental terms of all, it is nature. The alternative in each case is to submit and surrender to the enemy and guide or to enter into an encounter – an active engagement – that can lead, in the long run, through mastery to harmony and unity. One of her finest poems, "Beneath the Shadow of the Freeway" (1981), shows this process. On one level, it is a celebration of a multi-generational, all-women family. On another, related to it, it is a celebration of her own life and art, as she builds a home in the world for herself: a harmonious identity with nature, with one "gentle man," and with herself and her own needs. Linking the several forms of survival, homebuilding and harmony, are the images of birds that run through this complex piece. Playing on *pluma*, which in Spanish means both feather and pen, she links the notion of harmony, earned through struggle, to her own vocation as writer, maker of words and the making of this poem. In that way, the poem itself becomes an interlingual, intercultural signpost to survival, personal and communal.

In fiction, the appearance of a distinctively chicano literature was anticipated by the publication of *Pocho* by José Antonio Villareal (1924–2010) in 1959. Setting his story in the turbulent period from the Mexican Revolution of 1910–1920, when Mexican migrants flowed across the border, to the beginning of World War II, Villareal concentrates on two characters, Juan Rubio and his son Richard, to explore and celebrate the process of assimilation, the link of events that binds Mexican Americans to America and the American way of life. That message of assimilation meets its opposite in a novel published ten years after *Pocho, The Plum Pickers* (1969) by Raymond Barrio (1921–1996), which is set, as Villareal's book is, in the Santa Clara Valley of California, but sounds a note of radical resistance. *The Plum Pickers* is different from *Pocho* in formal terms. Highly experimental, it combines documentary realism with political allegory and satirical fantasy; sometimes, the prose breaks into a poetic riff or prophetic comment. It also differs in its conclusions. "Moving, moving, always moving," the central characters of *The Plum Pickers*, the migrant couple Manuel and Lupe Guitterez, experience California as "the newest of modern tortures." They are also dimly aware that the new world they encounter is a bizarre system of oppression. Manuel begins to feel "a thrill of power" as he stands up to his oppressors. Another, younger character called Ramino Sanchez, in turn, embodies a still firmer hope. "He would find a way, some way out," Ramino believes. And he begins to find that way through a will to action that does not stop short of violence – and that embraces both restoration of the past and revolution in the future. Working towards all this, he seems to link up with a myriad others involved in a struggle against oppression, "from prehistory into glassbright civilization." In an epic story of resistance, he is the rebel as culture hero.

Two books published shortly after *The Plum Pickers*, in the early 1970s, announced the arrival of chicano fiction as a major presence in American literature. The first was ...*y no se lo trágo la tierra/And the Earth Did Not Devour Him* (1971) by Tomás Rivera (1935–1984). The son of Mexican citizens who migrated to Texas in the 1920s, Rivera worked as a migrant farm laborer in the 1950s; and this experience, together with his working-class background, formed the basis of his writing. *Tierra* has profound social concerns, but it is not a work of social realism. Instead, in covering the ten years from 1945 to 1955, it offers a complex narrative of subjective impressions. Concentrating on the lives and wanderings of Mexican workers, and with the Korean War serving as an immediate backdrop, *Tierra* eschews chronological presentation and linear plot development. What it has instead is a structure reminiscent of Hemingway's *In Our Time*. Two vignettes frame the book. Within that frame are twelve brief stories or *estempas* common to Spanish and Latin American fiction, interspersed with thirteen sketches. The links between these different elements are tonal and thematic, as Rivera reveals a dawning sense of communal solidarity among the Mexican migrants. A central character, an unnamed boy, appears in many, but by no means all, of the sections. On one level, *Tierra* narrates an allegorical year in the life of this anonymous young farmworker; and, on this level, what the reader witnesses is the growth of a consciousness. The host of migrant workers, caught in the flow of their feelings and thoughts, gradually register their ability to sustain their own imagined community. As they do so, and in a related movement, the central narrative persona constructs an identity for himself that enables him to mediate between his Mexican past and neocolonial present. He also recognizes that this identity depends on identification with the people, the wretched of the earth who share his condition of wandering.

So, in its thematic inclination, *Tierra* is very different from *In Our Time*. The central character realizes himself with rather than without his people. Like the equally anonymous protagonist of Ralph Ellison's *Invisible Man*, it is his task to forge the uncreated conscience of his race. *Tierra* is a novel that does not work in the easy, polarized terms of assimilation or resistance. Instead, it explores and enunciates the complex, richly layered character of Mexican American identity, as the nameless narrator, the anonymous bearer of his race, becomes a spiritual voyager – open to constant transformation as the old struggles with the new. A similar awareness of ethnic identity as a borderland, a meeting place between different cultures, marks the other novel that announced the arrival of chicano fiction as a significant force, *Bless Me, Ultima* (1972) by Rudolfo A. Anaya (1937–). Rich in folklore, moving between memory, reality, and dream, the material, myth, and magic, the book focuses on the experiences of Antonio Marez as he begins school towards the end of World War II. The novel is attentive to the specifics of the culture where it is set, a fairly remote area of New Mexico: a culture rooted in the rich traditions of precolumbian aboriginal America and the Spain of the golden age. It also draws on the early experiences of its author. It reaches out beyond that, however, to map the border territory that, spiritually, all Mexican Americans inhabit – perhaps everyone, in a transcultural age. And, as Anaya himself has observed, Antonio is not so much a fragment of autobiography as a paradigmatic new world person, a cultural composite who "incorporates the Espanol and the Indio, the old world and the new."

As the last of four sons in the family, Antonio bears the burden of the increasingly desperate hopes of his parents. His mother is a Luna, a descendant of farmers and priests, his father a Marez, descended from sailors and vaqueros. Their family names sketch out their different allegiances. Both are alert to tradition. For the mother, though, tradition involves stillness. "It is the blood of the Lunas to be quiet," she tells Antonio. "They are quiet like the moon." For the father, it involves independence, adventure. "It is the blood of the Marez to be wild," the mother explains, "like the ocean from which they take their name, and the spaces of the llano which have become their home." "Oh, it was hard to grow up," Antonio comments, as he recalls struggling with the conflicting ambitions of his parents for him: to be a farmer or a priest, or a vaquero. And, in growing up, he turns to the tutelage of Ultima who "came to stay with us," Antonio remembers, "the summer I was almost seven." Ultima is "a curandera, a woman who knew the herbs and remedies of the ancients, a miracle worker." Through her, he learns of the cultures of the Indians of the region; he recovers an indigenous education in his cultural origins far more persuasive than the one offered in school. With her, he also learns what he calls "the secret of my destiny"; and he experiences a sense of unity with his surroundings. "Does one have to choose?" the young man asks, when he is told he must decide "between the god of the church, or the beauty that is here and now." And quietly Ultima reveals that he does not. As she tells Antonio, when she appears to him in a dream, existence is interdependence, communality. The task of the young protagonist, then, is not to choose between this or that, but to "take the llano and the river valley, the moon and the sea, the God of the church and the gods of aboriginal folklore and make something new": to realize his deepest potential, for himself and for his people, out of the cycle, the confluence of elements that is his being. As the dying Ultima blesses Antonio at the end of the novel, she tells him, "I shall be with you"; and she is still there with him, the reader infers, all the while he narrates this story. What Antonio has been blessed with, above all, is the power to liberate himself from the warring contraries of his inheritance by seeing and synthesizing them, then speaking of that synthesis here.

One of the distinctive features of chicano fiction of a more recent generation is that it acknowledges the movement of many Mexican Americans into new, urban environments. Another, even more distinctive feature is that it is very often written by women and, as with the poetry of Lorna Dee Cervantes, adopts a critical view towards the cult of machismo and the tensions between the sexes in the Mexican American community. A notable illustration of both these features is the fiction of Sandra Cisneros (1954–): *The House on Mango Street* (1980), then later *Woman Hollering Creek and Other Stories* (1991). Born in Chicago, Cisneros spent her early years moving backwards and forwards between the United States and Mexico with her family. Moving to the border state of Texas, she then began to write what she later described as "the stories that haven't been written . . . to fill a literary void." The eventual result was the collection *The House on Mango Street*, which established her reputation. In this volume, Cisneros developed the form used by other chicano/a writers, such as Rivera: a series of related stories and sketches, with a central character and narrator to provide them with a sense of continuity. The central character here is Esparanza Cordero, a young girl who moves into the house that gives the book its title. The trope of movement so rooted in chicano fiction is still there. However, this series of stories concentrates on Esparanza, her family, and the rundown neighborhood in Chicago where they live. "Here there is too much sadness and not enough sky," Esparanza observes. Giving her narrator an intimate idiom that moves between the colloquial and the lyrical, Cisneros explores the "sadness" of those lives and their gazing at the "sky," yearning for something better. Telling her story ("I like to tell stories," she confides), Esparanza confides in few people apart from the reader (whom she calls "my friend"). And her confidences begin to liberate her. By the end of the collection, she is beginning to realize that freedom.

The House on Mango Street addresses several forms of enclosure and liberation: opposites figured throughout the story in terms of the polarities of house and sky, room and window (so many women in these stories spend their time gazing from their windows), streets and trees. This is a series of stories about coming of age: Esparanza breaks slowly out into the adult world of high heels and womanly hips, jobs and kisses, sex and death. It is also about the ghetto, the urban enclosure inhabited by Mexican Americans, where, as Esparanza puts it, "we make the best of it," living in an exile that is cultural and also maybe linguistic – dreaming, perhaps, of "the ones left behind . . . far away." It is also about the imprisonment of women, denied the possibility of realizing their dreams even – especially – by their own men. Finally, it is about the mind-forged manacles from which the narrator is freed through her writing: literally so, since by the end of the book she is ready to depart. "One day I will go away," Esparanza explains, to a house of her own: a true house that is, in part, the house of fiction, like the book she is telling and Cisneros is writing. "They will not know I have gone away to come back," she says of the friends and neighbors she will leave. "For the ones I left behind. For the one who cannot out."

The fiction of Helena Maria Viramontes (1954–) measures the capacity for experiment shown by chicano/a writers, especially the more recent ones. It also reveals how permeable the barriers are between the chicano/a and the wider latino/a communities. In her short story collection, *The Moths and Other Stories* (1985), Viramontes uses a fractured narrative technique to disrupt our reading of the text. The effect is one of strangeness, disorientation, so that we, the readers, experience a disturbance analogous

to that felt by her characters, the immigrant workers entering a culture not their own –
and one that values them only intermittently, as useful tools. It is an effect that the
chicana poet Pat Mora (1942–) also achieves in poems like "Border Town: 1938"
(1986) and "Unnatural Speech" (1986). As readers, we are hurled here into forms of
broken speech and narration that imitate precisely the immigrant experience of shifting,
suspected, multiple identities. "An American/to Mexicans/a Mexican to Americans/"
as Mora observes, in one of the poems, "Legal Alien," from her first collection, *Chants*
(1984): this is "the discomfort/of being pre-judged/Bi-laterally," "sliding back and
forth/between the fringes of both worlds." Viramontes adds to the discomfort
announced and aroused by Mora, by subverting the traditional Mexican American
notion of "familia." This she does in two ways: by opening up concepts of the family and
community to feminist perspectives, and by enlarging those concepts to embrace "los
ores Americanos" – other refugees and immigrants from other hispanic cultures. Her
books cut across the boundaries between chicano and other hispanic cultures, not only
because they exploit the magical, experimental techniques of Latin American writers
like Gabriel Garcia Marquez, but because they incorporate people and memories from
countries like El Salvador. They remind us that there is a wider hispanic community to
which Mexican Americans belong: which is a community of the oppressed.

This is particularly true of those from Puerto Rico, who began coming to the
mainland in large numbers after World War I. One of the most outspoken writers, as far
as the Puerto Rican experience is concerned, is the poet Pedro Pietri (1944–2004). One
of the so-called Nuyorican poets who began to read at the Nuyorican Poet's Cafe in
New York City, Pietri is typical of these poets as a group. He uses a harsh, demotic
language, the street speech of African Americans and Puerto Ricans in the barrio, to
reflect the problems and the pride of "puertorriquenos." In a key text for Nuyorican
poetry, *Puerto Rican Obituary* (1973), Pietri even creates a mock epic about the Puerto
Rican community. The image of communal death is deployed here to denounce the
suffering of everyone in the barrio; men and women have died, the poet declares, and
will continue to die, "Always broke/Always owing/Never knowing/that they are a
beautiful people." Yet the poem concludes in a hopeful vein: with a vision of some place
where "puertorriquenas" can achieve peace. That place is "aquí," "here" within each
Puerto Rican man and woman. This is a vision of possible redemption that measures its
distance from mainstream millennialism, the American dream, precisely through its
bilingualism, the poetic use of English and Spanish – and what has been called
"Spanglish," a mixture of the two.

Tato Laviera (1951–) is another Puerto Rican poet who mixes languages to register
his mixed inheritance and uses a powerful orality to capture the rhythms of the street.
Laviera has published several volumes, including *La Carreta Made a U-Turn* (1976)
and *Mixturao and Other Poems* (2008), but he has always produced poems that are
meant to be sung or spoken. He celebrates the Puerto Rican community and his own
Puertoricanness. However, he also insists on the presence of a new ethnic identity, the
product of a convergence with other minority groups: with New York City as the
exemplary space in which this cultural mixing, or *mestijaze*, occurs. "We gave birth to a
new generation," Laviera announces in "AmeRican" (1985), and the title of this poem
is the term he uses to describe this "new generation": a new America with the accents of
many cultures. In his own way, Laviera is rewriting the vision of Whitman. His poems

often have the oracular sweep of "Song of Myself," with Laviera stirring in new influences, such as the oral traditions of Puerto Rico and Caribbean and Afro-Caribbean music. They equally often proclaim the arrival of a new dispensation in the new world, just as Whitman did. But this "new america, humane america, admired america, loved america, harmonious america" that Laviera conjures, with driving rhythms, speaks in the tongues of many languages, more than even Whitman ever imagined: among them, "the soul gliding talk of gospel boogie music" and "new words in spanglish tenements, fast tongue moving street corner . . . talk being invented at the insistence of a smile!" By comparison, Victor Hernández Cruz (1949–) is a more formal, introspective poet, whose work registers the influence of such different aesthetic movements as surrealism, concrete poetry, and minimalism. He is attentive to the subtleties of wordplay, as the title of his 1982 collection, *By Lingual Wholes*, illustrates – alluding as it does to bilingualism and the warring concepts of totality and absence. And he is interested in literary experiment. Nevertheless, Cruz is just as committted as Laviera and Pietri are to registering the truth of his culture. In "Mountain Building," past and present converge, as the mountains where the Indians once lived metamorphose into high-rise buildings where Puerto Ricans now live with other impoverished ethnic groups, among them later generations of Indians. "It is," the poet observes, "the same people in the windowed/Mountains."

The poetry of Cruz represents a transformation of literary English thanks to its contact with Spanish. Witty, often erudite, and sometimes violent, it exists at the intersection between English and Spanish literary cultures. So, in another way, do the poetry and prose of Aurora Levins Morales (1954–) and Judith Ortiz Cofer (1952–). Morales was born in Puerto Rico, brought up in Chicago and rural New Hampshire, and now lives in the San Francisco Bay area. Her ethnic origins are a similarly rich mix. "I am a child of the Americas,/," she writes in "Child of the Americas" (1986), "a light-skinned mostiza of the Caribbean,/a child of many diaspora, born into this continent at a crossroads." "I am a US Puerto Rican Jew," she adds in the same poem; "my first language was spanglish." To explain her life at the crossroads, she draws on several traditions: notably, Latin American writers like Pablo Neruda, American feminists such as Adrienne Rich, and the African American author Alice Walker. Morales identifies herself, not just with latina women, but American women of color. She uses the signs and symbols of her Puerto Rican and Jewish inheritances to link the experiences of her own body to the body politic: not just on a national but an international level – she is, for example, deeply concerned with the Middle East conflict. Transnational and transcultural in her concerns, she is also transgenerational: her 1986 book, *Getting Home Alive*, for instance, was co-authored with her mother Rosa; she has described it as a "cross-fertilization" between her mother's voice and her own.

"In American literature, I, as a Puerto Rican child, did not exist," the novelist and short story writer Nicholasa Mohr (1935–) has observed; "and I as a Puerto Rican woman do not exist now." That is a gap, an absence, Mohr herself has attempted to fill. So has Esmerelda Santiago (1940–) in her memoir *When I Was Puerto Rican* (1993) and her novel *América's Dream* (1996). In novels like *Nilda* (1974) and *Felita* (1979), and in the twelve stories of *El Bronx Remembered* (1976), Mohr focuses on the experiences of children and adolescents: to show how, as she puts it in the preface to *El Bronx Remembered*, Puerto Ricans are "strangers in their own country ... with a different language, culture, and racial mixture." A similar sense of difference, together with defiance, shines through the story of the immigrant woman América Gonzales, the central character in *América's Dream*. A hotel maid on the island of Vieques off the Puerto Rican coast, she is "not ashamed" of her job. "It's housework, women's work," she tells herself, "nothing to be ashamed of." Nevertheless, she seems trapped in a system of power: her identity and body controlled, not only by the work she is required to do, but by an abusive partner. By the close of the novel, however, América has made a new life for herself. Her partner killed by her when he abused her one time too often, she moves to a Puerto Rican section of the Bronx. She still bears the scars of the abusive relationship she has escaped. "They're there to remind her that she fought for her life, and ... has a right to live her life as she chooses it," the novel concludes. "It is, after all, her life, and she's the one in the middle of it." *América's Dream*, as its title implies, is a novel that reconstructs the American dream: as an act of resistance to both the machismo of the old culture and the neocolonial oppression of the new.

The largest source of new residents in New York City, for the past several decades, has not, however, been Puerto Rico but the Dominican Republic. Dominicans accounted for one out of every five immigrants to the city in the 1990s. They have also been the subject of two remarkable novels by Julia Alvarez (1950–), a Dominican who emigrated to the United States in the 1960s: *How the Garcia Girls Lost Their Accents* (1991) and *Yo* (1997). The narrative of the earlier and finer of these novels centers on political turmoil and flight, with the Garcia family escaping to the United States after being implicated in a failed plot against the Dominican dictator Trujillo. Its tripartite structure, in turn, moves back in time: from 1989 to 1972, then 1970 to 1960, then 1960 to 1956. The Garcia family arrive in America in a condition of "abrupt exile" and soon encounter an alien culture. Dr. Garcia, the father, never shakes off all the residues of his former life as a prominent member of the Dominican community, such as his accent and his assumption of patriarchal authority. He is enough of a realist, though, to assimilate himself to the American work ethic and an agenda of social mobility. He is also sufficiently successful in his new clinical practice to move the family out to Long Island eventually. Very soon, he is proudly proclaiming his new identity as "*un dominican-york*," and takes out American citizenship. The real center of the family is not Dr. Garcia, however, but his wife Laura. Her abrupt exile may initially lead her to recall her old home "through the lens of loss." But she soon becomes the "daughter of invention" in America. To her four daughters, she is "their Thomas Edison, their Benjamin Franklin Mom," the emotional matrix of their lives and their role model. Gathered together in an "invisible sisterhood," the four Garcia girls learn independence from her. One of the daughters, Yolanda, who turns to writing as a vocation, finds adjustment difficult. The central consciousness of the novel, as her nickname "Yoyo" implies, she finds herself yoyoing, oscillating between the old culture and the new in a way that the other Garcias do not. But, as the narrative makes clear, her reluctance to become simply American is not a sign of her identification with her old home. Rather, it is a symptom of her subtle reaction to the alchemy of exile; she, at least, understands that she must recreate herself out of the two cultures to which she is heir.

Another potent source of latino culture in the United States has been supplied by the successive waves of immigrants arriving from Cuba. In *The Mambo Kings Play Songs of Love* (1989), Oscar Hijuelos (1951–) centers his story on two Cuban brothers, Nestor and Cesar Castillo, who arrive in America a decade before the revolution in their homeland. It is 1949, and Latin American music is at the height of its popularity. "Part of the wave of musicians who had been pouring out of Havana," they are lured by the hope of fame and fortune. They love "the immensity of the United States," and they embrace the glamour of the metropolis. In New York City they also find themselves cheerfully at home in a community of immigrants, "apartments filled with travelers or cousins and friends from Cuba." Their music, a mix of Cuban and American influences, enables them to make sense of their new world and navigate their way through their divided allegiances. However, the novel is no simple success story. Even at the height of their fame, the songs of the Castillo brothers, full of the "sadness and torment of love," reflect their lingering attachment to a lost, lamented world. And with the passing of the fashion for Latin music, the Castillo brothers find their fame fading away. Not a simple success story, neither is *The Mambo Kings* a naturalist tale of failure and decline. It is a magically realist account of the way celebration and sadness are woven into the same tapestry. The story is structurally framed by the occasion when, at the apex of their fame, the Castillo brothers appear on the *I Love Lucy* television show. And it is emotionally framed by the Cuban American star of that show, Desi Arnaz, who invites them to appear after hearing, in their music, a poignant expression of "his own past love, his love for . . . his family down in Cuba and old friends he had not seen in a long time." Like the Castillo brothers, Desi remains torn between his old home and his new. Like them, too, he has shaped his life, and his art, out of the fusion between them.

"Cuba is a peculiar exile, I think, and island-colony," says the narrator of *Dreaming in Cuban* (1992) by Christine Garcia (1958–). "We can reach it by a thirty-minute charter flight from Miami, but never reach it at all." The dreamlike rhythm of longing and attachment, exile and return, is as fundamental to this novel as it is to *The Mambo Kings*. It describes the condition out of which here too, like the Castillo brothers, the characters must construct an authentic reality: in this case, the four women of the del Pino family. The idea of Cuba is a shifting, ambiguous dream for all four: the different ways in which they try to come to terms with that dream determine their lives and describe quite different strands in the Cuban American experience. The oldest of the four, Celia del Pino, for instance, stays in Cuba, where she transfers an unrequited passion for a lost love to "El Lider," Fidel Castro. Her daughter, Lourdes, on the other hand, moves to Brooklyn where she embraces American opportunity, becoming a successful entrepreneur, head of her own "Yankee Doodle Bakery" chain. The daughter of Lourdes, in turn, Pilar, the signature voice of the novel, experiences a dual exile, caught in the interstices between Cuban and American cultures. By the close of the story, she has returned to Cuba. Nevertheless, she realizes that "sooner or later" she will return to New York. "I know now," she says, "it's where I belong – not *instead* of here, but *more* than here." That strikes a recurrent chord in the fiction by and about Cuban Americans. Dreaming mostly in metropolitan spaces, the characters in this fiction may have trouble weaving their way between memory and longing. But they never entirely surrender their dreams; sometimes, they even manage to give them magical life.

Improvising America: Asian American writing

As late as 1960, there were less then 900,000 people of Asian descent in the United States. Thirty years later, there were more than seven million. The largest group, in terms of national origins, were and are Chinese Americans, followed by Filipinos, Japanese, Asian Indians, Koreans, Vietnamese and, lower down the numerical scale, Laotians, Cambodians, and Hmong. By the end of World War II, the Chinese American community was decimated, its ageing bachelor society waiting for an injection of new immigrants and a recovery of family life. *Eat a Bowl of Tea* (1961) by Louis Chu (1925–1970) is one of several novels to capture the tone of this bachelor society; others include *Chinatown Family* (1948) by Lin Yutang (1895–1976) and *The Flower Drum Song* (1957) by Chin Yang Lee (1917–). What has been remarkable, though, since the publication of the Chu novel, is not only the exponential growth in the Chinese American population, but also the proliferation of Chinese American writing: poetry, autobiography, and, above all, fiction. Among poets, the most notable has been Cathy Song (1955–). Song was born in Honolulu to a Chinese mother and Korean father. Her first book, *Picture Bride*, was published in 1983. Consisting of thirty-one poems divided into five sections, *Picture Bride* concentrates on autobiography to explore family and history – and, in particular, the equivocal nature of her own relation with the traditions of Asian culture. In "The Youngest Daughter," for example, Song delicately sketches out her relation with her mother, "the familiar silence" of their intimacy, her mother's unease about her and her own longing for flight. Other poems explore, with similar, mothlike precision, the routines of family life, a home where "there was always something that needed fixing" ("The Tower of Pisa" (1987)), the "magic island" of Hawaii where Song was born ("The Magic Island" (1988)), and a later generation – "We love them more than life,/" as the poet puts it in "The Binding" (1988), "these children that are born to us." Always, these poems hover gracefully between the old and the new, memory and adventure. As a result, the poetic persona that weaves her way through them seems to belong with the "beautiful iridescent" women whom the Japanese printmaker Utamuro depicted and whom Song celebrates in her poem, "Beauty and Sadness" (1983), as "creatures from a floating world."

As for prose, the three most notable Chinese American writers of the past few decades have all also been female: Amy Tan (1952–), Gish Jen (1956–), and Maxine Hong Kingston (1940–). All three are preoccupied with what Jen, in *Typical American* (1991), jokingly refers to as being "Chang-Kees" or "Chinese Yankees." All turn their attention, at times, to the first generation born and brought up in the United States and their poignant, often problematical relationship with their immigrant parents. Their strategies for dramatizing and dealing with the bilingual, bicultural dilemmas of their protagonists are, however, very different. So, in *The Joy Luck Club* (1989), then later *The Kitchen God's Wife* (1991) and *The Bonesetter's Daughter* (2001), Amy Tan concentrates on the relation between mothers and daughters, as a measure of changes and continuities that are both cultural and emotional. *The Joy Luck Club*, for instance, is a series of narratives telling the stories of eight women: the four original members of the Joy Luck Club of Gweilin and their four daughters, all born in the United States. The mothers initially met every week, despite deprivation and devastation, to devise their own moments of respite, gossip, and anecdote around the mah-jong table in China. In the United States, they continue to meet, to talk, praise, and complain about their daughters until one of the mothers dies. The novel makes two complete rounds of the table. As it does so, it explores the generational contests that form its core. "My mother believed you could be anything you wanted to be in America," one of the daughters, Jing-Mei "June" Woo, recalls. Despite such beliefs, the mother, Suyuan Woo, is outraged by the very American independence of her daughter. To begin with, Jing-Mei resists her mother's demand that she could and should mix "American circumstances and Chinese character." "Inside," she feels and her mother suspects, "– she is all American-made." But, like the other daughters, she eventually learns that, as one of the other mothers, An-Mei Hsu, puts it, "All of us are like stairs, one step after another, going up and down, but all going the same way." There is continuity, connection: something that Jing-Mei, in particular, discovers when, following her mother's death, she travels to China. "I am becoming Chinese," she reflects, as her mother had predicted and hoped. By retrieving the past, the history of her mother, the daughter learns how to balance her Americanized identity against the claims of tradition. She is, she now understands, both Chinese and American, Jing-Mei and June.

Gish Jen has similarly centered her stories around family, but in a much quirkier way. Her stories, many of them, and her novels, *Typical American* and *Mona in the Promised Land* (1996), are concerned with the Chang family: in particular, the father, Ralph Chang and the two daughters, Mona and Callie. "It's an American story," *Typical American* begins. Like Jen's 2005 novel, *The Love*, it is also a story told with ironic wit. Ralph, born with the name Yifeng, comes to America in 1947. On the boat from China, he composes a list of aims for himself that recalls the self-help program of Benjamin Franklin. Arriving in San Francisco, the "splendor" and "radiance" of the Golden Gate Bridge is wreathed in fog. That is the first sign of the paradoxical nature of the Golden Land he will encounter. As he then travels across the New World to New York City, "the whole holy American spectacle," "famous rivers, plains, canyons" "lumbered by," but he does not notice them. He is too immersed in his studies. He does, however, notice and admire New York. This, after all, is "the city of cities," Ralph tells himself: an intricate American machine, almost mythic in its mechanical grandeur and the opposite of his rural Chinese upbringing. Here, he embarks on his own eccentric quest to become a typical American: with a new name, given to him by a secretary at the university where he enrols and a gradually acquired new language. The quest, Jen suggests in a recurrent image, is like a roller-coaster ride: full of surprises, slow rises, sudden falls, then gradual recoveries. "Anything could happen, this was America," Ralph tells himself when he first arrives. "He gave himself up to the country, and dreamt." Just about anything and everything does then happen to him. As a result, he does appear to have learned his lesson, and begun to change, by the end of the novel. "Opposites begin in one another," Ralph's father once told him. Now, Ralph is starting to see how opposites begin in him, since Chinese past and American promise both form part of his character.

Maxine Hong Kingston is the most widely recognized contemporary Asian American writer. Her first book, *The Woman Warrior* (1975), is subtitled *Memoirs of a Girlhood Among Ghosts*. It is, however, not so much a memoir as an intentionally hybrid form, blending elements of several genres: myth, fiction, autobiography, and biography, as well as memoir. Negotiating both the sexism of traditional Chinese culture and the racism of white America, Kingston recounts the childhood experiences of a young girl. Interweaving adolescent confusion and uncertainty of perspective with ironic adult commentary, she describes someone caught between her Chinese inheritance and her American upbringing, Canton and California. The narrative as a whole is separated into five sections, each one pursuing the theme of the development of the young girl into the inspirational figure of the woman warrior. Each section, in turn, tells the story of a particular woman who has a formative influence on the protagonist, who is also the narrator. These maternal figures, who are both actual and mythical, gradually promote a growth from silence to speech. For what the book slowly discloses is the power of story to shape character and behavior: the opportunity, and even the necessity, to speak oneself into being and identity. To that extent, the woman warrior is the writer, the author of *The Woman Warrior*. Tellingly, the book opens with an injunction to silence. "You must not tell anyone what I am about to tell you," Kingston's mother warns her, before revealing the true story of Kingston's aunt's illegitimate pregnancy, shaming, and eventual suicide. This is the "no name woman" of the first movement. For Kingston, "deliberately forgetting" her aunt has been the cruelest punishment meted our to her by her family. Now, by "telling" about her she is redressing the balance. She knows the perils attendant on this. Her aunt, she recognizes, is an unquiet ghost who "does not always mean me well." But she is willing to take that risk in order to discover in the past what she needs for her own speech and survival.

The solution *The Woman Warrior* offers to the problem of being both a "Chinese 'I'" and an "American 'I'" is not to collapse these dualities and differences but to accommodate them. The final story, "A Song for a Barbarian Reed Pipe," offers an illustration of this. It is about an actual historical figure, Ts'ai Yen, who was captured and forced to live in "barbarian" lands for many years. A mother, warrior, and poet, to her "the barbarians were primitives," we are told. But she heard a strange music among them, made on reed flutes; and she learned how to sing in a way that somehow "matched the flutes." Returned to her own people at last, Ts'ai Yen "brought her songs back from savage lands." One of these is called "'Eighteen Stanzas for a Barbarian Reed Pipe,' a song that Chinese sing to their own instruments. It translated well." Clearly, Ts'ai Yen supplies an analogue for the author and narrator's own status as a woman warrior of words: using the instruments or forms at her disposal to "translate" her experiences, dramatize her own mixed heritage. Equally clearly, there is change here, since the old story is rewritten as it is retold, and there is also consistency – not least, because *this* version of the story is retold by both mother and daughter. "The beginning is hers," Kingston discloses, "the ending, mine." The young girl remembered in *The Woman Warrior* is someone who seems habitually stifled and silenced: her inability, in particular, to speak with confidence in English is linked to a crisis in identity. What she learns is what the narrator demonstrates: how to find refuge and redemption in telling, writing books like this one.

The book that followed *The Woman Warrior*, in 1980, *China Men*, also depends on family history. As its title implies, however, it concentrates on men and on a difficult, uncommunicative relationship between father and daughter. A hybrid, like its predecessor, it also draws on history and imaginative revisioning of historical fact. Her aim, Kingston said, was to "claim America" for Chinese Americans by showing how deeply in debt America is to the labor of Chinese men, her forebears among them, who cleared the land, built the railroads, and created fertile farmland out of desert and swamp. *Tripmaster Monkey: His Fake Book*, published in 1989, is more of a novel, recounting the exploits of Wittman Ah Sing. Wittman, a "Chinese beatnik" as he is called at one juncture in the story, is a protean figure, who gradually resolves his problems by embracing his immigrant past while singing the song of an American open road. And like its protagonist, the form of the book is fluid, with the borderlines between naturalism and myth constantly blurred. This may be the story of a beatnik playwright, a contemporary incarnation of Walt Whitman, living in Berkeley, California in the 1960s. It also alludes to Chinese legend and fantasy, however. One constant source of reference, for example, is the Chinese classic, *Monkey* or *Journey to the West*, the story of a magical, mischievous monkey who accompanies a monk to India for the sacred books of Buddhism. Resisting any monolithic notion of American identity, Wittman sees and names multiplicity as the core of personal and national selfhood. For him, as for his (almost) namesake, the author of "Song of Myself," America is a "teeming Nation of nations." Both Wittman and Whitman, in turn, echo Kingston here: who, in *Tripmaster Monkey* as in all her other writing, creates a multidimensional fictive space to express the American mosaic.

Unlike the Chinese, the Japanese had historically emigrated to America, before World War II, as families. They had no equivalent of the Chinese American "bachelor society." What Japanese Americans had with the outbreak of war, however, was far more traumatic. The attack on Pearl Harbor in 1941 created a mood of national hysteria, one consequence of which was the creation of internment camps for people of Japanese ancestry. It was a transformational moment, a radical displacement of humanity that became a dominant trope for Japanese American writers – as powerful for them as the trope of the Middle Passage was, and remains, for African American writers. Several Japanese American writers wrote highly critical retrospective narratives after the war, describing the experience of internment. These included two notable collections of short stories, *Yokohama, California* (1949) by Toshio Mori (1910–1980) and *Seventeen Syllables and Other Stories* (1985) by Hisaye Yamamoto (1921–), and the autobiographical *Nisei Daughter* (1953) by Monica Sone (1919–). The most remarkable book to come out of the Japanese American experience of the war, however, is *The No-No Boy* (1957) by John Okada (1923–1971). It is also a milestone, one of the first Japanese American novels. The "no-no boy" of the title is a twenty-five-year-old Japanese American, Ichiro Yamada. In 1943, all internees were given a "loyalty questionnaire" containing two unsettling questions: whether or not the internee would be willing to serve in the American military and whether or not they would deny allegiance to Japan. Ichiro, we learn, has answered "no-no" to these two questions; and when we meet him, at the beginning of the novel, he has just returned to Seattle, where his family lives, after two years in the internment camp and – following his refusal to be drafted – a further two years in a federal prison. He is no hero, but an alienated stranger in his own land, doubly marginalized and conflicted because he rejects his Japanese as well as his American identity. His family, similarly conflicted, offers no refuge. On the basic level of communication, there is division and confusion, since his parents "spoke virtually no English" while "the children, like Ichiro, spoke almost no Japanese." His father, a submissive, feminized reversal of traditional Japanese notions of patriarchy, seeks comfort in drink, while his mother is so disoriented by the war and internment that she firmly believes Japan was victorious and that ships will soon be arriving to take them home. Ichiro rejects the mythmaking of his mother, together with "her stories about gallant and fierce warriors" drawn from traditional Japanese lore. He cannot, and will not, embrace the foundation narratives – and, more specifically, the warrior values – of either America or Japan. So he becomes a wanderer. To use a trope that Okada weaves through the narrative, he is a traveler moving around without a map.

What compel *The No-No Boy* in new directions, gradually, are the relationships Ichiro has with his friend, Kenji, and his lover, Emi. Kenji is his foil and desired double. Kenji, a decorated and wounded war hero, is idolized, whereas Ichiro is despised; his family is brought together by the war, while the family of Ichiro is torn apart. Kenji offers Ichiro the chance of intimacy, the opportunity to break out of the descending spiral of his own hopelessness: not least, when Ichiro is required to witness, and share in, Kenji's suffering and dying. A similar chance, to break out and perhaps believe in "the great compassionate stream of life that is America," is offered by the woman to whom Kenji introduces him. Emi, whose father was repatriated to Japan and whose husband, a Japanese American soldier, has left her for a second tour of military duty and will never return, is freely compassionate and loving. Together with Kenji, she is vital to the protagonist's sometimes fainthearted "quest for completeness." That quest is never completed, to the extent that the narrative circles back on itself: with Ichiro, at the end, still in motion. But, at least, there is the sense, as the book goes on, that this *is* a quest: not just a wandering but a seeking. Ichiro extends his sympathies to a former enemy injured in a barroom brawl; his frozen emotional state starts to thaw; and his story closes, for us, on a carefully nuanced note of hope. The conclusion is not simply affirmative. What it is, is delicately shaded: Ichiro leaves the story journeying towards redemption, the elusive promise of a recovery that is both personal and cultural.

Janice Mirikitani (1942–) also experienced internment as a very young girl. It is an experience that supplies material for many of her poems. So do her memories of her mother and father, who were interned along with her. In "Breaking Silence" (1987), she even uses excerpts from her mother's testimony to the Commission on Wartime Relocation and Internment. The quotations reveal her mother's courage – and her resistance to the traditional imperatives of female submission and silence. That resistance is shared by the daughter. It has led Mirikitani to weave the lyrical and the political together, or sometimes be direct to the point of bluntness. It has also led her to celebrate rebellion as the only, true tradition that one generation of Asian American women should pass down to the next. "My daughter denies she is like me," Mirikitani says in "Breaking Tradition" (1987). "She mirrors my ageing,/" she adds. "She is breaking tradition." The daughter becomes like the mother in wanting to be unlike her. She reflects her, by insisting on being herself, doing things her own way.

Another accomplished Japanese American poet, Garrett Hongo (1951–), offers a different nuance on the idea of tradition. Hongo has a keen eye for what he has called the "specificities" that "bear culture." In a manner that is sometimes reminiscent of the Imagists, he presses the telling detail into service, the random gesture or casual habit that carries a whole freight of cultural meaning. So, "the essence/of garlic and black lotus root" can become a paradigm for the secrets of Japanese culture ("Who Among You Knows the Essence of Garlic?" (1982)). And the poet's own father, in "Off from

Swing Shift" (1982), betting on horse races with his constant dream that "maybe tonight" would be "his night/for winning, his night/for beating the odds," is made to epitomise, in an oddly heroic fashion, Japanese American suffering and stoicism. Hongo is adept, too, at secret histories. His anonymous characters voice their experiences of living "on the frontier" ("The Unreal Dwelling: My Years in Volcano" (1985)). As they do so, they reveal an irrepressible spirit that has plainly cultural, communal origins. In "Something Whispered in the *Shakukachi*" (1982), for instance, the speaker of the poem recalls his poverty in peacetime, internment in wartime, and subsequent survival. He is reminded, in particular, of the flutes he used to fashion out of the bamboo on his farm, and play, when he was much younger. It is an apt image of someone making something out of nothing, or very little. It is also a compelling portrait of the artist as Japanese American, making music out of his own territory and tradition.

Like the Japanese, many Korean immigrants traveled initially to Hawaii, escaping first from Japanese aggression at the beginning of the twentieth century and then, between 1930 and 1945, from Japanese occupation. Something of what Koreans had to contend with during the years of occupation is revealed in *Comfort Woman* (1997) by Nora Okja Keller (1965–). The novel is narrated from the perspective of Akiko, a Korean refugee who has fled to the United States, and her daughter by an American missionary, Beccah. And it tells the story of a search for stability, and a secure identity, framed by the mother's secret past as a "comfort woman," a prostitute in a "recreation camp" forced to service the Japanese military. Eventually, they stay in Hawaii. There it becomes Beccah's task to piece together the traumatic story of her mother. As Akiko struggles to come to terms with her past, she tries to find a place for herself in America. That place is never really found, not least because she sees the United States only as a "country of excess and extravaganza." Her daughter, too, experiences dislocation and disorientation. Still, by the end of the narrative, she is beginning to break out of "death thoughts" in a way that, understandably, her mother could never manage. With her mother dead, but the truth of her life and the love between them now acknowledged, Akiko seems to have achieved a kind of wholeness. Like the protagonists of so many stories of immigrant experience, Akiko ends with a beginning, by starting to understand and even cope with the diasporic currents of her life.

For Filipino Americans those currents are, if anything, more turbulent and conflicted than for most. Shaped by Spanish language, culture, and religion since the sixteenth century, the inheritors as well of the English language and American popular culture, Filipinos are arguably more Western in their orientation than other Asian immigrant groups. They certainly enjoy a richly heterogeneous racial heritage. The contribution of American mass culture, in particular, to this ethnic mix is marked in two novels by Jessica Hagedorn (1949–), *Dogeaters* (1991) and *The Gangster of Love* (1996). In *Dogeaters* (a pejorative term for Filipinos), Hagedorn tells the stories of a range of Filipino characters, among them a pimp, a freedom fighter, and a movie star. Told retrospectively by Rio Gonzaga, a young woman who as a teenager emigrates with her mother to the United States, these stories incorporate a variety of narrative forms, ranging from the discourses of history to vernacular forms such as gossip. What is remarkable, though, is the sense that the forms and imagery of the American media have penetrated Filipino culture so deeply that even memories of the Philippines are marked by it. The era of the Filipino dictator Ferdinand Marcos, for instance, is recollected as if it were a series of Hollywood scripts, some romantic, some comic, pornographic or the stuff of nightmare. Similarly, the protagonist of *The Gangster of Love*, Rocky Rivera, the member of a struggling rock band, admits that she is trapped in her "media-saturated, wayward American skin." The story she tells is appropriately disjunctive, mixing narrative with poetry, dramatic skits, and jokes. By the end, her careering backwards and forwards across America has brought her little beyond the dubious gift of being superficially Americanized. And, like many other immigrant protagonists, she makes the journey back to her old home in the hope that there she may be able to resurrect and retrieve her origins.

It was not until several decades after World War II that, for quite different reasons, the United States experienced significant immigration from Vietnam and South Asia. The exodus from Vietnam that followed the disastrous military engagement there is the narrative occasion of *Monkey Bridge* (1997) by Lan Cao (1961–), which tells the story of a mother and a daughter, and a people, not accustomed to "crossing boundaries" who suddenly have to do so. From farm life on the Mekong Delta to strategic hamlets to Saigon and then to Little Saigon in Virginia: the characters in this novel have to negotiate the perilous "monkey bridge" from one "shifting world" to another. They become wandering spirits, threatened with "the complete absence of identity, of history," looking for an "American future" but longing to "hang onto their Vietnam lives" – and learning, some of them, to "relocate one's roots and bend one's body in a new direction."

The arrival of South Asians in America in large numbers, in turn, has been the source and inspiration of a number of stories and novels published in the last two or three decades of the twentieth century. They include the work in shorter and longer narrative forms by the most significant South Asian American writer, Bharati Mukherjee (1940–). *Wife*, published in 1975, introduces one typical kind of Mukherjee protagonist: the immigrant woman who remains trapped inside her house, for fear of what lies outside, beyond the door. Dimple Dasgupta, the daughter of middle-class Indian parents, marries and emigrates to the Unite States. "Dimple Dasgupta had set her heart on marrying a neuro-surgeon," the novel begins with typical, ironic wit, "but her father was looking for engineers in the matrimonial ads." And it is with an engineer, eventually, that she makes her journey to the New World. Her expectations are high, and they are disappointed. Dimple encounters a world of, at best, indifference and, at worst, real prejudice. Her husband cannot get the work for which he is qualified. And she is frightened by what she sees as the perilous landscape of New York City. So, she retreats into the safety and security of her apartment. Faced by the challenge of the new, she opts for memories of the old, isolation and a form of cultural stalemate. The novel that Mukherjee published fourteen years after *Wife*, *Jasmine*, tells a different story and describes a quite different – but, in her own way, equally typical – heroine. The eponymous Jasmine Vijh is born and raised in rural India, named "Jyoti, Light" by her grandmother. She emigrates to the United States alone to escape her fate as a widow in a small village. There, she constantly reinvents and renames herself, as Jasmine, Jane, or Jase, confessing, "I changed because I wanted to." And pursuing what she calls a "zigzag route" across America, she leads a life of "adventure, risk, transformation"; "the frontier is pushing indoors through uncaulked windows," she declares triumphantly at the end of the novel, as she prepares to leave old home for new.

Jasmine is not, however, a simple celebration of American innovation and the national imperative to "shuttle between identities." It is more barbed than that. "I didn't know what to think of America," Jasmine confesses to herself prior to her arrival in the United States. "I'd read only *Shane* and seen only one movie." What she encounters, when she first arrives with a group of "outcasts" or illegal immigrants, is hardly the promised land. "The first thing I saw were the two cones of a nuclear plant," she remembered. A waste land is her entrance into what often appears to be an "underworld of evil." Washed up in America like so much flotsam and jetsam, Jasmine is confined and raped by a man called Half-Face, a paradigm of the disfigured landscape and perverted national myth. She has to kill Half-Face to escape: first to New York City, then to Iowa – which may seem rooted, reassuring, but has its own forms of poverty and violence, and is, besides, a place where people tend to regard her as "alien." Throughout her trials, however, what sustains Jasmine is her spiritual buoyancy, her eager response to what she terms "the fluidity of American character and American landscape." Not only that, she learns to find salvation eventually in a synthesis between old and new. Her newly acquired American belief in the reinvention of the self finds confirmation, it turns out, from her inherited Indian belief in reincarnation. She is able to connect up with the idea that she can be many women because she is committed to the notion of spiritual metamorphosis. Shuttling between each of her identities as if it were "a possible assignment from God," she combines the cosmic rhythms of ancient belief with the New World rhythms of mobility and adventure. So Jasmine is not so much a divided personality as a unified one, deriving her strength from the marriage between the cultures she is heir to. That strength enables her, as the novel closes, to strike out for a territory that inspires a connection with the oldest and newest of American stories. She is "heading West"; and, as she does so, she tells us, she is "greedy with wants and reckless from hope."

New and ancient songs: The return of the Native American

Writing of those white settlers who were headed west over a hundred years before Jasmine, the poet Simon Ortiz (1941–) observes: "It is a wonder/they ever made it to California./But of course they did." "And they named it success./Conquest./ Destiny./" he adds. Ortiz is from the Acoma Pueblo tribe. The cycle of poems from which these lines are taken, *From Sand Creek* (1981), weaves together autobiography and history, as Ortiz rehearses his experiences as a veteran in a military hospital, the wars white Americans fought to wrest the land from its original inhabitants, and the wars the tribes still have to fight in a society that is oblivious to their presence, let alone their needs. "I am a veteran of 30,000 years," Ortiz declares in another work, "The Significance of a Veteran's Day" (1992). Exploring personal and cultural dispossession, Ortiz finds the tools of survival in the oral traditions of the Acoma Pueblo people. "I am talking about how much we have been able/to survive insignificance," he explains. And the "we" here includes other Native American tribes since, as he observes wryly in another, earlier collection of poems, *Going for Rain* (1974), "You meet Indians everywhere." All Native Americans, Ortiz insists in this collection, must work against the "feeling of no self-esteem, insignificance, powerlessness." They can do so by rediscovering their connection with the land and with the myths of their peoples.

Only by such means can they make a place and presence for themselves and realize their dream of a true homeland. "That dream/shall have a name/after all," Ortiz prophesies in *From Sand Creek*, in words that offer a new variation on an old American theme.

A historical sense of dispossession, the search for a place and past rooted in the oral tradition, the presence and pleasure of a communal identity coextensive with the land, the transformative power of language: these themes sounded in the poetry of Simon Ortiz are common in contemporary Native American writing. The writers speak them, however, and other themes, in a variety of voices. The poetic voice of Roberta Hill Wideman (1947–), for instance, a member of the Oneida tribe, is quieter, more indirect and economical. "Indians know how to wait," she writes in "Lines for Marking Time" (1984); and her poems reveal the rewards of waiting, patient attention to a particular event or object – a house and museum ("In the Longhouse, Oneida Museum" (1984)), a familiar street ("Scraps Worthy of Wind" (1984)) – as a preliminary to emotional release and discovery. As the title of her collection, *Star Quilt* (1984), intimates, Wideman sees her project as a weaving together of the apparently trivial and mundane into significant pattern: a knitting together of the scraps and fragments of memory into forms that invite revelation.

While sharing certain themes in common with Ortiz and Wideman, the poetic voice of Wendy Rose (1948–) is, in turn, different from either. Of mixed Hopi, Miwok, English, Scottish, Irish, and German extraction, Rose also reaches out in her work to women of any race, although particularly to those of mixed-blood origin like herself. "Remember I am a garnet woman," one of her poems called "If I Am Too Brown or Too White for You" (1985) begins. Through a series of linked images, of woman, water, stories, and jewels, Rose then explores the fluid nature of her identity and the chance song gives her to celebrate what she calls here the "small light/in the smoke, a tiny son/in the blood." That light is a crystalline clarity of self that, for so many women like her, so often remains secret, unacknowledged. It is up to Rose, as she sees it, to lay bare the secret. Storytelling, Rose tells us in "Story Keeper" (1985), is something she learned from her family and her tribe. It offers a return to origins, and a means of rediscovering the personal by reconnecting it to the communal.

Joy Harjo (1951–), a poet born into the Creek Nation, also mixes Anglo and Native American influences in her work. Her poems deploy a free verse line that connects her with the tradition of Whitman; they are also marked, however, by a cadence that recalls the repetitions of the Indian ceremonial drum. There is song here, and chant, as Harjo describes Native American women living on a knife edge ("The Woman Hanging from the Thirteenth Floor Window" (1983)), the tragic past and grim present of most Native Americans ("New Orleans" (1983)), or rehearses her own memories and metamorphic sense identity. "Remember that you are all people and that all people/are you," she writes in "Remember" (1983). "The dance that language is" is, in effect, the key for Harjo: the way to unlock what Native Americans have been, are, and may become. Her work is packed with the dire particulars of Native American history, but it is also brimming over with visions. She is, she indicates, like her fellow Native American poets in her search for the right words that will enable her to tell the truth, the tale of her tribe.

"We are what we imagine," N. Scott Momaday (1934–) from the Kiowa tribe once wrote. "Our very existence consists in the imagination of ourselves.... The greatest tragedy that can befall us is to go unimagined." Momaday has also remarked that, when he began writing the novel that established his reputation, *House Made of Dawn* (1968), he did not know any other works of Native American fiction existed. To that extent, he was faced with an "unimagined" collective existence, the erasure of Native Americans from the national literature and life. And, although this was more a matter of perception than fact, it is nevertheless true that Momaday's remarkable first book helped to usher in a renaissance in Native American writing. Following its publication and critical and commercial success, a whole series of works, especially in prose, have helped establish the Native American presence and helped Native American readers in particular to see, and imagine, who they were and what they might become, ranging from the naturalistic fiction of James Welch (1940–2003) to the radically experimental writing of Gerald Vizenor (1934–). The core texts in this Native American renaissance in fiction, following Momaday, have, however, been the work of three writers: Leslie Marmon Silko (1948–), Louise Erdrich (1954–), and Sherman Alexie (1966–). Key workers in prose fiction, each of these three has produced work worthy to stand with *House Made of Dawn*. As remarkable as they are remarkably different, all of them together with Momaday have been instrumental in producing a body of work that deserves to stand in the front row of contemporary writing.

Momaday himself lived in several non-Indian communities as a child, as well as with several Southwestern tribes, especially the Jemez Pueblo. Diversity became a

Figure 5.4　Portrait of N. Scott Momaday, 2006. © Christopher Felver/Corbis.

characteristic, as a result, not just of his writing as a whole, but of individual texts. In *The Names: A Memoir* (1976), for example, he uses fictional techniques, as well as traditional autobiographical ones, to trace his rediscovery and reinvention of himself. The poems in his collections *The Gourd Dancer* (1976) and *In the Presence of the Sun* (1992) range wide: from forms recollecting Native American orality through traditional to free verse. His 1989 novel, *The Ancient Child*, mixes ancient Kiowa bear stories, the contemporary tale of a male artist's midlife crisis, and outlaw fantasies imagined by the young medicine woman who tries to cure the artist. More extraordinary still, his 1969 book, *The Way to Rainy Mountain*, welds together several genres. Here, Momaday collects stories from his Kiowa elders. To all but a few of these he attaches short historical and personal commentaries. He then arranges twenty-four of these triple-voiced movements into three sections titled "The Setting Out," "The Going On," and "The Closing In." Framed by two poems and three lyric essays that combine mythic, historic, and personal perspectives, the three sections dramatize several kinds of journey: the two foregrounded being the historical migration of the Kiowa and the personal entry of the author into his Kiowa identity. As these journeys continue, *The Way to Rainy Mountain* sounds the themes that resonate through all Momaday's writing: the uses of memory, imagination, and the oral in the formation of personal and communal presence, the land and language as extensions of being, the beauty and authority of the Native American sense of the sacred. And similarly resonant with these themes is the book that preceded *The Way to Rainy Mountain* by a year, that first established Momaday's reputation and remains his finest work: *House Made of Dawn*.

Set circularly in Walatowa, a fictional version of Jemez Pueblo, Los Angeles, and then by eventual return, the pueblo again, *House Made of Dawn* tells the story of Abel, a Pueblo Indian. After fighting in World War II, Abel returns alienated from white America and from Pueblo culture. Abel is described, several times, as "unlucky." In an interview, however, Momaday has described his hero as tragic. The trauma suffered by Abel, Momaday explained, was shared by a "tragic generation" of Indians who suffered "a dislocation of the psyche." What Abel has to do, and in the end manages, is to renegotiate his Indian identity through an empowering embrace of ritual and mythical precedent. And the prologue to the novel reveals how he will do it, as it anticipates the end by showing Abel running in a ceremonial race. As he runs, we are told, he appears to have become one with the "still and strong" land around him. The prologue also begins with the traditional invocation, *Dypaloh*, of a Walatowa or Jemez Indian storyteller. It then announces: "There was a house made of dawn. It was made of pollen and rain, and that land was very old and everlasting." The motif that gives the book its title is taken from the songs of the Navajo Nightway ceremony, a long healing ritual. From the beginning Momaday alludes in this way to traditions of storytelling and healing within quite separate Indian cultures of the Southwest. *House Made of Dawn* consequently becomes a continuation of each tradition, as well as, in its alternately terse and densely referential prose, a continuation of the more Anglo-American lines of Hemingway and Faulkner.

In the prologue, Abel is running seven years after the time of the first section, "The Longhair." Set in the pueblo in 1945, this, the first of four sections into which the book is divided, introduces Abel as he stumbles drunkenly off a bus bringing him home from military service. Haunted though he is by war memories, it is clear that his sense of separation from the pueblo community occurred before he entered the army. And his vulnerability to pressure is measured in two key experiences: his involvement with a privileged white woman who is attracted to his "primitive" masculinity, and his murder of an albino Indian whom he takes to be an incarnation of evil. The second section of the novel, "The Priest of the Sun," is set in a miasmic Los Angeles. After a trial in *"their* language," the language of a white society that does not begin to understand the terms and conditions of his life, Abel has been imprisoned and now relocated to the city. The third section, "The Night Chanter," begins with a Navajo Indian called Benally telling the tale of the departure of Abel from the city. Abel and Benally have become friends; and Benally has told Abel about the songs and chants associated with the Navajo healing ceremonies, the Beautyway and the Night Chant.

The final section of the book, "The Dawn Runner," turns the wheel of the narrative full circle. Abel awakes at dawn, only a week after his return from Los Angeles, to find his grandfather dead. The grandfather has taught his grandson about the land, its rhythms and rituals, he has acted as a guide into the mysteries of sex and death. He has also, over the years and over the night, helped to give Abel the right words, pointed a way for him to articulate and celebrate his being. Abel now prepares the body of his grandfather in the ritual fashion. He then hurries off to run after the men who have set off in the ceremonial race. Abel runs to the point where "he could see at last without having to think." What he sees are "the canyon and the mountains and the sky," "the rain and river and the fields beyond," and "the dark hills at dawn." Entering body and soul into a holistic harmony with the land that, from time immemorial, has sustained his people, Abel begins to sing "under his breath." Abel has at last found the right words: the words of the Night Chant that restore him to earth and community. The Walatowa term *Qtsedaba*, indicating that the story is over, seals the healing process, an experience of restoration of being that is also a restoration in saying and seeing. It is a defining moment in contemporary Native American writing: not least because, in responding to the ancient rhythms and rituals, the novel itself has entered into a new language along with its protagonist. In wedding the forms of American fiction to the songs and storytelling of the Native American oral tradition, Momaday has fashioned the right voice for himself, just as his hero Abel has done.

Like Momaday, Leslie Marmon Silko has a mixed ancestry. The family of her father was a mixture of Laguna and white; her mother came from a Plains tribe; and she also has some Mexican ancestors. As the title of her first book, *Laguna Woman* (1974), a collection of poems, indicates, however, it is the traditions and territory of the Laguna that have meant most to her. For Silko, as the title of her 1991 novel, *Almanac of the Dead,* intimates, fiction is a continuation of the oral tradition, in that it retells old tales, marrying the signs of the past to the settings of the present so as to make "the names sound different." "In the belly of this story/" the prologue to her finest novel, *Ceremony* (1977) announces, "the rituals and the ceremony/are still growing." Like "a good ceremony," a good story is curative because its element is growth; it enacts those repetitive, but constantly revitalized rhythms that are the determining characteristics of life.

Like *House Made of Dawn, Ceremony* has a World War II veteran as its protagonist. Tayo, a man of mixed blood, returns to postwar New Mexico feeling dispossessed and disoriented. During the war, he and other Native American combatants had felt "they belonged to America"; now he, and they, have lost that "new feeling." The place to which he returns is a disconcerting mix of the old and the new. There is poverty and homelessness, white tourism and "the dirty walls of the bars along Highway 66." There is significant tension, too, between the new, urban Indians cut off from their tribal cultures and the perpetuation of ceremonies by the medicine men. "I'm sick," Tayo admits. He goes to see a medicine man called Betonie: a man who, with all his allegiance to the ancient rituals, acknowledges the ineluctable nature of the new. "Ceremonies have always been changing" since the arrival of the whites, Betonie tells Tayo, and "only this growth keeps the ceremonies strong." As a man in search of healing, Tayo finds restoration in the hybrid rituals of Betonie, who teaches Tayo the difference between "witchery," red or white, that treats the world as "a dead thing," and ceremony through which Tayo comes to learn "the world was alive." A sign or symbol of witchery is the atomic bomb. The first atomic explosion occurred, historically, little more than a hundred miles from the Laguna; and in *Ceremony*, Tayo, whose grandmother saw that explosion, sees the bomb as uniting humanity under the threat of annihilation. The redemptive ceremony is the experience in the book, the one that Tayo undergoes, and the experience of the book, as it incorporates everything, old and new, into an inclusive vision of peace. Sitting among the rocks mined for uranium to make the atom bomb, Tayo sees in the stars a pattern of convergence with "no boundaries, only transitions through all distances and time." That pattern the protagonist sees is one that this narrative also performs, from its opening invocation to a close that repeats in a new key the old songs and chants: "Sunrise,/accept this offering,/Sunrise."

Louise Erdrich has devoted much of her career to writing a tetralogy. Of German and Chippewa descent, Erdrich grew up in the Turtle Mountain Band of Chippewa, in North Dakota. And in 1984 she published the first of four books set on and around a fictional Chippewa reservation in her homestate, *Love Medicine*, consisting of a series of free-standing narratives told by various members of two families, the Kashpaws and the Lamartines, living on the reservation between 1974 and 1984. This was followed by *The Beet Queen* (1986), *Tracks* (1988), and *The Bingo Palace* (1994). Erdrich is particularly adept, not only in weaving the stories of several people together into one densely layered tapestry, but also at linking story to history and the naturalistic to the magical. Nowhere is this more evident than in what is probably the finest of these four novels, *Tracks*. "We started dying before the snow," the novel begins, as one narrator, Nanapush, takes his audience back to 1912. This was a crucial time. The challenge of white disease killing Native peoples, which Nanapush refers to here, becomes a paradigm of cultural invasion and crisis. The spread of epidemic disease, we learn, land loss, confinement on reservations, forced assimilation, and intertribal conflicts: all had a traumatic effect on Indian communities. Covering the years from 1912 to 1924, *Tracks* then dramatizes the deep divisions between "conservative" and "progressive" members of these communities: that is, between those who were resistant to the pressure from the federal government to assimilate into white society and culture and those who were more positively responsive. Rather than dramatizing those divisions in conventionally historical terms, however, Erdrich, typically for her, turns to the personal. History, for her, is not so much a singular, objective, narrative, as a multidimensional, often magical one created out of the conflict between various, vibrant, and often fallible voices. The voices are many, but two matter, in particular, since the story is structured around two alternating narrators. One is Nanapush, the storyteller whose story begins the book.

His stance is clear from the fact that he refers to his people as the "Anishinabe," meaning First or Original People, the tribal name for itself, rather than "Chippewa," the name given by the United States government to the tribe in legal agreements. The other is a woman called Pauline Puyat, of mixed Chippewa and white ancestry, who tries to deny her Indian identity and leaves the Indian community to become a nun.

The life of Nanapush, as he recalls it, straddles the time from when the Chippewas still lived freely off the land to when they lived off government supplies on the reservation. *Tracks* captures the conflicted state in which the Chippewas live, now that their culture and even their character have been invaded by the whites, and their lives of hunting and gathering, living with the earth, all but lost to anything but memory. But it also conjures up the animistic world that people like Nanapush still inhabit. In this novel, "the spirits of the dead" accompany the living, people resort to magic and medicine to accomplish their aims, and a woman may drown three times and be three times saved – thanks, it seems, to the water spirit or manitou, Misshepeshu. The land may be subject to taxes, but it still seems alive; and, as Nanapush says, "land is the only thing that lasts from life to life." Nanapush may be a richly historical character, but he carries with him traces of Native American folktale and legend. His name links him, it turns out, with the Chippewa trickster Naanabozho, who appears in traditional oral narratives as a culture hero. Mediating between white and Indian society, even while he maintains his traditional view of the world, Nanapush is no more simply one thing or another – man or trickster, tied to old ways or captivated by the new – than *Tracks* is simply a record of cultural resistance or surrender. The strength of both the character and the novel lies, precisely, in their many dimensions, their density of texture. What is told here is a story of triumph not despite but through tragedy, the heroism of continuance against all the odds.

The fiction of Sherman Alexie maps a territory in which the mysticism of Silko and the mix of the ordinary and extraordinary that Erdrich favors coexist with the contemporary reality of casinos and sweatlodges, rock music and ancient ritual, landfill and sacred sites. Alexie's first novel is titled *Reservation Blues* (1996) and reservation blues music, we are told, is a "little bit of everything." It is a "tribal music" that cannibalizes elements from all kinds of distinctive idioms – delta blues, country and western, punk, heavy rock, American Indian traditions – to create "new songs" responsive to the crisscross "crossroads" culture Native Americans now inhabit. And it is the music of Alexie's stories. Alexei, who comes from the Spokane and Coeur d'Alene tribes, produced a substantial body of work even before he reached the age of thirty. There have been ten collections of poetry (including *The Business of Fancydancing* (1992) and *Dangerous Astronomy* (2005)), three volumes of short stories (among them, *The Lone Ranger and Tonto Fistfight in Heaven* (1998)), and three novels (*Reservation Blues, Indian Killer* (1997), *Flight* (2007)). Much of this work relates to the area in and around the Spokane reservation in the eastern part of Washington State. This is the setting for most of *Reservation Blues*. It is a divided territory that seems both disabling and empowering. A crossroads near Wellpinit, "the only town on the reservation," is appropriately the starting point for the story. The African American blues guitarist Robert Johnson miraculously arrives there. Having made a deal with the "Gentleman," or the Devil, to become a great guitarist, he has, he says, been on the run since faking his death in 1938. His guitar is taken up by a young Spokane Indian on the reservation called Victor Joseph. With two other young Spokane Indians, Junior Polatkin and Thomas Builds-the Fire, Victor then forms an "all-Indian rock and blues band," calling themselves Coyote Springs. Sticking to cover versions of songs by other musicians at first, they gradually turn to their own "new songs." At first, the band enjoys some success. They are even invited to New York by an outfit called Cavalry Records to make some demonstration tapes. The trip and the recording tryout are, however, both disastrous. The band falls apart. Victor sinks into alcoholism and apathy; Junior kills himself; and Thomas, who gradually emerges as the central character, leaves the "rez" for the city accompanied by Chess and Checkers Warm Water, two sisters from the Flathead reservation in Montana who had earlier joined the band. "Songs were waiting for them in the city," Thomas believes. He has become a mobile adventurer, who nevertheless takes the memories, even some of the mysticism, of the "rez" with him. Robert Johnson, meanwhile, chooses to stay where he is.

In dramatizing the fortunes of Coyote Springs, Alexie plays with several possibilities. The band and its music catch the tensions in contemporary Native American culture, convey ways of turning pain into poetry that are similar to Alexie's own, and concentrate the raw feeling and rough magic of the entire narrative. Also, in their rise and fall, the band connects up with history. After all, the record company that spurns Coyote Springs bears a name, Cavalry Records, that recalls earlier white interventions in Native American territory and culture. And, freewheeling between past and present, the narrative presents the executives of the company, called Wright and Sheridan, as all too substantial ghosts. They are the nineteenth-century military leaders, Colonel George Wright and General Philip Sheridan, living on into the late twentieth century. The link is clear, and clearly forged in its downbeat way, between the victimization of Native Americans in an earlier age and the exploitation of Native Americans now. Wright, in particular, is described as the man who in 1858 ordered the killing of hundreds of Spokane horses. And the spirits of those horses appear sporadically throughout the novel, in a kind of collective narrative memorializing of pain. After Coyote Springs fails to perform as required in the recording studio, Wright sees in the band "the faces of millions of Indians, beaten, scarred, by smallpox and frostbite, split open by bayonets and bullets." Gazing at his own hands, he sees "the blood stains there." That is the significant past that haunts him. The past that haunts the central Native American character Thomas and his traveling companions at the end of *Reservation Blues* is utterly different. As Thomas, Chess, and Checkers leave for the city in their van, they see shadows that become horses. "The horses were following, leading Indians toward the city," we are told. In the van, the three travelers begin to sing. "They sang together with the shadow horses: we are alive, we'll keep living. Songs were waiting for them up there in the dark." It is with this visionary mix of myth, the material, and magic that *Reservation Blues* ends: in an end that is no end at all. In the end is the beginning, it seems. The first Americans have not vanished; they are journeying on, transforming mourning into music, commemorating the "dead Indians" but also celebrating the living. Just like those generations that lived American lives for thousands of years before the arrival of Columbus, these are people turning their American world into their own American words. This is a new song perhaps, but it echoes an ancient one.

Index